AGRICULTURAL LAW

A Lawyer's Guide to Representing Farm Clients

**J. W. Looney □ Julia R. Wilder
Sam Brownback □ James B. Wadley**

Published in Cooperation with the
National Center for Agricultural Law
Research and Information
Robert A. Leflar Law Center
University of Arkansas School of Law

Section of General Practice

American Bar Association

Photo Credit: Peter Christopher/Masterfile

The material contained herein represents the opinions of the authors and editors and should not be construed to be the action of either the American Bar Association or the Section of General Practice unless adopted pursuant to the Bylaws of the Association.

Printed in the United States of America.

ISBN 0-89707-538-2

Discounts are available for books ordered in bulk. Special consideration is given to state bars, CLE programs, and other bar-related organizations. Inquire at Publications Planning & Marketing, American Bar Association, 750 North Lake Shore Drive, Chicago, Illinois 60611.

95 94 93 92 91   5 4 3 2 1

About the Authors

J. W. Looney is Dean of the University of Arkansas School of Law, where he has been a member of the faculty since 1980. He received a B.S.A. degree from the University of Arkansas in 1966, two M.S. degrees from the University of Missouri–Columbia: one in Animal Science (1968), and one in Agricultural Economics (1976). He received the J.D. degree from the University of Missouri–Kansas City in 1971. He taught at the University of Missouri, Virginia Tech, and Kansas State University and was in private practice in Mena, Arkansas. He is licensed to practice in Arkansas, Missouri, and Virginia and is a former president of the American Agricultural Law Association.

Julia R. Wilder received a B.A. from the University of California at Berkeley in 1976 (With Distinction), and an M.A. (1982) and J.D. (1984) from Indiana University at Bloomington, where she was a Note Editor for the Indiana Law Journal. Ms. Wilder has completed the coursework for an LL.M. in Agricultural Law at the University of Arkansas and is presently writing her LL.M. thesis on the topic of sustainable agriculture. She is a member of the Massachusetts bar and has worked in private practice in Boston.

Sam Brownback has been Kansas Secretary of Agriculture since 1986. He previously was in private practice in Manhattan, Kansas, and served as an Extension Specialist in Agricultural Law and as an Instructor in Agricultural Law at Kansas State University. He graduated from Kansas State University with a degree in Agricultural Economics (1979) and from the University of Kansas School of Law in 1982. He is a member of the Kansas Bar.

James B. Wadley is Professor of Law at Washburn University, where he has been on the faculty since 1979. He previously served as Director of the Eastern Water Law Center and of the Land Use Law Center at the University of Florida. He holds the B.S. (1969) and M.S. (1969) from Utah State University and is a 1972 J.D. graduate of Tulane University.

CONTENTS

CHAPTER 1

AGRICULTURAL LAW - AN OVERVIEW

I. Introduction to Agricultural Law

Agricultural law has become a recognized area of academic concentration within the legal community. This recognition confirms what many general practitioners of law have known for years - that the problems of their farm clients require unique legal treatment. Because the problems of farm clients are increasingly numerous and complex, it has become necessary for these practitioners to be familiar with the large body of specialized law which affects agriculture and to recognize the unique results that sometime occur when general legal concepts are applied to agriculture. In a sense this is what characterizes agricultural law as a specialty area - it emphasizes that body of law which is unique to agriculture and the results which occur when general legal concepts are applied to the agricultural sector. The purpose of this chapter is to present a conceptual overview of agricultural law.

The term "farm client" generally refers to a person who produces agricultural commodities or livestock (including poultry) on a farm where he or she resides. This person may either own or rent the land which they farm. The purpose of this book is to provide a guide to the areas of agricultural law which are most often encountered by lawyers who represent farm clients. While the book is designed for general practitioners, it may also be useful to others. For example, the information may be valuable to specialists who wish to review the legal concepts which relate to a specific area of agriculture and to non-lawyers who are seeking an overview of the legal problems which confront agricultural producers.

It should be noted that some areas of law which could be included within the scope of a book on agricultural law are not covered here. The most conspicuously absent areas of law are agricultural taxation and estate planning. Those topics are treated thoroughly in other sources.[1] Furthermore, this book does not focus on all agricultural law areas. Some areas are

1

omitted because they do not directly relate to the "farm client," as that term is defined above. For example, federal legislation related to agricultural marketing affects the operations of the agribusiness entities which handle, process, and market agricultural products. However, since the farmer client is only indirectly affected by these laws, they are not covered here. The focus is on the regulatory problems most often encountered by the individual "family farmer." The book outlines the practices and procedures which a lawyer must use when representing a farmer in a USDA administrative proceeding and gives some attention to other agencies of direct concern. However, it does not deal with all of the non-USDA agencies whose programs may affect farmers. Details on many of the related programs may be found in more extensive treatises and references.[2]

One major purpose of this book is to review the laws and regulations which govern the operations of United States Department of Agriculture (USDA) agencies. This includes the specialized rules of the respective agencies as well as the general USDA rules. These regulations, which govern the transactions between farmers and USDA agencies, are analyzed within the context of legislative history and case law. The rulemaking and adjudicatory procedures of USDA agencies are also outlined. Additionally, in chapter 2, the special provisions of laws such as the Freedom of Information Act, the Privacy Act, and the Equal Access to Justice Act are outlined for their use in conjunction with administrative proceedings.

Laws which relate to agriculture generally belong to one of three categories:

1. General law that is applied to both agricultural and non-agricultural matters;

2. Specialized law that has been developed to address the specialized needs of agricultural producers and which form an exception to general legal rules; and

3. Specialized law which comprises a system of government regulation of agriculture.

The first of these three categories, general law, will be only briefly examined. The second category, specialized exceptions to general law, is generally unknown, even to many lawyers, and therefore needs a more specific focus. It includes rules which are designed specifically for agricultural activities. This is a major area of agricultural law. A number of succeeding chapters deal with this category. The third category, specialized laws of government regulation, is also a major focus of contemporary agricultural law. It is introduced in this chapter and treated extensively in later chapters.

II. General Law as Applied to Agriculture

For many agricultural operations and activities, the applicable law is the same as that which applies to non-farmers and their activities. For example, a contract to purchase a farm or to hire farm labor is subject to the same basic rules of contract law as are non-farm related contracts. In areas such as these, the legal rules that are applied to agricultural activities do not differ merely because the subject matter involved is agricultural in nature. However, the effect upon the parties may be different when the general rules are applied to the agricultural operation. This is largely because the practical needs of farmers are often different from the needs of persons in other economic sectors of American society. As such, agricultural law includes many general rules of law which tend to create unique effects when applied to agricultural activities.

In order for a lawyer to effectively represent a farm client, he or she must have an understanding of the effect that the general legal rules may have on both the agricultural enterprise and the farm family. Since land is the most important productive asset of a farming operation, much legal inquiry is related to the effect of law on land use issues. For example, although the law which is applicable to farm business organizations, such as corporations or partnerships, is the same as that involving any other business, the effect of using a particular structure may differ since the major asset involved is land. As a result, the predominance of land as an asset in a family farm situation may call for a different legal strategy than what might be used for non-farm businesses or for non-farm families. Other examples of this distinction between farm and non-farm concerns include estate planning (with attention to special tax provisions applicable to farmland) and the buying and selling of products (with special attention to Uniform Commercial Code exceptions for farm products). This category of general law is discussed in several chapters. For example, Chapter 16 focuses

3

on liability issues associated with a farm business. In this area, the laws applicable to farmers are based upon the use of land as the primary asset of the enterprise. The applicable rules are basically the general rules of tort law.

III. Specialized Agricultural Law as an Exception to General Law

For a variety of reasons, many aspects of agricultural production have been viewed by the law as significantly different from other industrial enterprises. Therefore, in those situations the general legal rules have been deemed inappropriate for agriculture. For the most part, the law has created exceptions to the general rules to deal with those matters, rather than create a separate, specialized body of agricultural law. Several areas of specialized legal treatment for agriculture have been selected for discussion in succeeding chapters of this book. For example, farm employers are not subject to many federal labor laws and in many states are not included within the scope of state worker's compensation provisions. Labor and employment issues are discussed in Chapter 14. Agricultural cooperatives are generally exempt from federal anti-trust constraints and therefore can merge, fix prices and deliberately form monopolies through engaging in activities which are prohibited to non-farm businesses. These are addressed in Chapter 13.

The Uniform Commercial Code (U.C.C.) has special provisions for goods which are designated as "farm products." Various U.C.C. rules, such as implied warranties of fitness, do not apply to some farm livestock sales. Likewise, in many states, a farmer is not considered a merchant for many purposes under the U.C.C. Special U.C.C. matters affecting sales by farmers are addressed in Chapter 9. The unique laws which are applicable to the farmer as a borrower are addressed in Chapter 3. The application of bankruptcy law to agriculture is of special interest because a recently enacted chapter of the Bankruptcy Code, (Chapter 12), pertains solely to the financial insolvency of farmers. This subject, along with other matters involving financial distress, is addressed in Chapter 5.

A. Justifications for the Specialized Legal Treatment of Agriculture

Historically, a major premise of the American legal system has been that all similarly situated individuals and situations must be treated equally by the law. Any law which, by content or effect, appears to confer special favor, or to discriminate between particular individuals and groups, is generally seen as offensive. Indeed, a considerable body of law has developed which proscribes the "arbitrary, capricious, unreasonable or discriminatory" administration of law by courts and administrative agencies. A related body of law prescribes that all persons are guaranteed "equal protection of the law." Given the existence of these doctrines, it may seem surprising that persons and businesses which are associated with agriculture have been systematically excluded from the impact of many general legal rules. It is in fact a distinctive feature of agricultural law that agriculture is frequently affected by the exception to a legal rule rather than by the rule itself.

Certain reasons may be offered as an explanation for this divergent treatment. First, farming is viewed as a unique way of life which is dependent on natural forces which occur in an isolated rural environment. It is generally accepted that the success of a farming operation is dependent upon various factors which are beyond the farmer's control. These factors include matters such as the weather, the price and availability of production inputs, and variation in consumer demand for individual agricultural products. Farmers are also viewed as a uniquely stabilizing element in society because of their vital role in food and fiber production. Modern society continues to perceive small farms, and especially those identified as "family farms," as particularly desirable. These types of farms seem to epitomize and promote the American value of self-sufficiency. On a more pragmatic level, because farmers are such efficient producers, they enable most individuals in American society to participate in other areas of the economy. In other words, the majority of citizens are not required to participate in the task of food production since a small number of farm producers are so efficient. Lastly, farmland is a major source of aesthetically and psychologically pleasing open space, and is the locale for many non-farm recreational activities. Ironically, prime farmland is also the potential location for future commercial, industrial and residential development in many locales.

Despite these positive aspects of farming and farmland in contemporary society, farmers are a distinct minority in our country. They constitute about 2% of the United States population. They therefore must withstand the increasing problems and pressures that are associated with the fact that contemporary political and economic power is concentrated in a non-farm, urban-oriented constituency. In that sense, it is arguable that farmers receive specialized legal treatment as an attempt to protect them from the generally urban orientation of law and government. On the other hand, these legal distinctions are not entirely grounded in paternalism. There is considerable concern among urban dwellers that if farmers are not reasonably successful, food supplies in the cities may become scarce and more expensive. This is another factor underlying agricultural law and public policy.

The constitutionality of specialized rules for agriculture is determined by whether the special treatment has a rational basis, or whether the special treatment denies "equal protection of the law." As a basic rule, if the object of the law is viewed as a "discrete, insular minority," courts take the position that the minority is entitled to "heightened judicial scrutiny" and the state or federal government is required to show a "compelling public interest" in order to justify the disparate treatment of those individuals. Despite their minority status, farmers have never been recognized as the kind of minority for whose disparate treatment the compelling public purpose must be shown.[3]

Law pertaining to agriculture is analyzed under a rational basis test. This test supports the constitutionality of an otherwise discriminatory activity if there is a rational relationship between the goal to be accomplished and the regulation which is being administered. In most cases, the exceptions pertaining to agriculture have also been upheld upon an equal protection of the law analysis.[4]

B. How a Farmer May Qualify for the Exceptions

The initial objective for an attorney who represents a client in an agricultural matter is to determine whether the subject activity is within the scope of the legal definition of agriculture. This can present a difficult threshold problem because the definition of what constitutes a farming operation varies between jurisdictions and even varies between different statutes. Nevertheless, there are some general guidelines which are found within in the definition of "farming operation." For the most part, the definitions tend to incorporate the following factors:

a. whether the product of the enterprise is normally considered to be the product of farming operations;[5]

b. whether the resources used in the process are those normally associated with farming;[6]

c. whether the technical methods of production are those normally thought of as associated with farming;[7]

d. whether the economic organization of resource use is consistent with what is normally understood as farming;[8]

e. whether the farm operator bears the risks normally associated with farming; and

f. whether the farm operator and the farming operation are subject to the kinds of problems that the exception to the general rule was designed to address. It should be noted that, although this definition is associated with traditional perceptions of agriculture, courts are increasingly willing to find that additional or newer farming methods fit within that definition. For example, a recent bankruptcy court decision held that the breeding and sale of puppies on a farm is part of a farming operation for purposes of determining farm income.[9]

A relatively recent United States Supreme Court case, United States v. National Broiler Marketing Association,[10] illustrates the operation of the factors which define "agriculture" for legal purposes. National Broiler analyzed the Capper Volstead Act, which exempts agricultural cooperatives from some key restrictions of anti-trust law if the cooperative is comprised of farmers, planters, or ranchmen who are engaged in agricultural production.

In National Broiler, the Association was comprised of 35 vertically integrated broiler companies. With the development of vertical integration in the broiler industry, it has become common for the broiler marketing entity to own the broiler production facilities or to contract with individual producers to

7

raise the required broilers. In an antitrust action against the Association, the Supreme Court held that the Association was not a bona fide cooperative which was entitled to claim the Capper Volstead Act exemption to the anti-trust laws. The Court's holding was based on the findings that:

(1) six members of the Association did "not own or control any breeder flock whose offspring are raised as broilers;" and

(2) six members did not "own or control any hatchery where broiler chicks are hatched."

Therefore, the court concluded that not all members of the Association were farmers, and that the Act did not apply. The Court suggested that the loss of the agricultural exemption from anti-trust would occur if even one member was not properly qualified. The decision of the Fifth Circuit Court of Appeals, which was upheld by the Supreme Court, said, in reference to the definition of "farmer" that, "[W]hatever else farming may mean, an irreducible minimum must be either husbandry of animals or farm ownership."[11] However, even this statement does not limit the parameters of the term "agriculture" for legal purposes. For example, farm operators of leased land usually qualify as farmers. Attorneys who represent farm clients should operate on the premise that "agriculture" is inclusively defined by the courts. Therefore, an attorney may be able to establish that an operation is agricultural in nature under a variety of factual circumstances. A court's willingness to expand the scope of that term may depend somewhat on the type of relief that a farmer is seeking. For example, recent bankruptcy courts' decisions have arguably been quite sympathetic to farmers' insolvency and have made Chapter 12 relief readily available to farmers under wide variety of circumstances.

IV.   Specialized Law Regulating Agriculture

Beginning in the 1800's, agriculture has been the subject of highly specialized regulatory programs developed and ad-ministered by both federal and state governments. However, the federal government is the primary source of agricultural regula-tions. Federal regulation of agriculture is primarily adminis-tered through United States Department of Agriculture (USDA) administrative regulations. To a lesser degree, government regulation also involves state regulation of agriculture and joint federal-state regulatory programs.

A. Scope of Federal Regulation

The United States constitution authorizes a broad scope of federal agricultural regulation. Government regulation of interstate commerce is explicitly authorized under the Commerce Clause. Moreover, an intrastate activity may be federally regulated if the activity has an effect on interstate commerce. Even a minimal "effect" is sufficient justification for regulation. The United States Supreme Court decision in Wickard v. Filburn[12] illustrates the nature and extent of government regulation of agriculture. In Wickard, the Court upheld a federal regulation which limited the acreage a farmer could plant, and which penalized the farmer for excess production even though the harvest was allegedly intended for on-farm consumption by that farmer. The Court's justification for upholding the law was the congressional authority to regulate interstate commerce. Congress had enacted the law at issue for the purpose of controlling the overproduction of commodities which causes low prices. Even though the farmer argued that his activity had no impact beyond the farm itself, the Court stated that the governmental authority to regulate "extends to those activities intrastate which so affect interstate commerce, or the exercise of the power of Congress over it, as to make regulation of them appropriate means to the attainment of a legitimate end, the effective execution of the granted power to regulate intrastate commerce."[13] Once the matter was determined to be within the bounds of the commerce clause, the Court held that Congress may choose the means that it deems appropriate to effectively implement the legislative policy--provided that the means selected is not unreasonable, arbitrary, or discriminatory. It should be noted that, despite the potential breadth of the Wickard decision, Congress has been reluctant to directly mandate regulations which appear to be primarily intrastate in nature.

Much USDA program activity is directed toward research and development to create support services for farmers. This includes services pertaining to methods of production and marketing. Moreover, many of the programs develop, promote or protect international markets for farm products. The USDA programs which are directed at farmers attempt to control the correlated problems of overproduction and low prices. These price support programs are administered on a voluntary basis of participation. In contrast, marketing programs often directly regulate handlers and dealers rather than farmers. This is because farmers rarely market the commodities which they produce directly to consumers. The Packers and Stockyards Act regulations and the Perishable Agricultural Commodities Act regulations are examples of government programs which regulate the intermediary "handlers" of agricultural commodities. It should also be noted that many of the farm programs are actually designed to achieve consumer-oriented benefits virtually without regard to specific on-farm impacts.[14] This lack of farmer participation beyond the production stage of agriculture is arguably a contributing factor to their inability to attain adequate income.

Within the broad congressional power to regulate economic activity is included the power to delegate much of the regulatory function to administrative agencies. Courts will generally hold an agency's regulation to be a constitutional delegation of legislative power by Congress if a delegating statute contains a clear statement of the general purpose which Congress seeks to achieve through the administrative agency. This statement of purpose must be sufficient to enable a court to construe the delegated administrative power in the context of the legislative purpose. The delegation of adjudicatory power by Congress to an administrative agency is rarely successfully attacked.

Much of the current law which regulates agriculture was enacted during the New Deal in an effort to restore economic viability to the agricultural sector after the 1930's Depression. However, some federal agricultural statutes pre-date the New Deal by several years. For example, the Packers and Stockyards Act, which regulates the livestock industry, was enacted in 1921. Other examples include the Capper-Volstead Act, authorizing the antitrust exemption for agricultural cooperatives, and the Grain Futures Act, regulating commodity futures trading, each of which was enacted in 1922.

The Agricultural Adjustment Act of 1938, the successor

legislation to the Agricultural Adjustment Act of 1933, established the foundation for current federal regulatory policies pertaining to production control and price and income support. The Agricultural Act of 1949 is also a major source of current law in these areas. Many new legal provisions are enacted as amendments to the 1949 Act. Recently, the enactment of the Food Security Act of 1985 has established a new focus for many of the traditional USDA programs. A new major federal farm bill is expected to be enacted in 1990. In the area of agricultural marketing, the Agricultural Marketing Agreement Act, the Perishable Agricultural Commodities Act, the United States Grain Warehouse Act, the USDA inspection and quality control programs, all evolved during the 1930's period.

B. Federal Regulation vs. State Regulation

Agricultural production and marketing are regulated by both federal and state programs. Under the Tenth Amendment, states are responsible for maintaining the health and safety of their citizens. These "police powers" of the states are presumed to be valid and controlling in an area which is traditionally reserved to the state, unless Congress clearly expresses its intent to preempt state regulation.

The primary method by which states regulate agriculture is through the licensing of production and marketing processes. For example, grain and seed dealers are often regulated under state laws. Some states also administer inspection and quality control programs which affect agricultural marketing. In some areas, concurrent federal and state regulations exist. It may be difficult or impossible for a client to comply with conflicting federal and state regulations in the areas which are jointly regulated. When this conflict exists, the rules of federal preemption determine which law is controlling. In other words, when state and federal regulatory programs operate in conjunction with each other, the federal program takes precedence. However, a state may impose stricter guidelines than those imposed by federal law if the state regulations further the purposes of federal policy.

The doctrine of preemption is derived from the Supremacy clause of the United States Constitution. This doctrine authorizes a court to void the effect of a state statute which

11

directly conflicts with a federal statute. If a farmer's compliance with both federal and state regulations is impossible, federal law is controlling where the state regulation presents an obstacle to the accomplishment and execution of the full purposes and objectives of Congress.[15]

Where Congressional intent is an issue in determining whether a federal law either supersedes or pre-empts a state law, courts typically consider whether the federal law regulates an area of traditional federal concern, and whether the legislative history and subsequent interpretation of the law reveal the congressional intent to preempt state law. As a general rule, if a court finds that the federal law creates a pervasive regulatory scheme, or touches a dominant federal interest, the federal law will be held to prevail over the conflicting state law.

In many cases, it will not be clear from the text of a federal statute whether Congress intended the federal law to preempt a similar state law. Under that circumstance, a court will look for implied intent on the part of Congress to preempt state law. On the issue of implied intent, courts tend to focus on factors as whether the federal law promotes an interest that is traditionally held to be a state concern, whether the statute creates a pervasive regulatory scheme, and whether the state's regulation interferes with the accomplishment of the federal law's objectives. These factors are generally considered to be evidence of Congressional intent to preempt state legislation. Of these factors, the factor of traditional state concern seems the most compelling. As a general rule, if the regulated area is one of traditional state concern, courts are less inclined to allow federal law to displace or preempt a state law.[16]

As noted earlier, it is possible that both state and federal regulations may pertain to the same agricultural activity. Moreover, despite the fact that the federal government is pervasively involved in the regulation of agriculture, in some areas additional state regulation is needed. Therefore, in a preemption analysis, each case will have to be considered on the basis of its own facts and circumstances. Where it is clear that the federal legislation is intended to coexist with state legislation, state activity may be permitted. For example, in Rice v. Santa Fe Elevator Corp.,[17] which involved the regulation of grain elevators, the United States Supreme Court held that the eleva-

12

tor company could elect to be covered by either federal or state law, both of which shared the same field of licensing requirements. Under this holding, if the elevator company chose the federal law, the state law would not apply. On the other hand, if the company opted to be subject to state law, the provisions of the federal law might not apply in areas of conflict.

Other cases illustrate the preemption principle that federal law may altogether void the effect of a similar state law. For example, in <u>Michigan Canners and Freezers Association, Inc. v. Agricultural Marketing and Bargaining Board</u>,[18] the United States Supreme Court held that certain provisions of the Agricultural Fair Practices Act, which protects the right of producers to join or refrain from joining a producers association, preempted a similar state law. The state law designated a particular producers' association as the exclusive bargaining agent on behalf of producers of the specific commodity, regardless of whether the individual producers of the association were members of the association. The Court's rationale in finding preemption was that the state law stood as an "obstacle to the accomplishment and execution of the full purposes and objectives of Congress." Similarly, in <u>Florida Lime and Avocado Growers, Inc. v. Paul</u>,[19] the Court found that it was impossible for a producer to comply with both state and federal requirements, and held that state law was preempted by the federal law.

Finally, in some cases the federal and state laws are not designed to accomplish the same objective and can therefore both independently regulate the same activity. In <u>Medo-Bel Creamery v. State of Oregon</u>,[20] the Oregon Court of Appeals held that when Congress enacted the Agricultural Marketing Agreement Act, it did not intend to preempt the field to the extent of setting milk prices. The court reached this conclusion even though the state price was higher than the federal price. The court viewed these two laws as promoting compatible objectives.

In the case of <u>United States v. Kimball Foods, Inc.</u>,[21] the Supreme Court addressed the issue of whether a government security interest claimed by the Farmers Home Administration took priority over a private lien perfected under state law. In <u>Kimball</u>, the court found that there was no applicable federal rule even though the facts presented involved a definite and substantial federal interest. Therefore, the Court held that the state law, Article 9 of the Uniform Commercial Code, could be applied.

C. Federal Regulation of Agriculture

As noted earlier, the United States agricultural industry is pervasively regulated by federal law, and the United States Department of Agriculture (USDA) administers these laws through the promulgation and enforcement of its regulations. Interestingly, agriculture is the only United States industry which is regulated by a federal department which promotes the special needs of the industry separately from the general economic policies of the government. This is probably because the production and distribution of food in our economy is of fundamental importance to society. Therefore, USDA policies and programs can be viewed as constituting a societal infra-structure.

Despite a presumed high degree of agreement as to the importance of adequate food supplies to this country, there is much public debate about the role that government should exercise in the agricultural sector of the economy. Some of the issues in this debate involve complicated political and legal issues. As just indicated, the most pragmatic reasons for government regulation of the agricultural sector involve the fundamental need to protect national security and public health through the provision of a reliable supply of food and fiber. However, in a society as sophisticated as the United States, the availability of adequate food is sometimes taken for granted. Thus, the importance of the government's role in promoting and protecting United States food production and distribution is often minimized by those who criticize federal intervention in agricultural production and marketing.

The government's role in agriculture is largely designed to protect farmers and farming operations by providing price and income supports. Farm operators also receive direct subsidized benefits from programs in the areas of crop insurance, soil conservation, farm finance and credit, irrigation, flood control, and commodity exchange regulation. However, the law also extends a great deal of protection to consumers. Most of the federal programs exist to insure that adequate supplies of quality food products are consistently available to consumers at reasonable prices. This consumer protection role is certainly suggested by the wide range of concerns embraced by current programs such as marketing standards, inspections, animal and plant health, agricultural research, food safety and quality standards, and container standards. Methods such as price supports, marketing quotas, marketing agreements and orders, and export/import programs are extensively used to promote orderly marketing, and therefore also indirectly benefits consumers.

The context of these rules and regulations on wide-ranging subjects is distinctly agricultural. In this sense, it may be said that agricultural law relating to government regulation is a highly specialized body of law. Perhaps the most significant characteristic of this area of law is that it is mostly administrative law. This means that the relevant rules are not made by legislatures or judges but rather by United States Department of Agriculture (USDA) administrative agencies.

The USDA was created by an Act of Congress on May 15, 1862. Over the years, the USDA has been reorganized so that its agencies are more responsive to pressing farm problems. At present, it is organized into seven program areas. These include economics, food and consumer services, international affairs and commodity programs, marketing and transportation services, natural resources and environment, science and education administration, and small community and rural development. These Department areas are supported by a number of staff offices which include General Counsel, Budget Program Analysis, Governmental and Public Affairs, the Inspector General and Administration. All of this is administered at the executive cabinet level under the direction of the Secretary of Agriculture.

To deal effectively with administrative law, a lawyer must have an understanding of how those agencies function and how adverse agency decisions can be appealed. This primarily requires that a lawyer maintain access to the rules and regulations of the relevant agencies with which he or she deals. It also involves attaining knowledge of the specialized litigation practices which take place within the administrative agencies, including practices relating to agency enforcement actions and reparation proceedings.

The most likely direct contact of farmers with federal regulation is through the division of International Affairs and Commodity Programs or Marketing and Transportation Services within the USDA. These agencies administer what is popularly known as the "farm programs." The crops with which those programs deal are also commonly known as "program crops." These crops are wheat, feed grains, upland cotton, extra long staple cotton and rice.

Within the International Affairs and Commodity programs division of the USDA are (1) the Agricultural Stabilization and Conservation Service (ASCS), which administers the basic price support programs, (2) the Commodity Credit Corporation (CCC), which administers the price support loan programs (using the ASCS staff as administrators), (3) the Federal Crop Insurance Corporation, which administers the crop insurance program, and (4) the Foreign Agricultural Service, which is involved with the promotion of farm exports. These matters are addressed in detail in chapters 6 and 8.

Within the USDA Marketing and Transportation Services programs division are (1) the Agricultural Marketing Service, which administers the marketing orders and marketing agreement programs, (2) the Packers and Stockyards Administration, (3) the Perishable Agricultural Commodities Act, which provides the source of standardization for most inspection and grading services for commodities such as live cattle, swine, sheep, feed grains, fresh fruits and vegetables and other farm products. These programs are discussed in Chapters 10 and 11.

Another important USDA agency is the Farmers Home Administration (FmHA). This agency is located within the USDA Small Community and Rural Development division. FmHA is a primary source of credit to farm borrowers who are unable to secure credit from commercial sources such as banks, at rates they can afford. Within the USDA Natural Resources and Environment division, the Soil Conservation Service (SCS) administers programs through local conservation districts which are designed to assist farmers with soil and water conservation. These programs are the focus of Chapters 4 and 7, respectively.

Although the USDA administers a wide range of programs that affect agriculture, only areas that directly involve farmers have been selected for presentation here.

V.   Other Federal Agencies

While many people assume that USDA programs are the most important regulators of agriculture, many other agencies are also involved and may have a direct impact on individual farm clients.

In 1981 Congress authorized eleven federal agencies to conduct a National Agricultural Land Study. This study concluded that nearly a hundred government programs significantly affect the availability of land for agricultural use. These programs are found in a wide range of federal agencies in addition to the USDA. These agencies include the Department of Housing and Urban Development, the Economic Development Administration, the Veterans Administration, the Water and Power Resources Service, the Army Corps of Engineers, the Tennessee Valley Authority, the Department of Energy, and the Environmental Protection Agency. In addition, the Department of Labor, the Department of Commerce, the Department of the Interior, the Department of the Treasury (particularly the Internal Revenue Service), and the Department of Health and Human Services all have substantial regulatory programs which have a direct impact on farm businesses. As an additional example, some farmers are involved in trading commodity futures contracts in the organized contract markets (or boards of trade). These markets and the commodity professionals who involved in trading are regulated by the Commodity Futures Trading Commission (CFTC), not the USDA. This regulatory process is similar to that followed in some USDA programs but deserves special attention. It is discussed in Chapter 12. Thus, although the USDA is the primary federal agency responsible for farm-oriented programs, federal agricultural policy is actually administered by a multiplicity of federal agencies.

FOOTNOTES

1. For farm income taxation information see O'Byrne, John C. and Charles Davenport, Farm Income Tax Manual (Charlottesville: The Michie Co., 1988). For farm estate planning information see Kelley, Donald H. and David A. Ludtke, Estate Planning for Farmers and Ranchers (Colorado Springs: Shepard's/McGraw Hill, 1988) 2 vol. Both topics are also covered extensively in Harl, Neil Agricultural Law (New York: Matthew Bender, 1982) 15 vol. especially vol. 4-6.

2. See Davidson, John (ed.) Agricultural Law (Colorado Springs: Shepard's/McGraw Hill, 1981) 2 vol. Harl, Neil, Agricultural Law (New York: Matthew Bender, 1982) 15 vol. and Juergensmeyer, Julian C. and James Wadley, Agricultural Law (Boston: Little Brown and Company, 1982) 2 vol.

3. See, e.g., United States v. Garth, 733 F.2d 1469 (5th Cir. 1985).

4. See, e.g., Cueto v. Stahman Farms, 608 P.2d 537 (N.M. 1980).

5. See, e.g., K.S.A. § 17-1602a; K.S.A. § 2-3203.

6. See, e.g., K.S.A. § 50-624.

7. See, e.g., K.S.A. § 44-819.

8. See, e.g., K.S.A. § 65-185d.

9. In Re Maike, 77 Bankr. 832 (Bankr. D. Kan. 1987).

10. 436 U.S. 816 (1978).

11. 550 F.2d 1380, 1386 (5th Cir. 1977).

12. Wickard v. Filburn, 317 U.S. 111 (1942). See also Mulroy v. Block, 569 F. Supp. 256 (1983).

13. 317 U.S. 111, 124 (1942).

14. See Wadley, "Small Farms: The USDA, Rural Communities and Urban Pressures," 21 Washburn L.J. 478 (1982).

15. Rice v. Santa Fe Elevator Corp., 331 U.S. 218 (1946); Florida Lime & Avocado Growers v. Paul, 373 U.S. 132 (1963); L & L Started Pullets, Inc. v. Bourdine, 592 F. Supp. 367 (1984).

16. For further discussions, see, e.g., "Federal Preemption of State Food Standards; the Egg Products Inspections Act as a Case in Point, 11 U. Cal. Davis L.R. 511 (1978).

17. 331 U.S. 218 (1947).

18. 104 S. Ct. 2518 (1984).

19. 383 U. S. 132 (1963).

20. 673 P.2d 537 (Or. App. 1983). See also Parker v. Brown, 317 U. S. 341 (1943).

21. 440 U. S. 715 (1979).

CHAPTER 2

PRACTICE AND PROCEDURE IN
THE USDA ADMINISTRATIVE PROCESS

I.   USDA Process
The activities of USDA agencies may affect the client in
one of three ways. First, an agency may engage in rule making
procedures that affect the client. Second, the agency may
conduct an adjudicatory proceeding in which the Secretary
brings an action against or involving the client. Third, the
agency may conduct a reparations proceeding in which a private
individual brings an action against or involving the client.

Agency proceedings are usually governed by the USDA
general rules of practice which are authorized by the
Administrative Procedure Act (APA).[1] However, in some
USDA agencies and programs the general rules will be made
inapplicable by statute and specialized rules will be applied
instead. Furthermore, the agencies which conduct reparation
proceedings, the Packers and Stockyards Administration and the
Agricultural Marketing Service, have specialized rules of practice
for reparations proceedings. (These are discussed in Chapters
10 and 11.)

The primary source of legal information about the
details of USDA program operations is the Federal Register
and its annual codification, the Code of Federal Regulations.
Most of the rules and regulations of USDA agencies are
published on a daily basis in the Federal Register. This includes
regulations in their proposed, interim, and final forms.

The Code of Federal Regulations is published annually
by the office of the Federal Register, National Archives and
Records Administration, Washington, D.C., as a special edition
of the Federal Register. The Code of Federal Regulations is a
codification of the general and permanent rules which are
published in the Federal Register by the executive departments
and agencies of the federal government, including the USDA.
The Code of Federal Regulations is continually updated by the
individual, daily issues of the Federal Register. These two

publications must be used together to determine the latest version of any given USDA rule or regulation.

The contents of the Federal Register are required to be judicially noticed.[2] The Code of Federal Regulations is prima facie evidence of the text of the original documents.[3]

II.   Rules and Rulemaking

Agencies have the power to promulgate rules to govern the programs within their purview. USDA agencies promulgate their rules through the observance of specific rulemaking procedures. Each USDA agency has considerable discretion in determining the substantive content of the rules and regulations which it uses to administer the statutory authority delegated to it by Congress.

The USDA generally follows rulemaking procedures similar to those outlined in the Administrative Procedures Act.[4] The function of the APA rulemaking provisions is to insure substantive and procedural fairness in the rules which are promulgated.[5]   The Act outlines minimum mandatory procedures for the rulemaking process, including:

(1)   notice of proposed rules by publication in the Federal Register,[6]

(2)   public participation by written or oral comments on proposed rules, and

(3)   publication of final rules not less than 30 days prior to the effective date.[7]

The notice provisions of the APA do not apply in the following situations:

(1)   to interpretative rules, general statements of policy, or rules of agency organization, procedure or practice;

(2)   when an agency "for good cause finds (and incorporates the findings and a brief statement of reasons in the rules issued) that notice and public procedure are impracticable, unnecessary or contrary to the public interest",[8] or

(3)   "for good cause found and published with the rule."[9]

The USDA rulemaking procedures set out a similar process whereby the public is given notice of proposed rulemaking and is given the opportunity to give written submissions on the proposals.[10]

In an emergency situation, temporary regulations may be promulgated and made immediately effective without complying with the APA notice-and-comment procedure. However, in order for the regulations to become permanent, notice-and-comment procedures must be followed.[11]

Public participation through the notice and comment procedures is required in the APA and in USDA rulemaking processes unless there is an applicable statutory exception which excuses compliance. During the public comment process, each agency must provide an opportunity for any person to submit written data, opinions and arguments to the agency before the proposed rule becomes final and effective. The APA provides for oral presentations under certain circumstances, although there is usually no public evidentiary hearing required.[12] The agency must evaluate and consider all relevant data in its possession during the process of promulgating rules. In the final rule, the agency must incorporate a general statement of the basis and purpose of the rule. This facilitates judicial review of the rule and the manner in which it is administered by the agency.[13]

III.   Adjudicatory Procedures

The APA provides detailed rules which govern agency adjudicatory procedures.[14] In order to satisfy constitutional due process requirements, adjudicatory procedures must afford litigants proper notice and a hearing before an impartial fact-finder.[15] After the hearing, the agency must outline its written conclusions in an order.[16]

The rules of practice governing formal adjudicatory procedures within USDA are found at 7 C.F.R. § 1.130 et seq. (1988). These rules are applicable to all adjudicatory proceedings under the listed statutory provisions including (but not limited to):

Egg Products Inspection Act, Section 18 (21 U.S.C. 1047).
Federal Land Policy and Management Act of 1976, Section 506 (43 U.S.C. 1766).

Federal Meat Inspection Act, sections 4, 6, and 7(e), 8 and 401 (21 U.S.C. 604, 606, 607(e), 608, 671).
Federal Seed Act, Section 409 (7 U.S.C. 1599).
Packers and Stockyards Act, Sections 203, 312, 401, 502(b), and 505 (7 U.S.C. 1599).
Perishable Agricultural Commodities Act, Sections 3(c), 4(d), 6(c), 8(a), 8(b), 8(c), 9 and 13(a) (7 U.S.C. 499c(c), 499d(d), 499f(c), 499h(a), 499h(b), 499h(c), 499i, 499m(a). (The rules are not applicable to reparations proceedings under 6(c)).
Poultry Products Inspection Act, Sections 6, 7, 8(d), and 18 (21 U.S.C. 455, 456, 457(d), 467).
United States Grain Standards Act, Sections 7(a)(3), 9, 10, and 17A(d) (7 U.S.C. 79 (g)(3), 85, 86).
United States Warehouse Act, Sections 12 and 25 (7 U.S.C. 246, 253).[17]

The rules also apply to adjudicatory proceedings under the regulations promulgated under the Agricultural Marketing Act of 1946 (7 U.S.C. § 1621 et seq.) for the denial or withdrawal of inspection, certification, or grading services.[18]

Any interested person may provide an agency Administrator with information concerning apparent violations of the statutes listed in 7 C.F.R. § 1.131 or violations of a "regulation, standard, instruction, or order issued pursuant thereto."[19] Information concerning violations may be submitted by telegram, letter or by a preliminary statement of facts setting forth the details of the alleged violation.[20]

Once the Administrator of the appropriate agency has received the information, the agency will conduct whatever investigation is justified by the facts.[21] During the investigation, the agency will determine whether there is reason to believe that a violation has occurred, or is occurring. If there is reason to believe that a person has violated or is violating any provisions of a statute, regulation, standard, instruction or order, a complaint will be filed with the agency Hearing Clerk. If the investigation determines that no violation has occurred, no further action will be taken and the person who submitted the information will be informed.[22] If a complaint is filed the person who submitted the initial information is not a party to the proceeding but may be subpoenaed as a witness or deponent.[23]

Prior to the filing of the complaint the Administrator will attempt to settle the matter in an amicable and informal way by giving notice of the facts to the person involved and by allowing the person reasonable time in which to demonstrate or achieve compliance in those cases involving the possible withdrawal, suspension or revocation of a license.[24] A formal proceeding is instituted by the filing of a complaint with the agency Hearing Clerk as in other cases.

The complaint in formal proceedings must state the "nature of the proceeding, the identification of the complainant and the respondent, the legal authority and jurisdiction under which the proceeding is instituted, the allegations of fact and provisions of law which constitute a basis for the proceeding, and the nature of the relief sought."[25] The respondent must file a signed answer with the hearing clerk within 20 days after the service of the complaint.[26] This time period is 10 days in a proceeding under § 4(d) of Perishable Agricultural Commodities Act. The failure of the respondent to file an answer to the complaint with denials within the time specified constitutes an admission of the allegations in the complaint for purposes of the litigation.[27]

Any party may request a hearing on the facts before an administrative law judge appointed pursuant to 5 U.S.C. § 3105.[28] In general, the failure to request a hearing within the time in which an answer may be filed constitutes a waiver of the hearing.[29] The respondent's failure to file an answer, or the admission in the answer of all the material allegations of fact in the complaint, also constitutes a waiver of the hearing.[30] If the hearing is waived, the complainant must file a proposed decision accompanied by a motion for adoption of the decision. The proposed decision and motion will be served on the respondent by the Hearing Clerk. The respondent has 20 days after service in which to file objections to the proposed decision. If the Judge finds that meritorious objections have been filed, the complainant's motion will be denied with a statement of supporting reasons. If meritorious objections are not filed, the Judge must issue a decision without further proceeding or hearing. After the decision is entered in the record, it becomes final without further proceedings 35 days after the date of service of the decision upon the respondent, unless an appeal to the Judicial Officer is timely filed.[31]

If any material fact is denied in the respondent's answer, the matter may be set for hearing upon the request of the complainant or upon the Judge's own motion.[32] Hearings must be reported and transcribed verbatim.[33] The failure of either party to appear at a scheduled hearing "without good cause" is deemed to be waiver of an oral hearing and an admission of any facts which may be presented at the hearing.[34]

The Judge may order a prehearing conference upon motion of a party or upon the Judge's own motion.[35] Depositions may be ordered upon the motion of a party to the proceeding.[36] Subpoenas may be used to require the attendance and testimony of witnesses and the production of documentary evidence.[37]

The parties may file proposed findings of fact, conclusions of law and orders, as well as briefs in support thereof.[38] The Judge is required to prepare and file a decision within a reasonable time after the period allowed for filing these documents has elapsed.[39] The Hearing Clerk will serve a copy of the decision upon each of the parties. This decision is final and becomes effective 35 days after the date of service unless there is an appeal to the Judicial Officer.[40]

Within 30 days after receiving service of a decision, either party may appeal the decision to the Judicial Officer.[41] The Judicial Officer is an official of the USDA to whom appeal authority has been delegated by the Secretary. No agency decision is final for purposes of judicial review except a final decision of the Judicial Officer upon appeal.[42] A response to the appeal must be filed by the opposing party within 20 days after service of a copy of an appeal petition.[43] Either party may request oral argument before the Judicial Officer.[44] The failure to have requested a hearing on the facts before the Administrative Law Judge does not constitute a waiver of oral argument upon an appeal of the Judge's decision to the Judicial Officer.[45]

The parties may agree to submit their case for a decision on the basis of the appeal briefs which have been filed unless the Judicial Officer directs that appeals be argued orally.[46] Any argument on appeal is limited to the issues raised in the appeal or in the response to the appeal unless the Judicial Officer determines that additional issues should be argued.[47]

A petition to reopen a hearing held before The Administrative Law Judge to take further evidence may be filed with the Hearing Clerk at any time prior to the issuance of the decision of the Judicial Officer.[48] The petition must state the specific grounds relied upon, including the nature and purpose of the additional evidence and a good reason why the evidence was not presented at the hearing.[49]

A petition to rehear or to reargue a proceeding, or to reconsider the decision of the Judicial Officer, must be filed within 10 days after the date of service of the decision. The petition must state the specific matters claimed to have been erroneously decided and the alleged errors must be briefly stated.[50]

Within 20 days following the service of any of these petitions, any party may file a reply.[51] As soon as practicable after that, the Judge or the Judicial Officer, as the case may be, will grant or deny the petition. A decision is not final for purposes of judicial review until the petition is denied or the decision is affirmed or modified.

IV.   Judicial Review of Agency Action

After the administrative hearing process has been completed the affected parties may usually seek judicial review of agency decisions. The Administrative Procedures Act provides for judicial review of agency actions in the following circumstances: (1) if the action is made reviewable by statute and/or (2) if there is no adequate legal remedy other than judicial review of the final agency action.[52] The major legal issues pertaining to judicial reviewability focus on matters such as issue preclusion, exhaustion of administrative remedies, and the scope of review.

A. Preclusion

There is a general presumption of reviewability of agency action and most USDA actions involving clients are reviewable. However, review is precluded if it is expressly prohibited by statute or if the matter is committed to agency discretion by law.[53]

In construing the effect of the "preclusion" concept the United States Supreme Court, in <u>Block v. Community Nutrition Institute</u>[54] stated:

> Whether and to what extent a particular statute precludes judicial review is determined not only from its express language, but also from the structure of the statutory scheme, its objectives, its legislative history, and the nature of the action involved.[55]

B. <u>Exhaustion of Administrative Remedies</u>

The doctrine of exhaustion of administrative remedies prevents a court from exercising jurisdiction in a case until a final decision has been reached in the administrative process. In <u>United States v. Carroll</u>[56] the court summarized the concept of exhaustion of administrative remedies as follows:

> When agency action is subject to appeal to higher administrative authority, the administrative remedy obviously has not been exhausted until higher authority has acted. . . . It is elemental that the defendant is bound by an administrative decision from which he failed to appeal.[57]

C. <u>Scope of Review</u>

The APA sets forth specific grounds for judicial review. Upon review, a court may hold unlawful, and set aside, an agency action which it finds to be:

(1) arbitrary, capricious, an abuse of discretion or otherwise not in accordance with law;

(2) contrary to a constitutional right, power, privilege or immunity;

(3) in excess of statutory jurisdiction, authority or limitations or short of statutory rights;

(4) without observance of procedure required by law;

(5) unsupported by substantial evidence; or

(6) unwarranted by the facts to the extent that the facts are subject to trial de novo by the reviewing court.[58]

D. How to Achieve Review

Judicial review of most agency decisions is accomplished by direct appeal to the appropriate federal Circuit Court of Appeal as authorized by statute. Questions of reviewability may also arise in federal district court in situations where the agency seeks enforcement of its own orders through court action or when the affected party brings a direct action against an agency. For example, in U. S. v. Batson[59] the agency sought enforcement of its interpretation of rules involving various government programs and the recovery of payments alleged to have been improperly made. In Esch v. Lyng[60] farmers successfully brought an action against the agency to stop proceedings against the farmer and to compel the agency to carry out certain aspects of its programs. In Wescott v. USDA[61] the suit included a claim for damages against the agency on the grounds that the agency and its officials had acted beyond the scope of their authority.

V. Statutory Provisions Giving Rights to Those Who Deal With USDA

Three separate federal statutory provisions provide specialized assistance to the client who has transacted business with the USDA. These statutes are the Freedom of Information Act,[62] the Privacy Act[63] and the Equal Access to Justice Act.[64] The USDA has promulgated regulations which implement each of these statutes.

A. Freedom of Information

The Freedom of Information Act (FOIA), allows public access to non-privileged agency information.[65] The FOIA does not apply to Congress, the courts or states, even if they administer funds under federal programs.

The FOIA requires that agencies make information available to the public either by publication in the Federal Register or by making records available for inspection and copying. Substantive rules must be published in the Federal Register.[66] However, statements of agency policy and interpretations are not required to be published.[67]

The Office of Governmental and Public Affairs has the primary responsibility for administering the FOIA within the

USDA.[68] All agency records must be made promptly available to any person who submits a request in accordance with USDA regulations, except those records which are exempt from mandatory disclosure.[69] However, an agency may release records which are exempt from mandatory disclosure whenever it determines that such disclosure would be in the public interest unless the disclosure of information is specifically prohibited by an Executive Order, statute or regulation. Disclosure is in the public interest if the benefit to the public in releasing the document outweighs any harm likely to result from disclosure.[70]

Each USDA agency must make the following materials available for public inspection and copying, unless they are materials which are promptly published and offered for sale:

1. final opinions and orders made in the adjudication of cases;
2. statements of policy and interpretation which have been adopted by the agency and are not published in the Federal Register; and
3. Administrative staff manuals and instructions to staff that affect a member of the public.[71]

The agencies must also maintain and make available current indexes of all the above materials which have been issued after July 4, 1967.[72]

(1) Requests

Any person who wishes to inspect or obtain copies of record of any USDA agency must submit a written request addressed to the official designated in the regulations promulgated by the agency. The request may include a petition for a fee waiver if a charge for services is expected. All requests for records are deemed to have been made pursuant to FOIA, regardless of whether the Act is specifically mentioned in the request. To facilitate the processing of a request, the statement "FOIA REQUEST" should be placed in capital letters on the front of the envelope in which the request is mailed or submitted.[73]

A request must reasonably describe the records sought, providing specific information such as dates, titles, etc. which may help the agency to locate and identify the records. If the request relates to a matter which is involved in pending litigation, the court and its location should be identified. If the agency determines that a request does not reasonably describe the records, it must inform the requester of this fact and allow the requester an opportunity to clarify the request. More over, the requester must be allowed to confer promptly with knowledgeable agency personnel to attempt to identify the records he or she is seeking.[74]

The agency is allowed to respond to oral requests for information. However, if the requester is dissatisfied with the response, the agency official involved must ask the requester to submit a written request. Moreover, for recordkeeping purposes the agency is always entitled to ask for a written information request.[75]

If compliance with the information request involves the inspection of records by the requester rather than the forwarding of copies of the records by the agency, the agency response must include the name, mailing address and telephone number of the person within the agency to be contacted to arrange a mutually convenient time for the inspection to occur.[76]

Each agency provides public notice which specifies the person(s) to whom requests for information must be directed. For example, the Animal and Plant Health Inspection Service (APHIS) rules direct that information requests be made to the APHIS offices in Hyattsville, Maryland.[77]

USDA agencies charge uniform fees for record searches and copying services. The photocopying charge is 20 cents per page. There is a fee waiver provision if request is deemed in the public interest. The requesting party may wish to inspect records directly to avoid incurring copying and search charges.

The agency may also charge for assistance from its personnel. The charge may either be based on the employee's salary rate, or at a rate of $10.00 per hour for clerical time and $20.00 per hour for supervisory or professional time.[78]

(2) Agency Response

USDA agencies must comply with the time limits set forth in FOIA for responding to and processing requests for agency documents and appeals unless there are unusual circumstances.[79] However, if the agency is unable to comply with a time limit, it must notify the requester in writing and must continue processing the request as expeditiously as possible.[80] Each USDA agency must notify the requester of its determination regarding the information request within 10 days of the date of receipt of the request.[81] If the agency denies the request in whole or in part, it must immediately provide the requester with the following information:

1. the reasons for the denial;
2. the name and title of each person responsible for the denial of the request;
3. the requester's right to appeal the denial and the title and address of the official to whom the appeal should be made; and
4. the requirement that the appeal be made within 45 days of the date of the denial.[82]

If the records requested contain some portions which are exempt from mandatory disclosure and others which are not, the official responding to the request must insure that all nonexempt portions of the relevant records are disclosed, and that all exempt portions are identified according to the specific exemption(s) which are applicable.[83] If the reason for not fulfilling the request is that the records requested are in the custody of agency which is outside the USDA, the agency must inform the requester of this fact and forward the request to that agency for processing in accordance with its regulations.[84]

If a request for records or a request for a fee waiver under is denied by an agency, the person making the request has the right to appeal the denial. All appeals must be in writing and must be addressed to the official designated in the regulations promulgated by the agency which denied the request.[85]

Each USDA agency to which an appeal is submitted must notify the requester of its decision of the appeal within 20 days of the date it was received. If the appeal is denied, the agency must provide the requester with the following information:

1. the reasons for the denial;
2. the name and title of each person responsible for the denial of the appeal, and

3.   the right to judicial review of the denial.[86]

(3) Exemptions
The FOIA contains the following nine exemptions:
1.   matters that are specifically authorized under criteria established by an executive order to be kept secret in the interest of national defense or foreign policy;
2.   matters that relate solely to the internal personnel rules and practices of an agency,
3.   matters exempted from disclosure under other federal statutes provided that the statute requires that the matters to be withheld so as to leave no discretion to the agency on this issue, or establishes particular criteria for withholding or refers to particular types of matters to be withheld.
4.   trade secrets and commercial or financial information obtained from a person and which is privileged or confidential.
5.   inter-agency or intra-agency memorandums or letters which would not be available by law to a party other than an agency in litigation with the agency;
6.   personnel and medical files and similar files whose disclosure would constitute a clearly unwarranted invasion of personal privacy;
7.   investigatory records compiled for law enforcement purposes, but only to the extent that the production of the records would interfere with enforcement proceedings, deprive a person of a right to a fair trial, constitute an unwarranted invasion of personal privacy, disclose the identity of a confidential source or confidential information provided only by that confidential source, disclose investigative techniques or procedures, or endanger the life or safety of law enforcement personnel.
8.   matters contained in reports prepared by or for the use of financial institutions; and
9.   geological and geophysical information and data, concerning wells.[87]

33

B. Privacy Act

The Privacy Act of 1974[88] requires agencies to provide individuals access to records maintained by the agency which pertain to the individual. Moreover, the Act prohibits an agency from disclosing records to a person or agency unless it has the prior written consent of the person to whom the records pertain. Another purpose is to insure that the records which are kept are as accurate as possible.

The USDA has issued regulations which implement the Privacy Act. According to the regulations, no agency may release a record to anyone other than the party to whom the record pertains, unless that individual authorizes the release.[89]

(1) Requests for Records

Any individual who wishes to be notified if a records system maintained by an agency contains any record pertaining to him, or wishes to request access to such records, must submit a written request in accordance with the instructions set forth in the system notice for that system of records. The request must contain the name of the person making the request, the name of the person seeking access to records, and, must state whether he or she wishes to make a personal inspection of the records, or to be supplied with copies by mail.[90] An individual whose request for access to, or copies of, agency records is denied may appeal that denial to the head of the agency which maintains the system records to which the request relates.[91] If this appeal is denied, the requester may bring a civil action in federal district court to seek review of the denial.[92]

When an agency has granted a request for personal inspection of records, the requester must present sufficient personal identification prior to the inspection to verify that he or she is the individual to whom the records pertain. No identification is required when the records are ones whose disclosure is required by the FOIA.[93] The agency must provide copies of pertinent records to any individual who has made a personal inspection of records pertaining to him.[94] Copies of records will not be released through the mail until adequate personal identification is provided.[95]

The agency must acknowledge a request or appeal within 10 days of its receipt. Wherever practicable, the acknowledgement should indicate whether or not access to records will be granted. If access is granted, it should indicate when and where access to records will be granted. When access is granted, the agency should provide the access within 30 days of receipt of the request or appeal. If the agency is unable to meet this deadline, it must inform the requester of this fact, and state the reasons for its inability to do so and an estimate of the date on which access will be granted.[96]

The agency is not required to give the requester access to the physical record itself. Moreover, the regulations acknowledge that the form in which a record is kept or the content of the record may require that the record be edited or translated in some manner by the agency. However, the agency may not use either of these procedures to withhold information in a record about the requester.[97]

(2) Exempted USDA Records

No agency may deny a request for information concerning the existence of records about the requester, or deny any request for access to records about the requester, in any system of records which the agency maintains, unless that system is exempted from the requirements.[98]

Various systems of USDA records (or portions of them) are exempted from the provisions of the Act. These are listed at 7 C.F.R. § 1.123. If any agency receives a request for access to system records which are exempted, the system manager must determine whether to assert the exemption. If he or she determines to deny the request for records based on the exemption, the requester must be informed of that determination, the reason for the determination and the title and address of the agency head to whom the denial can be appealed.[99] If the head of an agency determines that an appeal is to be denied, he or she must inform the requester of that determination, the reason for the determination and must inform the requester of his or her right to seek judicial review of the denial in federal district court.[100]

(3) Correction or Amendment of Records

An individual who wishes to request a correction or amendment of a record pertaining to him which is contained in a system of records maintained by an agency must submit a written request in accordance with the instructions set forth in the system notice for that system of records.[101] The request must include sufficient information to allow the agency to apply standards set forth in the Act.[102] These standards require that agency records contain only information about a person that is relevant and necessary to accomplish an authorized purpose of the agency and that the agency must maintain those records so that their accuracy, relevance, timeliness and completeness are reasonably assured.[103] In making its decision, the agency must follow requirements outlined in the Act.[104]

An agency which receives a request for an amendment or correction of agency records must acknowledge that request within 10 days of receipt. The agency must either promptly make any correction, deletion or addition with regard to any portion of a record which the requester believes is not accurate, relevant, timely or complete, or inform the requester of its refusal to amend the record in accordance with the request. In the latter case, the agency must inform the requester of the reason for the refusal, the procedures whereby an appeal can be sought from the agency head and the title and business address of that official.[105] If the agency is unable to make a determination within 30 days of its receipt of a request for correction or amendment, it must notify the requester of that fact, and state the reasons for the delay, and the approximate date on which a determination will be reached.[106]

If the agency determines that it will grant all or any portion of a request for a correction or amendment, it must:

1. advise the requester of that determination;
2. make the requested correction or amendment; and
3. inform any person or agency outside the USDA to whom the record has been disclosed, and where an accounting of that disclosure is maintained, of the occurrence and substance of the correction or amendment.[107]

If the agency determines not to grant all or any portion of a request it must advise the requester of this fact and state the reasons for the denial. It must also inform the requester of his or her right to appeal the determination to the head of the agency which maintains the system of records, and must describe the appeal procedures, including the title and business address of the official to whom the appeal must be addressed.[108]

After an appeal concerning an initial adverse agency determination on a correction or amendment is received, the agency head must make a final determination within 30 days from the date on which the individual requests the review.[109] The agency head may extend this time period if good cause is shown the agency must notify the requester of the extension and give an estimate of the date on which a final determination will be made. An extension of time should be used only under exceptional circumstances and should not exceed 30 days.

The review of the appeal must be guided by the standards set out in the Act. If the agency head determines not to grant all or any portion of the appeal, he or she must inform the requester:

1. of this determination and the reasons therefore;
2. of the requester's right to file a concise statement of his or her reasons for disagreeing with the agency's decision:
3. of the procedures for filing the statement of disagreement;
4. that such statements of disagreement will be made available to anyone to whom the record is subsequently disclosed;
5. that prior recipients of the disputed record will be provided with a copy of the statement of disagreement; and
6. of the requester's right to seek judicial review of the agency's determination in a federal district court.[110]

The regulations do not permit access to information compiled in reasonable anticipation of a civil action or proceeding.[111]

An individual whose request for a correction or amendment is denied may appeal that denial to the head of the agency to which the request was made.[112] If the appeal is denied, the requester may bring a civil action in federal district court to seek a review of the denial.[113]

C. Equal Access to Justice Act

The Equal Access to Justice Act,[114] ("the Act"), provides for the award of attorney fees and other expenses to eligible individuals and entities who are parties to certain administrative proceedings (called "adversary adjudications") before the USDA. An eligible party may receive an award when it prevails over the USDA unless the position of the agency was substantially justified or special circumstances make an award unjust. The Act applies to most adversary adjudications pending or commenced before the USDA on or after August 5, 1985.[115]

The Act applies to adversary adjudications in which the position of the USDA is presented by an attorney or other representative who enters an appearance and participates in the proceeding.[116] It also applies to appeals of decisions made pursuant to the Contract Disputes Act of 1978 before the Agriculture Board of Contract Appeals.[117] Proceedings to modify, suspend, or revoke licenses are covered if they are otherwise "adversary adjudications."[118]

The proceedings covered are adversary adjudications under the statutory provisions listed below.

Agricultural Marketing Agreement Act of 1937 (7 U.S.C. 608c(15(A))
Animal Quarantine Act (21 U.S.C. 104)
Animal Welfare Act (7 U.S.C. 2149)
Archaeological Resources Protection Act (16 U.S.C. 470)
Beef Research and Information Act (7 U.S.C. 2912)
Capper-Volstead Act (7 U.S.C. 292)
Cotton Research and Promotion Act (7 U.S.C. 2111)
Egg Products Inspection Act (21 U.S.C. 1047)
Egg Research and Consumer Information Act (7 U.S.C. 2713, 2714(b))
Endangered Species Act (16 U.S.C. 1540(a))
Federal Land Policy and Management Act (43 U.S.C. 1766)
Federal Meat Inspection Act (21 U.S.C. 604, 606, 607(e), 608, 671)
Federal Seed Act (7 U.S.C. 1599)
Horse Protection Act (15 U.S.C. 1823(c), 1825)

Packers and Stockyards Act (7 U.S.C. 193, 204, 213, 218c, 221)
Perishable Agricultural Commodities Act (7 U.S.C. 499c(c), 499d(d), 499ff(c), 499h(a), 499h(b), 499h(c), 499h, 499m(a))
Plant Quarantine Act (7 U.S.C. 163)
Potato Research and Promotion Act (7 U.S.C. 2620)
Poultry Products Inspection Act (21 U.S.C. 455, 456, 457(d), 467)
Swine Health Protection Act (7 U.S.C. 3804(b), 3805(a))
U.S. Cotton Standards Act (7 U.S.C. 51b, 53)
U.S. Grain Standards Act (7 U.S.C. 79(g)(3), 85, 86)
U.S. Warehouse Act (7 U.S.C. 246, 253)
Virus-Serum-Toxin Act (21 U.S.C. 156)
Wheat and Wheat Foods Research and Nutrition Education Act (7 U.S.C. 3409).[119]

The failure of the USDA to identify a type of proceeding as an "adversary adjudication" does not preclude the filing of an application by a party who believes the proceeding is covered by the Act; whether the proceeding is covered will then be an issue for resolution in proceedings on the application.[120] If a proceeding includes both matters covered by the Act and matters specifically excluded from coverage, any award made will include only fees and expenses related to covered issues.[121]

(1) Eligibility of applicants

To be eligible for an award of attorney fees and other expenses under the Act the applicant must be a prevailing party to the adversary adjudication for which it seeks an award.[122] The types of eligible applicants are as follows:

(1) an individual with a net worth of not more than $2 million;

(2) the sole owner of an unincorporated business who has a net worth of not more than $7 million including both personal and business interests, and not more than 500 employees;

(3) a charitable or other tax-exempt organization described in section 501(c)(3) of the Internal

Revenue Code with not more than 500 employees;

   (4)   a cooperative association as defined in section 15 (a) of the Agricultural Marketing Act with not more than 500 employees; and

   (5)   any other partnership, corporation, association, unit of local government, or organization with a net worth of not more than $7 million and not more than 500 employees.[123]

The net worth and number of employees of an applicant shall be determined as of the date the proceeding was initiated.[124] The net worth and number of employees of the applicant and all of its affiliates are aggregated to determine eligibility.[125]

The employees of an applicant include all persons who regularly perform services for remuneration for the applicant, under the applicant's direction and control. Part-time employees shall be included on a proportional basis.[126]

(2) Standards for Awards

A prevailing party may receive an award for fees and expenses incurred in connection with a proceeding, or in a significant and discrete substantive portion of the proceeding, unless the position of the Department was substantially justified. In addition to the position taken by the Department in the adversary adjudication, "position of the Department" includes the action or failure to act by the Department upon which the adversary adjudication is based. The burden of proof that an award should not be made to an eligible prevailing applicant because the position of the Department was substantially justified is on the agency counsel.[127] An award will be reduced or denied if the applicant has unduly or unreasonably protracted the proceeding or if special circumstances make the award sought unjust.[128]

Awards will be based on rates customarily charged by persons engaged in the business of acting as attorneys, agents, and expert witnesses, even if the services were made available without charge or at reduced rate to the applicant.[129]

But, no award for the fee of an attorney or agent can ordinarily may exceed $75.00 per hour.[130] However, if warranted by an increase in the cost of living or by special

40

circumstances (such as limited availability of attorneys qualified to handle certain types of proceedings), the USDA may adopt regulations providing that attorney fees may be awarded at a rate higher than $75 per hour in some or all types of proceedings.[131] No award to compensate an expert witness may exceed the highest rate at which the Department pays expert witnesses.[132] However, an award also may include the reasonable expenses of the attorney, agent, or witness as a separate item.[133] The reasonable cost of any study, analysis, engineering report, test, project or similar matter prepared on behalf of a party may also be awarded.[134]

In determining the reasonableness of the fee sought of an attorney, agent, or expert witness, the adjudicative officer is to consider the following:

(1) His or her customary fee for similar services;

(2) The prevailing rate for similar services in the community in which the attorney, agent or witness ordinarily performs services;

(3) The time actually spent in the representation of the applicant; and

(4) The time reasonably spent in light of the difficulty or complexity of the issues in the proceeding.[135]

(3) Information Required From Applicants

An application for an award of fees and expenses under the Act must identify the applicant and the proceeding for which an award is sought. The application must indicate that the applicant has prevailed and identify the position of the USDA that the applicant alleges was not substantially justified and shall briefly state the basis for such allegation. If the applicant is not an individual , the application also must state the number of employees of the applicant and describe briefly the type and purpose of its organization or business.[136]

The application also shall include a statement that the applicant's net worth does not exceed $2 million (if an individual) or $7 million (for all other applicants, including their affiliates). However, an applicant may omit this statement if it attaches a copy of a ruling by the Internal Revenue Service that it qualifies as an organization described in section 501(c)(3) of the Internal Revenue Code or it states that it is a cooperative on which association as defined in section 15(a) of the Agricultural Marketing Act.[137]

An applicant, except a qualified tax-exempt organization or cooperative association, must provide with its application a detailed exhibit showing the net worth of the applicant and any affiliates (as of the date) when the proceeding was initiated.[138] Ordinarily, the net worth exhibit will be included in the public record of the proceeding. However, an applicant that objects to public disclosure of information in any portion of the exhibit and believes there are legal grounds for withholding it from disclosure may submit that portion of the exhibit directly to the adjudicative officer in a sealed envelope labeled "Confidential Financial Information," accompanied by a motion to withhold the information from public disclosure. The motion shall describe the information sought to be withheld and explain, in detail, why it falls within one or more of the specific exemptions from mandatory disclosure under the Freedom of Information Act. If the adjudicative officer finds that the information should not be withheld from disclosure, it shall be placed in the public record of the proceeding. Otherwise, any request to inspect or copy the exhibit shall be disposed of in accordance with the established procedures of this Department under the Freedom of Information Act.[139] The application also may include any other matters that the applicant wishes this Department to consider in determining whether, and in what amount, an award should be made.[140] The application shall be signed by the applicant or an authorized representative. It also must contain a written verification under oath or affirmation under penalty of perjury that the information provided in the application.[141]

The application must be accompanied by full documentation of the fees and expenses, including the cost of any study, analysis, engineering report, test, project, or similar matter for which an award is sought.[142] The documentation shall include an affidavit from any attorney, agent, or expert witness representing or appearing in behalf of the party, stating the actual time expended and the rate at which fees and other expenses were computed and describing the specific services performed.[143] The documentation also shall include a description of any expenses for which reimbursement is sought

42

and a statement of the amounts paid and payable by the applicant or by any other person or entity for the services provided.[144]

An application may be filed whenever the applicant has prevailed in the proceeding or in a significant and discrete substantive portion of the proceeding, but in no case later than 30 days after final disposition of the proceeding by USDA.[145] Final disposition means the date on which a decision or order disposing of the merits of the proceedings or any other complete resolution of the proceeding, such as a settlement or voluntary dismissal, become final and unappealable, both within the Department and to the courts.[146]

(4) Procedures for Considering Applications

Any application for an award must be filed and served on all parties to the proceedings in the same manner as other pleadings in the proceeding except for confidential financial information.[147]

Within 30 days after service of an application, agency counsel may file an answer. If agency counsel fails to timely answer or settle the application, the adjudicative officer, upon a satisfactory showing of entitlement by the applicant, may make an award for the applicant's allowable fees and expenses.[148] If agency counsel and the applicant believe that the issues in the fee applications can be settled they may jointly file a statement of intent to negotiate a settlement. The filing of this statement will extend the time for filing an answer for an additional 30 days, and further extensions amy be granted by the adjudicative officer upon request by agency counsel and the applicant.[149]

The answer must explain in detail any objections to the award requested and identify the facts relief on in support of agency counsel's position. If the answer is based on any alleged facts not already in the record of the proceeding, agency counsel shall include with the answer either supporting affidavits or a request for further proceedings.[150] Within 15 days after service of an answer, the applicant may file a reply. If the reply is based on any alleged facts not already in the record of the proceeding, the applicant shall include with the reply either supporting affidavits or a request for further proceedings.[151]

Ordinarily the determination of an award will be made

on the basis of the written record. However, on request of a party or on his or her own initiative, the adjudicative officer may order further proceedings, such as an informal conference, oral argument, additional written submissions or as to issues other than substantial justification (such as the applicant's eligibility or substantiation of fees and expenses) pertinent discovery or an evidentiary hearing. Whether the position of the Department was substantially justified shall be determined on the basis of the administrative record, as a whole which is made in the adversary adjudication for which fees and other expenses are sought.[152]

The adjudicative officer shall issue an initial decision on the application as expeditiously as possible after completion of proceedings on the application. Whenever possible, the decision shall be made by the same administrative judge or panel that decided the matter for which fees are sought. The decision must include written findings and conclusions on the applicant's eligibility and status as a prevailing party, and an explanation of the reasons for any difference between the amount requested and the amount awarded.[153]

Except with respect to Board of Contract Appeals, either the applicant or agency counsel may seek review of the initial decision on the fee application. If neither the applicant nor agency counsel seeks review, the initial decision on the fee application shall become a final decision of the Department 35 days after it is served upon the applicant.[154]

Judicial review of final agency decisions on awards may be sought.[155]

An applicant seeking payment of an award shall submit to the head of the agency administering the statute involved in the proceeding a copy of the final decision of the Department granting the award, accompanied by a statement that the applicant will not seek review of the decision in the United States courts. The agency is to pay the amount awarded to the applicant within 60 days, unless judicial review of the award or of the underlying decision of the adversary adjudication has been sought by the applicant or any other party to the proceeding.[156]

FOOTNOTES

1. 5 U.S.C. § 551 et seq.

2. 44 U.S.C. § 1507.

3. 44 U.S.C. § 1510.

4. 5 U.S.C. § 551 et seq.

5. 5 U.S.C. § 553.

6. 5 U.S.C. § 553(b).

7. 5 U.S.C. § 553(d).

8. 5 U.S.C. § 553 (b)(B).

9. 5 U.S.C. § 553(d)(3).

10. 7 C.F.R. § 1.27.

11. See American Federation of Government Employees-AFL-CIO v. Block, 655 F.2d 1153 (1981).

12. 5 U.S.C. § 553(c).

13. See Community Nutrition Institute v. Block, 749 F.2d 503 (1984).

14. 5 U.S.C. § 554-558.

15. 5 U.S.C. § 554, 556-557.

16. 5 U.S.C. § 557.

17. 7 C.F.R. § 1.131(a).

18. 7 C.F.R. § 1.131(b).

19. 7 C.F.R. § 1.133 (a).

20. 7 C.F.R. § 1.133 (a) (2).

21. 7 C.F.R. § 1.133(3).

22. 7 C.F.R. § 1.133(3).

23. 7 C.F.R. § 1.133 (a) (4).

24. 7 C.F.R. § 1.133 (b) (2).

25. 7 C.F.R. § 1.135.

26. 7 C.F.R. § 1.136 (c).

27. 7 C.F.R. § 1.136 (c).

28. 7 C.F.R. § 1.141(a).

29. 7 C.F.R. § 1.141(a).

30. 7 C.F.R. § 1.139.

31. 7 C.F.R. § 1.139.

32. 7 C.F.R. § 1.141 (a).

33. 7 C.F.R. 1.141(h).

34. 7 C.F.R. § 1.141(e).

35. 7 C.F.R. § 1.140 (a).

36. 7 C.F.R. § 1.148.

37. 7 C.F.R. § 1.149.

38. 7 C.F.R. § 1.142 (b).

39. 7 C.F.R. § 1.142 (c).

40. 7 C.F.R. § 1.142 (c).

41. 7 C.F.R. § 1.145(a); See 7 C.F.R. § 2.35(a) for delegation of appeal authority to the Judicial Officer.

42. 7 C.F.R. § 1.139.

43. 7 C.F.R. § 1.145 (b).

44. 7 C.F.R. § 1.145 (d).

45. 7 C.F.R. § 1.141(a).

46. 7 C.F.R. § 1.145 (h).

47. 7 C.F.R. § 1.145 (e).

48. 7 C.F.R. § 1.146 (a) (2).

49. 7 C.F.R. § 1.146 (a) (2).

50. 7 C.F.R. § 1.146 (a) (3).

51. 7 C.F.R. § 1.146(b).

52. 5 U.S.C. § 704.

53. 5 U.S.C. § 701.

54. 104 S. Ct. 2450 (1984).

55. 104 S. Ct. at 2454.

56. 203 F. Supp. 423 (1962).

57. 203 F. Supp. at 428.

58. 5 U.S.C. § 706.

59. 588 F. Supp. 871 (N.D. Tex. 1984).

60. 665 F. Supp. 6 (D.D.C. 1987).

61. 611 F. Supp. 351 (D. Neb. 1984); aff'd 765 F.2d 121 (8th Cir. 1985).

62. 5 U.S.C. § 552.

63. 5 U.S.C. § 552a.

64. 5 U.S.C. § 504.

65. 5 U.S.C. § 552.

66. 5 U.S.C. § 552(a)(1).

67. 5 U.S.C. § 552 (a)(2)(B).

68. 7 C.F.R. § 1.1.

69. See, 5 U.S.C. § 552(b); 7 C.F.R. § 1.17 (a).

70. 7 C.F.R. § 1.17 (b).

71. 7 C.F.R. § 1.5(a); 5 U.S.C. § 552(a)(2).

72. 7 C.F.R. § 1.5(b).

73. 7 C.F.R. § 1.6(a).

74. 7 C.F.R. § 1.6 (b).

75. 7 C.F.R. § 1.6 (d).

76. 7 C.F.R. § 1.8(f).

77. 7 C.F.R. § 370.

78. 7 C.F.R. Pt. 1, Sbpt. A, App. A.

79. 7 C.F.R. § 1.2 (a); 5 U.S.C. § 552(a)(6)(B).

80. 7 C.F.R. § 1.15.

81. 7 C.F.R. § 1.8(a).

82. 7 C.F.R. § 1.8(a).

83. 7 C.F.R. § 1.8(b).

84. 7 C.F.R. § 1.8(c).

85. 7 C.F.R. § 1.6(e).

86. 7 C.F.R. § 1.8(d).

87. 5 U.S.C. § 552(b).

88. 5 U.S.C. § 552a.

89. 7 C.F.R. § 1.119.

90. 7 C.F.R. § 1.112 (a).

91. 7 C.F.R. § 1.112(b).

92. 7 C.F.R. § 1.112(c).

93. 7 C.F.R. § 1.113 (b).

94. 7 C.F.R. § 1.113(d).

95. 7 C.F.R. § 1.113(e).

96. 7 C.F.R. § 1.114 (a).

97. 7 C.F.R. § 114 (b).

98. 7 C.F.R. § 1.114(c).

99. 7 C.F.R. § 1.114 (d).

100. 7 C.F.R. 1.114 (e).

101. 7 C.F.R. § 1.116 (a).

102. 7 C.F.R. § 1.116(b); 5 U.S.C. § 552a (e)(1) and (5).

103. 5 U.S.C. § 552a (e)(1) and (5).

104. 7 C.F.R. § 1.117(c); 5 U.S.C. § 552a (e)(1) and (5).

105. 7 C.F.R. § 1.117 (a).

106. 7 C.F.R. § 1.117(b).

107. 7 C.F.R. § 1.117(d).

108. 7 C.F.R. § 1.117(e).

109. 7 C.F.R. § 1.118(b).

110. 7 C.F.R. § 1.114.

111. 7 C.F.R. § 1.114(f).

112. 7 C.F.R. 1.116(c).

113. 7 C.F.R. § 1.116(d).

114. 5 U.S.C. § 504.

115. 7 C.F.R. § 1.182. The Act also applies to any adversary adjudication commenced on or after October 1, 1984, and disposed of finally before August 5, 1985, provided that an application for fees and expenses was filed with the agency within 30 days after August 5, 1985, and to any adversary adjudication pending on or commenced on or after October 1, 1981, in which an application for fees and other expenses was timely filed and was dismissed for lack of jurisdiction.

116. 7 C.F.R. § 1.183.

117. See, 41 U.S.C. § 605 and 607. The Act also applies to any hearing conducted under Chapter 38, Title 31 of the United States Code. 7 C.F.R. § 1.183(a).

118. 7 C.F.R. § 1.183(a)(2).

119. 7 C.F.R. § 1.183(a)(2).

120. 7 C.F.R. § 1.183(b).

121. 7 C.F.R. § 1.183 (c).

122. See, 5 U.S.C. § 551(3) for definition of "party". 7 C.F.R. § 1.184(a).

123. 7 C.F.R. § 1.184(b).

124. 7 C.F.R. § 1.184(c).

125. 7 C.F.R. § 1.184(f).

126. 7 C.F.R. § 1.184(e).

127. 7 C.F.R. § 1.185 (a).

128. 7 C.F.R. § 1.185(b).

129. 7 C.F.R. § 1.186(a).

130. 7 C.F.R. § 1.186(b).

131. 7 C.F.R. § 1.187.

132. 7 C.F.R. § 1.186(b). See, 7 C.F.R. § 1.150 for USDA expert witness fees.

133. 7 C.F.R. § 1.186(b).

134. 7 C.F.R. § 1.186(d).

135. 7 C.F.R. § 1.186(c).

136. 7 C.F.R. § 1.190(a).

137. 7 C.F.R. § 1.190(b).

138. 7 C.F.R. § 1.191(a).

139. 7 C.F.R. § 1.191(b).

140. 7 C.F.R. § 1.190(d).

141. 7 C.F.R. § 1.190(e).

142. 7 C.F.R. § 1.192(a).

143. 7 C.F.R. § 1.192(b).

144. 7 C.F.R. § 1.192(c).

145. 7 C.F.R. § 1.193(a).

146. 7 C.F.R. § 1.193(b).

147. 7 C.F.R. § 1.194.

148. 7 C.F.R. § 1.195(a).

149. 7 C.F.R. § 1.195(b). A proposed settlement by agency counsel and the applicant may be filed with the application itself. 7 C.F.R. § 1.198.

150. 7 C.F.R. § 1.195(c).

151. 7 C.F.R. § 1.196.

152. 7 C.F.R. § 1.199(a).

153. 7 C.F.R. § 1.200.

154. 7 C.F.R. § 1.201(a).

155. 7 C.F.R. § 1.202; 5 U.S.C. § 504(c)(2).

156. 7 C.F.R. § 1.203.

CHAPTER 3

FARM CREDIT

I.   Introduction

The American farmer has long been dependent upon credit to conduct or expand business operations. The availability of adequate credit is often a critical problem and, traditionally, farmers have had difficulty securing needed credit. In part, this has been because certain types of credit have been less available in rural areas than in urban areas. Furthermore, because much of the land actually farmed is rented rather than owned, a farmer may not have adequate collateral to secure the amount of financing needed. Finally, farmers have sometimes been at a disadvantage in dealing with creditors because of their lack of financial sophistication. There is a perceived unequal relationship between farm debtors and creditors which allegedly may cause some unfairness in the relationship.

In this chapter several of the important financial issues with which farmers must deal are discussed. This chapter focuses on the structuring of short and long term credit needs. It will not focus in detail on the problems of financial distress or on what happens when the debtor-creditor relationship irretrievably breaks down. Those questions are addressed in Chapter 5. This chapter also does not provide a detailed analysis of the myriad of problems which can arise when a farmer transacts business with the Farmers Home Administration (FmHA). Those issues are discussed in Chapter 4. Furthermore, no attempt will be made here to deal with the manifold tax issues that play an integral part of any farm financing arrangement.

A.   The Nature of the Debtor-Creditor Relationship

When a person borrows money, a relationship is created with the lender which is dual in nature. On the one hand, the parties may be bound personally to each other by promises made in the context of the loan agreement. These promises are enforceable under the principles of contract law. On the other hand, the creditor may receive a proprietary interest in some (or all) of the debtor's property. These rights and obligations are enforceable according to principles of property law. When the creditor has an interest in the debtor's personal property (such as farm machinery), the legal rules to be applied to the transaction will often be different from those applied in the situation where the creditor's interest is in real property (such as farmland). The presence of more than one set of rules in the debtor-creditor relationship considerably complicates that relationship. Moreover, it is sometimes difficult to determine which set of rules should be applied in a given situation.

The fact that two kinds of relationships exist, one contractual and one proprietary, also creates enforcement options for creditors. For example, when a purchase money mortgage is secured by real estate, but is not repaid when due, the creditor may elect to seek a contractual remedy, based upon promises made in the promissory note, or may utilize the remedy of enforcing the lien against the property itself, or both.[1]

B. The Nature of the Debtor-Creditor Relationship: Fiduciary and Other Duties

In recent years, it has been suggested that the relationship between a lender and a borrower creates a fiduciary relationship between them. It is perhaps hoped that if such a relationship exists, the farm debtor will be given defenses or protection which might mitigate the harsh results of foreclosure, repossession or liquidation.

Although the origins of the concept of fiduciary status are obscure, it is clear that the role a fiduciary is expected to play in a relationship is one of utmost care and fairness toward the other party. Self dealing is inimical to such a relationship. A variety of legal theories have been offered in support of the concept. Among the most widely held, for example, is the "unjust enrichment" theory which argues that, based on ethical considerations, a fiduciary relationship should be recognized when one person obtains property or another advantage which justice dictates should belong to another.[2] In contrast, the "commercial utility" theory requires that a fiduciary relationship be imposed in any legal relationship where it is necessary to hold a person or class of persons to a higher-than-average standard of ethics or care in order to protect the good faith expectations of the parties or to protect the integrity of a commercial enterprise.[3] Alternatively, the so-called "reliance theory" predicates fiduciary relationships upon the presence of trust or confidence placed by one person in another.[4] The "unequal relationship" theory imposes fiduciary duties on the basis of the unequal relationship (either as a matter of fact or law) between the parties which may result in the dominion of one by the other.[5] The "contractual" theory of fiduciary relationships proposes that such a relationship ought to exist whenever one person relies upon or trusts another and that trust or reliance has been accepted by that other person.[6] The "power and discretion" theory argues that a fiduciary relationship is created whenever one person has either the power to change the legal position of another or the discretion to exercise that power.[7] Combinations of the above principles have been suggested in an attempt to formulate a modern rationale for the fiduciary concept.[8]

Despite the above-stated rationale for finding a fiduciary relationship, courts have fairly consistently held that the mere presence of a debtor-creditor relationship, without more, does not create a fiduciary relationship. As a result, it becomes critical to identify the additional factors which must be present in the debtor-creditor relationship to justify the finding of a fiduciary status on the part of the lender. In the case of DePhillips v. Mortgage Associates, Inc.[9] the court observed that

> A fiduciary or confidential relationship exists where by reason of friendship, agency, business association and experience, trust and confidence are reposed by one person in another, who as a result, gains an influence and superiority over the other. The relationship of mortgagor and mortgagee does not of itself show the existence of confidential or fiduciary relationship. Where a fiduciary relationship does not exist as a matter of law, the relationship must be proved by clear and convincing evidence. (citations omitted and emphasis added)[10]

Nevertheless, at least one court has suggested that the relationship may be implied on the basis of the surrounding facts and circumstances.[11] Another court has held that the relationship need not be a formal one, but that the parties must understand that a special trust or confidence has been created between them.[12] Recent case law from a variety of jurisdictions has more precisely identified the most important factors involved in the determination. In <u>A. Gay Jenson Farms Co. v. Cargill, Inc.</u>,[13] for example, the court focused on the presence of creditor control over the farming operation itself. Although no one factor was deemed dispositive, the court paid particular attention to acts performed or decisions made by the bank that would normally be made by the debtor or the party actually in control of the operation. This included such matters as management decisions, hiring decisions, control over expenditures, and other operational decisions. The presence of restrictive covenants in the debt instruments, which involved restrictions on management, personnel or production, were also considered important.[14]

In several cases, the role of the creditor as a purchaser from, or seller to, the debtor has been explored in ways which suggest that total economic dependence by the debtor on the creditor is also a relevant factor.[15] Similarly, the absence of good faith in dealings governed by contract has been considered an important factor,[16] as well as the presence of oral promises[17] and customary dealings between the parties.[18] The primary message from the case law, taken as a whole, is that it is very difficult to establish the existence of a fiduciary duty toward the debtor on the part of the lender. Clearly, that relationship will not result from the mere status of the parties as debtor and creditor. This, of course, does not mean that creditors owe no duties to debtors beyond those actually contained in the particular agreement between the parties. For example, negligence may be the basis for recovery against creditors.[19] Likewise, the theory of economic duress has prevailed in at least one case.[20]

II.   General Sources of Credit

In some respects, it is more difficult for a farmer to obtain the credit needed to acquire and operate a farm than for a person to obtain a credit needed to establish a non-farm business. For one thing, lenders generally perceive that there are greater risks in farming than in other business enterprises. Moreover, it has been difficult to obtain outside capital investment in agriculture -- due in part to the fact that agricultural enterprises are not allowed to be operated as corporations in some states. As a result, operating capital for a farm will usually come from the capital contributions of the farmer, from intermediate and short term credit arrangements (usually chattel mortgages or security agreements) and from long term mortgages on the land. In some cases, equity financing from investors and financing leases may be available, but these arrangements are not nearly as common as in the non-farm sector.

A. Federal Involvement

To enhance the availability of credit in rural areas, the Federal government created the Farm Credit Administration, which is an independent agency in the executive branch of government which oversees the federal Farm Credit System. The Federal government also established the Farmers Home Administration within the United States Department of Agriculture. This agency acts as a lender of last resort for farmers who have been unable to secure credit from any other source. Other important sources of credit have included commercial banks, insurance companies, and other individuals or retail business entities.

1. Federal Farm Credit System

In an effort to bolster the availability of credit in rural areas, the federal government adopted the Farm Loan Act of 1916. This Act was designed to create, with federal capitalization, a permanent and dependable source of borrowed capital at reasonable rates and on terms which are suited to the needs of the agricultural sector. Under this Act, federal land banks were established and given the authority to make long term loans secured by mortgages on real estate. It eventually became apparent that other types of credit were needed. This resulted in the creation of Federal Intermediate Credit Banks. In 1933, Congress authorized the creation of Production Credit Associations to meet the short term credit needs of agricultural producers, and Banks for Cooperatives to meet the agricultural credit needs of agricultural cooperatives. These units comprise the federal Farm Credit System. They were initially capitalized by the federal government. By 1968, all of these institutions had repaid the "seed money" and had become completely owned by their borrowers. Nevertheless, they are still federally supervised under the auspices of the Farm Credit Administration, an independent agency within the executive branch of the Federal government. It should be noted that while there is some federal supervision of these credit institutions, most of the lending practices, as well as the debtor-creditor relationship itself, are subject to state law.

Historically, the Federal Land Banks, through Land Bank Associations, have serviced the long term credit needs of farmers while the Intermediate Credit Banks and Production Credit Associations have handled farmers' short term financial needs. In recent years, declining land values and other problems in the farm economy have made this system less viable. As a result, restructuring has taken place within the Farm Credit System. Both the Farm Credit Amendments Act of 1985[21] and the Agricultural Credit Act of 1987[22] have imposed stricter regulations in order to promote greater efficiency in operation of the system.

2. Farmers Home Administration

The Farmers Home Administration (FmHA) is an agency within the USDA which was principally established to provide for the credit needs of farmers who could not find adequate credit elsewhere at reasonable rates or on reasonable terms. FmHA administers a wide variety of loan programs, including operating loans and farm ownership loans. Farm ownership and farm operating loans are of two types: either insured (direct) loans or guaranteed loans. In the former case, FmHA loans federal money directly to qualified borrowers. In the latter case, a private source of credit actually supplies the money and FmHA guarantees repayment of up to 90% of the amount of the loan. In recent years, there has been a distinct policy trend in the direction of promoting the use of guaranteed loans. However, it is only with respect to the insured or direct loans that FmHA takes a security interest in the farmer's property, and is therefore in a position to take foreclosure action against the farmer-borrower upon default.

FmHA now requires the adoption of a Soil Conservation Service approved farm conservation plan as a condition for loan approval. Under the provisions of the Food Security Act of 1985,[23] farmers have until 1990 to develop and until 1995 to implement the necessary conservation plans relating to farming on highly erodible farm acreage. Chapter 4 discusses issues related to FmHA in detail.

C. ASCS Farm Storage Facility Loan Program
1. General Provisions

The Commodity Credit Corporation (the "CCC") provides a loan program by which farmers can finance the purchase of farm storage facilities or the remodeling of existing storage facilities.[24] The availability of this program may vary. It may be suspended at any time except in areas where the Secretary has determined that there is a deficiency of storage for grain.

The Cotton, Grain and Rice Support Division of the Agricultural Stabilization and Conservation Service (the "ASCS") administers this program through the ASCS State and County committees.[25] The Deputy Administrator of ASCS State and County Operations is responsible for immediate program supervision. He or she is authorized to make decisions on matters involving individual loans which would otherwise require the approval of the CCC Executive Vice-President.[26]

Program forms are distributed by the ASCS county offices.[27] Interested persons should refer to the procedures and forms which have been adopted by each state ASCS committee to assure proper compliance with relevant state law.[28]

2. Eligible Borrowers

According to the regulations, an "eligible borrower" is any person who is either a landowner, landlord, tenant or sharecropper, and who also:

1. produces one or more of the following commodities, which are designated as "facility loan commodities": corn, oats, barley, sorghum, wheat, and/or rice;
2. needs farm facilities for the storage of one or more

of those commodities, and

3.   participates in an acreage reduction program which is in effect for one of the facility loan commodities.[29]

The term "person" means any individual or individuals who are competent to enter into a binding contract. This may include a partnership, firm, joint stock company, corporation, association, trust, estate, or other legal entity, or a state, political subdivision of a state, or any agency thereof.[30]

3. Eligible Storage Facilities

Loans are only authorized for the purchase and installation of eligible storage facilities.[31] Loans are not available to provide storage for commercial use or for storing commodities which the borrower intends to purchase or to store for others. Eligible storage facilities may include the following:

(1) New or newly constructed conventional-type cribs, bins or flat structures designed and engineered for grain storage;

(2) Flat storage structures designed and engineered for multipurpose use which are adapted or modified for use as grain storage. These structures qualify on the condition that, if only a portion of the structure is for use as grain storage, the area or space used for grain storage must be isolated or closed off from other use areas and only the pro rata costs of the portion of space used for grain storage will be included in determining the amount of the loan;

(3) Oxygen-limiting and other upright silo-type structures designed for wet storage; and

(4) Used structures if the structure was either purchased from the CCC or sold by the CCC pursuant to the provisions of a security agreement.

4. Term of Loan

The maximum term of the loan is five years from the date of execution of the promissory note and security agreement.[32] The term of an individual loan, however, may be extended and reextended for terms of not to exceed one year each if the approving State or county committee determines in writing that the borrower is unable to meet the current payment when due because of conditions beyond the borrower's control.

5. Security for Loan

In all States except Louisiana loans must be secured by a promissory note and a security agreement which covers the farm storage facility.[33] The promissory note and security agreement must grant the CCC a security interest in the collateral and must constitute the sole security interest in that collateral except for prior liens on the underlying realty which by operation of law attach to the collateral if it is a fixture.[34] If any such prior lien on the realty will attach to the collateral, the CCC may require that a subordination agreement or a disclaimer be obtained in writing from each person, other than the borrower, who has any interest in the real estate on which the collateral is to be located.

In Louisiana all loans must be secured by a chattel mortgage covering the farm storage facility.[35] This mortgage must be filed or recorded as required by state law and must constitute the sole security interest in the collateral, except for prior liens on the underlying realty which by operation of law attach to the collateral if it is a fixture. If any such prior lien on the realty will attach to the collateral, the CCC may require that a severance agreement be obtained from each person, other than the borrower, who has any interest in the real estate on which the collateral is to be located.[36]

A lien on real estate is required for any loan, regardless of the loan amount, if the approving committee determines that additional security is needed to protect the CCC's interest.[37]

6. Amount of Loan

The amount of any farm facility loan, when added to the outstanding balance of any facility loan, must not create an aggregate outstanding balance in excess of $25,000, and must not exceed the smaller of:

(1) 70 percent of the net cost of the applicant's needed storage, or

(2) The prorated cost of the applicant's storage which is needed and suitable for the storage of the applicable commodities when a storage structure has a larger capacity than the applicant's needed capacity.[38]

7. Interest and Late Charges

Loans made under this program bear interest at the rate set forth in a notice published in the FEDERAL REGISTER.[39] If a loan installment is not paid when it is due and payable, a late payment charge will be applied against the delinquent debt.

8. Forms

The following forms must be used in connection with the Farm Facility Loan Program: CCC-185, Loan Application and Approval; CCC-186, Promissory Note and Security Agreement; CCC-187, Disbursement, Repayment and Inspection Record; CCC-298, Assumption Agreement; CCC-299, Certificate of Title; CCC-308, Supplier's Agreement; CCC-401, Bill of Sale; CCC-500, Repayment Record. These forms, and any other form required by State law, may be obtained in the ASCS State and County offices.[40]

III. Intermediate and Short-Term Financing

Article 9 of the Uniform Commercial Code (U.C.C.)[41] applies to any transaction which is intended to create a security interest in personal property or fixtures. As a result, when a farmer borrows money to purchase equipment and uses livestock or crops as security for the loan, the relationship will be regulated by Article 9.

The 1962 Official Text of the Uniform Commercial Code was prepared by the American Law Institute and the National Conference of Commissioners on Uniform State Laws. With a few exceptions, most states enacted the Uniform Commercial Code (U.C.C.) from the 1962 Official Text. Several amendments to the 1962 Official Text of the U.C.C. were made by the National Conference of Commissioners on Uniform State Laws. These amendments updated and streamlined the original Code, and have been adopted by many states in the form of the 1972 Official Text of the U.C.C.

A. Kinds of Collateral

The specific rights possessed by the holder of an Article 9 security interest are initially determined by the particular kind of collateral involved. The method by which the interest is perfected may vary with the classification. Collateral is classified as either:

Consumer goods - if the purchase or primary use of the property is for personal, family or household purposes;

Equipment - if the purchase or primary use is for business purposes (including farming);

Farm products - if the goods are crops or livestock or supplies used or produced in farming operations, or are the products of crops or livestock in their unmanufactured state and are in the possession of the debtor engaged in farming; or

Inventory - if the goods are held for sale or lease or are to be furnished under contracts of service, or are raw materials, work in progress or materials used or consumed in a business.[42]

Equipment, farm products and inventory are mutually exclusive categories. In other words, if goods qualify for one category they cannot be considered to fall within another category.

Virtually all personal property in the possession of the farmer-debtor which is used or produced in the farming operation will be classified as either "farm products" or "equipment". The definition of farm products is more comprehensive than that of equipment. Any personal property in a farmer's possession which does not meet the test of "farm products" will generally be classified as equipment. However, one common exception to this rule is where goods undergo a manufacturing process while in the hands of a farmer. When this occurs, the goods become inventory if they are held for sale. In most cases the proper classification of the collateral is readily apparent. However, when doubt exists, any action which is taken to perfect a security interest should be that which is appropriate for all possible classifications of goods involved. The determination as to the type of goods covered by a security agreement becomes important when questions arise concerning priority, place of filing and rights of purchasers of goods from debtors.

For example, a problem with the classification of the collateral arose in the case of Peoples State Bank of Cherryvale v. Clayton.[43] The collateral involved was dairy equipment installed in a barn. The sole issue on appeal was whether the collateral should be classified as "equipment" or "fixtures". The Uniform Commercial Code (U.C.C.) definition of fixtures provides:

> Goods are "fixtures" when affixing them to real estate so associates them with the real estate that, in the absence of any agreement or understanding with his vendor as to the goods, a purchaser of the real estate with knowledge of interests of others of record, or in possession, would reasonably consider the goods to have been purchased as part of the real estate.[44]

The court found the collateral to be equipment and not fixtures. In making that determination a three-pronged test to define fixtures was applied. This test focuses on: 1) how the goods are attached and how easily they may be removed, 2) the intent of the parties involved, and 3) how the goods are adapted to the use of the land. This test was found to be consistent with the U.C.C. However, a fourth requirement added by the statute is whether the average buyer would expect the goods to be included in the purchase of the land. In this case the court reasoned that since the equipment was easily removable, the barn could be used after its removal. Furthermore, there was no agreement that any improvements to the barn would remain after the sale. Since the bank had properly perfected the security interest in property as equipment, the bank's interest was protected.

Other primary differences in the rights which result from collateral classifications have been diminished by two relatively recent developments. Generally, security interests may be perfected by filing the financing statement. Interests in farm products, fixtures and consumer goods were perfected by filing locally with the Register of Deeds or a similar official of the county of the debtor's residence. Other places designated for filing are where the collateral is physically located, or if the interest involves growing crops, where the land on which they are growing or to be grown is located.[45] Interests in inventory and equipment are filed centrally with the Secretary of State or similar official. Some states have changed the filing requirements to provide that financing statements for farm products must also be filed centrally with the Secretary of State.

Under the U.C.C. the security interest of the lender attached to inventory, equipment and consumer goods may not apply to a purchaser in the ordinary course of business.[46] As a result, a buyer of any goods other than farm products could take those goods free and clear of the security interest. Under the U.C.C. rule the security interest of the lender remains applicable to farm products even if sold to a buyer in the ordinary course of business. However, Section 1324 of the Food and Security Act of 1985[47] statutorily preempted state law in regard to the farm products exception. Under the Federal statute, unless the buyer is notified in writing of the outstanding security interest within one year prior to the sale, or unless the state has an approved central filing system in which the buyer may participate, the lender's security interest may not apply to farm products after the sale. Chapter 11 contains an extensive discussion of this provision.

B. Creation of the Security Interest

The creditor's interest in collateral arises when it "attaches" to the property. Before a security interest can "attach" to the collateral, certain criteria must be met. The debtor has to have "rights in the collateral"[48] and the secured party must have given value in exchange for the interest.[49] There must be a valid agreement between the parties. This agreement is usually in the form of a security agreement. It represents the contract which creates the creditor's rights in the debtor's property. Another document, the financing statement, is a memorandum of the security agreement which is filed to give third parties "notice" of the transaction. The security agreement must be in writing and signed by the debtor, unless the creditor has possession of the collateral. Second, the collateral must be described in the financing statement with reasonable certainty. U.C.C. 9-110 provides:

> A statement of collateral in a financing statement is adequate if it generally identifies goods by one or more of the classifications listed in U.C.C. 9-109, or generally identifies other collateral by one or more of the following classifications: fixtures, documents, instruments, general intangibles, chattel paper or accounts.[50]

67

As a result, the security agreement will normally list each item of collateral specifically. The financing statement should use one or more of the classifications designated in the statute.

An additional description requirement is imposed when the collateral consists of growing crops. In this case, the financing statement must also include a description of the real estate on which the crops are growing. A legal description should be used if possible. Where this is not possible, the description should designate a particular parcel of land by either its location or by its common name, e.g. "Jones Farms", should identify the county in which it is located, and should specify the distance and direction to the nearest town from which the land may readily be located.

Most of the litigation over collateral description has focused on the sufficiency of the description of real estate once it is incorporated into the security agreement or financing statement. A leading case which held that a description used in a financing statement was insufficient as a matter of law is Chanute Grain Production Credit Assoc. v. Weir Grain Supply, Inc.[51] The court ruled that a financing statement which had described the crops and land on which the crops were grown as "annual perennial crops of whatever kind and description which are now growing or are hereafter planted, grown, and produced on land owned or leased by the debtor in Cherokee County, Kansas," was an insufficient description under the Kansas Uniform Commercial Code. The court conceded that U.C.C. 9-402 and U.C.C. 9-110 require something less than a legal description of land to apprise purchasers and creditors of the existence of a security interest in growing crops. However, a financing statement which describes the realty as "land owned or leased by the debtor in Cherokee County, Kansas," is insufficient to perfect a security interest in those crops. The court decided that the general description used by the secured party would impose too great a burden on other purchasers and creditors because they would be forced to make a detailed search of land records to determine all lands owned or leased by the debtor.

Once a security agreement is properly created, several important consequences result. First, the security interest is deemed to "attach" to the collateral. This, in effect, gives the creditor an "interest" in the property and makes the property subject to a lien in favor of the creditor. This "interest" or lien can be enforced by the creditor in order to repossess the property if the debtor defaults on the loan agreement. Second, the arrangement is binding on the debtor regardless of whether it is "perfected".[52] In other words, recording is not necessary for the security agreement to be valid as between the parties to the agreement. Third, if the security interest has been properly created, it may then be "perfected" by proper filing, in which case it becomes effective against most third parties.[53] Fourth, the creditor is entitled to claim an interest in the "proceeds" of the collateral. This includes whatever is received by the debtor from the sale, exchange, collection or other disposition of the collateral. U.C.C. Section 9-203(3) states:

Unless otherwise agreed, a security agreement gives the secured party rights to proceeds provided by 9-306.[54]

U.C.C. Section 9-306(1) provides that:

"Proceeds" includes whatever is received upon the sale, exchange, collection or other disposition of collateral or proceeds.[55]

A variety of problems have arisen with respect to what may be considered proceeds. With respect to warehouse receipts, the generally accepted view appears to be that the "exchange" of grain for a warehouse receipt is not the kind of exchange contemplated under the language of U.C.C. § 9-306. This is because the farmer retains certain rights in the crop, even though it is in the possession of the warehousemen. On the other hand, the attachment of the security interest to the warehouse receipt may occur if the lender has claimed an interest in documents of title as part of the collateral description.

At least one court has held that payments of insurance funds from crop casualty insurance policies are not "proceeds".[56] This suggests that it is vitally important that the creditor provide specific language in the security agreement which identifies those payments as being subject to the security agreement. One recommended course of action is to name the secured party as beneficiary to any policy, and require actual delivery of the policy into the secured party's possession.

Similar questions may arise as to whether federal farm program payments are valid "proceeds" under the U.C.C.[57] ASCS, the agency which administers the price and income support program, has specific requirements for the creation of security interests in payments issued under those programs. Any effort to create a security interest must be closely coordinated to comply with both state law and agency regulations.[58] As in most "proceeds" situations, obviously the best credit approach is to prevent a problem from occurring by placing a detailed description of the collateral in the security agreement.

The transformation of crops into other forms of farm products poses difficult problems. This is the case, for example, where the crops are used as feed for livestock or as seed for subsequent crops. In First National Bank v. Bostron and Colorado High Plains Credit Corp.,[59] the court concluded that grain consumed by cattle was not traceable to the livestock under U.C.C. Section 9-315, but rather that the collateral, "once eaten . . . not only loses its identity, but in essence it ceases to exist and thus does not become part of the mass in the sense that the Code (under section 9-315) uses the phrase." Where the collateral changes form to such a degree that it no longer exists, its new form may not necessarily be considered "proceeds".

Another problem sometimes arises in the creation of security interests where the collateral includes after acquired property. U.C.C. Section 9-204 provides:

1. Except as provided in subsection (2), a security agreement may provide that any or all obligations covered by the security agreement are to be secured by after-acquired collateral.

   . . .

3. Obligations covered by a security agreement may include future advances or other value whether or not the advances or value are given pursuant to commitment.[60]

The intent of the debtor to grant a security interest in after-acquired property should be determined by the specific language in the security agreement. The Official Comment to the U.C.C. states:

1. Subsection (1) makes clear that a security interest arising by virtue of an after-acquired property clause has equal status with a security interest in collateral in which the debtor has rights at the time value is given under the security agreement. That is to say: the security interest in after-acquired property is not merely an equitable interest; no further action by the secured party -- such as the taking of a supplemental agreement covering the new collateral -- is required.[61]

C. Perfection

As noted above, the attachment of the security interest to the collateral gives remedies to the creditor in the event of the debtor's default. Perfection of the security interest, on the other hand, serves to protect the creditor from competing claims against the debtor by third parties[62] and assists in determining the relative priority of competing creditor claims to the collateral. Perfection is generally achieved in one of three ways: by possession of the collateral, automatically by operation of law, or by filing a financing statement in the appropriate record.

Possession is the means of perfection which is required where the collateral is money, accounts or general intangibles. For negotiable documents of title, such as negotiable warehouse receipts, or for letters of credit, goods and chattel paper, perfection may be achieved either by possession or by filing.[63]

Perfection occurs by operation of law when collateral covered by a perfected security agreement is sold. The security interest automatically applies to the proceeds for a limited period of time. The automatic perfection of the proceeds ceases in 10 days for most collateral, and in 21 days for instruments or negotiable documents, unless specific steps are or have been taken by the creditor to perfect the interest in the proceeds.[64]

Filing is the most common way to perfect a security interest. This method requires the filing of a financing statement which has been signed by the debtor, and which contains the addresses of both the debtor and creditor and a description of the collateral. The security agreement, which creates the security interest between the parties, is not required to be filed. It is common practice to incorporate the security agreement by reference into the financing statement, or to use one document which serves as both a security agreement and a financing statement. In the latter case the security agreement is a part of the document which is filed.

The location for filing the financing statement will vary with the type of collateral. If the goods are consumer goods, the proper place to file is with the county Register of Deeds, or at a similar office in the County of the debtor's residence. If the debtor is a nonresident, the filing should be in the office of the Register of Deeds or a similar office in the county where the collateral is located. For all other types of collateral, filing is done centrally with the Secretary of State.[65] Perfection by filing lasts five years from the date of filing. This period may be extended if a confirmation statement is filed before the interest lapses.

As a general rule, third parties are bound by a properly perfected security agreement. This means that the creditor may pursue the collateral, or its proceeds, into the hands of third parties. However, there are important exceptions to this rule. First, under U.C.C. Section 9-306(2), a purchaser of the collateral is protected from prior perfected security interests when "the disposition was authorized by the secured party in the security agreement or otherwise . . . ." The language that has most often been subject of litigation is "or otherwise". The clearest line of cases favoring the purchaser focus mainly on the past actions of the secured party in similar situations.[66] In many instances, U.C.C. Sections 9-306 and U.C.C. 1-205 are construed as creating a "course of dealing" which may be relied upon by the seller and purchaser.

On the other hand, decisions such as Garden City PCA v. Lannon,[67] have found that a proper creditor authorization for a sale was lacking. In this case, the "course of dealing" approach was abandoned. As a result, the creditor's interest continued after the sale as provided in U.C.C. Section 9-307.

Creditors benefit from sales of collateral to the extent that those sales provide the debtor with income which is used to repay the debt obligation. To allow these sales to occur, while at the same time retaining control over the collateral and its disposition, lenders have used so-called "conditional authorization" clauses. These give the debtor permission to sell the collateral on certain conditions. These agreements require a specific written authorization for the sale of collateral and withhold authorization to dispose of the particular collateral in any other manner. Other approaches have been for the creditor to require the issuance of payment to the seller and secured party jointly or that a determination be made that no prior defaults have occurred before permission to sell will be granted.

Second, U.C.C. Section 9-307(1) provides that a buyer in the ordinary course of business (other than a purchaser of farm products) takes free of the security interest which is created by the seller and properly perfected, even though the purchaser is aware of its existence. To qualify as a buyer in the ordinary course of business, one must buy the goods from a person in the business of selling goods of that kind, the buyer must make the purchase in good faith and the security interest must have been created by the seller of the goods.

Finally, under U.C.C. Section 9-307 if the collateral is characterized as "farm products," the security interest continues to follow the property despite its sale to third parties. Since the enactment of the Food Security Act of 1985, the lender can enforce a security interest in the collateral against a subsequent purchaser only if the security interest is properly filed in an approved central filing system or if the buyer has been properly notified of the lender's security interest.[68]

D. Competing Claims In The Collateral

The status of competing claimants to the collateral is affected by a variety of factors, including whether the creditor has a perfected or attached interest, the basis for the security interest and the type of collateral involved. Determinations of priority may be complicated. It is possible, nevertheless, to identify some general rules that are used to determine priority between competing parties:

1) Federal law controls the federal government's priority rights. In the absence of a controlling federal law, state law may be used;[69]

2) As between perfected and nonperfected security interests, the perfected interest prevails unless the nonperfected

73

interest is given statutory priority;[70]

3) Where neither security interest has been perfected, the first to attach prevails;[71]

4) Purchase money security interests may take precedence over prior perfected security interests under a variety of circumstances, including the following:

> a) If the secured party properly files to perfect a purchase money security interest within 20 days after the collateral comes into the possession of the debtor, that interest will take priority over lien creditors whose interest arises after the time the security interest attaches and the time of filing;[72]

> b) A purchase money security interest in other than inventory prevails over a prior interest is the same collateral, which is claimed under an after acquired title clause in the earlier security agreement, provided that the purchase money security interest is perfected at the time or within 10 days after the debtor takes possession of the collateral;[73]

> c) A purchase money security interest in inventory generally prevails over prior conflicting interests if the requirements set forth in U.C.C. Section 9-312(3) are satisfied;[74] and

> d) A purchase money security interest in crops, which is taken to enable the debtor to produce the crops during the current season and which is given not more than 3 months prior to planting, takes priority over earlier perfected security interests covering the crops provided that the earlier interest is at least six months overdue at the time of planting.[75]

There may also be competing claims between those persons with a valid security interest and other parties with rights in the collateral. For example, buyers in the ordinary course of business will prevail over the holder of a security interest in all goods except farm products. With respect to farm products, the buyer will prevail over the secured creditor to the extent that proper notice is not given to the buyer under either the direct notification or central filing system requirements of Section 1324 of the Food Security Act.[76] In addition, where the security interest is attached to goods which will be installed or affixed to other goods which are already the subject of a security interest, the interest in the accessions will prevail over the prior interest in the whole provided the interest is properly created before the goods are affixed.[77]

E. Default

Before a creditor may undertake foreclosure or repossession of the collateral, the debtor must be in default of the loan agreement. The specific conduct which constitutes default is not defined by statute. As a result, the security agreement will determine the events which constitute default. Typically, an incident of default will involve the failure to make payment when due or the unauthorized disposition of the collateral.

In the absence of an "acceleration" clause in the security agreement only the obligations in default may be foreclosed.[78] This may be problematic when the obligation is to be repaid in installments and only one or a few payments are missed. Under those circumstances, the creditor's remedies would be limited to only those missed payments. To avoid this problem, "acceleration" clauses may be inserted in the security agreement. The impact of this clause is to allow the creditor to treat the entire remaining obligation immediately due upon the default of any one payment. U.C.C. Section 1-208 further provides that the agreement may allow the creditor to accelerate payment or performance, or that it may require additional collateral to be provided "at will" or "when the creditor deems himself insecure." These clauses may be invoked only in good faith. The burden of showing a lack of good faith is on the party against whom the clause applies.

F. Creditors' Remedies

If the security interest is properly perfected, the secured party has the right to repossess the collateral upon default by the debtor. In contrast, where the creditor is an unsecured creditor, a valid judgment against the debtor must be secured first and then the judgment may be executed by the sheriff upon any property belonging to the debtor.

Most repossessions constitute a "self-help" remedy. In

other words, court permission is not required in order for the creditor to take possession of the collateral.[79] This action will be permitted as long as there is "no breach of the peace" committed by the creditor in taking possession. Alternatively, the creditor may render the equipment unusable or dispose of the collateral on the debtor's premises. In order to properly repossess the property without judicial approval, the creditor must send written notice to the debtor which describes the default, indicating the amount due and informing the debtor of the right to "cure" by tendering performance within a reasonable time from the date of receipt of the notice of default.[80]

After default and proper notice, the creditor may sell, lease or otherwise dispose of the collateral to satisfy the indebtedness. Sale of the collateral is the most common form of disposition and any surplus proceeds beyond the outstanding debt must be returned to the debtor.[81] The sale must be conducted in a commercially reasonable manner including proper publication and notice.[82] However, a debtor may, after default, waive the right to notice of the sale. The purchaser of collateral under these circumstances takes free and clear of the security interest and of any other claims that do not take priority over the security interest of the creditor who is conducting the sale.[83] If the sale does not generate sufficient proceeds to satisfy the indebtedness, the creditor may still be entitled to the unpaid balance.[84]

Wrongful repossession of the collateral by the creditor may give the debtor a cause of action for conversion. In addition, the debtor may be able to recover from the creditor any losses caused by the creditor's failure to comply with the U.C.C. requirements for repossession, deposition and sale.[85]

G. Landlord and Other Similar Liens

In most states landlords are given a statutory lien on crops to secure the payment of rent.[86] This lien is superior to all other liens and security interests.[87] Since this lien arises by operation of law and does not require the consent of the parties, it is not subject to the provisions of Article 9. Therefore, it does not need to be "perfected" or recorded to be valid. For example, in Shell v. Guthrie[88] the Kansas Supreme Court stated that:

A landlord's lien on crops grown on his farm to secure
and satisfy the payment of the rent of his farm is
superior to that of the holder of a chattel mortgage
(security interest) on the tenant's share of the crops
grown thereon.[89]

Furthermore, although the landlord lien statutes often do not
specifically provide that a landlord's lien will be preferred over
other statutory liens, courts may give them preference. For
example, the Kansas Court stated in <u>Knapp v. Hines</u>,[90]

The landlord's lien is a long-standing rule of elementary
Kansas law. Almost everybody is aware of it, certainly
every country banker. No businessman of any prudence
will contract for any part of a crop grown by a tenant
farmer, without taking the precaution to assure himself
that the landlord's claim for rent (like the thresher's
claim for his labor) has either been paid or that
satisfactory provision has been made for its payment, so
that the crop he contracts will not be subjected to one
of these statutory liens.[91]

Since the landlord's lien under a crop share lease is
outside the scope of U.C.C. Article 9, it would not appear
necessary for the landlord to comply with the special notice or
filing notice requirements of Section 1324 of the Food Security
Act of 1985 in order to achieve priority over a purchaser of
farm products. However, some landlords have chosen not to
rely on the statutory landlord's lien for securing payment of rent
but rather have elected to create an Article 9 security interest
in the crops. If the landlord uses Article 9 to secure payment
of the rent, the notice requirements of the federal rule would
seem to apply. The landlord's lien would have to be properly
recorded in an approved central filing system or the landlord
would be required to give pre-purchase notification to all
possible purchasers of the crop. In that case, the landlord
would be able to trace the crop to purchasers under the U.C.C.
"farm products" rule.

It may be advisable for a landlord to create an Article 9
security interest in the crops for rent due as if it were a regular
credit transaction. This is particularly true if there is any
possibility that the tenant may be facing an imminent

bankruptcy. The reason for using this approach is that the trustee in bankruptcy has certain lien avoidance powers which extend to statutory liens, such as the landlord's lien. Having a validly perfected security interest would therefore protect the landlord's rights in the crops in the event of a tenant bankruptcy.

In addition to the landlord's lien, which is excluded from the operation of Article 9 by U.C.C. Section 9-104(b), other priority liens to secure the payment for various services are recognized by statute in many states. For example, U.C.C. Section 9-310 provides:

> When a person in the ordinary course of business furnishes services or materials with respect to goods subject to a security interest, a lien upon goods in the possession of such person which is given by statute or rule of law for such materials or services takes priority over a perfected security interest unless the lien is statutory and the statute expressly provides otherwise.[92]

Under this section a person who furnishes services or materials with respect to goods already subject to an Article 9 security interest may have a statutory lien which has priority over the security interest, unless the statute reverses the priority. To qualify for this priority lien, the services or materials must be furnished in the ordinary course of business and possession must be retained by the service provider.

There are specific statutes in many states which create possessory-type liens in agriculturally related transactions that prevail over Article 9 security interests. These include, for example, liens for materials and services, otherwise known as the artisan's lien and the agister's lien.[93] Other examples include the lien for threshing and husking,[94] and for seeding and baling broom corn and baling hay.[95] These are non-possessory liens since the party providing the services is not required to retain possession of the property in order to exercise the lien.

IV.   General Provisions of Long Term Financing

Usually when land is purchased on credit, the purchase and sale arrangement will be structured in one of two ways: with a mortgage (or an equivalent instrument, such as a deed of trust), or with a contract for deed or other mortgage substitute. The mortgage method of financing tends to be more common when institutional financing is used. The contract for deed and other substitutes are more common when private sources of financing are used.

A. Creation of Mortgages

A mortgage involves the exchange of an interest in land as security for the performance of a personal promise to repay a debt. In the typical situation, the mortgage will involve three elements: a debt, a promise to repay the debt and the use of real property as security for the repayment of the debt. The first two elements are contractual in nature and are personal to the debtor. The third, relates to the land and "runs" with the land until the underlying debt is repaid. In earlier times, the title to the real property was actually deemed to pass to the creditor at the time the agreement was executed, subject to a right of future divestiture if the debt was repaid. This approach was seen as rather harsh and is no longer the law in most jurisdictions. In most states, the interest of the creditor is merely a lien on the property to secure the loan.

The formalities required for the creation of a valid mortgage are similar to those required for deeds. These will include such things as the language of conveyance, title covenants, adequate consideration, property descriptions, the signature of debtor, etc. A statutory short form used in Kansas, for example, assures that these requisites will be present if the prescribed format is followed:

> Any mortgage of lands, worded in substance as follows: "A.B. mortgages and warrants to C.D. (here describe the premises), to secure the payment of (here insert the sum for which the mortgage is granted, or the notes or other evidences of debt, or description thereof, sought to be secured, also the date of payment)," the said mortgage being dated, and duly signed, and acknowledged by the grantor, shall be deemed and held to be a good and sufficient mortgage to the grantee, his or her heirs, assigns, executors and administrators, with warranty from the grantor and his or her legal representatives of a perfect title in the grantor, and against all previous

79

encumbrances; and if in the above form the words "and warrants" be omitted, the mortgage shall be good without warranty.[96]

It is not necessary that a particular form be used. In the case of Assembly of God v. Sangster,[97] the Supreme Court of Kansas held that:

Notwithstanding the fact there is a statute (G.S. 1949 67-303) which sets out a "short form" of mortgage, it has been held that in order to create a mortgage contract no particular "form" of instrument is necessary and no particular words are required. The "form" of an agreement by which security is given is unimportant if the purpose plainly appears. All that is necessary is that there be a debt and that the instrument creates a lien on real property as security for the payment of the debt.[98]

The property description required is the same as that required for land conveyances. It must describe the property with sufficient particularly so that it is distinguishable from all other tracts of land. In the alternative, the description as a minimum must provide within it an adequate means of identification of the land which is involved in the transaction. Tracts which have a regular shape and which constitute fractional parts of sections may properly be described in reference to the federal quadrangular survey system (e.g., NW 1/4 of the SE 1/4 of Section 21, Range R 15E, T4S). Irregularly shaped tracts are ordinarily described by survey or metes and bounds (e.g. begin at point A, thence East to Point B, thence South to point C, thence West to point D, thence north to point of beginning). For this type of description to be valid, the point of beginning for the description must be ascertainable and locatable and the description sequence must completely enclose the tract.

Informal descriptions may create difficulties in identifying the property. The difficulty with an informal description is that it may not contain enough specific location information to fully apprise others of the particular tract involved. In Luthi v. Evans,[99] the court held that so-called "Mother Hubbard" clauses, such as "all my land" contained within a general area, were not adequate to give notice to third persons.

A mortgage is binding between the parties if it is properly created, regardless of whether it is recorded.[100] However, to be binding on third parties, who may not have actual notice or knowledge of the purchase and sale arrangement, it is necessary to properly record the mortgage in the land records of the county in which the property subject to the mortgage is located.[101] In order to be recorded, the mortgage must be properly acknowledged[102] and the recording fees and taxes must be paid.[103]

B. Mortgage Substitutes

There is little opportunity for negotiation between the parties in regard to the specific terms of a mortgage. The lender usually controls the drafting of the mortgage documents in a mortgage transaction. For this reason, the law has been quite protective of borrowers in many instances. This has been reinforced by the fact that the borrower's rights of redemption have been protected in the foreclosure process. As a result, it has been a long established practice for lenders to seek financing devices that are not subject to the substantive law of mortgages. Specifically, these devices seek to avoid the problems of the foreclosure process. In several cases, particularly with trust deeds and installment land sales contracts, the law has not permitted lenders to completely avoid the foreclosure process. Nevertheless, it is useful to understand a few of the most common of these mortgage substitutes.

1. Installment Land Sales Contracts (Contracts for Deed)

An installment land sales contract is also known as a contract for deed. It provides for a series of payments during the contract term. Title to the property is conveyed to the buyer when the purchase price has been fully paid or at some earlier point as provided in the agreement or by operation of law. These arrangements have some advantages to the seller. For example, if the buyer defaults on the contract, there is no need for the seller to reacquire title to the property, since the seller retains it. Furthermore, the contract may provide that the seller may retain all amounts paid to the time of default as damages for the breach of contract. Contract remedies, such as specific performance, may be exercised by the seller.

The contract for deed may leave the buyer unprotected. In response, a number of jurisdictions have adopted statutes which mandate "grace" periods in which the debtor may cure the default before the forfeiture of prior payments will occur or before the debtor's rights in the property may be terminated. Courts have reasoned that buyers should have a reasonable time in which to cure the default and have characterized these arrangements as equitable mortgages.[104] As a result, either the seller may be forced to take specific legal steps to terminate the buyer's interests in the property or the buyer may seek protection by having the court establish an equitable redemption period.

2. Deeds of Trust

Deeds of trust are used as mortgage substitutes in many states. Virtually all jurisdictions now consider deeds of trust to be fully subject to mortgage law. Under this arrangement property is conveyed in trust pending the repayment of the debt. The trustee typically has the power to terminate the trust upon certain conditions such as non-payment. The trustee may extinguish the buyer's interest in the property according to the terms of the trust without regard to the legal requirements of foreclosure. In states which recognize only judicially supervised foreclosure, a power of sale provision in the deed of trust which purports to empower the trustee to immediately sell the property upon the default of the debtor would not be enforceable.

3. Other Devices

Other devices sometimes used as mortgage substitutes include the deed absolute, conditional sales and purchase money resultant trusts. The principle of a deed absolute is to structure the transaction as a conveyance of property to the lender but with an oral understanding that if the debt is repaid, the property will be reconveyed to the borrower. Obviously, such an approach may lead to problems. For example, while case law permits the introduction of parol evidence to establish the agreement that a reconveyance would occur, this evidence must

82

be clear and convincing.[105] In addition, the recording of the document of reconveyance would be necessary to bind third parties.

In some cases, the right of the borrower to have the property reconveyed will be in the form of an option to repurchase, or some other similar condition. The option will be expressed either in the original deed or in a collateral document. The problem, of course, is that the true intention of the parties is not reflected in the deed or the collateral document.

The purchase money resultant trust concept applies in the situation where, for example, A pays B to sell property to C who then is to reimburse A. If C does not repay A, A will want some recourse to the property. The purchase money resultant trust concept allows the law to treat C as holding the property in trust for A until the repayment occurs.[106]

C. Usury

Perhaps the biggest concern of borrowers with respect to real estate loans is the issue of interest rates. Another concern is with the procedure for determining variable interest rates. In most jurisdictions the law deals with this concept in the context of the principle of usury. By definition, usury is an unlawful charge for the use of money. It is statutory in nature. If a statute does not impose a limit on interest rates, there is no common law limit. Where interest rates are regulated by usury principles, four traditional elements must be shown: 1) a loaning of money; 2) a requirement that the debt be repaid; 3) excessive interest; and 4) the intent to collect the interest that is charged.

D. The Sale of Mortgaged Property

When property which is covered by a mortgage is sold or transferred, a question may arise as to what the obligations of the original mortgagor are following this sale. First, the new purchaser may take the property but not assume any of the personal obligations to the creditor under the original promissory note. In this case, the purchaser takes "subject to" the mortgage. Alternatively, the new purchaser may not only take the property but may also assume the primary personal responsibility of the original debtor to repay the debt (i.e., the obligations under the promissory note). In this case, the purchaser is said to "assume" the mortgage and in the process becomes the individual primarily responsible for repaying the debt. The original debtor in that situation assumes the status of a surety and is liable for repaying the debt if the new purchaser defaults and is unable to pay. Before the lender may seek recourse against the surety, however, he or she must first seek recovery from the primary debtor (the "assuming" purchaser). If it is not clear in the transaction which type of transfer is involved (i.e., "subject to" or "assumption"), the courts in most jurisdictions presume that the purchaser takes "subject to" the mortgage rather than on an "assumption."[107]

In recent years, it has become increasingly difficult to transfer property subject to a mortgage without the approval of the creditor (mortgagee). The most common devices to restrict the ability of property owners (mortgagors) to transfer mortgaged property are known as "due on sale" and "due on encumbrance" clauses in the original mortgage agreement. These clauses give the mortgagee the option of declaring the entire remaining balance due and payable if the mortgagor either transfers the property or encumbers it with additional liens without the consent of the mortgagee. Often, in exchange for the mortgagee's permission, a transfer fee or a higher interest rate will be charged. These clauses are more troublesome to mortgagors who wish to sell their property when interest rates are rising. The ability to pass on a lower rate may make the purchase of the property quite attractive, but the lender will wish to re-finance at a higher rate of interest.

The primary argument in favor of these clauses is that they permit the lender to obtain protection against the risk that the property will be sold to someone who poses a higher risk of default on the loan than the original borrower. On the other hand, it has been argued that these clauses are unreasonable restraints on the alienation of property. In recent years, case law[108] and federal legislation[109] appear to have resolved doubts in favor of the legitimacy of these clauses. The regulations which implement this legislation provide some protection to the selling mortgagor as well. First, when a lender has waived the right to accelerate the loan and has accepted the new purchaser as an "assuming" grantee, the lender is required to release the original borrower from personal liability. That is, the borrower is no longer a surety in the transaction.[110] Second, when a borrower requests the lender's approval for a transfer, the lender must respond in 30 days and give written notice of the decision and the reasons if the transfer is not approved.[111] The failure to respond in this manner prohibits the lender from being able to exercise the "due on sale" clause.

There is some question as to what types of property transfers are subject to a "due on sale" clause. It has been held, for example, that a sale by the mortgagor under an installment land contract constitutes a sale even though title does not immediately pass to the purchaser.[112] Similarly, where the property is conveyed and the seller/mortgagor either retains a second mortgage or a long term lease is entered into, arguably enough of a transfer has occurred to allow the "due on sale" clause to take effect. On the other hand, an involuntary disposition such as a probate transfer or a transfer to a spouse in a divorce proceeding would not permit the clause to become operative.[113]

In transactions which involve installment sale contracts, there has been a tendency for courts to construe these clauses narrowly against the seller[114] or to require that the seller demonstrate that his or her interest will be impaired by the transfer. This is primarily because forfeiture of the property may result from a default under the terms of such a contract. Furthermore, federal regulations apply only to indebtedness secured by a "lien on real property," which normally is not the case in a contract for deed situation.

E. Prepayment

On occasion, the debtor may be interested in paying off the debt earlier than the loan contract requires. It is often assumed that debtors, as a matter of law, have that right to prepay. On the contrary, the common law has long held that there is no right to prepay a debt secured by a mortgage.[115] This means that prepayment is a "privilege" which must be included in the loan agreement if it is to be asserted by the borrower. In fact, the lender will often impose a "prepayment penalty" for the privilege of exercising the option even when it is included in the agreement. Prepayment penalty clauses typically apply if the option is exercised within a specified time period (e.g., within the first five years), and specify the amount actually to be paid in penalty (e.g., 90 days interest on the amount prepaid). As a general rule, if these provisions are deemed reasonable, they will be enforced by the courts.[116]

As in the case of "due on sale" clauses, involuntary prepayment will generally not be subject to prepayment penalties. This includes payment as a result of casualty loss or the exercise of condemnation power by a unit of government. Similarly, case law in many jurisdictions has excluded those situations where the penalty is imposed as a result of the exercise of a "due on sale" clause.[117]

Virtually all mortgages include an "acceleration" clause which gives the lender the right to declare the entire debt due and payable upon a default in payment. As a general rule, these clauses are activated at the lender's option. Further, the debtor may cure the default before the lender elects to accelerate the debt. Unfortunately for the debtor, in most states, formal notice of acceleration to the debtor is not necessary. The filing of a petition to foreclose in the proper court is usually deemed sufficient notice that the lender has elected to accelerate.

Where the loan agreement includes an acceleration clause which would make the entire outstanding amount due upon default, it has been suggested that a debtor who wants to prepay could default and then pay the entire balance without prepayment penalty. This approach has not gained wide acceptability since acceleration clauses are inserted in mortgages for the benefit of the lender, not the borrower, and the lender cannot be forced to exercise rights under these clauses.[118]

F. Foreclosure
Often the lender under a mortgage or the trustee under a deed of trust has a power of sale which can be exercised upon default by the debtor. However, some states require that the sale be conducted under judicial supervision.[119] The remedy of foreclosure, in many jurisdictions, requires judicial supervision and is a lengthy process. Most procedural matters, such as service of process and pretrial discovery, are handled essentially

like other civil suits. Service of the complaint is usually permitted either by mail or by publication. In many default situations, foreclosure is not the mortgagee's preferred alternative. Therefore, alternatives to foreclosure should be explored. These include options such as workouts, deeds in lieu of foreclosure and pursuing rights under the promissory note.

First, the parties may use a "workout arrangement" to allow the debtor to overcome temporary financial difficulty. "Workout arrangements" may include such terms as payment adjustments, extensions of time, and waivers of late charges. These arrangements may be successfully negotiated if there is evidence of good faith on the part of the debtor and a reasonable prospect of success.

Second, if it is not possible for the mortgagor to overcome the default and either pay off the debt or bring it current within a reasonable period of time, the lender may be willing to accept a deed in lieu of foreclosure. In this case, the debtor may be released from the debt and the lender would have no further recourse against the debtor. This option, if the property is worth less than the amount of outstanding debt, would deprive the lender of the full value of the debt. Therefore, the lender cannot be forced to take the property. It may, however, choose to do so. Likewise, if the lender is willing to accept the property but not fully discharge the debtor, it has that option as well.

A third option for the lender is to pursue its rights under the promissory note without foreclosing the mortgage. In many states, the lender may proceed alternatively against the debtor on either the note or the mortgage.[120]

G. Redemption

The right of redemption was created by courts of equity to mitigate the harsh impacts of strict foreclosure. In early legal history, after default had occurred equity courts set a period of time in which the debtor had to cure the default or forever lose his right. If the debtor failed to repay the debt within the specified period, the lender received a fee simple absolute in the property. In many states, the redemption period is now governed by statute. Under those statutes, the debtor is generally given a specified period in which to redeem. If a

87

federal interest is involved and the interest holder is entitled to redemption rights, federal law prevails over state law and the federal period (generally one year) must pass before that right terminates.

The redemption period begins to run with the completion of the sale. During the running of the period of redemption, the debtor remains in possession of the property and is generally entitled to obtain the rents and profits from the property. This right is subject only to the limitation that the property cannot be subjected to waste.[121] The legal policy is to restore the property, in full title, to the debtor if possible. Thus, if the debtor redeems the property, the foreclosure process ends.

H. Priority Problems

A completed foreclosure action will terminate all rights of any party whose interest in the land is inferior to that of the lender if they are made a party to the proceeding. On the other hand, the foreclosure of a mortgage will not affect superior interests. Thus, when a second mortgage is foreclosed, the first mortgagee is not a required party and their interest will not be affected by the proceeding. Conversely, a foreclosure of a first mortgage will terminate a second mortgage and any other subordinate interest.

Frequently when a mortgage is foreclosed, the proceeds from the sale will be insufficient to fully pay all of the parties who have liens or claims against the property. Thus, it becomes necessary to establish a hierarchy of claims to insure that superior claims are paid before inferior ones.

In most cases, the resolution of priority problems will be based on which interest was created first. Furthermore, although the agreement between a debtor and a creditor is binding on the parties, it is not binding on others until they have notice of it. Notice may be either "actual" or "constructive". Constructive notice is based on the performance of some act which the law deems a sufficient basis upon which to give notice of the interest to third parties. The most common act that gives rise to constructive notice is the recording of the transaction in the public records. As a result, in most cases involving mortgages, priority will be determined upon the order in which the respective interests appear in the public records. There are several notable exceptions. These include certain purchase money mortgages, certain taxes, lis pendens, future advances, fixtures and mechanics liens.

1. Purchase Money Mortgages

Where money is advanced for the purpose of purchasing the property which is offered as security under the mortgage, a purchase money mortgage results. The law basically takes the position that since the money was loaned for the purpose of enabling the debtor to buy the particular property, that the property should be available to secure the repayment of that debt.[122] In most jurisdictions, the rule has been adopted that these purchase money mortgages take priority over any other claim or lien attaching to the property through the mortgagor, even though those other liens have arisen prior to the execution of the purchase money mortgage.

Where the transaction is financed by more than one lender, each may obtain a purchase money mortgage. For example, if a bank loans most of the money for a purchase, and the seller finances the remainder of the debt secured by a nominal "second" mortgage, most banks will require that the seller subordinate his or her interest to the bank to protect the priority of the bank.

2. Taxes

By statute, state and local property tax liens generally take priority over mortgages regardless of when they arise in relation to the creation of the mortgage.[123] On the other hand, federal income tax liens acquire priority over mortgages based upon the recording of the tax lien in the public records. Thus, they will prevail only over liens created subsequent to that recording.[124]

3. Lis pendens

Under the common law, a pending law suit is deemed to give constructive notice of the claims of the parties to the property which is a subject of the lawsuit. Therefore, anyone who took an interest in the property involved in the lawsuit did so at his or her peril and took subject to the subsequent judgment of the court. Under the common law, the act of filing the lawsuit is sufficient to preserve the priority of the claim. Many states now require by statute that a separate notice of the lawsuit be filed in the Registry of Deeds before it will be deemed to give this kind of notice.

4. Future Advances
Occasionally a lender will agree to advance additional funds to a borrower subsequent to the date of the creation of the mortgage. Statutory provisions give the same priority to these later advances as is accorded to the first loan, up to the amount stated in the original mortgage.[125] In the absence of statutory provisions, case law suggests that for the subsequent advances to be protected, they must be based on a future advancement clause in the mortgage and must be for similar purposes to that of the original mortgage.[126]

5. Fixtures
When equipment or materials are installed as improvements to property the issue arises as to whether the lender who has a mortgage on the land will prevail over the creditor who advanced the money to purchase the equipment or materials. This issue will be resolved by a determination of whether the equipment or materials constitute a fixture. According to the U.C.C., goods are fixtures when they become so related to particular real estate that an interest in them arises under real estate law.[127] If the equipment or materials are not related to the real estate to that degree, they will be treated as personal property, and will not be covered by the real property mortgage. Section 9-313 of the U.C.C. was designed to resolve this problem by allowing for the creation of a security interest in fixtures except for ordinary building materials incorporated into an improvement on the land.[128]

6. Mechanics Liens
Mechanics liens are created by statute in favor of those who supply labor or materials to a construction project. The lien is created by operation of law, and applies at least for a short time period to the materials which have been installed as a part of the construction project. Under the terms of the

typical statute, a mechanics lien has priority over any lien or claim that arises subsequent to the commencement of the furnishing of the labor, supplies or material. If the mechanics lien is properly filed and recorded, it is deemed to relate back to the time that the labor or materials were first furnished at the commencement of the buildings or improvements.[129]

7. Marshalling

Although technically not a rule of priority, the equitable concept of marshalling may apply in ways that might enhance the chances of a junior creditor getting full satisfaction of his or her mortgage. There are two main facets of the rule. First, the so-called "two funds" rule provides that if a senior creditor has a mortgage against more than one parcel of property while the junior creditor only a mortgage on one, the senior lienholder must enforce his claim in the way that will best preserve the value of the junior creditor's security. For example, under this rule the senior lienholder must seek the sale of the parcels that the junior does not have a claim on before enforcing the claim against the parcel on which both have an interest.[130]

The second facet is the so-called "sale in inverse order of alienation" rule. This usually applies only to subdivided land which has been sold in separate parcels without a release of the underlying mortgage on the land. If default on that mortgage occurs, this rule requires that land still retained by the mortgagor be sold before any of the lots previously sold are used to satisfy the claim. If it is necessary to use the lots previously sold, those that were sold first are to be used last.[131]

FOOTNOTES

1. See Rossiter v. Merriman, 80 Kan. 739, 104 P. 858 (1909).

2. See Shepherd, "Towards a Unified Concept of Fiduciary Relationships," 97 L.Q. Rev. 51 (1981).

3. 97 L.Q. Rev. at 56.

4. 97 L.Q. Rev. at 58.

5. 97 L.Q. Rev. at 61.

6. 97 L.Q. Rev. at 65.

7. 97 L.Q. Rev. at 69.

8. See Frankel, "Fiduciary Law," 71 Cal. L. Rev. 795 (1983).

9. 8 Ill. App. 3d 759, 291 N.E.2d 329 (1972).

10. 291 N.E.2d at 332-33.

11. First Bank of Wakeeney v. Moden, 235 Kan. 260, 681 P.2d 11 (1984).

12. Umbaugh Pole Building Co., Inc. v. Scott, 58 Ohio St. 2d 282, 390 N.E.2d 320 (1979).

13. 309 N.W.2d 285 (Minn. 1981).

14. See also Buck v. Nash-Finch Co. 78 S.D. 334, 102 N.W.2d 84 (1960); Umbaugh Pole Building Co., Inc. v. Scott, 58 Ohio St. 2d 282, 390 N.E.2d 320 (1979); Note "Agency--Creditors and Buyers as Principals: Beware of Too Much Control" 32 Kan. L. Rev. 497 (1984); Kunkel, "The Fox Takes over the Chicken House: Creditor Interference with Farm Management," 60 N.Dak. L.R. 445 (1984).

15. See, e.g., In re Prima Co., 98 F.2d 9521 (7th Cir. 1938); Edwards v. Northwestern Bank, 39 N.C. App 261, 250 S.E.2d 651 (1979); Commercial Credit Co. v. L.A. Benson Co., 170 Md. 270, 184 A. 236 (1936) (All cases held in favor of the bank).

16. See, e.g., Wagnar v. Banaon, 101 Cal. App. 3d 27, 161 Cal. Rptr. 516 (1980); KMC, Inc. v. Irving Trust Co., No. 3-82-365 (E.D. Tenn. 1983).

17. Wait v. First Midwest Bank of Danville, 491 N.E.2d 795 (Ill. App. 1986).

18. National Farmers Organization v. Kingsley Bank. 731 F.2d 1464 (1984).

19. See, e.g., Wagner v. Benson, 101 Cal. App. 3d 27, 161 Cal. Rptr. 516 (1980); Wait v. First Midwest Bank of Danville, 491 N.E.2d 795 (Ill. App. 1986); National Farmers Organization, Inc. v. Kingsley Bank 731 F.2d 1464 (1984).

20. Dennis v. BancOhio, No. 1873S, (Perry Co. Mar. 14, 1985).

21. Pub. L. 99-205, 99 Stat. 1678 (1985).

22. Pub. L. 100-233, 101 Stat. 1568 (1988).

23. Pub. L. 99-198, 99 Stat. 1354 (1985).

24. 7 C.F.R. § 1474.1.

25. 7 C.F.R. § 1474.1(a).

26. 7 C.F.R. § 1474.2(a).

27. 7 C.F.R. § 1474.2.

28. 7 C.F.R. § 1474.1, 14.72.2(c).

29. 7 C.F.R. § 1474.4(a).

30. 7 C.F.R. § 1474.4(a).

31. 7 C.F.R. § 1474.5.

32. 7 C.F.R. § 1474.6.

33. 7 C.F.R. § 1474.7(a).

34. 7 C.F.R. § 1474.7(a).

35. 7 C.F.R. § 1474.7(b).

36. 7 C.F.R. § 1474.7(b).

37. 7 C.F.R. § 1474.7(c).

38. 7 C.F.R. § 1474.8(b).

39. 7 C.F.R. § 1474.10.

40. 7 C.F.R. § 1474.18.

41. U.C.C. § 9-101 et seq.

42. U.C.C. § 9-109.

43. 2 Kan. App. 2d 438 (1978).

44. U.C.C. § 9-313(1)(a).

45. U.C.C. § 9-401(1).

46. U.C.C. § 9-307(1).

47. Pub. L. 99-198, 99 Stat. 1354 (1985). This central filing
system is independent of the filing system by which the security
interests are perfected. For further discussion, see Note, "Clear
Title: A Buyer's Bonus, A Lender's Loss--Repeal of U.C.C.
9-307(1) Farm products Exception by Food Security Act Sec.
1324 [7 U.S.C. 1631]," 26 Washburn L.J. 71 (1986).

48. It is not necessary that the debtor have "title" to the goods. See, U.C.C. § 9-202.

49. Generally, if the consideration will support a contract, it is adequate for a security agreement.

50. U.C.C. § 9-110.

51. 210 Kan. 181 (1972).

52. U.C.C. § 9-203.

53. See Kansas State Bank v. Overseas Motorsport, Inc. 222 Kan. 26, 563 P.2d 414 (1977).

54. U.C.C. § 9-203(3).

55. U.C.C. § 9-306(1).

56. Quigley v. Caron 247 A.2d 94 (Me. 1968).

57. See Rasor and Wadley, "The Secured Farm Creditor's Interest in Federal Price Supports: Policies and Priorities," 73 Ky. L.J. 595 (1984-85); Comment, "Bankruptcy, the U.C.C. and the Farmer: PIK Payments--Heads General Intangibles, Tails, Proceeds," 26 Washburn L.J. 178 (1986). But see United States v. Carolina Eastern Chem. Co. Inc., 638 F. Supp. 521 (D. S.C. 1986) reconsideration denied, 639 F. Supp 1420 (D. S.C. 1986).

58. See Hamilton, Securing Creditor Interests in Federal Farm Program Payments, 33 S.D. L.Rev. 1 (1987-88).

59. 564 P.2d 964 (Colo. App. 1977).

60. U.C.C. § 9-204(1),(3).

61. Official Comment to § 9-204(1).

62. One should note that a purchaser in the ordinary course of business will take free of the lien under most circumstances with respect to equipment and inventory and with respect to farm products to the extent permitted by Section 1324 of Food Security Act. It should also be noted that a secured interest in after-acquired property will not prevail over a later purchase money security in that collateral. Further, when disposition of the collateral is authorized by the creditor, the purchaser will take free and clear of the lien. Finally, there are a number of personal liens relating to agricultural production and harvesting that are given statutory priority over even a perfected security interest. See, e.g., K.S.A. 58-207 (lien for feed and care of livestock).

63. For most non-negotiable receipts, maximum protection may be secured by filing as to the goods covered, giving notification to the warehouse of the secured parties interest and having of the receipt issued in the names of the debtor and the creditor for negotiable receipts, clearly possession is safest. Where the collateral is accounts or general intangibles or goods which may be used in more than one jurisdiction, the proper location for filing is where the principal plan of business of the debtor is located.

64. U.C.C. § 9-306(3).

65. U.C.C. § 9-402.

66. See, e.g., Planter's PCA v. Bowles, 256 S.W.2d 654 (1974); Hedrick Sav. Bank v. Meyers, 229 N.W.2d 252 (Iowa 1975); Lisbon Bank & Trust Co. v. Murray, 206 N.W.2d 96 (Iowa 1973); North Cent. Kan. PCA v. Washington Sales Co., 557 P.2d 35 (Kan. 1978).

67. 186 N.W.2d 99 (Neb. 1971). See also Duvall-Wheeler Livestock Barn v. United States, 415 F.2d 226 (1969).

68. For discussion, see Note, "Clear Title: A Buyer's Bonus, a Lenders' Loss--Repeal of U.C.C. 9-307 (1) Farm Products

Exception by Food Security Act § 1324 [7 U.S.C. § 1631]," 26 Washburn L.J., 71 (Fall 1986).

69. United States v. Kimbell Foods, Inc., 440 U.S. 715 (1979). For an analysis of possible situations where state law may not be non-discriminatory as far as government price support payments are concerned, see Rasor and Wadley, The Secured Farm Creditor's Interest in Federal Price Supports: Priorities and Policies, 73 Ky. L.J. 595 (1984-85).

70. See, e.g., U.C.C. § 9-310.

71. U.C.C. § 9-203.

72. U.C.C. § 9-301(2).

73. U.C.C. § 9-312(4).

74. U.C.C. § 9-312(3) provides:
A perfected purchase money security interest in inventory has priority over a conflicting security interest in the same inventory and also has priority in identifiable cash proceeds received on or before the delivery of the inventory and also has priority in identifiable cash proceeds received on or before the delivery of the inventory to a buyer if,
> (a) the purchase money security interest is perfected at the time the debtor receives possession of the inventory; and
> (b) the purchase money secured party gives notification in writing to the holder of the conflicting security interest if the holder had filed a financing statement covering the same types of inventory (i) before the date of the filing made by the purchase money secured party, or (ii) before the beginning of the twenty-one day period where the purchase money security interest is temporarily perfected without filing or possession (subsection (5) of section 9-304); and
> (c) the holder of the conflicting security interest receives the notification within five (5) years before the debtor receives possession of the inventory; and

(d) the notification states that the person giving the notice has or expects to acquire a purchase money security interest in inventory of the debtor, describing such inventory by item or type.

75. U.C.C. § 9-312(2). A lender who takes a purchase money security interest (PMSI) in collateral such as livestock, may face substantial proof problems unless the livestock are permanently marked or physically separated from the rest of the herd since it may be impossible to separate them from the livestock covered in a prior security agreement. If the cattle are not separately marked or segregated, a PMSI lender should have the prior lender sign a subordination agreement in order to assure himself of priority.

76. See 7 U.S.C. § 1631.

77. U.C.C. § 9-314.

78. U.C.C. § 1-208.

79. U.C.C. § 9-503. See also Benschoter v. First National Bank of Lawrence, 218 Kan. 144, 542 P.2d 1042 (1975).

80. Some states have enacted the Uniform Consumer Credit Code which may provide for default for a specified period before further action may be taken. For example, see United Kansas Bank and Trust Co. v. Rixner, 4 Kan. App. 2d 662, 610 P.2d 116 (1980). But see Musil v. Hendricks, 6 Kan. App. 2d 196, 627 P.2d 367 (1981).

81. Reasonable expenses of retaking, holding, preparing for sale and selling the property, and reasonable attorney's fees and legal expenses may be deducted from the sale price. 84-9-504(1). It has been held that a mortgagee of growing wheat, after taking possession, was allowed to deduct the cost of harvesting, threshing and marketing the wheat. Exchange State Bank v. Kirwin State Bank, 119 K. 70, 237 P. 936 (1925).

82. U.C.C. § 9-504(3). If the collateral is perishable or will rapidly change in value the notice requirement may be avoided. The failure to get the best possible price is not necessarily evidence that the sale was not conducted in a commercially reasonable manner. See U.C.C. § 9-507(2).

83. U.C.C. § 9-504(4).

84. U.C.C. § 9-504(2).

85. U.C.C. § 9-507.

86. See, e.g., K.S.A. 58-2524.

87. See Bank v. Burr, 7 Kan. App. 197, 52 P. 704 (1898); Bank v. Equity Exchange, 113 K. 696, 216 P. 278 (1923); Shell v. Guthrie, 129 K. 632, 284 P. 420 (1930); Schmitz v. Stockman, 151 K. 891, 101 P.2d 962 (1940); Knapp v. Hipes, 159 K. 94, 152 P.2d 805 (1944).

88. 129 Kan. 632, 284 P. 420 (1930).

89. 284 P. at 420.

90. 159 Kan. 94, 152 P.2d 805 (1944).

91. 152 P.2d at 806.

92. U.C.C. § 9-310.

93. See, e. g., K.S.A. § 58-201 (artisan's) and K.S.A. § 58-220 (agister's).

94. See, e. g., K.S.A. § 58-203.

95. See, e. g., K.S.A. § 58-218.

96. K.S.A. § 58-2303.

97. 178 Kan. 678, 290 P.2d 1057 (1959).

98. 190 P.2d at 1059.

99. 223 Kan. 622, 576 P.2d 1063 (1978).

100. See, e. g., K.S.A. § 58-2223.

101. See, e. g., K.S.A. § 58-2222.

102. See also Hildebrant v. Hildebrant, 9 Kan. App. 2d 614 (1984).

103. See K.S.A. § 79-3102. See also Misco Industries, Inc. v. Board of Sedgwick County Commissioners, 235 Kan. 958 (1984).

104. Mustard v. Sugar Valley Lakes, 7 Kan. App. 340, 642 P.2d 111 (1981).

105. Saylor v. Crooker, 89 Kan. 51, 130 P. 689 (1913).

106. Many states have abolished this device. See, e. g., K.S.A. § 58-2406-2408.

107. See, e. g., 4th National Bank in Wichita v. Hill, 314 P.2d 312 (Kan. 1957).

108. See, e. g., Capital Federal Savings and Loan v. Glenwood Manor, Inc., 235 Kan. 935 (1984). See also Fidelity Federal Savings and Loan Assn. v. de la Cuesta, 102 S.Ct. 3014 (1982), holding that the Federal Home Loan Bank Board regulations permitting due on sale clauses preempted conflicting state laws.

109. See Section 341 of the Depository Institutions Act of 1982 (Pub. L. 97-320, 96 Stat. 1690)(codified in scattered sections of 12 U.S.C.).

110. See 12 C.F.R. § 591.5(b)(3). This is applicable to all lenders now.

111. 12 C.F.R. § 591.4(d)(3).

112. See, e.g., Century Savings Assoc. v. C. Michael Franke & Co. 9 Kan. App. 2d, 776 (1984); Terry v. Born, 604 P.2d 504 (Wash. App. 1979); Lipps v. First American Service Corp., 286 S.E.2d 215 (Pa. 1982).

113. See, e.g., Mills v. Nashua Federal Savings and Loan Assn., 433 A.2d 1312 (N.H. 1981). See also § 341(d) of the Depository Institutions Act of 1982.

114. See, e.g., Connor v. First National Bank & Trust Co. of Rockford, 439 N.E.2d 122 (Ill. App. 1982).

115. Nelson and Whitman, Real Estate Finance Law at 421-422 (West 1985).

116. See, e.g., Hartford Life Ins. Co. v. Randall, 538 P.2d 1126 (Or. 1978).

117. See, e.g., Slevin Container Corp. v. Provident Federal Savings and Loan Assn., 98 Ia. App. 3d 646, 424 N.E.2d 939 (1981); Tan v. Calif. Fed. Sav. & Loan Assn., 140 Cal. App. 3d 800, 189 Cal. Rptr. 775 (1983).

118. See, e. g., Peter Fuller Enterprises, Inc. v. Manchester Savings Bank, 102 N.H. 117, 152 A.2d 179 (1959).

119. See, e. g., K.S.A. § 58-2418, 2419, 2301; 60-2410 through 2416. But see Comment, "Validity of Power of Sale," 16 Kan. L. Rev. 611 (1968).

120. See, e. g., Rossiter v. Merriman, 80 Kan. 739, 104 P. 858 (1909); Lichty v. McMartin, 11 Kan. 424 (1873).

121. See First Federal Savings and Loan Association of Coffeyville v. Moulds, 202 Kan. 557 (1969); Broadhurst Foundation v. New Hope Baptist Society, 194 Kan. 40 (1964).

122. See Nelson and Whitman, Real Estate Finance Law, at 678-679 (West 1985). Historically, the notion was probably

grounded on concepts of fundamental fairness. <u>See</u> Tiffany, <u>Real Property</u> (3rd Ed.) § 1462.

123. <u>See</u>, <u>e. g.</u>, K.S.A. § 79-2111, 2801 <u>et</u> <u>seq.</u>

124. United States v. Union Central Life Ins. Co., 368 U.S. 291 (1961).

125. <u>See</u>, <u>e. g.</u>, K.S.A. § 58-2336.

126. <u>See</u>, Nelson and Whitman, <u>Real Estate Finance Law</u>, at 834-841 (West 1985).

127. U.C.C. § 9-313(1)(a).

128. U.C.C. § 9-313(2).

129. <u>See</u>, <u>e. g.</u>, Ark. Code Ann. § 18-44-111 (1987).

130. Nelson and Whitman, <u>Real Estate Finance Law</u> at 724 (West 1985).

131. Nelson and Whitman <u>Real Estate Finance Law</u> at 723 (West 1985).

CHAPTER 4

FARMERS HOME ADMINISTRATION

The Farmers Home Administration (FmHA) is an agency of the United States Department of Agriculture. FmHA was created in 1946 by the Farmers Home Administration Act. FmHA is authorized to make insured (direct) government loans and to guarantee loans made to farmers by banks and other lenders. FmHA replaced earlier federal farm loan agencies which had started direct lending to farmers during the 1930's Depression-era.

The main objective of FmHA's farm lending policy is to "provide credit and management assistance to farmers and ranchers to become operators of family sized farmers or continue such operations when credit is not available elsewhere."[1] In Curry v. Block,[2] the Federal District Court characterized FmHA legislation by stating that "[t]he object of the current FmHA legislation is to aid the underprivileged farmer, and [it] is therefore a form of social welfare legislation." FmHA borrowers are required to "graduate" to other sources of credit when the borrower is able to afford credit which other lenders offer at reasonable rates and terms.

The three main areas of FmHA programs are farmer programs, rural housing programs and rural community facility programs. The farmer loan program and the rural housing loan program are jointly administered by FmHA through the provisions of the Consolidated Farm and Rural Development Act. This chapter will concentrate on farmer programs which provide loans to eligible farm owners and operators. Beginning with Curry v. Block, courts have established significant due process rights for FmHA farmer-borrowers. These rights were first recognized in the rural housing loan program context and were subsequently applied to farmer loans. These rights were further expanded by the Agricultural Credit Act of 1987,[3] which extensively revised and expanded the loan servicing requirements and restricted FmHA's foreclosures rights. This Act also established a new FmHA appeals process and provided funding for state mediation programs.

A fundamental policy assumption of all FmHA farm
loan programs is that FmHA borrowers present more risk than
other farm borrowers. This is reflected in the eligibility criteria
for a FmHA loan that the applicant be unable to obtain credit
from other lenders. In general, there are two categories of
high-risk borrowers who receive FmHA loans: (1) beginning,
low-equity family farmers and (2) established farmers who have
expanded their farming operation.

The most prominent farmer direct loan programs are the
Farm Ownership Loan (FO), Operating Loan (OL), and the
Disaster Emergency Loan (EM). In addition, the guaranteed
Operating (OL), Soil and Water (SW) and Farm Ownership
(FO) loan programs are available. In the guaranteed loan
programs, the borrower receives the loan from a commercial
lender and the loan is guaranteed by the government. The
direct loan programs and the guaranteed loan program will be
discussed separately.

FmHA Structure
The FmHA administrative system is comprised of a
national office, state offices, district offices and county offices.
The FmHA national office plays a major role in interpreting
congressional intent for FmHA programs. It promulgates the
regulations for all FmHA programs. The national office also
supervises the implementation of FmHA programs at the state
and county level. In particular, the national office issues
administrative notices (AN's) to the state and local offices to
advise them of policy changes and new procedures. The
national office is headed by a National Administrator.

State offices are headed by an FmHA state director.
The state director administers all of the FmHA programs within
that state. This includes the farmer, housing, and community
facilities programs within his or her jurisdiction. Within the
state office there is a Chief of Farmer Programs. This person
has primary responsibility for administering the state's farmer
program loans. The Chief maintains regular communications
with District Directors and county level officials. The Chief is a
key FmHA official with whom lawyers who represent FmHA
borrowers may need to communicate. The state office issues

state "bulletins" or supplements to the county offices. They serve a similar informational function to that of the administrative notices issued by the national office, although they provide information unique to that state.

District offices are located in various regions of each state, to supervise and coordinate state programs within their region. The district director reviews the loan servicing methods used by county supervisors in handling the accounts of delinquent and problem borrowers and proposed liquidation proceedings. In some cases the district director may be the actual decisionmaker.

Within the county office, FmHA loan administration is handled by a County Committee and a County Supervisor. The County Committee is comprised of three members, two of whom are elected by farmers in the county and the third designated by the State Director. The County Committee determines the eligibility of applicants for FmHA's farmer loan programs. The County Committee must certify in writing that the applicant meets the eligibility requirements for the loan. The County Committee also classifies farm real estate property as being suitable or unsuitable; makes recommendations on resolving problem cases; confers with the County Supervisor concerning borrowers who should be referred to other credit sources; makes recommendations regarding the compromise or adjustment or cancellation of debts; gives advice, when requested by the County Supervisor, concerning voluntary debt adjustment; and attends appeal hearings, if necessary. The regulations which address County Committee elections and the composition and function of the committees are found at 7 C.F.R. Subpart W of Part 2054.

The County Supervisor is the FmHA loan approval officer for farmer loans. Upon a determination by the County Committee that an applicant meets the eligibility criteria, the County Supervisor must approve or disapprove the loan. Once a loan has been approved and loan funds have been advanced, the County Supervisor is responsible for servicing the loan.

Direct Loan Programs
FO Program
The basic objectives of FO loans are to assist eligible

applicants to become owner-operators of family-sized farms or to continue those operations when credit is not available elsewhere; to assist family-farm operators to make efficient use of land, labor and other resources; and to enable farm families to have a reasonable standard of living.[4] FmHA is required to provide supervision and management assistance to FO borrowers "to the extent necessary to achieve the objectives of the loan and to protect the interest of the Government. . .".[5]

The loan purposes which are explicitly authorized by the regulations include the purchase or enlargement of a farm; the construction, purchase, or improvement of buildings and facilities needed on or in close proximity to the farm; the purchase or improvement of land and water development, pollution control and energy saving measures; the acquisition of water supplies and rights, and conservation measures essential to the operation of the farm; to refinance debts, subject to certain conditions; to pay reasonable expenses incidental to obtaining, closing and making the loan; and to finance a nonfarm enterprise when it will provide another source of necessary income.[6]

OL Program
The primary objective of the OL program is "to provide the credit and management assistance necessary for farmers, ranchers and rural youth to conduct successful operations."[7] It is targeted to assist limited resource operators, new operators, and low-income operators.[8] As in the FO program, FmHA is required to provide management assistance to all OL borrowers "to the extent necessary to achieve the objectives of the loan."[9]

OL loans may be made for farm, forestry, recreation and nonfarm enterprises for purposes which are "essential to the operation."[10] The loan purposes which are explicitly authorized by the regulations include the purchase of farm machinery, farm equipment, livestock, poultry and other farm animals;[11] payment of annual operating expenses;[12] payment of family living expenses;[13] refinancing debts incurred for any authorized operating loan purpose other than FmHA debts;[14] purchase of membership and stock in a farm-related cooperative association;[15] purchase and repair of essential home equipment;[16] purchase of a milk base or milk quota with or

106

without cows;[17] the improvement or repair of real estate of not more than $7,500 in a fiscal year, if additional specified conditions are met;[18] payments to a creditor;[19] purchase of a franchise or contract when necessary to the operation of the planned enterprise;[20] partial payment for the purchase and construction of crop storage and drying facilities in certain situations;[21] payment of costs for training farmer program borrowers in record-keeping skills for farming and ranching operations;[22] and to plant softwood timber on marginal land which was previously used to produce an agricultural commodity or as pasture.[23]

There are certain limitations on the availability and use of an OL loan. The total outstanding principal balance on a direct OL loan may not exceed $200,000 at loan closing.[24] An OL loan may not be used to purchase real estate, to make principal payments on real estate or to refinance debts which were incurred for the purchase of real estate.[25] An OL loan also may not be used for any purpose that will contribute to excessive erosion of highly erodible land or to the conversion of wetlands to produce an agricultural commodity.[26] Furthermore, an OL loan may not be used to pay land lease costs under any arrangement other than cash rent.[27]

FmHA will restrict the making of OL loans for purposes that would conflict with the policies and objectives of other federal farm programs. For example, OL loans cannot be used to increase the production of a commodity when the USDA is taking action to reduce production of that commodity. Similarly, OL loan decisions must be coordinated with federal price support and subsidy programs.[28]

EM Loans

EM loans are available to applicants who have "qualified severe physical and/or production losses within a county named by FEMA (Federal Emergency Management Agency) as eligible for Federal assistance under a major disaster or emergency declaration by the President or under a natural disaster determination by the Secretary of Agriculture. . . and to applicants having qualifying severe physical property losses when, prior to action by the President or Secretary, the FmHA Administrator has determined. . .that such losses have occurred as a result of a natural disaster."[29]   For disasters occurring on or after May 31, 1983, all counties which are contiguous to the eligible county are also authorized to make EM loans to applicants whose operations have been substantially affected by the same disaster.[30]

The applicant must have sustained "qualifying physical loss" and/or "qualifying production loss" due to the disaster. "Qualifying physical loss" is a loss caused by damage to or destruction of physical property that is essential to the successful operation of the farm, and if it is not repaired or replaced the farmer would be unable to continue operations on a reasonably sound basis.[31]   "Qualifying production loss" is the equivalent to at least 30 percent loss of normal per acre or per animal production in any single enterprise which is a basic part of the farming operation.[32]

Loan Application Documents

A completed application for farmer program loans includes the submission of numerous documents. The necessary documents include Form FmHA 410-1, "Application for FmHA Services"; a brief narrative which describes the applicant's farm training and/or experiences; financial records for the past five years; five years of production and expense history; a brief narrative describing the proposed operation, if a new application; the projected production, income and expenses and loan repayment plan, the "Farm and Home Plan"; Form SCS CPA-26 and Form AD 1026 (obtained from the SCS office); a copy of any lease, contract, agreement, or option entered into which may be pertinent to the operation; Form FmHA 440-32, "Request for Statement of Debts and Collateral"; a legal description of all owned farm and other real estate and all rented crop land; written evidence from lenders which documents the applicant's inability to obtain other credit; a list of credit references; a verification of off-farm income (if applicable); and Form FmHA 1924-1, "Development Form."[33]

Loan Application Procedure

Any person who wishes to submit an FmHA loan application must be permitted to do so, even if funds for a particular program are not currently available.[34]   County office employees are responsible for receiving the applications and providing explanations of the types of assistance available.[35]

Completed applications are initially reviewed by the County Supervisor to determine if all the information necessary to determine eligibility has been received. The County Supervisor will also verify the information received.[36] Within 20 working days after receipt of the application, the applicant must be notified by letter if additional information is needed. The notice must explain to the applicant that additional information is needed and that the application cannot be processed until the information is received.[37]

The County Committee determines eligibility for all farmer program loans. The County Committee will not determine the applicant's projected repayment ability, the adequacy of collateral, or the feasibility of the proposed operation.[38] Written notice of eligibility or ineligibility must be sent to the applicant no later than 30 days after receipt of a completed application.[39] County Committee minutes must show the action taken on each application, including specific reasons for any unfavorable decisions. The factual justification for the unfavorable decision must be included in the written notice to the applicant.[40]

If the County Committee has determined that the applicant is eligible, the County Supervisor must make a determination as to whether or not the proposed operation is "feasible." Each application must be approved or disapproved within 60 days after receipt of a completed application. Moreover, the applicant must be notified in writing of the decision within that time period.[41] After a loan has been approved, funds must be released to the applicant within 15 days of the date the loan is approved by the county supervisor or within 15 days after sufficient funds become available.[42]

Applicants must be advised of their right to appeal unfavorable eligibility decisions made by the County Committee and/or unfavorable "feasibility" decisions made by the County Supervisor. Appeals will be processed pursuant to 7 C.F.R. Part 1900, Subpart B.[43]

Loan Approval Criteria

The eligibility requirements for an OL and FO loan are

109

found at 7 C.F.R. 1941.12 and 7 C.F.R. 1943.12, respectively. For individuals, the individual must:

(1) Be a citizen of the United States or an alien lawfully admitted to the United States for permanent residence;

(2) Possess the legal capacity to incur the obligations of the loan;

(3) Have sufficient applicable educational and/or on the job training or farming experience which indicates the ability necessary to assure reasonable prospects of success;

(4) Have the character (emphasizing credit history, past record of debt repayment and reliability) and industry to carry out the proposed operation;

(5) Honestly try to carry out the conditions and terms of the loan;

(6) Be unable to obtain sufficient credit elsewhere; and

(7) Be the owner-operator or tenant-operator of not larger than a family farm after the loan is closed.[44]

When considering an applicant's creditworthiness, the County Committee is prohibited from allowing any of the following occurrences to indicate an unacceptable credit history: foreclosure, judgments, or delinquent payments which occurred more than 36 months before the application, if no recent similar situations have occurred; isolated incidents of delinquent payments; "no history" of credit transactions; recent bankruptcy, foreclosure, judgment or delinquency payments when the applicant can demonstrate that the circumstances causing the above were temporary and were beyond the applicant's control; nonpayment of debts due to circumstances beyond the applicant's control; or previous FmHA debt settlements.[45]

Appraisals

An appraisal of the farm property is a key factor in the loan approval decision. The appraisal is a written statement that identifies the property and expresses an opinion about its value.[46] USDA regulations allow both the "agricultural value" and the "market value" to be considered in arriving at a recommended value of the property. "Agricultural value" is the amount a typical purchaser would be willing to pay, and be justified in paying for the farm, with the expectation of receiving earnings from the farm. "Market value" is the amount a typical purchaser, considering both agricultural and non-agricultural uses, would be willing to pay.[47]

An appraiser must make the following fundamental assumptions in appraising the property:

1. That the farm will be operated by a typical operator;
2. That the farm will be developed as planned;
3. That the crop yields are based on current practices and present farm technological methods which are in general use; and
4. That general economic conditions will remain stable.[48]

The purpose of the appraisal is to determine the appraiser's recommended market value as recorded on Form FmHA 422-1 (Part 7). The recommended market value is determined by a combination of the market data approach, the capitalization approach, and the summation approach, plus any final adjustments.[49] The market value approach uses the sale prices of comparable properties. The capitalization approach determines the amount a prudent investor would pay for the property based on future earnings and advantages. The summation approach adds the value of essential buildings and considers depreciation and physical deterioration.

Management Assistance

A central feature of FmHA loan programs is the agency's provision of management assistance to borrowers. Management assistance includes credit counseling,[50] long-term and annual production planning,[51] assistance with required recordkeeping systems,[52] supervision through farm visits and collateral inspections,[53] and analysis to assist borrowers in utilizing sound business planning and management practices.[54]

The Farm and Home Plan is one of the most fundamental documents in the annual production planning process. It provides the basic financial information which is used both in the initial loan approval decision and later loan servicing processes. The Farm and Home Plan serves as a balance sheet, a statement of financial conditions, a debt repayment plan, and as a projection of farm and family expenses and income. The Plan must set forth objectives which are realistic and achievable, using production and price projections that are based on verifiable data. The Farm and Home Plan must be "feasible." A feasible plan will show that a borrower will at least be able to pay all operating expenses and all taxes which are due during the projected period, meet necessary payments on debts, and provide for the essential living expenses for the family.[55]

The other form that is completed once each year and revised as needed is Form FmHA 1962-1, "Agreement for the Use of Proceeds/Release of Chattel Security." This form contains information which projects all property which will be sold during the year, the price at which it will be sold, the potential purchasers, and the use to which sale proceeds will be put. All sales proceeds must be paid to creditors with liens on the proceeds, in their order of priority. The form must provide for releases of proceeds so that the borrower can pay essential family living and farm operating expenses.[56] The borrower and the County Supervisor are required to work together to develop a plan for the disposition of property. Each is required to sign Form 1962-1 once an agreement on these matters has been reached.

If the borrower and the County Supervisor cannot agree on the initial plan for use of proceeds or any subsequently requested revision, the borrower has the right to appeal the County Supervisor's decision. While any appeal is pending, FmHA must make releases which would enable the borrower to meet essential family living and farm operating expenses which are average for the area.[57] In addition, FmHA must make releases for other items on which the borrower and the County Supervisor do agree.[58] After the appeal, the County Supervisor and the borrower will sign a form in accordance with the hearing officer's decision.[59] FmHA Form 1962-1 will be discussed in further detail in a later section.

Supervised Accounts
FmHA may require the use of a supervised bank account to control the disbursement of loan funds, but only in "rare instances."[60] These instances include the necessity of assuring

correct expenditures of the loan funds;[61] depositing funds from the sale of Economic Opportunity (EO) secured property or the proceeds from insurance on that property, to assure that funds will be available to obtain replacement property;[62] and when it is determined by the County Supervisor and requested or agreed to by the borrower that special supervision is needed to handle the borrower's financial affairs.[63] It is important to note that an account established for the latter reason can only be established upon the borrower's consent that special supervision is needed. The period of the account must not exceed one year, unless extended by the District Director.

Security Agreements

Each FO loan must be secured by real estate or by a combination of real estate and chattels or other security.[64] FmHA prefers to take a mortgage on the entire farm.[65] If adequate real estate is unavailable, chattel security may be utilized.[66] Additional security may include buildings, fixtures, water rights, fences, and other improvements.[67]

The security for an OL loan should be adequate to assure loan repayment. FmHA will want the loan secured by a first lien on any property or products acquired or produced with the loan proceeds.[68] FmHA may also require a lien on all or part of the borrower's real estate.[69] The regulations allow an income assignment to be taken as security.[70] Debtors are increasingly making assignments of, and granting security interests in, their federal farm program payments to creditors such as FmHA for purposes of securing loans. The regulations specify the forms to be used by the County Supervisor to obtain the borrower's interest in various government program payments.[71] The borrower and his or her representative should carefully review all security agreement forms prior to signing so the borrower fully understands whether federal program payments are included in the property which is being secured. If a dispute arises, the borrower should determine whether FmHA has executed the proper federal assignment and consent forms and state UCC forms necessary to have a valid security interest in farm program payment(s).

FmHA will accept real estate or chattel security for emergency disaster loans.[72] After a disaster, a farmer often

113

lacks adequate security. In that case, FmHA may assess the loan application on the basis of repayment ability. Loan approval on repayment ability will be conditioned on the loan becoming fully secured within 3 years of the date of loan closing.[73]

Disposition of Secured Property

A borrower must be aware of the distinction between "basic" security and "normal income" security in order to properly maintain FmHA security property. Basic security is equipment, real estate and foundation livestock which are the "basis" of the farming operation. "Basic security" livestock is typically comprised of breeding stock and dairy cattle. These are items that depreciate in value and produce income. In contrast to basic security, normal income security consists of the assets which are produced by the basic security. It includes crops, non-breeding livestock and other farm products which are sold in the ordinary course of business to provide cash flow for operating expenses.[74]

If a borrower wants to dispose of chattel security which is not listed on Form FmHA 1962-1 ("Agreement for the Use of Proceeds/Release of Chattel Security") or in a way not listed on that form, the borrower must obtain FmHA's consent before the disposition of the property occurs or before the proceeds are used. FmHA must give consent for the release of normal income security if the change in the agreement is necessary for the borrower to meet essential family living and farm operating expenses.[75]

In Coleman v. Block,[76] the court held that planned releases of income security proceeds for necessary living and operating expenses can not be terminated by FmHA without prior notice to the debtor and with an opportunity for a hearing. The court reasoned that a borrower's interest in the proceeds from the sale of normal income security is legally analogous to that of a worker's interest in his or her wages.[77] A Federal District Court in Colorado ordered FmHA to "refund" proceeds which were wrongfully seized in violation of the borrower's due process rights.[78] In 1986, the Coleman order was extended to provide due process protections to borrowers when FmHA refused to release security proceeds for necessary family living and farm operating expenses even though no Farm and Home Plan was in effect, and the borrower's expense was unplanned.[79]

Congress addressed both the above-discussed and other recurring borrower problems in the Agricultural Credit Act of 1987.[80] The Act and its accompanying regulations now require FmHA to release sufficient amounts from normal income security to pay for essential household and farm operating expenses, until the point at which FmHA accelerates a loan.[81] FmHA considers essential family living and farm operating expenses to be those which are "basic, crucial or indispensable".[82] Excess proceeds can be applied to the FmHA debt, used to purchase property better suited to the borrower's needs, used to preserve the security, or exchanged for better suited property. In certain circumstances, livestock security can be consumed by the borrower or crops used as security can be fed to livestock if this is preferable to direct marketing.[83]

Since a sale of security property is the primary source of a farmer's income, it is generally to FmHA's advantage to allow these sales to take place. FmHA will usually release its lien if the sale of collateral and use of proceeds are in accordance with Form 1962-1 and the Farm and Home Plan.

The borrower should carefully maintain and account for the security property in order to avoid difficulty with FmHA. The following practices are recommended to borrowers:

1. Maintain records of the disposition of the property and the actual use of the proceeds;[84]

2. Get prior FmHA consent before disposing of property not listed, disposing of property in a way not listed, or using proceeds in a way not listed, on the Form 1962-1;[85] and/or

3. Notify FmHA if property will be disposed of at a different time, the property will be sold or exchanged to a different person, disposed of in a different quantity, or sold at a different price, than that listed on the Form 1962-1.[86]

If the borrower disposes of chattel security in a manner not authorized by Form 1962-1, the County Supervisor is required to either request restitution or make a post-disposition approval of the sale. If the borrower refuses to make restitution, if the County Supervisor cannot make a post-disposition approval, or if the borrower makes a second unauthorized disposition of collateral, the County Supervisor must submit all relevant information to the State office. This information will in turn be submitted to the Office of Inspector General.[87]

The borrower's act of disposing of collateral without prior FmHA authorization may constitute conversion. FmHA has been filing an increasing number of conversion lawsuits against borrowers and their sales agents. FmHA may bring a civil action for conversion against a borrower who fails to account for secured property or may file a criminal action for conversion under 18 U.S.C. 658.[88]

A borrower who has been charged with conversion may attempt to characterize his or her sale of security as impliedly authorized on the basis that it fulfills the objectives of the Farm and Home Plan. This characterization could have arguable validity if the proceeds are used for farm operating and family living expenses. However, this defense has had limited success. For example, in United States v. Garth,[89] a farmer who was a criminal defendant in an FmHA conversion case unsuccessfully raised the Farm and Home Plan defense. This defense was unconvincing under the facts presented. Specifically, the farmer did not produce evidence that he had actually applied the proceeds of the unauthorized sales of FmHA security to payments for necessary farm operating or living expenses. However, the court noted that, even if this alleged application of the proceeds had been established, it would not be a sufficient defense as a matter of law.

The principles in Coleman v. Block,[90] are also relevant to a conversion action against an FmHA borrower. Coleman held that a borrower accused or convicted of conversion must nevertheless be given the opportunity to apply for deferral relief. However, FmHA regulations still treat conversion as an occurrence of default.[91]

Loan Servicing

7 U.S.C. 1981a provides that "the Secretary may permit, at the request of the borrower, a deferral of principal and interest on any outstanding loan made, insured, or held . . .[by

116

FmHA] . . . and may forego foreclosures of any such loan, for such period as the Secretary deems necessary upon a showing by the borrower that due to circumstances beyond the borrower's control, the borrower is temporarily unable to continue making payment of such principal and interest without duly impairing the standard of living of the borrower."[92] While this statute gave FmHA the discretion to defer payments on delinquent loans, FmHA had failed to promulgate regulations or to otherwise implement the provision. In Curry v. Block,[93] the Federal District Court held that Section 1981a confers substantive and procedural rights upon borrowers. The court found that while granting deferral on a specific case was within the Secretary's discretion, the Secretary must promulgate regulations and make deferral available to borrowers.

The Eighth Circuit Court of Appeals developed the doctrine of FmHA borrower's rights even further in Allison v. Block.[94] In Allison, farm operators brought an action seeking declaratory and injunctive relief against the Secretary of Agriculture and other officials to enjoin them from foreclosing various farm loans obtained from the Farmers Home Administration. The Court held that the Secretary was required to promulgate both procedural and substantive regulations to implement the loan deferral relief provisions of 7 U.S.C. 1981(a). As in Curry, the Court noted that this requirement existed notwithstanding the Secretary's discretion under the statute in making individual deferral decisions. Under this holding, the Secretary was enjoined from foreclosing the Allisons' farm until he had first complied with his responsibility to provide them with adequate notice of their deferral rights and to provide procedures under which they could demonstrate their eligibility for Section 1981a deferral relief.[95] The Allison Court also held that the foreclosure would be enjoined until uniform substantive regulations had been published.[96]

The Agricultural Credit Act of 1987 further instructed the Secretary of Agriculture with respect to FmHA loan servicing programs. Under the 1987 Act, FmHA is instructed to utilize write-down of loan principal and interest and debt-set aside when those procedures would enable the borrower to continue operating his or her farm or ranch and when the return to the government under the restructured debt is at least

117

as great as the return from involuntary liquidation.[97] FmHA was further instructed to use all primary loan servicing programs available to ensure that borrowers are able to continue their farming operations. FmHA has promulgated interim regulations which set forth the FmHA loan structures and loan servicing obligations under the 1987 Act.[98]

Loan servicing is considered a continuing process, not a single event. The new FmHA policy states that loan servicing has two objectives: 1. to help farmers to manage credit so that they can return to private sector credit sources; and 2. to minimize costs to the government.[99] FmHA loan servicing involves two separate areas: primary loan servicing and preservation loan servicing. Primary loan servicing takes place prior to foreclosure and includes consolidation, rescheduling, reamortization, interest rate reduction, deferral, soft-wood timber loans, conservation easements, and write-down of debt. On the other hand, preservation loan servicing actions take place both before and after foreclosure. These include the leaseback/buyback program and the homestead protection program.

An applicant for primary loan servicing programs must meet all of the following requirements:
1. The borrower's cash flow demonstrates that expenses and payments exceed available income and that this reduction in income is due to circumstances beyond the borrower's control;
2. The borrower has acted in good faith in meeting the agreements set forth in Form FmHA 1962-1 and other agreements made with FmHA; and
3. A feasible plan of operation can be developed through primary loan servicing.[100]

The primary loan servicing programs contain the following basic provisions:
1. Loan consolidation involves the combination of two or more of the same type of loans into one larger loan.
2. Loan rescheduling alters the payment schedule so that the borrower has a longer time to repay loans which are secured by equipment, livestock, or crops.

118

For example, repayment of an operating loan can be extended for up to 15 years. When a loan is rescheduled, the interest rate may be reduced.

3. Loan reamortization involves changing the payment schedule to give the borrower a longer time to repay loans which are secured by real estate. For example, an FO loan may be extended for up to forty years from the date the original loan agreement was signed. When a loan is reamortized, the interest rate may be reduced.

4. Interest rate reduction may be available to borrower who has an operating loan or a farm ownership loan. This involves qualifying for "limited resource loan" interest rates. For OL loans the "limited resource loan" rate is 3% below the regular rate. For FO loans, the "limited resource loan" rate is between 5% and an amount that depends on the cost to the government to borrow money.

5. Loan deferral involves the delay of payments of principal and interest for up to five years. The borrower must be able to show that he or she cannot pay essential living expenses, maintain their property and make their scheduled debt payments. The borrower must also be able to show that the ability to repay will exist at the end of the delay period. The interest rate will either be the current rate or the original rate on the loan, whichever is lower. The interest that accrues during the delay period will not be added to principal. This interest must be paid in equal yearly payments for the remainder of the loan term. Additionally, deferral will only be available if loan consolidation, rescheduling, reamortization, or interest reduction are not effective for the borrower.

6. The Soft-wood timber program allows marginal land to be planted in soft-wood timber. If the borrower is qualified, a debt of up to $1,000 per acre can be deferred for up to 45 years. Interest is charged during the deferral period. The debt must be repaid when the timber is sold.

7. Conservation easements involve highly erodible
    land, wetlands, and wildlife habitats which the
    borrower transfers to the Secretary on a voluntary
    basis. FmHA will reduce the borrower's debt by
    the value of the transferred land or by the
    difference between the value of the land and the
    amount the borrower owes, whichever is larger.
    The amount of land remaining with the farmer after
    the transfer must be enough to enable him or her
    to continue the farming operation.

8. Debt write-down involves the reduction of both
    debt principal and interest. The debt can be
    reduced to the net recovery value of the property.
    In order to qualify for debt write-down, the
    borrower must demonstrate that a "feasible" plan of
    operation exists. This means that he or she will
    have enough money to pay family living and
    farming operation expenses and scheduled debt
    payments, including payments on the FmHA loan
    that remains. FmHA will not write down more of
    the debt than is necessary to show a "feasible" plan.
    Debt write-down is available only when
    consolidation, rescheduling, reamortization, interest
    rate reduction, or loan deferral will not show a
    "feasible" plan of operation for the borrower.[101]

Five Loan Servicing Phases

The new regulations under the Agricultural Credit Act
of 1987 set forth five phases for servicing borrower's
accounts.[102] Phase One involves the accounts of borrowers
who, despite being current in their payments, anticipate that
they may be unable to meet their principal and/or interest
payment on the loan in the future. Rescheduling and
reamortization are available in this phase to meet the primary
objective of keeping the borrower in business and minimizing
losses to the government.

If the borrower is unable to meet regular payments, even
with a rescheduled or reamortized loan, the borrower enters
Phase Two of the loan servicing options. Phase Two utilizes
lower interest rates and deferrals. When these options do not

assist the borrower in preventing delinquency and when the borrower is 180 days delinquent, the borrower enters Phase Three of the loan servicing process. At this point FmHA must determine which of its available alternatives will provide the best net recovery value to the government. These alternatives are either to allow the farming operation to continue or to liquidate it. The primary loan servicing options are available at this stage. This includes consolidation, rescheduling, reamortization, interest rate reduction, deferral, softwood timber loans, conservation easements, and write-down of debt. Each of these loan servicing options will be measured against the net recovery value to the government. In Phase Three, if the government determines that it cannot restructure the loan, a Notice of Intent to Accelerate form will be sent to the borrower. This notifies the borrower of his or her right to a meeting with FmHA, the right to appeal, the right to request an independent appraisal, and the right to buy out the loan at net recovery value. If the borrower does not exercise these primary loan servicing or buy-out rights, the borrower is considered for preservation loan servicing programs, the leaseback/buyback and homestead protection options.

If the loan cannot be restructured and it is determined that the borrower is ineligible for preservation loan servicing options, or if the borrower does not request preservation loan servicing, liquidation is required. This is Phase Four of the loan servicing procedure. Lastly, Phase Five involves property once it is in the FmHA inventory and the borrower is being considered for preservation loan servicing options.

In applying the primary loan servicing regulations, the County Supervisor will calculate the value of the restructured debt and compare it to the net recovery value of the collateral. If the calculations show that the value of the restructured debt is equal to or greater than the net recovery value of the collateral, FmHA will restructure the debt. If it is determined that primary loan servicing options will not provide value greater equal to or greater than the value of the collateral, the borrower is entitled to the opportunity to retain the security property by paying FmHA the net recovery value of that property. FmHA will not provide the credit for this transaction. This purchase of the property at net recovery value

121

will not be available to the borrower if a feasible plan can be developed with one of the primary loan servicing programs.[103]

Net Recovery Buyout
Under net recovery buyout provisions the borrower has forty-five (45) days after receiving the notice of ineligibility for primary loan servicing to buy the property at the net recovery value. FmHA will not finance this buy-out.[104] A borrower who buys the property at net recovery value must enter into a Net Recovery Buyout Recapture Agreement.[105] This agreement requires a borrower who sells the property within two years of the buyout, and realizes a gain, to agree to pay the difference in the sale price and the net recovery value buyout amount to FmHA. During the two-year period, FmHA will have a lien against the property which will be subordinate to any purchase money security interest. The borrower's account will be credited with the amount paid. Concomitantly, a receivable account will be established in the amount equal to the difference between the net recovery value and the market value of the real estate.[106] If the property is not sold within the two-year period, the lien on the receivable account will automatically be extinguished.[107]

Preservation Loan Programs
Preservation loan programs will automatically be considered for a borrower who cannot develop a feasible plan through any of the primary loan servicing programs after the borrower has become at least 180 days delinquent on an FmHA loan. The borrower must be given notice of the availability of both the primary and preservation loan programs.[108] As noted earlier, the preservation loan programs are leaseback/buyback and homestead protection.

The purpose of the preservation loan programs is to give the borrower an opportunity to retain ownership of at least a portion of his or her land, or to lease it with an option to repurchase. An applicant can participate in the homestead protection program and finance the balance of the farm under the leaseback/buyback program. FmHA is authorized to enter into a leaseback/buyback or homestead preservation agreement with a farmer-borrower prior to foreclosure or voluntary liquidation. This agreement can be executed prior to the borrower voluntarily assigning the property to FmHA. It should be noted that, prior to the enactment of the 1987 Act, borrowers were put in the difficult position of voluntarily assigning the property to FmHA without knowing whether FmHA would later be willing to execute a leaseback/buyback or homestead agreement with the borrower.

Preservation loan servicing also is available to borrowers whose property has already been placed in the FmHA inventory. When FmHA acquires a farm property, the former owner is sent notification of preservation loan service programs within 30 days of the acquisition. The former owner has 180 days from the date FmHA acquires the farm to apply for leaseback/buyback, unless state law provides for a longer period.[109] A former owner must request homestead protection within 90 days of the date on which FmHA acquired the property.[110]

Leaseback/buyback

In the leaseback/buyback program the immediate previous owner of the acquired property will have the first opportunity to re-acquire it. If that person is not interested, the opportunity will be given to the spouse or child of the previous owner if the previous owner was an individual, to the entity members of a corporation, partnership, or joint operation if the previous owner was an entity, or to the immediate previous family-farm operator of the farmland which is/was security for the loan.[111]

Inventory property cannot be leased or sold until these individuals are given notice and opportunity to apply for the program. They must also have the opportunity to complete an appeal of any unfavorable decision on their application. FmHA will send notification to the immediate previous owner of the property or to the immediate previous operator if the previous owner or other eligible individuals choose not to participate in the program. The immediate previous owner is responsible for giving notice of this opportunity to his or her spouse or children.

The applicant must demonstrate that a feasible plan of operation can be developed.[112] The term of the lease can be from one to five years, with the lessee selecting the term of the

123

lease. If the lessee is able to pay the cash lease payment at the time the lease is executed, a feasible plan is not required.[113] All leases under the leaseback/buyback program will contain an option to purchase. The purchase price will be the lower of the capitalization value or market value at the time the option is exercised. The option to purchase may be exercised at any time during the period of the lease. All options expire when the lease term ends.[114] If the borrower wants to finance the buyback with FmHA credit, he or she must meet the eligibility criteria for an FmHA farm ownership (FO) loan.[115] The FmHA leaseback/buyback program encompasses the total farm property. Farm property will not be subdivided for lease or purchase.[116] Denial of applications or disputes about the terms and conditions of the lease or purchase agreement under the leaseback/buyback program may be appealed pursuant to 7 C.F.R. Part 1900, Subpart B.[117]

Homestead Protection

Homestead protection is available to a farmer-borrower whose former loan was secured by real property which contains the borrower's principal residence. The purpose of the homestead protection program is to permit an eligible borrower to continue to farm or resume farming by allowing him or her to retain their dwelling through a lease and/or purchase agreement.[118]

Property which is subject to homestead protection includes the borrower's principal residence, up to 10 acres of adjoining land that is used to maintain the borrower's family, and a reasonable number of farm buildings which are located on the land adjoining the residence.[119] The County Supervisor will review the proposed boundaries of the homestead protection property. If the borrower and the County Supervisor cannot agree on the proposed shape or size of the property, the County Supervisor will make a determination. This determination is subject to appeal by the borrower.[120]

An applicant for homestead protection must be an individual who is or was personally liable for the loan that was secured in part by the homestead protection property. The applicant must also be, or have been, the owner of the homestead protection property.[121] The applicant (and spouse,

124

if applicable) must have received gross farm income from the farming or ranching operation which was reasonably commensurate with the size and location of the farm. This income must also have been reasonably commensurate with local agricultural conditions in at least two calendar years during the six year period preceding the calendar year in which the application is made.[122]

Under the homestead protection regulations, the applicant (and spouse) must have received at least 60% of their gross annual income from the farming and ranching operation in at least two of the six calendar years preceding the calendar year of application. Furthermore, the applicant must have continuously occupied the homestead protection property during the six year period preceding the calendar year in which the application is made. An exception to this requirement may be allowed if the applicant had to leave the property for a period of time not to exceed 12 months during the six year period, due to circumstances beyond the applicant's control.[123] Lastly, the applicant must have sufficient income to make the rental payments for the term of the lease and have the ability to maintain the property in good condition.[124]

The homestead protection lease will contain an option to purchase.[125] The lessee may exercise the option in writing at any time prior to the expiration of the lease term. If the lessee exercises the option to purchase, the purchase price will be the current market value of the homestead protection property. The purchase price may be paid in cash or financed with credit. If the lessee seeks a credit purchase-and-sale, the County Supervisor must determine if the lessee has adequate repayment ability.[126] The terms for a credit sale of homestead protection property will not exceed 35 years with equal amortized monthly installments, if the lessee exercises the option to purchase and has qualified for a credit sale. No down payment will be required.[127]

The applicant can appeal an FmHA decision made with reference to a determination of ineligibility for homestead protection, a termination of the lease for failure to make lease payments, or a failure to maintain the property in good condition.[128]

Loan Servicing Decisionmakers

All loan servicing decisions will be made by the County Supervisor, except write-down. Only a State Director can approve the write-down of a borrower's debt. If subsequent rescheduling or reamortization of the debt is necessary, approval must be obtained in writing from the District Director.[129]

Special Notification Requirements

There are specific notification requirements for farm borrowers whose FmHA loan accounts were accelerated between November 1, 1985 and May 7,1987; other farmer program borrowers whose loan accounts have been accelerated; borrowers with bankruptcies pending on January 6, 1988 whose accounts had not been foreclosed or liquidated; and borrowers who had been discharged or had plans confirmed in bankruptcy prior to January 6, 1988 and who had not been foreclosed or liquidated prior to that date.[130]

For borrowers who are less than 180 days delinquent, the County Supervisor is required to contact a delinquent farmer program borrower within 30 days after the borrower's account becomes delinquent. A meeting to determine the reasons for the delinquency must be scheduled within 10 days. If it is determined that the borrower does not have the resources to bring the account current, the County Supervisor must consider primary loan servicing for the borrower.[131]

Program borrowers who are 180 days delinquent and who cannot develop a feasible plan which uses rescheduling, reamortization, limited resource rates, or deferral will be sent notice of the FmHA loan service programs by certified mail. Notice of the loan servicing programs must be provided to borrowers prior to FmHA initiation of liquidation action, acceptance of a voluntary conveyance of security property, the borrower's request to sell security property, accelerating payments on the loan, repossessing the borrower's property, foreclosing on the property, or taking any other collection action.[132] Borrowers who are sent the "Notice of Availability of Loan Service Programs" must request consideration of loan servicing options within 45 days after receipt of the notice. FmHA will proceed with liquidation if the borrower's request is not received within this time period, or if the borrower who

126

wishes to request a hearing does not do so within 30 days.[133]

Action on a Completed Borrower Application

Within 60 days of FmHA receipt of a completed application with the proper attachments for primary loan servicing programs, the County Supervisor must consider all primary loan servicing programs as possible options for the borrower. The County Supervisor will use the FmHA computer program, DALR$, to find the combination of loan servicing programs that will result in a feasible plan for the particular borrower.[134] If the County Supervisor determines that the borrower is not eligible for any of the primary loan servicing programs or that restructuring is not feasible because of debt held by other lenders, the borrower will be advised of the option of mediation, or a meeting of creditors. If mediation or the meeting of creditors does not result in a feasible plan, the borrower will be sent the FmHA Notice of Intent to Accelerate. This notice advises the borrower of his or her right to a meeting, the right to appeal, the right to an independent appraisal of the property involved, and the opportunity to buy the property at the net recovery value.

If the borrower appeals the denial of primary loan servicing, the appeal must be completed before FmHA begins any further processing of preservation loan service program requests. If an adverse decision is upheld on appeal and the borrower is determined eligible for preservation loan servicing programs, FmHA will complete the processing of the application for preservation loan servicing. No acceleration or foreclosure can occur until the appeal process for both primary and preservation loan servicing has been completed.[135]

Debt Settlement

Under certain circumstances a farmer-borrower may wish to seek adjustment, cancellation, or compromise of an outstanding indebtedness to FmHA. This usually occurs in situations where the farmer-borrower is no longer in possession of the collateral which secures the indebtedness, and has few or no other resources with which to pay the remainder of the debt. Debt adjustment is a form of debt settlement procedure, in which the debt is reduced, conditioned upon completion of payment on the adjusted amount at a specific future time(s). This can be applied either with or without the payment of any consideration when the adjustment offer is approved.[136] In contrast, cancellation of the debt is the final discharge of a debt without any payment on it.[137] Similarly, the compromise of a debt is the satisfaction of a debt or claim by the acceptance of a lump sum payment of less than the total amount owed on the debt or claim.[138]

A borrower who wishes to debt settle with FmHA should file Form FmHA 456-1, "Application for Settlement of Indebtedness." The County Committee is required to review these applications for settlement of indebtedness and to either approve or reject each application received. A settlement will not be approved if it is more favorable to the debtor than that which has been recommended by the County Committee.[139]

Upon a favorable recommendation by the County Committee, the request for debt settlement is referred to either the State Director or the National Administrator. District Directors and County Supervisors cannot approve debt settlement actions. State Directors have the discretion to either approve or reject debt settlement applications when the outstanding balance of the relevant indebtedness, less the amount of a compromise or adjustment offer, is less than $250,000. The State Director may also approve the cancellation of debts which were discharged in a Chapter 7 bankruptcy proceeding regardless of the amount of the outstanding indebtedness. The National Administrator (or his or her designee) will approve or reject the settlement proposal when the outstanding balance of the relevant indebtedness, less the amount of the compromise or adjustment offer, is $250,000 or more.[140]

Settlements may not be approved for one joint debtor unless approved for all joint debtors. The ability of each debtor to pay is evaluated in making a determination of the settlement of a debt by joint debtors.[141] A borrower whose debt settlement offer has been rejected may appeal the decision.[142]

The present and future repayment ability of a debtor will be the basis of determining whether the debt should be collected in full, compromised, adjusted, cancelled, or charged off. In regard to compromise and adjustment of debts, the amount offered must be reasonably related to the debtor's ability to pay, and must also bear a reasonable relation to the amount which could be recovered by enforced collection procedures. The debtor's total present income and nonsecurity assets are among the factors which determine eligibility for any settlement.[143] Debts may be compromised or adjusted for debtors who are able to pay in full but refuse to do so. However, the government will examine a wider scope of the debtor's assets to determine the likelihood of recovery by enforced collection procedures.[144]

Sale of Inventory Farmland

Inventory farmland may be classified as either "suitable" or "surplus" land. "Suitable" land is property that can be used to carry out the objectives of an FmHA loan program with financing provided through that program. "Surplus" land is either property that is not suitable for sale to eligible applicants, or suitable CONACT property which is not sold within three years of acquisition. CONACT property is property which is acquired or sold pursuant to the Consolidated Farm and Rural Development Act. "Suitable" property must be offered for sale to farmers who operate family-sized farms. In contrast, "surplus" property may be sold without regard to the size of the farming operation or the eligibility of the buyer for FmHA loans.

In the 1985 farm bill, Congress enacted provisions which require FmHA to reserve the sale of all FmHA inventory land to FmHA-eligible, family-sized farming operations. However, in many states FmHA had, in effect, circumvented this statutory requirement by classifying land as "unsuitable" for further FmHA loans. Under this approach, FmHA maintained that, as a result of this classification, it was entitled to sell the land as "surplus" property to ineligible borrowers. The Agricultural Credit Act of 1987 has addressed this situation by requiring that the County Committee classify farmland as being "suitable" for use in a farming operation unless the property cannot be used to meet any of the purposes found at Section 303 of the Consolidated Farm and Rural Development Act.[145]

Guaranteed Loans

In the mid-to-late 1980's, FmHA has made a policy transition from issuing direct loans to an emphasis on issuing guaranteed loans. A "guaranteed" loan is a loan which is made and serviced by a private lender and for which FmHA has issued a loan note guarantee. The loan note guarantee and contract of guarantee constitute obligations which are supported by the full faith and credit of the United States. These guarantees are incontestable except for fraud or misrepresentation of which the lender or holder has actual knowledge at the time the agreement is executed, or which a lender or holder participates in or condones.[146] A note which provides for the payment of interest on interest cannot be guaranteed.[147] The maximum percentage of the guarantee for all loans, except Business and Industrial loans, is 90%.[148]

A farmer-borrower and/or the lender may file either a preliminary application or a complete application. By filing a preliminary application, the prospective borrower or lender seeks an FmHA determination of eligibility, feasibility, or the availability of guarantee authority prior to determining whether to file a complete application.[149] If it appears that the applicant is eligible for the loan guarantee and loan guarantee funding authority is available, the County Supervisor will inform the lender and applicant of these determinations not later than 20 calendar days after receipt of the preliminary application. The County Supervisor will also request them to file a complete application.[150] If it appears that the applicant is not eligible, the County Supervisor must notify the loan applicant and the lender within ten (10) days of FmHA's decision of all the reasons for the decision. Any adverse decisions by FmHA in regard to loan guarantees are appealable by the lender and the applicant pursuant to 7 C.F.R. Part 1900, Subpart B.[151] The appeal must be a joint appeal unless the lender is appealing a denial or reduction of a final loss payment request.

Upon receipt of a complete application, the County Supervisor must evaluate the application to determine whether the proposed loan is for authorized purposes, whether there is reasonable assurance of a positive cash flow projection, and whether there is sufficient collateral and equity for the loan.[152] If this evaluation indicates that the guarantee may be approved, the County Supervisor will present the application to the County Committee for certification or rejection.[153] If the County Committee finds the applicant eligible, the members of the committee will sign a form which certifies the applicant's eligibility for assistance.[154]

A major distinction between FmHA direct loans and guaranteed loans is that all servicing of guaranteed loans is conducted by the lender. Although the applicable guaranteed loan regulations allow for consolidation, rescheduling, reamortization, deferral and debt write-down, respectively, if the respective criteria for each are met, these loan servicing options are permissive rather than mandatory. In other words, a private lender is not required to offer these loan servicing options.[155]

Appeals

The Agricultural Credit Act of 1987[156] requires the Secretary of Agriculture to establish a national appeals staff to hear and review appeals of FmHA adverse decisions.[157] Although the Act only requires that this system be provided to CONACT borrowers, FmHA has decided to use the national appeals system for all FmHA applicants and borrowers, and for holders of loans guaranteed by FmHA. The national appeals division is an independent branch within FmHA and has its own staff. The Director of Appeals reports directly to the administrator of FmHA.

The purpose of establishing an independent national appeals staff is to separate the hearing and review process from the initial decision makers or their immediate supervisors. Prior to the implementation of the national appeals system, the hearing officer in an FmHA appeal was usually a District Director. This was frequently a person who had participated in making the initial decision, or who was a District Director from a nearby area and was well acquainted with the employees whose decisions he or she was required to review.

Prior to issuing an adverse decision to an applicant or borrower, FmHA decision makers are required to ascertain that all documentation and calculations necessary to the determination are accurate, complete, and included within the administrative file. Any calculations or documentation which demonstrate the reasons for the decision should be provided

131

and carefully explained in detail to the applicant.[158]

A person against whom FmHA has issued an adverse action is entitled to an informal meeting with the decision maker before the appeal process begins.[159] The decision maker must give the applicant or borrower notice of her right to a meeting no later than 10 days after the adverse decision is rendered.[160] If the informal meeting results in a resolution of the issues, the decision maker must send the individual a letter within seven (7) days of the meeting setting forth the conclusions reached during the meeting. If the meeting does not result in a resolution of the issues, the decision maker must notify the individual within seven (7) calendar days of his or her right to an administrative appeal.[161]

When an applicant disputes the value of an FmHA-appraised property, FmHA must inform the applicant that he or she must request review of the appraisal by the FmHA State Director before an appeal is pursued. If the applicant or borrower seeks this review, the time for seeking an appeal will be extended until the State Director has acted on the request to review the appraisal. Appraisals which involve farmer program primary loan servicing may be appealed to the area supervisor of the national appeals staff without prior review by the State Director.[162] The appellant has the burden of demonstrating that the appraisal is in error. The appellant may submit an independent appraisal from a qualified appraiser. The independent appraisal must conform to the agency appraisal regulations for that particular loan program. If the independent appraisal and the FmHA appraisal vary by no more than 5 percent, the FmHA appraisal will be considered as the basis for the valuation.[163]

FmHA uses the following terms in its appeal process. The "appellant" is the individual who is directly and adversely affected by an administrative decision by FmHA, and who brings the appeal. The "hearing" is an informal proceeding at which an administrative appeal from an adverse decision is heard. The "decision maker" is the FmHA official who made the specific decision which is the subject of the appeal. This does not include officials who serve in an advisory capacity and who are not significantly involved in the decision. The "hearing officer" is the member of the national appeals staff who conducts the

132

administrative appeal hearing. This person has the authority to uphold, reverse, or modify the decision(s) of the decision maker. The "review officer" is the member of the national appeals staff who has the authority to uphold, reverse, or modify the decisions of the hearing officer.[164]

Once an individual has requested an appeal hearing, the area supervisor of the national appeals staff will verify whether the appeal was submitted within the authorized period. If not, the appellant's appeal rights are terminated unless the delay was beyond the appellant's control or for other good reason as determined by the area supervisor.[165]

The appellant's case file must be available to the appellant (or their representative) at the FmHA decision maker's office for 10 working days following the receipt of a request for an appeal. During this period the appellant has the right to inspect or receive copies of FmHA material concerning the case. The file is then forwarded to the hearing officer.

If, after review of the file, the hearing officer determines that the decision will be reversed, he or she will notify all parties. Otherwise, the hearing officer will arrange for a hearing. This will normally take place within 45 calendar days of receipt of the request for a hearing.[166] A hearing that results from a denial of a borrower's request for release of normal income security must be held within 20 days of the request, unless the borrower agrees to a longer time period.[167]

At any time, the appellant may waive the opportunity for a hearing and request the hearing officer to make a decision based on the file and any written evidence or statements the appellant may have submitted.[168]

The appeal hearings are informal proceedings. The appellant has the responsibility of showing why the initial decision should be modified or reversed. The appellant may present any evidence, witnesses, and arguments in support of the appeal. The appellant may also controvert evidence relied upon by FmHA, and may question all witnesses. Evidence may be received by the hearing officer without regard to whether the evidence would be admissable in judicial proceedings.[169]

The appeal hearing proceedings will be tape recorded by the hearing officer. Appellants may also tape record the proceedings at their own expense. At the time a decision is rendered, the appellant may request and receive a copy of the hearing tape at no expense. The appellant may also request a written transcript of the hearing. The appellant must pay the government's costs of transcription. Appellants may also make their own arrangements for a transcript of the hearing.[170]

The hearing officer must render a decision within 30 days of the date set for the hearing, unless additional materials or responses have been requested. Any hearing decision concerning farmer primary loan servicing programs must be made within 45 days of receipt of the appeal request.[171] The decision of the hearing officer should be based on facts presented at the hearing or in writing, rebuttal by the appellant and the decisionmaker of new evidence, additional information requested by the hearing officer, appropriate FmHA files, applicable statutes and regulations and the hearing officer's general knowledge of FmHA program functions.[172]

If the initial decision is upheld or modified but not reversed, the hearing officer must advise the appellant of the specific reasons for the decision. If the hearing officer renders an adverse decision, the appellant may request further review by a review officer. If the appellant does not make a written request for a review of the hearing officer's decision within the 30 day calendar period provided in the letter, the appeal will be considered concluded.[173] If the appeal request includes a request for an independent appraisal of property involved in the decision, the hearing officer must provide the borrower with a list of three appraisers who are approved by the County Supervisor for this purpose. The borrower must select an appraiser from this list and pay the costs of the appraisal. A copy of the appraisal must be provided to the borrower. If an independent appraisal is requested, the 45 day decision deadline will be extended as necessary to allow the completion of the appraisal.[174]

The review officer must render a decision within 45 days of receipt of the request. The review officer's decision will be based on the written facts presented, the certified record, any additional information requested by the review officers, any responses to the additional information, applicable statutes and regulations, and the review officer's general knowledge of FmHA program functions.[175]

The review officer's decision must be set forth in a written letter sent to the appellant. If the adverse decision is upheld, the letter must contain the statement: "This review concludes the administrative appeal of your case." If the State Director is the review officer, the appellant is entitled to further review rights before the Director of Appeals.[176]

When an appeal is concluded, the effective date of the action to be taken will be the date of the initial decision from which the appeal was taken. Foreclosure action will not be pursued by the agency until the time for appeal has expired or the appeal is terminated or resolved. Any loan made as the result of an appeal will bear interest at the lower of the interest rates in effect for that type of loan on the date of actual loan approval or loan closing.[177] A decision made when an appeal is concluded will be administratively final.[178] Appeal records will be maintained in the applicant's or borrower's case folder.[179]

Judicial Review

After a borrower has reached an unsuccessful outcome to his or her administrative appeal of an adverse FmHA decision, the borrower may want to consider pursuing judicial review of the agency action. There is no statutory provision within the FmHA organic act which establishes a right of judicial review. However, under the Administrative Procedure Act (APA)[180] Congress has provided an express statutory right to judicial review of most agency actions. The APA provides that "[a] person suffering legal wrong because of agency action, or adversely affected or aggrieved by agency action within the meaning of a relevant statute, is entitled to judicial review thereof."[181] The Administrative Procedure Act provides a right of judicial review to FmHA decisions "except to the extent that -- (1) statutes preclude judicial review; or (2) agency action is committed to agency discretion by law".[182]

In many, if not most, of the reported cases which have involved FmHA's handling of a borrower's account, the courts have found that FmHA actions are committed to agency discretion, and therefore unreviewable. On the other hand, courts have been more likely to find that an FmHA action was reviewable if it involved a systemic matter, such as FmHA's failure to promulgate borrower's rights regulations.

Under the first APA exemption noted above, courts presume that Congress intended to provide a right of judicial review in the absence of "clear and convincing evidence" that it meant to preclude such review.[183] Thus, unless a statute expressly denies a right of review, the first exemption will not apply. Moreover, the second exemption has been narrowly construed. The leading case in this area is <u>Citizens to Preserve Overton Park v. Volpe</u>.[184] According to <u>Overton Park</u>, APA Section 701 precludes judicial review only "in those rare instances where...there is no law to apply".[185] In the lower federal courts, the majority view appears to be that the determination of whether there is law to apply "necessarily turns on pragmatic considerations as to whether an agency action is subject to judicial review".[186] Under the "pragmatic considerations" test, courts are likely to find that agency action is unreviewable if the area of decisionmaking involves the application of agency expertise in a complicated area and the potential for a large number of agency actions to become subject to judicial review would substantially burden the agency in its functions, as well as burden the courts.

As noted earlier, it is generally difficult for a borrower to establish a right of judicial review for FmHA actions which involve individual borrower accounts. For example, in <u>Tuepker v. Farmers Home Administration</u>,[187] the farmer-borrower had sued FmHA after exhausting his administrative appeals in regard to FmHA's denial of his loan request. The Court of Appeals for the Eighth Circuit affirmed the lower court's determination that no judicial review was available. Specifically, the Court stated that each of the agency determinations which Tuepker contested were "a qualitative, subjective decision based on agency expertise within the bounds of the statutory directive" to make loans to persons who possessed reasonable prospects for successfully operating a farm.[188] The court noted that review would likely be available if the complaint had alleged that FmHA action(s) constituted a "substantial departure" from important procedural rights or if FmHA had seriously misconstrued its obligations to the borrower under the governing legislation.[189] Similarly, in <u>Woodsmall v. Lyng</u>,[190] the Court of Appeals for the Eighth Circuit held that FmHA's conclusion that the applicant lacked creditworthiness was a qualitative, subjective decision of the agency which was not subject of judicial review.

In contrast to <u>Tuepker</u> and <u>Woodsmall</u>, in <u>Allison v. Block</u>,[191] the Eighth Circuit Court of Appeals, while not addressing the issue of judicial review, held that FmHA abused its discretion by failing to promulgate loan deferral regulations pursuant to 7 U.S.C. 1981a. The court found that the Secretary had disregarded explicit Congressional intent by failing to promulgate those regulations. The court noted that this holding was notwithstanding the fact that the Secretary of Agriculture had the discretion to make individual deferral decisions on borrower's loan accounts.

It should be noted that in <u>Harper v. Federal Land Bank of Spokane</u>,[192] the Federal District Court held that the Agricultural Credit Act of 1987 conferred upon Farm Credit System borrowers an implied private right of action against Farm Credit institutions. In <u>Harper</u>, the borrowers established that their creditors violated the 1987 Act by continuing a foreclosure proceeding without first considering a restructuring of the debt involved. <u>Harper</u> may only be of limited use as authority for establishing a right of judicial review against FmHA. First of all, this case does not deal with the Administrative Procedure Act, which forms the matrix of borrower's rights of judicial review against FmHA. Secondly, the language of the case is expressly limited to the Farm Credit System, whose functions and policies are separate and distinct from FmHA. On the other hand, the <u>Harper</u> case does unequivocally stand for the proposition that the Agricultural Credit Act of 1987 should confer a private right of action upon the borrowers to whom its loan servicing provisions apply.

FOOTNOTES

1. 7 C.F.R. § 1941.2 (1988).

2. 541 F. Supp. 506 (S.D. Ga. 1982).

3. Pub. L. No. 100-233, 101 Stat. 1568 (to be codified at various Parts of 12 U.S.C. § 2001 et seq. and 7 U.S.C. § 1921 et seq., respectively.

4. 7 C.F.R. § 1943.2 (1988).

5. 7 C.F.R. § 1943.3 (1988).

6. 7 C.F.R. § 1943.16 (1988).

7. 7 C.F.R. § 1941.2 (1988).

8. 7 C.F.R. § 1941.2 (1988).

9. 7 C.F.R. § 1941.3 (1988).

10. 7 C.F.R. § 1941.16 (1988).

11. 7 C.F.R. § 1941.16(a)(1988).

12. 7 C.F.R. § 1941.16(b)(1988).

13. 7 C.F.R. § 1941.16(c)(1988).

14. 7 C.F.R. § 1941.16(d)(1988).

15. 7 C.F.R. § 1941.16(e)(1988).

16. 7 C.F.R. § 1941.16(f)(1988).

17. 7 C.F.R. § 1941.16(g)(1988).

18. 7 C.F.R. § 1941.16(h)(1988).

19. 7 C.F.R. § 1941.16(i)(1988).

20. 7 C.F.R. § 1941.16(j)(1988).

21. 7 C.F.R. § 1941.16(k)(1988).

22. 7 C.F.R. § 1941.16(l)(1988).

23. 7 C.F.R. § 1941.16(m)(1988).

24. 7 C.F.R. § 1941.17(a)(1988).

25. 7 C.F.R. § 1941.17(a)(1988).

26. 7 C.F.R. § 1941.17(a)(1988).

27. 7 C.F.R. § 1941.17(a)(1988).

28. 7 C.F.R. § 1941.17(b)(1988).

29. 7 C.F.R. § 1945.20 (1988).

30. 7 C.F.R. § 1945.20 (1988).

31. 7 C.F.R. § 1945.154(28)(1988).

32. 7 C.F.R. § 1945.154(129)(1988).

33. 53 Fed. Reg. 35673-54 (1988) (to be codified at 7 C.F.R. § 1910.4) and 53 Fed. Reg. 35678 (1988) (to be codified at 7 C.F.R. Part 1910, Subpart A, Exhibit A).

34. 53 Fed. Reg. 35672 (1988) (to be codified at 7 C.F.R. § 1910.3(a)).

35. 53 Fed. Reg. 35672 (1988) (to be codified at 7 C.F.R. § 1910.3(c)).

36. 53 Fed. Reg. 35673 (1988) (to be codified at 7 C.F.R. § 1910.4(a)).

37. 53 Fed. Reg. 35674 (1988) (to be codified at 7 C.F.R. § 1910.4(c)).

38. 53 Fed. Reg. 35675 (1988) (to be codified at 7 C.F.R. § 1910.4(g)).

39. 53 Fed. Reg. 35675 (1988) (to be codified at 7 C.F.R. § 1910.4(i)).

40. 53 Fed. Reg. 35675 (1988) (to be codified at 7 C.F.R. § 1910.4(j)).

41. 53 Fed. Reg. 35675 (1988) (to be codified at 7 C.F.R. § 1910.4(i)(1988)).

42. 53 Fed. Reg. 35676 (1988) (to be codified at 7 C.F.R. § 1910.6(e) and (f)).

43. 53 Fed. Reg. 35676 (1988) (to be codified at 7 C.F.R. § 1910.6(b) and (d)).

44. 53 Fed. Reg. 35685-86 (1988) (to be codified at 7 C.F.R. § 1941.12) & 53 Fed. Reg. 35694 (1988) (to be codified at 7 C.F.R. § 1943.12).

45. 53 Fed. Reg. 35675-66 (1988) (to be codified at 7 C.F.R. § 1910.5(c)).

46. 7 C.F.R. § 1809.1(a)(1988).

47. 7 C.F.R. § 1809.2 (1988).

48. 7 C.F.R. § 1809.3(a)(1988).

49. 7 C.F.R. § 1809.4 (1988).

50. 53 Fed. Reg. 35679 (1988) (to be codified at 7 C.F.R. § 1924.56).

51. 53 Fed. Reg. 35680-82 (1988) (to be codified at 7 C.F.R. § 1924.57).

52. 53 Fed. Reg. 35682 (1988) (to be codified at 7 C.F.R. § 1924.58).

53. 53 Fed. Reg. 35682 (1988) (to be codified at 7 C.F.R. § 1924.59).

54. 53 Fed. Reg. 35682-83 (1988) (to be codified at 7 C.F.R. § 1924.60 (1988)).

55. 53 Fed. Reg. 35680 (1988) (to be codified at 7 C.F.R. § 1924.57(c)(5)).

56. 53 Fed. Reg. 35784 (1988) (to be codified at 7 C.F.R. § 1962.17(b)(2)(i)).

57. 53 Fed. Reg. 35680 (1988) (to be codified at 7 C.F.R. § 1924.57(b)(2)).

58. 53 Fed. Reg. 35680 (1988) (to be codified at 7 C.F.R. § 1924.57(b)(2)).

59. 53 Fed. Reg. 35681 (1988) (to be codified at 7 C.F.R. § 1924.57(d)(3)).

60. 53 Fed. Reg. 35670 (1988) (to be codified at 7 C.F.R. § 1902.2(a); 7 C.F.R. § 1902.1(j)(1988)).

61. 53 Fed. Reg. 35670 (1988) (to be codified at 7 C.F.R. § 1902.2(a)(4)).

62. 53 Fed. Reg. 35670 (1988) (to be codified at 7 C.F.R. § 1902.2(a)(5)).

63. 53 Fed. Reg. 35670 (1988) (to be codified at 7 C.F.R. § 1902.2(a)(6)(1988)).

64. 53 Fed. Reg. 35697 (1988) (to be codified at 7 C.F.R. § 1943.19(a)).

65. 53 Fed. Reg. 35697 (1988) (to be codified at 7 C.F.R. § 1943.19(b)).

66. 53 Fed. Reg. 35698 (1988) (to be codified at 7 C.F.R. § 1943.19(c)).

67. 53 Fed. Reg. 35698 (1988) (to be codified at 7 C.F.R. § 1943.19(d)).

68. 53 Fed. Reg. 35688 (1988) (to be codified at 7 C.F.R. § 1941.19)).

69. 53 Fed. Reg. 35689 (1988) (to be codified at 7 C.F.R. § 1941.19(b)).

70. 53 Fed. Reg. 35689 (1988) (to be codified at 7 C.F.R. § 1941.19(c)).

71. 53 Fed. Reg. 35689 (1988) (to be codified at 7 C.F.R. § 1941.19(f)).

72. 7 C.F.R. § 1945.169(a)(1988).

73. 7 C.F.R. § 1945.169(d)(2)(1988).

74. 53 Fed. Reg. 35783 (1988) (to be codified at 7 C.F.R. § 1962.4).

75. 53 Fed. Reg. 35784 (1988) (to be codified at 7 C.F.R. § 1962.17(b)(5)).

76. 580 F. Supp. 194 (D.N.D. 1984).

77. 580 F. Supp. at 203 (citing Sniadach v. Family Finance Corp., 395 U.S. 337 (1969).

78. Payne v. Block, 622 F. Supp. 904, 907 (D.C. Colo. 1985).

79. <u>Coleman v. Block</u>, 632 F. Supp. 997 (D.N.D. 1986).

80. Pub. L. No. 100-233, 101 Stat. 1568 (1988).

81. Pub. L. No. 100-233, § 611, 101 Stat. 1673 (amending 7 U.S.C. 1985(f)).

82. 7 C.F.R. § 1962.17(b)(2)(iii)(A)(1988).

83. 7 C.F.R. § 1962.17(b)(2)(iii)(1988).

84. 7 C.F.R. § 1962.17(b)(3)(1988).

85. 53 Fed. Reg. 35784 (1988) (to be codified at 7 C.F.R. § 1962.17(b)(5)).

86. 7 C.F.R. § 1962.17(b)(4)(1988).

87. 7 C.F.R. § 1962.18 (1988).

88. 7 C.F.R. § 1962.4(e) and (f)(1988).

89. 773 F.2d 1469 (5th Cir. 1985).

90. 580 F. Supp. 194, 211 (D.N.D. 1984).

91. 7 C.F.R. § 1962.4(g)(3)(1988).

92. 7 U.S.C. § 1981a.

93. 541 F. Supp. 506 (S.D. Ga. 1982).

94. 723 F.2d 631 (8th Cir. 1983).

95. 723 F.2d at 636.

96. 723 F.2d at 638.

97. Pub. L. No. 100-233, § 615, 101 Stat. 1678 (1988) (to be codified at 7 U.S.C. § 2001).

98. 53 Fed. Reg. 35638 (1988)(to be codified at 7 C.F.R. Parts 1809, 1902, 1910, 1924, 1941, 1943, 1944, 1945, 1951, 1955, 1962 & 1965). The loan servicing regulations are found at 53 Fed. Reg. 35718 (1988) (to be codified at 7 C.F.R. Part 1951).

99. 53 Fed. Reg. 35718 (1988) (to be codified at 7 C.F.R. § 1951.902).

100. 53 Fed. Reg. 35723-24 (1988) (to be codified at 7 C.F.R. § 1951.909(c)(1),(2)&(3)).

101. 53 Fed. Reg. 35740 (1988) (to be codified at 7 C.F.R. Part 1951, Subpart S, Exhibit A, Attachment One).

102. 53 Fed. Reg. 35719-20 (1988) (to be codified at 7 C.F.R. § 1951.902)).

103. 53 Fed. Reg. 35719-20 (1988) (to be codified at 7 C.F.R. § 1951.902).

104. 53 Fed. Reg. 35729 (1988) (to be codified at 7 C.F.R. § 1951.909(h)(3)(iii)).

105. 53 Fed. Reg. 35746 (1988) (to be codified at 7 C.F.R. Part 1951, Subpart S, Exhibit C).

106. 53 Fed. Reg. 35737 (1988) (to be codified at 7 C.F.R. § 1951.913).

107. 53 Fed. Reg. 35746 (1988) (to be codified at 7 C.F.R. Part 1951, Subpart S, Exhibit C).

108. 53 Fed. Reg. 35731 (1988) (to be codified at 7 C.F.R. § 1951.911(a)(3)(i)); 53 Fed. Reg. 35730 (1988) (to be codified at 7 C.F.R. § 1951.911(a)(1)(i)).

109. 53 Fed. Reg. 35730 (1988) (to be codified at 7 C.F.R. § 1951.911(a)(1)(ii)).

110. 53 Fed. Reg. 35734 (1988) (to be codified at 7 C.F.R. § 1951.911(b)(2)(iii)).

111. 53 Fed. Reg. 35730 (1988) (to be codified at 7 C.F.R. § 1951.911(a)).

112. 53 Fed. Reg. 35732 (1988) (to be codified at 7 C.F.R. § 1951.911(a)(6)).

113. 53 Fed. Reg. 35732 (1988) (to be codified at 7 C.F.R. § 1951.911(a)(6)(i)).

114. 53 Fed. Reg. 35732-33 (1988) (to be codified at 7 C.F.R. § 1951.911(a)(6)(ii)).

115. 53 Fed. Reg. 35732 (1988) (to be codified at 7 C.F.R. § 1951.911(a)(5)(B)).

116. 53 Fed. Reg. 35733 (1988) (to be codified at 7 C.F.R. § 1951.911(a)(8)(i)).

117. 53 Fed. Reg. 35733 (1988) (to be codified at 7 C.F.R. § 1951.911(a)(8)(v)).

118. 53 Fed. Reg. 35734 (1988) (to be codified at 7 C.F.R. § 1951.911(b)(1)).

119. 53 Fed. Reg. 35734 (1988) (to be codified at 7 C.F.R. § 1951.911(b)(2)(i)(A)).

120. 53 Fed. Reg. 35734 (1988) (to be codified at 7 C.F.R. § 1951.911(b)(2)(i)(C)).

121. 53 Fed. Reg. 35734-35 (1988) (to be codified at 7 C.F.R. § 1951.911(b)(3)(i)).

122. 53 Fed. Reg. 35735 (1988) (to be codified at 7 C.F.R. § 1951.911(b)(3)(iii)).

123. 53 Fed. Reg. 35735 (1988) (to be codified at 7 C.F.R.
§ 1951.911(b)(3)(iv)&(v)).

124. 53 Fed. Reg. 35735 (1988) (to be codified at 7 C.F.R.
§ 1951.911(b)(3)(vi)).

125. 53 Fed. Reg. 35735 (1988) (to be codified at 7 C.F.R.
§ 1951.911(b)(8)(i)).

126. 53 Fed. Reg. 35736 (1988) (to be codified at 7 C.F.R.
§ 1951.911(b)(8)(ii)(A)-(D)).

127. 53 Fed. Reg. 35736 (1988) (to be codified at 7 C.F.R.
§ 1951.911(b)(9)).

128. 53 Fed. Reg. 35735 (1988) (to be codified at 7 C.F.R.
§ 1951.911(b)(5)).

129. 53 Fed. Reg. 35720 (1988) (to be codified at 7 C.F.R.
§ 1951.903(b)).

130. 53 Fed. Reg. 35721-22 (1988) (to be codified at 7 C.F.R.
§ 1951.907(a)-(d)).

131. 53 Fed. Reg. 35722 (1988) (to be codified at 7 C.F.R.
§ 1951.907)).

132. 53 Fed. Reg. 35722 (1988) (to be codified at 7 C.F.R.
§ 1951.907(e)).

133. 53 Fed. Reg. 35722-23 (1988) (to be codified at 7 C.F.R.
§ 1951.907(h)).

134. 53 Fed. Reg. 35723 (1988) (to be codified at 7 C.F.R.
§ 1951.909(a)).

135. 53 Fed. Reg. 35723 (1988) (to be codified at 7 C.F.R.
§ 1951.909(b)).

136. 7 C.F.R. § 1956.54(a)(1988).

137. 7 C.F.R. § 1956.54(b)(1988).

138. 7 C.F.R. § 1956.54(d)(1988).

139. 7 C.F.R. § 1956.57(f)(1988).

140. 7 C.F.R. § 1956.58(a)(1988).

141. 7 C.F.R. § 1956.57(j)(1988).

142. 7 C.F.R. § 1956.58(e)(1988).

143. 7 C.F.R. § 1956.66(a)(1988).

144. 7 C.F.R. § 1956.66(b)(1988).

145. Pub. L. No. 100-233, § 610, 101 Stat. 1669 (1988) (to be codified at 7 U.S.C. 1985(c)).

146. 7 C.F.R. § 1980.11 (1988).

147. 7 C.F.R. § 1980.11 (1988).

148. 7 C.F.R. § 1980.20 (1988).

149. 7 C.F.R. § 1980.113 (1988).

150. 7 C.F.R. § 1980.113(c)(1988).

151. 7 C.F.R. § 1980.113(c)(1988).

152. 7 C.F.R. § 1980.114 (1988).

153. 7 C.F.R. § 1980.114(b)(1988).

154. 7 C.F.R. § 1980.115(a)(1988).

155. 7 C.F.R. § 1980.124 (1988).

156. Pub. L. No. 100-233, 101 Stat. 1568 (1988).

157. Pub. L. No. 100-233, § 608, 101 Stat. 1667 (1988).

158. 53 Fed. Reg. 26408 (1988) (to be codified at 7 C.F.R. § 1900.53(a)(1988)).

159. 53 Fed. Reg. 26408 (1988) (to be codified at 7 C.F.R. § 1900.53(a)(3)).

160. 53 Fed. Reg. 26408 (1988) (to be codified at 7 C.F.R. § 1900.53(a)(3)).

161. 53 Fed. Reg. 26408 (1988) (to be codified at 7 C.F.R. § 1900.53(a)(4)).

162. 53 Fed. Reg. 26408 (1988) (to be codified at 7 C.F.R. § 1900.53(b)).

163. 53 Fed. Reg. 26408 (1988) (to be codified at 7 C.F.R. § 1900.53(b)).

164. 53 Fed. Reg. 26407 (1988) (to be codified at 7 C.F.R. § 1900.52(a),(b),(c),(e)&(f)).

165. 53 Fed. Reg. 26409 (1988) (to be codified at 7 C.F.R. § 1900.56(a)(1)).

166. 53 Fed. Reg. 26409 (1988) (to be codified at 7 C.F.R. § 1900.56.(3)).

167. 53 Fed. Reg. 26409 (1988) (to be codified at 7 C.F.R. § 1900.56).

168. 53 Fed. Reg. 26409 (1988) (to be codified at 7 C.F.R. § 1900.56(7)).

169. 53 Fed. Reg. 26410 (1988) (to be codified at 7 C.F.R. § 1900.57(a)).

170. 53 Fed. Reg. 26410 (1988) (to be codified at 7 C.F.R. § 1900.57(d)).

171. 53 Fed. Reg. 26410 (1988) (to be codified at 7 C.F.R. § 1900.57(h)).

172. 53 Fed. Reg. 26410 (1988) (to be codified at 7 C.F.R. § 1900.57(f)).

173. 53 Fed. Reg. 26410 (1988) (to be codified at 7 C.F.R. § 1900.57(k)).

174. 53 Fed. Reg. 26410 (1988) (to be codified at 7 C.F.R. § 1900.57(l)).

175. 53 Fed. Reg. 26410 (1988) (to be codified at 7 C.F.R. § 1900.58(c)).

176. 53 Fed. Reg. 26410 (1988) (to be codified at 7 C.F.R. § 1900.58(d)).

177. 53 Fed. Reg. 26411 (1988) (to be codified at 7 C.F.R. § 1900.59(a)).

178. 53 Fed. Reg. 26411 (1988) (to be codified at 7 C.F.R. § 1900.59(b)).

179. 53 Fed. Reg. 26411 (1988) (to be codified at 7 C.F.R. § 1900.60).

180. 5 U.S.C. 552 et seq.

181. 5 U.S.C. 702.

182. 5 U.S.C. 701(a).

183. Abbott Laboratories v. Gardner, 387 U.S. 136, 141 (1967).

184. 401 U.S. 402 (1971).

185. 401 U.S. at 410.

186. Natural Resources Defense Council, Inc. v. SEC. 606 F.2d 1031, 1043 (D.C. Cir. 1979); Tuepker v. Farmers Home Administration, 708 F.2d 1329 (8th Cir. 1983).

187. 708 F.2d 1329 (8th Cir. 1983).

188. 708 F.2d at 1332.

189. 708 F.2d at 1332.

190. 816 F.2d 1241 (8th Cir. 1987).

191. 723 F.2d 631 (8th Cir. 1983).

192. 692 F. Supp. 1244 (D.Or. 1988).

CHAPTER 5

FINANCIAL DISTRESS

During the 1980's, unusually severe financial problems confronted an unprecedented number of agricultural producers. This situation generated considerable public support for providing farmers with alternative measures of relief, in addition to those forms of relief traditionally available. As a general rule, a farmer who faces severe financial problems has few alternatives. In many cases, the lack of assets or lack of cash flow in a farm business is a practical problem which the law itself is powerless to solve. In most cases, the farmer is faced with one of three options: a) to negotiate with the lender(s) involved and to attempt to work out a satisfactory arrangement, including such measures as refinancing, interest deferral or rescheduling; b) to do nothing and allow the lender to foreclose on the defaulted obligation and attempt to redeem the property when it is sold; or c) to consider one of the possible bankruptcy alternatives -- voluntary liquidation under Chapter 7 or reorganization under either Chapter 11, 12, or 13, respectively.

I.   Deferral, Rescheduling and Other Loan Servicing
      Options
      In most situations, when the debtor cannot repay his or her loan installments on schedule, the lender will give serious consideration to initiating a foreclosure proceeding. This process is, of course, not an attractive alternative to the lender because of the costs and time delays involved in collecting the debt. Moreover, one possible outcome of foreclosure is that the lender will take title to the property and be confronted with problems and costs associated with the management or disposition of the property. Due to these factors, the lender may have a strong interest in avoiding foreclosure. Therefore, farmers have the realistic option of approaching the lender with the objective of negotiating an acceptable workout arrangement. The lender may agree to this arrangement if there is a reasonable prospect of success. One possible workout

arrangement is debt rescheduling. This approach may include a change in the repayment schedule, a reduction in the installment payment amount, or a temporary change in the interest rate, or other similar measures. The success of this approach will depend upon the facts of each situation and the particular lending policies of the financial institutions which are involved.

Prior to 1978, the ability of a farmer-borrower to negotiate rescheduling relief with the FmHA was virtually impossible. This was because FmHA's lending policy did not specifically recognize rescheduling as an option. However, the enactment of 7 U.S.C. 1981a mandated that farmers be given thorough due process consideration for deferral and rescheduling of loan payments.[1] The law now provides that the Secretary of Agriculture may defer payment of principal and interest on any FmHA farm loan. The deferral provisions constitute directives to the Secretary of Agriculture, and therefore only apply to lending programs which are administered by the Secretary. This limits the application to FmHA policies and programs. In addition to deferral relief, under current law FmHA borrowers may also qualify for other loan servicing options. These options include consolidation, rescheduling, reamortization, interest rate reduction, debt write-down, and softwood timber and conservation easement programs, respectively.[2]

The farmer must make a written request for this relief. To be eligible, the farmer generally must satisfy three (3) criteria: first, the farmer's inability to effect timely repayment of the loan must be caused by hardship due to circumstances beyond the farmer's control which have reduced the farmer's income and secondly, the farmer must have acted in good faith in his or her dealings with FmHA. Federal regulations provide that circumstances beyond the farmer's control may include matters such as unemployment; illness, injury or death of the borrower; natural disasters; and/or widespread economic factors. Thirdly, it must be shown that the borrower can develop a feasible plan of operation.[3] Under the Agricultural Credit Act of 1987,[4] FmHA is instructed to utilize loan servicing to enable borrowers to continue farming when the return to the government under the restructured debt is at least as great as the return from involuntary liquidation.

Prior to the enactment of the 1987 Act, there had been considerable litigation over the issue of whether the Secretary of Agriculture was required to allow farmers to apply for FmHA deferral relief.[5] In those cases, the courts began to establish "borrower's rights." They generally held that the law requires that farmers who request deferral and rescheduling relief from FmHA must be given adequate consideration. As a practical matter, this means that farmers must be allowed to file the application for relief and that the application be promptly processed to completion. Moreover, cases held that the law requires that farmers must be notified of the availability of loan servicing options.[6] Any doubts about the nature or extent of borrower's rights in the area of delinquent loan servicing were resolved by the enactment of the Agricultural Credit Act of 1987.[7] This Act has provisions that are applicable both to FmHA and Farm Credit System borrowers. The terms of the 1987 Act explicitly state that FmHA (or a Farm Credit System institution) must defer and reschedule the debtor's payments if this method would bring an equal or greater financial return to the institution that what it would attain through the foreclosure process.

When a farmer requests loan servicing from FmHA, it is the current practice for FmHA to consider rescheduling, consolidation, and reamortization before considering the deferral option. FmHA will grant a deferral for up to five years for all or part of the loan only if the projections demonstrate positive cash flow for the farm. One of the most important of the borrower's rights available to farmers is that FmHA must release family living and operating expenses according to previously approved Farm and Home Plans up until the time that the final appeal process on FmHA loan servicing has ended.[8]

FmHA may use a supervised bank account, but only in "rare instances".[9] These instances include to assure the correct expenditure of loan funds, and to assure that replacement property can be obtained after a sale of security property or the proceeds of insurance from such property.[10] An important right is now provided to the borrower in that the supervised account can only be established with the borrower's consent that special supervision is needed.[11]

Borrowers now have expanded rights even after foreclosure has occurred. The primary programs in this area are leaseback/buyback and homestead protection. The former owner of a farm has 180 days from the date on which FmHA acquired the farm to apply for leaseback/buyback, unless state law provides for a longer period.[12] Under leaseback/buyback, FmHA can lease the land to the previous owner (debtor) with an option to purchase if a reasonable prospect of success can be shown in a cash flow projection provided by the debtor. Under homestead protection, borrowers are given an opportunity to retain their home and a reasonable amount of adjoining land even though the larger farm parcel is being foreclosed. A former owner must request homestead protection within 90 days of the date on which FmHA acquired the property.[13]

A more detailed discussion of the various options available to FmHA borrowers is provided in Chapter 4.

Farm Credit System (FCS) institutions are covered by provisions of the Farm Credit Amendments Act of 1985 and the Agricultural Credit Act of 1987.[14] Under the 1985 law, the determination of whether FCS borrowers were able to secure a restructuring agreement similar to that afforded to FmHA borrowers depended upon the particular forbearance policies of each Farm Credit Bank district. Under the 1987 Act, new loan restructuring procedures have been implemented. Under restructuring, if a qualified lender determines that the potential cost to the lender of restructuring the loan in accordance with a proposed restructuring plan is less than or equal to the potential cost of foreclosure, the qualified lender "shall" restructure the loan in accordance with the plan.[15] In Harper v. Federal v. Federal Land Bank of Spokane,[16] the Federal District Court held that the Agricultural Credit Act of 1987 conferred an implied private right of action upon borrowers to enforce the restructuring policy against Farm Credit Institutions. In Harper, the borrowers established that their creditors had violated the 1987 Act by continuing a foreclosure proceeding without first considering restructuring the debt. The Court found that the legislative history demonstrated Congressional intent that a private right of action should exist for borrowers. According to the court, Congress was operating under the mistaken belief that a private right of action existed under the Farm Credit Act of 1971. Nonetheless, the fact that "Congress intended to maintain the broad right to bring suit in federal court that it believed already existed" was sufficient to create the private right of action.[17]

To get some historical perspective on this subject, it is interesting to note the following cases. In one case, DeLaigle v. Federal Land Bank of Columbia,[18] the court held that the Farm Credit forbearance regulations had the force and effect of law. However, the DeLaigle court was directly challenged on this point in the subsequent case of Smith v. Russellville Production Credit Association.[19] In Smith, the court held that the "policy" of forbearance did not have the force and effect of law and that there was no private right of action to enforce this policy. Therefore, forbearance was not a substantive rule. This same conclusion was reached in Farmers Production Credit Association of Ashland v. Johnson,[20] where the court held that the federal regulation was directed to agency policy and was not a substantive rule. The effect of these interpretations of the Farm Credit Act Amendments of 1985 was that FCS borrowers could not raise the defense of forbearance in a foreclosure action. Moreover, according to these decisions, borrowers from the Farm Credit System were not entitled to forbearance as a matter of right. In direct contradiction to these cases, the Agricultural Credit Act of 1987 now provides Farm Credit System borrowers with extensive rights.

Farm Credit Services Borrower's Rights Provisions under the Agricultural Credit Act of 1987.

The Agricultural Credit Act of 1987[21] contains eight Titles. Title Four of the Act contains the Borrower's Rights for Farm Credit Services borrowers. In essence, Farm Credit Services borrowers are given (1) the right to certain disclosures, (2) the right to administration of distressed loans with the objective of offering alternatives to foreclosure, (3) the right to notice of the action taken on applications for restructuring, (4) the right to reconsideration of certain actions, (5) the right to restructuring of distressed loans in accordance with guidelines established by the Act, (6) certain rights concerning a bank's differential interest rates, (7) the right of first refusal of the

155

previous owner to repurchase or lease foreclosed property, (8) the prohibition against a bank's requiring any borrower to provide additional collateral to secure a loan if the borrower is current in the payment of principal and interest on the loan, (9) the right of access to copies of appraisals, and (10) the borrower's right to the application of borrower's monies held in uninsured voluntary or involuntary accounts to be applied as payment against indebtedness of the borrower in the event of capital depletion or insolvency of a system institution holding the account.[22]

The regulations which implemented the Agricultural Credit Act of 1987 provisions for the Farm Credit Administration appear at 53 Fed. Reg. 35427 (1988)(to be codified at 12 C.F.R. Parts 614, 615, and 618). These are the final rules.

Right to Disclosure
Under the 1987 Act, Farm Credit Administration borrowers are entitled to meaningful and timely disclosure of the following information not later than the time of loan closing: (1) the current rate of interest on the loan; (2) if the loan is a variable or adjustable rate loan, the amount and frequency by which the interest rate can be increased during the term of the loan, and a statement of the factors taken into account by the lending institution in determining adjustments to the interest rate; (3) the effect of any loan origination charges or purchases of stock or participation certifications on the effective rate of interest; (4) any change in the interest rate; (5) a statement that stock which is purchased is at risk; and (6) a statement indicating the various types of loan options available to borrowers, with an explanation of the terms and rights that apply to each type of loan.[23]   Farm Credit banks generally have three categories of interest rates on loans. These rates are based on the creditworthiness of the borrower. The less risk involved in making the loan, the lower the interest rate. Most banks raise the interest rates on loans if the borrower becomes delinquent in the payment of principal and interest. This practice has caused severe hardship on many Farm Credit institution borrowers. Unfortunately, the 1987 Act does not forbid the practice but merely requires disclosure of the factors

which may cause an increase in the interest rate on the borrower's loan prior to the closing of the loan.

Administration of Loans

Under the 1987 Act there are important new borrower's rights provisions. Each Farm Credit district was required, within 60 days of enactment of the 1987 Act, to develop a policy to govern the restructuring of distressed loans.[24] The policies must include an explanation of the procedure for submitting an application for restructuring and an explanation of the right of borrowers with distressed loans who are family farmers to seek review by a credit review committee. Restructuring policies must include standards that take into consideration whether the cost to the Farm Credit institution of restructuring the loan is equal to or less than the cost of foreclosure. The policies must also examine whether the borrower is applying all income other than that necessary for reasonable living and operating expenses to the payment of primary obligations, whether the borrower has the financial capacity and the management skills to protect the collateral, and whether the borrower is capable of working out existing financial difficulties to reestablish a viable farming operation and repay the loan on a rescheduled basis. If the institution bank determines that the cost of restructuring the loan is equal to or less than the cost of foreclosure, the institution bank must restructure the loan.[25]

Before accelerating a loan or otherwise commencing a foreclosure proceeding on a distressed loan of a borrower who is a family farmer, the institution bank must notify the borrower in writing of the restructuring policy and that the borrowers loan may be suitable for restructuring. A restructuring application form should accompany the notice.[26] Any borrower who is a family farmer and submits an application for restructuring is entitled to prompt written notice of the action on the application, the reason for such action if the application is denied, and notice of the applicant's right to seek review of the decision by a credit review committee.[27]

Right of First Refusal

Under the 1987 Act certain agricultural real estate is

subject to a right of first refusal by a previous owner-borrower. This includes agricultural real estate that is acquired by a Farm Credit institution as a result of loan foreclosure or a voluntary conveyance by a borrower who did not have the resources to avoid foreclosure. The disposition of this real estate is subject to the right of first refusal of the previous owner to repurchase or lease the property.[28] The previous owner has the right to offer to purchase the property at its appraised fair market value or to offer to purchase the property at a price less than the appraised value. The Farm Credit institution may not sell the property to any other person at a price equal to, or less than, that offered by the previous owner, or on different terms and conditions than those that were extended to the previous owner without affording the previous owner the opportunity to purchase the property on those same conditions and terms.[29]

II.   State Mortgage Foreclosure Moratoria

Most states have enacted laws which place restrictions on the availability of foreclosure as the primary remedy available to the lender in the event of debtor default. Many of these laws have been held unconstitutional after court challenges.[30] For example, in 1986 Kansas enacted a statute, S.B. 696, which provided certain qualified farmers stay from the foreclosure of farm loans. In 1987, the Kansas Supreme Court declared the Act unconstitutional on the grounds that it violated constitutional restrictions on state impairment of contracts. Although S.B. 696 is no longer law, it serves as an instructive example of the legislative activities which states have attempted in this area.[31]

An example of a recent, valid law in this area is Iowa's mortgage moratorium statute, which lapsed on March 30, 1988 by the terms of the statute. The constitutionality of this law under the contracts clause was never challenged. This law provided for the continuation of court proceedings on the foreclosure of real estate mortgages, deeds of trust of real property, and contracts for the purchase of real estate.[32] Under this statute, the owner of real estate was entitled to appear in the foreclosure proceeding and file an answer. The answer was required to admit some of the indebtedness and a breach of the relevant mortgage instrument. If the court found that the application was made in good faith and supported by competent evidence, it could continue the foreclosure proceeding. The evidence was required to establish that the inability to pay was due to drought, flood, heat, hail, storms or other climatic conditions, or the infestation of pests. The law also applied in the event that the governor declared a state of economic emergency.[33] The period of the foreclosure continuance was determined on the basis of the circumstances presented.

It should be noted that the availability of state mortgage foreclosure moratoria varies from state to state.

III.   Bankruptcy

The current Bankruptcy Code[34] provides several alternatives to the farmer-debtor for relief from the problems of financial distress. The options available include Chapter 7 liquidation, Chapter 11 reorganization, Chapter 12 debt adjustment for family farmers with regular income, and Chapter 13 debt adjustment for individuals with regular income. If the farmer-debtor's financial situation appears to offer some prospects for improvement, the debtor may file a reorganization proceeding under either Chapter 11, 12 or 13 of the Bankruptcy Code. Otherwise, a Chapter 7 liquidation procedure may be most suitable for the debtor's situation. The threshold decision for the debtor, of course, is to choose the appropriate chapter under which to proceed. For farmers, the choice has been simplified somewhat by the addition of Chapter 12, which is specifically designed for farmers. Some farmer-debtors will, however, still choose to use Chapters 11 or 13. For those who choose Chapter 11, one of the crucial determinations to be made is whether the reorganization plan under Chapter 11 will give the debtor enough time to overcome the financial problems which he or she faces.

To be eligible for relief under any of these chapters of the Bankruptcy Code, a debtor must be a person who resides in the United States or who has a domicile, place of business, or property in the United States.[35] The term "person" includes individuals, partnerships, and corporations, but does not include governmental units unless the governmental unit acquires an asset from a person as a result of the operation of a loan guarantee agreement, or as a receiver or liquidating agent of a person.[36] Under the Code, the term farmer (except when that term appears in the term "family farmer") is defined as "a person that received more than 80 percent of such person's gross income during the taxable year of such person immediately preceding the taxable year of such person during which the case under this title was commenced from a farming operation owned and operated by such person".[37] A "farming operation", includes farming, tillage of the soil, dairy farming, ranching, production or raising of crops, poultry or livestock and production of poultry or livestock products in an unmanufactured state.[38] The terms "family farmer" and "family farmer with regular annual income" provide unique requirements for a farmer who elects to utilize the provisions of Chapter 12. These terms are defined and discussed later in this chapter.

For purposes of Chapters 7, 11 and 13, the determination of whether a debtor is a farmer actually involves a two-part test. First, the debtor must be personally engaged in a farming operation. Second, the debtor must derive the requisite percentage of gross income from that farming operation.[39] The primary significance of a person being considered a "farmer" as opposed to any other person under the Bankruptcy Code is that a farmer cannot be forced into involuntary bankruptcy.[40] Ordinarily, an involuntary bankruptcy can be commenced against a debtor under Chapter 7 or 11 by the filing of a petition by three or more creditors with aggregate claims of at least $5,000.[41] "Farmer" status must be pled and proved by the farmer in order to qualify for this exemption.

The commencement of a voluntary case under any chapter of the bankruptcy code constitutes an order for relief under that chapter.[42] Therefore, the act of filing a bankruptcy petition automatically and immediately creates certain rights and protections for the debtor. The filing of the petition provides an automatic stay which proscribes all creditor acts or proceedings to collect or enforce a debt. The debtor, debtor's property, and estate are all covered by this injunctive protection.[43] As a practical matter, the stay will generally be in effect until a bankruptcy discharge is granted or denied, or until the case is closed or dismissed.[44]

160

1. Chapter 7

The filing of a Chapter 7 petition creates a distinct legal estate which is comprised of the debtor's property. A trustee is appointed by the bankruptcy court to administer the estate. The trustee has broad statutory powers to draw assets into the estate, to liquidate the estate and to distribute the proceeds from the liquidation of the estate. The Chapter 7 bankruptcy involves a complete liquidation of the estate, except for exempt assets, and culminates in the distribution of the proceeds of the estate to creditors.

Bankruptcy law exempts certain of the debtors assets from the claims of creditors. This aspect of the law is based on the following policy objectives:

1) To allow the debtor to retain the property which is necessary to support his or her physical survival;
2) To protect the dignity and the cultural and religious identity of the debtor;
3) To enable the debtor to rehabilitate himself financially and to earn income in the future;
4) To protect the debtor's family from the adverse consequences of impoverishment; and
5) To shift the burden of providing financial support to the debtor away from society and to the debtor's creditors.[45]

State law will determine which property is actually exempt for bankruptcy purposes. State law may require that a specific state exemption list be used to determine which property is exempt. If state law requires that debtors must use the federal exemptions, the state exemption list does not apply. The Bankruptcy Code provides that either a state list or federal list of exemptions may be used.[46]

Section 522(d) of the Bankruptcy Code lists property which the debtor can exempt from the bankruptcy estate under the federal exemptions. The federal list is extensive but the value limit on some property items is restrictive. For example, the list includes an exemption for real or personal property used as a residence by the debtor or a dependent of the debtor. However, the value limit of this exemption is $7,500. For this reason, some states have restricted debtors to the state exemption list which may contain more liberal provisions. For example, debtors in Kansas may claim an exemption of 160 acres of farmland or one acre of land if it is located within city limits.[47] The exemption also includes all improvements made on that property regardless of the value of the improvements.

The election of the state exemptions by the debtor does not prohibit the claim of some additional exemptions under federal law. There are certain exemptions allowed under federal law that are permitted even when the state list is used.[48] These include:

- Foreign Service Retirement and Disability payments;
- Social Security payments;
- Injury or death compensation payments for war risk hazards, and the wages of fishermen, seamen, or apprentices;
- Civil Service retirement benefits;
- Longshoremens and Harbor Workers' Compensation Act death and disability benefits;
- Railroad Retirement Act annuities and pensions;
- Veterans' benefits;
- Special pensions paid to winner of the Congressional Medal of Honor; and
- Federal homestead lands on debts contracted before issuance of the patent.[49]

The debtor is not required to claim all of the listed exemptions, but is limited to the listed exemptions. When filing a petition for bankruptcy, the debtor must list all property which he or she claims is exempt from the estate. Notice must be given to all interested parties. The property is then deemed exempt unless a party in interest files a timely objection.

It should be noted that although exempt assets may be deemed exempt from creditor's claims, those assets are not released from security interests or mortgages which have attached to those particular assets. Thus, when a debtor receives a bankruptcy discharge and debts are cancelled, the pre-petition debts which were incurred with respect to exempt assets continue to the extent those assets are retained by the debtor. Thus, the debtor must chose between declaring the assets exempt and continuing to be subject to the debts that relate to those assets or the debtor may refrain from seeking exempt status for those assets and have the corresponding debts discharged.

It may be possible for a debtor to convert non-exempt assets into exempt assets. For example, an insolvent person could sell non-exempt property and invest the proceeds in a homestead, thereby placing the proceeds beyond the reach of creditors. The ability to shift assets in order to maximize the allowable exemptions has been held legal in the absence of circumstances such as fraud.[50]

According to the United States Supreme Court, for purposes of bankruptcy fraud must involve moral turpitude or intentional wrong on the part of the debtor. It does not include implied fraud which may exist without the imputation of bad faith or immorality.[51] Courts have consistently held that the shifting of assets from non-exempt to exempt status is not fraudulent per se.[52]

The final aspect of a Chapter 7 proceeding is the distribution of the assets of the estate. The following expenses and claims have priority over the claims of general secured and unsecured creditors:

1. administrative expenses;
2. debts incurred after the commencement of an involuntary case but before the appointment of the trustee;
3. unsecured claims for wages, salaries, and commissions;
4. unsecured claims for contributions to employee benefit plans;
5. unsecured claims of farmers who are engaged in the production or raising of grain, up to $2,000, against a debtor who owns or operates a grain storage facility, for grain or the proceeds of grain;
6. unsecured claims up to $900 of individual creditors who have paid for but not received certain property or services; and
7. unsecured claims for certain taxes;[53]

In addition to the claims against exempt property, some other debts are not dischargeable. For example, debts such as taxes, alimony and child support always survive the debtor's discharge in bankruptcy.[54]

2.   Chapter 11

A Chapter 11 bankruptcy involves a reorganization of the debtor's financial obligations without a liquidation of the debtor's assets. A Chapter 11 proceeding involves three somewhat separate stages. First, the debtor must file a petition to reorganize, accompanied by a statement of assets, liabilities and financial affairs. This petition invokes the automatic stay against actions by creditors to collect debts. Creditors may obtain relief from the automatic stay only under limited circumstances. The first circumstance is where the debtor fails to provide adequate protection for the creditor's interest. The second circumstance is where the debtor has no equity in the property in which the creditor has an interest and the property is not necessary to a successful reorganization.

The second stage in a Chapter 11 proceeding may be identified as the "pre-plan" stage. During this stage the reorganization plan is negotiated through meetings with creditors and then is drafted into the form in which it will be presented to the court for confirmation. The third stage of a Chapter 11 is the implementation of the plan, its confirmation, execution and discharge.

The requirements for a plan and its contents are specifically set out in the Bankruptcy Code.[55] In most cases, the plan will consist of four functional parts. First, the plan must organize all claims and interests into classes that are "substantially similar". Second, it must designate which classes are "impaired" under the plan. Third, it must specify the treatment of each claim or interest. Finally, the plan must provide adequate means for its successful execution. The types of "adequate means" which are legitimate are specifically listed in the Code.[56]

As a general rule, the plan must provide equal treatment to each creditor within a class. Moreover, the provisions for each class must be consistent with the interests of creditors, equity security holders and public policy. Section 1123 of the Code requires that the plan specify the treatment which will be afforded to each impaired class of creditors. As long as the individual members of each class are treated equally and are not discriminated against, the debtor is free to propose any method to repay the creditors of the impaired class.[57]

164

If a plan satisfies the criteria of the Code, the court must confirm the plan.[58] As a general rule, the plan does not qualify for confirmation unless each class accepts the plan or is unimpaired by it. "Acceptance" is determined by a vote of creditors within a class. Creditors who represent at least two-thirds of the allowed claims (by value of claims) or more than half of the claims (in terms of the number of creditors) may accept the plan on behalf of the class.[59] In some cases, the court can approve the plan despite the objections of one or more dissenting classes of creditors. The plan can be "crammed down" if at least one class of claims that is impaired has accepted the plan.[60] With respect to each impaired class of claims or interests, each claim holder or interest holder must either accept the plan or receive not less than what they would receive if the debtor were liquidated under Chapter 7.[61]

Chapter 11 bankruptcies tend to be expensive for the debtor because of the substantial administrative costs involved. It is also very time consuming for the debtor to work with the trustee (if one is appointed), the court and the various creditors. A Chapter 11 is most suitable for farmers whose problems are only temporary and who are strongly committed to remaining in farming.

3. Chapter 13

Although Chapter 11 and 7 bankruptcies can be filed involuntarily against debtors other than farmers, Chapter 13 is always a voluntary proceeding. Like Chapter 11, Chapter 13 involves a payment plan without liquidation of the debtor's assets. To qualify for relief under Chapter 13, the debtor must have sufficient regular income to pay all or part of the debts according to a plan submitted to the court.[62] The debtor will use a certain percentage of his or her wages to pay creditors on an installment payment plan which modifies original payment obligations. The advantage of a Chapter 13 proceeding in comparison to Chapter 7 bankruptcy is that no liquidation of assets is involved. Further, unlike Chapter 11, no creditor approval of the Chapter 13 plan is necessary. If difficulties arise in the execution of the plan it can either be modified with the court's approval or converted to a Chapter 7 proceeding.

A debtor may file a Chapter 13 bankruptcy petition only

if he or she:

   (1) is an individual;

   (2) has regular income (is an individual whose income is sufficiently stable and regular to enable such individuals to make payments under a plan), and

   (3) has noncontingent, liquidated unsecured debts of less than $100,000 and noncontingent, liquidated secured debts of less than $350,000.[63]

To initiate a Chapter 13 bankruptcy proceeding, the debtor must file a petition with the bankruptcy court. The debtor must file a Chapter 13 plan either when the petition is filed or within 15 days thereafter.[64] The plan must propose a method of payment and to whom the payments will be made. The plan must then be confirmed by the court.[65] The plan may be modified after confirmation, but before completion of payments under the plan, to achieve any one of the following objectives:

   (1) to increase or reduce the amount of payments on claims of a particular class provided for by the plan;

   (2) to extend or reduce the time for payments to be made; or

   (3) to alter the amount of the distribution to a creditor whose claim is provided for by the plan, to the extent necessary to take into account any payment of that claim other than under the plan.[66]

The plan may not extend for more than three years, although it may be extended for good cause to five years.[67] After payments under the plan are completed, the debtor is discharged.[68]

4.   Chapter 12

In 1986, Congress adopted legislation which created a new bankruptcy Chapter especially for farmers. The new Chapter 12, Adjustment of Debts of a Family Farmer with Regular Annual Income,[69] is designed to give farmers the benefits of Chapter 11 without some of the limitations.[70] Specifically, the "Chapter 11-type" benefit is that the debtor remains in possession of the property which comprises the farming operation and can continue to manage and operate the farm.[71] However, the debtor is supervised by a trustee.

166

Under Chapter 12, a "family farmer" is defined as:
(A) individual or individual and spouse engaged in a farming operation whose aggregate debts do not exceed $1,500,000 and not less than 80 percent of whose aggregate non-contingent, liquidated debts (excluding a debt for the principal residence of such individual or such individual and spouse unless such debt arises out of a farming operation), on the date the case is filed, arise out of a farming operation owned or operated by such individual or such individual and spouse, and such individual or such individual and spouse receive from such farming operation more than 50 percent of such individual's or such individual and spouse's gross income for the taxable year preceding the taxable year in which the case concerning such individual or such individual and spouse was filed; or (B) a corporation or partnership in which more than 50 percent of the outstanding stock or equity is held by one family or by one family and the relatives of the members of such family, and such family or such relatives conduct the farming operation, and (i) more than 80 percent of the value of its assets consist of assets related to the farming operation; (ii) its aggregate debts do not exceed $1,500,000 and not less than 80 percent of its aggregate non-contingent, liquidated debts (excluding a debt for one dwelling which is owned by such corporation or partnership and which a shareholder or partner maintains as a principal residence, unless such debt arises out of a farming operation), on the date the case is filed, arise out of the farming operation owned or operated by such corporation or such partnership; and (iii) if such corporation issues stock, such stock is not publicly traded.[72]

A "family farmer with regular annual income" is separately defined to mean a family farmer whose annual income is sufficiently stable and regular to enable that person to make payments under a Chapter 12 plan.[73]

"Family farmer" is the key

To obtain the specialized relief that Chapter 12 provides to debt-ridden farmers, a farm debtor must meet the Chapter 12 definitional requirements of "family farmer," "farming operation," and "regular annual income."[74] The ability of Chapter 12 to provide effective relief to farm debtors have been briskly challenged by creditors who have filed motions to dismiss alleging that the debtor does not qualify as a "family farmer."[75] Thus, the "family farmer" definition has emerged as the threshold test facing the farmer-debtor in pursuit of a confirmed Chapter 12 plan.

It should be noted that the fifty percent income requirement is imposed upon the "individual" family farmer, with no corresponding income requirement imposed upon the corporate or partnership family farmer entity. Instead, a rigid requirement is imposed upon the corporation or partnership that eighty percent of its assets be "related to the farming operation." Presumably, the explanation for this discrepancy is that the gross income test would not be a meaningful indicator for corporate or partnership family farm entities because the test could take into account the diversified (non-farming) interests of a corporation or the personal interests of the partners.

Aside from the income and assets requirements, a key term included in the "family farmer" definition is "farming operation."[76] A farming operation "includes farming, tillage of the soil, dairy farming, ranching, production or raising of crops, poultry, or livestock, and production of poultry or livestock products in an unmanufactured state."[77]

If the threshold "family farmer" requirement of 11 U.S.C. section 101(17) is met (which includes the "farming operation" requirement), the farmer-debtor may file a petition for relief under Chapter 12. Before the plan is confirmed, the "family farmer" must establish the requisite "regular annual income," which is defined as income that is "sufficiently stable and regular to enable such family farmer to make payments under a plan under Chapter 12."[78] Generally, the requisite financial information about the debtor will be collected and/or verified at the creditor's committee meeting.[79] In particular, the trustee presiding at the meeting will examine the debtor regarding information contained in the schedules filed in the case. If the debtor can meet the requirements of 11 U.S.C. Section 101(18), the plan would be eligible for confirmation.

The term "family farmer" is a new term in the Bankruptcy Code.[80] It defines a special sub-category of "farmer," a term which was introduced into federal bankruptcy law in 1898.[81] Prior to the enactment of Chapter 12, farmer-debtors engaged in bankruptcy proceedings had to meet the requirements imposed by section 101(17) ("farmer") and section 101(18) ("farming operation"). Both of these definitions remain intact after the advent of Chapter 12. However, the "family farmer" requirement of section 101(17) supercedes the previous "farmer" requirement of section 101(17) (now section 101(19)) for the purpose of qualifying a farmer for Chapter 12 relief). The distinction between these key threshold terms - "farmer" and "family farmer" - indicates Congressional intent to limit Chapter 12 relief to debtors who actively operate relatively small-scale (and relatively high risk) farming operations, whether they are operated as a sole proprietorship (including a husband and wife "sole proprietorship"),[82] or as a corporation or partnership.[83] Congress enacted the "family farmer" provision to "ensure that only family farmers - not tax shelters or large corporate entities - will benefit."[84]

The "farming operation"

As stated above, a "family farmer" must satisfy the "farming operation" definition. The cases under Chapters 7, 11, and 13 which construe the terms used in Chapter 12, or analogous terms, are instructive for purposes of interpreting the scope, or suggested scope, of Chapter 12 terminology. In Chapter 11 cases which have construed "farming operation," the "risk-laden" nature of farming has frequently been the criterion applied. For example, in Armstrong v. Corn Belt Bank,[85] the debtor had ceased active farming and had cash leased his land when a creditor began involuntary bankruptcy proceedings against him. The court held that since the debtor received cash rent on an unconditional basis, he did not bear any risk and therefore was not engaged in a farming operation. The court stated that the term "farmer" in the Bankruptcy Code indicates Congressional intent "to protect only those whose income is derived from operations that are subject to climate, farm price fluctuation, and uncertain crop production."[86]

The issue of risk has also been a key criterion applied by the courts to the "farming operation" issue in Chapter 12. For example, in In re Mary Freese Farms, Inc.,[87] Chapter 12 protection was denied to a corporate debtor whose sole source of revenue was cash rent from farmland. The Mary Freese court found that the necessary "risk" was lacking because the debtor-landlord under the cash lease arrangement was protected by a statutory crop lien.[88] Interestingly, the Mary Freese court did allude to the possibility of recognizing a non-participatory lease as a phase of farming when it noted its consideration of the fact that there was "no evidence that any family member intends to engage in any farming operation in the foreseeable future."[89]

In In re Tim Wargo & Sons, Inc.,[90] the court's opinion undermines the notion that the risk factor is solely determinative of the "farming operation" issue. In Wargo, after the Wargo family had personally farmed 440 acres of farmland for many years, they leased the land to a tenant farmer under a one-fourth crop share agreement. The farm was leased when the bankruptcy petition was filed. The Wargo court stated that "the fact that an entity derives its income from an activity that is subject to the same risks faced by farmers does not necessarily determine that such activity constitutes a "farming operation."[91] The Wargo opinion was based on the court's finding that the debtor had relinquished control over the manner in which the tenant operated the farm and therefore did not have an active role in the farming operation.[92] To the extent that the risk standard was applied, the debtor was found to be insulated from the risks of financial loss associated with farming since Arkansas law provides the debtor-landlord with a statutory lien for rent against the crops.[93]

Some courts have recognized that, irrespective of the issue of risk, farmers have traditionally leased part or all of their land and farming operations to others. For example, in First National Bank & Trust Co. v. Beach,[94] the court observed that "acres personally cultivated and those occupied by tenants are phases and aspects of a unitary calling."[95] While the facts in Beach involved a person who was actively farming one-fourth of his land and renting the remainder to other farmers, the court's reasoning suggests a liberal application to facts such as those in which, although a farmer has ceased farming, he or she remains committed to farming by perpetuating the activity as a lessor.

Liberal relief for family farmers

While some courts have limited the scope of Chapter 12 through a restrictive interpretation of "farming operation," others have used their substantial equity powers to more liberally promote the extraordinary objectives of Chapter 12. These courts have adopted a stance more sympathetic to the needs and circumstances of financially-stressed farmers. They appear to be more familiar with how farms operate and are able to more accurately construe the scope of activities pursued by a "family farmer" or in a "farming operation." This knowledge includes familiarity not only with how farms traditionally operate in times of relatives prosperity but also recognizes the warranted adjustments that farmers are forced to make during times of financial stress.

Courts taking this approach have determined that a cutting back or "farming out" of crop or livestock production constituted either (1) the reality of traditional farming in certain parts of the country, or (b) special efforts being made by a farmer to survive the "farm crisis." This is important because many of the Chapter 12 cases present facts which reasonably might suggest an abandonment of farming or a diversification into non-farming sources of income. Two separate non-Chapter 12 opinions from cases arising in Minnesota are illustrative. In the first of these cases, In re LaFond,[96] the Eighth Circuit Court of Appeals recognized that the requirement that debtors meet the eighty percent test in the Chapter 7 Code definition of "farmer" would unfairly preclude many debtors legitimately engaged in farming from utilizing the section 522(f) lien avoidance remedy in the manner Congress intended. The court affirmed the view, espoused and held by both the bankruptcy and district courts below, respectively, that:

> [a] more realistic definition [of farmer] should take into account the intensity of a debtor's past farming activities and the sincerity of his intentions to

continue farming, as well as evidence that [the] debtor is legitimately engaged in a trade which currently and regularly uses the specific implements or tools exempted and on which lien avoidance is sought.[97]

The debtors had successfully moved to avoid a lien of the local PCA on certain large items of farm equipment. The PCA appealed the affirmation by the district court, arguing that the LaFonds did not qualify as farmers for the reasons that (a) they lost money farming, and (b) Mr. LaFond's primary occupation was as a policeman.

The court found sufficient evidence to support the conclusion that Mrs. LaFond was engaged in the trade of farming and that, notwithstanding the fact that Mr. LaFond derived income from outside employment, the debtors were making a bona fide effort to earn a living as farmers. The court observed that "given the economics of small-farm agriculture under the harsh climatic conditions of Northeastern Minnesota, it is nearly impossible for most farmers to subsist without outside employment."[98]

Similarly, in Middleton v. Farmers State Bank of Fosston,[99] the court denied the debtors' request, pursuant to 11 U.S.C. section 522(f)(2)(B), to avoid certain non-possessory, non-purchase money liens held by a bank on the debtors' farm machinery and equipment. On appeal, the judge remanded the case to determine whether the appellants were farmers, i.e. either that they were farming at the time they filed the complaint or that they intended to farm again in the future.[100]

The debtors in Middleton, wife and husband, began farming in early 1974. The court found that both debtors had been actively engaged in the farming operation as equal partners. Because of financial losses, the husband was forced to assume off-farm employment in 1983. The wife remained "on the farm as a farmer" up until the livestock and farm equipment were auctioned. The husband testified that farming was his preferred means of earning a living and that if at all possible he intended to resume farming in the future.[101]

Addressing the section 101(17) definition of "farmer," the court stated that "one may be a farmer without meeting the defined requirements."[102] The standard to be applied is that the debtor "must be engaged in farming at the time the exemption is claimed or at some point in the future."[103] The court emphatically stated:

> If the 80% income was the only test, many debtors legitimately engaged in farming could be excluded from taking advantage of the needed benefits. They would be deprived of the benefits afforded to farm debtors by the Code because they are hardworking and produce income for (sic) sources other than farming. Each case must be judged upon its own particular facts and circumstances.[104]

In comparison, the court in Matter of Haschke,[105] viewed the debtors' actions in a manner which precluded examination of the debtors' future plans. In Haschke, on the date the Chapter 12 petition was filed, all of the debtors' farmstead was leased to others, except their personal residence. They also had sold all of their farm equipment and were therefore physically incapable of farming. They were strictly engaged in receiving cash rent for their land. The only link with crops maintained by the debtors was that they were still storing and marketing crops that they had produced. The court held that the mere storing and marketing of crops does not constitute "production or raising of crops" pursuant to section 101(20).[106] Thus, the debtors were deemed to have abandoned or ceased farming.

Chapter 12 cases have held also that the scope of "family farmer" and "farming operation" definitions must be liberally construed in order to properly administer Chapter 12. In In Re Welch,[107] creditors challenged whether the debtors met the income requirements of 11 U.S.C. section 101(17)(A) at the date of filing the petition. The court determined that the debtors were qualified "family farmers" at the time they filed their petition by examining the debtors' activities over a course of years prior to the filing of the petition. The court recognized a certain "equity" in the fact that the debtors had engaged in dairy and grain farming for nearly fifteen years. Thus, they were found to have worked as farmers, working their own farmland and suffering the financial distress common to many farmers. That put them within the class of farmers for which Congress designed Chapter 12.

In In re Maike,[108] the bankruptcy court held that Chapter 12 debtors who derived a majority of their income from the breeding, raising, and sale of puppies were family farmers. In order to carry out the legislative intent that fueled the enactment of Chapter 12, the court applied a "totality of circumstances" test to determine the existence of a "farming operation."[109] The court applied that test so as not to limit relief to farm enterprises that fall within a "single test of farming." Instead, the court reasoned, Chapter 12 should afford relief to debtors whose farms reflect modern changes in agricultural enterprises. Thus, analogizing the debtor's business enterprises to a cattle feedlot, the Maike court stated that "if feeding and maintaining other people's cattle for ultimate resale is a farming operation, the same services performed with respect to dogs should also be considered farming."[110]

Maike sets forth an analytical method in which nontraditional activity will be characterized as a "farming operation" if it is reasonably analogous to any of the traditional farming operations prescribed in the Bankruptcy Code. Therefore, the type of produce and its eventual market should be a factor in defining the farming operation.[111] The court also recognized that many farmers are beginning to diversify by growing crops not traditionally associated with farming in the state of the court's location. The court should not eliminate those products from the "farming operation" definition.[112]

"Regular annual income"

As stated earlier, the "regular annual income" requirement of Chapter 12 is relevant to the confirmation of the plan, and is not a threshold requirement to be satisfied at the time the petition is filed. The determination of whether a "family farmer" has adequate annual income to fund the plan is made at the confirmation hearing.[113] In re Hoskins[114] examined the income requirement imposed by the section 101(18) definition of "family farmer with regular annual income." 11 U.S.C. § 101(18). The issue was of first impression. Noting that the language of Chapter 12 is similar, if not identical, to the language employed in the analogous definition in Chapter 13, 11 U.S.C. § 101(29), the court stated that the meaning of section 101(18) can be determined by examining the meaning of section 101(29).[115] In Chapter 13, the debtor is allowed to use various sources of income, including wages and income from property and capital, to meet the test. The court held that the Chapter 12 debtor should be similarly accommodated. Thus, in making the determination of whether the Chapter 12 debtor has sufficiently stable and regular income, the income to be calculated should include income from both farming operations and non-farming sources.

In conclusion, the Chapter 12 debtor must meet the definitional requirements of "family farmer," "farming operation," and "regular annual income," in order to obtain a confirmed plan. As suggested by the above, meeting each of these requirements will likely present unique challenges in each Chapter 12 case.

The Chapter 12 Plan

Under Chapter 12, the debtor must propose a plan within 90 days after the date of filing of the petition, which constitutes the order for relief.[116] The plan must submit a portion of the debtor's future earnings or income to the appointed trustee for the execution of the plan and to pay, in deferred installments, all priority claims.[117] The plan must classify claims and provide the same treatment to all claims within the came class.[118] The plan may not discriminate unfairly against any class. In the plan, the debtor may propose measures such as the modifying of certain rights of secured creditors, the curing of defaults and providing for the sale of property.[119]

The plan is subject to confirmation at a hearing which must be held not later than 45 days after the filing of the plan.[120] The bankruptcy court must confirm the plan if the following conditions are met:

1) the plan complies with all the requirements of Chapter 12;
2) the plan is proposed in good faith;
3) the payment of fees which are required to be paid before confirmation have been paid;
4) unsecured creditors will be paid at least as much as they would receive in a Chapter 7 liquidation;
5) secured creditors have accepted the plan, they

175

retain their liens during the pendency of the plan and the value of the lien is not less than the allowed amount of the claim, or the debtor surrenders the secured property to the creditor; and

6) the debtor will be able to make all payments under the plan.[121]

If the trustee or an unsecured creditor objects to the plan, it may not be confirmed unless either (1) the value of property to be distributed under the plan is not less than the amount of the dissenting claim or (2) the plan provides that all of the debtor's projected disposable income for the next three years (or longer if the court permits) is applied to payments under the plan.[122] Upon confirmation, the plan binds the debtor and each creditor or equity holder to the terms of the plan and vests all the property in the estate of the debtor.[123]

Upon completion of the payments under the plan, the debtor will be discharged of remaining debts except those specifically reserved (such as debts not yet due)[124] or those which are generally not dischargeable in bankruptcy.[125] In the event that the debtor fails to complete the plan, a discharge will be allowed only if:

1) the failure to complete the plan results from circumstances for which the debtor should not be held accountable:

2) the value of the property actually distributed to unsecured creditors is not less than what they would receive under a Chapter 7 liquidation; and

3) modification of the plan under Section 1229 of the Code is impracticable.[126]

A discharge may be revoked upon the request of a party in interest within one year after the date of discharge if the discharge was obtained through fraud and the requesting party did not know of the fraud at the time of discharge.[127]

The plan may be modified after confirmation and before the completion of payments. This may be done to increase the amount of payments, to extend or reduce the time for payments, or to alter the amount of property to be distributed.[128] Modification can be requested by the debtor, the trustee or the holder of an unallowed unsecured claim.[129] Alternatively, the debtor may voluntarily convert the case to a Chapter 7

176

liquidation proceeding.[130] However, the case can be involuntarily converted into a Chapter 7 bankruptcy upon the occurrence of fraud.[131] The debtor also has the right to file a motion requesting that the proceeding be dismissed.[132] Similarly, any party in interest may move for a dismissal of the case for cause, including:

1) unreasonable delay, or gross mismanagement by the debtor that is prejudicial to creditors;

2) the nonpayment of any fees and charges required under Chapter 13 of the Code;

3) the failure to timely file a plan under Section 1221 of the Code;

4) the failure to commence making timely payments which are required by a confirmed plan;

5) the denial of confirmation of a plan under Code Section 1225 and the denial of a request made for additional time for filing another plan or a modification of a plan;

6) the occurrence of a material default by the debtor with respect to a term of a confirmed plan;

7) the revocation of the order of confirmation under Code Section 1230 and denial of confirmation of a modified plan under Code Section 1229;

8) the termination of a confirmed plan by reason of the occurrence of a condition specified in the plan; or

9) continuing loss to or diminution of the estate and the absence of a reasonable likelihood of rehabilitation.[133]

Adequate Protection

One of the major advantages of Chapter 12 is the fact that the concept of "adequate protection" for the creditor has been modified. Under general bankruptcy law, the creditor is entitled to adequate protection.[134] In proposing plans under Chapter 11, it has been particularly difficult for farmers to succeed in attaining a confirmed plan because courts have interpreted adequate protection to mean that the creditor must be compensated for "lost opportunity" costs. Those "lost opportunity" costs are usually considered to be equivalent to the interest that an undercollateralized creditor could earn by reinvesting an amount of money equal to the value of the collateral. More specifically, according to the Code, the creditor must receive "the indubitable equivalent of such entity's interest in such property" in order to be adequately protected.[135] Section 1205 of the Code provides that adequate protection under Chapter 12 does not include the obligation to compensate the creditor for lost opportunity costs.[136] Under Chapter 12, a creditor is given "adequate protection" if the plan:

1) requires the trustee to make cash payments or periodic payments to the extent that the collateral has decreased in value; or

2) gives the creditor a replacement lien or additional lien to the extent of the decrease in value; or

3) pays the creditor a reasonable rent for the use of the farmland based on the rental value, net income and earning capacity of the property; or

4) gives such other relief "as will adequately protect the value of the property".[137]

Conclusion

Chapter 12 may be a practical solution for some farmers, although it is possibly more expensive than a Chapter 11 reorganization. Realistically, Chapter 12 will only be useful to farming operations that have a strong likelihood for financial success based on factors such as debt-asset ratio and the ability to generate positive cash flow. A well-drafted Chapter 12 plan may provide these farms with the protection they need. On the other hand, it is doubtful that Chapter 12 will significantly help farms which are extremely debt-ridden. For those very serious cases, the filing of a Chapter 12 at best offers the debtor a temporary enhancement of the debtor's negotiating and bargaining position with creditors. Alternatively, it provides the debtor with sufficient respite from creditor actions to allow the debtor to adjust to the phase-out of the farming operation.

5. Special Note On Foreclosure In Bankruptcy

Since the filing of a petition in bankruptcy operates as a stay of all creditors' actions against a debtor,[138] the petition's impact on a prepetition foreclosure action is an important issue.

The creditor who has filed a foreclosure action will be likely to seek relief from the bankruptcy stay. This relief may be granted on motion, after a hearing, where the creditor faces the threat of irreparable injury, loss or damage.[139] In addition, the creditor may request "adequate protection" to preserve the creditor's present position and to guard against diminution or loss of the value of the creditor's interests.[140] The creditor may seek to have the property released from the bankrupt's estate on the ground that the debtor does not have equity in the property and that the property is not necessary for the effective reorganization of the estate.[141]

When the bankruptcy petition is filed after the initiation of foreclosure but before judgment, there is authority (at least in the context of a Chapter 13 bankruptcy) that the debtor can still cure the default.[142] Where the bankruptcy is filed after judgement but before sale, applicable case law suggests that the debtor has no right to cure.[143]

Where bankruptcy is filed after mortgaged property has been sold as a result of foreclosure, the situation is different. If the bankruptcy is filed before the end of the redemption period, most courts have taken the position that the redemption period is not lengthened. The Code provides that the bankruptcy estate (not the debtor) has redemption rights for a period of at least 60 days after the filing of the petition.[144]

FOOTNOTES

1. 7 U.S.C. § 1981a. Section 1981a provides that, in addition to any other authority that the Secretary may have to defer principal and interest and forego foreclosure, the Secretary may permit, at the request of the borrower, the deferral of principal and interest on any outstanding loan made, insured, or held by the Secretary under this chapter, or under the provisions of any other law administered by the Farmers Home Administration, and may forego foreclosure of any such loan, for such period as the Secretary deems necessary upon a showing by the borrower that due to circumstances beyond the borrower's control, the borrower is temporarily unable to continue making payments of such principal and interest when due without unduly impairing the standard of living of the borrower. The Secretary may permit interest that accrues during the deferral period on any loan deferred under this section to bear interest during or after such period: Provided, that if the security instrument securing such loan is foreclosed such interest as is included in the purchase price at such foreclosure shall become part of the principal and draw interest from the date of foreclosure at the rate prescribed by law.

2. 53 Fed. Reg. 35718 (1988) (to be codified at 7 C.F.R. § 1951.901).

3. 53 Fed. Reg. 35724 (1988) (to be codified at 7 C.F.R. § 1951.909(c)).

4. Pub. L. No. 100-233, § 615, 101 Stat. 1678 (1988) (to be codified at 7 U.S.C. § 2001).

5. See, e.g, Allison v. Block, 723 F.2d 631 (8th Cir. 1983); United States v. Garner, 767 F.2d 104 (5th Cir. 1985); Shick v. FmHA, 748 F.2d 35 (1st Cir. 1984); United States v. Hamrich, 713 F.2d 69 (4th Cir. 1983); Payne v. Block, 622 F. Supp. 904 (D. Colo. 1985); United States v. Servaes, 608 F. Supp. 775 (E.D. Mo. 1985); United States v. Trimble, 86 F.R.D. 435 (S.D. Fla. 1980). See also Lyng v. Payne, 476 U.S. 926, 90 L.Ed. 2d 921, 106 S.Ct. 2333 (1986).

6. See, e.g., Coleman v. Block, 562 F. Supp. 1353 (D.N.D. 1983); Curry v. Block, 541 F. Supp. 506 (S.D. Ga 1982); Allison v. Block, 723 F.2d 631 (8th Cir. 1983).

7. Pub. L. No. 100-233 § 615, 101 Stat. 1678 (1988) (to be codified at 7 U.S.C. § 2001).

8. Coleman v. Block, 580 F. Supp. 192 (D.N.D. 1984); Payne v. Block, 622 F. Supp. 904 (D.C. Colo. 1985). See also 53 Fed. Reg. 35680 (1988) (to be codified at 7 C.F.R. 1924.57(b)(2)).

9. 53 Fed. Reg. 35670 (1988) (to be codified at 7 C.F.R. § 1902.2(a)).

10. 53 Fed. Reg. 35670 (1988) (to be codified at 7 C.F.R. § 1902.2(a)(4) & (5)).

11. 53 Fed. Reg. 35670 (1988) (to be codified at 7 C.F.R. § 1902.2(a)(6)).

12. 53 Fed. Reg. 35730 (1988) (to be codified at 7 C.F.R. § 1951.911 (a)(1)(ii)).

13. 53 Fed. Reg. 35734 (1988) (to be codified at 7 C.F.R. § 1951.911(b)(2)(iii)).

14. Farm Credit Amendments Act of 1985, Pub. L. No. 99-205, 99 Stat. 1678 (1985) (amending 12 U.S.C. § 2001 et seq.); Agricultural Credit Act of 1987, Pub. L. No. 100-233, 101 Stat. 1568 (1988), (amending 12 U.S.C. § 2001 et seq.).

15. Pub. L. No. 100-233, § 102, 101 Stat. 1574 (1988) (codified at 12 U.S.C. § 2202a(e).

16. 692 F. Supp. 1244, 1248-49 (D.Or. 1988).

17. 692 F. Supp. at 1248-49.

18. 568 F. Supp. 1432 (S.D. Ga. 1983).

19. 777 F.2d 1544 (11th Cir. 1985).

20. 24 Ohio St.3d 69, 493 N.E.2d 946 (1986).

21. Pub. L. No. 100-233, 101 Stat. 1568 (1988) (codified at 12 U.S.C. § 2001 et seq.)

22. Pub. L. No. 100-233, §§ 101-110, 101 Stat. 1572 (1988)(codified at various sections of 12 U.S.C. § 2001 et seq.).

23. Pub. L. No. 100-233, § 103, 101 Stat. 1579 (1988) (amending 12 U.S.C. § 2199).

24. Pub. L. No. 100-233, § 102, 101 Stat. 1574 (1988) (amending 12 U.S.C. § 2202).

25. Pub. L. No. 100-233, § 102, 101 Stat. 1574 (1988) (amending 12 U.S.C. § 2202).

26. Pub. L. No. 100-233, § 102, 101 Stat. 1574 (1988) (amending 12 U.S.C. § 2202).

27. Pub. L. No. 100-233, § 105, 101 Stat. 1579 (1988) (amending 12 U.S.C. § 2201).

28. Pub. L. No. 100-233, § 108, 101 Stat. 1582 (1988) (amending 12 U.S.C. Section 2219a).

29. Pub. L. No. 100-233, § 108, 101 Stat. 1582 (1988) (amending 12 U.S.C. Section 2219a).

30. See, e.g., Home Builders and Loan Assoc. v. Blaisdell, 290 U.S. 398 (1933).

31. Under S.B. 696, in cases commenced after May 8, 1986, the farmer who met specific criteria set forth in this Act could apply to the court by motion, within 20 days prior to the foreclosure trial, for protection under the Act. Within 10 days of filing the motion, the farmer had to serve all parties with a schedule of assets and liabilities, verified under oath. A hearing was to be held on the motion to enable the court to make a determination of the current fair market value of the property (as a whole and by parcel). The court would also determine whether the farmer was insolvent, under the terms of the Act.
Under S.B. 696, if the court found the farmer was entitled to protection under the Act, the court was empowered to order a stay of execution of the foreclosure judgment for 30 days. Within that 30 day period, the farmer had to deposit with the court in cash or by certified check either (1) an amount equal to the interest for one year on the fair market value of the land or parcel or (2) one year's interest depreciation if property other than land were involved. This payment could have been modified by the court into semi-annual or quarterly payments. At that point the foreclosure action would be ordered stayed for one year. There was a provision for an additional one year stay to be ordered for a second and third year upon similar conditions being met by the farmer. Under this law, the failure to make a payment would automatically end the stay and the judgment would be enforced. In exchange for this protection, the Act required the farmer to waive the right to redeem the property, except according to the terms of the Act. To redeem under the Act, the farmer had to pay an amount equal to the fair market value of the property as determined at the time the order was entered. Lastly, rights to protection under the Act could be waived by the debtor in a debt restructuring agreement only when the waiver was fairly given and not unconscionable.

32. Iowa Code § 654.15 (1987).

33. Iowa Code § 654.15(1) & (2) (1987).

34. 11 U.S.C. § 101 <u>et</u> <u>seq</u>.

35. 11 U.S.C. § 109.

36. 11 U.S.C. § 101(35).

37. 11 U.S.C. § 101(19).

38. 11 U.S.C. § 101(20).

39. <u>See</u>, <u>e.g.</u>, In re Blanton Smith, 7 Bankr. 410 (Bankr. M.D. Tenn. 1980), in which a debtor whose entire gross income during the pre-filing years was derived from processing, packaging and marketing eggs was held to be a farmer.

40. 11 U.S.C. § 303(a).

41. 11 U.S.C. § 301(b)(1).

42. 11 U.S.C. § 303.

43. 11 U.S.C. § 362(a); <u>see</u> <u>also</u> § 1201 of Chapter 12, Adjustment of Debts of a Family Farmer with Regular Annual Income.

44. 11 U.S.C. § 362(c).

45. Resnick, "Prudent Planning or Fraudulent Transfer? The Use of Non-Exempt Assets to Purchase or Improve Exempt Property on the Eve of Bankruptcy," <u>Rutgers L.Rev.</u> 615, 621 (1978).

46. 11 U.S.C. § 522(b)(1).

47. K.S.A. § 60-2301.

48. 11 U.C.C. § 522(b)(2)(A).

49. These same items appear in the federal exemption list of 11 U.S.C. § 522(d).

50. See, e.g., Metz v. Williams, 149 Kan. 647 (1939).

51. Neal v. Clerk, 95 U.S. 704, 709 (1877).

52. See, e.g., In re Aldman, 541 F.2d 999 (2nd Cir. 1976); In re Jackson, 472 F.2d 589 (9th Cir. 1973).

53. 11 U.S.C. § 507(a).

54. 11 U.S.C. § 523 for a complete list.

55. 11 U.S.C. § 1123.

56. 11 U.S.C. § 1123(5).

57. 11 U.S.C. § 1123(a)(4).

58. 11 U.S.C. § 1129.

59. 11 U.S.C. § 1126.

60. 11 U.S.C. § 1129(a)(10).

61. 11 U.S.C. § 1129(a)(7).

62. 11 U.S.C. § 1321-1330 outlines the requirements for the plan.

63. 11 U.S.C. § 109(e).

64. Rule 3015, Bankruptcy Rules.

65. 11 U.S.C. § 1324.

66. 11 U.S.C. § 1329.

67. 11 U.S.C. § 1322.

68. 11 U.S.C. § 1328.

69. 11 U.S.C. § 1201 et seq.

70. 11 U.S.C. § 1203.

71. 11 U.S.C. § 1203.

72. 11 U.S.C. § 101(17).

73. 11 U.S.C. § 101(18).

74. 11 U.S.C. § 101.

75. 11 U.S.C. § 101(17).

76. 11 U.S.C. § 101(20).

77. 11 U.S.C. § 101(20).

78. 11 U.S.C. § 101(18).

79. 11 U.S.C. § 431.

80. Pub. L. No. 99-554, § 251, 100 Stat. 3104 (1986).

81. 30 Stat. 544.

82. 11 U.S.C. § 101(17)(A).

83. 11 U.S.C. § 101(17)(B).

84. 132 Cong. Rec. S15076 (daily ed. Oct. 3, 1986) (statement of Sen. Grassley).

85. 55 Bankr. 755 (Bankr. C.D. Ill. 1985).

86. 55 Bankr. at 761.

87. 73 Bankr. 508 (Bankr. N.D. Iowa 1987).

88. 73 Bankr. 510.

89. 73 Bankr. at 509.

90. 74 Bankr. 469 (Bankr. E.D. Ark. 1987).

91. 73 Bankr. at 473-74.

92. 74 Bankr. at 473.

93. 74 Bankr. at 474, n. 6.

94. 301 U.S. 435 (1937), quoted in In re Maike, 77 Bankr. 832, 837 (Bankr. D. Kan. 1987).

95. 301 U.S. at 440.

96. 791 F.2d 623 (8th Cir. 1986).

97. 791 F.2d at 626.

98. 791 F.2d at 626.

99. 45 Bankr. 744 (Bankr. D. Minn. 1985).

100. 45 Bankr. at 747.

101. 45 Bankr. at 746.

102. 45 Bankr. at 747.

103. 45 Bankr. at 747.

104. 45 Bankr. at 747.

105. 77 Bankr. 223 (Bankr. D. Neb. 1987).

106. 77 Bankr. at 225.

107. 74 Bankr. 401 (Bankr. S.D. Ohio 1987).

108. 77 Bankr. 832 (Bankr. D. Kan. 1987).

109. 77 Bankr. at 839.

110. 77 Bankr. 839.

111. 77 Bankr. 839.

112. See 77 Bankr. at 839.

113. See In re Welch, 74 Bankr. 401, 405 (Bankr. S.D. Ohio 1987).

114. 74 Bankr. 51 (Bankr. C.D. Ill. 1987).

115. 74 Bankr. at 53.

116. 11 U.S.C. § 1221.

117. 11 U.S.C. § 1222(a).

118. 11 U.S.C. § 1222(a)(3).

119. 11 U.S.C. § 1222(b).

120. 11 U.S.C. § 1224.

121. 11 U.S.C. § 1225.

122. 11 U.S.C. § 1225(b)(1).

123. 11 U.S.C. § 1227.

124. 11 U.S.C. § 1222(b)(5) & (b)(10).

125. 11 U.S.C. § 1228, 11 U.S.C. § 523(a).

126. 11 U.S.C. § 1228(b).

127. 11 U.S.C. § 1228(d). See also 11 U.S.C. § 1230.

128. 11 U.S.C. § 1229.

129. 11 U.S.C. § 1229(a).

130. 11 U.S.C. § 1208.

131. 11 U.S.C. § 1208(d).

132. 11 U.S.C. § 1208(b).

133. 11 U.S.C. § 1208(c).

134. See 11 U.S.C. §§ 361, 362, 363(a), 364.

135. 11 U.S.C. § 361(3).

136. 11 U.S.C. § 1205.

137. 11 U.S.C. § 1205(b).

138. 11 U.S.C. § 362.

139. 11 U.S.C. § 362(d).

140. See 11 U.S.C. § 361.

141. 11 U.S.C. § 362(d)(2). See also In re Monroe Park, 6 CBC 2d 139 (D.C. Del. 1982); In re Robson, 10 B.R. 362 (B.C. N.D. Ala. 1981); In re Parnell, 12 B.R. 51 (B.C. E.D. Pa. 1981).

142. See In re Davis, 15 B.R. 22 (B.C. Kan. 1981). See also, In re Taddeo, 9 B.R. 299 (B.C. E.D. N.Y. 1981), aff'd, 685 F.2d 24 (2 Cir. 1982).

143. In re Elliott, Case No. 82-10940 (B.C. Kan. 1983, distinguishing In re Davis).

144. See, 11 U.S.C. § 108(b).

CHAPTER 6

FEDERAL FARM PROGRAMS AND THE ASCS

This chapter will review the various federal government programs for price and income support which directly affect United States agricultural production and marketing. United States Department of Agriculture (USDA) programs and regulations often have a major effect on individual farming operations. These programs are administered within the International Affairs and Commodity Programs Division of the USDA by the Agricultural Stabilization and Conservation Service (ASCS). The focus of this chapter is on the price and income support programs. This chapter will not discuss the Farm Storage Facility Loan Program administered by the ASCS. That discussion appears in chapter 3.

I.   Program Administration: The CCC and the ASCS
        The Commodity Credit Corporation (CCC) was created by executive order in 1933 and is incorporated in Delaware. It was initially capitalized by funds appropriated by Congress. In 1948 it was re-incorporated as a wholly-owned government corporation. The CCC charter authorizes it to buy, sell and lend, to stabilize prices, increase production, insure adequate commodity supplies and to facilitate their distribution. It is authorized to borrow from the United States Treasury and private lending institutions.[1]
        The CCC administers the agricultural price support activities of the USDA. However, because the CCC does not have an administrative staff, it has delegated the operation of the price and income support programs to the Agricultural Stabilization and Conservation Service (ASCS). Therefore, ASCS actually administers all of the USDA price and income support programs. Local farmers elect ASCS county committees which determine the eligibility of individual farmers and farming operations for the various farm programs. The county committee also administers all of the other aspects of those programs, in addition to eligibility determinations. Any

191

"producer or participant" affected by any decision of the county committee is entitled to appeal that decision.[2]

II.   Price and Income Support
        Federal programs which provide price and income support for farmers have been in existence for over fifty years. Price instability and chronic over-production of agricultural commodities have contributed to the need for price and income support for farmers.

        In many respects, the major concepts involved in current price and income support programs (including those of the most recent farm bill adopted by Congress) are not new. In a significant sense, the basic price and income support structure is an outgrowth of the economic depression of the 1930's. As currently (and historically) structured, federal price and income support programs have two basic objectives: to raise farm incomes to parity levels while insuring the availability of food and fiber at a reasonable cost to consumers; and to stabilize the agricultural sector of the economy by preventing severe volatility in farm prices.

        At the inception of the federal programs, government intervention was directed toward market price supports for individual commodities to achieve increased income. Since price supports could serve as an incentive for production, methods of controlling production were introduced along with price supports to counteract excess supplies of commodities. These production control programs provide government subsidies to encourage producers to remove a portion of their farmland acreage from crop production. The purpose of the programs is to control overall crop yield in the specific commodities. The programs also help to conserve soil and to protect marginal lands. Although participation in price and income support programs was made voluntary, the availability of government payments has given producers an incentive to participate in acreage control programs. However, under the federal program structure, those who choose to face the risks associated with market price fluctuations by not participating in the price support programs are under no obligation to participate in acreage control programs.

        During the nineteen seventies the target price/deficiency

192

payment system was also implemented. Target prices are established and adjusted by law. The target price programs for wheat, feed grains, cotton and rice allow government support payments to fluctuate in accordance with market prices. At present, soybeans, rye, flax, fruits, nuts and vegetables are not included in the deficiency payment program. For the commodities which are included, if market prices drop below a certain level producers receive some protection in the form of a price guarantee at the target price level. In contrast, if prices rise above the target price level some stabilization in supply can occur through the return of reserves to the market. The exact terms and provisions of these price support programs change periodically. However, the programs consistently adhere to the basic concept of a price corridor within which prices move as market conditions change.

The availability of price and income support programs has an effect on the marketing decisions which farmers make. For example, the farmer's decision about how much of a particular crop to grow will be influenced by whether a particular crop is eligible for price support. The farmer may decide to expand production of a particular crop if the minimum price in the government program is favorable in relation to the production costs for that crop. If a farmer refrains from participating in target price programs, he or she is not constrained by government acreage restrictions, such as the land set-aside provisions. However, the farmer would then be ineligible to receive deficiency payments in the event of low market prices at harvest time. Therefore, the farmer who elects not to participate takes a calculated risk that market prices at harvest will be adequate to cover production costs and to allow a profit.

III.   Development of Support Programs

In developing the statutory programs to provide price and income support, considerable attention has been directed toward the most appropriate level of that support. The debate has often focused on the concept of "parity price". The term "parity price" was made popular by the Agricultural Adjustment Act of 1938.[3] The term is used to identify a price that would enable a farmer, at any given point in time, to receive for his

193

commodity output the value necessary to enable him to purchase the same quantity of other products as he could have purchased during the specified based period (1910-1914). The parity concept has largely been abandoned for most commodities. Instead, support prices are directly set by statute or made in reference to average prices for particular commodities.

The Agricultural Adjustment Act of 1933[4] was the first major farm legislation. The 1933 Act provided for voluntary reduction in commodity production in exchange for direct payments to farmers. It also established price supports through nonrecourse loans. This has become the primary price support mechanism for most commodities. A farmer who participates in the non-recourse loan program places commodities in reserve while retaining ownership of them. Loan rates are set at market clearing levels and serve as the floor price which the farmer can receive. If the market price drops below the loan rate, the loan amount effectively becomes the price for the commodity. Thus, the CCC loan rate serves as a minimum price.

In U.S. v. Butler,[5] the United States Supreme Court invalidated certain of the 1933 Act's provisions. In response to this ruling, Congress enacted the Agricultural Adjustment Act of 1938.[6] The 1938 Act established price support loans for designated commodities, as well as parity payments, farm acreage allotments and marketing quotas. The 1938 Act also created the Federal Crop Insurance Corporation. In the Agricultural Act of 1949[7] Congress modified some of the prior programs and established provisions that still serve as the foundation for current price and income support programs.

Generally, the price and income support programs which were promulgated in the 1938 Act remained in use until the 1960's. The programs eventually became ineffective, however, due to the excessive commodity supplies which resulted both from the production incentives provided by the programs and by the development of improved agricultural technology. The production incentives resulted because price support levels were often above market prices.

The 1973 Agriculture and Consumer Protection Act[8] addressed this problem by introducing the target price and deficiency payment concepts. For most feed and food grains, income support is achieved through the provision of "deficiency payments" designed to make up the difference between a national average market price and a higher "target price" which is set either by Congress or the Secretary of Agriculture. The "target price" is intended to be a price level at which the farmer is assured of a fair return for his or her product. In this sense, deficiency payments guarantee that the farmer will receive at least the target price for the commodity. However, the payment is not determined by any specific price an individual farmer marketing his or her product might receive. Rather, deficiency payments are issued only when the national average market price received by farmers for the first five months of the marketing year falls below the established target price. These payments are calculated by multiplying the payment rate times the farm's established yield times the number of acres planted for harvest. This figure then may be multiplied by any applicable allocation factors. These concepts provide flexibility for determining price support payments in relation to actual market conditions. The target price and deficiency payment concepts have been a part of all price support programs since 1973.

The Food Security Act of 1985[9] established price and income supports for the 1986-1990 crop years. The loan program covers the commodities of wheat, feed grains, upland and extra long staple cotton, rice, soybeans and sugar. The Act also provides deficiency payments for wheat, feed grains, upland and extra long staple cotton and rice. The already-existing price supports for milk, wool and mohair were continued through 1990. A peanut program, which operates through two tiered marketing quotas, was continued with minor changes. Honey is also supported by a loan program.

Statutory guidelines of the 1985 Act determine the commodity amounts and the terms and conditions of price and income support programs. With certain commodities the Secretary has the discretion to implement programs above a minimum level. The factors which must be considered by the Secretary in deciding whether to implement discretionary support programs include:

(1) the relationship of supply and demand for the

195

commodity;

(2) the price levels at which other commodities
are being supported, and, in the case of feed
grains, the feed values of those grains in relation
to corn;

(3) the availability of funds;

(4) the perishability of the commodity;

(5) the importance of the commodity to agriculture and
the national economy;

(6) the ability to dispose of stocks acquired
through price-support operations;

(7) the need to offset temporary losses of export
markets;

(8) the ability and willingness of producers to
keep supplies in line with demand; and

(9) in the case of upland cotton, changes in the
cost of producing the cotton.[10]

The Secretary must also determine the level at which support
should be undertaken. Where support is mandatory these
factors also guide the determination of support levels in excess
of the statutory minimum.

IV.   Current Program Provisions

A. Price Support

Price support is administered by the ASCS through non-
recourse loans and purchase programs. As noted earlier, there
is a clearly discernible production control element in these
programs. The objective of production control is to keep prices
within a controlled range by the use of grain reserves and
cropland set-aside practices. Payments under price support
programs have tended to be one of two types, loans or
purchases.

1. Loans

For feed and food grains, oil seeds and oils, fibers,
manufactured milk products, honey, gum navel stores, tobacco,
peanuts, and dry edible beans, the primary price support
mechanism is the post-production loan. Although administered
by the ASCS, these loans are actually made by the Commodity
Credit Corporation. The ASCS acts as the CCC agent in

administering CCC programs, since the CCC has no staff. To participate in the loan program, producers place the particular harvested commodity in an approved storage facility.

There are two basic loan programs: regular loans and reserve loans. Regular loans are made at a national loan rate and are typically of nine-months duration. They are to be repaid by the farmer at any time prior to the final maturity date of the loan through payment to the CCC of the outstanding loan amount plus any interest that has accrued. In contrast, reserve loans, while made to producers at generally the same rate as regular loans, are for a much longer time period. This induces the farmer to keep the grain off the market until the price reaches a pre-set level at which the farmer will be deemed to receive a fair return for the stored commodity. Farmers are contractually bound not to dispose of their commodities during the loan period. When the average national market price reaches a particular level (currently 125 percent of the national loan rate) and remains there for a specified period (currently five days), the commodity is released from its reserve status and may be sold by the farmer and the loan repaid. If the national market price drops below the "release price" without being sold, the commodity may then be returned to reserve status and will continue to be kept off the market. If the national average market price reaches and remains at a generally higher level, the loan may be called and the farmer will have no choice but to repay the loan. When this occurs, the farmer is then completely free to dispose of the commodity in the marketplace.

Both of these types of loans are typically "non-recourse" in nature. This means that producers are not obligated to bear the loss resulting from any decline in the market price below the national loan rate. For example, if at the end of the regular nine-month loan period, the national market price for the commodity has not reached the national loan level, the grain may be forfeited to the CCC. The CCC takes title to the commodity as full payment of the loan and interest charges and the loan obligation is discharged in full. The CCC has no recourse against the debtor beyond the proceeds of the forfeited commodity itself.

2. Purchases

In many cases, the CCC will directly purchase the commodity from the farmer. To accomplish this, the producer must apply at the ASCS county office for the option of selling a quantity of his or her commodity to the CCC. In some cases, as with manufactured milk products, the CCC may be legally obligated to purchases commodities in order to keep excess supplies from causing prices to drop. The price to be paid for the commodity is generally established by USDA regulation. The CCC will purchase at that price whatever quantity a particular producer wishes to sell, up to a maximum amount eligible under the program.

B. Income Support

Income support is provided by direct payments, target prices and deficiency payments, marketing loans and loan deficiency payments.

1. Direct payments

Sometimes income support is achieved through direct payments to individual producers. These include indemnity payments to producers for losses (e.g. to honey producers for bees killed by a farmer's insecticides), or which constitute a production incentive (e.g. in the case of wool and mohair).

Disaster payments are provided in situations where Congress authorizes assistance due to special circumstances. For example, the Disaster Relief and Assistance Act of 1988[11] was designed to provide much needed relief to farmers following the drought which occurred during the summer of 1988. Moreover, emergency livestock feed programs and relief for disaster-related losses of program crops are usually available. These programs are discussed in more detail in Chapter 8.

The most frequently used of the incentive payment programs is for producers of wool and mohair. This program pays the producer an amount based on the difference in average market price and a specified support level.

2. Target Prices and Deficiency Payments

For wheat, feed grains, upland and extra long staple cotton, and rice, the primary means of income support is through the target price/deficiency payment program discussed earlier. Under this program a target price is set either by Congress or by the USDA through its administrative authority. If the market price falls below the target price, the farmer receives a deficiency payment from the government for the difference in price. When market prices exceed the target price a "release price" may be reached. If so, CCC reserves are released into the market. This serves to lower the market price.

A special provision may allow a producer to receive some deficiency payments for grain not planted under the so called "92/50" or "92/0" provisions. These allow payment based on 92% of permitted acreage to a producer who reduces plantings on up to 50% (or even on 100% in some wheat programs) of the acreage.

3. Marketing Loans

In those situations in which the farmer has obtained a CCC non-recourse loan and the market price is actually below the loan rate, the farmer has the option of forfeiting the grain as repayment of the loan. This has, in the past, led to the accumulation of a surplus of government-owned commodities and has effectively set a "floor" under the world market price. To avoid these problems the 1985 Food Security Act[12] introduced the concept of the marketing loan. Under this concept the producer must still repay the CCC loan but may do so by selling the commodities at the market price and paying off the loan at the market price (not at the original loan rate). The difference (received by the producer earlier) is a subsidy to the producer. This program is authorized for wheat, feed grains, soybeans and honey and is required for rice and cotton if the world market price is below loan levels. The Secretary has not chosen to use the authority for all crops, but has for upland cotton, honey, and rice.

4. Loan Deficiency Payments

The Secretary will announce whether loan deficiency payments will be made available to farmers for a specific crop during a crop year.[13] This payment constitutes a subsidy for farmers who refrain from participating in the marketing loan program when it is in effect.

199

Loan deficiency payments are currently available for wheat, feed grains, rice and upland cotton. In order to be eligible to receive a loan deficiency payment, the producer of the relevant commodity must:

    1. Comply with all of the program requirements to be eligible to obtain loans or purchases, in accordance with price support programs (7 C.F.R. Part 1421) or cotton loan and payment programs (7 C.F.R. Part 1427);

    2. Agree to forego obtaining those loans or purchases; and

    3. Otherwise comply with all program requirements.[14]

The loan deficiency payment is to be computed by multiplying the "loan payment rate" by the quantity of the crop the producer is eligible to pledge as collateral for a CCC loan.

The loan payment rate for crops (other than upland cotton) is the amount by which the level of the price support loan originally determined for the crop exceeds the level at which the CCC has announced that producers may repay their price support loans.[15] With respect to upland cotton, the loan payment rate is an amount not to exceed one-half of this payment. With respect to rice, an amount not to exceed one-half of that payment must be made.[16]

C. Production Control

Various methods are used under current law to restrict production and to control the levels of CCC inventories of various commodities. The most common of these programs is the cropland set-aside which was initiated in the Agricultural Act of 1970.[17] The set-aside program requires producers of feed and food grains and of cotton to withhold a specified percentage of acres from production as a condition of receiving government payments. In addition, the farmer may be required to plant an approved cover vegetation or use conservation practices on the idled acres.

Cross compliance, or offsetting compliance, may also be required. That is, if a farmer farms more than one farm or raises more than one kind of the crops which are covered by the program, farmers must participate in the set-aside program for all set-aside crops on a farm to be eligible for benefits (cross compliance). Or, they must insure that normal crop acreage is not exceeded on non-participating farms (offsetting compliance). A more recent supply management program is the acreage reduction program which was first authorized by the Agriculture and Food Act of 1981.[18] Under this program, acreage is taken from the individual crop acreage base for individual farms based on the actual plantings of the previous year. This acreage, like set-aside, is to be devoted to conservation uses. Participation may be required as a condition of eligibility for support and cross compliance may be mandated.

The Secretary of Agriculture has the authority to initiate paid diversion programs for certain commodities. Through the diversion program farmers are induced to take acreage out of designated crop production in exchange for a specified payment. In most cases, the amount of payment will be based on the established yield for the farm multiplied by the acreage diverted and the per-unit payment amount.

1. Cropland Set-Asides

If supply forecasts for wheat or feed grains indicate that supplies are in excess of demand, eligible farmers may be required to set-aside a percent of their total planted acreage and manage it through designated conservation practices to be eligible for government loans and deficiency payments. The amount of acreage which is to be set-aside is based on total plantings from previous years but is not based on the specific crop history for a given farm. The Secretary will announce pertinent information each year, including whether a set-aside requirement is in effect for a crop year for a specific crop of feed grains or wheat, the percentage of the planted crop acreage that is required to be set-aside, and other requirements of the program for the year.[19] To qualify for program benefits, producers of the applicable crops must devote an acreage equal to the set-aside requirement to conservation uses, not knowingly exceed the authorized crop acreage and otherwise comply with all program requirements.[20]

2. Acreage Reductions (ARP)

A farmer may also be required to participate in an

acreage reduction program (ARP) as a condition of eligibility for support. The amount of acreage which is removed from production under this program is determined from the individual crop acreage base as determined from records of previous years' plantings. Based on guidelines in the 1985 Food Security Act,[21] a normal crop acreage (NCA) is established for each farm. The Secretary will announce whether an acreage reduction program (ARP) is in effect for a specific crop during the crop year, the percentage reduction to be applied to the crop acreage base to determine the amount of required reduction, and other requirements of the program for the year.[22] Producers of the applicable crop(s) must devote the reduced acreage to conservation uses or, as determined in accordance with instructions issued by the ASCS Deputy Administrator, a proportionately smaller acreage if the planted acreage is smaller than the permitted acreage, and otherwise comply with all production restrictions and other program requirements.[23]

3. Paid Acreage Diversion

Under this program farmers are paid to voluntarily take acreage out of production. Unlike the set-aside and ARP programs, diversion is not necessarily a condition of eligibility for other government program benefits. The Secretary may determine whether compliance with the land diversion requirement is required in order for the producer on the farm to be eligible for loans, purchases and payments for the crop. The Secretary will announce whether a paid acreage diversion program is in effect for a crop year for a specific crop, the percentage of the planted crop acreage or of the crop acreage base that producers must divert from crop production under the program, the payment rate, and whether advance program payments will be available.[24] In order to be eligible for any paid acreage diversion payment, producers of the applicable crop or crops must devote an acreage which is equal to the required diverted acreage to conservation uses and meet all other program requirements.[25]

4. Bid Diversion Program

For major agricultural commodities, the Secretary may

open the program to participating producers for the purpose of accepting bids for the diversion of acreage planted to that crop.[26] The CCC will announce the manner in which bids for participation in the program must be made and the manner in which the program will be conducted.[27] This information will include the following: (1) The period of time during which bids may he submitted; (2) The form of the bid, i.e. whether the bid should be as a percentage of the farm program payment yield for the farm, as a number of pounds or bushels per acre, or such other form as may be determined and announced; (3) The basis for evaluating bids, including any limitation upon the number of acres that may be accepted; (4) The manner in which payments will be made to the producers whose bids are accepted; and (5) Other requirements of the program.[28]

The operator or producer on a farm may submit to the local ASCS office a contract bid on a form prescribed by the CCC. To be eligible to submit a bid, the operator and any other producers on the farm must be parties to a contract in which that farm participates in the program for the applicable commodity in that crop year.[29]

The contract to participate in the bid diversion program may contain requirements as to the eligibility of acres planted to the crop, the time and manner by which any growing crop must be destroyed, limitations on the use of the acreage and the crop residue, provision for assessing liquidated damages in the case of violation of the contract, and any other provisions which are necessary for the effective operation of the program.[30]

If a bid diversion program is offered for more than one commodity, the operator and any other producers may select the commodities to be included in the bid, except that the CCC may require that the bid include either both crops or neither crop of corn and grain sorghum, or barley and oats.[31]

After the final date for submitting bids, the bids in each county will be ranked for each commodity. The CCC may elect to treat corn and grain sorghum or barley and oats as single commodities, on the basis of the percentage of the farm program payment yield, with the lowest percentage being ranked highest.[32] In the case of identical bids, the bids must be ranked in the order received. Where an appointment procedure was utilized by the county ASCS office during the time in which producers submitted bids, a lottery will be conducted to determine the order by which those bids should be ranked. The bids for each commodity must then be accepted in rank order. The CCC may establish the number of acres for which bids will be accepted for each commodity in each county.[33]

To the extent practicable, any questions about the content of the bid will be resolved by the county committee when the bids are opened.[34] Any decision by the county committee may be appealed. If an appeal is resolved in the producer's favor, the bid may then he accepted without regard to whether accepting the bid would result in exceeding the maximum number of acres which may be enrolled in the program as established for the county.[35]

5. Inventory Reduction Program

The Secretary will announce to farmers whether an inventory reduction program is in effect for a crop year for a specific crop.[36] In order to be eligible for any inventory reduction payments, the farmer must:

1. Comply with all of the program requirements to be eligible to obtain a loan or purchase agreement;
2. Agree to forego obtaining those loans or purchases;
3. Agree to forego receiving deficiency payments;
4. Limit the acreage of the crop planted for harvest to the crop acreage base reduced by one-half of the acreage required to be diverted from production, in accordance with any acreage reduction and/or land diversion program for the crop; and
5. Otherwise comply with all program requirements.[37]

6. Acreage Conservation Reserve (ACR)

Land that is designated for the set-aside, ARP or any of the diversion programs must be managed in accordance with the rules for the Acreage Conservation Reserve (ACR). Under the Acreage Conservation Reserve (ACR) program the operator and each producer on the farm agree that they will devote an eligible acreage of land to approved conservation uses as may be required by the commodity program for that crop. The operator must agree to timely file an accurate report of acreage on Form ASCS-578. This form lists the ACR acreage and the

204

planted acreage of the program crop(s).[38] In exchange, the CCC agrees that the harvested crop will be eligible for loans and purchases. The CCC also agrees that deficiency payments will be made to the operator and producers.[39]

D. Conservation Reserve Program (CRP)

Farmers must submit bids to the government for the opportunity to participate in the unique soil conservation program known as the Conservation Reserve Program (CRP). Under the CRP, the Secretary of Agriculture is authorized to enter into contracts with eligible owners and operators of highly erodible cropland to assist them in conserving and improving the soil and water resources on their farms and ranches. This is achieved by converting the participating land to permanent vegetative cover in accordance with an approved conservation plan. Participating farmers are required to place highly erodible cropland under designated conservation practices for the term of the contract. In exchange, the farmer receives annual rental payments. The farmer also receives a 50% cost sharing payment to partially cover the cost of planting the necessary vegetative cover.

The objectives of the CRP are to:
1. reduce water and wind erosion;
2. protect the long-term U.S. capability to produce food and fiber;
3. reduce sedimentation;
4. improve water quality;
5. create better habitat for fish and wildlife through improved food cover;
6. curb production of surplus commodities, and
7. provide needed income support for farmers.[40]

The maximum acreage in a county which may be placed in the CRP may not exceed 25% of the total cropland in the county unless the CCC determines that such action would not adversely affect the economy of the county.[41]

1. Eligibility

To be eligible to enter into a CRP contract, a person must be the owner or operator of eligible cropland. The operator must also have operated the cropland for the period

205

beginning not less than 3 years prior to the close of the applicable sign-up period and must provide satisfactory evidence that the person will continue to be the operator of the cropland during the CRP contract period.[42] The owner of eligible cropland must have owned the cropland for not less than 3 years prior to the close of the applicable sign-up period. An exception to this rule is provided if the new owner acquired the cropland by will or succession as a result of the death of the previous owner, or if it is determined that the new owner did not acquire the cropland for the purpose of placing it in the CRP.

To be eligible for the CRP, a field must:

1. have been annually planted in a crop other than orchards, vineyards or ornamental plantings in 2 of the 5 crop years from 1981-1985;
2. have the physical capability to be planted to produce a crop other than orchards, vineyards, or ornamental plantings; and
3. consist primarily of soils which are "highly erodible cropland" as defined in the regulations.[43]

The CRP applicant must develop a conservation plan in consultation with the Soil Conservation Service.[44] If applicable, the State Forester will develop a tree planting plan to be included with the conservation plan.[45] All conservation plans must be approved by the state Conservation District (CD), or by a representative of the Soil Conservation Service (SCS) if the land area is not located within a CD.[46] Eligible conservation practices are those practices specified in the conservation plan that meet all quantity and quality standards needed to establish permanent vegetative cover. This cover may include introduced or native species of grasses and legumes, forest trees, permanent wildlife habitat, field windbreaks, and shallow water areas for wildlife that will provide adequate erosion control for the contract period.[47]

2. Contracting Procedure

The CRP is administered through a contract between the owner or operator and the CCC. In order to enter into a CRP contract, the applicant must submit an offer to participate on Form CRP-1 at the local county ASCS office during the announced sign-up period for the applicable crop year.[48] This offer is irrevocable for a period of 30 days subsequent to the close of the applicable sign-up period.[49] The applicant will be assessed liquidated damages if he or she revokes an offer prior to the expiration of this period.[50] The CCC has complete discretion to reject any and all offers to place land into the CRP.[51]

After the CCC acceptance of an offer, participants in the CRP must:

1. carry out the terms and conditions of the CRP contract for a period of 10 crop years from the date the contract is executed;
2. implement the conservation plan in accordance with the timetable and conservation practices prescribed by the plan;
3. agree to a reduction in the aggregate total of crop acreage bases, allotments and quotas which is derived from the ratio between the total cropland acreage on the farm and the total acreage on the farm subject to the CRP contract;
4. not undertake any action on other land under the participants control during the contract periods that would tend to defeat the purpose of the CRP;
5. not knowingly or willingly allow grazing, harvesting or other commercial use of any crop from the cropland subject to the CRP contract except for those periods of time in accordance with instructions issued by the Secretary in response to drought or similar emergency;
6. not knowingly or willing allow grazing, harvesting, as Christmas trees or nursery stock, of any trees planted during the contract period on land subject to the CRP contract;
7. maintain the vegetative cover and the required conservation practices on the land subject to the CRP contract and take other actions that may be required by the CCC to achieve the reduction in soil erosion necessary to maintain the production capability of the soil throughout the CRP contract period, and
8. comply with the noxious weed laws of the applicable

state on land subject to the CRP contract.[52] The participant and each other person who signs the CRP contract are jointly and severally responsible for compliance with the CRP contract.[53]

The CCC must, subject to the availability of funds:
1. share with the participant the cost of establishing eligible conservation practices;
2. pay the participant an annual rental payment in the amount which is specified in the CRP contract; and
3. provide the technical assistance which is necessary to assist the participant in carrying out the CRP contract.[54]

3. Payments

Cost-share payments can only be issued after a determination by the CCC that the eligible conservation practice, or an identifiable unit thereof, has been established in compliance with the standards and specifications prescribed for eligible conservation practices.[55] The CCC will share up to 50 percent of the actual or average cost of establishing the eligible conservation practices specified in the conservation plan. Cost-share payments may be authorized for the replacement or restoration of conservation practices for which cost-share payments have been previously allowed only if:
1. replacement or restoration of the practice is needed to achieve adequate erosion control; and
2. the failure of the original practice was not due to the lack of proper maintenance by the participant.[56]

The maximum amount of rental payments which a person may receive under the CRP for any fiscal year must not exceed $50,000.[57] Payments for CCC cost-share or rental obligations may be made in cash, in-kind, in commodity certificates or by any combination of those methods.[58] CRP program payments may be offset by claims or liens held by agencies of the U.S. government but not by any other creditor.[59]

4. Contract Modification

Under certain circumstances a CRP contract may be

subject to modification. The CCC and the CRP participant may modify the contract by mutual agreement in order to:

1. decrease the acreage placed in the CRP;
2. permit the production of an agricultural commodity during a crop year on all or part of the land subject to the CRP contract; or
3. facilitate the practical administration of the CRP.[60]

However, the concurrence of the SCS, the State Forester where applicable and the CD are necessary when modifications of a CRP contract involve a technical aspect of the conservation plan.[61]

The CCC may modify CRP contracts to add, delete, or substitute conservation practices when:

1. the installed conservation practice has failed to adequately control erosion through no fault of the participant;
2. the installed method deteriorated because of conditions beyond the control of the participant; or
3. another conservation practice will achieve at least the same level of erosion control.[62]

5. Transfer of Ownership

In the event that a new owner or operator purchases or assumes occupancy of the land subject to a CRP contract, the new owner or operator may assume the existing CRP contract or may offer to enter into a new CRP contract which covers the transferred land.[63] If the new owner or operator does not become a CRP participant, the original participant:

1. must forfeit all rights to any future annual rental or cost-share payments;
2. must refund all or part of past payments plus interest, as determined by the CCC. The participant may be allowed to retain whatever portion of the payment represents the achievement of desired conservation benefits for an acceptable period; and
3. must pay liquidated damages as specified in the CRP contract.[64]

6. Violation of Contract

If the participant violates any of the terms and

conditions of the CRP contract the CCC may, after considering the recommendations of the CD and the SCS, terminate the contract.[65] If the CCC terminates the CRP contract, the participant must forfeit all rights to future payments under the contract, refund all payments received together with interest thereon as determined by CCC and pay liquidated damages in the amount specified in the CRP contract.[66]

The policy reason for imposing liquidated damages as a CCC remedy upon the breach of a CRP contract is explained in the regulations, as follows:

> Once a CRP contract has been entered into between CCC and the owner or operator, CCC and other segments of the agricultural community will act based on the assumption that the CRP contract will be fulfilled and the reduction in erosion and production will be obtained. CCC's action includes budgeting and planning for the CRP in subsequent crop years. A participant's failure to carry out the terms and conditions of the CRP contract undermines the basis for these actions, damages the credibility of CCC's programs with other segments of the agricultural community and requires additional expenditures in subsequent crop years in order for the required levels of acreage to he placed in the CRP and in order for an adequate reduction in acreage to be obtained. While the adverse affects on CCC of the participant's failure to comply with the CRP contract is obvious, it would be impossible to compute the actual damage suffered by CCC.[67]

If the participant fails to carry out the terms and conditions of the contract, but the CCC determines that the failure does not warrant termination of the CRP contract, the CCC may require that the participant refund contract payments received or accept adjustments in payments that CCC determines to be appropriate.[68] If, after a CRP contract is approved on behalf of the CCC, it is discovered that the contract is not in conformity with the program regulations as a result of a misunderstanding of the program procedures by a signatory to the contract, a modification of the contract may be made by mutual agreement. If an agreement can not be reached, the contract will be terminated and all payments paid or payable will be forfeited or refunded to the CCC.[69]

7. Other Provisions

A USDA representative must be given the right of access to land which is the subject of a CRP offer or contract and has the right to examine any other cropland under the applicant's or participant's control. This right of access is for the purpose of determining whether the land is highly erodible and whether the farmer is in compliance with the terms and conditions of the CRP.[70]

Payments received under a CRP contract must be divided fairly and equitably among all participants to the contract. The regulations contain guidelines relating to the division of payments and the rights of tenants and sharecroppers.[71]

The CRP participant is entitled to a review of any administrative determination made under the CRP program. Appeals are brought in accordance with the ASCS appeal regulations.[72] However, any program determination made by the SCS or a CD may be reviewed in accordance with the SCS appeal regulations.[73]

E. Methods of Program Payment

Prior to 1985, most government payments were made in cash. However, the Food Security Act of 1985[74] authorized various non-cash methods of payment. The regulations authorize non-cash methods of payment for program payments and loans made by the Commodity Credit Corporation (CCC) or the Agricultural Stabilization and Conservation Service (ASCS).[75] The decision to make a non-cash payment is at the sole discretion of the CCC.[76] The regulations authorize the following non-cash forms of payment:

1. By delivery of a commodity to a person at a warehouse or other similar facility;
2. By transfer of negotiable warehouse receipts;
3. By the issuance of commodity certificates;
4. By the acquisition and use of commodities pledged as collateral for CCC price support loans;
5. By the use of commodities owned by the CCC; and
6. By any other method which the CCC deems appropriate,

particularly methods which assure that the producer receives the same total return as if the payments had been made in cash.[77] The value of the non-cash payments is determined exclusively by the CCC.

A farmer who is a member of a marketing cooperative which is eligible to receive the farmer's price support payment (in accordance with 7 C.F.R. Part 1425), may qualify for a special arrangement whereby the CCC makes the non-cash payment directly to the cooperative.[78]

The two major forms of non-cash payments are commodity certificates and in-kind payments.

1. Commodity Certificates

While the CCC authority for non-cash payments is broad, the most popular form of payments other than in cash has been by the issuance of commodity certificates.[79] Once the commodity certificates are issued, farmers can use them to acquire CCC stocks or to reacquire commodities pledged as collateral under the government loan programs. The certificates may also be used to reacquire commodities which were pledged as collateral under the government loan programs. Moreover, they may be used to reacquire commodities under the farmer owned grain reserve program.[80]

The commodity certificates are "generic". This means that, while they have a fixed dollar face value, they are not commodity specific and can be exchanged for various program commodities. They have an 8 month life which begins at the end of the month of issuance.

Commodity certificates bear a fixed face value in a dollar denomination. They may be transferred, exchanged for CCC inventory or exchanged for cash.[81] A commodity certificate may be transferred to any other person. The transfer must be in the full amount of the certificate. This transfer can be effected only by a restrictive endorsement on the back of the certificate.[82] Generally, any holder of a commodity certificate may exchange the certificate, either singly or in combination with other commodity certificates, for commodities which are made available by the CCC.[83] Information regarding the commodities which are available for exchange, and the

212

procedures for the exchange, may be obtained from the Kansas City Commodity Office, ASCS-USDA, Kansas City, MO 64141-0205.

The CCC reserves the right to require or permit holders of commodity certificates to exchange the certificates for commodities owned by the CCC which are stored by the certificate holder, without making those commodities or kinds of commodities available to other holders of commodity certificates.[84] The value of CCC-owned commodities made available to certificate holders will be determined exclusively by the CCC.[85] The title to commodities owned by the CCC is transferred when a person submits commodity certificates.[86] The person who submits the certificates to the CCC is responsible for all costs incurred in transferring title to the commodity. The transfer of title is not subject to any state law or claim pursuant to a creditor's lien against the commodity or its proceeds. However, the transfer is subject to any United States government liens which arise pursuant to a federal statute. The CCC has the option to discount or refuse to accept any commodity certificate which is presented for exchange after the expiration date stated on the certificate.[87]

Generally, a holder of a commodity certificate may use the certificate to receive commodities pledged as collateral for CCC loans made to that person.[88] A certificate holder who wishes to exercise this option must redeem and sell to the CCC a quantity of the commodity which is equal in value to the dollar denomination of the certificate. This value determination is made exclusively by the CCC. The purchase price will be set at a value equivalent to the cost of liquidating the loan or the portion of the loan for which the commodity is pledged as collateral.

In order to receive the commodity, the certificate holder must endorse the certificate to the CCC and submit it to the ASCS office which issued the loan. If the CCC determines that the certificate holder does not have pledged collateral for CCC loans equal in value at the dollar denomination of the certificate, the CCC may, at its discretion, pay the difference to the person either by check or in the form of a new commodity certificate. No person may use a commodity certificate to receive a quantity of tobacco, peanuts, or extra long staple

213

cotton which has been pledged as collateral for a CCC loan.[89]

2. Payment in Kind

The Food Security Act of 1985[90] expanded the payment-in-kind (PIK) program, a concept which was first introduced during the 1983 crop year when the government had excessive commodities in storage. The programs in which PIK certificates are used include acreage reduction, paid land diversion, the Conservation Reserve Program, rice marketing loans, disaster programs and emergency feed programs. Under the PIK program, persons eligible for certain program benefits are paid by the CCC in a form other than cash. The decision to make a non-cash payment is at the sole discretion of the CCC.[91] The certificates are transferable. Farmers may sell them to commercial entities such as warehouses or to other farmers.[92] Transfers of certificates must be in the full amount of the certificate and the transfer must be effected by a restrictive endorsement.[93]

One of the primary uses which farmers have for PIK certificates is to redeem loan collateral which is held in government storage under the CCC non-recourse loan program. Farmers benefit from this practice because any interest expenses they otherwise would have incurred are waived. Under certain conditions the certificates may be exchanged for a loan commodity at a very advantageous price. The price advantage occurs when there is a price differential between the "posted county price" (PCP), which the CCC establishes for the commodity at a given time, and the loan rate. If the PCP is below the cash price an advantage may also exist regarding the price differential. The amount of a commodity which will be redeemed is based upon the announced PCP on the day the certificate is redeemed.

F. Payment Limitation

The concept of a payment limitation for farm program benefits evolved during legislative discussions of agricultural policy in the late 1960's. In recent years the limitation has been set at $50,000 for combined deficiency and diversion payments. These limitations were continued in the Food Security Act of 1985[94] as applied to crops of wheat, feed grains, upland cotton, extra long staple cotton and rice. However, the 1985 Act greatly increased the potential for individual farmers to receive more than $50,000 in payments because various types of payments were expressly excluded from the payment limitation provisions. Payments not subject to the limitation in the 1985 Act include the additional wheat or feed grain deficiency payments which result from any downward adjustment in loan rates by the Secretary of Agriculture under the so-called "Findley Amendment."[95] Other types of payments not included in the $50,000 limit include payments for disaster relief, marketing loan gains, loan deficiency payments, inventory reduction payments, resource adjustment payments and compensation for public access for recreation. As a consequence of these exclusions and the particular price relationships that could evolve in the crop years after 1985, the potential existed for individual farmers to receive benefits in an amount much greater than $50,000.

The payment limitation provisions were amended in 1986 to impose an overall $250,000 limitation effective for the 1987 crop.[96] This applies to all direct payments, including the items excluded from the $50,000 limit. Presumably, large operators could reach the $250,000 limit as a result of gains realized from the marketing loan program alone. However, most smaller operators are primarily concerned with the basic $50,000 payment limitation.

1. Regulatory Approach

The payment limitations have been implemented through regulations which attempt to define the term "person" and to determine whether multiple individuals or other entities constitute one or more separate persons. The regulations which implement the 1985 Act attempted to define "person" to include all possible legal entities, including an individual, a joint stock company, a corporation, an association, a trust, an estate or any other legal entity.[97] To be deemed a separate person under the rules a person had to meet the following criteria: (a) Have a separate and distinct interest in the land or the crop involved; (b) Exercise separate responsibility for that interest; and (c) Be responsible for the cost of farming related to such interest from a fund or account separate from that of any other individual or entity. Under these criteria many farmers could benefit from participation in multiple farming entities, each of which could qualify as a separate person for payment limitation purposes. Congress perceived this as an unintended opportunity for farmers to avoid the constraints of payment limitations. Family farmers and their affiliates were often uncertain of whether their honest attempts to profit at farming were viewed as legitimate combinations for purposes of payment limitations.

To clarify some of the confusion surrounding typical family businesses, Congress adopted the Agricultural Reconciliation Act as a part of the Omnibus Budget Reconciliation Act of 1987.[98] This 1987 Act amended the 1985 Food Security Act with respect to the maximum payment limitation for specified payments. Under the 1987 Act new regulations from USDA were proposed in April of 1988 and issued as final regulations on August 1, 1988.[99]

2. Definition of Person

The primary regulatory approach to achieve restrictions in program payments has been through the definition of the term "person". According to the statutory terms, the payment limitation applies to the total amount of payments which a person should be entitled to receive. Under the 1987 Act "person" includes an individual, an individual participating as a partner, a participant in a joint ventures, a grantor of a revocable trust, a joint stock company, a corporation, a limited partnership association, a charitable organization or other similar entities.[100] To be considered a separate person the individual or other legal entity must: (a) Have a separate and distinct interest in the land or the crop involved; (b) Exercise separate responsibility for that interest; and (c) Maintain funds or accounts separate from that of any other individual or entity for such interest.[101]

Under the regulatory authority the Secretary is directed to provide a "fair and reasonable application" of the payment limitation.[102] The Secretary had arguably attempted to do so in the prior regulation, Part 795, by addressing requirements for entities, joint operations, corporations, estates and trusts. In addition, special regulations were established relating to minor children, husbands and wives, leases and custom farming operations. The economic incentive of meeting the requirements, while also qualifying for participation through a greater number of "persons", caused farmers to undertake efforts at restructuring farm business with multiple entities. As noted earlier, a major focus of the 1987 Act is directed at constraining farmers from attaining "multiple person" status.

The 1987 Act restricts a person who receives farm program payments from holding, directly or indirectly, a substantial beneficial interest in more than two entities engaged in farming operations which also receive payments as separate persons. A person who does not receive direct payments may hold a substantial beneficial interest in no more than three entities that receive payments as separate persons. The regulations define "substantial beneficial interest" as an interest of 10% or more.[103]

3. Actively Engaged in Farming Requirement

The 1987 Act limits program payments to persons who are "actively engaged in farming," starting with the 1989 crop year.[104] For individuals this means that the following criteria must be met: (a) the individual must make a significant contribution of capital, equipment or land and active personal labor or active personal management based on the total value of the farming operation; (b) the individual's share of profits or losses must be commensurate with the contribution to the operation; and (c) the individual's contribution must be at risk.[105]

According to the regulations, the determination of whether an individual is contributing a significant amount of active personal labor or active personal management must take into account factors such as the types of crops produced, the normal and customary farming practices in the area and the total hours necessary to provide adequate personal management and personal labor for the farming operations.[106]

It is important to note that the contribution of capital, equipment or land, separately, is no longer a sufficient basis for a person to be considered as "actively engaged in farming". Either personal labor or personal management is now also required.

Members of joint operations such as general

217

partnerships, joint ventures or similar business arrangements may be considered to be actively engaged in farming if the member makes the required significant contribution of capital, equipment on hand (or combination thereof) and either provides active personal labor or active personal management (or a combination of both).[107] For corporations, limited partnerships and other similar entities the actively engaged in farming requirement means that: (a) the entity must separately make a significant contribution of capital, equipment or land or a combination of capital equipment and land based on the total value of the farming operation; (b) the stockholders, partners or members collectively must make a significant contribution of active personal labor or active personal management whether compensated or not; (c) the share of profits or losses must be commensurate with the contribution to the operation; and (d) the contributions must be at risk.[108]

For limited partnerships and corporations, the regulations impose additional restrictions with regard to the providing of active personal labor or active personal management. In such cases the combined "beneficial interest" of all partners or stockholders who provide the active personal labor or active personal management must be at least 50%.[109]

Similar requirements apply to both irrevocable and revocable trusts and to estates. In these cases, as with partnerships and corporations, the entity must make a separate contribution of land, capital or equipment. For irrevocable trusts the income beneficiaries must make a significant contribution of active personal labor or active personal management. For a revocable trust, the contribution must be from beneficiaries. This is not limited to income beneficiaries. The contribution may be made by either the personal representative or the heirs of an estate.[110] Special provisions were included in the 1987 Act for landowners who contribute land to a farming operation. The owner is not considered to be actively engaged in farming if in return for the contribution of land, the owner receives cash rent or a crop share guaranteed as to the amount of the commodity to be paid in rent.[111]

On the other hand, a landowner may be considered actively engaged in farming if the following criteria are met: (1) if the rent or income is based on the land's production or the results of the operation; (2) if the landowner's share of profits or losses is commensurate with the contribution to the operation; and, (3) if the contribution is at risk.[112]

For tenants the new rules under the 1987 Act mean that: (a) the tenant must make a significant contribution of active personal labor and capital, land or equipment, or active personal management and equipment; (b) the tenant's share of profits and losses must be commensurate with the contribution to the operation; and, (c) the contribution must be at risk. The law requires that a tenant make a contribution of active personal labor or active personal management combined with a contribution of land, capital or equipment (specifically equipment if active personal management is contributed).[113] It should be emphasized that this provision is for tenants. By reading this provision in conjunction with the provision for landowners, a properly designed rental agreement could allow both the landowner and the tenant to be actively engaged in farming. By contrast, the landlord who receives cash rent or on a share basis which is guaranteed by the amount of the commodity to be paid in rent is not considered to be actively engaged in farming.

The 1987 Act specifically provides for custom farming services. The person who receives those services may be separately eligible for payment limitation purposes if he or she is actively engaged in farming according to the tests set out for individuals or entities. No other rules are applicable.[114]

Special problems commonly arise in family situations where more than one family member is involved in the farming operation. According to the 1987 Act individual adult family members may be considered actively engaged in farming if: (a) they make a significant contribution of active personal management or active personal labor; (b) the share of profits or losses is commensurate with the contribution of each to the operation; and, (c) the contribution of each is at risk. The category of adult family members includes lineal descendants, lineal ancestors, or siblings, including spouses of those not themselves making a significant contribution.[115]

G. Contracting Procedures/Program Compliance
 1. Sign up
Eligible producers may offer to enter into a farm
program contract with the CCC by executing a contract and
submitting it to the ASCS office in the county where the
records for the farm are maintained. This must be done not
later than the date specified in the announcement of the
program.*116*

 2. Producer eligibility
The producer must be a person who shares in the risk
of producing the program crop in the current year, shares in its
proceeds, or would have shared in the crop if it had been
produced on that farm in the current year.*117* This must occur
on the farm for which the contract is submitted. The ASCS
county committee must determine producer eligibility for
program benefits. The county committee must also determine
who is a "person" for the purposes of payment limitations.

 3. Participation Contract
Program restrictions and requirements are included
within the contract the producer signs to participate in any of
the programs. This contract consists of Form CCC-477 plus
Appendix and any addendum. The contract may contain any
provisions which the CCC determines to be appropriate for
administering its programs and incorporates by reference the
regulations for the various programs.*118* The contract must
include a liquidated damages clause.*119* This is because the
objective of an acreage reduction, set-aside, land diversion, or
wheat grazing and hay program is to obtain a reduction of
acreage of the applicable crops. This objective is to achieve the
total national acreage of those commodities at desirable levels.
Once a contract has been entered into between the CCC and a
producer, the USDA and other segments of the agricultural
community act based upon the assumption that the contract will
be fulfilled and the reduction in acreage will be obtained. The
actions of CCC include budgeting and planning for programs in
subsequent crop years. A producer's failure to comply with a
contract undermines the basis for these actions, damages the
credibility of the USDA programs with other segments of the

agricultural community, and requires additional expenditures in subsequent crop years to offset the effect of the increased production in the current crop year. According to USDA policy, even though the adverse effects on the CCC of the producer's failure to comply with a contract are obvious, it would be impossible to compute the actual damages suffered by the CCC.

If the farmer fails to comply with the contract, the farmer will be disqualified for program benefits. In addition, the farmer may incur penalties. If the violation is in the amount of acres planted, the farmer can destroy the crop to reduce it back to the permitted amount of acreage up to the certification date without penalty. After that time, the farmer must pay liquidated damages and will declared ineligible for participation in the program. The formula for calculating liquidated damages varies with the particular commodity but is designed to reflect an amount sufficient to deter noncompliance. Where the failure to comply with the contract is not based on a failure to abide by the production limits, participation in the program will not necessarily be terminated. In this type of case, the penalty generally may not be imposed until after the farmer is given an opportunity to explain to the county committee the reason for his or her failure to comply and the committee determines that the reason for the failure is unacceptable. Penalties of this type are assessed by the county committee and therefore vary from county to county.

4. Incomplete Performance Based Upon an Action or the Advice of an Authorized ASCS Representative

A special provision exists to protect farmers from any adverse consequence which results from their good faith reliance upon either an action or the advice of an authorized ASCS representative relative to the provisions of any ASCS price support program. According to this provision, any performance which is rendered by a farmer in reliance upon the action or advice of the ASCS representative may be accepted by the ASCS as meeting the requirements of the applicable program.[120] Specifically, the ASCS may extend price support or make a payment in accordance with that action or advice to the extent it is deemed necessary to do so in order to provide fair and equitable treatment to the farmer.

This provision only applies if a farmer relied upon the action or advice of the ASCS representative in rendering a performance which the farmer in good faith believed was sufficient to meet the requirements of the applicable program.[121] Similarly, this provision does not apply in cases where the farmer either knew, or had sufficient reason to know, that the action or advice of the ASCS representative upon which he or she relied was improper or erroneous. It also does not apply in cases where the farmer rendered a performance in reliance upon his or her misunderstanding or misinterpretation of the relevant program provisions, notices or advice.

The determination of whether to accept a farmer's performance in accordance with this provision can be made by any one of the following individuals:

1. the ASCS Administrator (CCC Executive Vice President);
2. the ASCS Associate Administrator (CCC Vice President); or
3. the ASCS Deputy Administrator for State and County Operations (CCC Vice President).[122]

However, the state committee may, in accordance with an instruction issued by the ASCS Deputy Administrator for Programs, exercise the authority to honor this provision in cases where the total amount of price support and payments does not exceed $1,500.00.[123]

A farmer who wishes to seek consideration for the benefit of this provision should file his or her request with the local county committee.[124]

5. Authority to Make ASCS Payments When There Has Been A Failure to Comply Fully With A Program

The Deputy Administrator of state and county operations has the discretion to authorize the making of loans, purchases or payments in a case in which a farmer failed to fully comply with the terms and conditions of the relevant program. This provision is applicable only to farmers who made a good faith effort to comply fully with the terms and conditions of the program and who actually did render a substantial performance.

This authorization is allowable for loan or payment amounts which are determined to be equitable in relation to the seriousness of the failure to comply with the program regulations.[125] This provision of the regulations is applicable to the ASCS wheat, feed grain, upland cotton, and rice programs, and to other programs made applicable by individual program regulations.[126]

H. ASCS Appeal Regulations

Any producer or participant may obtain reconsideration and review of ASCS determinations which are made by the county committee, county office, state committee, or Deputy Administrator under the following programs:

1. Agricultural Conservation Program (7 CFR Part 701);
2. Land Use Adjustment Program (7 CFR Part 751);
3. Soil Bank Program (except matters classified as violations which are governed by separate regulations) (7 CFR Part 750);
4. Allotment Programs for Cotton (7 CFR Part 722), Tobacco (7 CFR Parts 724 and 725), Wheat (7 CFR Part 728), Peanuts (7 CFR Part 729), and Rice (7 CFR Part 730), except when the matter being appealed involves a marketing quota, in which case review is conducted pursuant to 7 CFR Part 711;
5. Feed Grain Program (7 CFR Part 775);
6. Wheat Stabilization Program (7 CFR Part 776);
7. CCC Loan and Purchase Programs (7 CFR Parts 1421, 1427, 1434, 1443, 1446, 1474);
8. Sugar Programs (7 CFR Parts 849, 85O, 855, 856, 857, 861, 862, 863, 864, 866, 867, 868, 891, 892, 893, 894, 895);
9. Wool and Mohair Programs (7 CFR Parts 1468, 1472);
10. Livestock Feed Program (7 CFR Part 1475);
11. Wheat Diversion Program (7 CFH Part 728);
12. Farm Wheat Marketing Certificate Program (7 CFR Part 728);
13. 1964 and 1965 Cotton Domestic Allotment Program (7 CFR Part 1427);

14. Upland Cotton and Extra Long Staple Cotton Programs (7 CFR Part 722);
15. Regional Agricultural Conservation Programs (7 CFR Part 755); and
16. All other programs to which this part is made applicable by individual program regulations.

1. Filing the Appeal

Any producer or participant who is dissatisfied with any determination initially made by the county committee, county office, state committee or the Deputy Administrator, may obtain a reconsideration of the determination through an informal hearing by filing a request for reconsideration with the county committee.[127] If a producer or participant is dissatisfied with the redetermination made by the county committee of its initial determination, he or she may obtain a review of the determination with an informal hearing by filing an appeal with the State committee.[128]

Except as to certain matters any producer or participant who is dissatisfied with the determination of the State committee, either upon reconsideration of its determination or upon appeal from a determination of the county committee, may obtain a review by the Deputy Administrator of the determination. This may include an informal hearing. This review may be obtained by filing an appeal with the Deputy Administrator.[129]

Each request for reconsideration or appeal must be in writing and signed by the producer or participant or by their authorized representative. The request must be supported by a written statement of facts.[130] This statement of facts may be submitted with the request or at any time prior to the hearing. The producer or participant may either request an informal hearing or may request that the determination be made without a hearing on the basis of the written statement submitted by him or her and on the basis of other information available to the reviewing authority.

A request for reconsideration or appeal must be filed within 15 days after the written notice of the determination is mailed to or otherwise made available to the producer or participant.[131] The request is considered to be filed when it is either personally delivered or when it is postmarked, if mailed. If the final date for filing falls on a Saturday, Sunday or legal holiday, the time for filing is extended to the close of business on the next working date.[132] A late filing of a request will be accepted if the reviewing authority believes that circumstances warrant that action.[133] A request or appeal which is mistakenly filed with an inappropriate reviewing authority will not be denied because of the error or because the error delays the receipt of the request or appeal by the appropriate reviewing authority.[134]

2. Hearing

The reviewing authority will designate the time and place of the hearing.[135] The reviewing authority must conduct the hearing in the manner "most likely to obtain the facts relevant to the matter in issue".[136] The producer or participant must be advised of the issues involved. The reviewing authority may confine the presentation of evidence to pertinent matters and may exclude irrelevant, material, or unduly repetitious evidence, information, or questions. However, compliance with formal rules of evidence is not required.

The producer or participant has the right to give a full presentation of relevant facts and information. This may be done through the use of oral or documentary evidence.[137] The reviewing authority has the discretion to request or permit persons other than the producer or participant (or their representative) to present information or evidence at the hearing. If this occurs, the authority may permit the producer or participant to question those persons.

A verbatim transcript of the hearing may be taken by the hearing authority if the producer or participant requests that a transcript be made prior to the hearing and also agrees to pay for the expense involved.[138] The reviewing authority may sua sponte take a transcript if he or she believes that the nature of the case makes such a transcript desirable. If the producer or participant or their representative fails to appear at the scheduled hearing, the reviewing authority may elect between two courses of action. He or she may either close the hearing or may accept information and evidence submitted by the other persons who are present at the hearing.

Prior to making a determination, the reviewing authority may request that the producer or participant produce additional relevant evidence. In the alternative, the reviewing authority may develop additional evidence from other sources.[139] The producer or participant, and each other affected person, must be notified in writing of the determination. The notification must clearly set forth the basis for the determination. The reviewing authority may, upon its own motion or that of a producer or participant, reopen a hearing for any reason it deems appropriate unless the matter has been appealed to or reconsidered by a higher reviewing authority.[140]

3. Limitations on Appeal Review

Determinations made by the Deputy Administrator are not appealable.[141] Certain determinations made by a State committee are not appealable. These include:

1. the establishment of farm yields for wheat, feed grain, and cotton;
2. the establishment of wheat allotments;
3. the establishment of farm feed grain allotments;
4. the establishment of upland cotton base acreage allotments;
5. matters arising under the tobacco discount variety program;
6. eligibility provisions of the livestock feed program;
7. the disaster provisions of the wheat, feed grain, and upland cotton programs where there is a finding that a loss on a farm was due in whole or in part to causes other than the natural disaster or conditions beyond the control of the producer;
8. the establishment of rice allotments, and
9. crop appraisals by the Agricultural Stabilization and Conservation Service (ASCS) and by the Federal Crop Insurance Corporation for the ASCS.[142]

Certain matters are binding on the reviewing authority.[143] These include matters arising under the (1) Agricultural Conservation Program which involve a finding or certification by a technician of the Soil Conservation Service or Forest Service, or (2) appraisal redeterminations under the

226

wheat, feed grain, upland cotton, or rice programs by the Federal Crop Insurance Corporation or Agricultural Stabilization and Conservation Service.

Nothing precludes the ASCS Administrator, (Executive Vice President, CCC), or his or her designee, on their own motion, from determining any question arising under the programs to which these regulations apply or from reversing or modifying any determinations made by a State or county committee or the Deputy Administrator.[144]

I. Cases Interpreting ASCS Administrative Procedures
1. State Law

The terms in a CCC loan agreement are not altered by state law to the contrary. For example, in Buckeye Sugars, Inc., v. Commodity Credit Corporation,[145] the CCC loan agreement contained a provision which relieved the CCC of the obligation to account to borrowers for surplus proceeds from the sale of loan collateral. This loan term was contrary to state law provisions under Uniform Commercial Code (UCC) Sect. 9-504. This UCC section requires a secured party to account to a debtor for any surplus proceeds after the secured party has sold the collateral following the debtor's default.

2. Due Process

Farmers who execute contracts with the ASCS to receive payments or benefits are entitled to an adjudicatory hearing prior to any denial of benefits by the ASCS.[146] In Prosser v. Butz,[147] the court held that due process entitles the farmer to:

(1) Notice of the specific charges or allegations which form the basis of the denial of benefits within a reasonable time prior to the hearing in order to allow the farmer to prepare a defense;

(2) the right to retain private counsel and be represented by counsel at the hearing;

(3) the right to present a reasonable quantum of argument and evidence at a hearing on the charges;

(4) the right to confront and cross-examine adverse witnesses at the hearing;

(5) the right to be provided with a brief written statement of the reasons and evidence relied upon by ASCS in

support of the committee's decision; and

(6) the right to be heard before an impartial adjudicative body.

The court also noted that the existence of administrative appeal rights does not constitute an adequate remedy for a due process deficiency which stems from an agency's failure to satisfy the rights to notice and hearing.[148]

The Prosser court held that due process considerations require that farmers be informed of the basis for the agency determination which adversely affects them. Moreover, administrative or judicial appeals must be determined on the basis of the record. It is therefore very important that the administrative record be complete.[149]

3. Limitations on Judicial Reviewability

There is some controversy as to whether all ASCS decisions are reviewable by courts. 7 U.S.C. Sect. 1385 provides that certain factual determinations made by the ASCS "shall be final and conclusive and shall not be reviewable by any other officer or agency of the Government. . ." These include the factual determinations which form the basis for any Soil Conservation Act payment, any payment under the wheat, feed grain, upland cotton and rice programs authorized by the Agricultural Act of 1949, any loan or price support finding, when these matters are officially determined in conformity with the applicable regulations prescribed by the Secretary or by the Commodity Credit Corporation.

Some courts have interpreted the finality provisions of Sect. 1385 to preclude judicial review of any ASCS factual determination which constitutes the basis for any payment or denial of a payment.[150] However, there are usually legal issues involved in ASCS determinations in addition to the factual matters. Accordingly, some courts have held that the finality provision of Sect. 1385 does not prevent judicial review of the legal questions involved in the agency's determination.[151] Furthermore, other courts have held more generally that Sect. 1385 merely limits, but does not preclude, judicial review of agency action. For example, in Garvey v. Freeman,[152] the court held that Sect. 1385 did not preclude judicial review to determine whether the agency's finding of fact was in conformity with the applicable regulations. In <u>King v. Bergland</u>,[153] the court, in reference to the <u>Garvey</u> decision, held that Congress did not intend to preclude judicial review when it drafted the finality provision of Sect. 1385. Thus, according to <u>King</u>, the scope of judicial review, rather than the availability of review, is the true issue. As to the standard of review, the <u>King</u> court said that judicial review is limited to determining whether the agency considered all relevant factors and whether its decision has a rational basis.[154]

Other courts have held that Sect. 1385 does not allow judicial review of the procedures employed by the agency in making its factual determinations.[155] These cases indicate that Sect. 1385 provides the ASCS with limited protection from judicial review of its actions. However, an attorney who represents a farmer who has been the subject of an adverse determination should assess:

    (1) whether the procedures used by the ASCS provided adequate due process, and

    (2) whether the record developed by the ASCS enables the court to review the adequacy of the process which was used in making the agency's determination.

4. Immunity for ASCS Officials

In <u>Westcott v. USDA</u>,[156] the Federal District Court held that ASCS county committees which relied on the ASCS rules in rendering decisions did not act outside the scope of their authority. Furthermore, the committee members were held to be within the scope of governmental immunity while in the course of performing discretionary acts. In <u>Gross v. Sederstrom</u>,[157] governmental immunity was also held to extend to members of a county ASCS committee.

FOOTNOTES

1. 15 U.S.C. § 714(c).

2. 7 C.F.R. Part 780, Appeal Regulations.

3. Pub. L. No. 75-430, 52 Stat. 31 (1938).

4. 48 Stat. 31 (1933).

5. 297 U.S. 1 (1936).

6. Pub. L. No. 75-430.

7. Pub. L. No. 81-439.

8. Pub. L. No. 93-83.

9. Pub. L. No. 99-198, 99 Stat. 1354 (1985).

10. 7 U.S.C. § 1421(b).

11. Pub. L. No. 100-387, 102 Stat. 924 (1988) to be codified at 7 U.S.C. § 1421 et seq. and at other sections of Title 7.

12. Pub. L. No. 95-198, 99 Stat. 1354, (1985).

13. 7 C.F.R. § 713.55(a).

14. 7 C.F.R. § 713.55 (b)(1).

15. 7 C.F.R. § 713.55(d).

16. 7 C.F.R. § 713.55(e).

17. Pub. L. No. 91-524, 84 Stat. 1358 (1970).

18. Pub. L. No. 97-98, 95 Stat. 1213 (1981).

19. 7 C.F.R. § 713.52(a).

20. 7 C.F.R. § 713.52(b).

21. Pub. L. No. 99-198, 99 Stat. 1354 (1985).

22. 7 C.F.R. § 713.51(a).

23. 7 C.F.R. § 713.51(b).

24. 7 C.F.R. § 713.53(a).

25. 7 C.F.R. § 713.53(b).

26. 7 C.F.R. § 713.58(a).

27. 7 C.F.R. § 713.58(b).

28. 7 C.F.R. § 713.58(b).

29. 7 C.F.R. § 713.58(c).

30. 7 C.F.R. § 713.58(d)(1).

31. 7 C.F.R. § 713.58(d)(2).

32. 7 C.F.R. § 713.58(d)(3).

33. 7 C.F.R. § 713.58(d)(3).

34. 7 C.F.R. § 713.58(d)(4).

35. 7 C.F.R. § 713.58(d)(4).

36. 7 C.F.R. § 713.56(a).

37. 7 C.F.R. § 713.56(b)(c).

38. 7 C.F.R. § 713.49(a).

39. 7 C.F.R. § 713.49(h).

40. 7 C.F.R. § 704.1 (1988).

41. 7 C.F.R. § 704.5.

42. 7 C.F.R. § 704.6(a).

43. 7 C.F.R. § 704.7(a).

44. 7 C.F.R. § 704.9(a).

45. 7 C.F.R. § 704.9(c).

46. 7 C.F.R. § 704.9(d).

47. 7 C.F.R. § 704.10(a).

48. 7 C.F.R. § 704.11(c).

49. 7 C.F.R. § 704.11(c)(1).

50. 7 C.F.R. § 704.11(c)(2).

51. 7 C.F.R. § 704.11(f).

52. 7 C.F.R. § 704.12(a).

53. 7 C.F.R. § 704.12(b).

54. 7 C.F.R. § 704.13(a).

55. 7 C.F.R. § 704.14(b).

56. 7 C.F.R. § 704.14(d).

57. 7 C.F.R. § 704.16(c).

58. 7 C.F.R. § 704.17.

59. 7 C.F.R. § 704.19.

60. 7 C.F.R. § 704.20.

61. 7 C.F.R. § 704.20.

62. 7 C.F.R. § 704.20(c).

63. 7 C.F.R. § 704.21(a).

64. 7 C.F.R. § 704.21(b).

65. 7 C.F.R. § 704.22(a)(1).

66. 7 C.F.R. § 704.22(a)(2).

67. 7 C.F.R. § 704.22(3).

68. 7 C.F.R. § 704.22(c).

69. 7 C.F.R. § 704.23.

70. 7 C.F.R. § 704.25.

71. 7 C.F.R. §§ 713.109 and 713.150.

72. 7 C.F.R. Part 780.

73. 7 C.F.R. Part 614.

74. Pub. L. No. 99-198, 99 Stat. 1354 (1985).

75. 7 C.F.R. § 770.1.

76. 7 C.F.R. § 770.2(a).

77. 7 C.F.R. § 770.2(b).

78. 7 C.F.R. § 770.2(d).

79. 7 C.F.R. § 770.2.

80. 7 C.F.R. § 770.4.

81. 7 C.F.R. § 770.4(a).

82. 7 C.F.R. § 770.4(c).

83. 7 C.F.R. § 770.4(d).

84. 7 C.F.R. § 770.4(d)(3).

85. 7 C.F.R. § 770.4(d)(4).

86. 7 C.F.R. § 770.4(d)(5).

87. 7 C.F.R. § 770.4(d)(6).

88. 7 C.F.R. § 770.4(e)(1).

89. 7 C.F.R. § 770.4(e)(2).

90. Pub. L. No. 99-198, 99 Stat. 1354 (1985).

91. 7 C.F.R. § 770.2(a).

92. 7 C.F.R. § 770.4(c).

93. 7 C.F.R. § 770.4.

94. 7 U.S.C. § 1308.

95. 7 U.S.C. § 1308(2)(B).

96. 7 U.S.C. § 1308(2)(A).

97. 7 C.F.R. Part 795, now superseded by Part 1497, 1498.

98. Pub. L. No. 100-203, 101 Stat. 1330 (1988) amending 7 U.S.C. § 1308.

99. 7 C.F.R. Part 1497, 1498.

100. 7 C.F.R. § 1497.3(b).

101. 7 C.F.R. § 1497.3(b).

102. 7 U.S.C. § 1308(5)(A).

103. 7 C.F.R. § 1497.3(b).

104. Pub. L. No. 100-203 § 1302.

105. 7 C.F.R. § 1497.6(d).

106. 7 C.F.R. § 1497.6(c).

107. 7 C.F.R. § 1497.8.

108. 7 C.F.R. §§ 1497.6, 1497.9(a)(1), (2).

109. 7 C.F.R. § 1497.9(a)(2).

110. 7 C.F.R. §§ 1497.10, 1497.11, 1496.12.

111. 7 C.F.R. § 1497.17.

112. 7 C.F.R. § 1497.13.

113. 7 C.F.R. § 1497.16.

114. Pub. L. No. 100-203 § 1302.

115. 7 C.F.R. § 1497.14.

116. 7 C.F.R. § 713.50(a).

117. 7 C.F.R. § 713.50(b)(1).

118. 7 C.F.R. § 713.49(c).

119. 7 C.F.R. § 713.49(d).

120. 7 C.F.R. § 790.2(a).

121. 7 C.F.R. § 790.2(b).

122. 7 C.F.R. § 790.2(a)j.

123. 7 C.F.R. § 790.3.

124. 7 C.F.R. § 790.4.

125. 7 C.F.R. § 791.2.

126. 7 C.F.R. § 791.1.

127. 7 C.F.R. § 780.3.

128. 7 C.F.R. § 780.4.

129. 7 C.F.R. § 780.5.

130. 7 C.F.R. § 780.7.

131. 7 C.F.R. § 780.6(a).

132. 7 C.F.R. § 780.6(b).

133. 7 C.F.R. § 780.6(c).

134. 7 C.F.R. § 780.6(d).

135. 7 C.F.R. § 780.8(a).

136. 7 C.F.R. § 780.8(b).

137. 7 C.F.R. § 780.8(c).

138. 7 C.F.R. § 780.8(d).

139. 7 C.F.R. § 780.9(a).

140. 7 C.F.R. § 780.10.

141. 7 C.F.R. § 780.9(a).

142. 7 C.F.R. § 780.11(a).

143. 7 C.F.R. § 780.11(c).

144. 7 C.F.R. § 780.12.

145. 744 F.2d 1240 (6th Cir. 1984).

146. Prosser v. Butz, 389 F. Supp. 1002 (N.D. Iowa 1974).

147. 389 F. Supp. 1002, 1005 (N.D. Iowa 1974).

148. 389 F. Supp. at 1006.

149. Also see, King v. Bergland, 517 F. Supp. 1363 (D. Col. 1981).

150. See Aycock Lindsey Corp. v. U. S., 171 F.2d 518 (5th Cir. 1948). Also see, U. S. v. Gomes, 323 F. Supp. 1319 (E. D. Cal. 1971) and U. S. v. Gross, 505 F.2d 1271 (Ct. Cl. 1974).

151. Aycock, Prosser and Gomes, supra.

152. 397 F.2d 600 (10th Cir. 1968).

153. 517 F. Supp. 1363 (D. Colo. 1981).

154. 517 F. Supp. at 1365-66.

155. See, Prosser supra.

156. 611 F. Supp. 351 (D.C. Neb. 1984).

157. 429 F.2d 96 (8th Cir. 1970).

CHAPTER 7

SOIL CONSERVATION PROGRAMS

Soil erosion is widely recognized as a major environmental problem in the United States. Recent estimates suggest that the annual soil loss through sheet and rill erosion is two billion tons per year on the 413 million acres of land which are designated as agricultural cropland. Two-thirds of this loss is estimated to occur on the prime farmlands that comprise the bulk of the United States cropland resource. There are places in the United States where the entire top soil layer has been lost through erosion in the span of only 50 to 100 years of cultivation. A recent United States Department of Agriculture (USDA) study has projected that if current levels of erosion are allowed to continue for the next 50 years it would cause a reduction in the production capacity of that land equivalent to the loss of 23 million acres, or eight percent of the total land base used in the calculation. In another study, it was suggested that the sole factor of wind erosion in the ten Great Plains States will cause a loss of productivity equivalent to the loss of another 62 million acres of cropland over the next 50 years.[1]

I.   <u>Federal Response to Soil Erosion Problems</u>
The history of the federal response to the soil erosion problem originates during the 1930's, when the Soil Conservation Service (SCS) was established. The SCS was actually a modification of an earlier agency, the Soil Erosion Service, which was established in 1933. Today, the SCS administers its programs through conservation districts at the county level throughout the United States. These conservation districts provide technical help to landowners who want to implement conservation measures. In recent years, the SCS has been involved in a wide variety of programs designed to prevent soil erosion. For example, under the Soil and Water Resources Conservation Act of 1977,[2] the SCS has major responsibility for appraising the status and condition of soil and water resources.

In addition, the SCS administers the federal responsibilities in relation to the National Cooperative Soil Survey. It is through this survey that the "prime farmland" concept has been developed. This concept was incorporated in the Surface Mining Control and Reclamation Act of 1977[3] to identify land to which special reclamation rules apply. The SCS also administers a number of programs which involve waterways, flood prevention, and small watershed projects.

Over the years, major efforts have been made to give special protection to the most fragile farmlands in the United States. For example, Congress enacted the Soil Bank Act as a part of the Agricultural Act of 1956.[4] This Act was designed to augment and stabilize farm income and to protect soil, water, forest, and wildlife resources from waste and depletion. To protect these resources, the Act's provisions gave farmers an incentive to divert cropland from agricultural production. This provided conservation assistance and also stabilized prices through production control. Although this program has been repealed, except for the Great Plains Conservation Program,[5] recent legislation has restored into use some of the same basic concepts. For example, under the 1985 Food Security Act[6] a Conservation Reserve Program (CRP) was established. (This is discussed in Chapter 6.) Under the CRP, landowners agree by contract to implement conservation measures on their land in exchange for an annual rental payment from the government. Landowners may bid to participate in this program. The government participates in the cost of the conservation measures through a "cost-share" agreement. In addition, as discussed below, the 1985 Act provides that persons who convert "highly erodible" lands or wetlands to cropland use are denied participation in federal price support programs.[7] In other federal legislation, the Tax Reform Act of 1986 enables a farm operator to elect between deducting soil and water conservation expenses and capitalizing those expenses on the condition that the expenses are consistent with SCS approved soil and water conservation plans for the area.[8]

II.   Response of the Courts

In most cases, the decision by a farmer or rancher to undertake soil conservation efforts will be based upon economic factors. These factors include the cost of the measures and the loss of productivity from the idled land. Each of these factors is examined in comparison to the benefits estimated to be derived from the conservation practices. Some recent case developments have focused attention on local government and conservation district efforts to compel farmers to implement specified measures regardless of the farmer's economic situation.

For example, in 1971 Iowa conservation districts were given statutory authority to establish soil loss limits for all land in the state. In 1974, a farmer filed a complaint with the soil conservation district which alleged that his property was being damaged by the soil erosion occurring on neighboring farms.[9] The district officials inspected the area, found the erosion level in the area to be higher than the state law standard and ordered the neighboring farmers to reduce soil erosion within six months to the statutory limit. Under the Iowa statute, the district was required to pay 75 percent of the cost of the conservation practices required to be undertaken by the neighboring farms. Nonetheless, neither of the neighbors involved complied with this order. As a result, the conservation district petitioned the District Court for an order to require immediate compliance with the conservation district's order. In the district court suit, the defendant farmers argued that enforcement of the soil loss limits was an unconstitutional exercise of the state's police power. The District Court agreed with the defendants and held that the soil loss limits constituted an unconstitutional taking of property in violation of the Fifth and Fourteenth Amendments.

On appeal, the only issue considered by the Iowa Supreme Court was the "taking" question. The Court evaluated the taking problem in terms of a balancing test to determine whether the statutory benefits to the public outweighed the specific restraints imposed on the farmers. The court was concerned with the economic impact of the regulation on farmers, particularly to the extent which the regulation interfered with their distinct, investment backed expectations. The Iowa Supreme Court found no denial of use or enjoyment of property sufficient to support the trial court's finding of unconstitutionality. The court held that the state had a right to require the financial burden caused by compliance with the district's order.

In a related case, Moser v. Thorp Sales Corp.,[10] the Iowa Supreme Court dealt with the issue of the liability of a farm tenant to the landlord for damage to the land caused by soil erosion. The erosion damages allegedly were accelerated by the particular cultivation practices employed by the tenant farmer. The court held that liability could be found under these circumstances. This case establishes the rule that a tenant farmer, in Iowa, who abuses the land can be held liable by the landowner for the damage done to the soil.

At the federal level, case law suggests that mandatory conservation practices are within the legitimate scope of public regulatory authority. Under the Surface Mining Control and Reclamation Act of 1977,[11] Congress required that strip mined land be returned to the equivalent of its prior productivity level. Specifically, under the Act mine operators are required to remove soil layers separately, and upon completion of the strip mining, to return the soil layers to the same order as before they were taken out. The mine operator is required to work with the soil until it reaches the same levels of production as the surrounding unmined soil. This constitutes, in effect, a complete soil restoration process. This provision of the Act was challenged in the case of Hodel v. Indiana.[12] In Hodel, the United States Supreme Court held that the rules contained in the prime farmlands provision did not violate the commerce clause or the Tenth Amendment. It also held that the Act did not, on its face, effect an unconstitutional taking of private property. Arguably, if the federal government may impose requirements on how the soil is returned to the land after being mined, it could similarly require that specific land use practices be undertaken to minimize soil losses through erosion.

III. Current Legislative Programs

As noted above, soil conservation practices are a required condition for federal price and income support payments under some circumstances. The relevant provisions are contained in the Food Security Act of 1985.[13]

A. Conservation Compliance

At present, when a farmer participates in support programs, erosion must be controlled on "highly erodible" acres.

A provision to this effect is contained in Form CCC-477 which a farmer must sign in order to receive commodity or other program benefits. Furthermore, the farmer must have drafted a written soil conservation plan for the highly erodible cropland by January 1, 1990 and have it fully implemented by 1995.[14] The conservation plans must serve to limit erosion for the full rotational period, not just in each individual year, and must be approved by the local conservation district. It should be noted that if even one field of highly erodible land which is owned or operated by a farmer does not have a written plan, the entire farming operation becomes ineligible for program benefits. This includes all other farming operations in which the farmer has at least a 20% financial interest.[15]

The definition of highly erodible cropland focuses on potential soil loss. Thus, a plan is required even if erosion is already being controlled by methods such as terraces, strip cropping or conservation tillage. Furthermore, whether a particular land parcel is highly erodible is determined by both the kind of soil and the slope.[16] This may require that a soil survey be undertaken. Where the land has not already been surveyed, the farmer has two years after the completion of a survey to finish the conservation plan.[17] The Soil Conservation Service technicians will inform a farmer by mail that he or she owns highly erodible land. If the farmer disagrees with the classification of the land, a reconsideration can be requested. If the farmer still disagrees, the matter can be appealed to the area SCS office, then to the state office and, finally, to the national headquarters.[18]

B. Highly Erodible Land and Wetland Conservation
The rights and obligations of farmers in relation to highly erodible land and wetland conservation practices were promulgated in the Food Security Act of 1985.[19] The primary rule is that after December 23, 1985, a person who produces an agricultural commodity on highly erodible land or converted wetland is considered ineligible for certain USDA program benefits.[20] These restrictions are intended to remove certain incentives for persons to produce agricultural commodities on highly erodible land or converted wetland. The stated purposes of this policy are:

243

(1) to reduce soil loss due to wind and water erosion;
(2) to protect the nation's long-term capacity to produce food and fiber;
(3) to reduce sedimentation and improve water quality;
(4) to assist in preserving the nation's wetlands; and
(5) to curb production of surplus commodities.[21]

1. Determination of Ineligibility for Government Program Benefits

A person who produces an agricultural commodity on a field in which highly erodible land is predominant, or on converted wetland, will be deemed ineligible for the following government benefits relating to any commodity produced during that crop year:

(1) any type of price support payment;
(2) a farm storage facility loan;
(3) a disaster payment;
(4) a crop insurance indemnity payment; or
(5) a farm loan made, insured or guaranteed by the FmHA, if FmHA determines that the proceeds of the loan will be used for a purpose that will contribute to the excessive erosion of highly erodible land or to the conversion of wetland for agricultural commodity production.[22]

The law also prohibits payments for the storage of an agricultural commodity owned by the CCC. A determination of ineligibility for program benefits is made by the USDA agency to which the person has applied for benefits.[23]

The Soil Conservation Service (SCS) is responsible for making the relevant land-use determinations in administering these provisions. It determines whether a field contains either a predominance of highly erodible land or converted wetland.[24] A different agency, the Agricultural Stabilization and Conservation Service (ASCS), is responsible for making the relevant crop and land ownership determinations. For example, the ASCS determines whether a person is or was entitled to share in the crops available from a particular tract of land,[25] and determines that the land is or was planted to an agricultural commodity during the year for which a person is requesting benefits.[26]

244

In order for a person to be determined eligible for USDA program benefits,

(1) the SCS must determine whether any farm in which the person applying for benefits has an interest contains highly erodible land, wetland or converted wetland;

(2) the person applying for the benefits must certify in writing on Form AD-1026 that no agricultural commodity will be produced on highly erodible land or converted wetland during the crop year in which the person is seeking benefits;

(3) the person applying for a FmHA insured or guaranteed farm loan must certify that he or she will not use the proceeds of the loan for a purpose that will contribute to excessive erosion on highly erodible land or to the conversion of wetlands to agricultural production; and

(4) the person applying for the benefits must authorize and provide USDA representatives with access to all land in which the person has an interest for the purpose of verifying any certification made.[27]

(a) Agricultural Stabilization and Conservation Service (ASCS)

The portions of the soil erosion provisions which are applicable to the ASCS will be administered by both the state ASCS committee (STC) and the county ASCS committees (COC).[28] The Deputy Administrator of the ASCS may determine any question pertaining to the ASCS which arises under these regulations. He or she may reverse or modify any determination of eligibility for ASCS programs which has been made by any ASCS official.[29]

The ASCS is responsible for making the following determinations:

(1) whether a person produced an agricultural commodity on a particular field;

(2) the establishment of field boundaries;

(3) whether land was planted to an agricultural commodity in any of the years, 1981-1985;

(4) whether to allow a person to exchange certain crop acreage bases (CAB) between CAB's with crops that leave a high residue, if recommended by the SCS for

245

inclusion in the conservation plan;

(5) whether land was set-aside, diverted or otherwise not cultivated under a program administered by the Secretary to reduce production of an agricultural commodity;

(6) whether the production of an agricultural commodity on highly erodible land or converted wetland by a landlord's tenant or sharecropper is required under the terms and conditions of the agreement between that landlord and tenant or sharecropper;

(7) whether the conversion of a particular wetland was commenced before December 23, 1985; and

(8) whether the conversion of a wetland was caused by a third party.[30]

A representative number of farms are routinely selected, in accordance with instructions issued by the Deputy Administrator, to be inspected by an authorized ASCS representative to determine compliance with the requirements for obtaining farm program benefits.[31]

(b) Soil Conservation Service (SCS)

The portions of the soil erosion provisions which are applicable to the SCS are administered by the Chief of the SCS. They are implemented by the state conservationist, area conservationist and district conservationist.[32]

The SCS is responsible for making the following determinations:

(1) whether land is either highly erodible, a wetland or a converted wetland;

(2) whether highly erodible land is predominant on a certain field;

(3) whether the conservation plan that a person is actively applying is based on the local SCS field office technical guide and is approved;

(4) whether the conservation system that a person is using has been approved as adequate for the production of an agricultural commodity on highly erodible land;

(5) whether the production of an agricultural commodity on a wetland is allowable because natural conditions protect

246

the wetland characteristics from the actions of the farmer; and

(6) whether the actions of a person in producing an agricultural commodity on converted wetland would have only a minimal impact on the hydrological and biological aspects of the wetland.[33]

A person may obtain a highly erodible land or wetland determination by making a written request on Form AD 1026. The SCS must put its determination in writing, and a copy will be provided to the person who made the request.[34] A determination of whether or not an area meets the highly erodible land or wetland criteria may be made by the district conservationist without an on-site inspection. The determination may be based upon existing records or other information.[35] This determination will be made within 15 calendar days after receipt of the written request, if practicable.

An on-site determination as to whether an area meets the highly erodible land or wetland criteria will be made under either of the following circumstances:

(1) if the person is in disagreement with the determination; or

(2) if adequate information is not otherwise available to the district conservationist with which to make a determination.[36]

When the need for an on-site determination is applicable, it must be made as soon as possible and no later than 60 calendar days after the request for a determination was made. However, when site conditions are unfavorable for the evaluation of soil or vegetation, the determination can be postponed until site conditions permit an adequate evaluation.[37]

If an area is continuously inundated or saturated for long periods of time during the growing season, to the extent that access by foot to make a determination of the predominance of hydric soils or the prevalence of hydrophytic vegetation is not feasible, the area will be determined to be a wetland.[38]

Persons who are adversely affected by a determination made by the SCS and who believe that the regulations were improperly applied may appeal the determination in accordance with 7 C.F.R. Part 614.[39]

(c) Farmers Home Administration

The portions of the soil erosion and wetland provisions which are applicable to the Farmers Home Administration (FmHA) are administered under the general supervision of the FmHA Administrator through FmHA's state, district and county offices.[40] FmHA will determine whether the proceeds of a farm loan which is made, insured or guaranteed by FmHA will be used for a purpose that will contribute to excessive erosion of highly erodible land or to the conversion of wetland.[41] A person who is denied program benefits as the result of an FmHA determination may obtain a review of the determination in accordance with 7 C.F.R. Part 1900.[42]

(d) Federal Crop Insurance Corporation

The portions of the soil erosion and wetland provisions which are applicable to the Federal Crop Insurance Corporation (FCIC) are administered under the general supervision of the FCIC Manager.[43] A person who is denied program benefits as the result of an FCIC determination may obtain a review of the determination in accordance with 7 C.F.R. Section 400.90.[44]

2. Exemptions for Highly Erodible Cropland

A person will not be determined to be ineligible for farm program benefits as the result of the production of an agricultural commodity on any highly erodible land that was either:

1) planted to an agricultural commodity in any year 1981 through 1985; or
2) set-aside, diverted or otherwise not cultivated in any of those crop years under a USDA program to reduce production of an agricultural commodity.[45]

This exemption ends on the later of January 1, 1990, or on the date that is two years after the date the cropland on which an agricultural commodity is produced was surveyed by the SCS to determine if the land is highly erodible. With respect to the production of an agricultural commodity on any land exempt under this provision, if, as of January 1, 1990, or the date that is 2 years after the date the SCS has completed a soil survey of the cropland on the tract or farm, whichever is later, a person is actively applying a conservation plan based on the local SCS field office technical guide, and approved by the CD, in consultation with the local ASCS committees and SCS, that person will have until January 1, 1995, to fully comply with the plan without being determined to be ineligible for benefits.[46]

A person will not be determined ineligible for benefits as the result of producing an agricultural commodity on highly erodible land if the production is in compliance with an approved conservation plan or conservation system.[47] Furthermore, a person is not ineligible for program benefits as the result of producing an agricultural commodity on highly erodible land and in an area under a conservation system that has been approved by the CD, after the CD determines that the conservation system is in conformity with technical standards set forth in the SCS field office technical guide for that district; or if not within a CD, under a conservation system that has been approved by the SCS as adequate for the production of that agricultural commodity on highly erodible land.[48]

3. Exemptions for Wetland

A person will not be determined to be ineligible for program benefits as the result of the production of an agricultural commodity on:

(i) Converted wetland, if the conversion of the wetland was commenced or completed before December 23, 1985; or

(ii) An artificial lake, pond or wetland created by excavating or diking non-wetland to collect and retain water for purposes such as water for livestock, fish production, irrigation (including subsurface irrigation), a settling basin, cooling, rice production, or flood control; or

(iii) A wet area caused by a water delivery system, irrigation, irrigation system, or application of water for irrigation; or

(iv) Wetland on which the production of an agricultural commodity is possible as a result of a natural condition, such as drought, and is possible without action by the person that destroys natural wetland characteristics; or

(v) Converted wetland if the SCS has determined that the actions of the person with respect to the production of an agricultural commodity on the converted wetland, individually and in connection with all other similar actions authorized by SCS in the area, would have only a minimal impact on the hydrological and biological aspects of the wetlands; or

(vi) Wetlands converted by the actions of persons other than the person applying for USDA program benefits or any of the person's predecessors in interest after December 23, 1985, if the conversion was not the result of a scheme or device to avoid compliance with the regulations. Further drainage improvement on those lands is not permitted without loss of eligibility for the USDA program benefits, unless the SCS determines that further drainage activities applied to those lands would have a minimal effect on any remaining wetland values. In applying this regulation, converted wetlands will be presumed to have been converted by the person applying for USDA program benefits, unless the person can show that the conversion was caused by a third party with whom the person was not associated through a scheme or device. In this regard, activities of a water resource district, drainage district or similar entity will be attributed to all persons within the jurisdiction of the district or other entity who are assessed for the activities of the district or entity. Accordingly, where a person's wetlands are converted due to the actions of the district or entity, the person will be considered to have caused or permitted the drainage.[49]

The conversion of a wetland is considered to have been completed before December 23, 1985 if before that date, the draining, dredging, leveling, filling or other manipulation, (including any activity that resulted in impairing or reducing the flow, circulation, or reach of water) was applied to the wetland and made the production of an agricultural commodity possible without further manipulation. This applies where the agricultural production on the wetland would not otherwise have been possible.[50]

The conversion of a wetland is considered to have been commenced before December 23, 1985 if before that date the activities toward conversion were actually started on the wetland; or the person applying for benefits has expended or legally committed substantial funds to the conversion project.[51]

The purpose of the determination of conversion commencement is to implement the legislative intent that those persons who had actually started conversion of wetland or obligated funds for conversion prior to the effective date of the Act (December 23, 1985) would be allowed to complete the conversion so as to avoid unnecessary economic hardship.

4. Affiliated Persons

For purposes of determinations regarding program benefits, certain persons are considered to be "affiliated persons." The actions of those affiliated persons are considered to be the actions of the person who has requested benefits from a USDA program.
Affiliated persons are:

(1) The spouse and minor child of the person and/or guardian of that child;

(2) Any corporation in which the person is a stockholder, shareholder, or owner of more than a 20 percent interest in the corporation;

(3) Any partnership, joint venture, or other enterprise in which the person has an ownership interest or financial interest; and

(4) Any trust in which the person applying for benefits or other affiliated person is a beneficiary or has a financial interest.[52]

If the person who has requested benefits from the Department is a corporation, partnership, or "other joint venture," any participant or stockholder therein, except for persons with a 20 percent or less share in a corporation, must also be considered to be the person applying for benefits from the USDA.[53]

5. Scheme or Device

All or any part of the benefits which are otherwise due a person from the USDA may be withheld or required to be refunded if the person adopts or participated in adopting any scheme or device designed to evade, or which has the effect of evading, the soil conservation and/or wetland regulations. Such acts may include, but are not limited to, concealing from the USDA any information which has a bearing on the application of the regulations, submitting false information to the USDA or creating entities for the purpose of concealing the interest of a person in a farming operation or to otherwise avoid compliance with these regulations. These acts also include acquiescence in, approval of or assistance to acts which have the effect of, or the purpose of, circumventing these regulations for the production of an agricultural commodity.[54]

6. Landlords and Tenants

The ineligibility of a tenant or sharecropper for benefits will not cause that person's landlord to be ineligible for benefits for which the landlord would otherwise be eligible. This applies with respect to commodities produced by the landlord on lands other than those in which the tenant or sharecropper has an interest.[55]

However, this provision is not applicable to a landlord if the production of an agricultural commodity on highly erodible land or converted wetland by the landlord's tenant or sharecropper is required under the terms and conditions of the agreement between the landlord and that tenant or sharecropper, of if the landlord has acquiesced in the disqualifying activities of the tenant or sharecropper.[56]

C. Soil Conservation Service (SCS) Appeal Regulations

An owner or operator of farmland may seek reconsideration of, or appeal from, certain decisions made by officials of the Soil Conservation Service (SCS) regarding eligibility for participation in the Conservation Reserve Program (discussed in Chapter 6) or regarding the applicability of the compliance requirements of the highly erodible land and wetland conservation provisions.

Requests for reconsideration or appeals under these procedures are limited to the following determinations:

1. Highly erodible land determinations:
    (i)   The land capability classification of a field or a portion thereof;
    (ii) The predicted average annual rate of erosion for a field or a portion thereof;
    (iii) The potential average annual rate of erosion for a field or a portion thereof;
2. Wetland determinations:
    (i)   The determination that certain land is a "wetland", as defined by the Act;

(ii) The determination that certain land is a "converted wetland", as defined by the Act; and

(iii) The determination of whether the conversion of wetland for the production of an agricultural commodity on the converted wetland will have a minimal effect on the hydrological and biological aspects of the wetland.

3. The determination by a conservation district, or by a designated conservationist in those areas where no conservation district exists, that a conservation system or a conservation plan should not be approved.[57]

1. Agency Determinations

All initial determinations must be in writing and must inform the owner or operator of the right to reconsideration, the procedures for requesting reconsideration and pursuing that request, and the effect of failing to request reconsideration. The determination document must be mailed or hand delivered to the owner or operator.[58]

Any determination made as a result of a reconsideration must set forth the determination, the basis for the determination, including all factors, technical criteria, and facts relied upon in making the determination; and must inform the owner or operator of their right to appeal, if applicable, and the procedures for requesting and pursuing the appeal. Determinations upon reconsideration must be mailed or hand delivered to the owner or operator.[59]

Any owner or operator who is adversely affected by a determination made by a conservation district or a designated conservationist may request a reconsideration by the person who made the initial determination.[60] The request for reconsideration must be in writing, must set forth the reasons for the request and any supporting statements or evidence, and must be mailed or filed with the office making the initial determination within 15 days after the written notice of the determination was mailed or otherwise made available to the owner or operator.[61]

If a request for reconsideration is not filed, the initial determination of the conservation district or designated conservationist cannot be appealed.

2. Filing Appeals of Agency Determination

Any owner or operator who is adversely affected by an initial determination of the conservation district or designated conservationist, which has been reconsidered, may appeal to the area conservationist or, in states without area conservationists, to the state conservationist.[62] Any owner or operator who is adversely affected by the determination of the area conservationist, may appeal to the State conservationist.[63] Any owner or operator who is adversely affected by the determination to the State conservationist, may appeal that determination to the Chief.[64] Determinations by the Chief are the final decisions of the Department of Agriculture from which there is no further administrative review.[65]

A request for reconsideration or appeal from any determination must be filed within 15 days after the written notice of the determination is mailed to or otherwise made available to the owner or operator. An appeal is to be considered "filed" when it is personally delivered or, if mail is used, when it is postmarked.[66] If the final date for filing a request for reconsideration or appeal falls on a Saturday, Sunday, legal holiday, or other day that the office to which the appeal is sent is closed, the time for filing will be extended to the close of business on the next working day.[67]

A request for reconsideration or appeal which is filed with a reviewing authority other than the appropriate one will not be denied because of the misdirection of the request.[68]

Each request for reconsideration or appeal must be in writing and signed by the owner or operator or authorized representative. It must be supported by a written statement of facts, which may be submitted with or as a part of the request for reconsideration or appeal.[69]

In the case of reconsideration, the owner or operator may request an informal meeting. In the case of an appeal, the owner or operator may either request an informal hearing or request that a determination be made by the reviewing authority without a hearing on the basis of the written statement submitted and other information available to the reviewing authority.[70] All appeals to the Chief must be based upon the administrative record developed in previous proceedings and relevant written statements. Informal hearings will not be held at the Chief's level.[71]

3. Appeal Hearings

The appeal hearing will be held at the time and place designated by the reviewing authority.[72] The hearing must be conducted by the reviewing authority in the manner which it deems most likely to obtain the facts relevant to the matter at issue. The owner or operator must be advised of the issues involved. Moreover, the reviewing authority may confine the presentation of facts and evidence to pertinent matters.[73]

The owner or operator or authorized representative must be given full opportunity to present facts and information relevant to the matter at issue. This may be achieved through the presentation of oral or documentary evidence.[74] The reviewing authority may request or permit persons other than those appearing on behalf of the owner or operator to give information or evidence at the hearing. In such event, the owner or operator may be permitted to question those persons.[75]

The reviewing authority must prepare a written record of the hearing which contains a clear, concise statement of the facts asserted by the owner or operator and the material facts found by the reviewing authority.[76] The names of interested persons appearing at the hearing must be included. Any documents presented in evidence should be identified. A verbatim transcript may be taken if:

1. The owner or operator requests before the hearing begins that the reviewing authority make a transcript and agrees to pay the expense thereof, or
2. The reviewing authority feels that the nature of the case makes the taking of a transcript desirable.[77]

If, at the time scheduled for the hearing, the owner or operator is absent and no representative appears on their behalf, the reviewing authority may, after a reasonable period of time, close the hearing. The reviewing authority may also exercise the option of accepting information and evidence submitted by other persons at the hearing.[78]

The reviewing authority, prior to making a determination, may request the owner or operator to produce additional evidence deemed relevant, or may develop additional evidence from other sources.[79] Upon completing the review and within program authorities, the reviewing authority may affirm, modify, or reverse any determination the reviewing authority made initially, or a lower reviewing authority made, or may remand the matter to a lower reviewing authority for such further consideration as is deemed appropriate.[80]

The owner or operator must be notified in writing of the determination. The notification must clearly set forth the basis for the determination and must inform the owner or operator of the right to further appeal, if any, and of the procedures for pursuing such appeal. Copies of documents, information, or evidence upon which a determination is made or which will form the basis of the determination, must be made available to the owner or operator upon request.[81]

The reviewing authority may, upon its own motion or upon the request of the owner or operator, reopen any hearing for any reason it deems appropriate unless the matter has been appealed to or considered by a higher reviewing authority.[82]

FOOTNOTES

1. See, R. Sampson, <u>Farmland or Wasteland: A Time to Choose</u>, pp. 110-152 (1982).

2. 16 U.S.C. 2001-2009.

3. 30 U.S.C. 1201-1328.

4. Act of May 28, 1956, c. 327, 70 Stat. 188.

5. 7 U.S.C. 590.

6. Title XII, Food Security Act of 1985, PL 99-198.

7. 16 U.S.C. § 3811.

8. I.R.C. § 175.

9. Woodbury County Soil Conservation Dist. v. Ortner, 279 N.W.2d 276 (Iowa 1979).

10. 312 N.W.2d 277 (Iowa 1981).

11. 30 U.S.C. § 1201-1328.

12. 101 S. Ct. 2376.

13. 16 U.S.C. § 3801-3845.

14. 7 C.F.R. § 12.4.

15. 7 C.F.R. § 12.8.

16. 7 C.F.R. § 12.21.

17. 7 C.F.R. § 12.5(b).

18. 7 C.F.R. § 12.22.

19. 16 U.S.C. § 3801-3845.

20. 7 C.F.R. § Sec. 12.1(a).

21. 7 C.F.R. § 12.1(b).

22. 16 U.S.C. § 3801.

23. 7 C.F.R. § 12.6(a).

24. 7 C.F.R. § 12.4(b)(1).

25. 7 C.F.R. § 12(b)(2).

26. 7 C.F.R. § 12.4(b)(3).

27. 7 C.F.R. § 12.7(a).

28. 7 C.F.R. § 12.6(b).

29. 7 C.F.R. § 12.6(b)(2).

30. 7 C.F.R. § 12.6(b)(3).

31. 7 C.F.R. § 12.6(b)(4).

32. 7 C.F.R. § 12.6(c).

33. 7 C.F.R. § 12.6(c)(2).

34. 7 C.F.R. § 12.6(c)(4).

35. 7 C.F.R. § 12.6(c)(4)(i).

36. 7 C.F.R. § 12.6(c)(4)(ii).

37. 7 C.F.R. § 12.6(c)(4)(iii).

38. 7 C.F.R. § 12.6(c)(4)(iv).

39. 7 C.F.R. § 12.6(c)(5) and § 12.12.

40. 7 C.F.R. § 12.6(d)(1).

41. 7 C.F.R. § 12.6(d)(2).

42. 7 C.F.R. § 12.12.

43. 7 C.F.R. § 12.6(e).

44. 7 C.F.R. § 12.12.

45. 7 C.F.R. § 12.5(a).

46. 7 C.F.R. § 12.5(b)(1).

47. 7 C.F.R. § 12.5(b).

48. 7 C.F.R. § 12.5(b)(3)(i) & (ii).

49. 7 C.F.R. § 12.5(d)(1).

50. 7 C.F.R. § 12.5(d)(2).

51. 7 C.F.R. § 12.5(d)(3).

52. 7 C.F.R. § 12.8(a).

53. 7 C.F.R. § 12.8(b).

54. 7 C.F.R. § 12.10.

55. 7 C.F.R. § 12.9(a).

56. 7 C.F.R. § 12.9(b).

57. 7 C.F.R. § 614.1(b).

58. 7 C.F.R. § 614.3(a).

59. 7 C.F.R. § 614.3(b).

60. 7 C.F.R. § 614.4(a).

61. 7 C.F.R. § 614.4(b), and 614.6.

62. 7 C.F.R. § 614.5(a).

63. 7 C.F.R. § 614.5(b).

64. 7 C.F.R. § 614.5(c).

65. 7 C.F.R. § 614.5(e).

66. 7 C.F.R. § 614.6(a).

67. 7 C.F.R. § 614.6(b).

68. 7 C.F.R. § 614.6(c).

69. 7 C.F.R. § 614.7(a).

70. 7 C.F.R. § 614.7(b).

71. 7 C.F.R. § 614.7(b).

72. 7 C.F.R. § 614.8(a).

73. 7 C.F.R. § 614.8(b).

74. 7 C.F.R. § 614.8(c).

75. 7 C.F.R. § 614.8(c).

76. 7 C.F.R. § 614.8(d).

77. 7 C.F.R. § 614.8(d).

78. 7 C.F.R. § 614.8(e).

79. 7 C.F.R. § 614.9(a).

80. 7 C.F.R. § 614.9(b).

81. 7 C.F.R. § 614.9(c), (d), (e).

82. 7 C.F.R. § 614.10.

CHAPTER 8

SPECIAL PROTECTIONS FOR FARMERS

This chapter will address special Federal programs that provide income and other forms of support for farmers whose crops have been damaged, or whose livestock is threatened, by adverse weather conditions. The programs addressed are federal crop insurance, livestock feed programs and other forms of extraordinary relief, such as that provided by the Disaster Assistance Act of 1988.

I. Federal Crop Insurance
    The Federal Crop Insurance Program is administered by the Federal Crop Insurance Corporation (FCIC) which was created by the Federal Crop Insurance Act ("the Act").[1] The FCIC offers crop insurance to farmers through two methods. First, the FCIC offers an insurance contract directly to the insured.[2] Second, private companies offer contracts which contain substantially the same terms and conditions as the FCIC contract. These private contracts are reinsured by the FCIC.[3]

    A. Limits on Coverage
    There is a limit to the FCIC insurance coverage that a farmer may carry in a given crop year. Specifically, no person may have in force more than one contract on the same crop for that crop year, whether it is issued by the FCIC or by a company which is reinsured by the FCIC.[4] If a person has more than one contract under the Act outstanding on the same crop for the crop year, all of those contracts will be voided for that crop year. Moreover, the person who purchased the contracts will be liable for the premium on all of the contracts.[5] However, this provision will not apply if the farmer can show to the satisfaction of the FCIC that the multiple insurance contracts were inadvertent and that the farmer was not at fault. Moreover, if the multiple insurance is found to be inadvertent, the contract with the earliest application date will be deemed valid and the other contracts will be cancelled without liability

to the farmer.[6]

Any farmer who wishes to participate in the FCIC program must submit an application for insurance on a form prescribed by the FCIC.[7] The farmer may participate in the program in order to cover his or her share in the insured crop as either a landlord, owner-operator or tenant. The insurance application must be submitted to the FCIC at the FCIC service office on or before the applicable sales closing date on file in the service office.

B. Applications and the Insurance Contract

The FCIC manager is authorized to extend the sales closing date in any crop year by placing a notice in the Federal Register and placing the extended date on file in the applicable service offices.[8] However, if adverse conditions develop during this period the FCIC will immediately discontinue the acceptance of applications.

All applicants for insurance under the Act must advise the FCIC in writing, at the time of application, of any previous applications for insurance under the Act and the present status of any existing applications or insurance contracts.[9] At the time that the application for insurance is made, the applicant must elect an amount of insurance or a coverage level and price from among those contained in the actuarial table for the crop year.[10] The FCIC may reject applications, or discontinue the acceptance of applications, in any county or from any individual upon its determination that the insurance risk is excessive.[11]

The insurance contract will become effective upon the acceptance by the FCIC of a duly executed insurance application on the standard FCIC form.[12] The contract will cover the crop as provided in the policy and in the crop endorsement. The contract itself is comprised of the application, the policy, the crop endorsement and any amendments thereto, and the county actuarial table. No indemnity payments will be made to the farmer unless he or she complies with all of the terms and conditions of the contract.

The provisions of the General Crop Insurance Policy are found at 7 C.F.R. Section 408(d). These administrative provisions are applicable only to the following crops, whose

264

respective endorsements are found in the regulations, as follows:

Wheat Endorsement   Sect. 401.101
Winter Coverage Option for Wheat   Sect. 401.102
Barley Endorsement   Sect. 401.103
Winter Coverage Option for Barley   Sect. 401.104
Oat Endorsement   Sect. 401.105
Rye Endorsement   Sect. 401.106
Hybrid Sorghum Seed Endorsement   Sect. 401.109
Almond Endorsement   Sect. 401.110
Corn Endorsement   Sect. 401.111
Corn Silage Option   Sect. 401.112
Grain Sorghum Endorsement   Sect. 401.113
Canning and Processing Tomato Endorsement   Sect. 401.114
Soybean Endorsement   Sect. 401.117
Cotton Endorsement   Sect. 401.119
ELS Cotton Endorsement   Sect. 401.121
Rice Endorsement   Sect. 401.120
Safflower Seed Endorsement   Sect. 401.123
Sunflower Seed Endorsement   Sect. 401.124
Malting Barley Option   Sect. 401.135

There are two special endorsements available for certain crops. First, the Late Planting Agreement Option is available for wheat, barley, oats and rye. This agreement must be executed before the "final planting date" which is contained in the actuarial table on file in the FCIC service office.[13] The agreement provides insurance on acreage planted for up to 20 days after the applicable final planting date. The "production guarantee" is the guaranteed amount of production under the provisions of the applicable crop insurance endorsement.[14] Under the late planting agreement, this guarantee will be reduced by 10 percent for each 5 days that the acreage is planted after the final planting date.[15] Second, the Prevented Planting Endorsement is available for barley, corn, cotton, ELS cotton, grain sorghum, oats, rice and wheat. To qualify for this endorsement, a farmer must participate in the ASCS Acreage Reduction or Set-Aside Program.[16] The insurance covers the risk of the farmer being unavoidably prevented from planting insurable acreage of either the above crops ("eligible crops") or any other crop ("non-conserving crops").

C. Denial of Insurance

The Food Security Act of 1985[17] requires that crop insurance which is either issued or reinsured by the FCIC be denied to persons who are determined to have engaged in certain prohibited practices. These prohibited practices are:

1. Conviction under federal or state law for planting, cultivating, growing, harvesting or storing a controlled substance. Ineligibility is imposed during that crop year and during the four succeeding crop years,[18]

2. Producing an agricultural commodity on a field on which highly erodible land is predominant, unless the farmer is exempt (under the provisions of 7 CFR Section 12.5). Ineligibility is imposed for that crop year,[19] and/or

3. Producing an agricultural commodity on converted wetland, unless the farmer is exempt (under the provisions of 7 CFR Section 12.5). Ineligibility is imposed for that crop year.[20]

Each applicant for FCIC insurance is required to certify on Form AD-1026, prior to the sales closing date for the crop to be insured, that the applicant will not produce an agricultural commodity on highly erodible land or converted wetland during that crop year.[21] This provision is not applicable if the production is exempt in accordance with 7 CFR Section 12.5.

D. Insurance Programs Available

There are separate FCIC insurance programs, complete with their own respective regulations, for each of the following crops:

	7 C.F.R. Part
Raisin crop	402
Peach (fresh) crop	403
Western United States apple crop	404
Apple crop	405
Eastern United States apple crop	408
Arizona-California citrus	409
Florida citrus crop	410

266

A late planting agreement option is available for many of these crops.[22]

E. Reliance on Agents

In general, a farmer who purchases a FCIC crop insurance policy is protected against liability arising from good faith reliance on misrepresentation(s) made to him or her by an agent of the FCIC. The farmer is protected from:
1. indebtedness to the FCIC for additional premiums; or
2. for crop losses which are not insured or are not indemnified because of the failure of the insured to comply with the terms of the insurance contract.[23]

This provision applies in cases which involve $100,000.00 or less, upon a finding by the FCIC Board of Directors or Manager that:
1. An FCIC agent or employee did in fact make the misrepresentation, give erroneous advice or take erroneous action;
2. the insured relied thereon in good faith; and
3. to require the payment of the additional premiums or to deny indemnity would be unfair and inequitable.[24]

F. Appeals of Determinations

Regulations are issued pursuant to the Federal Crop Insurance Act to prescribe the procedures under which a person may obtain review of determinations which are made by the FCIC.[25]

The right to appeal an FCIC determination is available to the following persons:

(a) Any person who has been determined to be indebted to the FCIC as a result of:
   (1) Overpaid indemnities; or
   (2) Non-payment of a premium;
(b) Any person whose claim for indemnity under insurance obtained pursuant to the Act has been denied;

(c) Any person whose request for insurance pursuant to the Act has been denied;

(d) Any party to a contract who has received notification of a determination by the FCIC regarding any terms or conditions of the contract between the person and the FCIC which the party disputes;

(e) Any person whose request for relief under the good faith reliance on misrepresentation provisions of the crop insurance regulations has been denied in whole or in part; or

(f) Any party to a crop insurance contract with a multi-peril insurance company whose contract has been reinsured by the FCIC, provided that the appeal is related to yield and coverage issues based upon actuarial data furnished by the FCIC which the party disputes. In such cases, the FCIC must notify the multi-peril insurance company of the appeal request and that company must be offered an opportunity to participate in the appeal hearing; and

(g) Any person who has <u>not</u> been notified by the FCIC that, because of actions of the person concerning the present or a previous federal crop insurance contract, or reinsured crop insurance contract, such person is ineligible to purchase crop insurance from the FCIC and that the FCIC will not reinsure any crop insurance contract issued to such person by a private insurance company.[26]

1. Requesting an Initial Hearing

Written requests for an initial hearing must be received by the Director, Kansas City Operations Office, Federal Crop Insurance Corporation, P.O. Box 293, Kansas City, Missouri, 64141, within forty five days of the date of notification by the FCIC of the determination or action being appealed from.[27] The request for the hearing must be signed by the appellant; and contain 1. statement of the facts which comprise the matter on which the hearing is sought; and 2. a statement of the appellant's reasons for believing that the FCIC determination(s) or other matter being appealed from is incorrect.

Written notice of the time and place of the hearing must be given to the appellant by certified mail, return receipt requested, at least thirty days prior to the date of the hearing unless waived by the appellant.[28] The appellant may elect to waive his or her appearance at a hearing and request that a determination be made on the basis of written material submitted by the appellant and other information available to the hearing officer.[29]

If, at the time scheduled for a hearing, the appellant is absent, the hearing officer may, after the lapse of a reasonable period of time, dismiss the hearing.[30] In the alternative, the hearing officer may accept information and evidence submitted by other persons who are present at the hearing.

2. Authority of the Hearing Officer

The hearing officer is authorized to:

(1) Rule upon motions and requests;

(2) Adjourn the hearing from time to time and change the time and place of hearing;

(3) Receive evidence;

(4) Admit or exclude evidence;

(5) Hear oral arguments on facts or law;

(6) Do all acts and take all measures necessary for the maintenance of order at the hearing and for the efficient conduct of the proceeding; and

(7) Make a written determination based upon evidence submitted at the hearing.[31]

The hearing officer does not have the authority to compromise claims or to waive provisions of the FCIC regulations or contracts unless the appeal is from a determination made under the good faith reliance on misrepresentation provisions of the crop insurance regulations.[32]

3. Initial hearing

The initial hearing will be conducted by the hearing officer at a time and place which, although designated by the hearing officer, takes into consideration the convenience of the appellant.[33] The hearing is to be informal and conducted in a manner deemed most likely to obtain the facts relevant to the issues. The hearing officer will restrict the hearing to pertinent matters under consideration and may exclude irrelevant, immaterial or unduly repetitious evidence.[34] The appellant will be given a full opportunity to present relevant evidence through oral or documentary information. Persons other than those

270

appearing on behalf of the appellant may be permitted to present information. All persons who appear at the hearing to present information may be questioned by the appellant.

A transcript of the hearing may be taken if the following conditions are met:
(1) The appellant advises the hearing officer at least ten days prior to the hearing, makes arrangements with a certified court reporter or equivalent individual or company for the transcript to be made at the appellant's expense, and agrees that the FCIC may obtain a copy of the transcript at the FCIC's expense. If the appellant wants the transcript to be considered a part of the record of the hearing, the appellant must supply a copy for that purpose unless the FCIC purchases a copy; or
(2) The hearing officer feels that the nature of the case would make a transcript desirable. Under this circumstance a copy of the transcript will be made by the FCIC and provided to the appellant at the appellant's expense.[35]

After the close of the hearing, the hearing officer must promptly prepare a written determination which contains a clear and concise statement of the appellant's and the FCIC's contentions and which lists the material facts as found by the hearing officer.[36] The report must also contain a delineation of the issues and the hearing officer's determination on each of those issues. The determinations must generally be based upon information or evidence which was presented at the hearing or otherwise made known to the appellant and made a part of the record of the hearing.[37] The appellant must be given the opportunity to examine and respond to all evidence presented prior to the determination of the hearing officer. The determination of the hearing officer must be mailed to the appellant by certified mail, return receipt requested.[38]

4. Appeal hearing

The regulations which are applicable to the initial hearing are also applicable to the appeal hearing.[39] The appellant may appeal from the determination of the hearing officer which results from an initial hearing by doing so in writing within forty five days of the date of the determination.[40] This request should be delivered to the Deputy Manager, FCIC,

United States Department of Agriculture, Washington, DC 20240. The hearing officer who is designated to hold the hearing must not be a person who participated in the decisions or determinations from which the appellant is appealing. The hearing will be scheduled in Washington, DC, or at another place, and at the time which the FCIC designates, after taking into consideration the interests of the appellant.

The appeal hearing will be de novo.[41] However, the record of the initial hearing will be admitted at the appeal hearing and considered by the hearing officer in making a determination. The record at the initial hearing may be supplemented by the FCIC and/or and the appellant. Evidence which duplicates written evidence or transcribed testimony which appears in the record of the initial hearing will not be admitted by the hearing officer absent a showing of good cause.

The determinations of the hearing officer at the initial hearing will not be considered by the hearing officer at the appeal hearing.[42] However, the hearing officer at the appeal hearing may adopt relevant portions of the initial hearing officer's determinations if the appeal hearing officer agrees with those portions after having conducted an independent examination of the record.

Nothing in the regulations precludes the Manager of the FCIC from determining any question which arises under the programs to which the regulations apply, or from revising or modifying any determination which has been made by a hearing officer.[43]

II.   Livestock Feed Programs
        The Livestock Feed Program and the Emergency Livestock Feed Program will be discussed separately.

        A. Livestock Feed Program
        The objective of the Livestock Feed Program ("LFP")[44] is to provide assistance to eligible livestock owners through reduced-price sales of feed grain for eligible livestock. The purpose of this assistance is to prevent widespread liquidation or undue culling of livestock because of flood, drought, fire, hurricane, storm, tornado, earthquake, disease, insect infestation or other catastrophe.[45] The program is administered by the

Agricultural Stabilization and Conservation Service (ASCS) and the Commodity Credit Corporation (CCC).[46]

1. Livestock Eligibility

For the purposes of this program, "livestock" is defined as all classes of beef and dairy cattle, sheep, goats and swine.[47] "Eligible livestock" is defined as livestock which have, for at least six months prior to the date of the application to purchase feed, been owned or leased under a contractual agreement which requires that the lessee furnish the feed for the livestock, and which provides that the lessee has a beneficial interest in the livestock. This beneficial interest may be evidenced by the right of the lessee to market a share of the increase. Eligible livestock must either have been located in the emergency area on the date the area was designated, as determined by the state committee, or were moved into the area in accordance with the owner's normal livestock operation, such as rotation grazing. Cattle, sheep, goats, and swine are eligible for emergency feed if they were purchased by the applicant as replacement breeding stock according to his or her customary breeding operations. Eligible livestock also includes livestock which was inherited by an applicant, or purchased by an applicant as part of a complete farming operation, other than through foreclosure. The offspring of eligible livestock are also eligible for emergency feed.[48]

2. Owner Eligibility

An owner may be approved to purchase feed grain for eligible livestock if the emergency has caused a reduction of the feed normally produced by the owner such that the owner must purchase substantially more feed than normal.[49] In addition it is required that at the time the owner applies for feed grain, he or she does not have, and is unable to obtain, sufficient feed for their eligible livestock through normal channels of trade without incurring undue financial hardship.[50] "Undue financial hardship" means that, under prevailing local standards, the owner's financial resources are such that if he or she attempted to obtain the required feed from normal suppliers it would jeopardize the continuation of the farming operation. This "jeopardization" could include defaulting on existing financial

273

obligations, unsound new borrowing or excessive disposal of livestock. In making this determination, officials must give especially close scrutiny to applicants who are customarily regarded in their locality as being wealthy, having large financial reserves, or as having substantial non-farm sources of income. If the approving officials are uncertain as to whether the applicant meets the eligibility requirements, they may request whatever factual information they need to make a determination.[51]

If the applicant is a partnership, the resources of the partnership and all the partners must be taken into consideration in determining the partnership's eligibility for assistance.[52] If the applicant is a family corporation, the resources of the corporation must be considered in conjunction with the resources of the individuals who are considered to be a "person" with the corporation.[53]

3. Application and Approval

An owner of eligible livestock who fulfills the requirements of the regulations may file an application under this program. Upon application, the applicant must execute a certification that he or she is eligible for feed.[54] An application must be filed at the county office in which the majority of the livestock shown on the application are usually located.[55] Applications for feed grain may be filed at any time during the program period on the condition that sufficient time exists for the use of the feed grain prior to the ending date of the program period.[56]

The County committee is responsible for reviewing each application which it receives. The County committee is authorized to approve or disapprove all applications except where the applicant is an ASCS committee member or an ASCS employee.[57] The State committee or its designee is authorized to approve or disapprove the applications of county committee members and ASCS employees,[58] and DAP or its designee may approve or disapprove applications from State committee members.[59]

No application may be approved unless the owner meets all of the eligibility requirements.[60] Information which is furnished by the applicant and other information, including

274

knowledge of the County and State committee members concerning the owner's normal operations, must be taken into consideration in making relevant recommendations and determinations. If information which has been furnished by the owner is incomplete or unclear, additional information which is deemed necessary may be requested from the applicant before a decision is made.

The owner must be notified in writing of:

(i) the action taken on his or her application by the approving officials; and

(ii) his or her right to appeal the decision.[61]

4. Quantities of Feed Grain Approved

Prior to the purchase of feed grain under this program, the owner must repay the principal and interest on all of his or her commodity loans which cover certain grains. This involves grains which are designated by the Secretary as feed grains and which were obtained after the program was available for use and are determined by the County committee to be stored within reasonable hauling distance of the owner's livestock operation.[62] This provision does not apply to warehouse-stored loan grain which is delivered by rail, or certain other grain.[63] In the case of a commodity loan made jointly to the owner of the eligible livestock and another producer, the owner must repay the principal and interest on the portion of the loan represented by his or her share of the collateral.[64]

The net approved quantity is the net feed grain allowance, which will be computed for the entire feeding period.[65] The net feed grain allowance is the smallest of:

(i) The feed grain gross allowance less the total quantity of feed (feed grain, hay, silage, pasture and range) determined by officials to be available to the owner for feeding his or her eligible livestock during the feeding period; or

(ii) The quantity that officials determine to be adequate considering the total quantity of feed available to the owner for feeding his or her eligible livestock during the feeding period; or

(iii) The amount of livestock feed lost by the owner as a result of the emergency. If the applicant purchases oats, the net allowance may be increased by up to 20 percent.[66]

The feed grain gross allowance must not exceed the smaller of 10 pounds per day, or whatever lesser quantity is established by the State committee or County committee, times the number of days in the feeding period times the eligible animal units.[67] The total quantity of feed available to the owner will be the quantity owned by the owner plus feed sold or contracted for sale by him or her after a date(s) established by the State committee. Purchased feed will not be considered as feed available.[68]

Sales of feed grains will be made in quantities which would permit feeding the grain to eligible livestock up until the final date of the program period.[69]

5. Financial Arrangements

When an owner wishes to purchase grain pursuant to an approved application, he or she must make payment to the County committee by means of an acceptable remittance for the quantity of grain purchased. Delivery will not be allowed until this payment has been made.[70] The sale price of feed grain is 100 percent of the applicable CCC county loan rate for the county in which the commodity is delivered.[71]

Inadvertent overdelivery to an owner of the total approved quantity stated in the application may be settled between the owner and the CCC at the applicable sales price for the grain delivered. However, overdeliveries in excess of the total approved quantity which are caused by warehouses, handlers or dealers and are not the result of error by the CCC, must be settled between those intermediaries and the owner.[72]

No feed grain, except the owner's loan grain of the kind designated by the Secretary as feed grain, may be sold to an owner until a particular condition is met. This condition is that all of the owner's loan grain, which the County committee has determined to be within reasonable hauling distance of the owner's livestock operation, must first be redeemed or purchased by him or her.[73] In other words, grain which an applicant has under loan must be utilized to fulfill feed grain requirements under an approved application.

6. Loan Grain

In making feed grain available which the applicant has

under a farm stored loan, the CCC must meed the following five conditions:

(i)   it must accelerate the maturity date of the entire loan or that portion of the loan which is needed to meet the approving requirements (notwithstanding any provisions of the loan documents to the contrary);

(ii)   it must require delivery of the grain to the CCC on the farm where it is stored, with settlement to be made on the basis of the producer's loan documents;

(iii)   it must require the owner to purchase the quantity of the grain referenced in the application at the applicable price under this program;

(iv)   it must redeliver the grain to the applicant on the farm where it is stored; and

(v)   it must make additional grain available to the applicant from CCC stocks, if the quantity needed is in excess of that which the applicant has under loan.[74]

Storage payments will be based on the storage period ending in the month which precedes the month in which the commodity is delivered to the CCC in satisfaction of the loan.[75]

If there has been a conversion of the grain which secures the loan, settlement must be made in accordance with commodity loan regulations. Under these circumstances, the owner will be declared ineligible to participate in the Livestock Feed Program.[76]

In making feed grain available which the applicant has under a warehouse stored loan, the CCC must do the following:

(i)   it must accelerate the maturity date of the entire loan or that portion of the loan which was made on a warehouse receipt(s) representing a quantity of grain not exceeding the quantity and quality of grain needed to meet the approved requirements;

(ii)   it must acquire title to this grain;

(iii)   it must credit the loan with the settlement value of the quantity and quality of the grain, with settlement to be made on the basis of the producer's loan documents and price support regulations;

(iv)   it must require the owner to purchase the grain under the approved application at the applicable price under this program; and

(v) it must deliver the warehouse receipt(s) representing the grain to him or her. Liquidation of part of a receipt will not be permitted.[77] This applies only to warehouse storage loans on grain which has not been delivered by rail.[78]

7. Sales of CCC-owned Grain

The CCC must designate the delivery point and kind of CCC-owned grain to be sold under this program. The delivery of grain will be authorized after payment is received by the CCC.[79] Delivery will be effected by the issuance of non-transferable delivery orders which state the kind and quantity of grain to be delivered. Quantities authorized by delivery orders may not exceed the quantity of grain that can normally be fed between the expected date of delivery and the end of the program period.

The title and risk of loss to the grain specified in the delivery order and stored at a warehouse or handler facility will pass to the owner upon the issuance of the delivery order.[80] Settlement for differences in quality or quantity between the grain delivered to the owner and the grain described in the delivery order should be made between the owner and the warehouseman or handler. However, in cases where there is a substantial underdelivery in quantity, the owner should not make settlement with the warehouseman or handler but instead should promptly notify the County office. After such notification is received, a revised delivery order will be issued to the owner.

Where CCC-owned grain is not available in the area in which the owner lives and there are no approved handlers or dealers available, the CCC will ship and consign the required grain to the County committee.[81] The title and risk of loss will pass to the owner either (a) upon delivery of the grain into his or her conveyance, or (b) whenever he or she takes possession of the grain. The sale price will not be subject to adjustment for the grade and quality actually delivered.

If any feed grain delivered by the CCC to an owner is not of a quality fit for feeding livestock, he or she must advise the County office of this fact. Arrangements will then be made for delivery of substitute feed grain.[82]

8. Custom Processing

An owner who wishes to have grain pelletized, ground, rolled, custom mixed, or otherwise processed may do so under certain circumstances. This is allowable if (a) the feed is processed from the grain purchased from the CCC or (b) the feed accepted from the processor is processed from the same kind of grain of grade number 3 or better.[83] The CCC is not responsible for any charges which involve processing, bagging or added freight incurred for processing in-transit. Any owner who prefers to purchase processed feed grain from the stocks of an approved dealer may do so upon proper request at the county office.[84]

9. Disposition of Grain and Adjustment of Sales Price Feed for Livestock

The total quantity of feed purchased under the Livestock Feed Program must be fed to the owner's livestock within the program period.[85] The County committee may consider feed grain as being fed within the program period where the failure to timely feed all of the grain was unavoidable. The amount of remaining grain which may be considered as being timely fed may not exceed a 10 day supply.

If the owner does not feed the grain to eligible livestock, he or she will be required to pay to the CCC, as liquidated damages, the difference between the price paid for the feed grain and its market price.[86] The market price will be determined by the CCC, on the date of the delivery order, warrant, or other delivery authorization applicable to the last acquisition of the feed grain. If an owner has failed to report a livestock change he or she must pay to the CCC the price difference for any grain which he or she purchased in excess of the quantity that the CCC would have approved if the report had been made.[87]

If an owner suffers losses of, or disposes of, or transfers any of their eligible livestock, he or she must report this fact promptly to the County office from which feed grain was purchased under the program.[88] Similarly, if the owner fails to use the feed for eligible livestock, he or she must report this fact promptly to the applicable County office.

10. Violations

If the owner is unable to utilize the quantity of feed purchased under the program, it is imperative that he or she should not dispose of the grain.[89]   The owner will be subject to both civil penalties and criminal liabilities, under applicable federal statutes, if the feed grain acquired from the CCC is disposed of to any other person, or if a delivery order or warrant is used for obtaining other than feed grain.[90]

An owner, warehouseman, handler, dealer or any other person may be suspended from participation in this program in accordance with the CCC regulations if that person has falsely certified, represented or reported any information under these regulations, or has failed to comply with any provisions of these regulations or of any contracts entered into under these regulations.[91]   The making of fraudulent representations will render such person liable under applicable federal civil and criminal statutes.

11. Appeals

Any owner who is dissatisfied with a Livestock Feed Program determination as to:

(a) personal eligibility or livestock eligibility; or

(b) the quantity of feed grain approved for eligible livestock, may elect between two legal options. He or she may either make a request for reconsideration of the determination, or may appeal the determination in accordance with the procedures set forth in the ASCS appeal regulations.[92]   However, determinations which are made by a State committee are not appealable.

B. Emergency Livestock Feed Program

The objective of the Emergency Livestock Feed Program ("ELFP"), of the Food and Agriculture Act of 1977,[93] is to pay eligible livestock owners a portion of the cost of feed which they purchased during an emergency. An emergency is deemed to exist if the livestock owner suffered a substantial loss of feed production for his or her livestock due to a natural disaster.[94] The program is administered by the ASCS State and County committees.[95]

1. Livestock Eligibility

"Livestock" is defined as beef and dairy cattle, horses, mules, sheep, goats, swine and poultry. Buffalo and beefalo are also included when maintained on the same basis as beef cattle in support of the beef industry.[96]

"Eligible livestock" is defined as livestock (excluding poultry) which have been owned by the applicant for at least six months prior to the date of application. Livestock maintained in a feedlot will be considered to be eligible livestock only if the feedlot is owned by the applicant, and all the cattle in the feedlot are owned by the applicant. Eligible livestock may include livestock (excluding poultry) which have been owned less than six months or poultry owned less than three months when inherited by the applicant or born as offspring of eligible livestock. Work horses and mules may be considered to be eligible livestock only if they are used for pulling equipment or for riding purposes necessary to the applicant's agricultural operations. Eligible livestock does not include horses and mules kept in excess of the number needed to produce food and fiber on the applicant's farm. Eligible livestock includes poultry which are chickens, turkeys, geese and ducks and which are owned by the applicant for at least three months prior to the date of application for assistance under the program.[97]

2. Owner Eligibility

The owner may be approved to purchase feed for eligible livestock if the following eligibility criteria are met:

(1) The disaster has caused a substantial loss of production of the feed normally produced for the owner's livestock on the farm owned or operated by the owner;

(2) the owner does not have sufficient feed that has adequate nutritive value for the owner's particular type(s) of livestock; and

(3) the owner is required to purchase a quantity of feed greater than normal during the crop year.[98]

"Substantial loss of production" means that the amount of feed produced on the farm (including pasture, forage and feed in storage) during the crop year is at least 40 percent below that considered by the approving officials as being normal production for the farm, and which constitutes a loss of feed

281

caused by a natural disaster. Any loss of feed production which the approving official considers to be attributable to overgrazing or farming practices which are not recognized as being normal in the area will not be included in determining loss of production.[99] All of the applicant's holdings must be considered in determining eligibility, regardless of its location. This includes land, feed produced, feed on hand, etc.[100]

3. Application and Approval

Any owner of livestock may file an application under this program.[101] An application must be filed at a County ASCS office in the county where the records covering the major portion of the applicant's holdings are located, or in a county which is agreed to by both the applicant and the County committees.[102] The owner must certify that he or she meets the requirements of the program.[103] The deadlines for filing an application for feed assistance depends on when the production losses occurred. If the losses occurred between the beginning of the crop year and the end of the calendar year, the application must be filed by December 31 of that year. However, if the losses occurred between January 1 and the end of the crop year, the application must be filed within 30 days after the disaster occurs.[104]

The ASCS County committee will review each application which it receives.[105] The State committee or its designee is authorized to approve or disapprove applications of County committee members and ASCS employees; and DASCO or its designee may approve or disapprove applications of State committee members.[106]

No application will be approved unless the owner meets all eligibility requirements.[107] Information which has been furnished by the applicant and other information, including knowledge of the County and State committee members con- - cerning the owner's normal operations, will be taken into consideration in making recommendations and approvals. If the information which was furnished by the owner is incomplete or unclear, the application will not be approved until sufficient additional information is provided by the owner.

The owner must be notified in writing of:

(i)   the action taken on the application by the

approving officials and

(ii) the applicant's right to appeal the decision.[108]

4. Determining Loss of Production

The current crop year acreage and yield of crop(s) used to feed eligible livestock, including pasture and the normal yield for such crop(s), will be converted to grain equivalent and used in arriving at the amount of feed lost because of the disaster.[109] Loss of production may include feed stocks which were produced on the farm in the current crop year and which were damaged in storage. Feed stocks which were not totally destroyed must be appraised for their remaining value as livestock feed.[110] Any loss of production otherwise computed will be reduced:

(i) by the amount of loss attributable to pasture acreage for which any deferred grazing payment may have been earned in the current crop year;

(ii) by the amount of any disaster payments received in the crop year for feed grain; and

(iii) by the amount of any benefits received through insurance or any other indemnification for current year feed which was lost either in storage or during production.[111]

5. Determining Feed Available and Amount of Assistance

The total quantity of feed available to the owner will be the quantity owned and on hand as of the date of application, in grain equivalent, plus any prior or current crop year feed, which was sold or contracted for sale during the current crop year. This includes any grain under loan.[112]

The amount of feed otherwise determined to be on hand will be reduced by the amount of any purchased feed on hand, or any feed which is determined by the County committee to be unsuitable for the owner's livestock. On the other hand, it will be increased by the amount of any disaster payments which were received in the crop year for feed grain and the amount of any benefits received through any Federally subsidized insurance for current year for feed which was lost either in storage or during production.[113]

The determination of feed on hand will exclude any feed

grain reserved specifically for consumption by the applicant's ineligible livestock, or which is reserved for use as seed to plant crops on the owner's farm(s) for the next harvest. It will also exclude any feed grain of the prior crop year which was placed in storage under a CCC loan, or used as collateral for a loan and any feed (hay, grain, etc.,) purchased for resale.[114] Feed utilized in a feedlot for the commercial feeding of livestock is not considered feed purchased for resale and is included as feed available.

The gross feed allowance may not exceed the smaller of 10 pounds per day per animal unit, or whatever lesser quantity is established by the State committee or County committee, times the number of days in the feeding period times the eligible animal units.[115]

The net feed allowance is the smaller of:

(i)   The gross feed allowance less the total quantity of feed (feed grain, hay, silage, pasture and range converted to feed grain equivalent) determined by the approving officials to be available to the owner for feeding eligible livestock during the feeding period, or

(ii)   The quantity which the approving officials determine to be adequate considering the total quantity of feed available to the owner for feeding eligible livestock during the feeding period because of the emergency.[116]

Based on the presentation of acceptable evidence of purchase, the owner will be reimbursed with commodity certificates at the rate of 50 percent of the cost of eligible feed purchased, but not to exceed 5 cents per pound of feed grain equivalent.[117]   In no case may assistance be provided in an amount greater than the total feed allowance computed as outlined above.

Acceptable evidence of purchase will be limited to appropriate sales documents or receipts which are signed by the seller.[118]   Eligible costs of purchased feed are limited to the purchase price at the point of possession.[119]

6.   Disposition of Feed and Adjustment of Net Allowance

Feed obtained under this program may not be exchanged for other services, cash, credits, or any other thing of value.[120]

284

An amount of feed equal to that acquired under the program must be fed to the applicant's eligible livestock.[121]

If there is a reduction in the number of the owner's eligible livestock, the owner must promptly report this fact to the County office.[122] If additional feed becomes available to the owner from production on the farm during the feeding period, including from pasture, this fact must be promptly reported to the county office.[123]

7. Violations

Any person who disposes of any feed for which reimbursement is made under this program in any manner other than as authorized by the Secretary, will be subject to a penalty equal to the market value of the feed involved. This amount may be recovered by the Secretary in a civil suit. In addition, the person will be subject to criminal liability which may result in a fine of not more than $10,000 or imprisonment of not more than one year, or both.[124] The issuance of a false sales document, the changing of dates or data on a sales document, or the making of a false statement in an application for assistance or other document, for the purpose of enabling the applicant to obtain payment to which the applicant is not entitled, may subject a person to liability under applicable Federal civil and criminal statutes.[125]

The County committee may deny cost share assistance under this program to any person for the current crop year if it is determined the person knowingly made a false statement for the purpose of obtaining benefits under the program.[126]

8. Appeals

Any owner may obtain both reconsideration and review of determinations which affect his or her participation in the program, in accordance with the ASCS appeal regulations.[127]

9. Limitations of Authority/Misinformation

Performance by an owner which is based on misaction or misinformation will be handled in accordance with 7 CFR Part 790 if the performance was rendered in good faith and in reliance upon the action or advice of a County or State committee or their authorized representative.[128]

State and county committees do not have the authority to modify or waive any of the provisions of the regulations in this program.[129] The State committee may take any action which the regulations authorize or require to be taken by the County committee, when such action has not been taken by the county committee.[130] The State committee may also:

(1) correct, or require a County committee to correct, any action taken by the county committee which is not in accordance with these regulations; or

(2) require a County committee to refrain from taking any action which is not in accordance with these regulations. Id.

No delegation to a State or County committee under these regulations will preclude DASCO or its designee from determining any question arising under the regulations or from reversing or modifying any determination made by a State or County committee.[131]

10. Setoffs/Overpayments/Assignments

If any indebtedness of the producer to any agency of the United States is listed on the county claims control record, payments due to the producer under these program regulations will be applied to that indebtedness as provided in the Setoff Regulations located at 7 CFR Part 13.[132] USDA compliance with the provisions of this section will not deprive the producer of any right the producer would otherwise have to contest the justness of the indebtedness involved in the setoff action, either by administrative appeal or by legal action.[133]

A producer will be liable for repayment of the amount by which any payment disbursed to the producer exceeds the amount of the payment which is authorized under these regulations.[134] An applicant must not make an assignment of any payment which is due or will come due under the regulations of this program.[135]

11. Records and Inspection

The producer must maintain books, records, and accounts which support any information furnished to the County committee for the purposes of this program.[136] This also applies to any other person who furnishes information to the producer or to the County committee for the purpose of enabling the producer to receive a payment under this program. These records must be preserved for three years following the end of the year during which the application for payment was filed. The producer or other person must permit authorized USDA representatives and General Accounting Office representatives to inspect, examine, and make copies of such books, records, and accounts during regular business hours.

III.   Federal Disaster Relief
There are Federal disaster relief provisions contained in most of the major farm bills. For example, in the Food Security Act of 1985 there are relief provisions for farmers with crop losses in relation to the program crops of rice, upland cotton, feed grains, and wheat. Under these provisions, the Secretary of Agriculture is authorized to issue payments to a farmer whose crop losses have created an "economic emergency" for that farmer. Compensation is allowed for losses attributed to prevented planting and reduced yields, respectively. These adverse crop conditions must have been caused by drought, flood, or other natural disaster, or other condition beyond the control of the farmer. These payments can only be made if crop insurance indemnity payments under the Federal Crop Insurance Act and other forms of assistance made available by the Federal government to the farmer are insufficient to alleviate the economic emergency.[137]

In addition to these standard disaster relief provisions, the occurrence of a natural disaster will often cause Congress to enact specialized relief provisions for that particular disaster. These provisions may apply to either a regional or national area. For example, the "Disaster Assistance Act of 1988" was enacted on August 11, 1988 in response to the drought which afflicted farmers throughout much of the United States during 1988.[138] This Act includes provisions on such diverse drought-related subjects as food prices, rural business, forward contracting, agricultural exports, migrant and seasonal workers, water management for rural areas, Reclamation States drought assistance, disaster credit and forbearance, conservation assistance, emergency livestock assistance, emergency crop loss assistance, crop quality reduction disaster benefits, commodity stock adjustment, sale of corn to ethanol producers, and federal crop insurance provisions.

In summary, a farm client whose crop or livestock production has been disrupted by a natural disaster may decide to file a claim for a Federal relief payment(s). Most of the Federal disaster relief programs are administered by the Agricultural Conservation and Stabilization Service (ASCS) county offices. While disaster relief payments are generally characterized as a gratuity, and not an entitlement, an adverse payment decision may usually be appealed by the farmer.

FOOTNOTES

1. 7 U.S.C. § 1501 et seq.

2. The contract may be found at 7 C.F.R. § 401.8.

3. 7 C.F.R. § 401.2(a).

4. 7 C.F.R. § 401.2(c).

5. 7 C.F.R. § 401.2(d).

6. 7 C.F.R. § 401.2(e).

7. 7 C.F.R. § 401.8(a).

8. 7 C.F.R. § 401.8(b).

9. 7 C.F.R. § 401.2(h).

10. 7 C.F.R. § 401.3(b).

11. 7 C.F.R. § 401.8(b).

12. 7 C.F.R. § 401.7.

13. 7 C.F.R. § 401.107(c)(1) & (2).

14. 7 C.F.R. § 401.107(c)(3).

15. 7 C.F.R. § 401.107(c)(2).

16. 7 C.F.R. § 401.108(b).

17. Pub. L. No. 99-198, 99 Stat. 1354 (1985).

18. 7 C.F.R. § 400.47(a).

19. 7 C.F.R. § 400.47(b).

20. 7 C.F.R. § 400.47(c).

21. 7 C.F.R. § 400.49.

22. The Applicable crops are listed at 7 C.F.R. § 400.4.

23. 7 C.F.R. § 401.6(a).

24. 7 C.F.R. § 408.6(b).

25. 7 C.F.R. § 400.90.

26. 7 C.F.R. § 400.92.

27. 7 C.F.R. § 400.93.

28. 7 C.F.R. § 400.94.

29. 7 C.F.R. § 400.95.

30. 7 C.F.R. § 400.96.

31. 7 C.F.R. § 400.97(a).

32. 7 C.F.R. § 400.97(b).

33. 7 C.F.R. § 400.98(a).

34. 7 C.F.R. § 400.98(b).

35. 7 C.F.R. § 400.98(c).

36. 7 C.F.R. § 400.99(a).

37. 7 C.F.R. § 400.99(b).

38. 7 C.F.R. § 400.99(c).

39. 7 C.F.R. § 400.100(a).

40. 7 C.F.R. § 400.100(b).

41. 7 C.F.R. § 400.100(c).

42. 7 C.F.R. § 400.100(c).

43. 7 C.F.R. § 400.101.

44. Pub. L. 86-299, as amended, and sections 407 and 421 of the Agricultural Act of 1949, as amended.

45. 7 C.F.R. § 1475.1.

46. 7 C.F.R. § 1475.2.

47. 7 C.F.R. § 1475.3(r).

48. 7 C.F.R. § 1475.3(s).

49. 7 C.F.R. § 1475.4(a).

50. 7 C.F.R. § 1475.4(b).

51. 7 C.F.R. § 1475.4(b).

52. 7 C.F.R. § 1475.4(b).

53. 7 C.F.R. § 1475.4(b). For the definition of a family corporation see 7 C.F.R. § 1475.3(g).

54. 7 C.F.R. § 1475.5(a).

55. 7 C.F.R. § 1475.5(b).

56. 7 C.F.R. § 1475.5(c)(2).

57. 7 C.F.R. § 1475.5(e)(1)(i).

58. 7 C.F.R. § 1475.5(e)(1)(ii)

59. 7 C.F.R. § 1475.5(e)(1)(iii).

60. 7 C.F.R. § 1475.5(e)(2).

61. 7 C.F.R. § 1475.5(e)(3).

62. 7 C.F.R. § 1475.5(d)(1).

63. 7 C.F.R. § 1475.5(d)(1); also see 1475.9(c)(1).

64. 7 C.F.R. § 1475.5(d)(1).

65. 7 C.F.R. § 1475.5(d)(2).

66. 7 C.F.R. § 1475.5(d)(3).

67. 7 C.F.R. § 1475.5(d)(4).

68. 7 C.F.R. § 1475.5(d)(5).

69. 7 C.F.R. § 1475.6.

70. 7 C.F.R. § 1475.7.

71. 7 C.F.R. § 1475.8(a).

72. 7 C.F.R. § 1475.8(b).

73. 7 C.F.R. § 1475.9(a).

74. 7 C.F.R. § 1475.9(b)(1).

75. 7 C.F.R. § 1475.9(b)(2).

76. 7 C.F.R. § 1475.9(b)(3).

77. 7 C.F.R. § 1475.9(c)(1).

78. 7 C.F.R. § 1475.9(c)(2).

79. 7 C.F.R. § 1475.10(a).

80. 7 C.F.R. § 1475.10(b).

81. 7 C.F.R. § 1475.10(c).

82. 7 C.F.R. § 1475.10(d).

83. 7 C.F.R. 1475.10(e).

84. 7 C.F.R. § 1475.11.

85. 7 C.F.R. § 1475.12(a).

86. 7 C.F.R. § 1475.12(b)(1).

87. 7 C.F.R. § 1475.12(b)(2).

88. 7 C.F.R. § 1475.12(c).

89. 7 C.F.R. § 1475.14(a).

90. 7 C.F.R. § 1475.14(a).

91. 7 C.F.R. § 1475.14(b).

92. 7 C.F.R. § 1475.16.

93. 91 Stat. 913 (1977).

94. 7 C.F.R. § 1475.50.

95. 7 C.F.R. § 1475.51.

96. 7 C.F.R. § 1475.52(1).

97. 7 C.F.R. § 1475.52(m).

98. 7 C.F.R. § 1475.54(a)(1)-(3).

99. 7 C.F.R. § 1475.52(j).

100. 7 C.F.R. § 1475.54(b).

101. 7 C.F.R. § 1475.55(a).

102. 7 C.F.R. § 1475.55(b).

103. 7 C.F.R. § 1475.55(c)(1).

104. 7 C.F.R. § 1475.55(c)(2).

105. 7 C.F.R. § 1475.55(g).

106. 7 C.F.R. § 1475.55(g)(1).

107. 7 C.F.R. § 1475.55(g)(2).

108. 7 C.F.R. § 1475.55(g)(3).

109. 7 C.F.R. § 1475.55(d)(1).

110. 7 C.F.R. § 1475.55(c)(1).

111. 7 C.F.R. § 1475.55(d)(3).

112. 7 C.F.R. § 1475.55(e)(1).

113. 7 C.F.R. § 1475.55(e)(2).

114. 7 C.F.R. § 1475.55(e)(3).

115. 7 C.F.R. § 1475.55(f)(1).

116. 7 C.F.R. § 1475.55(f)(2).

117. 7 C.F.R. § 1475.56(a).

118. 7 C.F.R. § 1475.56(b).

119. 7 C.F.R. § 1475.56(c).

120. 7 C.F.R. § 1475.57(a)(1).

121. 7 C.F.R. § 1475.57(a)(2).

122. 7 C.F.R. § 1475.57(b)(1).

123. 7 C.F.R. § 1475.57(b)(2).

124. 7 C.F.R. § 1475.58(a).

125. 7 C.F.R. § 1475.58(b).

126. 7 C.F.R. § 1475.58(c).

127. 7 C.F.R. § 1475.60.

128. 7 C.F.R. § 1475.61. 7 C.F.R. Part 790 applies to all situations under ASCS programs where action or advice of authorized representatives results in incomplete performance.

129. 7 C.F.R. § 1475.63(a).

130. 7 C.F.R. § 1475.63(b).

131. 7 C.F.R. § 1475.63(c).

132. 7 C.F.R. § 1475.65(a).

133. 7 C.F.R. § 1475.65(b).

134. 7 C.F.R. § 1475.66.

135. 7 C.F.R. § 1475.62.

136. 7 C.F.R. § 1475.68.

137. See, e.g., 7 U.S.C. § 1441-1; 7 U.S.C. § 1444-1; 7 U.S.C. § 1444e; 7 U.S.C. § 1445b-3.

138. Pub. L. No. 100-387, 102 Stat. 924 (1988)(7 U.S.C. § 1421 et seq. (Statutory Notes) and at the Statutory Notes of various other Sections of Title 7 of the United States Code).

CHAPTER 9

SALES OF AGRICULTURAL PRODUCTS

I.   Introduction
      The primary objective of an agricultural enterprise is the production of a marketable product. This product will either be crops or livestock which are produced in a farming operation. The marketing of these products in the aggregate is affected by an array of federal and state regulations. However, individual sales of the products are governed by the state law which is applicable to contracts and torts. Therefore, state law provides the major source of law regarding the rights and obligations of individual buyers and sellers of farm products.

II.   Sales of Farm Products and the U.C.C.
      The Uniform Commercial Code (U.C.C.) has been adopted by most states as the basic law regarding commercial transactions. The adoption of Article 2 of the U.C.C. was specifically intended to facilitate and modernize the law of sales. Initially, Article 2 sought to codify existing law. However, as the code has evolved, it has become a new source of comprehensive law which governs most forms of sales transactions.
      For purposes of sales, goods are classified under the U.C.C. as "all things which are movable" other than money, investment securities and choses in action. This category includes farm products such as livestock, poultry, the unborn young of animals and growing crops.[1] The U.C.C. does not govern sales of land.
      U.C.C. Article 2 primarily addresses problems associated with the formation of sales contracts which involve merchants and with the rights and duties of the parties to those contracts. Most sales contracts which involve farm products or farm supplies will be subject to the provisions of U.C.C. Article 2.
      Merchants are often held to higher standards of conduct than other participants in sales transactions.[2] This makes merchant status a vital issue in dealing with sales problems. In a sales dispute, a critical issue will often be whether a farmer is

297

dealing with a merchant or is considered to be a merchant himself.

A. Farmers as Merchants

In commercial transactions where the farmer is the seller a critical issue is whether he or she is a merchant. The resolution of this issue often determines whether specific duties are imposed. It may even determine whether the transaction itself is valid or enforceable. The determination of whether farmers are merchants for purposes of the U.C.C. has been a hotly contested issue -- particularly where farmer-sellers have been involved in "forward contracts."

A "forward contract" is an agreement by which the seller promises to deliver a particular product at some agreed upon future date in exchange for a designated price. In the typical situation, the price and quantity will have been agreed upon orally. This price and agreement will then be confirmed by the buyer, who is often a grain elevator, in a written memorandum to the seller. The seller often does not sign the memorandum. In a situation where the price of the grain goes up, the farmer will have an economic incentive to form a new sales contract at that higher price. Consequently, the farmer may assert that he or she is not bound by the first contract since no written agreement was signed.

The U.C.C. provision which applies to this situation provides that a contract for the sale of goods at a price of $500 or more will not be enforceable unless it is evidenced by a writing signed by the party against whom enforcement is sought or by his or her authorized agent or broker.[3] An important exception applies to a transaction between merchants. This exception provides that, if a written memorandum is sent to confirm the agreement between merchants within a reasonable time after the contract is entered into, the party receiving it becomes bound by the contract unless he or she objects in writing to the memorandum within 10 days after it is received.[4]

As a result of this provision, a "merchant" will be bound by an oral agreement if he or she does not timely object in writing to a written confirmation of that agreement sent by the other party. Furthermore, under the U.C.C., an offer by a "merchant" to buy or sell goods in a signed writing which gives

298

assurance that the offer will be held open is not revocable for lack of consideration. Rather, it will be considered irrevocable for the period of time stated in the offer, or if no time is stated, it is irrevocable for a reasonable time.[5]

The U.C.C. further provides that a definite expression of acceptance which is sent to a "merchant" within a reasonable time operates as an acceptance even though it states terms additional to or different from those contained in the offer.[6] These additional terms may be considered part of the contract if the agreement is between merchants.[7] However, if the contract is otherwise than between merchants, the additional terms are only construed as proposals for an addition to the agreement.

Given these provisions, the critical issue in many cases is whether a farmer is a merchant. If he or she is found to be a merchant, then the law provides that the merchant is bound by the memorandum or additional terms in the memorandum sent by the purchaser even though the merchant does not sign it. Although the legal rule seems clear, courts dealing with this issue have reached varying conclusions in determining whether a farmer is a merchant.[8]

Two Kansas cases illustrate the confusion surrounding this issue. In Decatur Cooperative Association v. Urban,[9] the Kansas Supreme Court found that the farmer was not a "merchant" for the purpose of using the Statute of Frauds as a defense to an oral contract. In the second decision, Musil v. Hendrich,[10] the Kansas Court of Appeals distinguished the farmer in Decatur and found that the farmer was a "merchant" under the facts of the case.

The presence of conflicting opinions has prompted the following comment to be included with Section 84-2-104 of the Kansas version of the U.C.C.:

> The question of whether a farmer is a merchant has not been easy for the Kansas courts . . . [t]he question . . . remains unsettled, and the courts apparently will have to decide the question for each context in which it arises.

Upon closer examination, however, there may be less conflict than appears between the two decisions. In Decatur, the Kansas Supreme Court specifically considered the U.C.C. definition of "merchant" and concluded that there were various

ways in which the criteria of the definition could be satisfied.[11]
The court stated:

> . . . [i]t appears there are three separate criteria for determining merchant status. A merchant is (1) a dealer who deals in the goods of the kind involved, or (2) one who by his occupation holds himself out as having knowledge or skill peculiar to the practices or goods involved in the transaction, even though he may not actually have such knowledge, or (3) a principal who employs an agent, broker or other intermediary who by his occupation holds himself out as having knowledge or skill peculiar to the practices or goods involved in the transaction (Citation omitted). <u>Professionalism, special knowledge and commercial experience are to be used in determining whether a person in a particular situation is to be held to the standards of a merchant</u>. (Emphasis added)

On the specific facts of <u>Decatur</u>, the court found that Urban was not a "dealer", as that term is used in the U.C.C. It more particularly found that Urban had not held himself out "as having knowledge or skill peculiar to the practices or goods involved in the transactions." Although a farmer naturally has knowledge or skill with respect to the raising of his crop, the farmer must also be a "professional" with regard to selling the crop to be considered a merchant. Urban sold his wheat crop only once a year. The court did not feel this was sufficient to qualify Urban as a "professional" in the sense that the Code required.

In <u>Musil v. Hendrich</u>,[12] the court applied the criteria developed in <u>Decatur</u> to find that the farmer was a "dealer" in regard to the buying and selling of hogs. The court found that since the farmer had been in the hog business for 30 to 40 years and had sold 50 to 100 pigs per month during that time, he qualified as a "dealer". Further, the Court found that the farmer had held himself out as having the knowledge and skill peculiar to the practices and goods involved.

B. Contract Interpretation

As a general rule, a properly executed contract becomes binding between the parties to the contract. A variety of concerns may arise when a contract is executed. These concerns may involve issues of contract formation or issues involving the content of the contract. This issue particularly arises as to matters not specifically considered at the time the agreement was made. The U.C.C. imposes rules to determine how these gaps in the agreement are to be filled. The application of these rules may result in the imposition of unanticipated obligations upon either or both of the parties. In most cases, the critical issue will be the intent of the parties at the time the agreement was made.

In George v. Tate,[13] the United States Supreme Court held that the actual intent of the parties, at the time a contract is made, is to be deduced from the entire contract. This may include such factors as the subject matter of the contract, the purpose of its execution, and the circumstances of the parties when they executed the contract. This actual intent may prevail over the words of the instrument unless the implied intent runs counter to the plain meaning of the words of the agreement.

The U.C.C. generally adopts the common law of contracts[14] regarding contract formation. However, it also provides statutory guidelines to assist with the interpretation of provisions or the filling of gaps. These guidelines include factors such as custom and usage of the trade and the course of dealing between the parties. The U.C.C. defines "usage of trade" as a "practice or method of dealing having such regularity of observance in a place, vocation or trade as to justify an expectation that it will be observed" in a particular transaction.[15] The burden of proof as to a particular usage of trade is upon the party which asserts it. The existence of the factor of usage of trade is considered to be a question of fact. On the other hand, a "course of dealing" is defined as "a sequence of previous conduct between two parties to a particular transaction which is fairly to be regarded as establishing a common basis of understanding for interpreting their expressions and other conduct."[16] When several of the above factors present inconsistent interpretations, the U.C.C. establishes a priority of these factors, as follows: the express terms of the contract, course of performance, course of dealing, and usage of trade.[17]

C. Parol Evidence Considerations

Once a contract is reduced to writing, the general rule is that the writing becomes the best evidence of the bargain. In that case it is very difficult to contradict or refute provisions in the written agreement. U.C.C. Section 2-202 provides that when the parties to a contract intend that the writing serve as a "final expression of their agreement with respect to such terms as are included therein," the writing "may not be contradicted . . . but may only be explained or supplemented." Parol evidence is evidence found outside the terms of the written agreement. In most cases, parol evidence will be allowed to assist in interpreting an agreement only to the extent the contract provisions are ambiguous. Where an ambiguity is found, evidence may be introduced concerning usage of trade, course of performance, etc. In contrast, where the contract is clear and complete by its terms, it generally cannot be changed or supplemented by parol evidence.

D. Contract Performance

It is a general rule of contract law that the parties must act in good faith. This requirement is one which cannot be disclaimed either expressly or impliedly. With forward contracts the particulars of performance may be negotiated at a date later than the date of execution. Courts have given open term contracts a liberal application in situations where the purchaser had the sole right to determine if the quantity of goods was adequate, and whether the quality of goods was acceptable. Thus, such agreements will be upheld on the basis of their commercial reasonableness. Too many open terms, however, may render a contract void.[18]

When parties execute a contract they generally do so with the expectation that the contract will be fully performed. However, when performance becomes uncertain the U.C.C. provides that a potentially aggrieved party may demand assurances of due performance. If those assurances are not given within a reasonable time, not exceeding thirty days, the party's failure to give the assurance may be considered a repudiation of the contract.[19]

As the date for contract performance arrives, the seller-farmer has a duty to tender delivery of the goods specified in the contract. This is a condition precedent to the buyer's duties of acceptance and payment.[20] To "tender" the delivery the seller-farmer must "put and hold conforming goods at the buyer's disposition," and give him or her reasonable notice that the goods are available.[21] These requirements are based on the obligations of good faith of the parties and the custom of general dealing in the trade.[22] The place of delivery, absent contract terms to the contrary, is at the seller's place of business or his residence.[23]

When the contract requires that the farmer ship the goods to the market, or contains other provisions regarding shipment, he or she must "put the goods in the possession of such a carrier and make such a contract for their transportation as may be reasonable having regard to the nature of the goods. . . ." The farmer-seller must also obtain and tender the proper documents which enable the buyer to take possession of the goods.[24]

Upon proper tender or delivery of the goods, several rights and duties on the part of the buyer arise. First, the buyer is under a duty to accept conforming goods and to pay for them by any means or in any manner "current in the ordinary course of business unless the seller demands payment in legal tender . . . ."[25] Prior to acceptance, the buyer, of course, has a right to inspect the goods[26] unless the contract provides otherwise.[27] Generally the buyer must take affirmative steps to reject the goods. Either affirmative acceptance or acquiescence deprives the buyer of the right to further reject.[28] After that point, to reject the goods the buyer must prove that the goods do not conform to the contract, and that, as a result, the contract is substantially impaired.[29]

E. Breach of Contract

Under the U.C.C. the seller must exactly comply with the requirements of the contract or be in breach of the contract.[30] Although the U.C.C. does not define the term breach, it recognizes the terms in the agreement which may define what occurrences constitute a breach of that particular contract. In addition, anticipatory repudiation occurs when "one

303

party to the agreement disables himself or gives notice that he will not fulfill" the contract.[31] Anticipatory repudiation is a form of breach of contract.

As a general rule, it has been difficult for farmers in breach of contract cases to raise the defense that non-performance is excused due to the occurrence of a natural disaster which has resulted in crop failure. In general, the failure to produce a crop as a result of crop failure will not excuse performance of the contract. The seller will be in breach of the contract unless the promised commodity is obtained from another source and delivered to the buyer. The exception to this rule is if the parties expressly provided that performance would be excused in the event of adverse weather. U.C.C. Section 2-615 provides that the seller under these adverse conditions can terminate the contract without breach only if the conditions which cause the failure of performance were considered basic to the contract when it was made. A breach may also be excused if it is the result of a governmental regulation that makes performance impossible.

There are very few cases to illustrate how commercial law applies to crop failures. Moreover, the reported cases are not uniform in their conclusions.[32] Comment 9 to U.C.C. Section 2-615 relates specifically to farmers and indicates that the U.C.C. provides relief only to the extent that the contract identifies crops which are to be grown on particular designated land. Where performance is impossible because of crop failure, a farmer who has contracted to sell crops to be grown on designated land may be regarded as falling either within the section on casualty to identified goods or within U.C.C. Section 2-615. The farmer's performance may be excused, when there is a failure of the specified crop, because of the destruction of the identified goods or because of the failure of a basic assumption underlying the contract.

F. Remedies

When a seller or purchaser breaches obligations under the contract they may be subject to certain remedies available to the aggrieved party. In this respect, the U.C.C. provides for the liberal administration of remedies in order that the aggrieved party be put in as good a position as if the other party had fully performed.[33] For example, when the seller has breached, the buyer may cancel the contract and obtain restitution and/or damages. Either party may seek to have the contract specifically performed where the other party has defaulted. Furthermore, the contract may provide for liquidated damages.

III.   Sale of Diseased or Defective Livestock
        The production and sale of livestock is a very significant segment of American agriculture. If the animals which are sold are subsequently discovered to be diseased or otherwise defective, the question arises as to the extent to which the seller may be liable for the loss. Since animals are living things, it is possible that the cause of the defect is attributable to the natural but unfortunate characteristics of the animal itself, rather than to the seller. On the other hand, the defect may be the result of a lack of care on the part of the seller, or perhaps the defect was known to the seller prior to the sale, and was not disclosed to the buyer. Alternatively, the defect may be the result of something that occurred after the sale and is therefore the buyer's responsibility. Determinations with respect to these matters may be critical to the issue of liability. This is a particularly difficult matter when the defect or disease does not appear until after the sale takes place.
        Although federal and state health regulations provide an incentive for sellers to sell healthy animals, these rules and regulations do not typically address the question of liability when a disease or defect is detected in an animal. As a result, the fact that a seller was not be in full compliance with an applicable health regulation will be only one of several relevant facts that must be considered. Furthermore, it will usually be necessary to find another legal basis upon which the disappointed buyer may base his or her liability claim. Several legal theories have been developed to deal with this situation. These include approaches such as breach of contract, including breach of warranties, and negligence.

        A. U.C.C. Theories
        Perhaps the most commonly used theories by which liability is imposed on livestock sellers are the warranty theories available under the Uniform Commercial Code.[34]

1. Express Warranties

A livestock seller can create an express warranty, either oral or written, by making an affirmation of fact or promise which relates to the animals which he or she is selling. This affirmation of fact or promise is considered to be a part of the basis of the bargain and thereby creates an express warranty that the animals sold will conform to the affirmation or promises. Similarly, a seller creates an express warranty in the description of the animals to be sold. This also is treated as part of the basis of the bargain and has the impact of warranting that the animals will conform to the description. Finally, an express warranty is assumed when the seller asserts or promises that a particular animal is representative of all the animals he or she is selling. Here, no formal language or specific intention is needed to form a warranty. However, oral warranties can later be excluded if the agreement is reduced to writing and is intended to be the final agreement between the parties.

For example, in the case of Naaf v. Griffitts,[35] the court upheld a livestock seller's liability for breach of an express warranty on the basis of advertisements. These advertisements claimed that the heifers were "to calf September, October". Moreover, express oral representations were also made. The buyer told the seller that he wanted heifers that could calve. In response, the seller reaffirmed that the heifers were pregnant, based on tests conducted by a veterinarian.

It should be noted that express warranties will not be subject to exclusion or modification in the same manner as implied warranties. In fact, once it has been made, an express warranty can rarely be disclaimed. According to U.C.C. Section 2-316(1), words or conduct which tend to negate express warranties are to be construed as consistent with the warranty and disregarded to the extent that such construction is unreasonable. For example, in the case of Young & Cooper v. Vestring,[36] the court found that the buyer's acceptance of the herd without testing for brucellosis did not override the express warranties that appear to have been made by the seller. Likewise, in Wege v. Harris,[37] the fact that the buyer was an experienced buyer and had seen and inspected the cattle three times prior to the purchase was not sufficient to overcome express warranties.

306

2. Implied Warranties

The U.C.C. provides that two implied warranties may be recognized in contracts for the sale of goods.[38] These warranties are the implied warranty of fitness for a particular purpose and the implied warranty of merchantability, respectively. The warranties are imposed by operation of law for the protection of the buyer, and are generally construed liberally in favor of the buyer.

(a) Implied Warranty of Merchantability

The warranty of merchantability implies that the goods will "pass without objection in the trade under the contract description and are fit for the ordinary purposes for which such goods are used."[39] This implied warranty is created only in contracts for the sale of goods where the seller is a merchant, unless the warranty is expressly excluded or modified.[40] Furthermore, U.C.C. Section 2-314 states that "unless excluded or modified . . . a warranty that the goods shall be merchantable is implied . . . if the seller is a merchant with respect to goods of that kind." As a result, a seller must be a merchant with respect to the livestock before the warranty can be implied. Both livestock sale auctioneers and farmers have been held to be merchants for warranty purposes.[41]

(b) Implied Warranty of Fitness For a Particular Purpose

The implied warranty of fitness for a particular purpose is a more specific implied warranty. This warranty guarantees that goods subject to the contract are reasonably fit for the particular purpose for which the buyer purchased the goods. Whether a particular defendant knows of the purpose for which animals may be bought and whether the plaintiff relied on the skill and judgment of the defendant are questions of fact for the jury. Unlike the warranty of merchantability, which is implied where one party is a merchant, the implied warranty of fitness for a particular purpose can be imposed on anyone, regardless of their merchant status. In other words, under this section the farmer need not be a merchant to be liable. The legal obstacle to imposing liability under this theory is that reliance must be present. To impose the implied warranty of fitness, the buyer must show that the seller had "reason to know" the purpose for which the purchased goods were to be used. It is also not necessary to allege that the seller had knowledge of the defect. The courts have liberally construed this section to protect the buyer. In other words, courts typically find almost any "purpose" to be a particular purpose for the purchase of livestock. They have not required that the buyer show that the seller had actual knowledge of the buyer's purpose. For example, in Young & Cooper v. Vestring,[42] the Kansas Supreme Court found breeding to be a particular purpose when the buyer makes a purchase of breeding stock.

Reliance has also been found by the courts with little or no consideration given to how reasonable the reliance was. In Young & Cooper v. Vestring,[43] the seller stated prior to sale that the cattle had not been tested for brucellosis. Brucellosis was subsequently detected in the cattle. The Kansas Supreme Court imposed liability for breach of the implied warranty of fitness even though the seller had disclosed the fact that there had been no test for brucellosis conducted prior to the sale.

(c) Damages

As a general rule, the measurement of damages for livestock which are infected with a disease is either the difference in the value of the livestock, as warranted, less their value in a diseased condition, or the difference between the contract price and the value of the livestock in a diseased condition. The seller has also been held liable for the return of the buyer's purchase money under certain circumstances. This includes where the sale was in violation of a statute forbidding the sale of animals infected with disease or where the animals' diseased condition rendered them so worthless and caused the sale to be unsupported by consideration.

Special or consequential damages typically involve the interruption of the buyer's business, the loss of products produced by the livestock, the loss of the purchased animals' market value, the loss of future breeding, the costs of treating the diseased animal, the costs of protecting healthy animals against the disease, the loss from the spread of the disease to healthy animals, the loss from the spread of the disease to humans, the cost of destroying diseased carcasses and disinfecting premises, and the cost of transporting the livestock from the place of purchase to the place where the buyer intended to keep the animals. Approaches vary as to the seller's liability for these types of damages. For example, in Cudmore v. Tjoms-land,[44] the court affirmed a judgment based on a breach of a warranty that cattle were free of disease. However, the court did not allow a veterinarian's bill as an item of special damage because there was no evidence that the charge was reasonable. On the other hand, sellers have been held liable for costs associated with the treatment of diseased animals where courts have found that the seller knew or should have known that the animals were diseased.

Where expenses have been incurred to protect healthy animals from disease and to treat other animals that were affected by the spread of the disease, it has been held that the costs were too remote to allow recovery. The cost of disease protection devices, such as erecting or renting stables to isolate the healthy animals from the diseased ones, have occasionally been allowed as damages. In a non-U.C.C. case, Brouquet v. Tripp,[45] the Kansas court held that the buyer's consequential damages could properly include losses attributable to the fact that lambs born to the purchased diseased ewes had also been afflicted with the disease. The buyer had purchased a flock of sheep for breeding purposes under a warranty for fitness for a particular purpose. The court said the damages were recoverable if the lambs naturally and necessarily became diseased by running with the flock of diseased sheep. The court concluded that the death of lambs born prematurely because of the disease, or the death of the ewes during birth because of weakness from the disease, would also be recoverable as consequences of the seller's breach.

However, in a subsequent case, Lunger v. Colhouer,[46] the court narrowed the above holding. In Lunger, the court held that the purchaser of diseased hogs could recover for damage to his original herd only to the extent that the buyer had taken all reasonable actions, including the possibility of selling the original hogs on the market, to reduce damages. In addition, the court found the seller liable for costs incurred to disinfect the contaminated premises. The court relied upon sufficient proof that the seller knew or should have known the

309

animals sold were infected with the disease.

(d) Modifications of Implied Warranties

Efforts have been made to mitigate the seller's liability under implied warranties in livestock sales transactions and shift more risk to the buyer. The most commonly used approach has been for the seller to disclaim or to modify the implied warranty. As a general rule, such disclaimers of implied warranties have not been favored. They tend to be strictly construed against the seller. In most jurisdictions, the implied warranty of merchantability can be excluded or modified only if the language of the disclaimer uses the word "merchantability" and is conspicuous.[47] An exclusion of the implied warranty of fitness for a particular purpose also must be in writing and must be conspicuous.[48] An implied warranty could also be excluded or modified by course of dealing, course of performance or usage of trade.[49] The party which pleads these factors must show that the practice is done with regularity and that persons normally engaging in that trade or vocation would be aware of the practice.[50] The U.C.C. Comments also require that the usages be "currently observed by the great majority of decent dealers."[51]

In Fear Ranches v. Berry,[52] the Tenth Circuit Court of Appeals remanded a case to determine whether by trade custom there was no implied warranty that cattle were free from brucellosis. Similarly, in Kincheloe v. Geldmeier,[53] a Texas court found that the evidence supported the conclusion that a purchase of cattle was "as is" by usage of the trade. This exposed the buyer to the risk that the cattle were not free of disease. The court found that this practice was fully accepted by the buyers in the area.

An implied warranty may also be excluded or modified by the circumstances. This includes the circumstance where the buyer, before entering into the contract of sale, has had the opportunity to examine the goods or the sample or model, or has refused to examine the goods.[54] In that case, no implied warranty would be deemed to exist with regard to defects which an examination would have revealed. It should be noted, however, that this modification or exclusion of warranty could only occur when the buyer unreasonably fails to examine the goods before they are used and the resulting injuries are therefore attributable to the buyer's own inaction.

U.C.C. Section 2-316 has been modified in a number of states. A typical modification provides:

[W]ith respect to the sale of livestock, other than the sale of livestock for immediate slaughter, there shall be no implied warranties, except that the provisions of this paragraph shall not apply in any case where the seller knowingly sells livestock which is diseased.[55]

The impact of this provision is that sellers of livestock are not considered as having made any implied warranties of merchantability or of fitness for a particular purpose unless the sale is for immediate slaughter or the seller knows the animals are diseased.

Although the statutory exclusion of implied warranties prevents the buyer from seeking redress against the seller in many cases, it would appear that there will still be situations in which the implied warranties will be made by a seller and can be relied on by the buyer. Furthermore, the amendment of U.C.C. Section 2-316 is specifically confined to implied warranties. It has no impact on other remedies which are based on express warranty or on tort theories such as negligence, fraud, misrepresentation or strict liability. Furthermore, the buyer is clearly not deprived of other U.C.C. remedies, such as the right to reject nonconforming goods or remedies for breach of express warranty.

B. Alternative Theories
    1. Animal Disease Control Statutes

One of the most important functions of a state Department of Agriculture is the prevention and control of livestock and animal diseases. Since the economic well-being of the animal industry depends on the effectiveness of identification and prevention of animal diseases, states are held to have extensive police power authority in this area. With the cooperation of the federal government, states have traditionally exercised the primary role in animal disease control efforts. State disease control programs typically consist of the following general elements:

    1. The appointment of a specific agency to administer the

disease control effort;

2. The authorization of disease control programs which may involve the inspection, testing, quarantine, destruction and treatment of animals or premises, as necessary. Specialized control programs generally exist for particular diseases such as bovine brucellosis, bovine tuberculosis, swine brucellosis, pseudorabies, equine infectious anemia, mange, Spanish fever, hog cholera, Bang's disease, and vesicular exanthema in swine;

3. The prohibition of any acts by individuals which would be considered violations of the diseased stock or quarantine regulations, including:

   a. the possession of domestic animals with any contagious or infectious disease;

   b. knowingly allowing the animals to become infected or diseased;

   c. permitting the diseased animals to run at large;

   d. keeping the animal where other animals may be exposed to the disease; and/or

   e. selling, shipping, driving, trading or giving away the diseased or infected animals (except to a regularly licensed disposal plant);

4. The establishment of a mechanism for appraising and paying indemnification claims to owners of diseased livestock which are legally required to be destroyed;

5. The creation of a system of inspection and control to regulate the movement of animals into and through the state;

6. The establishment of entry requirements for animals shipped from other states and provisions for the issuance of health certificates;

7. The requirement that infectious, contagious or communicable diseases be properly reported;

8. The allowance that public sales of animals may be regulated and subjected to identification and record keeping requirements; and

9. The requirement that dead animals be properly disposed of and that businesses which dispose of dead animals be properly licensed.[56]

Although the diseased animal control statutes do not specifically create a basis for a legal action by the buyer against the seller, these statutes are relevant to the issue of liability in two respects. First, the statutory terms often provide that the statutes may not be construed in a manner which prevents the recovery of damages in civil actions.[57] These provisions indicate that the measures taken against sellers under the statutory program are not intended to be the exclusive remedy by which the problem may be resolved. Thus, these statutes neither preempt nor bar separate civil actions for damages. Second, it may be argued that a violation of a statutory program, particularly its criminal provisions, is itself evidence of negligence per se.

2. Packers and Stockyards Act

Section 308 of the Packers and Stockyards Act,[58] makes anyone who violates the Act, or any order by the Secretary of Agriculture relative to the sale, purchase or handling of live-stock under the Act, liable to injured persons for the full damages which result from the violation. The Act provides a basis for imposing liability upon sellers who sell through posted stockyards. Claims for damages pursuant to the Act may be made either through a complaint to the Secretary or by an action in a Federal district court.

When a complaint is made to the Secretary, the petition must be sent within 90 days after the cause of action accrues. The defendant is then given a reasonable time to satisfy or answer the complaint. If the complaint is not satisfied, the Secretary is required to conduct an investigation. After a hearing, the Secretary may order that reparation be paid to the injured person. If the defendant does not pay damages by the date set in the order, a suit may be brought in the appropriate U.S. Federal district court to enforce the order. The order constitutes prima facie evidence of the facts in the District Court proceeding.

An example of how the Packers and Stockyards Act may be used by the buyer of diseased livestock is found in the reparations case of Steven P. Russell v. R.L. Schmidt, DVM. et. al.[59] In Russell, a complaint was filed claiming $4,870.23 allegedly due as a result of the sale of sick cattle. The facts revealed that 250 cattle were consigned to the Miami County Livestock Company, which operated as a market agency in a posted stockyard in Paola, Kansas. The sale of the animals was prohibited by the attending veterinarian, who determined that the animals were sick. The visibly sick animals were separated from the other animals. The next day, the seller, with the active assistance of the Livestock Company, transported the 215 not-visibly-sick animals and consigned them for sale at the Kansas City stockyards. The agent for the complainant purchased a total of 70 heifers, including 46 of the not-visibly-sick animals that were prohibited from being sold in Paola the day before. In granting a reparation award, the judicial officer relied on general principles of misrepresentation to hold that the livestock company had engaged in fraud and that direct misrepresentation had occurred. The opinion quoted with approval the court in Barton v. Dours,[60] which stated that "if a fact known by one party and not the other is so vital that if the mistake were mutual the contract would be voidable and the party knowing the fact also knows that the other does not know it, non-disclosure is not privileged and is fraudulent." The officer then took official notice that the "custom of the trade" in a livestock marketing business would call for disclosure that the animals were subject to a probability of infection. Since the disease factor was not disclosed, there had been a direct misrepresentation. The measure of damages was calculated to be the difference between the market value of the goods at the time and place of acceptance and the value they would have had if they had been in the condition as represented. The reparations procedure under the Packers and Stockyards Act is discussed in more detail in Chapter 11.

3. Tort Theories

Several tort theories may be used as a basis for imposing liability upon sellers. These include the theories of negligence, fraud and strict liability.

The tort of negligence consists of an act or omission on the part of the defendant (seller) which breaches a duty of care owed to the plaintiff (buyer), which causes the plaintiff to be damaged or harmed. The duty of care owed by the seller may either be a special duty imposed by statute or case law, or a general duty to act as a reasonable person under the circumstances.

In the sale of livestock, the negligence theory of liability generally requires that a defect which caused the damage must exist in the livestock before the sale. Furthermore, it is necessary that the defect be the result of the failure on the part of the seller to take the steps which might be reasonably expected to prevent the defect.

The specific standard of care may be determined by custom as well as by specific statute. For example, in the case of <u>Olson v. Molacek Bros. of Calloway, Minn.</u>[61] it was alleged that the sale of animals infected with infectious bovine rhinotracheitis in violation of state livestock statutes constituted negligence <u>per se</u>. The court suggested that liability under the statute on a negligence theory was not preempted by the adoption of the Uniform Commercial Code and its warranty theories.

Similarly, negligence was asserted as the basis for liability in <u>Dekalb Hybrid Seed Co. v. Agge,</u>[62] with respect to the purchase of diseased baby chicks. In this case, the seller prevailed because the buyer was unable to prove the specific acts on the part of the seller which would constitute negligence. On the other hand, in <u>Anderson v. Blackfoot Livestock Commission. Co.,</u>[63] the plaintiff prevailed on a negligence theory. The court found that under the circumstances presented, the animals must have become infected while under the seller's control.

Fraud is a more difficult theory to establish than negligence since the plaintiff generally must show a false representation of fact, known to be false and made with the intent to induce the plaintiff to rely on the fact, to the plaintiff's damage. In the case of <u>Citizens State Bank v. Gilmore,</u>[64] the court considered the liability of a seller for fraud when a bank had taken a security interest in the cattle to finance the sale. When the buyer went bankrupt, the bank acquired the cattle and discovered that they were infected with brucellosis. Moreover, it was proven that the cattle had been quarantined at the time of sale. The court held that the bank could base its claim on fraud if the seller knew that the buyer would secure a loan from the bank based on the seller's representations as to the health of the cattle. On the other hand, the failure to disclose material facts relating to the transaction is at least intentional misrepresentation and would

315

be considered fraud.

As a general rule, strict liability is not available to buyers of defective livestock. In most cases, courts have been reluctant to apply the concept to animals. The strict liability concept is largely a judicial reaction to the difficulty and unfairness of requiring a plaintiff to prove negligence under circumstances in which it has been nearly impossible to demonstrate the specific manner in which the defendant has acted to create a defective product.

The strict liability theory imposes an absolute duty on the manufacturer to provide a product that is free of any unreasonably dangerous defect. As far as the sale of animals is concerned, courts have taken the position that animals are not "products" in the same sense as are manufactured goods. Furthermore, with respect to the condition of the animals, the position generally taken by the courts is that it is unfair to impose on the seller the risks which are associated with guaranteeing a disease-free animal.

For example, in the case of Two Rivers v. Curtiss Breeding Service,[65] the court refused to apply the theory of strict liability where semen sold by the seller allegedly caused syndactylism in the offspring. The claim was predicated on the argument that the seller had sold a genetically defective product that was unreasonably dangerous. The court held that because of difficulties in the legal characterization of "product" and "defect," the case was governed by rules of commercial law rather than products liability. Moreover, the court reasoned that even if the bull semen was defective, it could not be considered unreasonably dangerous. Finally, the court was persuaded that by custom, the risk of a genetic defect falls on the owner of the herd, not upon the seller of the semen.

The court in Anderson v. Farmer's Hybrid Companies, Inc.[66] also rejected the strict liability argument. In Anderson, the critical issue was whether hogs could be characterized as "products" for purposes of the products liability doctrine, including strict liability. The court observed that the definition of "products" was construed quite narrowly to avoid inclusion of things whose character is easily susceptible to changes outside the control of the seller.

Living creatures, such as the swine in the instant

316

case, are by their nature in a constant process of
internal development and growth, and they are also
participants in a constant interaction with the
environment around them as part of their development. Thus, living creature have no fixed nature in
the same sense as the blood or the mushrooms
[involved in prior cases] can be said to have a fixed
nature at the time they enter the stream of
commerce.[67]

Using this rationale, it could be argued that the semen
in the Two Rivers case, noted above, had a fixed nature when it
was sold (or offered for sale) and therefore could have been a
"product" for purposes of the doctrine of strict liability.
Conversely, it could be argued that the genetic composition of
semen constitutes a "living creature" and is therefore excluded
from the definition of a "product."

There has been a discernible trend towards using the
concept of strict liability in agricultural products liability cases.
This is true particularly for animal food, drugs and for products
which cause personal injuries.[68] In a case involving a sale of
animals, Bever v. Aquarium Supply Co.[69] the court refused to
dismiss a strict liability claim. In Bever an employee contracted
a disease from handling sick hamsters. The court stated that,
"[T]here is no reason why a breeder, distributor or vendor who
places a diseased animal in the stream of commerce should be
less accountable for his actions that one who markets a
defective manufactured product." The risk presented to human
well being by a diseased animal is as great and probably greater
than that created by a defective manufactured product and in
many instances, for the average customer, a disease in an animal
can be as difficult to detect as a defect in a manufactured
product.

IV.   Sale of Diseased or Defective Seed

Since 1939, purchasers of agricultural seeds have been
the beneficiaries of the Federal Seed Act,[70] which regulates the
interstate marketing of agricultural seeds. This Act is specifically designed to protect buyers against purchasing defective or
contaminated seed. It also requires that purchasers be informed
of the contents of the seed being marketed. To accomplish this,

the Act imposes labeling and disclosure requirements on seed producers and distributors of lawn seed, forage and field crop seed and vegetable seeds "used for seeding purposes in the United States," which are transported or delivered for transportation in interstate commerce.[71]

The labeling requirements prohibit interstate shipments of improperly labeled seed. Generally, the labels must disclose the name and kind or variety of the seed contained in the package, and the percentage by weight of the variety of seed represented in the total weight of the container. If the seed is a hybrid, that also must be stated on the label. Furthermore, the label must contain the lot number, origin of the seed, percentage by weight of weed seeds, the kind and rate of occurrence of noxious weed seeds, the percentage of germination, the date of the germination test and the date after which any inoculant used on the seed is not claimed to be effective.[72]

The Act prohibits any person from distributing seed pursuant to false advertisements.[73] The term "advertisements" is broadly defined to include all representations, other than those on the label, relating to the seed. When the labels contain warranties relating to the quality of the seed, the Act's advertisement restrictions apparently protect the farmer only as to misrepresentations concerning plant variety. The Act does not protect the farmer as to misrepresentation concerning seed performance.

Violations of the Act may result in administrative action by the Agricultural Marketing Service. However, the Act does not expressly provide a private civil remedy for the seed purchaser who is harmed by a violation of the Act. As a result, redress must be sought against the producer or distributor under general tort or contract law. On the other hand, if the injury stems from the failure of the producer or seller to comply with the Federal Seed Act, that fact may serve as the basis for a negligence action or to create warranties which can serve as the basis of relief.[74]

The labeling requirements of the Act provide the best potential basis for relief to the purchaser. The federal label requirements may serve as the basis for a claim of express warranty or may create express warranties of merchantability and fitness for a particular purpose. The label itself may be regarded as an express warranty as to certain matters since it must specifically disclose seed variety, germination, weed seed content and similar matters. However, sellers frequently attempt to limit liability for breach of warranty to the purchase price of the seed. The Act does not prohibit the use of disclaimers in invoices, advertising or labeling but it does provide that these are not a good defense on any prosecution or other proceeding under the Act.[75] However, the attempts to disclaim or limit liability are generally not effective since the express warranty and attempted disclaimer are inconsistent. Furthermore, the U.C.C. provides that "negation or limitation is inoperative to the extent that such construction is unreasonable."[76] Some courts have found that disclaimer or limited liability efforts were inconsistent with required descriptions of seed.[77] Others have found alternate approaches to avoiding the effect of a disclaimer, particularly if negligence or intentional violation of the law could be shown.[78] In addition, some courts have found a violation of the statutes to constitute negligence per se.[79]

If disclosures or limited liability provision are used to exclude or modify implied warranty provisions they must strictly comply with the U.C.C. provisions which permit exclusion or modifications.[80] If they are not disclaimed they may serve as the basis for liability.[81]

V.   Special Problems in Dealing With Grain
When grain is delivered to an elevator, the grain is weighed and the farmer will be issued either a weight ticket or scale ticket. These documents reflect both the quantity and grade of the grain received. The manner in which the grain is held by the warehouse is determined by whether the grain is considered sold at the time it is received by the elevator. If the grain is sold to the elevator, the scale ticket will be exchanged for a sales contract. The sales contract may contain a definite price term and contemplates that payment will be made at a future date. In the alternative, the contract may leave the sale price to be decided at some future time. The agreement may also reflect that no sale is intended and that the grain is only to be stored. This creates a bailment relationship between the farmer and the elevator. If this is the case, a warehouse receipt

319

will be issued to replace the scale ticket. If no receipt is issued, the grain is treated as being in open storage and the scale ticket will be the evidence of the farmer's title interest in the grain.[82]

In cases where grain is sold to the elevator prior to actual delivery, such as under a forward contract, the farmer may demand that the elevator give adequate assurance that it will perform its obligations under the contract.[83] If this assurance is not given, the farmer may treat the contract as repudiated by the elevator. The farmer may also refuse to tender the grain except in exchange for cash.[84] Finally, the farmer may seek to have the contract specifically enforced.[85]

The relationship with the grain elevator is more difficult for the farmer where the grain is sold on a deferred pricing basis and the elevator becomes insolvent or is declared bankrupt. In this situation, the seller has only a limited right to reclaim the grain. The U.C.C. provides that:

> Where the seller discovers that the buyer has received goods on credit while insolvent he may reclaim the goods upon demand within 10 days after the receipt, but if misrepresentation of solvency has been made to the particular seller in writing within 3 months before delivery, the 10 day limitation does not apply.[86]

Upon the occurrence of insolvency or bankruptcy, the farmer is an unsecured creditor of the elevator and has lower priority than most other claimants.

Recent amendments to the Bankruptcy Code[87] provide some additional protection to the farmer who has placed bailed grain in an insolvent or bankrupt elevator operation. Under Section 546(c) of the Bankruptcy Code, the trustee of the bankruptcy estate is subordinated to the seller's right to reclaim the grain. If reclamation of the grain is properly sought, the court can deny the farmer the right to repossess the grain only if it is secured with a lien. If reclaiming the grain is not possible, the court may give the seller's claim priority status as an administrative expense of the bankruptcy proceeding.

In an attempt to give farmers even more protection, the 1984 amendments to the Bankruptcy Reform Act[88] provided that farmers may be given priority status against the elevator to the extent of $2,000 per individual. This is a distinct benefit to farmers whose status would otherwise be that of unsecured creditors. Furthermore, the court is given authority to expedite the determination of the respective interests in the grain.

A farmer whose grain has merely been placed in storage is treated as a tenant in common with others who claim an identical interest in the stored grain. All of these farmers share pro rata in a superior interest in the grain to that of the elevator. However, since these claimants share proportionately in the stored grain, they usually will not receive the full amount of the grain represented by the scale tickets or warehouse receipts.[89] Furthermore, the farmer's interest in the grain may be defeated by someone who has purchased the grain and taken physical delivery of it as a "holder in due course". This is because U.C.C. Section 7-205 provides:

> A buyer in the ordinary course of business of fungible goods sold and delivered by a warehouseman who is also in the business of buying and selling such goods takes free of any claim under a warehouse receipt even though it has been duly negotiated.[90]

Section 7-205 applies to farmers, according to the official comments to this section:

> Purposes. The typical case covered by this section is that of the warehouseman-dealer in grain, and the substantive question at issue is whether in case the warehouseman become insolvent the receipt holders shall be able to trace and recover grain shipped to farmers and other purchasers from the elevator. This was possible under the old acts, although courts were eager to find estoppels to prevent it. The practical difficulty of tracing fungible grain means that the preservation of this theoretical right adds little to the commercial acceptability of negotiable grain receipts, which really circulate on the credit of the warehouseman. Moreover, on default of the warehouseman, the receipt holders at least share in what grain remains, whereas retaking the grain from a good faith cash purchaser reduces him completely to the status of general creditor in a situation where there was very little he could do to guard against the loss.[91]

FOOTNOTES

1. For purposes of financing the purchase of goods, goods are classified as consumer goods, equipment, inventory, and farm products. See U.C.C. § 9-109. This classification is mutually exclusive in that if goods are deemed to be in one class, they will not be in another. Farm products are defined as crops or livestock or supplies used or produced in farming operations in the possession of a debtor engaged in raising, fattening, grazing or other farming operations.

2. See, e.g., U.C.C. § 1-203, good faith obligations; § 2-201(2), formal requirements of the statute of frauds; § 2-205, firm offers; § 2-207, additional terms on acceptance or confirmation; § 2-209(2), modification, rescission and waiver; § 2-314, implied warranty; § 2-326, sale on approval, sale or return; § 2-402, rights of seller's creditors against goods sold; § 2-403(2), power to transfer; § 2-509(3), risk of loss in absence of breach; § 2-603, duties to rightfully reject goods; § 2-605(1)(b), waiver of objection by failure to particularize; § 2-609(1) and (2), right to adequate assurance of performance.

3. U.C.C. § 2-201.

4. U.C.C. § 2-201(2).

5. U.C.C. § 2-205.

6. U.C.C. § 2-107.

7. U.C.C. §§ 2-207(2), 84-2-104(3).

8. The following cases have held farmers not to be merchants: Cook Grains Inc. v. Fallis, 395 S.W.2d 555 (Ark. 1965); Oloffson v. Coomer, 296 N.E.2d 871 (Ill. App. 1973); Loeb & Co. v. Schreiner, 321 So. 2d 199 (Ala. 1975); Rush Johnson Farms Inc. v. Mo. Farmers Assn, 555 S.W.2d 61 (Mo. App. 1977); Terminal Grain Corp. v. Freeman, 270 N.W.2d 806 (S.D. 1978); Lish v. Compton, 547 P.2d 233 (Utah 1976); Pierson v.

Arnst, 534 F. Supp. 360 (D. Mont. 1982). The following cases have held farmers to be merchants: Ohio Grain Co. v. Swisshelm, 318 N.E.2d 428 (Ohio App. 1973); Campbell v. Yokel, 313 N.E.2d 628 (Ill. App. 1974); Sierens v. Clawson, 328 N.E.2d 559 (Ill. 1975); Continental Grain Co. v. Harbach, 400 F. Supp. 695 (D. Ill. 1975); Cargill v. Gaard, 267 N.W.2d 22 (Wis. 1978); Bradford v. Northwest Ala. Livestock Assn, 379 So. 2d 609 (Ala. App. 1980).

9. 219 Kan. 171, 547 P.2d 323 (1976).

10. 6 Kan. App. 196, 627 P.2d 367 (1981).

11. 219 Kan. at 176-177.

12. 6 Kan. App. 2d 196, 627 P.2d. 367 (1981).

13. 102 U.S. 564 (1880).

14. U.C.C. § 1-103.

15. U.C.C. § 1-205(2).

16. U.C.C. § 1-205(1).

17. U.C.C. §§ 1-205(4), 1-208(2).

18. See, e.g., Price v. Wiesner, 83 Kan. 343, 111 P. 439 (1910).

19. U.C.C. § 2-609(1).

20. U.C.C. §§ 2-301, 2-507(1).

21. U.C.C. § 2-503(1).

22. U.C.C. § 2-204. See, e.g., Bossemeyer Bros. v. Woodson County Grain Co., 108 Kan. 534, 196 P. 431 (1921).

23. U.C.C. § 2-308.

24. U.C.C. § 2-504.

25. U.C.C. §§ 2-301, 2-511(2).

26. U.C.C. § 2-513.

27. U.C.C. § 2-512.

28. U.C.C. § 2-606.

29. U.C.C. § 2-608.

30. U.C.C. § 2-601.

31. Moore v. Security Trust and Life Ins. Co., 168 F. 496 (C.C.A. Kan. 1909).

32. See, e.g., Low's Ezy-Fry Potato Co. v. J. A. Wood Co., 26 Ag. Dec. 583, 4 UCC Rptr 483 (1967) where U.S.D.A. determined that:

> when "parties contemplate a sale of all or a certain part of the crop of a particular tract of land, and . . . the crop fails . . . non-performance is . . . excused; the contract, in the absence of express provision controlling the matter, being considered as subject to an implied condition (of success). . . ." See also Holly Hill Fruit Products Co. Inc. v. Bob Staton, Inc., 275 So. 2d 583 (Fla. 1973) (U.C.C. not mentioned), where seller was excused from performance of a contract for the sale of oranges based upon loss due to frost. The court in this case excused performance without regard to when the crops were grown, indicating that excuse is not limited to circumstances in which a farmer contracts based on crops of his own land, but is excused regardless of the source of the crops. Other cases have denied excuse because of failure to specify that crop came from the farmer's land. See Bunge Corp. v. Miller, 381 F. Supp. 176 (W.D. Tenn. 1974), (the court wouldn't submit the issue to the jury of whether the contract intended that the particular crop came from farmer's land); Bunge

Corporation v. Reeker, 519 F.2d 449 (1975) (boilerplate contract indicating beans to be grown in continental U.S. was construed to prevent farmer from utilizing excuse because the farmer had the ability to fulfill the contract obligation by purchasing beans elsewhere. No parol evidence allowed to show the parties intended otherwise.

33. U.C.C. § 2-711.

34. U.C.C. §§ 2-314, 2-315, 2-316.

35. 201 Kan. 64, 439 P.2d 83 (1968).

36. 214 Kan. 311, 521 P.2d 281 (1974).

37. 420 S.W.2d 255 (Tex. Civ. App. 1967).

38. U.C.C. § 2-314 (implied warranty of merchantability); U.C.C. § 2-315 (implied warranty of fitness).

39. U.C.C. § 2-314.

40. U.C.C. § 2-314.

41. In the case of Powers v. Coffeyville Livestock Sales, Co., 665 F.2d 311 (10th Cir. 1981), the court found that an auctioneer was a merchant within the meaning of the Kansas Uniform Commercial Code, and remanded the case for a further determination of the impact of that fact on implied warranties. In the case of Musil v. Hendrich, 6 Kan. App. 2d 1961, 627 P.2d 367 (1981), the court found that a farmer seller of hogs could be considered a merchant under the UCC, and as such, made an implied warranty of merchantability.

42. 214 Kan. 311, 521 P.2d 281 (1974).

43. 214 Kan. 311, 521 P.2d 281 (1974).

44. 266 P.2d 1058 (Wash. 1954).

45. 36 Kan. 700 (1887).

46. 130 Kan. 385, 286 P. 203 (1930).

47. U.C.C. § 2-316(2).

48. U.C.C. § 2-316(2).

49. U.C.C. § 2-316(3)(c).

50. See, e.g., Holcomb v. Cessna Aircraft Co., 439 F.2d 1150 (5th Cir. 1971).

51. See Comments to U.C.C. § 2-213.

52. 470 F.2d 905 (10th Cir. 1972).

53. 619 S.W.2d 272 (Tex. Civ. App. 1981).

54. U.C.C. § 2-316(3)(a),(b).

55. This modification appears in K.S.A. § 84-2-316 but is identical or similar to that in many other states. See Uchtmann, Sarhan, and Charalambous, "Do Statutory Exclusions of Implied Warranties in Livestock Sales Immunize Sellers from Liability?" 8 Okla. City U. L. Rev. 21 (1983).

56. For a specific statutory example see the Kansas program at K.S.A. § 47-601 et seq.

57. See, e.g., K.S.A. § 47-644.

58. 7 U.S.C. § 209(a).

59. P & S Docket No. 5877, decided Aug. 10, 1982 (41 A.D. 1571).

60. 285 S.W. 988 (Mo. 1926).

61. 341 N.W.2d 375 (N.D. 1983).

62. 293 S.W.2d 64 (Tex. App. 1956).

63. 375 P.2d 704 (Idaho 1962).

64. 226 Kan. 662, 603 P.2d 605 (1979).

65. 624 F.2d 1242 (5th Cir. 1986).

66. 408 N.E.2d 1194 (Ill. 1980).

67. 408 N.E.2d at 1199.

68. See Note, Strict Liability and UCC Warranties Down on the Farm, 21 S. Dak. L. Rev. 669 (1976).

69. 404 N.Y.S.2d 778 (1977).

70. 7 U.S.C. § 1551 et seq.

71. 7 U.S.C. § 1561(7)(A).

72. 7 U.S.C. § 1571.

73. 7 U.S.C. § 1575.

74. See, Wadley, "The Federal Seed Act; Regulation of Seed Sales and Remedies Available to the Seed Purchaser" 27 S. Dak. L. Rev. 453 (1982).

75. 7 U.S.C. § 1574.

76. U.C.C. § 2-316(a).

77. See, e.g., Walcott & Steele, Inc. v. Carpenter, 436 S.W.2d 820 (1969); Mallery v. Northfield Seed Co., 264 N.W. 573 (1936).

78. Agricultural Serv. Ass'n v. Ferry-Morse Seed Co. 551 F.2d 1057 (6th Cir. 1977); Dessert Seed Co. v. Drew Farmers Supply, Inc., 248 Ark. 858, 454 S.W.2d 307 (1970).

79. Gibson v. Worley Mills, Inc., 614 F.2d 464 (5th Cir. 1980); Klein v. Asgrow Seed Co., 246 Cal. App. 2d 87, 54 Cal. Rptr. 609 (3rd Dist. 1966).

80. U.C.C. § 2-316(2).

81. See Ganthier v. Bogard Seed Co., 377 So. 2d 1290 (La. Ct. App. 1980) where the court recognized implied warranties as the basis for the claim but found insufficient evidence of breach. Also see, Agricultural Services Ass'n, Inc. v. Ferry-Morse Seed Co., Inc., 551 F.2d 1057 (6th Cir. 1977).

82. See Flour Mills of America, Inc. v. Burrus Mills, 174 Kan. 709, 258 P.2d 341 (1953); K.S.A. 84-2-107.

83. U.C.C. § 2-609.

84. U.C.C. § 2-702.

85. U.C.C. § 2-716. But see, In re Cox Cotton Co., 8 B.R. 682 (Bankr. E.D. Ark. 1981).

86. U.C.C. § 2-702(2).

87. 11 U.S.C. § 546(c)(2).

88. 11 U.S.C. § 507.

89. See, e.g., United States v. Luther, 225 F.2d 449 (10th Cir. 1955).

90. U.C.C. § 7-205.

91. U.C.C. § 7-205.

CHAPTER 10

MARKETING OF FRUITS, VEGETABLES AND MILK

I.   Introduction

Producers of fruits, nuts, vegetables and milk are subject to federal legislation which affects the marketing of those commodities in ways considerably different from the laws which regulate the major program crops. The two (2) major federal laws which regulate this area of agricultural commerce are the Agricultural Marketing Agreement Act of 1937 and the Perishable Agricultural Commodities Act. These two legislative programs are the focus of this Chapter. The provisions of the Agricultural Marketing Agreement Act of 1937[1] authorize the Secretary of Agriculture to enter into marketing agreements, after notice and a hearing, with producers, processors, and others who are engaged in the handling of agricultural commodities which are in commerce or affect commerce. These marketing agreements are exempt from antitrust laws. In appropriate situations, marketing orders may be used instead of marketing agreements.[2] An order may be issued after notice and a hearing when the Secretary of Agriculture has reason to believe that the issuance of an order will tend to effectuate the declared policy of the 1937 Act. The declared purpose of the Act is to promote the interests of producers and consumers by maintaining an orderly flow of commodities during their normal marketing season in order to avoid unreasonable fluctuations in supplies and prices. The constitutionality of the 1937 Act and its market regulation under the Fifth and Fourteenth Amendments was upheld by the United States Supreme Court in U.S. v. Rock Royal Coop., Inc.[3] In Rock Royal, the Court also held that the Act was a proper delegation of legislative power to the Secretary of Agriculture, and to the producers and cooperatives who participated in the order.

Producers of certain perishable agricultural commodities (fresh fruits and vegetables), are provided with important protections in the Perishable Agricultural Commodities Act (PACA).[4] PACA was enacted in 1930 to suppress unfair and fraudulent practices in the marketing of those commodities and to promote their orderly flow in interstate commerce. Aside from the regulation of the marketing of these commodities, PACA provides a reparations procedure whereby buyers and sellers of perishable commodities may claim money damages which result from PACA violations through an administrative proceeding as an alternative to court litigation.

II.   Marketing Agreements and Orders
Marketing orders provide a method whereby farmers regulate the marketing of their products through the auspices of a government marketing program. Farmers use marketing orders to establish control over the quantity and quality of the product to be marketed. Marketing orders specify various marketing conditions that must be maintained in order for a farmer to market the product. Marketing orders constitute a voluntary program in the sense that they are operated through a referendum procedure. Once established, the orders have a mandatory effect on all designated crops within the designated production or marketing areas. This means that certain producers will be required to comply with the orders on an involuntary basis.

A.   Authorized Products
Marketing orders have been promulgated for approximately 50 fruit, vegetable and specialty crops, and for milk. (See 7 CFR Part 900 for a list of the orders which are in effect). The orders affect both price and supply through quality and quantity control, respectively. Quality and quantity control for agricultural commodities other than milk may be achieved by use of the terms and conditions which are authorized in the 1937 Act.[5]

The Act authorizes a marketing agreement and order to be issued "for such production or marketing areas as are practicable."[6] Marketing orders provide information to regulated parties which encourages fair trade practices. Moreover, marketing orders reduce the risk of price instability. Some commentators contend that marketing orders increase the prices received by producers.[7]

330

1. <u>Marketing Orders for Fruits, Nuts and Vegetables</u>

The following fruits, nuts and vegetables and their products may be covered in a marketing order:

1. fruits (including filberts, almonds, pecans and walnuts);
2. apples produced in Washington, Oregon, Idaho, New York, Michigan, Maryland, New Jersey, Indiana, California, Maine, Vermont, New Hampshire, Rhode Island, Massachusetts, Connecticut, Colorado, Utah, New Mexico, Illinois, and Ohio;
3. pears, olives, grapefruit, cherries, cranberries, and apples from the states listed above except Washington, Oregon and Idaho, for canning and freezing;
4. vegetables, not including those for canning and freezing, except asparagus, and not including potatoes for canning, freezing and other processing;
5. grapefruit for canning and freezing if the order is approved by processors having canned or frozen more than 50% of the total by volume of the commodity canned or frozen during a representative period;[8]
6. Cherries, apples and cranberries for canning or freezing are subject to orders only if 50% of the processors by volume who have engaged in canning or freezing or marketing the commodity in a particular area vote to approve the order.

Orders may also be made applicable to other fruits and vegetables and their products. Milk, hops, tobacco, naval stores, and honey are also authorized for coverage in a marketing order. However, potatoes which are used for canning, freezing, or other processing are not eligible for marketing orders.[9]

While the Secretary is authorized to fix a minimum price for milk through a marketing order, there is no authorization to fix prices for any other commodity covered by the Act. Instead, the Secretary may only employ market controls in an effort to effectuate the declared policies of the Act.[10]

2. <u>Milk Marketing Orders</u>

Marketing orders for milk and milk products specify minimum prices for fluid milk which must be paid to producers, who are usually organized as cooperatives. Orders are

331

promulgated by a rulemaking procedure consistent with the Administrative Procedure Act guidelines. An order becomes effective upon the required approval of producers through a referendum procedure. The orders establish a system for classifying milk prices and distributing the proceeds of milk sales.[11] The system is designed to impose the financial loss created by surplus milk supplies equally on all producers.[12] This is accomplished by a nationwide or individual handler pooling of milk. The classification of milk, which determines the minimum price, is based upon the handler's use of the milk. Milk used for fluid milk products is given the highest price and is designated as Class I. Class II includes lower priced milk that is used to manufacture dairy products. Class III includes milk used to produce storable milk products.

One effect of milk marketing orders is that the prices paid to all handlers are uniform. Adjustments are made for the volume, market, and production differentials which are customarily applied by handlers. Adjustments are also made for the grade of milk, and the locations at which milk is delivered to handlers.[13]

In addition, the orders may contain provisions which specify standards regarding the qualifications of handlers and cooperatives to participate in the marketing order program, the reporting and accounting of the net proceeds of sales, and the establishment of research and development projects to promote domestic milk consumption and production.[14]

The provisions which specify the terms and conditions of milk marketing orders were intended to remedy the problems associated with disorderly marketing conditions. Another objective of the marketing order program is the elimination of low prices which were caused by "a basic two-price structure that permits a higher return for the same product, depending on its ultimate use, and the cyclical characteristics of production."[15] The typical milk marketing order will designate a marketing area and define the terms of the milk trade within the area.

Before the terms in any milk marketing order are prescribed, the Secretary of Agriculture must determine the parity price of the commodity. If the Secretary finds that parity prices of the commodity are unreasonable in view of feed prices and other economic conditions, he must establish a price that will insure a sufficient quantity of pure and wholesome milk.[16]

B. Adopting a Marketing Order

The Secretary of Agriculture or any other person, including a producer, may propose a marketing order.[17] If the Secretary believes that the order "will tend to effectuate the declared policy" of the Act, he must give notice of and an opportunity for a hearing on the proposed order.[18] A hearing is required to determine whether the issuance of the proposed order will tend to effectuate the purposes of the Act. This is known as a "tendency determination".[19]

The notice of the hearing on the proposed order commences the proceedings.[20] The notice must state the authority under which the order is proposed, define the scope of the hearing, the terms of the proposed order, the class of regulated persons, the time and place of the hearing, and the place where copies of the order may be examined. Any interested person has a right to be heard and to present relevant information at the hearing.[21] The Secretary has the authority to determine the reasonable scope of the rulemaking proceeding in which the order is promulgated. According to precedent in this area, courts will generally uphold the Secretary's determination unless the determination is found to be "arbitrary and capricious."[22] The public hearing is conducted on the record, and all parties are given an opportunity to cross-examine sworn witnesses for full disclosure of the facts.[23] A grant of a request for oral argument is within the judge's discretion.[24] Briefs, proposed findings and conclusions, and any objections to the judge's rulings may be filed by any interested party.[25]

In formulating the terms of the marketing order, only factual determinations made at the hearing or subject to official notice may be considered.[26] The Administrator must file with the hearing clerk a recommended decision on the order which contains a history of the proceedings, the material issues of fact, proposed findings and conclusions, a ruling upon each proposed finding or conclusion, and a marketing order which effectuates his or her recommendations.[27]

The Administrator, after filing his or her recommended decision, must give public notice of this decision by publication in the Federal Register. The public must subsequently have an opportunity to file exceptions to the recommendations. Any interested person may file written exceptions to the proposed marketing order with the hearing clerk.[28]

After the expiration of the period for filing exceptions or upon request of the Secretary, the record of the proceedings will be submitted to the Secretary, accompanied by any filed exceptions.[29] After the Secretary considers the record, he or she must render a decision which contains a statement of the Secretary's findings and conclusions, and other information.[30]

C. Issuance of the Marketing Order

If the Secretary and handlers execute a marketing agreement, the Secretary will issue and make effective a marketing order. First, the Secretary must determine that the order will tend to effectuate the purposes of the Act. Secondly, he or she must determine that the order has been approved by producers as required by the Act.[31]

Handlers of not less than 50% of the volume of the covered commodity produced in the area covered by the marketing order must sign the marketing agreement. Additionally, the marketing order must be approved by at least 2/3 of producers who have been engaged in production of the relevant commodity in the area designated in the order. In the alternative, the order may be approved by a group of producers who represent 2/3 of the producers of the commodity or who have, in the aggregate, produced and sold 2/3 of the volume of the commodity produced in the area.[32] (There is an exception to the requirements for California citrus.) The process of approving an order is a democratic process which is intended to reflect the collective will of the producers. The Supreme Court has held that there is no authority for the courts to inquire into the influences which caused the producers to favor the order.[33]

If the required group of handlers fails to sign the marketing agreement, the Secretary has the authority to issue a marketing order without a marketing agreement.[34] In a situation where the required representation of handlers who produce more than 50% of the commodity refuse to sign a marketing agreement, the marketing order will become effective if the Secretary determines that certain conditions are met.

Specifically, the Secretary must determine that the handlers' refusal to sign the agreement tends to prevent the effectuation of the Act's policy. The Secretary must also determine that the order is the only practical means of advancing the producers' interests. Last, the Secretary must determine that the appropriate producer approval has been given. This approval may be given by a group which represents at least 2/3 of the producers who have been engaged in the production of the commodity. In the alternative, the group may consist of producers who represent 2/3 of the volume of the commodity produced and sold within the marketing area.[35] The Act does not require an additional hearing in regard to the refusal of handler approval and the necessity of the order.[36] These determinations are within the Secretary's discretion and are nonreviewable.[37]

The marketing order is effective no less than 30 days after its publication in the Federal Register, unless the Secretary fixes an earlier effective date. To become effective, the order must be filed with the Office of the Federal Register. In the alternative, those persons who will be obligated to comply with the terms of the order must receive actual notice of it.[38]

D. Terms of Marketing Orders

All marketing orders must contain one or more of the following terms and conditions:

1. a prohibition of unfair methods of competition and trade;
2. a provision that the commodity or its products must be sold by the handlers in the manner set forth in the order;
3. provisions for various matters including agency selection to administer the order, the making of rules and regulations to effectuate the order, and provisions for the investigating and reporting of complaints of order violations to the Secretary, and to recommend amendments to the order to the Secretary; and
4. provision for other terms incidental to, and not inconsistent with, the terms and conditions specified in the Act.[39]

At least one of the following terms and conditions must be included in non-milk marketing orders. These include:

1. A limit on the quantity each handler may market in a specified period;
2. An allotment of the amount of the commodity or product subject to the order that each handler may purchase from or handle on behalf of producers during a specified period;
3. An allotment of the amount of the commodity or product each handler may market;
4. A provision for control and disposition of surplus commodities;
5. The establishment of reserve pools;
6. A required inspection of the commodity or product;
7. A provision of specific terms for hops and their products;
8. A provision of a method for fixing the size, capacity, weight, dimensions, or pack of the containers used in packaging, transportation, sale, shipment or handling or fresh or dried fruits, vegetables, or tree nuts;
9. The establishment of production research, marketing research, and development projects to improve and promote marketing distribution and consumption, and efficient production of the commodity or product; and/or
10. A provision for certain terms and conditions for pears used in canning or freezing.[40]

E. Modification and Challenges to Marketing Orders

A challenge to a marketing order is required to be undertaken in an administrative proceeding before the Secretary. A handler may petition the Secretary in writing for the modification of, or an exception from, a marketing order on the grounds that the order is "not in accordance with the law."[41] A handler may file a separate application with the hearing clerk to postpone the effective date of a marketing order or to suspend the application of a marketing order, or any provision of the order, pending final determination of the proceeding.[42]

1. Petition

A handler's written petition to the Secretary must be

filed with the hearing clerk.[43] The handler must carefully draft the petition. In the event that the petition does not comply with the content requirements of the regulation, or the petition is not filed in good faith, the Administrator may file a motion to dismiss the petition, or parts of it.[44] The Administrative Law Judge must issue an order pursuant to the motion to dismiss. This order becomes final unless it is appealed.[45] The petitioner must file a written application for an oral argument. Otherwise, the right to have an oral argument is waived.[46]

The Administrator must file an answer to the petition within 30 days after the filing of the petition, unless a motion to dismiss the petition has been filed. If this motion is made, the answer must be filed within 15 days after the filing of the order of the Administrative Law Judge which denies the motion or which grants the motion with respect to a portion of the petition.[47]

2. Hearing

The Administrative Law Judge has the discretion to determine the time and place of the hearing, and must file a notice of the hearing with the hearing clerk.[48] The petitioner may appear in person or by counsel or other representative.[49] If the petitioner, after having been sent proper notice, fails to appear at the hearing, he or she is deemed to have authorized the dismissal of the proceeding.[50] The hearing must be publicly conducted, with the opportunity for all parties to present evidence, in the form of witnesses, depositions and affidavits, and to make objections to the admission or rejection of evidence.[51] Subpoenas may be issued upon a showing of the grounds, necessity, and reasonable scope of the subpoena.[52] Transcripts of the hearing must be made available in the office of the hearing clerk.[53]

3. Decision

Within 10 days after the transcript of the hearing has been filed with the hearing clerk, each party may file proposed findings of fact, conclusions of law, and proposed orders with supporting briefs.[54] Within a reasonable time after the termination of the time period allowed for submission of the parties' proposed findings, the Administrative Law Judge must file his or her initial decision with the hearing clerk. Copies of the initial decision will then be served upon each party.[55] This decision becomes final 35 days after the date of service, unless an appeal of the initial decision is made to the Secretary before that date. A final decision of an appeal which has been issued by the Secretary is considered a final decision for purposes of judicial review.[56]

4. Appeals

A party which disagrees with the decision of the Administrative Law Judge may appeal the decision to the Secretary. Moreover, a party which is aggrieved by a marketing order must seek a remedy from the Secretary of Agriculture prior to seeking legal relief in a court.[57] An appeal petition must be filed with the hearing clerk within 30 days after service of the decision upon the party. The petition must separately set forth each issue and argument and must state the citations relied upon in the argument.[58] The party filing the appeal must make a written request for an oral argument before the Secretary. Otherwise, he or she will be deemed to have waived oral argument.[59] The appeal is limited to the issues raised in the petition. However, the Secretary has the discretion to raise additional issues.[60] Any other party must file its response to the appeal within 20 days after service of the appeal.[61]

As soon as practicable, the Secretary must rule on the appeal. If the Secretary agrees with the decision of the Administrative Law Judge, the Secretary may adopt the judge's decision as final. This is a final determination of which the appellant may seek judicial review.[62] The Secretary's final order is filed with the hearing clerk, who serves it upon the parties.[63]

Any party may request the reopening of the hearing, or a rehearing, reargument, or reconsideration of an order. A party who wishes to exercise one of these options must address a petition to the Secretary and file it with the hearing clerk. The petition must specifically state the grounds relied upon in making the request.[64] The opposing party must file an answer with the hearing clerk within 10 days following service of the petition.[65]

F. Judicial Review

1. Judicial Review of Adoption of Marketing Orders

The United States District Courts have jurisdiction to review and enforce final determinations made by the Secretary.[66] Generally, handlers have the right to judicial review of marketing orders in addition to administrative review.[67] However, standing is a necessary prerequisite to review. For handlers, a financial interest in the challenged action is the fundamental requirement for standing. In U.S. v. Rock Royal Coop Inc.[68], handlers were held to lack standing to challenge the effect of a producer settlement fund because the handlers were found to have no financial interest in the fund.

In addition, producers are entitled to judicial review under certain circumstances. For example, the Fifth Circuit Court of Appeals permitted producers to challenge a marketing order in Suntex Dairy v. Bergland.[69] Producers may attain substantive review of the Secretary's "tendency" determination. Discretionary determinations made by the Secretary, such as the "necessity" determination, may be challenged on the grounds that the agency lacked jurisdiction, that the decision was made under impermissible influence, or that the decision violated constitutional, statutory, or regulatory guidelines. The standard of review in Suntex Dairy was limited to whether the Secretary's decision was "arbitrary, capricious, an abuse of discretion or otherwise not in accordance with the law, or unsupportable by substantial evidence."[70]

The court in Suntex Dairy examined two separate decisions of the Secretary. First, the Secretary's determination that the order tended to effectuate the policy of the Act was found to be supported by substantial evidence and was not arbitrary, capricious, or an abuse of discretion. Second, the Secretary's decision that the lack of handler approval prevented the effectuation of the Act's policy and that the order was "necessary" as the only practical means of advancing producers' interests, was found to be within the discretion of the Secretary and not subject to judicial review.

In Stark v. Wickard,[71] the Supreme Court held that milk producers had standing to challenge the Secretary's deduction from a fund which protected the producers' minimum price. The court held that the Act conferred judicially enforceable "definite personal rights" to producers in regard to minimum milk prices.[72]   Unlike handlers, who have an administrative remedy for review, producers could seek direct judicial review because no administrative remedy is available to them in the Act.

The Fifth Circuit Court of Appeals in Consolidated-Tomoka Land Co. v. Butz[73] rejected the contention that the availability of judicial review for handlers precluded an action by producers to challenge the procedure by which the order was adopted. The producers were held to have standing "to seek a judicial determination of whether such order was issued in accordance with law."[74]

However, in Pescosolido v. Block,[75] the Ninth Circuit Court of Appeals held that producers of naval oranges who sought to compel the Secretary to terminate a marketing order lacked standing to bring claims outside the administrative remedies of the Act. The producers alleged that the marketing order failed to achieve and maintain parity prices for naval orange producers. The Court referred to the opinion in Community Nutrition Institute v. Block,[76] which held that consumers lacked standing to challenge marketing orders. Accordingly, the Pescosolido Court held that judicial review is available only to handlers.[77] The court refused to permit producer challenges outside the statutory administrative remedy absent special circumstances.

The facts in Pescosolido did not establish any exception which would allow judicial review outside the statutory provisions. This holding signifies that producers, under these circumstances, are not being denied any procedural rights. The interests of the producers in Pescosolido were found to be sufficiently similar to handlers interests so that judicial review was unwarranted.

2. Judicial Review Concerning Amendments To Marketing Orders

If 1/3 or more of the members of the relevant producer group file a written request for a hearing on a proposed amendment of a marketing order, the Secretary must schedule a hearing.[78] The hearing may be held in less than 15 days, but may not be held less than 3 days after publication of notice in the Federal Register.[79]

In Smyser v. Block,[80] independent milk producers challenged the validity of the Secretary's amendment to a regional milk marketing order, which added transportation credits to the order. The Third Circuit Court of Appeals held that these amendments clearly exceeded the scope of the Secretary's authority.

In another case, Lehigh Valley Farmers v. Block,[81] the Secretary's decision to amend milk marketing orders by adding 20 counties to the marketing areas was held to be not supportable by substantial evidence. As a result, the dairy farmers and cooperatives who were subject to the order were granted a permanent injunction which prohibited the Secretary from implementing the amendment.

G. Violation of a Marketing Order

Any handler or any officer, director, agent, or employee of the handler, who violates any provision of the marketing order to which he or she is subject (other than payment of a pro rata share of expenses), may upon conviction be fined not less than $50 or more than $5,000 for each violation. Each day during which a violation continues is treated as a separate violation.[82] However, if the court finds that a petition was filed with the Secretary stating that the order is not in accordance with law and asking for modification, no penalty will be imposed for violations occurring between the date the petition was filed and the date on which notice of the Secretary's ruling was given.[83]

The Administrator is authorized to investigate any handler whom he or she has reason to believe has violated, or is violating, the provisions of marketing order. After an investigation and after notice to the handler, the Administrator may conduct a hearing to find the facts. If the Administrator and the General Counsel believe that legal action is warranted, the General Counsel will refer the matter to the Attorney General for further legal proceedings.[84]

Enforcement proceedings for violations of marketing orders and marketing agreements are authorized by the Agricultural Marketing Agreement Act.[85] The Act confers jurisdiction upon the United States District Courts "to enforce and to prevent and restrain any person from violating any order, regulation, or agreement" under the Act. The Secretary may seek an injunction to compel compliance with an order, to require handlers to file reports and to pay future assessments.[86] Any person who exceeds quota or allotment provisions in marketing agreements or orders may face forfeiture of a financial amount equal to the market value of the excess commodity sold.[87]

4. Termination of a Marketing Order

The Secretary must terminate or suspend marketing orders which fail to effectuate the declared policy of the Act.[88] However, the Secretary is not authorized to terminate a marketing order for a commodity which is not covered by a federal price support program, unless the Secretary gives timely notice of the proposed termination to both the Committee on Agriculture, Nutrition and Forestry of the Senate and the Committee on Agriculture of the House of Representatives. This notice must be accompanied by an explanation of the justification for the termination.[89] The marketing order must be terminated if a majority of producers who have engaged in production within the marketing area favor termination.[90] Termination becomes effective at the end of the current marketing period.[91]

As stated above, in <u>Pescosolido v. Block</u>,[92] producers of naval oranges attempted to compel the Secretary to terminate a marketing order because the order had allegedly failed to achieve parity prices. In that opinion, the Ninth Circuit Court of Appeals recognized that parity is a "goal" rather than a fixed entitlement. The Secretary may terminate the order only after making a finding that the order obstructs or does not tend to effectuate the purpose of the Act. The Court held that an action of mandamus does not lie to compel the Secretary to make such findings.[93] Moreover, the court noted that the statute itself provides a self-executing remedy to the producers. The court was referring to the fact that a vote of the majority of the producers will terminate the order, which is less than the 2/3 approval necessary to approve the order.

III.   The Perishable Agricultural Commodities Act
The Perishable Agricultural Commodities Act (PACA)[94] is administered by the PACA Branch, Fruit and Vegetable Division, Agricultural Marketing Service, USDA. PACA was enacted in 1930 to suppress unfair and fraudulent practices in the marketing of perishable agricultural commodities and to promote the orderly flow of perishable commodities in interstate commerce. Most administrative cases under PACA are either disciplinary cases or reparation proceedings for money damages between buyers and sellers of commodities. Disciplinary cases ordinarily involve a party's failure to pay promptly or in full, the failure to properly account, or the misbranding of a commodity. Reparations cases involve a wide range of disputes. The reparations procedure is designed to provide an informal and inexpensive method by which disputes can be adjudicated. The reparation procedure provides an alternative forum for producers who suffer losses as a result of violations of PACA.

A. Unfair Conduct
The purpose of PACA is to prohibit various types of unfair conduct by commission merchants, dealers and brokers and to provide practical remedies to small farmers and growers who have to deal with the "sharp practices" of the "financially irresponsible and unscrupulous."[95] The types of conduct prohibited by PACA include such things as failure to pay fully; rejection of produce without reasonable cause; failure to pay promptly; failure to make good delivery without reasonable cause; failure to account truly and correctly; to discard, dump or destroy produce on consignment without reasonable cause; to ship produce which is misbranded or misrepresented as to grade, quality, weight, or state of origin; to alter inspection certificates or to make false or misleading statements.[96]

For example, in American Fruit Purveyors, Inc. v. United States,[97] the use of post dated checks was not considered prompt payment especially where several were returned for insufficient funds. In Cove Valley Packers, Inc. v. Pilgram Fruit Co.,[98] the buyer's rejection of a shipment of perishable agricultural commodities without reasonable cause rendered the buyer liable for damages.

What is often at issue is whether the broker, dealer or

343

commission merchant has engaged in unfair trade practices. A number of cases have established that the following practices are unfair under the provisions of the PACA:

(1) misrepresentations as to quality or quantity;
(2) tampering, removal, or alteration of labels;
(3) substitution or changes in content;
(4) rejection or discarding of shipments without reasonable cause;
(5) failure to ship according to the sales contract;
(6) failure to deliver the quality or quantity required;
(7) the refusal to ship; and
(8) the use of false and misleading packing statements.

B. Regulatory Approach

The basic regulatory approach of PACA is through the licensing of commission merchants, dealers and brokers who are engaged in transactions involving perishable agricultural commodities. A "commission merchant" is any person who is engaged in receiving any perishable agricultural commodity for sale, on commission, or for or on behalf of another. These persons are covered by the Act regardless of the volume of their business.[99] However, both "dealers" and "brokers" must meet "invoice value" tests for certain transactions. For example, a person who is engaged in the business of buying and selling perishable agricultural commodities in "wholesale or jobbing quantities" is considered a dealer. However, if that person buys solely for sale at retail he or she is a dealer only when the "invoice cost" of purchases exceeds $230,000. The sale of commodities which a person has raised does not make that person a dealer.[100]

A similar rule applies to persons who are considered to be brokers. A broker is a person who is engaged in the business of negotiating sales and purchases of perishable agricultural commodities for or on behalf of the vendor or purchaser. However, a person does not qualify as a broker if the sales are negotiated independently for the vendor and involve frozen fruits and vegetables with an "invoice value" of under $230,000 in any calendar year.[101] Of course, to be covered by the Act all of the activities of commission merchants, dealers and brokers must be in interstate or foreign commerce.[102]

Some transactions are not covered by PACA. For example, claims resting on transportation contracts are outside the jurisdiction of PACA. In <u>Grand Prairie Produce Brokerage, Inc. v. Royal Packing Co.</u>,[103] an operator was not considered to be a "broker" where he was not engaged in the business of negotiating either sales or purchases when he sold the crops.[104]

C. Licensing

Under PACA, any person who wishes to act as a dealer, commission merchant or broker in the interstate commerce of perishable agricultural commodities must secure a license from the Secretary of Agriculture. The threat of license revocation is intended to serve as a deterrent against licensed persons' engaging in the activities which cause losses to farm producers.

1. Refusal of License

The Secretary must refuse to issue a license to an applicant if he finds that the applicant is a person who is or was responsibly connected with a person who:

(a) has had his license revoked within two years prior to the date of the application or whose license is currently under suspension;

(b) within two years prior to the date of application has been found, after notice and opportunity for hearing, to have committed flagrant or repeated violations of the Act;

(c) within two years prior to the date of the application, has been found guilty in a federal court for having violated PACA provisions which relate to the prevention or destruction and dumping of farm produce; or

(d) has failed, except in the case of bankruptcy and subject to his right of appeal, to pay any reparation order issued against him within two years prior to the date of the application.[105]

A person cannot legally engage in the business of a commission merchant, dealer or broker without obtaining a license from the PACA Branch of the AMS, USDA and paying the appropriate licensing fee.[106] Business may be conducted under more than one trade name or under a different name without obtaining a new license. However, if the use of a trade name would be deceptive, misleading or confusing to the public

345

the name may be disapproved.[107] The Act provides for
suspension of the license for violations of the Act and for
revocation of the license if the violation is flagrant or
repeated.[108]

2. Prohibition of Employment of Those "Responsibly Connected"

The Act prohibits a licensee from employing any person
who has been found to have committed flagrant or repeated
violations of the Act or against whom there is an unpaid
reparation award. This prohibition extends to any person
"responsibly connected" with such persons.[109] For example,
under this provision the Agricultural Marketing Service (AMS)
could prohibit a licensee from employing a person who was
"responsibly connected" with a company which had an unpaid
reparations award outstanding. In this case, the person was
"responsibly connected" because he was the treasurer and a
board member of the company, and also owned more than 10%
of the company's outstanding shares of stock.[110] On the other
hand, the presumption that a person is "responsibly connected"
with a licensee if he is affiliated as an officer is rebuttable and a
former officer may be entitled to prove his officership was only
nominal.[111] However, in Pupillo v. United States,[112] the
Eighth Circuit Court of Appeals followed a per se rule and
expressly rejected the rebuttable presumption approach.

3. Suspension or Revocation

To invoke the authority to suspend or revoke a license
the Secretary must determine that a violation of the Act has
occurred.[113] A specific complaint and investigation procedure
is provided in the Act.[114] In addition, notice and an
opportunity for hearing is specifically required for a finding of
"flagrant or repeated" violations.[115] The regulations specifically
provide for notice and hearing in regard to a license suspension
or revocation.[116] Special rules are applicable to a finding of
"responsibly connected."[117]

An action of the Secretary in suspending a license for
violations of the Act will not be overruled upon judicial review
if the suspension was conducted in accordance with
constitutional and statutory standards and unless it is

346

"unwarranted in law without justification in fact."[118]

D. Record and Account Keeping Requirements

The Act is also enforced through record and account keeping requirements. According to the Act, licensed parties must keep records, accounts and memoranda that fully and correctly disclose all transactions involved in the business. The failure of a licensee to keep the required records may result in suspension of the license.[119] Apparently, the Secretary may examine the records at any time. In Cusimano v. Block,[120] the Fifth Circuit Court of Appeals upheld an unannounced, warrantless search of a dealer's records against a challenge that it violated the dealer's Fourth Amendment rights. The court said that there is no reasonable expectation of privacy in this area because it is so pervasively regulated by the government.

The Act also empowers the Secretary to employ and license inspectors who may inspect and certify the class, quality and condition of commodity shipments. This inspection may be done without regard to whether a complaint is filed under the Act and may serve as the basis for a license suspension or other disciplinary actions.[121]

E. Disciplinary Actions

The Secretary is given the authority to investigate complaints and to proceed with appropriate actions, either in a disciplinary or a reparation proceeding, in addition to any license suspension or revocation that may result from the findings.[122] In Finer Foods Sales Co. v. Block,[123] the court found that it was not necessary for a disciplinary complaint to be preceded by an informal complaint or a reparation complaint. Moreover, it was not necessary that the institution of the disciplinary proceeding be preceded by a hearing to determine whether the violation was willful.

Under PACA, administrative disciplinary actions include warning letters; monetary penalties in misbranding and misrepresentation cases; and the suspension or termination of a license in a number of situations.[124] For minor violations a warning order may be used instead of formal disciplinary proceedings. Warning letters are sent prior to a suspension or revocation of a licensee, except where the Act provides for automatic suspension or revocation. A warning order is necessary except where the termination or suspension is automatic or if the violating conduct is willful.[125] However, under the interpretation of the term "willful," a formal complaint, based on the same violation, may be instituted later. A violation is willful if the violator intentionally commits an act which is prohibited, irrespective of evil motive or reliance on erroneous advice, or acts with careless disregard of statutory requirements. The term "willful" may refer to either intentional conduct or conduct that was merely careless or negligent if the violator acts with careless disregard of statutory requirements.[126]

Formal disciplinary proceedings may either evolve from reparation actions, from a complaint by industry or state officials or from an investigation by the department. Disciplinary orders (not cease and desist orders) may include suspending the license, revoking the license or a finding of flagrant or repeated violation.[127] Disciplinary orders may also be issued if the PACA violation is committed by a person who is responsibly connected to the licensee. Disciplinary actions are handled in accordance with the uniform Rules of Practice of the Secretary of Agriculture.[128]

F. Reparations

The Act establishes a reparations forum for claims which involve a violation of the Act and consequent loss to the complainant.[129]

1. Jurisdiction

The jurisdiction of the agency in reparations actions involves four requirements - a matter involving a perishable agricultural commodity,[130] interstate commence,[131] a matter which is subject to licenses or a licensee under the Act[132] and the petition must be filed within 9 months of the time when the cause of action accrues.[133] The cause of action accrues when the event occurs, not when it is discovered.[134] This limitation also applies to counterclaims or affirmative defenses which are not the subject of the original complaint.[135] The Agricultural Marketing Service is able to adjudicate terms of contracts which were made before the complaint was filed as long as the complaint is filed within the statutory period after the cause of action accrues.[136]

The first of these requirements deals with the basic definitional question of whether a perishable agricultural commodity is involved in the dispute. The Agricultural Marketing Service issues a list of commodities covered by PACA based on the definition of "perishable agricultural commodity" in Section 1 of the Act, as follows:

> The term 'perishable agricultural commodity'
>
> (a) means any of the following, whether or not frozen or packed in ice: fresh fruits and fresh vegetables of every kind and character; and
> (b) includes cherries in brine as defined by the Secretary in accordance with trade usages.[137]

> By regulatory definition "fresh fruits and vegetables" are: all produce in fresh form generally considered as perishable fruits and vegetables, whether or not packed in ice or held in common or cold storage, but does not include those perishable fruits and vegetables which have been manufactured into articles of food of a different kind or character. The effects of the following operations shall not be considered as changing a commodity into a food of a different kind or character: Water or steam blanching, chopping, color adding, curing, cutting, dicing, drying for the removal of surface moisture; control, ripening and coloring; removal of seed, pits, stems, calyx, husk, pods, rind, skin, peel, et cetera; polishing, precooling, refrigerating, shredding, slicing, trimming, washing with or without chemicals; waxing, adding of sugar or other sweetening agents; adding ascorbic acid or other agents used to retard oxidation; mixing of several kinds of sliced, chopped, or diced fruits or vegetables for packaging in any type of containers; or comparable methods of preparation.[138]

2. Procedure for Complaint

The procedure for a reparations complaint under the

349

Perishable Agricultural Commodities Act permits any interested person to file a complaint. If the complaint contains a request for damages it must be filed within nine months of when the cause of action accrues.[139] The informal nature of the proceeding is illustrated by the fact that the complaint may be by telegram, letter, or by a preliminary statement of facts which set forth the essential details of the transaction.[140] The Division of Fruits and Vegetables of the Agricultural Marketing Service will conduct an investigation and, if the situation warrants, will try to achieve an amicable or informal adjustment of the matter.[141] If this is not successful the person who filed the informal complaint may file a formal complaint which sets forth the same information as in the informal complaint, including a statement of the damages claimed.[142] The Division will serve a copy on the respondent and serve both parties with copies of any investigative report.[143] Within 20 days an answer must be filed,[144] and then the matter is docketed.[145]

3. Hearing

If the amount in controversy is $15,000 or less an oral hearing will not be held unless the Division deems it necessary or desirable. An oral hearing can be granted upon application of either party if it appears proper to the agency.[146] A shortened procedure is available and serves in lieu of an oral hearing in many cases.[147] In the shortened procedure the pleadings, the report of the investigation, as well as written proof in support of any claim in the form of verified statements or depositions, are considered as the evidence in the proceeding.[148] If the parties consent, this shortened procedure may also be used in cases where the claim exceeds $15,000.[149]

Where the amount in controversy exceeds $15,000, any party may request an oral hearing on the facts. Failure to file such a request in a timely fashion constitutes a waiver of the oral hearing and the matter may be decided upon a record formed according to the shortened procedure.[150] Guidance for the development of the proposed orders and final decisions, as well as rehearing matters, are detailed in the regulations.[151]

350

4. Appeals and Enforcement

The entry of a reparation order by the Judicial Officer may be appealed to a U.S. District Court within 30 days from the date of entry of the order.[152] The suit in District Court is a trial de novo. However, the Judicial Officer's findings of fact and orders are prima facie evidence of the facts stated.[153]

If the reparation order is not appealed or paid within the time specified in the order, the complainant may file suit to enforce the order in a U.S. District Court.[154] These suits are treated like other civil suits for damages except that the Judicial Officer's findings of fact and orders are prima facie evidence of the facts stated.

The reparations provision does not repeal the law of sales and any rights under state law are still applicable.[155] In other words, reparations provides an additional remedy to those provided under other applicable statutes or under the common law.[156] However, once an choice of forum has been made the party is limited to any remedies available in that forum, i.e. the remedies are not cumulative. For example, the AMS may not proceed on an reparation order once a court decision has been entered in regard to the subject matter.[157]

In a reparations proceeding the findings of fact of the agency are prima facie evidence and will prevail upon judicial review unless there is a preponderance of evidence which overcome the findings.[158]

The reparation order can be enforced only against parties to the reparation proceeding. Any findings of the agency would not be prima facie evidence against those not a party to the proceeding.[159]

When a reparation order has been affirmed on appeal, the prevailing party is entitled to a reasonable allowance for costs and attorney fees.[160]

G. Statutory Trust

In 1984 PACA was amended to create a statutory trust for the benefit of unpaid suppliers or sellers of perishable agricultural commodities or their agents and on all inventories of food or other products derived from perishable agricultural commodities. This trust applies until full payment for commodities has been received.[161] This provision is designed

351

to protect unpaid suppliers, sellers and their agents in those circumstances where commission merchants, dealers or brokers encumber or give lenders a security interest in those commodities or in the inventories of products derived from the commodities.[162]

To obtain the benefit of the trust, the unpaid supplier, seller or agent must give written notice to the commission merchant, broker or dealer and file the notice with the Secretary within 30 days after the specified time for payment has elapsed.[163]

FOOTNOTES

1. 7 U.S.C. § 601 et seq.

2. 7 U.S.C. § 608c(1).

3. 307 U.S. 533, 59 S. Ct. 993 (1939).

4. 7 U.S.C. §§ 499a - 499s.

5. 7 U.S.C. § 608c(6).

6. U.S. v. Rock Royal Coop. Inc., 307 U.S. 533, 576, 59 S. Ct. 993, 1014 (1939).

7. E.M. Babb, "Marketing Orders and Farm Structure", in Structure Issues of American Agriculture USDA, Agr. Econ. Rpt. 438 (1979) at 251.

8. 7 U.S.C. § 608c(2).

9. 7 U.S.C. § 608c (2).

10. 7 U.S.C. § 608c. See Pescosolido v. Block, 765 F.2d 827 (9th Cir. 1985).

11. 7 U.S.C. § 608c(5).

12. Smyser v. Block, 760 F.2d 514 (3rd Cir. 1985).

13. 7 U.S.C. § 608c(5)(A).

14. 7 U.S.C. § 608c(5)(I).

15. Zuber v. Allen, 39 U.S. 168, 172, 90 S. Ct. 314, 317 (1969).

16. 7 U.S.C. § 608c(18).

17. 7 C.F.R. § 900.3(a).

18. 7 U.S.C. § 608c(3).

19. 7 U.S.C. § 608c(3).

20. 7 C.F.R. § 900.4.

21. 7 C.F.R. § 900.8(b).

22. See, Marketing Assistance Program, Inc. v. Bergland, 562 F.2d 1305, 1307 (D.C. Cir. 1977).

23. 7 C.F.R. § 900.8(d).

24. 7 C.F.R. § 900.9(a).

25. 7 C.F.R. § 900.9(b).

26. 7 C.F.R. § 900.9(b).

27. 7 C.F.R. § 900.12(a), (b).

28. 7 C.F.R. § 900.12(c).

29. 7 C.F.R. § 900.13.

30. 7 C.F.R. § 900.13(a).

31. 7 C.F.R. § 608c(8).

32. 7 U.S.C. § 608c(8).

33. U.S. v. Rock Royal Coop., Inc., 307 U.S. 533, 559 (1939).

34. 7 C.F.R. § 900.14(c).

35. 7 U.S.C. § 608c(9).

36. 7 U.S.C. § 608c(9).

37. Suntex Dairy v. Bergland, 666 F.2d 158, 164 (5th Cir. 1982).

38. 7 C.F.R. § 900.14(d).

39. 7 U.S.C. § 608c(7).

40. 7 U.S.C. § 608c(6).

41. 7 U.S.C. § 608(15)(A).

42. 7 C.F.R. § 900.70(a).

43. 7 C.F.R. § 900.52(a).

44. 7 C.F.R. § 900.52(c). The petition must contain specific items of information set forth in 7 C.F.R. § 900.52(b).

45. 7 C.F.R. § 900.52(2).

46. 7 C.F.R. § 900.52(3).

47. 7 C.F.R. § 900.52.

48. 7 C.F.R. § 900.60(a).

49. 7 C.F.R. § 900.60(b).

50. 7 C.F.R. § 900.60(b)(3).

51. 7 C.F.R. § 900.60(d).

52. 7 C.F.R. § 900.62.

53. 7 C.F.R. § 900.60(f).

54. 7 C.F.R. § 900.64(b).

55. 7 C.F.R. § 900.64(c).

56. 7 C.F.R. § 900.64(c).

57. U.S. v. Ruzicka, 329 U.S. 287, 67 S. Ct. 207, (1946).

58. 7 C.F.R. § 900.65(a).

59. 7 C.F.R. § 900.65(b).

60. 7 C.F.R. § 900.66(b)(2).

61. 7 C.F.R. § 900.66(c).

62. 7 C.F.R. § 900.66(a).

63. 7 C.F.R. § 900.66(b).

64. 7 C.F.R. § 900.68(a)(1).

65. 7 C.F.R. § 900.68(b).

66. 7 U.S.C. § 608c(15)(B).

67. Stark v. Wickard, 321 U.S. 288, 64 S.Ct. 559.

68. 307 U.S. 533, 59 S. Ct. 993 (1939)

69. 666 F.2d 158 (5th Cir. 1982).

70. 666 F.2d at 162.

71. 321 U.S. 288, 64 S.Ct. 559 (1944)

72. 321 U.S. at 303

73. 498 F.2d 1208 (5th Cir. 1974)

74. 498 F.2d at 1210, citing Freeman v. Hygeia Dairy Co., 326 F.2d 271, 273 (5th Cir. 1964).

75. 765 F.2d 827 (9th Cir. 1985)

76. 467 U.S. 340, 104 S. Ct. 2450 (1984).

77. 765 F.2d at 831.

78. 7 U.S.C. § 608c(17).

79. 7 C.F.R. § 900.4(a).

80. 760 F.2d 514 (3rd Cir. 1985)

81. 829 F.2d 409 (3rd Cir. 1987)

82. 7 U.S.C. § 608c(14).

83. 7 U.S.C. § 608c(14).

84. 7 C.F.R. § 900.201.

85. 7 U.S.C. § 608a(6).

86. Naval Orange Admin. Comm. v. Exeter Orange Co., Inc., 722 F.2d 449 (9th Cir. 1983).

87. 7 U.S.C. § 608a(5).

88. 7 U.S.C. § 608c(16)(A)(i).

89. 7 U.S.C. § 608c(16)(A)(ii).

90. 7 U.S.C. § 608c(16)(B).

91. 7 U.S.C. § 608c(16)(B).

92. 765 F.2d 827 (9th Cir. 1985).

93. 765 F.2d at 830.

94. 7 U.S.C. §§ 499a - 499s.

95. Chidsey v. Guerin, 443 F.2d 584 (6th Cir. 1971); Rothenberg v. Rothstein & Sons, 183 F.2d 524 (3rd Cir. 1950).

96. 7 U.S.C. § 499b.

97. 630 F.2d 370 (5th Cir. 1980).

98. 297 F. Supp. 200 (D.C. Mass. 1969).

99. 7 U.S.C. § 499a(5).

100. 7 U.S.C. 499a(6).

101. 7 U.S.C. § 499a(6).

102. 7 U.S.C. § 499a. See Iwater v. Western Fruit Growers, Inc., 90 F.2d 575 (9th Cir. 1937); Consolidated Citrus Co. v. Goldstein, 214 F. Supp. 823 (Pa. 1963).

103. 34 Ag Dec 1580 (1975).

104. Also see, United States v. Bourlon, 574 F.2d 202 (5th Cir. 1978).

105. 7 C.F.R. § 499d(b).

106. 7 U.S.C. § 499c(a), (b).

107. 7 U.S.C. § 499c(c).

108. 7 U.S.C. § 499h.

109. 7 U.S.C. § 499h(b).

110. Birkenfield v. U.S., 369 F.2d 491 (3rd Cir. 1966).

111. Quinn v. Butz, 510 F.2d 743 (D.C. Cir. 1975).

112. 755 F.2d 638 (8th Cir. 1985).

113. 7 U.S.C. § 499h(a).

114. 7 U.S.C. § 499f.

115. 7 U.S.C. § 499h(b).

116. 7 C.F.R. § 46.35 (suspension and revocation).

117. 7 C.F.R. § 47.47-47.68 ("responsibly connected" determinations.)

118. J. Acevedo & Sons v. U.S., 524 F.2d 977 (5th Cir. 1975); Eastern Produce Co. v. Benson, 278 F.2d 606 (3rd Cir. 1960); Melvin Beene Produce Co. v. Agricultural Marketing Service, 728 F.2d 347 (6th Cir. 1984).

119. 7 C.F.R. § 499i.

120. 629 F.2d 1025 (5th Cir. 1982).

121. 7 C.F.R. § 499n.

122. 7 U.S.C. § 499f.

123. 708 F.2d 774 (D.C. Cir. 1983).

124. 7 C.F.R. § 46.45 (warning letters and penalties); 7 U.S.C. § 499c, 499d, 499h, 499i and 499m (license suspension or revocation).

125. 5 U.S.C. § 558(c); Warning orders are used by PACA Regulatory Branch where misrepresentation or misbranding is alleged. 7 C.F.R. § 46.45(e)(3).

126. In re Shatkin, 34 Agric. Dec. 296 (1975).

127. See, 7 U.S.C. § 499c, 499d, 499h, 499i and 499m for various circumstances that may remit in suspension or revocation.

128. 7 C.F.R. § 1.130-.151.

129. 7 U.S.C. § 499e-g.

130. 7 U.S.C. § 499a(4).

131. 7 U.S.C. § 499a(8).

132. 7 U.S.C. § 499b(a).

133. 7 U.S.C. § 499f(a).

134. Maggio, Inc. v. First Nat. Stores, Inc. 39 Ag. Dec. 1179 (1980).

135. Kaplan's Fruit & Produce Co. v. Jim Weatherford Co. 37 Ag. Dec. 812 (1978).

136. Cooper v. Caro and Longo Wholesale Produce Co. Inc., 40 Ag. Dec. 454 (1981).

137. 7 C.F.R. § 499a(4).

138. 7 C.F.R. § 46.2(u).

139. 9 C.F.R. § 47.3.

140. 9 C.F.R. § 47.3(a)(2).

141. 9 C.F.R. § 47.3(b).

142. 9 C.F.R. § 47.6.

143. 9 C.F.R. § 47.6, 47.7.

144. 9 C.F.R. § 47.8.

145. 9 C.F.R. § 47.10.

146. 9 C.F.R. § 47.15.

147. 9 C.F.R. § 47.20.

148. 9 C.F.R. § 47.20(a).

149. 9 C.F.R. § 47.20(b).

150. 9 C.F.R. § 47.19.

151. 9 C.F.R. § 47.19.

152. 7 U.S.C. § 499g(c).

153. 7 U.S.C. § 499g(c).

154. 7 U.S.C. § 499g(b).

155. A.J. Conroy, Inc. v. Weyl-Zucherman & Co., 39 F. Supp. 784 (D.C. Cal. 1941); California Fruit Exchange v. Henry, 89 F. Supp. 580 (D.C. Pa. 1950) aff'd 184 F.2d 517 (3rd. Cir. 1950); Cohen v. Frima Products Co., 181 F.2d 324 (5th Cir. 1950).

156. Rothenberg v. H. Rohnstein & Sons, 183 F.2d 524 (3rd Cir. 1950); 21 A.L.R. 2d 832.

157. Adams Bros. Produce Co. v. Peeples, 37 Ag. Dec. 1216 (1978).

158. Barker-Miller Distributing Co. v. Berman, 8 F. Supp. 60 (D.C. NY 1934); California Fruit Exchange v. Henry, 89 F. Supp. 580 (D.C. Pa. 1950), aff'd 184 F.2d 517 (3rd Cir. 1950); Consolidated Citrus Co. v. Goldstein, 214 F. Supp. 823 (D.C. Pa. 1963).

159. Swanee Bee Acres, Inc. v. Fruit Hill, Inc., 597 F. Supp. 322 (N.D. Ill. 1984).

160. 7 U.S.C. § 499g. WS Westcott Co. v. York Rubis & Son, 122 F. Supp. 888 (D.C. Pa. 1954); C.F. Smith, Inc. v. Bushala, 232 F. Supp. 178 (D.C. Cal. 1964); Growers Marketing Service, Inc. v. Dino Produce, Inc., 38 Ag. Dec. 1599 (1979).

161. 7 U.S.C. § 499e(c)(2).

162. 7 U.S.C. § 499e(c)(1).

163. 7 U.S.C. § 499e(c)(3).

CHAPTER 11

MARKETING OF LIVESTOCK AND POULTRY

The marketing system for livestock and poultry in the United States is extensive and diverse. Marketing alternatives for livestock and poultry vary considerably depending on the type of animal and the stage of the production process involved. Specialized markets exist for sales which occur at the different stages of an animal's life. For example, fed cattle sold for slaughter are marketed separately from weaning age calves sold as feeders.

I.   Marketing of Livestock
       Terminal markets once placed a significant role in the marketing system for slaughter livestock. However, terminal markets have declined in relative importance. At present, most marketing of livestock is conducted through direct sales or auction markets.
       Fed cattle, hogs and sheep are primarily marketed by direct sale on a live weight per pound or per head basis. Often this involves sales agreements between a feedlot and area packers. Packers have found it more convenient and cost effective to locate slaughtering operations near the feedlots where the cattle are fattened. Packers generally prefer to ship meat rather than live animals. Auctions play a significant role in the marketing of non-slaughter livestock, such as stocker and feeder cattle, to feedlots. These animals may be marketed several times before actually reaching the feedlot.
       In addition to direct sales, forward contracting also plays a significant role in the marketing of livestock, especially feeder calves. In these transactions, the parties agree on a price and a date of future delivery under specified conditions. Payment is usually on a per pound basis. The contract generally includes very specific terms concerning delivery, weighing procedures, and other aspects of the transaction. Forward contracting is used to offset the risk of price fluctuation.

A. Overview of Regulation
Both livestock and poultry marketing are regulated at the federal and state levels. The Packers and Stockyards Act[1] forms the basis of federal regulation. It governs the marketing activities of packers, stockyards, market agencies, livestock dealers, and live poultry dealers and handlers. The Act prohibits various unfair trade practices and is a significant force in shaping industry practices. The other major federal programs affecting meat and poultry marketing are the inspection programs for meat, poultry and eggs and the federal programs relating to disease control.

Federal involvement in livestock marketing also affects the farmer in two other primary areas. One area is the federal "check-off" program which raises funds from beef producers to finance various promotional activities for beef sales. The other is the "federal version" of Uniform Commercial Code Section 9-307 which governs sales of mortgaged livestock.

State regulation of livestock marketing is also significant. The most important state laws are those related to disease control, branding practices and the UCC provisions which cover warranties in livestock sales.

B. Packers and Stockyards Act
1. Purpose of Act
The Packers and Stockyards Act of 1921 promotes fair trade practices in the livestock and meat packing industries.[2] The Act protects farmers, ranchers and consumers from economic harm resulting from unfair, monopolistic or discriminatory marketing practices. The Packers and Stockyards Act is enforced by the Agricultural Marketing Service's Packers and Stockyard Administration within the USDA. The purpose of the Act was considered by the Supreme Court in the case of Stafford v. Wallace,[3] to be the promotion of

[T]he free and unburdened flow of livestock from the ranges and farms of the West and Southwest through the great stockyards and slaughtering centers on the borders of that region, and hence, in the form of meat products, to the consuming cities of the country in the Middle West and East, or still as livestock, to the feeding places and fattening farms in the Middle West or East, for further preparation for the market.[4]

As such, the Act has been considered "remedial legislation," which should be liberally construed "to secure to patrons of stockyards prescribed stockyard services at just and reasonable rates",[5] to prohibit certain trade practices considered to be unfair and not in the public interest,[6] to prevent "economic harm to the 'growers' and the 'consumers' through the concentration in a few hands of the economic function of the middleman",[7] and "to impose upon stockyards the nature of public utilities."[8]

2. Administration of the Act

For purposes of regulation, suppliers of services targeted by the Act are divided into either packers or stockyards. The Act establishes the regulatory framework in separate subchapters for Packers;[9] Stockyards and Stockyard Dealers[10] and Live Poultry Dealers and Handlers.[11] Separate subchapters set out definitional provisions[12] and general provisions applicable to all persons who are covered by the Act.[13] The Packers and Stockyards Administration has promulgated extensive regulations to implement the regulatory program.[14]

The Packers and Stockyards Administration consists of a headquarters in Washington, D.C., and 12 regional offices. The Washington office includes the Office of the Administrator, the Packer and Poultry Division and the Livestock Marketing Division.

The Administrator is responsible for the general direction and supervision of Packers and Stockyards programs. The Administrator directs economic studies of the structure and performance of the livestock, meat, and poultry marketing, processing, and wholesale industries. The results of these studies influence the development of federal policy on antitrust matters.

The Packer and Poultry Division maintains a working relationship with the meat packing and poultry industries and performs numerous functions. It determines the applicability of the Act's provisions to individual packer and poultry operations and monitors those operations. It investigates complaints and initiates formal proceedings to correct illegal practices. These responsibilities are implemented through the Livestock

Procurement Branch, Meat Merchandising Branch, and Poultry Branch.

The Livestock Marketing Division deals with stockyard owners, market agencies, and dealers. Its responsibilities include the following areas: 1. jurisdiction, bonding, financial and trade practices in individual operations; 2. the installation, maintenance, and testing of scales; 3. the surveillance and investigation of stockyards, market agencies, and dealers; 4. the initiation of formal proceedings to correct illegal practices; and 5. the maintenance of working relationships with producer and industry groups. These responsibilities are implemented through the Financial Protection Branch, Marketing Practices Branch, and Scales and Weighing Branch.

The field services of the Packers and Stockyards Administration are divided into 12 regional offices. These offices are responsible for the supervision of the operations of stockyard companies, market agencies, dealers, packers and live poultry dealers and handlers to assure compliance with the Act.

The addresses and the States covered by these regional offices are as follows:
Atlanta - Room 338, 1720 Peachtree Street, NW, Atlanta, Georgia 30309 (Alabama, Florida, Georgia, South Carolina.)
Bedford - Turnpike Road, Box 101E, Bedford, Virginia 25423 (District of Columbia, Delaware, Maryland, North Carolina, Virginia, West Virginia.)
Denver - 208 Livestock Exchange Building, Denver, Colorado 80216 (Colorado, Montana, New Mexico, Utah, Wyoming.)
Fort Worth - Room 8A36, Federal Building, 819 Taylor Street, Fort Worth, Texas 76102 (Oklahoma, Texas.)
Indianapolis - Room 434 Federal Building and U.S. Courthouse, 46 E. Ohio Street. Indianapolis, Indiana 46204 (Illinois, Indiana, Kentucky, Michigan, Ohio.)
Kansas City - 828 Livestock Exchange Building, Kansas City, Missouri 64102 (Kansas, Missouri.)
Lawndale - 15000 Aviation Boulevard, Room 2W6, P. O. Box 6102, Lawndale, California 90261 (Arizona, California, Hawaii, Nevada.)
Memphis - Room 459, Federal Building, 167 Main Street, Memphis, Tennessee 38103 (Arkansas, Louisiana, Mississippi,

Tennessee.)
North Brunswick - 825 Georges Road, Room 303, North
Brunswick, New Jersey 08902 (Connecticut, Maine,
Massachusetts, New Hampshire, New Jersey, New York,
Pennsylvania, Rhode Island, Vermont.)
Omaha - 909 Livestock Exchange Building, Omaha, Nebraska
68107 (Iowa, Nebraska.)
Portland - 9370 S. W. Greenburg Road, Suite E, Portland,
Oregon 97223 (Alaska, Idaho, Oregon, Washington.)
South St. Paul - 208 Post Office Building, Box 8, South St.
Paul, Minnesota 55075 (Minnesota, North Dakota, South
Dakota, Wisconsin.)

3. Freedom of Information Act Requests

The Packers and Stockyards Administration maintains
and makes available for public inspection and copying current
indexes of all material required to be made available under the
Freedom of Information Act and the implementing regulations
of USDA.[15] These indexes are not published because the
USDA believes that the material is voluminous and does not
change often enough to justify the expense of publication.

The facilities for public inspection and copying of the
records and indexes are provided by the Packers and Stockyards
Administration during normal office hours. Requests for this
information should be made to the Freedom of Information Act
Officer (FOIA Request), Packers and Stockyards Administration,
United States Department of Agriculture, Washington, D.C.
20250.[16] Copies of these materials may be obtained in person
or by mail. Applicable fees for copies will be charged in
accordance with the regulations prescribed by the Director of
Information, Office of Governmental and Public Affairs, USDA.

The Freedom of Information Officer of the Packers and
Stockyards Administration makes initial determinations
regarding requests for information. The FOIA Officer is
authorized to receive requests and to (1) grant or deny initial
requests; (2) extend the administrative deadline; (3) make
discretionary release of exempt records; and (4) make
determinations regarding charges pursuant to the fee schedule.[17]

Any person whose request for information is denied has
the right to appeal the denial. Appeals should be addressed to

the Administrator, Packers and Stockyards Administration, U.S. Department of Agriculture, Washington, D.C. 20250.[18]

C. Packers
1. Definition
"Packers" are currently defined in the Act as persons "engaged in the business (a) of buying livestock in commerce for purposes of slaughter, or (b) of manufacturing or preparing meats or meat food products for sale or shipment in commerce, or (c) of marketing meats, meat food products, or livestock products in an unmanufactured form . . . ."[19] This provision has been broadly construed so as to include not only wholesalers or slaughterers but others involved in some phase of meat marketing and distribution as well. For example, the term "packer" has been considered by courts to include a corporation preparing meat or meat products for sale and shipment in commerce. In United Corp. v. Federal Trade Commission,[20] the Fourth Circuit Court of Appeals found a corporation which marketed canned meat products prepared for it by two licensed packers to be a packer under the Act.

The definition of the term "packer" broadly includes businesses that purchase and resell processed meat.[21] The 1976 amendments to the Packers and Stockyards Act extended the Act's coverage. In Peterman v. USDA,[22] a business person who sold meat products to consumers in a "meat locker" operation was held to be a packer. In Bruhn's Freezer Meats of Chicago, Inc. v. USDA,[23] freezer plant operators whose business included cutting sides and quarters of beef into consumer cuts, wrapping beef cuts, and freezing the meat cuts, were held to be packers. Nationwide supermarket chains which engage in meat processing activities were held to be packers in Safeway Stores Inc. v. Freeman.[24]

2. Prohibited Conduct
Packers (and live poultry dealers and handlers) are prohibited from engaging in the following practices with respect to livestock, meats, meat food products, livestock products in unmanufactured form, poultry, and poultry products:

(1) using unfair, discriminatory, or deceptive practices;

(2) giving unreasonable preference or advantage,

prejudice or disadvantage to any person or locality;

(3)   selling to or buying from another packer so as to affect supply, thereby restraining commerce or creating a monopoly;

(4)   doing anything that would result in manipulating or controlling prices, creating a monopoly, or restraining commerce; or,

(5)   conspiring to apportion territory or sales, to manipulate prices, or to aid another in any of the specified unlawful acts.[25]

This section has been held to prohibit a wide variety of practices. For example, in DeJong Packing Co. v. USDA,[26] packers conspired to force auction stockyards to alter sales terms. As a result, sales of slaughter cattle were made subject to satisfactory government inspection rather than on an "as is" basis. This was regarded as an unfair practice under this section. In Swift & Co. v. U.S.,[27] a packing company's practice of refraining from bidding against a particular dealer in fat lamb sales and then procuring most of the company's fat lambs from that dealer was held to be an unfair practice. In Wilson & Co. v. Benson,[28] a meat packer's price cutting activities were found to constitute unfair, unjustly discriminatory and deceptive practices. In Wilson, the packer sold meat products for less than the standard market price. This resulted in a loss for its operations in a particular area. Similarly, in Swift & Co. v. U.S.,[29] an agreement between a meat packer and a hog buyer to split the purchase price of hogs, with the intent to eliminate competition, was held to be a violation of the Act. The operation of a scale which was improperly balanced, resulting in false and incorrect weights, is also a violation of the Act.[30]

3.   Violations of the Act

The Secretary of Agriculture is authorized to take action against a packer whom he has reason to believe has violated, or is violating, any of the provisions of the Act.[31] The Packers and Stockyards Administration initiates the complaint process by serving a complaint on the packer. The matter must be set for hearing and the packer is required to testify at the hearing.[32] Civil penalties of up to $10,000 per violation may be assessed upon a finding of liability.[33] A packer who is subject to a

369

USDA order which results from this procedure is entitled to file an appeal. The appeal must be filed in the Federal circuit court of appeals for the circuit in which the packer's principal place of business is located.[34] This appeal proceeding has the status of a "preferred cause" and must be expedited by the Circuit Court.[35] The Court may affirm, modify, or set aside the order of the Secretary. The Court may take additional evidence if the case requires.[36]

The provisions of Section 192 list prohibited conduct which apply to packers and live poultry dealers and handlers.[37] However, the enforcement procedure outlined above applies only to packers.[38] This means that the Secretary is not authorized to use the cease and desist procedures, which require notice and a hearing, with respect to live poultry dealers and handlers.[39]

4. Prompt Payment Provisions/Statutory Trust

In 1976, Congress amended the Packers and Stockyards Act in an attempt to assure full and prompt payment. The Act now provides that each packer, dealer or market agency must deliver to the seller of livestock (or his authorized representative) the full amount of the purchase price for the livestock before the close of the next business day following the transaction unless the parties expressly agree otherwise.[40] In effect, this provision entitles the seller of livestock, in transactions covered by the act, to next-day payment unless that right is knowingly waived by the seller. For an agreement which waived the right to next-day payment to be effective, it must be in writing and not be procured by deceptive means. A copy or other evidence thereof must appear in both the dealer's and purchaser's records and be contained in documents issued by the purchaser relating to the transaction.[41] Furthermore, any attempt on the part of the dealer, market agency or packer to delay the payment of those sale proceeds is deemed to be an unfair practice under the Act.[42]

To further protect livestock sellers from insolvent packers, Congress added a statutory trust provisions to the Act in 1976.[43] Although this section applies only to those packers whose annual purchases exceed $500,000 and is applicable solely to cash sales, it establishes a statutory trust under which all

370

meat inventories, receivables and proceeds are to "be held . . . in trust for the benefit of all unpaid cash sellers" until they have been paid in full for their livestock.[44] This provision was deemed necessary to avoid a problem that livestock sellers faced under the Uniform Commercial Code (UCC). If a seller sold livestock to a packer or other party subject to the Act and was not immediately paid cash for the animals, the seller would have a claim against the packer. However, that claim would generally be an unsecured claim because it would not normally be "perfected" under the UCC (which requires the execution of a security agreement and the filing of a statement with the Secretary of State identifying the amount owed). This meant that notwithstanding the fact that federal law gave the seller a right to next day payment, state law (which was considered to apply in this situation) required that the secured creditors would be paid first in the event the packer was insolvent and the seller, as an unsecured creditor, would share whatever was left after that with other unsecured creditors.

Under the statutory trust provision, a packer holds livestock purchased in cash sales and all "inventories of, or receiving products derived therefrom," in trust for the benefit of unpaid cash sellers of the livestock until full payment has been received by the seller.[45] The sale of livestock constitutes a "cash sale" unless the seller has specifically signed a credit agreement to the contrary.[46] The seller's acquiescence in accepting late payments for purchases is not an express extension of credit by the seller to the packer.[47]

To receive the benefit of the trust provision, notification of a claim under this section must be made within 30 days of the final date set for payment (if no payment is received at all) or within 15 days of learning that a payment instrument has been dishonored. The unpaid seller must notify both the packer and the Secretary of Agriculture.[48]

D. Stockyards and Stockyard Dealers
1. Definition
The Act has two sections which prohibit certain activities by stockyard owners and market agencies.[49] One section is also applicable to dealers.[50] The Act contains a registration procedure for stockyards, market agencies and dealers. It also

prohibits certain activities from being conducted prior to registration.[51] The Secretary must make an initial determination that a particular business fits the statutory definition of "stockyard." The definition of "stockyard" is: "...any place, establishment, or facility commonly known as stockyards, conducted, operated, or managed for profit or nonprofit as a public market for livestock producers, breeders, market agencies, and buyers, consisting of pens, or other enclosures, and their appurtenances, in which live cattle, sheep, swine, horses, mules, or goats are received, held, or kept for sale or shipment in commerce."[52] A "market agency" is any person engaged in the business of either buying or selling livestock on a commission basis, or furnishing stockyard services such as "marketing, feeding, watering, holding, delivery, shipment weighing, or handling" livestock.[53] A market agency may also be required to register under the Act.[54] A dealer is a person engaged in the business of buying or selling livestock either on his or her own account or as the employee or agent of the seller or purchaser, and who is not a market agency. The activities of a dealer must also be "in commerce."[55]

Feedlots are not currently included within the definition of "stockyard" although the USDA has taken the position that they should be. In <u>Solomon Valley Feedlot, Inc. v. Butz</u>,[56] the Tenth Circuit Court of Appeals held that a feedlot was not a stockyard because the selling activity was an accommodation to owners, without charge, and the only profit to the feedlot was derived from the feeding of the cattle. The opposite result was reached in <u>In re Sterling Colorado Beef</u>[57] where the Judicial Officer found a feedlot to be a "dealer" (not a stockyard) because of the services provided. In this case a fee was charged for feeding the cattle and for handling purchases and sales. The Judicial Officer noted that even without a fee these services would have been sufficient to regard the feedlot as a dealer.[58]

Once the Secretary determines that a particular stockyard satisfies the definition, he notifies its owner(s) and gives public notice by "posting" the stockyard. After that has occurred, the stockyard is subject to the provisions of the Act.[59] Once a stockyard has been posted, market agencies and dealers have 30 days to register with the Secretary or cease doing business at that stockyard.[60] Market agencies and dealers must also have written authorization from the stockyard owner if they are to continue in business after a stockyard has been posted.[61] The Act authorizes the Secretary to require that market agencies and dealers post bond.[62] The bonding requirement has been held to be a prerequisite to registration.[63]

2. Prohibited Conduct

The services which are furnished by a stockyard or a market agency must be "reasonable and nondiscriminatory." Services must not be refused to any person for any reason that is unreasonable or unjustly discriminatory.[64] Moreover, the rates charged for stockyard services furnished by either a stockyard or market agency must be "just, reasonable, and nondiscriminatory."[65] Stockyard owners and market agencies doing business at posted stockyards must file all schedules of rates and charges with the Packers and Stockyards Administration. These schedules are open to public inspection at the stockyard.[66] When a new rate or charge schedule is filed, the Packers and Stockyards Administrator may "upon complaint or upon his own initiative without complaint" conduct a hearing to determine the lawfulness of the rate, charge, or regulation or practice affecting any rate or charge. The Administrator has the power to suspend the operation of a schedule, defer the use of the rate or charge, and following a hearing, to issue any appropriate orders.[67]

Stockyard owners and market agencies have a legal duty to "establish, observe, and enforce" regulations and practices that are "just, reasonable, and nondiscriminatory."[68] The stockyard owner has the "responsibility and right" to require those persons who are engaged in or attempting to engage in the "purchase, sale, or solicitation of livestock" at the stockyard to conduct their operations in a manner "which will foster, preserve or insure an efficient, competitive, public market."[69]

If, in the Secretary's opinion, any rate, charge, regulation or practice is unjust, unreasonable or discriminatory the Secretary may prescribe appropriate rates, charges, regulations or practices as are needed in a particular situation.[70]

The Act prohibits stockyard owners, market agencies and dealers from using "any unfair, unjustly discriminatory, or deceptive practice or device" in connection with a determination of whether a person is to be authorized to operate the stockyards, or is suitable to be "receiving, marketing, buying, or selling.... feeding, watering, holding, dealing, shipment, weighing or handling of livestock."[71] A violation of this section carries a potential penalty of $10,000 for each violation. The Secretary may also issue "cease and desist" orders. These sanctions may only be applied following notice and a hearing.[72]

It is a violation of the Act for a stockyard owner, market agency or dealer to violate an order of the Secretary under Section 211 (orders related to rates, charges, regulations or practices); Section 212 (orders related to rules and practices involving discrimination between interstate and intrastate commerce); or Section 213 (orders related to unfair, unjustly discriminatory or deceptive practices). Civil penalties of $500 per day may be imposed for the violation of an order.[73]

If a stockyard, market agency or dealer violates any provision of the Act, or an order of the Secretary which is related to the purchase, sale or handling of livestock, Section 209 imposes liability for the full amount of any damages resulting from the violation.[74] Liability can be assessed through a private cause of action in one of two ways. One is through litigation in a U.S. District court. The other is through an agency reparations proceeding.[75]

E. Reparations
In a reparation proceeding, a private party seeks to enforce the terms of the Act through a private cause of action for money damages. The Secretary is not a party of record in a reparations proceeding.[76]

1. Commencing a Reparations Proceeding
The filing of a complaint commences the reparations proceeding. Any interested person may file a complaint regarding actions which were committed or omitted by any stockyard owner, market agency, or dealer in violation of the Packers and Stockyards Act.[77] A reparations proceeding may also be used upon the violation of an order issued by the Secretary.[78]

The complaint must be in writing and may be in any of the following forms: (1) a printed form supplied by the

374

agency; (2) a formal litigation document; (3) a letter; (4) a mailgram; or (5) a telegram. It may be typewritten or handwritten.[79]

The complaint should include the following information:
(1) the date and place where the alleged violation of the Act occurred;
(2) the quantity and quality of the livestock involved;
(3) whether a sale is involved and, if so, the date, sale price, and amount actually paid and received;
(4) whether a consignment sale is involved and, if so, the date, and reported gross and net proceeds;
(5) the amount of reparation claimed, and method of computation;
(6) the name and address of each person involved, including any agent representing either the complainant or the respondent in the relevant transaction;
(7) the name and address of each partner or member, if a partnership or joint venture is involved;
(8) other material facts, including the terms of any contracts involved; and
(9) an appendix containing true copies of all available papers relating to the transaction complained of, including shipping documents, letters, telegrams, invoices, manifests, accounts of sales, and special contracts or agreements and checks and drafts.[80]

The complaint should be filed either at the agency headquarters in Washington, D.C., or at any regional office. Alternatively, the complaint may be delivered to any full time employee of the agency, wherever found.[81] The complaint must be received by the agency within 90 days after the accrual of the cause of action.[82]

The complaint may be amended without leave of the agency prior to the close of an oral hearing or prior to the filing of the last evidence in a written hearing.[83] However, the following exceptions apply:
(1) An amendment cannot add a respondent if it is filed more than 90 days after the accrual of the cause of action against that respondent;
(2) An amendment cannot state a new and different cause of

action if it is filed more than 90 days after the accrual of that new and different cause of action; and

(3) After the first amendment of the complaint, or after the filing of an answer by the respondent, an amendment may not be filed (a.) without the written consent of the respondent, or (b.) without leave of the presiding officer, or (c.) if the proceeding has not yet been docketed, without leave of the agency head.[84]

An amendment must be filed in writing and signed by the complainant or his or her representative. If an amendment is filed after service of the complaint, it must be served on the respondent.[85]

A complainant reserves the right to withdraw a complaint and thereby terminate the reparation proceeding.[86] However, this action would not terminate any pending counterclaims or crossclaims. If a complainant fails to cooperate with the Secretary in the conduct of the reparations proceeding, the complainant may be deemed to have withdrawn the complaint.[87] This deemed withdrawal would become effective after the parties have been served with written notice of the complainant's failure to prosecute and after the complainant has had reasonable opportunity in which to respond.[88]

2. Agency Evaluation of Complaints
   a. Informal Disposition

The agency head is authorized to conduct an initial evaluation of complaints which have been filed. This investigation will be conducted if there appears to be any reasonable ground for doing so.[89] If the agency head reasonably believes that there are not sufficient facts to form a basis for further proceedings, the matter may be discontinued without prejudice to subsequent court action on the same cause of action. If the matter is dropped, the person who filed the complaint will be informed of that fact.[90]

The agency may, in its discretion, prepare a report of its investigation. This report may be served on the parties and made a part of the record of the proceeding. The decision to prepare a report or to serve it on the parties and to make the report a part of the record, is reserved to the discretion of the

376

agency head. The information in the report will be considered to be evidence in the proceeding to the extent that the information is relevant and material.[91] Any party may submit evidence in rebuttal of the information in the report. The factfinder must give credible oral testimony greater weight as evidence than the information in the report.[92]

After reviewing the case, the agency head may attempt to obtain the consent of the parties to an amicable or informal adjustment of the case. This is permissible if the statements in the complaint and the information obtained in the investigation seem to warrant such action.[93] This informal adjustment may be achieved through oral or written communications with the parties or their representatives.[94]

b. Formal Disposition
If the complaint is not disposed of informally at the initial stage, the complaint must then be served on the respondent with notice that an answer is required to be filed.[95]

c. Filing of Documents
All documents and papers other than the initial complaint must be filed with the agency prior to the docketing of the proceeding. After docketing has occurred, all documents and papers must be filed with the hearing clerk. Each document or paper must be filed in quadruplicate with an extra copy for each party in excess of two. Any document or paper not filed in the required number of copies, except an initial complaint, may be rejected and returned to the party filing it.[96]

Any document or paper other than the initial complaint will be deemed filed at the time it reaches the headquarters of the Department in Washington, D.C. However, if it is authorized to be filed with an officer or employee of the Department at any place outside the District of Columbia, it is deemed to be filed at the time it reaches the office of the officer or employee.[97]

A reasonable extension of the time for filing a document or paper other than an initial complaint, may be granted upon request at any time prior to docketing. The extension will be made by the agency head, presiding officer, or judicial officer. Notice of an extension of time must be served on all parties.

After a proceeding has been docketed, an extension will only be granted after notice and an opportunity to be heard.[98]

Saturdays, Sundays, and federal holidays are included in computing the time allowed for the filing of any document or paper. However, when the time period expires on a Saturday, Sunday, or federal holiday the time is extended to include the following business day.[99]

d. Service of Documents

All documents or papers required to be served prior to docketing will be served by the agency head. After docketing, all documents or papers will be served by the hearing clerk.[100]

Service of any document or paper must be made by mailing a copy by registered or certified mail, addressed to the person to be served at their last known residence, principal office, place of business, or other mailing address.[101] Except in the case of a complaint, if the document or paper sent by certified or registered mail is returned undelivered because the addressee refused or failed to accept delivery, service can be made by remailing by regular mail. Proof of service must be made either by the return registered or certified mail receipt, or by the certificate of the person who mailed the paper(s) by regular mail.[102] The proof of service must be filed as a part of the record in the proceeding.[103] An order of a presiding officer which is made on the record at an oral hearing and shown in the transcript is deemed to be served on all parties present or represented at the hearing.[104]

e. Filing of Responsive Pleadings

Within 20 days after service of a complaint or its amendment on a respondent, he or she must file an answer in writing. The answer must be signed by the respondent or their attorney or representative. If an answer or amended answer is filed, it must be served on the complainant. If a respondent desires an oral hearing, a request for the hearing should be included with the answer.[105]

If a respondent desires to make a defense, the answer should contain a precise statement of the facts which constitute the grounds of the defense, and must specifically admit, deny, or explain each of the allegations of the complaint. However, the

378

answer may state that the respondent is without knowledge sufficient to respond to an allegation. If a respondent does not wish to defend, the answer must contain an admission of all the allegations of the complaint, or an admission of liability in the full amount claimed by the complainant.[106] An answer may be stricken for failure to comply with these requirements, but the respondent will be given an opportunity to comply with the rules.[107]

(1) Failure to file

If a respondent fails to file an answer as required above, he or she will be deemed to have admitted all the allegations in the complaint or cross-claim filed against that person. The respondent will also be deemed to have consented to the issuance of a final order in the proceeding, based on all evidence in the record.[108]

(2) Setoff, Counterclaim or Crossclaim

The answer may assert a setoff, counterclaim, or crossclaim. A counterclaim or crossclaim may only be pled if it is based on a violation for which the Act authorizes reparation to be ordered, and if it is filed within 90 days after the accrual of the cause of action alleged therein. However, a counterclaim may be filed after the 90-day period has elapsed if it is based on a transaction complained of in the complaint. A crossclaim must be served on the co-respondent. Within 20 days after such service, the co-respondent must file an answer thereto in compliance with the requirements for an answer to a complaint.[109]

(3) Reply to Counterclaim or Setoff

If the answer asserts a counterclaim or a setoff, the complainant may file a reply in writing within 10 days after the answer has been served. If any reply or amended reply is filed, it must be served on the respondent.[110]

The reply must be confined strictly to the matters alleged in the counterclaim or setoff. It must contain a precise statement of the facts which constitute the grounds of defense to the counterclaim or setoff. It must also specifically admit, deny, or explain each of the allegations in the counterclaim or setoff. However, if the complainant is without knowledge sufficient to allow a reply to an allegation, the reply must state that.[111] If no reply is filed, the allegations of the counterclaim or setoff are automatically regarded as denied.[112]

f. Docketing of the Proceeding
The agency head must transmit all of the papers which have been filed in the proceeding to the hearing clerk. This must be done promptly after the answer or the reply has been filed, or following the expiration of the period of time prescribed above for the filing of the answer or the reply. Thereafter, the hearing clerk must promptly transmit all of these papers to the Office of the General Counsel for assignment to a presiding officer.[113]

g. Discovery
(1) Taking of Depositions
A party may file an application for an order to allow the taking of testimony by deposition. This may be done at any time after the docketing of a proceeding and before the close of an oral hearing or the filing of that party's evidence in a written hearing. The application must contain the following information: (1) the name and address of the proposed deponent; (2) the name and address of the person before whom the proposed examination is to be made; (3) the reason(s) why the deposition should be taken, which must show that it will qualify for use as set forth in the regulations; (4) whether the proposed examination is to be on interrogatories or oral; and (5) if oral, a suggested time and place where the proposed examination should take place. This application should be in writing unless it is made orally on the record at an oral hearing.[114]

If an application for a deposition is made orally on the record, each party present at the hearing may respond orally to the application. If an application is in writing, it must be served on each party. Each party served has 10 days from the date of service to file a written response to the application.[115]

If the presiding officer is satisfied that there is good cause for taking the deposition, it may be ordered. The order must be served on the parties and must include the following information: (1) The name and address of the officer before whom the examination is to be made; (2) the name of the deponent; (3) whether the examination will be oral or on interrogatories; and (4) if the examination will be oral, the time, which must be not less than 10 days after the issuance of the order, and place where it will be held. The officer, time, and place need not be the same as those requested in the application.[116]

A deposition must be made before an officer authorized to administer oaths. An officer may not be a relative, employee, attorney, or representative of any party or who is financially interested in the result of the proceeding.[117] Testimony which is taken by deposition, to the extent credible, must be given greater weight as evidence than that contained in affidavits or other statements.[118]

The deponent must be examined under oath or affirmation, and the testimony of the deponent must be recorded by the officer. If the examination is oral, the deponent must be examined first by the party at whose instance the deposition is taken, and must be subject to cross-examination by any other party or their representative. The officer must propound any interrogatories which were filed by parties not present or represented at the examination.[119]

(2) Interrogatories

If the presiding officer so directs, or the parties agree, a deposition may be taken by means of written interrogatories. A deposition must be taken by interrogatories if the presiding officer finds that a party has a principal place of business or a residence more than 100 miles from the place of the examination and that it would constitute an undue hardship to be present or represented at an oral examination. Under these circumstances, the deposition, if taken, must be taken by means of interrogatories. If the applicant does not timely file the proposed interrogatories, the application may be denied.[120]

After the interrogatories are filed, they must promptly be served on all other parties. The other parties must be given not less than 10 days after the dates on which they are served with interrogatories, to file cross-interrogatories in writing. If any cross-interrogatories are timely filed, they must promptly be served on all parties. If the examination will be oral, parties who will not be present or represented at the examination may file interrogatories in writing with the officer prior to the time for the examination.[121]

(3) Transcripts
The officer must certify on the transcript that the deponent was duly sworn by the officer and that the transcript is a true record of the deponent's testimony, with such exceptions as the certificate may specify. The officer must mail appropriate originals and transcripts by registered or certified mail to the presiding officer.[122]

After the transcript is received by the presiding officer, it must promptly be served on all parties. Any party may file a written motion proposing corrections to the transcript within 10 days after service of the transcript. Any motion must be served on each party. Those parties then have 10 days to file a written response to the motion. All portions of the transcript which are not referred to in the motion will be presumed to be accurate.[123]

The transcript of a written deposition may be made a part of the record upon written motion. If any portion of a deposition transcript is made a part of the record, any other party may make the remainder, or any other portion, of the transcript a part of the record.[124]

(4) Expenses
Fees and reimbursements payable to an officer taking a deposition must be paid by the party at whose instance the deposition is taken.[125]

h. Pre-hearing Conferences
The presiding officer, at any time prior to the commencement of the hearing, may request that the parties or their counsel appear at a conference before the presiding officer to consider:
(1) The simplification of issues;
(2) The necessity of amendments to pleadings;
(3) The possibility of obtaining stipulations of fact and of the authenticity, accuracy, and admissibility of

documents, which will avoid unnecessary proof;
(4) The limitation of the number of expert or other witnesses;
(5) The negotiation, compromise, or settlement of issues;
(6) The exchange of copies of proposed exhibits;
(7) The identification of documents or matters of which official notice may be requested;
(8) A schedule to be followed by the parties for completion of the actions decided at the conference; or
(9) Such other matters as may expedite and aid in the disposition of the proceeding.[126]

There is no requirement that a transcript of the conference be made. However, the presiding officer must prepare and file for the record a written summary if any action is taken at the conference. The summary must incorporate any written stipulations or agreements made by the parties at the conference or following the conference. If the circumstances are such that the parties' appearance at a conference is impracticable, the presiding officer may conduct the conference by telephone conference call, or request that the parties correspond with the presiding officer for the purpose of accomplishing the objectives of a pre-hearing conference. Correspondence in these negotiations may not be made a part of the record.[127]

    i. <u>Hearings</u>
(1) <u>When Required</u>
An oral or written hearing must be held unless:
(1) Each respondent admits or is deemed to admit sufficient allegations of the complaint to support the full amount claimed by the complainant as reparation;
(2) Each respondent admits liability to the complainant in the full amount claimed by the complainant as reparation;
(3) Before a hearing has been completed the parties agree in writing that the proceeding may be decided on the basis of the record as it stands at the time that the agreement is filed; or
(4) Before a hearing has been completed the parties

settle their dispute or the complainant withdraws the complaint.[128]

(2) Representation

Any party may appear in an oral hearing, or file evidence in a written hearing, either in person or by counsel or other representative.[129] For unethical or contumacious conduct in or in connection with a proceeding, the presiding officer may preclude a person from further acting as the attorney or representative for any party to the proceeding. An appeal to the Judicial Officer may be immediately taken from any such order.[130]

(3) Oral Hearings

The hearing must be oral if: $10,000 or more is in controversy and any complainant or respondent files a written request for an oral hearing. If less than $10,000 is in controversy, the presiding officer has the discretion to determine, upon written request by any party, that an oral hearing is necessary to establish the facts and circumstances giving rise to the controversy.[131]

If $10,000 or more is in controversy and a party has timely filed a request for oral hearing, that party may withdraw the request at any time prior to completion of an oral hearing. If the withdrawal leaves no pending request for oral hearing in the proceeding, each other party must be served with notice of this and must be given 10 days to request an oral hearing. If any party files a request for oral hearing within that time, the request must be granted.[132] A party which is entitled to an oral hearing may withdraw its request for the oral hearing on the condition that only depositions be used if a written hearing is held.[133]

(4) Time and Place of Oral Hearing

If an oral hearing is to be held, the presiding officer must set a time and place for it, giving careful consideration to the convenience of the parties. When all parties have their principal places of business or residence within a single unit of local government, a single geographic area within a State, or a single State, the oral hearing must held as near as possible to

384

those places of business or residence.[134] A notice which states the time and place of the oral hearing must be served on each party.[135] If any party to the proceeding, after being duly notified, fails to appear at the oral hearing in person or by counsel or other representative, that party will be deemed to have waived the right to add any further evidence to the record in the proceeding, or to object to the admission of any evidence. If the parties who are present are all adverse to the absent party, they may elect to present evidence, in whole or in part, in the form of oral testimony, affidavits, or depositions.[136]

(5) Conduct of Oral Hearing
At the oral hearing the presiding officer must permit oral argument by the parties or their counsel to the extent that the presiding officer deems it necessary for the expeditious or proper disposition of the case.[137] The complainant is entitled to proceed first, if he or she is present at the commencement of the oral hearing.[138] Any party which is present or represented at an oral hearing, who wishes to file a written argument or brief, proposed findings of fact, conclusions of law, proposed order, or a statement of objections to rulings made by the presiding officer, must inform the presiding officer of this at the oral hearing. Upon being so informed, the presiding officer must set a reasonable time for the filing of those documents, and state it on the record at the oral hearing.[139]

(6) Evidence
The testimony of witnesses at an oral hearing must be on oath or affirmation and is subject to cross-examination. Any witness other than a party may be examined separately and apart from all other witnesses, in the discretion of the presiding officer. The presiding officer must exclude evidence which is immaterial, irrelevant, or unduly repetitious, or which is unreliable.[140]

If a party objects to the admission of any evidence or to the limitation of the scope of any examination or cross-examination or to any other ruling of the presiding officer, that party must state briefly the grounds of the objection, and the presiding officer must rule on it. Objections which are not timely made before the presiding officer may not subsequently

385

be relied on in the proceeding.*141*

Whenever evidence is excluded by the presiding officer, the party offering that evidence may make an offer of proof. If the evidence consists of a brief oral statement, it must be included in full in the transcript. If the evidence consists of an exhibit, it must be marked for identification and inserted in the record. In either event, if the judicial officer decides that the presiding officer's ruling in excluding the evidence was erroneous and prejudicial, the evidence will be admitted as part of the record.*142* A true copy of any written entry in any record of the Department, made by an officer or employee in the course of official duties, and relevant to the issues involved in the hearing, is admissible as prima facie evidence of the facts stated therein, without the production of the officer or employee.*143*

For each exhibit offered by a party, copies in addition to the original must be filed with the presiding officer. The copies are for the use of all other parties to the proceeding, except where the presiding officer finds that the furnishing of copies is impracticable.*144*

If the testimony of a witness refers to any document, the presiding officer must determine whether it must be produced at the hearing and made a part of the record as an exhibit, or whether it may be incorporated in the record by reference.*145*

If relevant and material matter is included in a document which also contains irrelevant or immaterial matter, the irrelevant or immaterial matter must be designated by the party offering the document in evidence, and must be segregated and excluded, insofar as practicable.*146*

(7) Use of Subpoenas

The attendance and testimony of witnesses at the place designated for an oral hearing, and the production of documentary evidence, may be compelled from anywhere in the United States by subpoena. Subpoenas may be issued by the presiding officer on a written application filed by a party, showing the grounds and necessity thereof. With respect to subpoenas for the production of documentary evidence, the application must show their competency, relevancy, and materiality and the necessity for their production. Subpoenas may be issued on the motion of the presiding officer.[147]

A subpoena may be served by any natural person over the age of 18 years. The party for whom a subpoena is issued is responsible for serving it. However, at the request of the party the Secretary will attempt to serve it. Service and proof of service must be properly made. If the person who delivers or mails a subpoena is not an employee of the Department or a U. S. Marshall or his deputy, proof of service must be by the affidavit of the person making service, or by a statement of that person under penalty of perjury.[148]

(8) Transcript of Oral Hearing

Parties who wish to secure copies of the transcript of the oral hearing may make arrangements with the reporter. The reporter must furnish and deliver copies directly to those parties, upon receipt of payment for them, at the rate per page provided by the contract between the reporter and the Department for reporting services.[149]

As soon as practicable after the close of the oral hearing, the reporter must transmit to the presiding officer the original transcript of the testimony, and copies for the Washington and area offices of the Agency. The reporter must also transmit a copy of the transcript to each party who has arranged and paid for it. Upon receipt of the transcript, the presiding officer must attach to the original transcript a certificate stating that, to the best of the presiding officer's knowledge and belief, the transcript is a true, correct, and complete transcript of the testimony given at the hearing. This certificate must also state that the exhibits mentioned in it are all the exhibits received in evidence at the hearing, with whatever exceptions the certificate specifies. This certificate must be served on each party and a copy must be attached to each copy of the transcript received by the presiding officer.[150]

(9) Written Hearings

In proceedings which involve a written hearing, the complainant must be served with notice of an opportunity to file evidence. Within 20 days after service, the complainant may file his or her evidence. Whatever evidence the complainant files in response to that notice must be served promptly on the respondent.[151]   After expiration of the time in which the complainant's evidence may be filed, the respondent must be served with notice of the opportunity to file evidence. Within 20 days after service, the respondent may file evidence. Whatever evidence the respondent files in response to that notice must be served promptly on the complainant.[152]

If the respondent files any evidence, the complainant must be served with notice of an opportunity to file evidence in rebuttal of what the respondent has filed. Within 10 days after service, the complainant may file his or her evidence. This evidence must be confined strictly to rebuttal of what the respondent has filed. Whatever evidence the complainant files in response to that notice must be served promptly on the respondent.[153]   The failure of a party to file any evidence within the time prescribed, constitutes a waiver of the right to file such evidence.[154]

After the filing of the last evidence in a written hearing, notice must be served on each party to the effect that the party may file, within 10 days after service, a written argument or brief, proposed findings of fact, conclusions of law, and/or a proposed order.[155]

j. Report of Presiding Officer
The presiding officer must prepare a report on the basis of all of the evidence in the record. This includes the investigation report and any admissions and stipulations. The report must be prepared in the form of a final order for signature by the Judicial Officer, and must be filed with the hearing clerk. The report must not be served on the parties until it is signed by the Judicial Officer.[156]

The report and the record must be filed simultaneously. The record should include: pleadings, motions and requests filed and rulings thereon; the investigation report; the transcript of an oral hearing, and exhibits received, if an oral hearing was held; evidence filed by the parties if a written hearing was held; documents filed in connection with pre-hearing conferences; any proposed findings of fact, conclusions of law and orders, statements of objections, and briefs; any stipulations; and proofs of service.[157]

k. Decision

When the hearing clerk reasonably believes that the record is complete and in proper order, the record and the report must be submitted to the Judicial Officer for final decision.[158] As soon as practicable after receiving the record and report, the Judicial Officer must issue an order on the basis of the record. This order must be served on the parties.[159]

If the Judicial Officer deems it advisable to do so, the order may be issued in tentative form. In that event, a presiding officer will be assigned and the tentative order will be served on each party. The parties will then have 20 days in which to file written exceptions to it, and arguments or briefs in support of those exceptions. If no party timely files exceptions, the tentative order will automatically become the final order, and notice of that fact will be served on the parties.[160]

l. Petition to Reopen A Hearing

Any party may file a petition to reopen a hearing to take further evidence, at any time prior to the issuance of the final order, or prior to a tentative order becoming final. The petition must state the nature and purpose of the evidence to be offered, show that it is not merely cumulative, and state a good reason why it was not offered at the oral hearing, or filed in the written hearing.[161] Similarly, any party may file a petition to rehear or reargue a proceeding or reconsider an order of the Judicial Officer, at any time within 20 days after service of the order on the party. The petition must specify the matters claimed to have been erroneously decided, and the basis for the petitioner's claim that the matters were erroneously decided.[162]

Any respondent against whom an order is issued by the Judicial Officer, and who failed to file an answer, may file a petition to set aside the order. This must be done within 20 days after service of the order on the respondent. The petition must state a good reason why an answer was not filed.[163] If a petitioner wishes to file a brief or memorandum of law in support of his or her petition, it must be filed with the petition.[164]

A presiding officer will be assigned upon the filing of a petition, or upon notice to the hearing clerk that the party intends to file a petition. The petitioner has the burden of establishing that the petition should be granted. If a petition to reopen is timely filed, the order must not be issued pending the decision whether to grant or deny the petition. If a petition to rehear, reargue or reconsider, or to set aside a default order, is timely filed, the effect of the order will be automatically stayed pending the decision whether to grant or deny it. If the petition is not timely filed, operation of the order will not be stayed unless the Judicial Officer determines otherwise.[165]

A petition, including the brief or memorandum of law in support of it, must be served on each party. Each party must file an answer to the petition within 20 days after service. If a party wishes to file a brief or memorandum of law in support of its answer, it must be filed with the answer. The answer, including the brief or memorandum of law in support of it, must be served on each party to the proceeding. A petition may be denied if proper service is not made.[166]

The presiding officer must prepare a recommendation with respect to the petition, and submit it to the Judicial Officer for decision. This recommendation must be prepared in the form of a final order for signature by the Judicial Officer. It must not be served on the parties unless and until it is signed by the Judicial Officer. The order of the judicial officer must be served on the parties.[167] If the judicial officer decides to reopen a hearing to rehear or permit reargument of a proceeding, or to set aside a default order, a presiding officer will be assigned.[168]

m. Authority of Presiding Officer

The presiding officer who is assigned to any proceeding has the authority to:

(1) Set the time and place of a prehearing conference and an oral hearing, adjourn the oral hearing, and change the time and place of the oral hearing;

(2) Administer oaths and affirmations;

(3) Issue subpoenas requiring the attendance and testimony of witnesses and the production of documentary evidence at an oral hearing;

(4) Summon and examine witnesses and receive evidence at an oral hearing;

390

(5) Take or order the taking of depositions;
(6) Admit or exclude evidence;
(7) Hear oral argument on facts or law; and
(8) Do all acts and take all measures necessary for the maintenance of order and the efficient conduct of the proceeding, including the exclusion of contumacious counsel or other persons.[169]

The presiding officer is authorized to rule on all motions and requests filed prior to the submission of the presiding officer's report to the Judicial Officer. However, a presiding officer is not authorized to dismiss a complaint. The submission or certification of any question to the Judicial Officer, prior to submission of the report, is in the discretion of the presiding officer.[170]

A person may not be assigned to act as a presiding officer in any proceeding if that person (1) has any material pecuniary interest in any matter or business involved in the proceeding; (2) is related within the third degree by blood or marriage to any party to the proceeding; or (3) has any conflict of interest which might impair the person's objectivity in the proceeding.[171]

A party may file a petition for disqualification of the presiding officer. It must set forth with particularity the grounds for the alleged disqualification. A petition must be filed with the hearing clerk, who must immediately transmit it to the Judicial Officer and inform the presiding officer. The record of the proceeding also must immediately be transmitted to the Judicial Officer. After any investigation or hearing which is deemed necessary, the judicial officer must either deny the petition or direct that another presiding officer be assigned to the proceeding. The petition, and notice of the order of the judicial officer, must be made a part of the record and served on the parties.[172]

n. Witness Fees

Witnesses who are subpoenaed before the presiding officer, and witnesses whose depositions are taken, are entitled to the same fees and mileage as are paid for like services in the courts of the United States. Fees and mileage must be paid by the party at whose instance the witness appears or has their deposition taken.[173]

o. Judicial Notice

Official notice must be taken of the matters which are judicially noticed by the courts of the United States and of any other technical or scientific fact of established character. However, parties must be given notice of the matters which are noticed, and must be given adequate opportunity to show that the facts are erroneously noticed.[174]

p. Petition To Intervene

At any time after the docketing of a proceeding and before commencement of an oral or written hearing, the presiding officer may permit any person to intervene in the proceeding if good cause is shown. The petition must state with preciseness and particularity: (a) the petitioner's relationship to the matters involved in the proceeding: (b) the nature of the material the petitioner intends to present in evidence; (c) the nature of the argument the petitioner intends to make; and (d) the reasons why the petitioner should be allowed to intervene. This petition, and notice of the order thereon, must be served on the parties and made a part of the record in the proceeding.[175]

q. Ex parte communications

In the time period between the docketing of a case and the issuance of the final decision, the presiding officer or judicial officer must not discuss ex parte the merits of the proceeding with any party, or attorney or representative of a party. Procedural matters are not be included within this limitation.[176]

If the presiding officer or Judicial Officer receives an ex parte communication in violation of this section,the one who receives the communication must place the following in the record of the proceeding:

(1) The document if it is written communication, or a memorandum stating the substance of the communication if it is oral; and

(2) A copy of any written response or a memorandum stating the substance of any oral response thereto.[177]

II. Marketing of Poultry

The poultry marketing system differs from the livestock marketing system in that it operates primarily through vertically integrated companies. Under this arrangement, growers (farmers) raise company-owned birds under a production contract. This contract is essentially a bailment agreement between the grower and the company. The company supplies the birds, and inputs such as feed and medication, to the growers. The company also supervises the production process. Once the birds reach the stage of development which corresponds to marketing specifications, the company regains possession of the birds. It then processes them and markets the finished poultry products.

A. Live Poultry Dealers and Handlers

The Packers and Stockyards Act defines a "live poultry dealer" as "any person engaged in the business of buying and selling live poultry in commerce for purposes of slaughter either on his own account or as the employee or agent of the vendor or purchaser."[178] In contrast, a live poultry handler is not explicitly defined in the Act. In Bunting v. Perdue, Inc.,[179] a vertically integrated poultry producer, which raised poultry through contract growers, was held not to be a live poultry dealer or handler. The key facts in Bunting were that the poultry producer did not engage in independent purchases and sales and did not serve as a "middleman" in poultry sales transactions. A small amount of sales activity with live poultry will cause a person to be classified as a dealer. For example, in U.S. v. Perdue Farms, Inc.,[180] the definition of "live poultry dealer" was held to apply to a wholesaler of ready-to-cook poultry where 0.5% of its business was from the sale of live birds.

The procedures which the Secretary may use to assess penalties against live poultry dealers for violations of the Act are more limited than the procedures available in the livestock industry. For example, the procedures outlined in Section 193 for packer violations are apparently not applicable to live poultry dealers and handlers. In Arkansas Valley Industries v. Freeman,[181] the Eighth Circuit Court of Appeals held that Section 192, the section applicable to packers, does not apply to live poultry dealers or handlers. Therefore, the cease and desist order, which was brought against the defendant for violating Section 192, was vacated. The holding in <u>Arkansas Valley Industries</u> was adopted by the Fifth Circuit Court of Appeals in <u>Davis v. U.S.</u>[182] The <u>Davis</u> court held that live poultry dealers and handlers are not "packers." Therefore, the Secretary is not authorized to issue cease and desist orders against them. Actions against live poultry dealers and handlers may be brought under the general provisions of the Act,[183] licensing provisions if applicable,[184] or by the Secretary's complaint to the Attorney General.

B. The Poultry Producers Financial Protection Act of 1987

The Poultry Producers Financial Protection Act of 1987 (the "Act"), an amendment to the Packers and Stockyards Act, was enacted on November 23, 1987.[185] It became effective on February 22, 1988. The Act's key provisions include the extension of "unlawful practices" liability to live poultry dealers and handlers, the establishment of a statutory trust to insure payment to growers under cash sale and poultry growing arrangements, and the requirement of prompt payment by dealers who purchase poultry. The Act's provisions are closely analogous to other Packers and Stockyards Act provisions that regulate purchase payment obligations of livestock dealers and handlers.[186]

The Act defines the following key terms:

(a) Poultry grower: "Any person engaged in the business of raising and caring for live poultry for slaughter by another, whether the poultry is owned by such person or by another, but not an employee of the owner of such poultry."[187]

(b) Poultry growing arrangement: "Any growout contract, marketing agreement, or other arrangement under which a poultry grower raises and cares for live poultry for delivery, in accord with another's instructions, for slaughter."[188]

(c) Live poultry dealer: "Any person engaged in the business of obtaining live poultry by purchase or under a poultry growing arrangement for the purpose of either slaughtering it or selling it for slaughter by another..."[189]

(d) Cash sale: "A sale in which the seller does not

expressly extend credit to the buyer."[190]

The statutory trust is intended to remedy the obstruction to commerce which is caused by financing arrangements in which live poultry dealers grant a security interest in poultry which they obtain by cash purchase or poultry growing arrangements. The trust applies to all poultry obtained by a live poultry dealer, whether by cash purchase or by a poultry growing arrangement.

The trust assets include all inventories of, or receivables or proceeds from, poultry obtained by the dealer, or the products derived therefrom. The grower-seller is protected from the risk of non-payment as an "unsecured creditor" under a cash sale because the value of the trust assets is held for the benefit of all unpaid cash sellers or poultry growers until they have received full payment.[191] In addition to failure to tender payment, payment is considered not to have occurred if the cash seller or poultry grower receives a payment instrument that is dishonored.[192]

Live poultry dealers are exempt from the statutory trust provisions if they (a) have $100,000 or less in average annual value of live poultry, or (b) have $100,000 or less in average annual value of live poultry obtained by purchase or by a poultry growing arrangement.[193]

Concomitantly, live poultry dealers must make prompt payment for poultry. Specifically, a dealer must deliver the full payment amount due to the seller-grower (a) before the close of the next business day following the purchase of poultry, in the case of a cash sale, or (b) by the close of the fifteenth day following the week in which the poultry is slaughtered, in the case of poultry obtained under a poultry growing arrangement.[194]

Furthermore, the following actions are to be considered "unfair practices" in violation of the Act: any attempt by a live poultry dealer to delay making payment due under the Act, or any actual delay in making payment, and any attempt made by the dealer for the purpose of, or resulting in, an extension of the normal payment period.[195]

If after a hearing, the Secretary finds that a live poultry dealer has violated either the statutory trust or prompt payment provisions of the Act, he or she must issue a cease and desist order against the dealer.[196] The Secretary may also assess a civil penalty of up to $20,000 for each such violation. However, the regulations provide that "in no event can the penalty assessed by the Secretary take priority over or impede the ability of the live poultry dealer to pay any unpaid cash seller or poultry grower.[197]

III.   Inspection and Disease Control Programs

Livestock and poultry marketing is greatly affected by various federal inspection programs designed to control the spread of communicable disease and to protect public health. These programs are administered under the authority of the Animal and Plant Health Inspection Services (APHIS) of USDA. These programs include those directed at preventing the introduction and dissemination of communicable animal diseases;[198] the Meat Inspection Act;[199] the Poultry Production Inspection Act;[200] and the Egg Products Inspection Act.[201]

A. Disease Prevention and Control

Congress empowered the USDA to "make such regulations and take such measures" as deemed necessary and proper to prevent the introduction or dissemination of contagious, infections or communicable diseases in animals and live poultry.[202] Commensurate with this responsibility, the USDA has the duty to prepare rules and regulations for the "speedy and effectual suppression and extirpation" of these diseases. It must also certify its rules and regulations to state authorities who are invited to cooperate in administering the programs. If a cooperative agreement is reached with a state, USDA expenditures can support measures to prevent the spread of disease.[203]

1. Interstate Movement

A major focus of disease control is the placing of restrictions on interstate movement of diseased animals. The transportation of livestock or poultry with any known "contagious, infectious, or communicable disease" is prohibited.[204] However, animals which react to a brucellosis test may be shipped or transported from one state to another for the purpose of immediate slaughter in accordance with

USDA regulations.[205] USDA is authorized to quarantine animals or poultry affected with contagious, infectious, communicable disease or where the risk of dissemination exists.[206] Transportation or movement of animals from a quarantined area is generally prohibited.[207] The Secretary may establish rules and regulations to govern "inspection, disinfection, certification, treatment, and handling and manner of delivery and shipment" of animals from quarantined areas.[208] Movement of contaminated animals in violation of USDA rules and regulations is illegal.[209] In U.S. v. Parks,[210] the government successfully prosecuted an experienced livestock dealer who moved cattle from Missouri to Arkansas without the health certificate required by the regulations.

2. Seizure and Quarantine

Congress enacted provisions which authorize the seizure, quarantine and disposal of livestock or poultry which are moving, being handled, or have been moved or handled in interstate or foreign commerce contrary to any law or regulation for the prevention of any communicable disease found in livestock or poultry. This provision applies to animals which are moving into the U.S. or in interstate commerce which are "affected with or have been exposed to" disease and to any animals which were affected or exposed to disease at the time of movement.[211]

An emergency exists if animals are determined to be affected with or exposed to any dangerous communicable disease. Under that circumstance, seizure, quarantine and disposal of any animal in the United States is authorized in order to prevent an outbreak of the disease. This authority extends to the carcasses of those animals and to any products or articles related to the animals if they are likely to spread the disease. Under this section, the USDA may seize, quarantine, and dispose of diseased animals and products only if the state is not taking adequate measures to control the disease.[212] Notice and compensation to the owner is required.[213] However, payment is not required if the owner has moved the animal, carcass, product or article in knowing violation of law or regulation.[214] In Cumberland v. USDA,[215] a farmer was awarded compensation for swine which were destroyed after they had been moved in interstate commerce. In <u>Cumberland,</u> the farmer had unknowingly violated the regulations. The compensation under this section is limited to the fair market value of the animals at the time of their destruction. Compensation does not extend to post-destruction profits, costs associated with cleaning and disinfecting the premises, or additional costs above that of other producers which are the result of special circumstances.[216]

3. Inspection of Conveyances and Facilities

Regulations govern the inspection, cleaning and disinfecting of conveyances and other facilities used in the movement of animals.[217] The movement of animals is regulated, if the animals are or have been affected with or exposed to communicable disease, vaccinated or treated for such disease or otherwise likely to introduce or disseminate any disease.[218] The Act expressly authorizes inspections of conveyances without a warrant. It also authorizes entry with a warrant upon premises to conduct the inspection. The seizure of an animal, carcass, product or article subject to disposal is also authorized.[219]

4. Importation

The USDA is authorized to promulgate rules and regulations to control the export of livestock and poultry from the United States to foreign countries.[220] Importation of diseased animals is generally prohibited.[221] Quarantine is authorized for cattle, sheep, and other ruminants and swine.[222] Importation, except at designated ports, is prohibited.[223] Inspection of all imported animals is required.[224]

B. Inspection Programs

The USDA administers three separate livestock and poultry inspection programs which affect the marketing of those commodities: (1) the programs for meat inspection, (2) poultry and poultry products inspection and (3) egg and egg products inspection.

1. Meat Inspection

The Federal Meat Inspection Act,[225] protects the health

and welfare of consumers by attempting to ensure that meat and meat products are "wholesome, unadulterated, properly marked, labeled, and packaged."[226] This law has a direct effect on livestock marketing. Pre-slaughter inspection is required of cattle, sheep, swine, goats, horses, mules, and other equine animals before they are allowed entry into a slaughtering facility.[227] States are encouraged to enact state meat inspection programs in cooperation with the federal program. State programs must adopt the federal standards as a minimum standard.

All animal carcasses must be inspected, including all body parts which are capable of being used as human food. Inspections must take place at any "slaughtering, meat canning, salting, packing, rendering or similar establishment."[228] This includes the inspection of carcasses or parts brought in to these establishments,[229] and meat food products prepared in any such establishment.[230] It also includes the inspection of establishments for sanitary conditions.[231] Inspection is specifically authorized for both nighttime and daytime slaughter.[232]

The law specifically prohibits the slaughter or preparation of articles for human food, except in compliance with the provisions of the Act. It also prohibits the sale, transport, offering for sale or transport, or receiving for sale or transport of any articles capable of use as human food if adulterated or misbranded unless the articles have passed inspection. Any action which has the effect or is intended to cause the articles to be adulterated or misbranded is prohibited.[233] Humane methods of slaughter are also required.[234]

Carcasses intended for export must be inspected and receive a certificate of condition.[235] In addition, carcasses, parts of carcasses, meat and meat food products may not be imported if they are adulterated or misbranded. Compliance with all inspection, building construction standards and other provisions of the meat inspection law is required.[236] Annual reports must be made to Congress as to compliance by foreign processing plants exporting these products to the United States, as well as on the programs carried out to assure compliance.[237]

Exemption from the various inspection requirements is granted for personal slaughtering of animals which are raised for personal, household, guest and employee use. The inspection requirements do not apply to the custom slaughtering of animals. The Secretary is authorized to issue regulations for custom slaughtering establishments.[238] Inspection is not required for establishments which do not intend that articles be used for human food. However, regulations requiring denaturing or identification may be issued.[239]

2. Poultry and Poultry Product Inspection

A comprehensive Federal inspection program has been established for poultry and poultry products. The Federal law is intended to encourage states to develop poultry product inspection programs which adopt Federal standards as a minimum standard.[240] The objective of the Federal poultry products inspection program is to protect the health of consumers, by ensuring that marketed poultry is unadulterated and that it is properly labeled.

Ante mortem inspection of poultry in establishments which process poultry or poultry products is required.[241] Post mortem inspection of the carcass of each bird processed is also required.[242] Condemnation, segregation and reinspection may be required. Any carcasses or products for human consumption found to be adulterated must be condemned and destroyed.[243] Specific prohibitions exist with regard to the processing, marketing, and sale of poultry and poultry products.[244]

The inspection requirements apply to a poultry producer with respect to raised poultry if the producer slaughters more than 1,000 poultry other than those raised on their own farms.[245] Certain establishments are exempted from specific provisions of the inspection requirements. The exemption applies to retail dealers whose poultry operation merely involves cutting up poultry products for sales to consumers.[246] Persons who slaughter, process or handle poultry or poultry products as required by recognized religious dietary laws are also exempted.[247] The Secretary is authorized to exempt any person whose slaughter of poultry is limited to poultry of her own raising, if it is processed and used exclusively by her, her household, and employee.[248] This exemption applies on the conditions that the custom slaughtering of poultry is by the owner for his or her own use, and that the custom slaughterer does not engage in the buying or selling of poultry products capable of use as human food.[249]

Additional exemptions may be granted by the Secretary to poultry producers or other persons who slaughter or process no more than 20,000 poultry per year and who do not slaughter or process at a facility used by any other person.[250] Exemptions apply to the slaughtering and processing of the producer's poultry if it is raised on his own premises and distributed only within that jurisdiction.[251] Also exempted are poultry producers who distribute directly to household consumers, restaurants, hotels and boarding houses for use in their own dining rooms solely within the jurisdiction.[252] These exemptions do not apply if the producer engages in buying and selling of any products other than as specified in these exemptions. The Secretary is authorized to grant other exemptions if they will not defeat the purposes of the Act.[253]

Imported poultry, and the parts or products of imported poultry, must comply with the standards for domestic poultry and poultry products. Imported poultry are subject to the same inspection, sanitary, quality, species verification and residue standards applied to domestic poultry and must be processed in facilities which maintain the conditions required for products processed domestically.[254]

3. Eggs and Egg Products Inspection

Eggs and egg products intended for use as human food constitute an important source of food which moves in interstate commerce. Congress has determined that inspection of these products is necessary to avoid adulteration and misbranding. The maintenance of product standards and restrictions upon the disposition of inferior grades of eggs are the central focus of quality control. The Act covers many types of egg products: shell eggs, egg products intended for human food, egg products not intended for human food, and imported eggs and egg products.[255]

Continuous inspection of egg processing operations is required. Any food manufacturing establishment, institution or restaurant which uses eggs that do not meet specific requirements is deemed to be a "plant processing egg products" and inspection is required.[256] Inspection is not required for plants which process egg products not intended for use as human food. However, such products must be appropriately denatured or identified to prevent their use as human food.[257] Exemptions are authorized for the sale, transportation, possession, or use of eggs which contain "no more restricted eggs than are allowed by the tolerance in the officials standards of United States consumer grades for shell eggs."[258] Also exempt is the activity at processing plants where the facilities and operating procedures meet sanitary standards prescribed by the Secretary.[259] The sale of eggs by a poultry producer from his or her own flocks directly to household consumers, the processing of eggs or egg products by a producer from eggs of his own flocks for sale directly to household consumers, and sales by shell egg packers on their own premises directly to household consumers are all exempt.[260] The sale of eggs by a producer who maintains annual egg production from a flock of hens numbering 3000 or less is also exempt.[261]

Imported egg products capable of being used as human food must be processed under an approved continuous inspection system and must otherwise comply with the standards set for the domestic egg program.[262]

IV.   Protection for Buyers of Livestock
    A.   Overview of Federal Preemption of the Uniform
          Commercial Code
In the Food Security Act of 1985[263] Congress in effect amended Section 9-307 of the Uniform Commercial Code which governs the sale of mortgaged agricultural products, including livestock. This change, which became effective on December 23, 1986, altered the UCC in most states. Under "old" Section 9-307, the "farm products exception", a secured creditor's valid security interest in farm products was not extinguished by the sale of those products in the ordinary course of business. Thus, "old" section 9-307 allowed the secured creditor to enforce liens against a purchaser of farm products, even though the purchaser was unaware that the sale violated the terms of an agreement between the seller and the secured creditor. As a result, under the old rule, purchasers of farm products, including marketing

agencies, were subjected to double payment liability in conversion actions brought by secured creditors.

Under the new federal provisions a buyer of farm products in the ordinary course of business receives the products free of any security interest created by the seller, even though the interest was perfected under the UCC and the buyer knew of the security interest.[264] An exception to the application of this rule is available to creditors if they comply with one of two options presented under federal law.[265] One option allows the creditor to give direct notice of the security interest to potential buyers of the farm products. The direct notice must contain essential information concerning the security interest, such as the description of the products, names and addresses of the parties, and the debtor's social security number. The buyer takes subject to the security interest if the buyer has, within the 12 months prior to the purchase date, received from the secured party or seller written notice of the secured party's interest in the products. A commission merchant or selling agent is also subject to this rule.[266]

The second option is available to creditors in states which have established a central filing system. If a state central filing system exists, a buyer takes purchased farm products subject to a security interest in those goods if the secured party has filed a financing statement with the Secretary of State's office which lists the products being sold.[267] Sellers must provide the creditor with a list of potential buyers. Moreover, buyers may register with the Secretary of State prior to purchasing farm products. The buyer takes purchased farm products subject to a creditor's security interest if the buyer has received written notice from the Secretary of State which lists the seller's name and the products which are subject to the creditor's financing statement. A buyer who has failed to register, and therefore has not received actual notice, takes subject to the security interest.[268]

The notice form, which lists all of the legally-binding information regarding security interests, must be distributed regularly to each buyer, commission merchant and selling agent whose names are on the list which is maintained by the Secretary of State.[269] After the potential buyer has received notice of the creditor's security interest in goods, the buyer should make payment checks jointly payable to the seller and the secured party. Otherwise, the buyer should require the seller to produce proof of a waiver or release of the security interest by the creditor.

A seller of farm products may be penalized if he or she sells goods to a party whose name is not on the list which was furnished to the creditor.[270] Therefore, the seller should provide the creditor with a list of potential buyers, selling agents or commission merchants which is as complete as possible. When a sale is made to a person whose name is not on the list, a farmer has two options to avoid being subject to sanctions under the Act. One is to provide the secured party with a written statement of the identity of the proposed buyer, selling agent or commission merchant whose name was not on the original list. This must be done at least 7 days prior to the date of sale. The second option is for the seller to account to the secured party for the proceeds of the sale not later than 10 days after the sale is completed.[271]

B. State Central Filing Systems

The Secretary of Agriculture has designated the Packers and Stockyards Administration as the lead agency in the development of regulations to govern state central filing systems. The regulations are found at 9 CFR Part 205. These regulations outline the requirements that a state must meet in order to obtain certification of its central filing system and detail the requirements for effective financing statements and the registration of buyers.

A State may elect to establish a system for specified products and not for others. A state which establishes a system only for specified products will be deemed to be "a State that has established a central filing system" as to the specified products, and will be deemed not to be a central filing state as to other products.[272]

1. Effective Financing Statement (EFS) - Minimum Information

The minimum information necessary on an EFS is:

(1) the pertinent crop year unless every crop of the farm product in question is to be subject to the particular

security interest for the duration of the EFS;

(2) the farm product name;

(3) the name of each county or parish in the state where the farm product is produced or to be produced;

(4) the name and address of each person who is subjecting the farm product to the security interest, whether or not a debtor;

(5) the social security number of each such person or, if other than a natural person, the applicable IRS taxpayer identification number;

(6) further details of the farm product subject to the security interest if needed to distinguish it from other quantities of the product which is owned by the same person(s) but which is not subject to the particular security interest; and

(7) the secured party's name and address.

A requirement of additional information on an EFS is discretionary with the state.

In addition, whether one EFS is permitted to reflect multiple products, or products in multiple counties, is discretionary with the state.[273]

An EFS is not required to be the same as a financing statement or security agreement under the Uniform Commercial Code or any successor state law, but can be an entirely separate document. According to the legislative history, "[T]he bill would not preempt basic state law rules on the creation, perfection, or priority of security interests."[274] An EFS must be a paper document since it must be signed.[275]

On both the EFS and the master list, the "amount" of farm products and the "reasonable description of the property including county or parish," need not be shown on every entry.[276] When an EFS and master list entry identifies a product but does not show an amount, this constitutes a representation that all of the product owned by that person is subject to the security in interest in question.[277]

When an EFS and master list entry identifies each county or parish in the same state where the product is or is to be produced but does not show any further identification of the location of the product, this constitutes a representation that all of the product produced in each such county or parish which is owned by that person is subject to the security

405

interest.[278] The need to supply additional information arises only where some of the product owned by a particular person is subject to the security interest and some is not.[279]

The additional information about the amount and the property description must be sufficient to enable a reader of the information to identify what product owned by that person is subject to the security interest and what is not. The precision needed in the description of the amount and location can vary from case to case.[280]

2. Registration of Buyer, Commission Merchant, or Selling Agent
(a) Minimum Information

The minimum information necessary to register a buyer, commission merchant, or selling agent is:

(1) the name and address of the buyer, commission merchant, or selling agent;

(2) the farm product or products in which the registrant is interested; and

(3) if the registrant is interested only in a product or products produced in a certain county or parish, or certain counties or parishes, in the same state, the name of each such county or parish. A registrant, if not registered for any specified county or parish, or counties or parishes, must be deemed to have registered for all counties and parishes shown on the master list.[281]

(b) Master List

The master list must include all of the information which is contained in the EFS's which are filed in the system. This information must be arranged so that it is possible to deliver to any registrant all of the information which relates to any product, produced in any county or parish covered by the system for any crop year. The system must be able to deliver this information either in alphabetical order by the word appearing first in the name of each person subjecting a product to a security interest, in numerical order by the social security number of each such person (or, if other than a natural person, IRS taxpayer identification number), or in both alphabetical and numerical orders, as requested by the registrant.[282] The portion to be distributed must be in "written or printed form." This means a recording on paper by any technology which can be read without special equipment.[283]

After the distribution of a portion of a master list, a supplement can be distributed which shows only changes from the previous one. However, if this is done, cumulative supplements must be distributed often enough that readers can find all the information given to them for any one crop year in no more than three distributions.[284]

The provisions in the regulations in regard to registration of "buyers of farm products, commission merchants, and selling agents," "regular" distribution of "portions" of the master list, and the furnishing of "oral confirmation . . . on request," must all be read together.[285] The regulations do not require these persons to register. However, if a person does not register they are subject to security interests shown on that system's master list whether or not they have actual knowledge of them. This rule applies whether they are inside or outside the State covered by that system. Thus, for their own protection, unregistered persons will need to query the system operator about any seller with whom they deal who is "engaged in a farming operation," in regard to a farm product which is produced in the State covered by that system.[286]

The effect of registration is that persons who register with a particular system are placed on the list for regular distribution of portions of that system's master list. Those persons who register are subject only to security interests which are shown on the portions which they receive, and are not subject to interests which are shown on the master list but not shown on portions which they receive. Moreover, if a particular security interest is shown on the master list, but has been placed on it since the last regular distribution of portions of that list to registrants, registrants would not be subject to that security interest.[287]

The regulations require "regular" distribution of portions of the master list to registrants, as amended from time to time by the filing of EFS's and amendments to EFS's.[288] The legislative history shows that buyers, commission merchants, and selling agents are not intended to be liable for errors or other inaccuracies which may be generated by the system.[289]

3. Effect of EFS Outside State in Which Filed

If an EFS is filed in one state, notice of it can be filed in another state and shown on the master list for the second state. There is nothing in the regulations to prevent this, but it would serve no purpose.[290]

The regulations provide only for the filing of an EFS which covers a given product in the system of the state in which it is produced. Upon such filing, buyers, commission merchants and selling agents who are not registered with that system are made subject to the security interest in that product whether or not they know about it, even if they are outside that state.[291] Persons who are registered with that system are subject to a security interest if they receive written notice of it even if they are outside that state. All of these provisions apply only where an EFS is filed in the system for the state in which the product is produced. They do not apply to a filing in another state's system.

4. Conclusion

The current version of UCC Section 9-307 affects the activities of commission merchants and selling agents who engage in livestock marketing. Since these persons engage in a large volume of trade, they will receive dozens of direct notices of security interests in livestock. In states which use a central filing system the commission merchant and selling agent should register with the Secretary of State and receive copies of the Secretary's lists of secured creditors' interests in that jurisdiction. As noted earlier, it is advisable for selling agents and commission merchants to protect themselves from possible conversion liability by issuing checks for purchased livestock which are jointly payable to the seller and the secured creditor. Buyers should exercise caution in private treaty sales by asking the seller for evidence of the creditor's waiver or release of the security interest.

Under the current provisions of the federal law, a buyer who is not directly notified of a security interest in farm products, either by a secured creditor or through the central filing system, will be protected from conversion liability to the secured creditor.

V.   Beef Promotion and Research - The "Check Off"
      Program

Since the early 1980's, beef producers have been confronted by a declining consumer demand for beef. There are many factors that have reduced public demand for beef. The increased production of meats such as pork and chicken at relatively lower prices than beef has had an impact on the quantity of beef purchased by consumers.[292] In particular, low poultry prices have significantly affected competition for beef sales to consumers. Additionally, beef production and sales have slowed while poultry production and sales have grown because of consumer concerns about health factors. Shifts in consumers' tastes away from beef have occurred due to public concern about fat, cholesterol, and food additives.

In an effort to promote the production and marketing of U. S. beef, Congress passed the Beef Promotion and Research Act of 1985.[293] The Act requires a one dollar per head assessment to be collected when cattle are sold. This revenue is used to finance a program of beef promotion and research which was established by order of the Secretary of Agriculture on October 1, 1986.[294] The program is administered by a Cattlemen's Beef Promotion and Research Board. Certain purchasers and selling agents are designated as "collecting persons". Their role is to collect assessments from the producers and to remit the assessment proceeds to the Beef Board. The Board is comprised of beef producers appointed by the Secretary of Agriculture. The Board uses the assessment revenues to finance promotional activities for U.S. beef such as research, advertising, and the publication of consumer and producer information.

Under the Act the Secretary of Agriculture was to conduct a referendum among beef producers within 22 months after the effective date of the Act. The purpose of the referendum was to enable the producers to decide whether the program should be continued. In June, 1988 producers voted to continue the program. Upon the request of 10% or more of the producers who voted in the referendum approving the order, the Secretary must hold a referendum to determine whether the producers want the order to be continued. If a majority of producers voting in the referendum do not approve of the

409

continuation of the program, the Secretary must terminate the program.[295] An individual producer can request a refund of his or her assessment under the designated procedures of the Act.[296] The Act states that "any producer...who is not in favor of supporting the program...shall have the right to demand and receive from the Beef Board a refund of such assessment..."[297] In order to receive a refund, the producer must complete a form before 60 days after the end of the month in which the transaction occurred and give proof to the Beef board that the producer actually paid the assessment.[298]

The constitutionality of the Beef Promotion and Research Act was upheld in U.S. v. Frame.[299] The opinion stated:

> ...this is not a statute in which Congress has exceeded its broad authority under the constitution; rather it reflects Congress' view that a coordinated response is needed to reverse the recent declines in the beef industry.[300]

FOOTNOTES

1. 7 U.S.C. § 181-229.

2. 7 U.S.C. § 181-229.

3. 258 U.S. 495 (1922).

4. 258 U.S. at 514.

5. U.S. v. Morgan, 307 U.S. 183 (1938).

6. Wilson & Co. v. Benson, 286 F.2d 891 (7th Cir. 1961).

7. Safeway Stores, Inc. v. Freeman, 369 F.2d 952 (D.C. Cir. 1961).

8. United States Fidelity & Guar. Co. v. Quinn Bros. of Jackson, Inc., 384 F.2d 241 (5th Cir. 1967).

9. 7 U.S.C. §§ 191-196.

10. 7 U.S.C. § 201-217a.

11. 7 U.S.C. § 218-218d.

12. 7 U.S.C. §§ 181-183.

13. 7 U.S.C. § 221-229.

14. 9 C.F.R., Parts 201, 202, and 203.

15. 7 C.F.R. 1.2(a).

16. 7 C.F.R. § 204.6(a).

17. 7 C.F.R. § 204.6 (c).

18. 7 C.F.R. § 204.7.

19. 7 U.S.C. § 192.

20. 110 F.2d 473 (4th Cir. 1940).

21. U.S. v. Jay Freeman Co., 473 F. Supp. 1265 (E. D. Ark. 1979).

22. 770 F.2d 888 (10th Cir. 1985).

23. 438 F.2d 1332 (8th Cir. 1971).

24. 369 F.2d 952 (D.C. Cir. 1966).

25. 7 U.S.C. § 192(a).

26. 618 F.2d 1329 (9th Cir. 1980) cert. den. 101 S. Ct., 449 US 783 1061, 66 L. Ed. 2d 603 (1980).

27. 393 F.2d 247 (7th Cir. 1968).

28. 286 F.2d 891 (7th Cir. 1961).

29. 308 F.2d (7th Cir. 1962).

30. Burruss v. USDA, 575 F.2d 1258 (8th Cir. 1978).

31. 7 U.S.C. § 193.

32. 7 U.S.C. § 193(a).

33. 7 U.S.C. § 193 (b).

34. 7 U.S.C. § 194.

35. 7 U.S.C. § 194(d).

36. 7 U.S.C. § 194 (e), (f).

37. 7 U.S.C. § 192.

38. 7 U.S.C. § 193 (a).

39. See Davis v. U.S., 427 F.2d 261 (5th Cir. 1970); Arkansas Valley Industries, Inc. v. Freeman, 415 F.2d 713 (8th Cir. 1969).

40. 7 U.S.C. § 228b(a).

41. 7 U.S.C. § 228b(b).

42. 7 U.S.C. § 228b(c).

43. 7 U.S.C. § 196.

44. 7 U.S.C. § 196(b).

45. 7 U.S.C. § 196(b).

46. See In re Gotham Provision Co., Inc. 669 F.2d 1000 (5th Cir. 1982) cert. den. 103 S.Ct. 129, 459 U.S. 858, 74 L.Ed 2d 111 (1982).

47. In re G & L Packing Co., Inc., 20 Bankr. 789 (Bankr. NDNY 1982), aff'd 41 Bankr. 903 (NDNY 1984).

48. 7 U.S.C. § 196(b).

49. 7 U.S.C. § 203, 208.

50. 7 U.S.C. § 203.

51. 7 U.S.C. § 203.

52. 7 U.S.C. § 202.

53. 7 U.S.C. § 201(c).

54. 7 U.S.C. § 203.

55. 7 U.S.C. § 201(d).

56. 557 F.2d 717 (10th Cir. 1977).

57. 39 Agric. Dec. 184 (10th Cir. 1980).

58. 39 Agric. Dec. at 226.

59. 7 U.S.C. § 202.

60. 7 U.S.C. § 203.

61. 7 U.S.C. § 203.

62. 7 U.S.C. § 204.

63. U.S. v. Wehrein, 332 F.2d 469 (8th Cir. 1964).

64. 7 U.S.C. § 205.

65. 7 U.S.C. § 206.

66. 7 U.S.C. § 207(a).

67. 7 U.S.C. § 207(e).

68. 7 U.S.C. § 208(a).

69. 7 U.S.C. § 208(b).

70. 7 U.S.C. § 211.

71. 7 U.S.C. § 213(a).

72. 7 U.S.C. § 213(b).

73. 7 U.S.C. § 215.

74. 7 U.S.C. § 209(a).

75. 7 U.S.C. § 209.

76. 9 C.F.R. § 202.102(i).

77. 7 U.S.C. § 209.

78. 9 C.F.R. § 202.103(a).

79. 9 C.F.R. § 202.103(b).

80. 9 C.F.R. § 202.103(c).

81. 9 C.F.R. § 202.103(d).

82. 9 C.F.R. § 202.103(e).

83. 9 C.F.R. § 202.103(f).

84. 9 C.F.R. § 202.103(f).

85. 9 C.F.R. § 202.103.(f).

86. 9 C.F.R. § 202.103.(g).

87. 9 C.F.R. § 202.103.(f).

88. 9 C.F.R. § 202.103(g).

89. 9 C.F.R. § 202.104.(a).

90. 9 C.F.R. § 202.104(a).

91. 9 C.F.R. § 202.104(c).

92. 9 C.F.R. § 202.104(c).

93. 9 C.F.R. § 202.104(a).

94. 9 C.F.R. § 202.104(a).

95. 9 C.F.R. § 202.104(b).

96. 9 C.F.R. § 202.105(a).

97. 9 C.F.R. § 202.105(b).

98. 9 C.F.R. § 202.105(c).

99. 9 C.F.R. § 202.105(d).

100. 9 C.F.R. § 202.105(e)(1).

101. 9 C.F.R. § 202.105(e)(2).

102. 9 C.F.R. § 202.105(b).

103. 9 C.F.R. § 202.105(e)(2).

104. 9 C.F.R. § 202.105(e)(4).

105. 9 C.F.R. § 202.106(a).

106. 9 C.F.R. § 202.106(b).

107. 9 C.F.R. § 202. 106(b).

108. 9 C.F.R. § 202.106(d).

109. 9 C.F.R. § 202.106(c).

110. 9 C.F.R. § 202.107(a).

111. 9 C.F.R. § 202.107(b).

112. 9 C.F.R. § 202.107(c).

113. 9 C.F.R. § 202.108.

114. 9 C.F.R. § 202.109(a).

115. 9 C.F.R. § 202.109(b).

116. 9 C.F.R. § 202.109(d).

117. 9 C.F.R. § 202.109(e).

118. 9 C.F.R. § 202.113(a).

119. 9 C.F.R. § 202.109(f).

120. 9 C.F.R. § 202.109(c).

121. 9 C.F.R. § 202.109(c).

122. 9 C.F.R. § 202.109(g).

123. 9 C.F.R. § 202.109(h).

124. 9 C.F.R. § 202.109(i).

125. 9 C.F.R. § 202.109(j).

126. 9 C.F.R. § 202.110(a).

127. 9 C.F.R. § 202.110(b).

128. 9 C.F.R. § 202.111(a).

129. 9 C.F.R. § 202.111(e).

130. 9 C.F.R. § 202.111(e).

131. 9 C.F.R. § 202.111(b).

132. 9 C.F.R. § 202.111(c).

133. 9 C.F.R. § 202.113(a).

134. 9 C.F.R. § 202.112(a).

135. 9 C.F.R. § 202.112(b).

136. 9 C.F.R. § 202.112(c).

137. 9 C.F.R. § 202.112(g).

138. 9 C.F.R. § 202.112(d).

139. 9 C.F.R. § 202.114(a).

140. 9 C.F.R. § 202.112(e).

141. 9 C.F.R. § 202.112(e)(2).

142. 9 C.F.R. § 202.112(e)(3).

143. 9 C.F.R. § 202.112(e)(5).

144. 9 C.F.R. § 202.112(e)(6)(i).

145. 9 C.F.R. § 202.112(e)(6)(ii).

146. 9 C.F.R. § 202.112(e)(6)(iii).

147. 9 C.F.R. § 202.112(f)(1).

148. 9 C.F.R. § 202.112(f)(2).

149. 9 C.F.R. § 202.112(h).

150. 9 C.F.R. § 202.112(i).

151. 9 C.F.R. § 202.113(c).

152. 9 C.F.R. § 202.113(d).

153. 9 C.F.R. § 202.113(e).

154. 9 C.F.R. § 202.113(p).

155. 9 C.F.R. § 202.114(b).

176. 9 C.F.R. § 202.122.(a).

177. 9 C.F.R. § 202.122(c).

178. 7 U.S.C. § 218(b).

179. 611 F. Supp. 682 (E.D.N.C.1985)

180. 680 F. 2d 277 (2nd Cir. 1982)

181. 415 F. 2d 713 (8th Cir. 1969).

182. 427 F. 2d 251 (5th Cir. 1970).

183. 7 U.S.C. § 221-226

184. 7 U.S.C. § 218(a).

185. 7 U.S.C. § 181 et. seq.

186. See, e.g., 7 U.S.C. §§ 196 and 228b (West Supp. 1987).

187. 7 U.S.C. § 182.(8).

188. 7 U.S.C. § 182(9).

189. 7 U.S.C. § 182(10).

190. 7 U.S.C. §§ 197 and 228b-1.

191. 7 U.S.C. § 187.

192. 7 U.S.C. § 197(c).

193. 7 U.S.C. § 197.

194. 7 U.S.C. § 228b-1.

195. 7 U.S.C. § 228b-1.

196. 7 U.S.C. § 228b-2.

197. 7 U.S.C. § 228b-2.

198. 21 U.S.C. § 111-135b.

199. 21 U.S.C. § 601-95.

200. 21 U.S.C. § 451-70.

201. 15 U.S.C. § 633, 1301.

202. 21 U.S.C. § 111.

203. 21 U.S.C. § 114.

204. 21 U.S.C. § 115.

205. 21 U.S.C. § 114a-1.

206. 21 U.S.C. § 123.

207. 21 U.S.C. § 124.

208. 21 U.S.C. § 125.

209. 21 U.S.C. § 126.

210. 455 F.2d (C.A. Ark. 1972).

211. 21 U.S.C. § 134a(a).

212. 21 U.S.C. § 134a(b).

213. 21 U.S.C. § 134a(c) and (d).

214. 21 U.S.C. § 134a(e).

215. 537 F.2d 959 (7th Cir. 1976).

216. Julius Goldman's Egg City v. U. S., 697 F.2d 1051 (CA Fed. 1983) <u>cert. den.</u> 104 S. Ct. 68, 464 U.S. 814, 78 L.Ed. 83.

217. 21 U.S.C. § 134(b).

218. 21 U.S.C. § 134(c).

219. 21 U.S.C. § 134(d).

220. 21 U.S.C. § 120.

221. 21 U.S.C. § 104.

222. 21 U.S.C. § 102.

223. 21 U.S.C. § 103.

224. 21 U.S.C. § 105.

225. 21 U.S.C. § 601-95.

226. 21 U.S.C. § 602.

227. 21 U.S.C. § 603(a).

228. 21 U.S.C. § 604.

229. 21 U.S.C. § 605.

230. 21 U.S.C. § 606.

231. 21 U.S.C. § 608.

232. 21 U.S.C. § 609.

233. 21 U.S.C. § 610.

234. 21 U.S.C. § 610(b).

235. 21 U.S.C. § 615, 616, 617.

236. 21 U.S.C. § 620(a).

237. 21 U.S.C. § 620(e).

238. 21 U.S.C. § 623.

239. 21 U.S.C. § 641.

240. 21 U.S.C. § 454.

241. 21 U.S.C. § 455(a).

242. 21 U.S.C. § 455(b).

243. 21 U.S.C. § 455(b)(c).

244. 21 U.S.C. § 458.

245. 21 U.S.C. § 464(c)(4).

246. 21 U.S.C. § 464(a)(1).

247. 21 U.S.C. § 464(a)(3).

248. 21 U.S.C. § 464(c)(1)(A).

249. 21 U.S.C. § 464(c)(1)(B).

250. 21 U.S.C. § 464 (c)(3).

251. 21 U.S.C. § 464 (c)(1)(c).

252. 21 U.S.C. § 464(c)(1)(D).

253. 21 U.S.C. § 464(c)(3).

254. 21 U.S.C. § 466 (d).

255. 21 U.S.C. § 1032.

256. 21 U.S.C. § 1034.

257. 21 U.S.C. § 1039.

258. 21 U.S.C. § 1044(a)(1).

259. 21 U.S.C. § 1044(a)(2).

260. 21 U.S.C. § 1044(a)(3)(4)(5).

261. 21 U.S.C. § 1044(a)(7).

262. 21 U.S.C. § 1046.

263. Pub. L. No. 99-198, 99 Stat. 1535 (1985); 7 U.S.C. § 1631.

264. 7 U.S.C. § 1631(d).

265. 7 U.S.C. § 1631(e).

266. 7 U.S.C. § 1631(g).

267. 7 U.S.C. § 1631(e).

268. 7 U.S.C. § 1631(e).

269. 7 U.S.C. § 1631(c).

270. 7 U.S.C. § 1631(h).

271. 7 U.S.C. § 1631(h).

272. 9 C.F.R. § 205.206(c).

273. 9 C.F.R. § 205.103

274. House Committee Report on Pub. L. 99-198, No. 99-271, Part 1, September 13, 1985, at 110.

275. 9 C.F.R. § 205.202.

276. 9 C.F.R. § 205.207(a).

277. 9 C.F.R. § 205.207(b).

278. 9 C.F.R. § 205.207(c).

279. 9 C.F.R. § 205.207(d).

280. 9 C.F.R. § 205.207(e).

281. 9 C.F.R. § 205.104.

282. 9 C.F.R. § 205.105(a).

283. 9 C.F.R. § 205.105(b).

284. 9 C.F.R. § 205.105(c).

285. 9 C.F.R. § 205.208(a).

286. 9 C.F.R. § 205.208(b).

287. 9 C.F.R. § 205.208(c).

288. 9 C.F.R. § 205.208(f).

289. See Nov. 22, 1985 Cong. Rec., Senate, pg. S16300, and Dec. 18, 1985 Cong. Rec., House, at H12523.   9 C.F.R. § 205.208(g).

290. 9 C.F.R. § 205.210(a).

291. 9 C.F.R. § 205.210(b).

292. Agricultural Outlook, USDA, Sept. 1987, at 13.

293. 7 U.S.C. § 2901 et seq.

294. 7 C.F.R. § 1206.101 et seq.

295. 7 U.S.C. § 2909.

296. 7 U.S.C. § 2911.

297. 7 U.S.C. § 2911.

298. 7 U.S.C. § 2911.

299. 658 F. Supp. 1476 (E.D. Pa. 1987).

300. 658 F. Supp. at 1483.

CHAPTER 12

HEDGING AND SPECULATION: COMMODITY FUTURES
TRADING AND REGULATION

I. Introduction to Commodity Trading

During the 1980's there has been increased participation
in the trading of commodity futures contracts, and the options
on those contracts, by an expanded group of persons. These
persons include farmers, handlers, shippers, dealers, millers, and
others whose businesses involve agricultural commodities and
their by-products. They use commodity trading to hedge
themselves against possible loss which may occur as the result
of price fluctuations. This increased participation in commodity
trading has occurred for several discernable reasons. First,
whereas in the past the futures markets have had a rather
negative public image, there has been a dramatic increase in the
commercial understanding that futures markets can be utilized
for positive and legitimate economic reasons. This development
is reflected in greater use of futures markets by agricultural
producers to hedge their price and income returns. Agricultural
lenders have also encouraged their borrowers to use hedging.

Second, during the 1980's the number of commodities
which are traded in the organized contract markets has been
significantly expanded. Perhaps the most significant expansion
is the area of the trading financial instruments. Today a person
can trade futures in everything from gasoline to plywood, from
90-day Treasury bonds to gold, in addition to the various
agricultural commodities.

Third, an aggressive regulatory entity, the Commodity
Futures Trading Commission (CFTC), was created in 1974, with
an expansive legislative endorsement. During the 1980's, the
CFTC has broadly interpreted its regulatory mission. This has
increased public confidence in commodities trading.

There is a strong likelihood that lawyers who represent
farm clients will encounter commodity futures law in their
practice. Certain premises affect the scope and orientation of
the coverage in this chapter. These premises are that:

- Most practitioners have had only limited experience with, or knowledge of, commodity trading matters.
- Practitioners who do become involved in legal matters which involve commodity futures will probably be representing a private individual rather than handling a regulatory matter which addresses the structure and function of the commodities marketplace.
- The client will probably be a customer of a brokerage firm rather than someone registered with the CFTC as a broker or an associated person.
- The representation of a client is likely to involve alleged fraudulent activity by a brokerage firm against its customer.

A. Basic Description of Commodity Trading

Commodity trading is the buying and selling of futures contracts on regulated exchanges which are registered with the Commodity Futures Trading Commission (CFTC). These exchanges are usually designated as a "board of trade" or "mercantile exchange". There is no over-the-counter trading of future contracts. In fact, it is illegal for commodity trading to occur outside of a contract market which is registered with the CFTC.

A futures contract is a standardized agreement. All of its terms, except for the price, are set by the relevant board of trade. The contract obligates a party to deliver (sell) or take delivery of (buy) a specified quantity and quality of a specified commodity at some designated time in the future. The price of the futures contract is established by a bidding process when the transaction is made. Most futures contracts are for a term of 6-18 months. With agricultural commodities this term often bears a relation to the crop year of the commodity being dealt in.

The purpose of commodity futures trading is to provide a mechanism whereby many different interests in society can benefit from spreading the risk of fluctuations in the price of different commodities. In addition, commodity trading plays an important function in price discovery. In other words, it establishes what the price of a commodity is likely to be at a given time in the future.

There are two main types of commodity traders, hedgers and speculators. Hedgers are individuals, such as producers or processors, who intend to eventually engage in a cash transaction of the physical commodity which underlies the futures contract. They use futures contracts to establish a price for the commodity which they wish to buy or sell. This shifts the risk of price fluctuations to others. In contrast to hedgers, speculators are individuals who have no actual need for the physical commodity which underlies the futures contract. Rather, they use the buying and selling of futures contracts as an investment, and hope to profit by taking advantage of favorable price fluctuations.

While speculators tend to be criticized as being little more than gamblers, this is not an accurate characterization. The risk of price fluctuation exists as a natural part of a capitalist system. Commodity speculators play an essential function in the operation of commodity markets by removing that risk from hedgers. Without the market liquidity provided by speculators, the commodity markets could not effectively provide the hedging function that they are designed to perform.

B. How a Farmer Might Use Commodity Trading

There are two basic ways for a farmer to use futures trading in the farm business. The primary use of futures trading for farmers is the hedging function, whereby the farmer can use the futures market to lock in a price and transfer the risk of price fluctuations to others. A farmer may use hedging to set the price at which he or she will sell a crop. Hedging may also be used by a large farming operation to set the price at which it can purchase supplies. For example, a cattle feeding operation could lock in the price of its feed purchases through the futures markets. In sum, hedging can be used by producers who wish to sell a physical supply of a commodity or by processors and others who will wish to purchase a commodity. It should also be noted that producer cooperative associations are entitled to trade futures, and to become a member of a board of trade.

The basic formula for profit in the futures markets is to "buy low and sell high," regardless of the order in which those transactions take place. The commercially rational choice for a

429

person who believes that prices will increase in the future would be to hedge "long". Being "long" indicates that the person holds a buying position in the futures market. In this example, the party holding the "long" position will offset the position by taking physical delivery of the commodity from a party who holds a "short" or selling position in the market. However, the alternative to dealing in the physical commodity is to offset the long or short position by simply trading one's position on paper through the exchange. About 97% of all futures contracts are offset in that manner. Thus, only about 3% of all futures contracts are settled by actual delivery.

The actual commodities which underlies a futures contract are referred to as "actuals" or "physicals". One of the benefits of futures trading is that a loss on the physical commodity market can be offset by the gain in the futures contract. For example, persons who raise cattle and are concerned that the price of the cattle might go down in the future can hedge short. In other words, they can sell contracts on the futures market for the months in which the cattle will be marketed. They are guaranteed to receive that price for their cattle in the month of delivery. By this method, any loss on the sale of the cattle on the spot (cash) market can be offset by gains on the short futures contracts.

It should be noted that several factors distinguish hedging from perfect price insurance. These include the costs of commissions and the fact that the basis, which is the difference between the local market price and the futures price, may fluctuate.

As just noted, hedging enables a farmer to lock in the price that he or she will pay or receive for a commodity. Of course, a farmer forgoes the opportunity to gain in the open market if the price changes. However, the hedger also avoids the uncertainties associated with uncontrolled risk of losses due to changes in the market price for commodities. For this reason, some lenders encourage farmers to hedge their commodity production to protect the lender's account with the borrower.

The expertise and understanding of a lender may be needed to conduct a sound hedging program. Many knowledgeable lenders are equipped to work with clients on hedging their crop production. They may even have developed special hedging loans. The cooperation of the lender is especially needed since the maintenance of a losing hedge may require substantial sums to cover margin calls. A lender would need to understand that the losses will be offset by gains on the physical commodities in the cash market in order to be willing to provide funding to meet margin calls. It must be noted that any farmer who is not hedging his or her crop production is in effect speculating with their physical inventory of the agricultural commodity.

An important legal aspect of lender financing of hedging is the protection of the lender's interest in the hedger's futures trading accounts. Lenders will need a special security agreement which notifies other creditors of the lender's interest in the borrower's futures accounts. Typically the lender's security interest would be subordinate to that of the commodity exchange and brokerage firm. Lenders protect their security interest by requiring the receipt of a copy of all account statements which are issued by the broker as to purchases and sales and margin calls in the farmer's account. The lender may specify this requirement, and any others it deems necessary, in the hedging loan agreement. For instance, the lender may obtain the farmer's authorization to pay margin calls directly in the event that the farmer cannot be located in a timely manner to pay the margin himself. This is important since, on many boards of trade, a margin call must be met within one (1) hour of issuance. Moreover, a broker has broad discretion to liquidate a customer's account if a margin call is not timely met.

A farmer may also play the role of speculator in hopes of guessing which way prices will move and establishing positions to benefit by those moves. The use of speculation for most farm clients is limited because of the fact that most farmers would not want to place their assets at the risk level that is presented by speculation.

It should be noted that farmers who operate small, family farming operations may find that the purchase of futures options (known as "options") offers more advantages to their business than the purchase of futures contracts. These options are traded much like futures contracts. Their availability is more limited in scope than futures, however. As the name implies, the option gives its owner the opportunity to determine the direction of price movement in a market before making the decision of whether to purchase the future (by exercising the option). The option is a unilateral contract. The holder of the option is not required to exercise it, although the broker who sold it is legally obligated to perform if the option is exercised. The price of the option is called a "premium". The price at which the option holder is entitled to acquire the underlying futures contract is called the "strike price".

A detailed discussion of options trading is beyond the scope of this chapter. It is suggested that further information on options trading may be obtained by written request to the CFTC or to a board of trade (see addresses, infra).

C. Key Definitions
A brief discussion of certain key terms used in commodities trading is useful in providing a minimum understanding of the mechanics of trading.

FUTURES CONTRACT: A contract for the purchase and sale of a commodity for future delivery. The contract must be obtained on an organized exchange ("board of trade") which is registered with the CFTC. The contract is subject to all of the terms and conditions which are included in the rules of that exchange.

LONG: The buying side of an open futures contract. A person who holds a long position must take delivery of the cash commodity at the end of the contract period, which is known as the "delivery month," unless the contract is offset with a sale of a futures contract through the futures market.

SHORT: The selling side of an open futures contract. A person who holds a short position must deliver the cash commodity unless the contract is offset with the purchase of a futures contract through the futures market.

OFFSET: The liquidation of a long or short futures position by an equal and opposite futures transaction. Open positions can be offset at any time during the life of a futures contract.

ROUND TURN: The completion of both a purchase and an offsetting sale, or a sale and an offsetting purchase.

HEDGING: Either the sale of a futures contract(s) as

432

protection against a price decline, or the purchase of futures as protection against a price increase. These transactions are utilized, respectively, as protection against adverse price movement in the open market.

SPECULATING: Entry into the trading of futures contracts for any purpose other than hedging.

BASIS: The difference between the price of the cash commodity and the price of a designated futures contract for that commodity. Some cash commodities are priced and traded in relation to futures prices, i.e. "basis plus ten cents".

INITIAL MARGIN: Customers' funds which are advanced as security for a guarantee of contract fulfillment, as defined by the rules of the exchange. Margin is analogous to earnest money or a performance bond.

MAINTENANCE MARGIN: Additional funds required to be deposited by customers as the price of the futures contract(s) bought or sold moves in a direction which is adverse to the customer. Margin requirements are defined by the rules of the exchange.

CONTRACT MARKET: The Exchange or Board of Trade where a particular futures contract is traded. The Board of Trade must be designated as the contract market for a commodity in order to legally conduct trading of that particular commodity. In other words, an exchange will function as numerous contract markets.

CLEARING HOUSE: The separate agency, which is associated with a futures exchange, through which futures contracts are offset or fulfilled. The Clearing House performs the function of financial settlement for each futures contract. (also known as a CLEARING ASSOCIATION).

CLEARING MEMBER: A member of the Clearing House or Association. Each clearing member must also be a member of the exchange. Each member of the exchange, however, need not be a member of the clearing association. All trades must be registered and eventually settled through a clearing member.

FUTURES COMMISSION MERCHANT: Individuals, associations, partnerships, corporations and trusts who engage in soliciting or in accepting orders for the purchase or sale of any commodity for future delivery on and subject to the rules of any contract market. This is the only entity which is legally authorized to maintain margined accounts for customers.

ASSOCIATED PERSON: An individual who is associated with a futures commission merchant in any capacity which involves soliciting or accepting customer orders or the supervision of other persons who are so engaged.

BROKER: A person who executes the buy and sell orders of a customer for a commission. There are two types of brokers. An introducing broker is a person who solicits and accepts orders for the purchase or sale of a futures contract, and who is not an associated person of a futures commission merchant and does not accept margin or other payments. A floor broker is a person who actually executes orders for the purchase and sale of commodity contracts on the trading floor (or pit). Many floor brokers trade on their own accounts, as well as for customers' accounts.

COMMODITY TRADING ADVISOR: A person who, for compensation or profit, advises others as to the value or advisability of trading in any futures contract. This may be done directly, or through publications or electronic media. Certain persons are exempt from this definition, including lawyers.

COMMODITY POOL OPERATOR: A person who solicits and receives funds from others which are at least partially used for the purchase or sale of commodity futures contracts which are held by the customers as a group. A commodity pool is analogous to a stock mutual fund.

DISCRETIONARY ACCOUNT: A customer account in which buying and selling orders can be placed by a broker or other person, without the prior consent of the customer for each individual trading order. The customer must give written authorization to the broker, usually in the form of a Power of Attorney, in order for discretionary trading to be legal.

SPREAD: This can occur in two (2) separate forms. The first form is the price difference represented by the purchase of one futures contract against the sale of another contract in a different month, a different commodity, or a different market. The second form is the price difference between two futures in the same or different markets. This is one aspect of what is commonly referred to as "arbitrage".

STRADDLE: The simultaneous purchase of one futures month

and the sale of another, either in the same or different commodity or exchange. This is one aspect of what is commonly referred to as "arbitrage".

CFTC: The Commodity Futures Trading Commission, which is the federal agency responsible for the regulation of commodity exchanges and the enforcement of the Commodity Exchange Act (and its amendments).

D. Commodity Account Documents

When a customer opens a commodity trading account there are several important documents which he or she must sign. These documents comprise the terms and conditions of the contractual relationship between the customer and the futures commission merchant. To a large extent, these documents determine the customer's rights in the event of a subsequent dispute with the futures commission merchant. It is important that an attorney who is representing a commodity customer be familiar with these documents. They may significantly affect the remedies available to the client. Moreover, improper documentation of the account may itself provide a cause of action to the customer. An example of this would be the failure of the broker to obtain a separate, signed Risk Disclosure Statement from the customer when opening the account.

1. Customer Agreement

This document is the basic agreement that is used to establish a customer account with a futures commission merchant. It generally contains several pages of provisions that establish the rights and duties of the parties to the agreement. A breach of this agreement may provide the basis for a common law breach of contract action in state court.[1]

One common provision of a customer agreement is that the customer is deemed to have ratified a trade if he or she does not object to a trade within a certain period of time after the trade was executed and the customer has notice of it. The agreement will probably also contain a consent to jurisdiction clause and an authorization to transfer funds between any multiple accounts which the customer has with the futures commission merchant. There may also be clauses in the

435

agreement whereby the customer agrees to pay commissions and to hold harmless the futures commission merchant under certain circumstances. There must also be a risk disclosure statement (discussed infra) attached as a rider to the agreement.

Needless to say, there is a tendency for the language of customer agreements to be slanted in favor of the futures commission merchants. However, at least one court has held that if the effect of all the various clauses is such that the customer is absolutely liable for any losses, then those provisions are void as being unconscionable and against public policy.[2] Likewise, the Federal District Court in <u>Poplar Grove Planting and Refining Co. Inc. v. Bache Halsey Stuart, Inc.,</u>[3] held that as a matter of public policy the defendant brokerage firm could not exculpate itself from all liability for unauthorized trading on the basis of a ratification provision in a customer agreement.

2. Risk Disclosure Statement
There is a high degree of risk inherent in commodities trading. The CFTC mandates that it is the duty of a commodity professional to disclose this risk to a potential client. In fact, fiduciary duties are owed to a potential customer by a registered commodity professional at the onset of communication with that potential customer. The CFTC has promulgated a regulation which requires that a customer be given and must sign a Risk Disclosure Statement as a separate document from the customer agreement.[4] This regulation specifies the exact language which the Risk Disclosure Statement must contain in order to comply with the law. Since a failure to use this language verbatim is in itself a violation of the law, an attorney for a farmer who is engaged in commodities trading should investigate the exact language that was used with his or her client. As just noted, a risk disclosure statement must be separately endorsed by the customer. In other words, if the statement is contained within a larger agreement the customer must sign the risk disclosure statement in addition to the larger agreement.

3. Other Documents
There are several other documents that will be involved

in certain types of commodity trading relationships. The CFTC rules may specify requirements for each respective document. For instance, as is discussed <u>infra</u>, a pre-dispute arbitration agreement may be signed by the futures commission merchant and the customer. This arbitration agreement must be voluntary and must be separately endorsed. It must contain language which notifies the customer of his or her right to rescind the arbitration agreement through the filing of a reparations complaint. It also must put the customer on notice of the other dispute resolution mechanisms which he or she might use and that certain rights may be waived by signing the arbitration agreement.[5]

Other important documents are the purchase and sale confirmation statements and the monthly account statement that a customer receives from the futures commission merchant. These documents notify the customer as to exactly what has occurred in his or her account. This information is very important in that it enables a customer to determine whether churning or unauthorized trading have occurred in the account.

E. <u>Important Addresses</u>

1. <u>Commodity Futures Trading Commission</u>

<u>Headquarters</u>

CFTC
2033 K St., N.W.
Washington, D.C. 20581
Ph: (202)254-6387

<u>Eastern Region</u>

1 World Trade Center
Suite 4747
New York, NY 10048
Ph: (212)791-0790

Central Region

CFTC
233 South Wacker Dr.
46th Floor
Chicago, IL 60606
Ph: (312)353-6642

Southwestern Region

CFTC
4901 Main St.
Room 208
Kansas City, MO 64112
Ph: (816)758-2994

2. Names and Addresses of Prominent Commodity
Exchanges

Chicago Board of Trade
141 West Jackson Boulevard
Chicago, IL 60604

Chicago Mercantile Exchange
444 West Jackson Boulevard
Chicago, IL 60606

Kansas City Board of Trade
4800 Main St., Suite 303
Kansas City, MO 64112

New Orleans Commodity Exchange
308 Board of Trade Place
New Orleans, L.A. 70130

New York Cotton Exchange
37 Wall St.
New York, NY 10005

II.	Regulation of Commodity Trading
	A.	Regulatory Powers of the Commodity Futures
		Trading Commission

Prior to the establishment of the CFTC, commodity futures trading was regulated by the United States Department of Agriculture. In 1974, Congress enacted the Commodity Futures Trading Commission Act[6], an amendment to the Commodity Exchange Act.[7] The 1974 Act provided for the establishment of the Commodity Futures Trading Commission (CFTC), an independent five (5) member regulatory commission. The 1974 Act granted the new CFTC broad regulatory powers to supervise and regulate the sale of commodity futures contracts.[8] The CFTC has three principal units. These are the Division of Trading and Markets, the Division of Enforcement, and the Office of Surveillance and Analysis.

	B.	The Exclusive Jurisdiction of the Commodity
		Futures Trading Commission

The CFTC is given broad powers to regulate commodity futures trading. This includes powers relating to the designation of a board of trade as an authorized exchange, the designation of a board of trade as a particular contract market, the enforcement of exchange rules, the supervision of the enforcement of exchange rules by registered futures associations, the declaration of emergencies to prevent price manipulation, the exercise of investigatory powers and the enforcement of customer protection rules. Another important function of the CFTC is the registration of commodity trading professionals. Currently the CFTC administers registration procedures for five classes of trading professionals:

1.	brokerage firms, known as futures commission merchants (FCM's);
2.	associated persons, who are the sales and supervisory personnel of the FCM's;
3.	floor brokers, the persons who trade on the floor of the exchange and who execute orders for the public and for themselves;
4.	commodity trading advisors, who advise customers on commodity trading decisions; and

5. commodity pool operators, who manage commodity
investment pools similar to mutual funds.

Under Section 2 of the Commodity Exchange Act,
Congress gave the CFTC "exclusive jurisdiction with respect to
accounts, agreements, . . . and transactions involving contracts of
sale of a commodity for future delivery, traded or executed on a
contract market designated pursuant to section 7 of this title
. . . or subject to regulation by the Commission . . . ".[9] Section
2 was enacted because of Congressional concern over the
proliferation of state laws dealing with the regulation of
commodity futures and because of continuing confusion in the
courts over the distinction between "commodities" and
"securities."
It is generally accepted, and has been interpreted by the
courts, that Section 2 of the Commodity Exchange Act
preempted state regulation of commodities trading. For
instance, in an Arkansas case, International Trading Ltd. v.
Bell,[10] the Arkansas Supreme Court held that the exclusive
jurisdiction provision of the Commodity Exchange Act (CEA)
preempted the Arkansas State Securities Commissioner from
using the Arkansas Securities Act to sue a company involved in
the fraudulent sale of "London Commodity Options." The court
ruled that the language of Section 2 "seems to express a clear
intention to vest exclusive jurisdiction of the regulation of
commodities options in the Commodity Futures Trading
Commission and to supercede the jurisdiction of all state and
federal agencies."[11] Similarly, the United States District Court
for the Northern District of Alabama held that the CEA
preempted the application of an Alabama gambling statute to
the sale of commodity futures.[12]

C. Common Law State Court Actions
The grant of exclusive jurisdiction to the CFTC contains
several provisions, including a savings clause which provides that
"nothing in this section shall supercede or limit the jurisdiction
conferred on the courts of the United States or any state."[13]
As will be discussed later, this provision probably preserves state
court jurisdiction over suits involving commodity trading in
which the claims are based on common law theories such as

contracts or torts.[14]

D. State Enforcement of Federal Law

While the Commodity Exchange Act (CEA) may preclude state regulation of commodity futures transactions, Congress in 1978 amended the law to allow state assistance in the enforcement of the CEA. The change was in response to the CFTC view that it needed state assistance to adequately enforce the Act. This was felt to be especially true because of the proliferation of fraudulent "commodity options" dealers. The 1978 amendment of the CEA allows states to bring parens patriae suits under the CEA and criminal actions under the state criminal antifraud laws. The CEA explicitly authorizes state suits in federal court to enforce the Act, including the provision that the CFTC is to be notified of the pending state action.[15] This provision can be used by a state attorney general or a state securities commissioner to bring an action to protect commodity customers who reside within that state. This process offers an alternative remedy to customers who believe they have been defrauded. However, the commodities customers are limited to those legal actions which the Attorney General (or securities commissioner or other authorized state official) is willing to pursue.

E. The Commodities - Securities Distinction

The Commodity Exchange Act contains a savings clause which relates to the jurisdiction of the Securities Exchange Commission (SEC). This clause states that Section 2 of the CEA does not supercede or limit the jurisdiction of the SEC. The issue of overlapping jurisdiction between commodities and securities has been a controversial one. The SEC maintains an abiding unwillingness to cede any of its regulatory authority to the CFTC in regard to futures contracts which involve securities. The issue has become more focused with the development of futures trading in financial instruments and other investments that, arguably, more closely resemble securities than do futures contracts which involve agricultural commodities. An example of commodities trading which arguably would involve the joint regulatory jurisdiction of the SEC and the CFTC is futures and options contracts on the

Standard and Poor's 500 Stock Index.

This jurisdictional debate continues, and is firmly
embedded in the relationship between the SEC and CFTC.
However, the courts have almost consistently favored the CFTC
as the designated regulatory authority whenever they have
reviewed this jurisdictional question.[16] During consideration of
the 1978 amendments to the CEA, the SEC proposed an
amendment that would have given the SEC jurisdiction over
futures contracts when the underlying commodity was a security.
Congress rejected any change in the "exclusive jurisdiction"
provision but did mandate communication between the CFTC
and the SEC in order to facilitate proper regulation of
securities-related futures.[17]

III.   How Practitioners May Encounter Commodity Futures
        Law
        There are two major areas in which an attorney might
typically represent a client whose interests are affected by
commodity futures law. The first would involve representing a
client in litigation where the client claims that his or her
futures commission merchant or broker engaged in fraudulent
activity. In this situation there are two initial determinations
which the attorney must make. These are 1) the cause(s) of
action which are implied by the facts and 2) which of the
available forums provides the most appropriate procedures
and/or remedy for the client.
        The second main area of legal work involving commodity
matters is in connection with the income tax consequences of
commodities trading. In this situation, the initial determination
which must be made by the attorney is whether the client's
trades are classified as hedging or speculation. A discussion of
commodities taxation is beyond the scope of this chapter.[18]

        A. Commodity Litigation
            1. Private Remedies - Choice of Forum
        Once an attorney has determined that a cause of action
exists, there are essentially four (4) forums in which the action
could be brought:
                a) an arbitration proceeding;
                b) a reparations action within the CFTC;

c) a civil action in federal court; and/or

d) a common law action in state court.

Each of these forums has its own advantages and disadvantages, in regard to strategy and available remedies. For example, while arbitration provides prompt resolution of disputes, the arbitration process is relatively informal in comparison to the other options. Arbitration is even less formal than a reparations proceeding. Similarly, reparations is a more informal process than civil litigation. It was designed to allow customers to pursue their actions on a pro se and expedited basis, if they so choose.

(a) Arbitration

The 1974 amendments to the CEA require that contract markets provide an arbitration procedure for the resolution of disputes.[19] In 1976 the CFTC enacted regulations which are intended to provide a "fair and equitable procedure for arbitration."[20] While arbitration procedures have not been well-accepted as a remedy in all types of legal disputes, those procedures may offer a relatively swift and effective method for resolving certain commodity trading disputes. It may be particularly useful under circumstances where the docket of reparations cases has created serious delay in the hearing of cases.

The arbitration procedure provides that jurisdiction is limited to claims of $15,000 or less and that counterclaims can be heard. Moreover, the customer may retain counsel at any point in the procedure.[21] The regulations also contain a significant provision which states that the use of pre-dispute arbitration agreements must be voluntary. In other words, a customer cannot be required to sign a pre-dispute arbitration clause as a condition of doing business with a commodity futures merchant.[22] Moreover, the customer must be advised in writing that he or she has the right to seek reparations by an election that can be made within 45 days after either party has filed the intent to arbitrate.[23] Furthermore, the arbitration agreement must contain specific cautionary language which is designed to protect the customer from inadvertently waiving any rights. This cautionary language must be separately endorsed by the customer.[24]

443

The provision which requires that the customer be advised of the right to rescind the arbitration agreement was designed to prevent commodities futures merchants from requiring customers to sign predispute arbitration agreements as a condition of doing business. This was a common practice before 1974. If this practice had been allowed to continue, reparations procedures would, as a practical matter, be generally unavailable to customers. A key case which upholds the Commission's position on this issue is <u>Bache Halsey Stuart Inc. v. French</u>[25]. Moreover, in <u>Curran v. Merrill Lynch, Pierce, Fenner and Smith, Inc.</u>,[26] the Fifth Circuit Court of Appeals held that the CFTC rule which requires that the pre-dispute arbitration agreement be contained in a separate document and contain warnings in large print, could be applied retroactively.

Of course, there are certain disadvantages to arbitration, including the unavailability of discovery and the right of appeal, respectively. However, arbitration does offer prompt resolution of disputes and the CFTC rules insure that the customer receives fair treatment in the procedure.

(b) <u>Reparations</u>

One of the most significant features of the 1974 Act was the establishment of a reparations procedure for customer complaints against commodity professionals who are registered under the CEA.[27] Only actual damages may be awarded in a reparations proceeding. A reparations award is enforceable in a U.S. District Court. The reparations forum is designed to provide customers with a just, speedy and inexpensive adjudication of their claims. Certain changes were made in the reparations proceeding by the Futures Trading Act of 1982.[28] The current CFTC reparations regulations are found at 17 C.F.R. Part 12.

A significant feature of a reparations proceeding is that it only provides a forum for complaints against persons who are either registered or required to be registered under the CEA. Furthermore, only actions based on violations of the CEA, or its rules and regulations, can form the basis of a reparations action. Thus, one major limitation of reparations is that claims based on common law causes of action are precluded from being heard in that forum, unless they are brought as a counterclaim.[29] An additional disadvantage for practicing attorneys is that reparations decisions are only reported in the CCH Commodity Futures Law Reporter25. The exception is the few cases which are reviewed by a U.S. Court of Appeals, and which are reported.

A reparations complaint must be drafted in conformity with the requirements which are specified in the regulations.[30] The Director of the Office of Proceedings within the CFTC will review each complaint which has been filed to determine its sufficiency in stating a claim for which relief can be granted. If, in the opinion of the Director, the facts set forth in the complaint warrant the action which is requested against any of the named registered persons, the Director will approve the complaint for service upon those registered person(s).[31] If the Director finds that the facts alleged do not state a claim which is cognizable under the Commodity Exchange Act, no further proceedings will be held on the complaint. This decision is not appealable. However, this termination of the complaint as to any registered person is regarded by the Commission as without prejudice to the right of the complainant to seek other forms of relief.[32]

When a complaint is approved by the Director for further proceedings, a respondent may satisfy the complaint either by paying the full amount claimed or an amount which the complainant will accept in satisfaction of the claim. Alternatively, the respondent must file an answer within 45 days of service of the complaint.[33] An answer may include a motion for reconsideration of the Director's determination to forward the complaint to the respondent.[34] The reparations rules allow for counterclaims to be filed. However, there is no third party practice available, i.e. no third party complaints or crossclaims are allowed.

When a person files a reparations complaint, they must elect one of the three (3) reparations procedures which are available. These procedures are the voluntary, the summary, and the formal, respectively. The rights of the parties to such basic procedures as discovery and oral hearings are determined by which of the three (3) reparations procedures is being used. Moreover, the parties' rights of appeal are also determined by which procedure is used. The simplest of the three (3) procedures is the voluntary procedure. This procedure is available regardless of the amount claimed or counterclaimed, but only if all parties agree to its use. By electing the voluntary procedure, all parties waive the opportunity for an oral hearing. They also waive their right to receive a written statement of the findings of fact upon which the final decision is based, the right to prejudgment interest, and the right to appeal the final decision either to the CFTC or to a U.S. Court of Appeals.[35] Discovery is allowed in a limited form. Each party may submit verified testimony and documents, verified testimony and documents of non-party witnesses, and other documents and tangible evidence. Absolutely no oral testimony is allowed, either by the parties or their witnesses.[36]

The second type of reparations procedure is the summary procedure. This procedure is limited to claims and counterclaims which do not exceed $10,000. As with the voluntary procedure, the primary form of evidentiary proof consists of the parties' filing verified statements of facts and verified statements from non-party witnesses. However, the Judgment Officer has the authority to allow an oral hearing upon motion by a party.[37] The Officer also can determine whether to hold a predecision conference to narrow the issues to be litigated and to encourage the settlement of the entire case.[38]

Under the summary procedure, the parties are not allowed to file proposed findings of fact or rulings of law.[39] The Judgment Officer will issue an initial decision which contains both the Officer's findings of fact and rulings of law. The initial decision becomes the final decision and order of the Commission thirty (30) days after it has been served on the parties, unless an appeal to the Commission is timely filed and perfected.[40]

The third type of reparation procedure is the formal procedure. This is available in cases where the amount claimed or counterclaimed exceeds $10,000. This procedure provides the parties with a complete administrative hearing process. The initial decision can be appealed to the Commission, in the first instance, and subsequently to a U.S. Court of Appeals. The discovery process available to the parties is much like that available in the courts. Therefore, disputes are likely to arise as to the proper scope and timing of discovery. Under the formal procedure, the Proceedings Officer has the authority to receive and rule upon motions for protective orders, motions to compel discovery, motions for leave to serve written interrogatories in excess of thirty (30), motions to enlarge the time permitted for discovery, and other similar motions.[41] The Proceedings Officer also has the discretion to hold a predecisional conference.[42]

Under the formal procedure, the case is decided by an Administrative Law Judge. The Judge will examine the evidence submitted by the parties during discovery and determine whether to hold an oral hearing for the disposition of the case.[43] Generally, an oral hearing will be provided. After all the evidence is submitted in the case, the Judge will issue an initial decision. This decision will include findings of fact and conclusions of law. The initial decision will become the final decision and order of the Commission unless a timely appeal is filed and perfected within thirty days of the date of service of the initial decision.[44]

(c) Implied Private Right of Action

Prior to 1974 there was an implied private right of action for a violation of the substantive provisions of the Commodity Exchange Act.[45] However, in a 1975 decision, Cort v. Ash[46], the United States Supreme Court established a more restrictive rule for finding an implied private right of action under federal regulatory statutes. Therefore, the Cort v. Ash decision raised some temporary doubt as to the availability of the private right of action.

In 1982 this matter was resolved by the United States Supreme Court in Merrill Lynch, Pierce, Fenner and Smith, Inc. v. Curran,[47] which accepted for review four (4) different cases that presented the question of the existence of a private right of action under the CEA. In Merrill Lynch v. Curran, the Supreme Court held that an implied private right of action under the CEA existed prior to 1974 and that it survived the 1974 amendments to the Act. Most importantly, Congress created an express private right of action in the Futures Trading Act of 1982.[48] Therefore, violations of the Commodity Exchange Act may be litigated in a federal district court, provided that federal jurisdictional requirements are met.

(d) State Court Common Law Action
Pursuant to the exclusive jurisdiction provisions of the
CEA, state courts are generally preempted from deciding cases
that are based on violations of the CEA. In addition, state
courts are generally preempted from enforcing state regulatory
provisions that are alleged to apply to commodities trading.[49]
However, state courts retain their jurisdiction over commodity
disputes that are framed in terms of common law claims, such
as breach of contract, fraud, negligence or breach of fiduciary
duty. For example, the Iowa Supreme Court, in Iowa Grain v.
Farm Grain & Feed Co.[50], allowed recovery against a brokerage
company for a violation of exchange rules. The Iowa Grain
holding was based on the theory that the broker's action was a
breach of the customer agreement, a contract between the
parties. The alleged breach of this contract stated a common
law claim. As a general rule, while state courts cannot hear
claims based on the terms and provisions of the CEA, virtually
all types of violations of the customer protection rules which
are codified in the CEA can also be brought under the above-
stated common law theories.

2. Causes of Action
There are several basic causes of action under the CEA
that an attorney can pursue, depending upon the nature of the
facts involved in the controversy.

(a) Fraudulent Activity - Violation of Section 6b
One of the basic causes of action is fraudulent activity
which violates Section 6b. Section 6b of the CEA provides
that:

> It shall be unlawful (1) for any member of a
> contract market, or any correspondent, agent or
> employee of any member, in or in connection with any
> order to make, or the making of any contract of sales of
> any commodity in interstate commerce, made, or to be
> made, on or subject to the rules of any contract market,
> for or on behalf of any other person, or (2) for any
> person, on or in connection with any order to make or
> the making of, any contract of sale of any commodity for
> futures delivery, made or to be made, on or subject to

the rules of any commodity market for or on behalf of any other person if such contract is for future delivery or may be used for (a) hedging any transaction in interstate commerce in such commodity or the products or by-products thereof, or (b) determining the price basis of any transaction in interstate commerce in such commodity or (c) delivering any such commodity sold, shipped, or received in interstate commerce for fulfillment thereof--

    (A) to cheat or defraud or attempt to cheat or defraud such other person;

    (B) willfully to make or cause to be made to such other person any false report or statement thereof, or willfully to enter or cause to be entered for such person any false record thereof;

    (C) willfully to deceive or attempt to deceive such other person by any means whatsoever in regard to any such order or contract or the disposition or execution of any such order or contract, or in regard to any act of agency performed with respect to such order or contract for such person; or

    (D) to bucket such order, or to fill such order by offset against the orders or orders of any other person, or willfully and knowingly and without the prior consent of such person to become the buyer in respect to any selling order of such person, or become the seller in respect to any buying order of such person.[51]

Section 6b provides the basis for many types of actions. The activities that might violate Section 6b generally can be categorized as the following types of activity:

    1) Churning;

    2) Unauthorized trading;

    3) Nondisclosure of Material Facts;

    4) Misuse of Customer Funds;

    5) Material Misrepresentations;

    6) Improper Order Executions; and/or

    7) Inaccurate Determination of Customer Suitability to Trade.

In a claim based on any of the above theories, it is necessary that the complaint be drafted in a manner that corresponds with the language of Section 6b. The "cheat or defraud" provisions of Section 6b provide a rather expansive basis for causes of action brought under the theory of fraud. The primary analysis within Section 6b actions is an examination of the standard of care owed to a customer by a trading professional, and whether the duty to maintain that standard of care was breached.

Enforcement actions to regulate and sanction trading professionals may be brought by the CFTC.[52] Private actions may also be brought by individual customers who believe that their commodity futures merchant or broker has engaged in fraudulent activity which is violative of Section 6b.[53]

(1) Requirement of Scienter Under Section 6b

A significant and unresolved issue concerning Section 6b actions is the nature of the intent required to constitute a violation of Section 6b. The courts and the Commission have examined scienter or bad faith as possible standards of intent in a commodity fraud case. Several cases have held that bad faith is not required for a violation of Section 6b.[54] However, these cases contradict cases decided prior to the establishment of CFTC,[55] and also contradict the United States Supreme Court's ruling in the well-known securities fraud case, Ernest & Ernest v. Hochfelder.[56] In Hochfelder, the scienter standard was applied. It was defined to consist of a mental state which involves the intent to deceive, manipulate or defraud. It is notable that a Ninth Circuit case, CFTC v. Savage,[57] required scienter for a violation of Section 6b but not Section 6o(1), which regulates the conduct of commodity trading advisors (CTA's), commodity pool operators (CPO's), and their associated persons (discussed infra).

The CFTC appears to favor a relatively low standard of intent for Section 6b actions. The conscious performance of an action probably provides the necessary intent. Administrative law judges have also generally taken this expansive view of Section 6b. In a CFTC decision involving a reparations award, Gordon v. Shearson Hayden Stone, Inc.,[58] the Commission distinguished the Hochfelder securities case from commodities

450

futures cases involving Section 6b. The <u>Gordon</u> case involved an alleged violation of Section 6b(A) by an associated person who failed to disclose the risk of a spread trading investment program to a customer. The Commission noted that the absence of "willful" as a modifier of the Section 6b(A) definition of fraud, and the legislative history of the antifraud provisions, compelled the conclusion that a negligent violation of a fiduciary duty is a violation of Section 6b(A). Of course, the breach of a fiduciary duty may automatically constitute constructive fraud, regardless of whether actual fraud exists.

The issue of whether scienter is necessary in a Section 6b action is not completely resolved. This may be one of the most difficult issues that a lawyer will deal with in a fraudulent activity case.

(2) Conduct Which Violates §6b

Several factors may influence the determination of whether specific conduct violates Section 6b:

    a) Whether the action is a reparation procedure, a CFTC enforcement action, or a private cause of action;

    b) Whether the broker's activities are alleged to be a violation of Section 6b(A) or another subsection of Section 6b; and

    c) Whether the violation of Section 6b(A) can be characterized as a breach of fiduciary duty.

(b) Churning

A claim of churning is based on the allegation that a broker engaged in excessive trading in an account in order to generate commissions for herself at the expense of the customer's best interest. There are two primary factors in the determination of churning:

    1. it must be shown that the broker had sufficient <u>control</u> over the customer's account; and

    2. it must be shown that the customer's account was traded excessively.[59]

(1) Control

It may be difficult to prove that the broker exercised

sufficient control over a customer's account. This proof problem is mitigated if the account is a discretionary account, i.e. one that is traded at the broker's discretion under a Power of Attorney. Through various decisions, the Commission has enumerated certain factors to be considered in determining control. Among the factors which tend to demonstrate control are 1) a lack of customer sophistication; 2) a lack of prior commodity trading experience on the part of the customer and a minimum of time devoted by him to his account; 3) a high degree of trust and confidence reposed in the associated person by the customer; 4) a large percentage of transactions entered into by the customer based on the recommendations of associated persons; 5) the absence of prior customer approval for transactions entered into on his or her behalf; and 6) customer approval of recommended transactions where the approval is not based upon full, truthful and accurate information supplied by the associated person.

When a nondiscretionary account is involved, the complainant bears the burden of showing that the broker had de facto control over the volume and frequency of trading. This is also described as the existence of broker dominance over the customer. It is not necessary to show that there was a formal vesting of discretion in the broker to establish this control or dominance. To determine the requisite control, the courts or the Commission will look to factors such as customer reliance on the broker's advice and the customer's lack of trading sophistication. The customer's experience in both commodities and securities trading will be used to determine a customer's sophistication. In other words, a customer who has engaged in substantial securities trading may be deemed to possess sophistication in regard to commodities trading even if he or she has little experience in commodities trading.

(2) Excessive Trading

The second element of churning, excessive trading, may also be difficult to prove. The courts and the Commission have held that no single quantitative indicator can conclusively establish excessive trading. Instead, the fact finder will take an overall view of the transactions in examining the customer's trading needs and objectives. The finding as to needs and

452

objectives is used in the determination of whether the broker disregarded the customer's interest in order to generate commissions. In general, the fact finder will determine whether excessive trading exists by examining the ratio of commissions generated to the amount of the customer's investment.

The courts have "borrowed" certain concepts from securities law to review churning claims. These concepts include the "turnover rate" of the customer's account, and the ratio of the broker's commissions to the average net equity in the customer's account. A certain type of trading activity is viewed as inherently indicative that churning may have occurred. This is known as day trading or short-term in-and-out trading. This is the type of activity that usually results in minimal gains and losses for the customer but which generate a steady flow of commissions for the broker.

(3) Defenses to Churning Allegations

The most obvious defenses available to a broker who has allegedly churned a customer's account is to prove that he or she either lacked the requisite control over the account, or that the trading was not excessive, or both. Another defense is to show that the broker or futures commission merchant was trading according to a mechanized (or computerized) system that triggered the individual trades, and controlled the trading pattern. Many speculators trade on the basis of technical factors which are entered into a trading system. The use of a mechanized trading system may provide a defense for a broker, particularly if the system was disclosed to the customer and the customer authorized its use.

(c) Unauthorized Trading

Perhaps the most common complaint brought by commodity customers is that the broker or futures commission merchant conducted unauthorized trading, i.e. made trades in conflict with the explicit instructions of the customer or made trades without specific authorization. It has been held in numerous cases that it is a violation of Section 6b of the CEA for an account executive in the brokerage business to execute trading transactions which have not authorized by her customers. For example, in Haltmier v. CFTC,[60] an account executive traded a customer's account in a number of commodities even though the customer had given specific instructions to trade only in long soybean contracts. In assessing liability, the court also noted that the agency status of associated persons provides clear authority for attributing the unauthorized trading liability of an employee to his or her employer.

In Poplar Grove Planting and Refining Co. Inc. v. Bache Halsey Stuart, Inc.,[61] it was held that the unauthorized trading activities of an account executive were attributable to the brokerage firm that employed him. In Poplar Grove, the court also held that it was against public policy for the defendant to be allowed to exculpate itself from the effects of the intentional acts of its agent by the use of a limitation of liability provision.[62]

Moreover, the court held that the burden of proving ratification is on the broker or commodity futures merchant. In that particular case, the customer had met margin calls on unauthorized trades. However, the court found that the customer took that action because he feared that the accounts involved would be liquidated if he did not maintain the margin requirements. Based on that finding, the court held that the customer's action did not constitute a ratification.[63]

One of the practical difficulties with the occurrence of unauthorized trading is that the illegal activity may be difficult to detect. Moreover, the broker's defense of customer ratification may be readily available in many cases. This will generally be a successful defense if the customer, through his or her actions, failed to notify the broker immediately upon receiving notice of the alleged unauthorized trade. Moreover, this defense may also be available if the customer paid extra margin upon receiving a margin call for alleged unauthorized trades, or if the customer accepted profits from unauthorized trades. Most customer agreements expressly provide that upon receipt of account statements which contain purchase and sale confirmations, the customer must notify the broker within a set period, usually 2-10 days, if it is believed that a trade was made without authorization or there is otherwise a discrepancy in the account. The customer's failure to promptly report his or her protest is treated as a ratification of the disputed trade. This type of provision is usually also contained in the purchase and sale documentation that a customer receives.

The CFTC has promulgated rules to provide that a futures commission merchant or associated person can not effect a commodity transaction for a customer's account without the specific authorization of the customer.[64] This applies to both the type and the amount of the commodity to be traded. The Commission has held that an investor has an absolute right not to incur liability for any trade not authorized by him or her. The Commission's position is that if a trade is executed without proper authorization, the contract interest will accrue to the futures commission merchant instead of the customer.[65] The obvious exception to this rule is the discretionary account, in which the customer has delegated trading authority to the broker.

(d) Margin Rule Violations

A cause of action exists when a customer is damaged because a broker has failed to comply with exchange rules which address margin calls and the liquidation of undermargined accounts. All exchanges have a rule which requires the liquidation of undermargined accounts within a set period or a reasonable time. In addition, the customer agreement that is signed when the account is opened contains a provision that all trades will be executed in compliance with exchange rules. The Iowa and Nebraska Supreme Courts have held, respectively, that a broker's failure to comply with exchange rules in regard to the liquidation of undermargined accounts is a breach of a contractual duty owed to the customer.

In Iowa Grain v. Farmers Grain and Feed Co.,[66] the Iowa Supreme Court held that a broker's failure to follow a Chicago Board of Trade rule which prohibited undermargined accounts was a breach of contract. Therefore, the customer was entitled to bring a counterclaim against the broker's action to collect a debit in the account. Based on the finding that there would have been a credit in the account if it had been liquidated properly, the customer was awarded a $60,000 judgment on its counterclaim. The Court distinguished other reparations decisions which had held that a breach of an exchange margin rule does not give rise to a private cause of action unless fraud is involved. In reference to this point, the Court in <u>Iowa Grain</u> stated that the cause of action presented was not based on the breach of the margin rule, but rather on the breach of the customer agreement.[67]

In <u>First Mid America Inc., v. Palmer</u>,[68] the Nebraska Supreme Court held that, under the facts presented, the broker had failed to follow exchange rules regarding the liquidation of undermargined accounts. This case involved the customer's explicit instructions regarding the handling of an undermargined account. Based on the broker's failure to properly liquidate the undermargined account, the customer prevailed in its counterclaim against the broker's claim for a $31,000 debt. The broker in <u>First Mid America</u> raised the defense that the customer agreement contained provisions that required the customer to satisfy all deficiencies. Therefore, the broker argued that he had been given the discretion as to when to liquidate the account. The broker also argued that the failure of the customer to object to any of the trades listed in the account statements within two days after their receipt served as a ratification of those trades. The Nebraska Supreme Court stated that the customer agreement would be an unconscionable contract if those provisions could be interpreted to mean that the customer was absolutely liable for any action taken by the broker.

There are cases which have ruled in favor of the broker on the issue of margin rule violations. For example, in <u>Lincoln Commodity Services v. Meade</u>,[69] the court held that the broker's breach of the exchange's margin rule did not excuse the customer from his obligation to indemnify a broker for losses in an account.

(e) <u>Other Causes of Action</u>

There are several other types of conduct that could constitute violations of Section 6b and may render a commodity professional liable to a customer. First, it is fraudulent for a commodity profession to make a material misrepresentation of fact to a customer (or potential customer) which induces that customer to open a trading account. This could involve such matters as misrepresenting the risks involved in commodities trading or assuring the customer that he or she would receive large profits from trading. Second, it is fraudulent for a commodity professional to misuse customer funds, which includes such matters as the conversion of funds and the failure or delay of the commodity futures merchant or broker to remit customer funds upon demand.

Generally, a major category of improper conduct by commodity brokerage firms involves the breach of fiduciary duties which those firms and their associated persons owe to the customer. The CFTC has taken a strong stand in regard to proscribing conduct which violates fiduciary duties. The Commission has also attempted to provide some definitive guidelines as to the types of conduct which constitute a breach of those duties.

The specific fiduciary duty which a trading professional owes to a customer depends upon their relationship and the type of account that is being traded. Importantly, in <u>Gordon v. Shearson Hayden Stone, Inc.</u>,[70] the CFTC established that no intent to defraud is required for a violation of Section 6b(A). As noted earlier, under the CFTC view, a breach of fiduciary duty, even if committed negligently, constitutes fraud as provided by Section 6b(A) of the Act. In <u>Gordon</u> the Commission held that, under the facts presented, the commodity professional who had advised the customer had "a duty to know all material market facts which are reasonably ascertainable in connection with a customer's trading decision" and that the advisor had a duty to disclose those facts.[71]

Generally, in order to establish a violation of Section 6b(A), it must be shown that a fiduciary relationship existed between the broker and the customer (or prospective customer) and that a fiduciary duty within that relationship was breached. Of course, to recover on a breach of fiduciary duty claim, it is necessary to show that the customer was damaged as a result of the breach. Thus, for example, an unauthorized trade by a broker which yields a profit to the customer would not be compensable in damages. In sum, where there is difficulty in a broker-customer relationship, the fact finder will need to examine each individual trade which occurred in the customer's account to determine its character and results.

3. Actions by Commodity Pool Operators and Commodity Trading Advisors

There are separate statutory provisions which apply to commodity pool operators and commodity trading advisors. The existence of these separate provisions illustrates that these two (2) categories of commodity professionals play a role in futures trading that is significantly different from the roles played by futures commission merchants, brokers and their respective associated persons. The primary difference is that there is an advisory role inherent in the functions of pool operators and commodity advisors, respectively. Because of their role in advising customers and prospective customers about commodity trading decisions, commodity pool operators and commodity trade advisors are held to a strict fiduciary standard. In contrast, the role of a broker is oftentimes simply to accept and execute customer orders which are based on the independent decision of the customer. The fiduciary duties of a person who serves in an advisory role with a customer, such as a commodity pool operator or a commodity trading advisor, will generally be more strict than those which apply to a broker, who serves as a mere conduit for customer orders.[72]

Congress determined that the respective activities of commodity pool operators and commodity trading advisors take place by the use of the mails and other means and instrumentalities of interstate commerce. Furthermore, Congress found that their activities are directed toward and cause the purchase and sale of futures contracts.[73] Therefore, the CEA provides that commodity pool operators and commodity trading advisors must generally register with the CFTC as a condition of doing business.[74]

Unless a person who meets the definition of a commodity pool operator or commodity trading advisor has registered with the CFTC, it is unlawful for that person to use the mails or any means or instrumentality of interstate commerce in connection with his or her business.[75] However, there are exceptions to the registration requirement for certain commodity trading advisors. This includes persons who, during the course of the proceeding twelve months, did not furnish trading advice to more than fifteen persons and do not hold themselves out to the public generally as a commodity trading

458

advisor.[76]

There are statutory anti-fraud provisions which apply to commodity pool operators and commodity trading advisors. These are contained in Section 6o(1) of the Commodity Exchange Act. Under these provisions it is unlawful for a commodity trading advisor, a commodity pool operator, or their respective associated persons by use of the mails or any means of instrumentality of interstate commerce directly or indirectly, to employ any device, scheme, or artifice to defraud any client or participant or prospective client or participant; or to engage in any transaction, practice, or course of business which operates as a fraud or deceit upon any client or participant or prospective client or participant.

Furthermore, it is unlawful for any registered commodity trading advisor, commodity pool operator, or their respective associated persons to represent or imply in any manner that they have been sponsored, recommended, or approved, or that their abilities or qualifications have in any respect been passed upon, by the United States or any of its agencies or officers. This does not preclude any of those registered commodity professionals from representing that he or she is registered with the CFTC if that fact is indeed the case and if the effect of the fact of registration is not misrepresented.[77]

Several cases reported by the CFTC provide the general guidelines for assessing claims of fraudulent activities under Section 6o.[78]

FOOTNOTES

1. See, e.g., Iowa Grain v. Farmers and Feed Co. Inc., 293 N.W.2d 22 (Iowa 1980).

2. See, First Mid America Inc. v. Palmer, 248 N.W.2d 30 (Neb. 1976).

3. 465 F. Supp. 585 (D. La. 1979).

4. 17 C.F.R. § 1.55 (1988).

5. 17 C.F.R. § 180-3(6) (1988).

6. Pub.L.No. 93-463, 88 Stat. 1389 (1974).

7. 7 U.S.C. §§ 1-24.

8. For examples of recent decisions dealing with the scope of CFTC powers, see, Board of Trade of the City of Chicago v. CFTC, 605 F.2d 1016 (7th Cir. 1979), and CFTC v. Hunt, 591 F.2d 1211 (7th Cir. 1979).

9. 7 U.S.C. § 2.

10. 262 Ark. 244, 556 S.W.2d 420 (1977), cert. denied 436 U.S. 956 (1978).

11. 556 S.W.2d at 423.

12. Paine, Webber, Jackson and Curtis, Inc. v. Conaway, 515 F. Supp. 502 (1981). See also, Clayton Brokerage Co. v. Mover, 531 S.W.2d 805 (Sup. Ct. Tex. 1975).

13. 7 U.S.C. § 2.

14. See, e.g., Iowa Grain v. Farmers Grain and Feed Co., Inc. 293 N.W.2d 22 (Iowa 1980). See generally, Johnson, "The

Commodity Futures Trading Commission Act: Preemption as Public Policy," 29 Vand. L. Rev. 1, 32-36 (1976).

15. 7 U.S.C. § 13a-2(1).

16. See, e.g., SEC v. American Commodity Exchange, 546 F.2d 1361 (10th Cir. 1976).

17. 7 U.S.C. § 4a (g)-2 (i). Useful discussions of this subject can be found in several law review articles, including Bromberg, "Securities Law Relationship to Commodity Law", 35 Bus. L. 787 (1980), and Hewitt, "The Line Between Commodities and Securities," 1 Agric. L.J. 291 and 473 (2 parts) (1979).

18. For a discussion of the tax aspects of commodities trading, see, O'Byrne and Davenport, Farm Income Tax Manual (Charlottesville: The Michie Co., 1988) § 331.

19. 7 U.S.C. § 7a (11).

20. 17 C.F.R. Part 180 (1988).

21. 17 C.F.R. § 180.2 (1988).

22. 17 C.F.R. § 180.3(6) (1988).

23. 17 C.F.R. § 180.3(6) (1988).

24. 17 C.F.R. § 180.3(6) (1988).

25. 425 F. Supp. 1231 (D. D.C. 1977).

26. 622 F.2d 216 (5th Cir. 1980).

27. 7 U.S.C. § 18.

28. Pub. L. No. 97-444, 96 Stat. 2294 (1982).

29. 7 U.S.C. § 18(a); CFTC v. Schor, 478 U.S. 833 (1986).

30. 17 C.F.R. § 12.13(b) (1988).

31. 17 C.F.R. § 12.15(a) (1988).

32. 17 C.F.R. § 12.15(b) (1988).

33. 17 C.F.R. § 12.16 (1988).

34. 17 C.F.R. § 12.18(b) (1988).

35. 17 C.F.R. § 12.100(b) (1988).

36. 17 C.F.R. § 12.105 (1988).

37. 17 C.F.R. § 12.201(g) (1988).

38. 17 C.F.R. § 12.206 (1988).

39. 17 C.F.R. § 12.210(a) (1988).

40. 17 C.F.R. § 12.210(d) (1988).

41. 17 C.F.R. § 12.301 (1988).

42. 17 C.F.R. § 12.303 (1988).

43. 17 C.F.R. § 12.311 (1988).

44. 17 C.F.R. § 12.314(d) (1988).

45. See, e.g, Booth v. Peavy, 430 F.2d 132 (8th Cir. 1970).

46. 422 U.S. 66 (1975).

47. 456 U.S. 353, 102 S.Ct. 1925 (1982).

48. Pub. L. No. 97-444, 96 Stat. 2294 (adding § 22(a)(1) to the CEA) (presently codified at 7 U.S.C. § 25).

49. See e.g., International Trading Ltd. v. Bell, 556 S.W.2d 420 (1977).

50. 293 N.W.2d 22 (Iowa 1980).

51. 7 U.S.C. § 6b.

52. 7 U.S.C. § 13a-1.

53. 7 U.S.C. § 18, § 25.

54. See, e.g., Haltmier v. CFTC, 554 F.2d 556 (2d Cir. 1977), and Silverman v. CFTC, 549 F.2d 28 (7th Cir. 1977).

55. See, e.g., McCurrin v. Kohlmeyer & Co., 347 F. Supp. 573 (E.D. La. 1972), aff'd 447 F.2d 113 (5th Cir. 1973).

56. 425 U.S. 185 (1976).

57. 611 F.2d 27 (9th Cir. 1979).

58. 1980 Comm. Fut. L. Rep. ¶21,016 (CFTC 1980).

59. See, e.g., Booth v. Peavy, 430 F.2d 132 (8th Cir. 1970) and Hecht v. Harris, Upham & Co., 283 F. Supp. 417 (N.D. Cal. 1968), mod. on other grounds, 430 F.2d 1202 (9th Cir. 1979).

60. 554 F.2d 556 (2d Cir. 1977).

61. 465 F. Supp. 585 (M.D. La. 1979).

62. 465 F. Supp. at 593. See also, Silverman v. Commodity Futures Trading Commission, 549 F.2d 28 (7th Cir. 1977).

63. Poplar Grove Planting and Refining Co., Inc. v. Bache Halsey Stuart, Inc., 465 F. Supp. 585, 595-96 (M.D. La. 1979).

64. 17 C.F.R. § 166.2 (1988).

65. See, Sherwood v. Madda Trading Co., 1977-1980 Transfer Binder Comm. Fut. L. Rep. ¶20,728 at 23,014 (CFTC 1979).

66. 293 N.W.2d 22 (Iowa 1980).

67. 293 N.W.2d at 24-25.

68. 248 N.W.2d 30 (Neb. 1976).

69. 558 F.2d 469, 473 (8th Cir. 1977).

70. See, Gordon v. Shearson Hayden Stone Inc., 1980 Comm. Fut. L. Rep. ¶21,016 (CFTC 1980).

71. Gordon, 1980 Comm. Fut. L. Rep. ¶21,016 at 23,981.

72. For the proposition that the scope of fiduciary duties are determined in large part by the advisory nature of the relationship, see Gordon, 1980 Comm. Fut. L. Rep. § 21,016 at 23,981.

73. 7 U.S.C. § 6l(1)&(2).

74. 7 U.S.C. § 6n.

75. 7 U.S.C. § 6m.

76. 7 U.S.C. § 6m.

77. 7 U.S.C. § 6(o)(2).

78. Beshara v. Spath, 1978 Comm. Fut. L. Rep. § 20,616; Tejeda v. Knight, 1978 Comm. Fut. L. Rep. § 20,647; R.H. Bartels v. Economic Systems, Inc., 1979 Comm. Fut. L. Rep. § 20, 889.

CHAPTER 13

FARM COOPERATIVES

I.   Introduction
     For decades cooperative associations have been an
integral and important part of American agriculture. Most
farmers are members of at least one cooperative. These
associations are designed to secure for farmers the economic
advantages of group action in the production and marketing of
agricultural commodities.
     Until the mid-1870's, farmers operated as independent
economic units. This began to change after the National
Grange developed a policy for effecting cooperation among
farmers at its 1875 annual convention.[1]   This policy enunciated
a number of factors as basic requirements for cooperatives.
These factors were derived from the Code of the English
Weavers Cooperative and included such principles as open
membership, one-person one-vote, cash trading, membership
education, political and religious neutrality, no unusual risk
assumption, limited interest on stock, the sale of goods at
regular retail prices, limitations on number of shares owned,
services offered to members at cost, and profits distributed to
members according to patronage. These factors are still relied
upon today to identify cooperatives and to distinguish them
from other business entities.
     In 1929 Justice Brandeis observed that "no one plan or
organization is to be labeled as truly cooperative to the
exclusion of others".[2]   However, most cooperatives are identified
by the criteria derived from these early roots in the National
Grange. Accordingly, cooperatives are held to embody the
following attributes:
     1. The basic purpose of a cooperative is to render
economic benefits to its membership;
     2. The risks, costs, and benefits of the cooperative are
shared "equitably" among members;
     3. The cooperative is democratically controlled and is
organized to serve the mutual interests of its members;

465

4. The cooperative is a non-profit enterprise in the sense that it is organized for the economic benefit of members on the basis of their use of the cooperative's services, and is not established for the primary purpose of making profits for the cooperative as a legal entity or for its members as investors;

5. The cooperative members are obligated to patronize the cooperative; and

6. Most of the cooperative's business is done with its members.[3]

II.   The Nature of Cooperatives

Cooperatives are voluntary business organizations which are created by statute. The cooperative form enables persons to join together for mutual help, including joint purchasing and marketing. A cooperative is usually a "non-profit" enterprise. Cooperatives tend to be specialized as one of three types: marketing, supply or bargaining cooperatives. As its name signifies, the marketing cooperative is designed to assist members in marketing the products grown or produced by them. Supply cooperatives exist to secure the supplies and equipment needed by its members at the lowest possible cost per unit.

The bargaining cooperative is organized expressly to act as a bargaining agent for its farmer-members. This may include collective bargaining in setting the prices to be charged by all members for their products.[4] This implies a monopolistic economic function of the cooperative.

A.   Marketing Cooperatives

Marketing cooperatives generally function in one of two ways. First, the cooperative may buy the products of members at the prevailing market rate. At the end of the annual or fiscal year, the results of the cooperative's activities will determine whether any net savings have been realized. These net savings are the equivalent of profits. These savings are allocated to each member-patron on the basis of his or her percentage of marketings. In other words, the member receives a proportionate share of the "profits." Alternatively, the cooperative may function as a marketing agency. In this case, the member-producer contracts with the cooperative to sell the product. In this transaction, a set amount based on volume is

466

deducted from marketing costs. All of the commodity production for a particular season is then "pooled" and marketed by the cooperative. The net savings which are generated through marketing are divided among the members of the cooperative based on the volume marketed by each member.

As a general rule, marketing contracts will be upheld as valid if they conform to the usual requirements of contract law.[5] Under either agency contracts or purchase and sale contracts, the cooperative's contractual obligation to its members is to sell the commodities (or other product) and to return the sale price to the member, after deducting expenses and other costs as set forth in the marketing agreement. In the agency contract, the cooperative is obligated to sell the member's product at the best price obtainable by it under market conditions. In contrast, under a purchase-and-sale agreement, the price paid to the member will normally be the resale or market price. Courts have recognized an implied requirement of good faith on the part of the cooperative in carrying out its obligation under the contract.[6] Furthermore, the relationship between each member and the cooperative has been viewed as creating fiduciary duties on the part of the cooperative toward the member.[7]

B. Supply Cooperatives

A supply cooperative purchases the supplies needed by its members. This typically includes inputs such as machinery, fertilizer, feed, or petroleum products. This bulk purchasing arrangement makes these supplies available to members at prices which are at or below the prevailing market price. Net savings at the end of the accounting period will be distributed to each member based upon the volume of business the member transacted with the cooperative.

C. Membership in Cooperatives

As a general rule, cooperatives are relatively free to determine who may become members. Usually, a person may obtain membership in a cooperative by entering into an agreement with the organization and, perhaps, through the purchasing of at least one share of stock. A typical agreement provides that the member will either market products through the cooperative or will take services and supplies from it. By

467

statute in most states, cooperative marketing contracts may require members to sell all or any specified part of their agricultural commodities exclusively to or through the cooperative.[8]

In most states[9] the cooperative may admit as members or issue voting common stock only to persons engaged in the production of agricultural products.[10] One agricultural cooperative association may generally become a member or stockholder of another cooperative.[11]

Membership in a cooperative continues until there has been a valid transfer, redemption or forfeiture of the stock. Consequently, it is generally impossible for a member to terminate membership simply by resigning from the cooperative. Similarly, the mere termination of a marketing contract or the cessation of further business transactions with the cooperative will not be sufficient to terminate membership.[12] On the other hand, it may be difficult for the cooperative to expel a member without proper notice and an opportunity for the member to be heard.[13]

III. Cooperative Finance
      A. Member Contributions to Financing
Members contribute financially to the cooperative in a number of ways. Forms of capital to the cooperative include stock subscriptions, membership fees, member loans, voluntary contributions and mandatory assessments. The ownership interest which a member acquires in exchange for these contributions may take a variety of forms. The most common forms of membership interest acquired are non-cash or deferred patronage refunds and unallocated capital reserves or surplus. Non-cash or deferred patronage refunds are evidenced by certificates such as shares of stock, revolving fund certificates, book credits (called allocated capital reserves or retains) or other certificates of equity.

Although most cooperatives generate capital by using many of the standard methods which are available to other businesses, the financial needs of cooperatives are also largely met through methods that are unique to cooperatives. In many cooperatives, the most practical way to accumulate capital is through capital retains. As was noted earlier, the "net proceeds"

468

or "net margin" of the cooperative is the remainder which is left after the cooperative deducts its expenses from the proceeds of the sale of members' products. When the cooperative calculates its "net proceeds" or "net margin" at the end of the year, it may return a portion of the amount it would otherwise have distributed as patronage dividends.

In some marketing cooperatives, equity certificates may be issued to validate per-unit capital retains in addition to, or instead of, retained net savings. Per-unit retains are the amounts that are deemed to be invested in the cooperative. These amounts are deducted from the actual sale of the patron's products, on a per bushel or per hundredweight basis.

Member contributions which involve retained patronage refunds are the amounts due to all customers of the cooperative association, regardless of stock ownership. They represent a proportional amount of the net proceeds based on the amount of business transacted by the member with or through the cooperative. On the other hand, equity credits or patronage credits represent the patronage dividends which are allocated by the cooperative to its patrons. However, these dividends are not paid out in cash or other medium of payment, but rather are retained by the cooperative to increase its capital. Therefore, these retained equity credits reflect the ownership interest of the patrons in the capital of the cooperative. The equity credits will actually be paid out to members at some future date. In most cases, the equity credits will be retained without a scheduled time for redemption. From the cooperative's standpoint, fixed equity obligations with a fixed repayment date are avoided because they offer the least flexibility. Capital retains without a fixed repayment date provide desired flexibility since redemption plans may be structured to meet the specific financial needs of the cooperative.

Unallocated assets are generally accrued as the result of investments made by the cooperative, business done with non-members, and value derived from the general appreciation of cooperative assets. Cooperatives generally have considerable latitude in determining how these assets will be divided among the membership. Typically, these investments may be placed in a revolving capital fund. When the cooperative has generated adequate capital, the fund will be revolved and the oldest investments will be redeemed to the members.

B. Members' Rights in Equity Credits

In cases which involve the rights of cooperative members to receive the equity credit payment, courts have suggested that these rights are governed either by statute, by the articles of incorporation or bylaws of the association, or by the contracts or agreements between the association and its members. A considerable amount of discretion is given to the cooperative as to when the retains will be refunded.[14]

Most states have not adopted specific statutory provisions to establish the time and manner in which equity credits must be redeemed. State laws do not generally require redemption even upon the member's death, retirement or upon the termination of his or her business. Instead, most states have allowed the individual associations to set up their own guidelines and procedures in their corporate bylaws. For example in Claassen v. Farmers Grain Cooperative,[15] the Kansas court took the position that although it could review the board of directors' determination not to pay patronage credits, it did not have the authority to become involved in the financial structure of the association for the purpose of determining whether the directors had acted reasonably under the circumstances. A similar view was expressed in Driscoll v. East-West Dairymen's Ass'n.,[16] where the court said:

> . . . The legislature, in adopting the provisions setting up a voluntary non-profit organization, would not ordinarily cast the mandatory provisions in permissive form. If it had been the legislative intent to set up a rule of conduct for all such associations and to prescribe and limit the rights and liabilities accruing through membership therein, it would have done so without the unnecessary mechanics of separate by laws for each organization to be thereafter formed.[17]

Where the articles of incorporation or bylaws contain provisions relating to the redemption of credits, these provisions govern.[18] In the absence of express provisions in the organizational or governing documents of the cooperative or in contracts between the association and the members, courts generally treat the matter as one of directors' discretion. For example, in a North Dakota case, <u>Evenenko v. Farmers Union Elevator</u>,[19] the court addressed bylaws which provided that, in the event of the death of a member, the board of directors could exercise discretion to terminate his membership, determine the value of his shares of the common stock, and pay his heirs or legal representative the value of the stock. This amount would be paid in addition to any patronage or other dividends accrued and unpaid, less any indebtedness due from the member to the association. In <u>Evenenko</u>, the court held that the right of a member's representative to collect accrued patronage credits in the name of the deceased member was subject to the discretionary power of the cooperative directors to withhold payment for the purpose of maintaining the financial stability of the cooperative. The court suggested that unpaid patronage credits to the account of a member are not the type of cooperative debt that can be collected by a patron or his representative upon demand. Rather, the patronage credits constitute a contingent interest which is not immediately payable. This interest becomes vested only when the board of directors, in the exercise of its sound discretion, determines that such cash payment could be made without imposing undue financial hardship on the cooperative. The court also stated that the board of directors would have the authority, if the financial condition of the cooperative warranted such action, to declare a deceased's patronage credits due as of the date of the member's death. However, it held that the board could not be compelled to jeopardize the financial status of the cooperative by being forced to make such payment, as a matter of law, on the death of any member. This rule applies in the absence of a showing of abuse of discretion by the board of directors.

On occasion, stockholders have sought to characterize their relationship to the cooperative as one of debtor and creditor. This has been done in an effort to compel the redemption of equity credits. These efforts have generally not been successful. For example, in <u>Placerville Fruit Growers Assoc. v. Irving</u>,[20] the California Appellate Court held that the relationship between a cooperative and its members was far different from the conventional relationship of debtor and creditor. The court made this statement with respect to the sale proceeds of the members' produce which had been retained by the association in a revolving fund account and for which revolving fund credits had been issued to the members. The court reached this holding notwithstanding a provision in the cooperative's bylaws which stated that the revolving fund credits should be deemed to evidence an indebtedness of the association to the respective persons to whom they were credited. The court reasoned that, although the credits might be taken to evidence an obligation similar to a debt, the property interest of the members whose funds had been retained by the cooperative was "remarkably analogous" to the property interest of shareholders in an ordinary corporation. The court noted that the operation of the fund was virtually the same as that which governs the declaration and payment by a corporation of dividends to its stockholders. This includes the determination of the time when withdrawals from those funds would be made, as well as the conditions under which withdrawals should be made. The court concluded that other than a right to expect, and under extreme conditions to enforce, the payment of surplus in recoupment of the amount's retained, the members had no control over a decision to use surplus funds for the payment of the revolving fund credits.

The power of the cooperative directors is not entirely without limitation. The court in <u>Claassen v. Farmers Grain Coop.</u>[21] suggested that there are circumstances under which a court may review the directors' determination not to repay patronage credits. Furthermore, stockholders of a cooperative association are always entitled to insist that the directors comply with charter provisions and bylaws which address the payment of dividends and the retirement of outstanding stock.[22]

Finally, stockholders may recover damages against directors under certain circumstances. These include circumstances where the directors have adopted a method of distributing the profits of the cooperative in a manner which has not specifically been authorized by the bylaws, or which has resulted in the payment of large patronage bonuses to the directors or other members. This also includes circumstances where preferred stockholders have rights which have been violated by the failure of the directors to declare dividends on the stock or by their failure to establish a revolving fund for the retirement of the stock as required by the bylaws.[23]

Membership interests may also be affected by whether the cooperative is insolvent. In the event of a dissolution, liquidation, or bankruptcy of the cooperative, courts have generally held that the members of the association are entitled to receive their pro rata share of the funds or assets which remain after the association's debts, losses, and expenses have been paid.[24] There is authority to suggest that members are entitled to their pro rata shares of the per-unit retains (from the proceeds of the sale of the particular member's products) after deductions for operating expenses have been made by the association prior to the distribution of the association's assets among its other obligees.[25] On the other hand, it was held in Clark v. Pargeter,[26] that the cooperative should not be permitted to deal with its shareholders in a manner that provides those shareholders preferential rights to the assets of the cooperative to the detriment of the general creditors.

IV.   Liability of Cooperative Directors to Shareholders and Others

The cooperative directors are responsible for managing the affairs of the cooperative, supervising the operation, and developing the operating policies. The directors may be held liable for the consequences of their actions in these areas.

Under the common law, directors may be sued for violations of specific recognized duties. First, directors are deemed to owe a fiduciary duty to both the cooperative and to its members. This duty requires that the directors exercise undivided loyalty to the cooperative. The directors may not engage in matters in which the director's personal interests conflict with the interests of the cooperative. This fiduciary duty also requires that the director refrain from taking personal advantage of opportunities which rightfully belong to the association. Similarly, the directors must act in an honest and good faith manner toward the cooperative and its members. The directors must also exercise due care to carry out their responsibilities with the degree of skill, diligence and care that are required by the circumstances and by the custom and usage in the business in which the cooperative is engaged. Finally, the directors are obligated to faithfully carry out the provisions of the association's charter or bylaws and any statutes or contracts to which the association is subject.[27]

Second, directors may be held liable under negligence theory for acts or omissions which cause injury to the association or to third parties. This applies where there is a duty of conduct imposed on the director and the harm or damage is caused by the director's breach of that duty. If negligence cannot be proven the director may also be held liable if he or she has intentionally caused harm, either to the association or to third parties.[28]

Directors may also be held criminally liable when their actions or omissions violate a statute or regulation. A number of specific acts which may affect a director's conduct are proscribed by statute. For example, the activities of the director may violate federal or state securities regulations, environmental regulations, health and safety regulations, marketing restrictions, or similar legislation.[29]

In many cases, a shareholder's complaint against the directors will relate to the distribution or payment of dividends. In this situation, liability will generally depend upon whether the directors have complied with pertinent provisions in the association bylaws which give directors discretion in internal financial matters. Although not common, directors have been held liable for abuse of discretion.[30] In general, however, where directors have acted in good faith, it is difficult to assess liability against them for errors in judgment.

Where an action is brought against the directors, the directors often will be indemnified for liability and reimbursed for some of the expenses incurred in defending the lawsuit. Indemnification is regulated by statute. These statutes typically condition indemnification upon whether the director, employee or agent acted in good faith and in a manner which he or she reasonably believed to be in the best interest of the cooperative. This also applies if the director's conduct was alleged to be criminal, whether or not he or she had reasonable cause to believe that the conduct was unlawful. Indemnification will generally not be paid when the director is found to be liable for negligent or willful misconduct.[31]

V.	Antitrust Exemptions For Cooperatives

A.	Antitrust Regulation

To promote competition among businesses, several federal statutes attempt to eliminate devices or practices which either create monopolies, restrain trade or commerce, restrict competition or obstruct the course of trade. The primary federal statute in this field of regulation is the Sherman Antitrust Act.[32]	Section 1 of the Sherman Antitrust Act provides:

> Every contract, combination in the form of trust or otherwise, or conspiracy, in restraint of trade or commerce among the several States, or with foreign nations, is hereby declared to be illegal. Every person who shall make any contract or engage in any combination or conspiracy hereby declared illegal shall be deemed guilty of a felony, and, on conviction thereof, shall be punished by fine not exceeding one million dollars if a corporation, or, if any other person, one hundred thousand dollars, or by imprisonment not exceeding three years, or by both said punishments, in the discretion of the court.[33]

Furthermore, section 2 of the Sherman Act states:

> Every person who shall monopolize, or attempt to monopolize, or combine or conspire with any other person or persons, to monopolize any part of the trade or commerce among the several states, or with foreign nations, shall be deemed guilty of a felony, and, on conviction thereof, shall be punished by fine not exceeding one million dollars if a corporation, or, if any other person, one hundred thousand dollars, or by imprisonment not exceeding three years, or by both said punishments, in the discretion of the court.[34]

Generally speaking, Section 1 deals with controlling the "means" which tend to create monopolies and Section 2 deals with the "ends" or the actual monopolistic results. Section 1 forbids all means of monopolistic trade. This includes all contracts and combinations which have the effect of restraining trade. Section 2 condemns the result which is achieved, rather

475

than the form of the combination or means used to achieve the result. The provisions of Sections 1 and 2 provide comprehensive coverage which reaches most conceivable acts which come within the spirit or purpose of the Sherman Act, regardless of the form in which the conduct is attempted.

In enforcing these and other restrictions, the government may impose criminal sanctions, enjoin offensive conduct and secure damages for injuries to businesses or property. Private individuals who are harmed by the prohibited activities have a private right of action under the Sherman Act. They may be awarded treble damages for violations of the Act. In addition, a prevailing plaintiff is entitled to recover costs, including reasonable attorney's fees.[35]

B. Antitrust Exemptions

A cooperative, by its very terms, can be construed under the Sherman Antitrust Act as a combination or conspiracy in restraint of trade. However, Congress has provided exceptions to the Sherman Act for agricultural cooperatives. These major exceptions are found in the Clayton Act.[36] The Clayton Act, in part, provides that antitrust laws are not to be construed to forbid the existence and operation of agricultural or horticultural organizations which are instituted for the purposes of mutual help. This exception is limited to cooperatives which do not have capital stock and are not conducted for profit. The Clayton Act provides that those organizations or their members may not be held to be illegal combinations or conspiracies in restraint of trade. Without this provision farmers could not legally form cooperative associations.

Subsequently, the Capper-Volstead Act[37] was enacted to clarify the Clayton Act exemption for agricultural organizations and to extend the exemption to cooperatives which have capital stock. In addition, the Cooperative Marketing Act[38] authorizes agricultural producers and associations to acquire and exchange pricing, production and marketing data.

The Robinson-Patman Act[39] authorizes agricultural cooperatives to make internal payments of net earnings on surplus to their members. Finally, the Agricultural Adjustment Act, as re-enacted and amended by the Agricultural Marketing Agreement Act,[40] exempts from monopoly status certain

476

agreements between the Secretary of Agriculture and parties who are involved in the handling of agricultural products.

It should be noted that agricultural cooperatives are not per se excluded from the scope of the antitrust laws. Rather, they must qualify for immunity from antitrust liability by organizing and conducting business in a manner which will place them within the realm of the various statutory exemptions.

C. Qualification for Antitrust Exemptions

Under the Capper-Volstead Act, a cooperative qualifies for the antitrust exemption if it is comprised of:

> Persons engaged in the production of agricultural products as farmers, planters, ranchmen, dairymen, nut or fruit growers may act together in associations, corporate or otherwise, with or without capital stock, in collectively processing, preparing for market, handling, and marketing in interstate and foreign commerce, such products of persons so engaged. Such associations may have marketing agencies in common; and such associations and their members may make the necessary contracts and agreements to effect such purposes: provided, however, That such associations are operated for the mutual benefit of the members thereof, as such producers, and conform to one or both of the following requirements:
>
> First, that no member of the association is allowed more than one vote because of the amount of stock or membership capital he may own therein; or,
>
> Second, that the association does not pay dividends on stock or membership capital in excess of 8 per cent per annum. And in any case to the following;
>
> Third, that the association shall not deal in the products of nonmembers to an amount greater in value than such as are handled by it for members.[41]

The justification for this exemption is that the business in which agricultural producers are engaged is different in nature from other businesses. Agricultural producers are perceived to be in a more precarious economic position due to forces beyond their control, such as the weather. The United States Supreme Court noted this difference between agricultural and other businesses in Tigner v. Texas,[42] where it stated:

> These large sections of the population--those who labored with their hands and those who worked the soil--were as a matter of economic fact in a different relation to the community from that occupied by industrial combinations. Farmers were widely scattered and inured to habits of individualism; their economic fate was in large measure dependent upon contingencies beyond their control. In these circumstances legislators may well have thought combinations of farmers . . . presented no threat to the community, or, at least the threat was of a different order from that arising through combinations of industrialists and middlemen.[43]

1. Activities Prohibited

As a result of these exemptions, agricultural cooperatives may engage in some activities which would otherwise constitute price fixing. Similarly, they may merge with other cooperatives and form monopolies. However, while the cooperative exemptions from antitrust provisions are liberally construed, cooperatives are not entirely free of antitrust regulations. In United States v. Borden Company,[44] the first major case interpreting cooperative immunity, the Supreme Court held that a Capper-Volstead cooperative loses its antitrust immunity when it combines, conspires or merges with a non-cooperative entity. The Borden case involved a conspiracy between dairymen, labor officials, municipal officers, local distributors and others to maintain the price of milk at artificially high prices. While the court recognized that the Capper-Volstead Act had authorized farmers to jointly market their products, it held that Capper-Volstead did not authorize farmers to combine or conspire with non-farmers in restraint of trade.

In United States v. Maryland Cooperative Milk Producers, Inc.,[45] a Federal district court also held that cooperatives could not conspire with non-cooperatives.

However, this holding limited the application of Borden by stating that cooperatives could conspire with other cooperatives. In the Maryland Cooperative case two defendants were charged with unlawfully conspiring to fix prices for milk sold to distributors. The government argued that Borden should be extended to prohibit a cooperative from conspiring with any person, including another cooperative. The court rejected this argument, holding that the fact that there was more than one cooperative involved in the conspiracy was irrelevant.

In Maryland and Virginia Milk Producers Association, Inc. v. United States,[46] the United States Supreme Court reaffirmed Borden and expanded that opinion further by holding that a cooperative is not completely immune from monopoly liability, if the cooperative either conspires with non-cooperatives or engages in predatory practices. The court drew an analogy to the fact that a cooperative is not immune from liability under Section 1 of the Sherman Act. In the Maryland and Virginia case, the Justice Department brought an action against an agricultural marketing association of 2,000 dairy farmers which accounted for 86% of the milk sold in the Washington D.C. area. The association acquired the assets of Embassy Dairy, which was the association's chief competitor. As part of the acquisition agreement, the association required Embassy owners to execute a covenant not to compete in the market area for ten years. It is also required Embassy to attempt to persuade its dairy suppliers to affiliate with the association. The court determined that neither the acquisition nor the contract were exempt from the Sherman and Clayton Acts. This was because the arrangement involved a non-agricultural party which was not entitled to the exemptions. The court also found the association guilty of combining or conspiring with others to eliminate competition, in violation of Section 3 of the Sherman Act. The acquisition was enjoined since it was determined that it would lessen competition and would tend to create a monopoly in violation of Section 7 of the Clayton Act.

The scope of prohibited predatory practices has been enlarged by federal decisions to include boycotts and concerted refusals to deal,[47] unilateral refusals to sell,[48] and practices such as interference with supply contracts between processors and non-affiliated producers, restrictive tying contracts,[49] price manipulation devices designed to eliminate competition,[50] predatory exercises of monopoly power,[51] unreasonably restrictive membership and marketing agreements,[52] and discriminatory pricing.[53]

2. Prohibited Structures

In Case-Swayne Co., Inc. v. Sunkist Growers, Inc.,[54] the United States Supreme Court held that whenever a cooperative includes "non-producer" members, the cooperative loses all of its immunity under Section 6 of the Clayton Act and the Capper-Volstead Act. In Case-Swayne, the court found that Sunkist included 12,000 growers of citrus fruit in Arizona and California and that it was divided into local associations which separately operated packing sheds to prepare the fruit for market. About fifteen percent of the local associations were private corporations and partnerships which owned and operated the packing houses for profit. The relationship between these private for-profit associations and the growers was governed by a contract other than a cooperative agreement. This made it possible for certain members to assert control over the association even though they were not producers. The court found a Sherman Act violation, holding that the legislation which granted antitrust immunity was intended only to benefit farmers in their capacity as producers. Therefore, if no production was generated by the members, antitrust protection could not be granted. As a result, the entire Sunkist organization lost its antitrust immunity because of the non-producers who were involved in its operation. This holding was extended by the Supreme Court in National Broiler Marketing Assn. v. United States,[55]. National Broiler held that in a vertically integrated industry, all members must either own the farm, lease the production facilities, or participate in the production activities with the farmer as a joint venture to fully qualify as a member.

In Treasure Valley Potato Bargaining Association v. Ore-Ida Foods, Inc.,[56] the plaintiff potato grower bargaining associations sued two potato processors under the Sherman Act for alleged price-fixing in connection with pre-season contracts and other alleged practices in restraint of trade. The defendants counterclaimed, charging that the bargaining association had combined and conspired in restraint of trade by meeting prior to the negotiations and agreeing to seek similar prices and terms in their contracts with the defendant. In Treasure Valley, the Ninth Circuit Court of Appeals employed a liberal construction of the "marketing agency" exemption of the Sherman Act. It held that the statute did not contain a requirement that the marketing agencies must also engage in the sale of potatoes to qualify for the antitrust exemption. In interpreting the word "marketing," the court used the common definition and held that "marketing" is, "[t]he aggregate of functions involved in transferring title and in moving goods from producer to consumer, including among others buying, selling, storing, transporting, standardizing, financing, risk bearing, and supplying market information." In applying this definition no antitrust violation was found.

More recently, in Fairdale Farms, Inc. v. Yankee Milk, Inc.,[57] the Second Circuit Court of Appeals declared that the Capper-Volstead Act gave associations of cooperatives the right to fix prices, and that a cooperative association organized for the sole purpose of forming a monopoly to fix prices was entitled to Capper-Volstead protection.

FOOTNOTES

1. See generally, R. Hofstadter, The Age of Reform, 112-13 (1955), at 112-113.

2. Frost v. Corporation Commission, 278 U.S. 515 at 564, dissenting opinion, (1929).

3. See generally, Hulbert & Neely, Legal Phases of Farmer Cooperatives, FCS Information 100, Farmer Cooperative Service, USDA (1976) and Juergensmeyer & Wadley, Agricultural Law (1982), at 207.

4. Treasure Valley Potato Bargaining Assn. v. Ore-Ida Foods, Inc., 497 F.2d 203 (9th Cir. 1974) cert. den. 419 U.S. 999 (1974); Northern California Supermarkets, Inc. v. Central Cal. Lettuce Producers Cooperative, 413 F. Supp. 984 (N.D. Cal. 1976) aff'd per curium 480 F.2d 369 (9th Cir. 1978) cert. den. 99 S.Ct. 873 (1979).

5. See, Rifle Potato Growers Co-op Assn. v. Smith, 78 Colo. 171, 240 P. 937 (1925).

6. Arkansas Cotton Growers Co-op Assn. v. Brown, 179 Ark. 338, 16 S.W.2d 177 (1929).

7. Rhodes v. Little Falls Dairy Co., Inc., 230 App. Div. 571, 245 N.Y.S. 432 (1930) aff'd 256 N.Y. 559, 177 N.E. 140 (1931).

8. See, e.g., § K.S.A. 17-1616.

9. See, e.g., § K.S.A. 17-1606.

10. The typical statute defines "Person" to include corporations. See, e.g., K.S.A. § 17-1602(b).

11. Some restrictions apply. The estate of a deceased stockholder is not eligible for membership, Hill v. The Partridge Co-operative Equity Exchange 174 Kan. 5, 254 P.2d 278 (1953),

nor may a county Farm Bureau. <u>See</u>, State ex rel Franklin County Farm Bureau, 172 Kan. 179, 239 P.2d 570 (1951).

12. <u>See</u>, <u>e.g.</u>, Picatora v. Gulf Cooperative Co., 68 Misc. Rep. 331, 123 NYS 980 (1910); Burley Tobacco Growers Coop. Assoc. v. Tipton, 227 Kan. 297, 115 W.2d 119 (1928).

13. <u>See</u>, Pacific Stationary & Printing Co. v. Northwest Wholesale Stationers, Inc., 715 F.2d 1393 (9th Cir. (1983)).

14. <u>See</u>, Claassen v. Farmer's Grain Cooperative, 208 Kan. 129, 490 P.2d 376 (1971).

15. 208 Kan. 129, 490 P.2d 376 (1971).

16. 122 P.2d 379 (Cal. App. 1942).

17. 122 P.2d at 381.

18. <u>See</u>, <u>e.g.</u> Loch v. Paola Farmers Union Co-op Cremery & Store Ass'n, 130 Kan. 136, 285 P. 523 (1930) <u>reh.</u> <u>den.</u> 130 Kan. 522, 287 P. 269 (1930).

19. 191 N.W.2d 258 (1971).

20. 135 Cal. App. 2d 731, 287 P.2d 793 (1955).

21. 208 Kan. 129, 490 P.2d 376 (1971).

22. <u>See</u>, <u>e.g.</u>, Driver v. Producers Co-op, Inc., 233 Ark. 334, 345 S.W.2d 16 (1961).

23. <u>See</u> Fee and Hoberg, "Potential Liability of Directors of Agricultural Cooperatives" 37 <u>Ark. L. Rev.</u> 60 (1983).

24. Hulbert and Neely, <u>Legal Phases of Farmer Cooperatives</u> FCS Information 100, Farmer Cooperative Service, USDA (1976) at 108-109.

25. See generally Hulbert and Neely, at 213-219, and cases cited therein.

26. 142 Kan. 781, 52 P.2d 671 (1935).

27. Hoberg and Fee "Potential Liability of Directors of Agricultural Cooperatives" 37 Ark. L. Rev. 61 (1983) at 63-69.

28. 37 Ark. L. Rev. at 69-73.

29. 37 Ark. L. Rev. at 75-80.

30. See, Claassen v. Farmers Grain Coop., 208 Kan. 129, 490 P.2d 376 (1971).

31. See Associated Milk Producers v. Parr, 528 F. Supp. 7 (E.D. Ark. 1979).

32. 15 U.S.C. §§ 1 - 7.

33. 15 U.S.C. § 1.

34. 15 U.S.C. § 2.

35. 15 U.S.C. § 15.

36. 15 U.S.C. § 17.

37. 7 U.S.C. §§ 291m, 292.

38. 7 U.S.C. § 455.

39. 15 U.S.C. § 13(b).

40. 7 U.S.C. § 608b.

41. 7 U.S.C. § 291.

42. 310 U.S. 141, (1940).

43. 310 U.S. at 145.

44. 308 U.S. 188 (1939).

45. 145 F. Supp. 151 (D.DC 1956).

46. 362 U.S. 458 (1960).

47. Case-Swayne Co. v. Sunkist Growers, Inc., 369 F.2d 449, 459 (9th Cir. 1967) rev'd. on other grounds, 389 U.S. 384 (1967).

48. Sunkist Growers, Inc. v. Winkler & Smith Citrus Products Co., 284 F.2d 1 (9th Cir. 1960) rev'd on other grounds, 370 U.S. 1962), reh. den. 390 U.S. 930 (1968).

49. Case-Swayne Co. v. Sunkist Growers, Inc., 369 F.2d 449, (9th Cir. 1967), rev'd on other grounds, 389 U.S. 384 (1967), reh. den. 390 U.S. 930 (1968).

50. Knuth v. Erie-Crawford Dairy Cooperative Ass'n., 395 F.2d 420 (3rd Cir. 1968) cert. den. 410 U.S. 913 (1973).

51. North Texas Producers Ass'n. v. Mezger Dairies, Inc., 348 F.2d 189 (5th Cir. 1965).

52. United States v. Associated Milk Producers, Inc., 5 Trade Reg. Rep. # 45,072 (W.D. Tex. 1972).

53. Bergjans Farm Dairy Co. v. Sanitary Milk Producers, 241 F. Supp. 476 (E.D. Mo. 1965).

54. 389 U.S. 384 (1967), reh. den. 390 U.S. 930 (1968).

55. 436 U.S. 816 (1978).

56. 497 F.2d 203 (9th Cir. 1974) cert. den. 419 U.S. 999 (1974).

57. 635 F.2d 1037 (2nd Cir. 1980), cert. denied 454 U.S. 818 (1981).

CHAPTER 14

AGRICULTURAL EMPLOYERS AND EMPLOYEES

I.   Introduction
        Agriculture has had a long history of exclusion from
statutes which regulate employers and employees. This has
been justified as a policy that was necessary to subsidize farming
or to relieve farmers of the administrative burdens that would
result from the inclusion of agriculture within the scope of
employment regulations. Other arguments against agricultural
labor regulations have raised such matters as the seasonal
nature of farm work, the impracticability of organizing farm
laborers, and the differences between agriculture and other
industrial sectors of the economy. Historically those justifi-
cations have been considered by the courts as sufficient to
uphold the generally exempt status of agriculture from labor
regulations. However, the recent industrialization of agriculture
and the dilution of the political strength of the agricultural
sector has brought with it a gradual extension of labor
legislation to agriculture. As a result, certain farm workers and
employers are now subject to a wide range of regulations at
both the Federal and the State level. These regulations
generally only apply to agricultural operations which meet the
threshold requirements of a minimum number of workers or
minimum payroll amount.

II.   Definition of Agriculture and Agricultural Workers
        Statutory exemptions to the regulation of agricultural
labor are limited to certain persons and situations. An
examination of agricultural exemptions under the National
Labor Relations Act (NLRA),[1] provides insight into the unique
treatment of agriculture. The NLRA provides collective
bargaining rights to employees. When the NLRA was enacted
in 1935, it provided that the term 'employee' does not include
an individual who is employed as an agricultural laborer.
However, the Act did not define "agriculture". Early cases
which interpreted the NLRA incorporated the definitions of

agriculture from other federal acts, including the Social Security Act, the Internal Revenue Code and the Fair Labor Standards Act (FLSA). These various definitions of agriculture are quite broad. In 1946, the Fair Labor Standards Act was amended for the purpose of providing a definition of agriculture for the NLRA. This was somewhat narrow, yet flexible enough to accommodate changes in agriculture. This definition provides that:

> "Agriculture" includes farming in all its branches and among other things includes the cultivation and tillage of the soil, dairying, the production, cultivation, growing, and of any agricultural or horticultural commodities . . . the raising of livestock, bees, furbearing animals, or poultry, and practices (including any forestry or lumbering operations) performed by a farmer or on a farm as an incident to or in conjunction with such farming operations, including preparation for market, deliver to storage or to market or to carriers for transportation to market.[2]

Judicial construction of this definition has resulted in the division of agriculture into two distinct categories.[3] First, agriculture consists of those things which are specifically enumerated in the definition, including activities such as the cultivation of the soil, the raising of livestock, and the growing and harvesting of agricultural commodities. Labor performed within the scope of these pursuits is deemed agricultural per se and is therefore exempt from NLRA coverage. However, there are a large number of tasks that may be performed by a farmer or a farmworker that are indirectly connected with the farming operation. These tasks will be considered to be agricultural if they are the kind of activities that are ordinarily and customarily performed by a farmer or on a farm and if they are part of agricultural production rather than a part of separately organized, independent activities such as preparation of the produce for market, transportation, packaging, etc.

In many cases, the line of demarcation between the first category and the second will not be clear. More importantly, it may be difficult to determine whether the activity at issue is sufficiently a part of the farming operation to cause the worker to be characterized as a farmworker as a threshold matter. There is a tendency in the case law to determine farmworker status on the basis of the specific activity in which the performance is rendered. As a result, it is possible that an employee will be considered a farmworker in some contexts and not in others. This variation may be problematic. In a non-NLRA case, one court observed that "there is no basis for distinguishing the work of a laborer who drives a truck at a factory from a laborer who drives one on the farm, or for any one of numerous other labor activities on the farm, as distinguished from the same activity in industry, wholesaling, retailing or building."[4] In notable contrast, at least one other recent non-NLRA case has suggested that farm labor status should be determined on the basis of the general character of the employee's work rather than by the nature of the specific task at issue. The theory behind this is that the constant shifting of employee status by specific task would make the administration of labor law impracticable. It also might discourage employers from making effective use of employees in order to avoid exposure to liability under a determination of non-farm employee status.[5]

III. Major Federal Labor and Employment Related Statutes Which Affect Agricultural Labor
   A. Fair Labor Standards Act
   The Fair Labor Standards Act (FLSA)[6] was enacted in 1938 to correct and eliminate "labor conditions detrimental to the maintenance of the minimum standard of living necessary for (the) health, efficiency and general well being of workers."[7] The Fair Labor Standards Act is primarily concerned with imposing limitations on minimum wages, maximum hours and child labor.

   1. Minimum Wage Provisions
   Minimum wage provisions of the FLSA require that employers:
   1. Pay at least the statutory minimum wage to each employee, in any work week, who is engaged in commerce or in the production of goods for commerce;[8]
   2. Refrain from wage discrimination between employees on

the basis of sex except where payment is made pursuant to either a seniority system, a merit system, a system in which payment is based on rate of production or on the basis of factors other than sex;[9]

3. Keep certain records on all employees and make reports to the administrator, as required. These records must be kept for a specific period (currently 3 years) and must include specified information on wages, hours worked and other conditions and practices within the employment relationship.[10]

2. Maximum Hours Provisions

The employer must limit the employee's work week to not more than 40 hours per week. An exception from this requirement is allowed if additional compensation is given at a rate of not less than one and one half times the rate at which the employee is paid for the 40 hour week.[11] A 1985 amendment to the Fair Labor Standards Act repealed the provisions which had authorized a 48 hour work week and a 10 hour per day seasonal employment before overtime compensation had to be paid.

3. Child Labor Provisions

The Fair Labor Standards Act prohibits or restricts:
1. oppressive child labor;[12]
2. the employment of minors under sixteen years of age;[13]
3. the employment of minors under sixteen years of age during school hours;[14] and
4. the employment of minors under sixteen years of age in occupations in agriculture that have been declared to be particularly hazardous.[15]

The Fair Labor Standards Act exempts from the child labor provisions any employee who is employed in agriculture under the following circumstances:
1. if the employee is employed by an employer who did not, during any calendar quarter during the preceding calendar year, use more than 500 man-days of agricultural labor;
2. if the employee is the parent, spouse, child, or other member of his employer's immediate family;
3. if the employee (a) is employed as a hand harvest laborer and is paid on a piece rate basis in an operation which has

490

been, and is customarily and generally recognized as having been, paid on a piece rate basis in the region of employment, (b) commutes daily from his permanent residence to the farm on which he is so employed and (c) has been employed in agriculture less than 13 weeks during the preceding calendar year;

4. if the employee (other than an employee described in #3 above):

> (a) is sixteen years of age or under and is employed as a hand harvest laborer, is paid on a piece rate basis in an operation which has been, and is customarily and general recognized as having been, paid on a piece rate basis in the region of employment;
>
> (b) is employed on the same farm as his parent or person standing in the place of his or her parent; and
>
> (c) is paid at the same piece rate as employees over age sixteen are paid on the same farm; or

5. if the employee is principally engaged in the range production of livestock.[16]

The Fair Labor Standards Act also exempts from the child labor provisions certain child laborers, 12 and 13 years of age, who are employed with written parental consent on a farm where the parents or guardians are employed, and who are exempt from the federal minimum wage laws.[17] Finally, upon application to the Department of Labor, restrictions may be waived for children 10 and 11 years of age to work in harvesting short season crops, provided that the employer does not use restricted pesticides and complies with minimum re-entry times for specified chemicals.[18]

B. Migrant and Seasonal Agricultural Worker Protection Act

The Migrant and Seasonal Agricultural Worker Protection Act (MSPA)[19] was enacted in 1983. It substantially amended the Farm Labor Contractor Registration Act to "assure necessary protections for migrant and seasonal workers, agricultural associations, and agricultural employees". The Act regulates parties who recruit, solicit, hire, employ, furnish or transport any person who meets the Act's definition of a "migrant" or "seasonal" worker.

Under the Act, as under the old law, anyone who is engaged in farm labor contracting activity must register under the Act. Moreover, under the expanded scope of the MSPA, no one may hire, employ or use any individual to perform farm labor contracting activities unless that individual has a certificate of registration either as a farm labor contractor or as a farm labor contractor employee.[20]

Several classes of persons are exempt from the registration provisions of the Act. These include:

1. family farm businesses, including processing establishments, packing sheds, nurseries, etc., where the labor is performed only for the particular operation and exclusively by the individual employed (or an immediate family member);
2. small businesses which hire fewer than 500 man days of agricultural labor as provided under the Fair Labor Standards Act;
3. common carriers;
4. certain labor organizations;
5. non-profit charitable organizations;
6. non-profit public or private educational institutions;
7. custom combine, hay, harvesting or sheep shearing operations;
8. anyone who engages in farm labor contracting solely within a 25 mile radius of the contractor's permanent place of residence and for not more than 13 weeks per year;
9. custom poultry harvesting and related businesses; and
10. certain part-time labor contractors who supply student and other laborers whose full time occupations are not agricultural employment. This type of non-regulated labor may be furnished for certain specific kinds of agricultural operations such as stringing or harvesting shade-grown tobacco.[21]

To secure the proper certificate under the MSPA, the applicant must submit an application to the Secretary of Labor which describes the type of activity to be engaged in, the kind of vehicle to be used in transporting the workers, the permanent place or residence of the contractor and a description of the housing to be used. In the case of housing registration, documentation must be furnished to establish that the relevant housing is in compliance with the standards set forth in the Act. Lastly, the applicant must submit a set of fingerprints.[22]

The application may be refused (or a renewal denied or the license revoked or suspended), if the applicant:

1. has knowingly made any misrepresentation in the application for the certificate;

2. is not the real party in interest in the application or certificate of registration, and the real party in interest is a person who has been refused the issuance or renewal of a certificate, or has had a certificate suspended or revoked, or does not qualify for a certificate;

3. has failed to comply with the Act or any regulation under the Act;

4. has failed either:

    a.   to pay any court judgment obtained by the Secretary or any other person under the Act, or any regulation under the Act, or under the Farm Labor Contractor Registration Act of 1963 or any regulation under that Act, or

    b.   to comply with any final order issued by the Secretary as a result of a violation of the Act, or any regulation under the Act, or a violation of the Farm Labor Contractor Registration Act of 1963 or any regulation under that Act; or

5. has been convicted within the preceding five years:

    a.   of any crime under state or Federal law relating to gambling, or to the sale, distribution or possession of alcoholic beverages, in connection with or incident to any farm labor contracting activities; or

    b.   of any felony under state or Federal law involving robbery, bribery, extortion, embezzlement, grand larceny, burglary, arson, violation of narcotics laws, murder, rape, assault with intent to kill, assault which inflicts grievous bodily injury, prostitution, personage, or smuggling or harboring individuals

493

who have entered the United States illegally.[23]

The protected workers under the MSPA are classified as either migrant or seasonal workers.

1. Migrant Worker Protections

The Act requires that migrant workers be provided with housing that meets safety and health standards, and that their wages be paid when due. Furthermore, labor contractors are prohibited from requiring that the migrant worker purchase goods or services solely from the contractor, or from a person affiliated with the contractor. The contractor and employer must keep records regarding the place of employment, wage rates, kinds of activities engaged in, housing and other benefits provided, including any costs associated with the services that are provided to the workers, etc.[24]

Labor contracts must provide basic written information to the workers in English, or in Spanish or another language which is common to the workers who are not fluent or literate in English. This basic written information must include:

1. the basis on which wages are paid;
2. the number of piecework units earned, if payment is on a piecework basis;
3. the number of hours worked;
4. the total pay period earnings;
5. specified sums which are withheld and the purpose for which each sum was withheld; and
6. the net pay.[25]

The Act prohibits acts of intimidation, threats, coercion, blacklisting by the labor contractor or employer, or the discharge of a worker who, with just cause, takes legal or administrative action to protect his or her rights under the Act.[26] Furthermore, any agreement between a worker and the labor contractor or employer which purports to waive the worker's rights under the Act are deemed void as contrary to public policy.[27]

Finally, the contractor must provide safe transportation for workers between work sites and must carry at least the amount of insurance which is required for common carriers of passengers.[28]

2. Seasonal Worker Protections

Most of the rights and protections noted with regard to migrant workers also apply to seasonal workers. Employers of seasonal agricultural workers are required to keep similar records and disclose similar information as is required in regard to migrant workers. In addition, the seasonal workers are given the same protections with regard to their right to receive wage payments when they are due and to not be compelled to purchase goods or services solely from the contractor or an affiliate of the contractor. Since the major difference between the two groups is that seasonal workers are not required to be absent overnight from their permanent place of residence, labor contractors and employers of seasonal workers are not subject to the regulations in regard to housing.[29]

The Act may be enforced by the Secretary of Labor or by any person aggrieved under the Act. A criminal conviction under the Act may result in the imposition of a fine of not more than $10,000 or a prison term of not more than three years or both. The Secretary may also impose administrative sanctions of not more than $1,000 per violation. A private suit for damages may result in an award of actual damages suffered or statutory damages of up to $500 per violation, as well as equitable relief.[30]

The Act is considered to supplement, rather than supersede, any state laws which address the rights of migrant and seasonal workers. It should be noted that a violation of the Migrant and Seasonal Agricultural Workers Protection Act may also result in liability being imposed under the Fair Labor Standards Act and other federal labor laws. In a recent case, the court held that migrants were "employees" for purposes of the Fair Labor Standards Act, noting that the same individual might be exempted from that status for purposes such as liability under the Internal Revenue Code.[31]

C. Immigration Law and its Effect on Agricultural Operations
1. The 1986 Immigration Reform and Control Act-- An Overview

With the 1986 enactment of the Immigration Reform and Control Act (IRCA),[32] Congress recognized the continuing

495

need for foreign workers in certain sectors of agriculture and attempted to balance that need with increased control over illegal immigration into the United States. The Act has caused significant changes in the Federal immigration laws.

The major focus of the new legislation is to impose sanctions on employers who hire illegal aliens, to require that employers verify worker identity and worker authorization to work, and, at the same time, to accelerate legalization for certain classes of undocumented aliens. Special provisions of the law give favorable treatment to agriculture. These provisions include the Special Agricultural Worker (SAW) Amnesty Program, the Replenishment Agricultural Worker (RAWs) Admission Program, the Non-Immigrant (H-2A) Temporary Guestworker Program, and a new search warrant requirement.

2. Employer Sanctions

Under the legislation employers can be subject to civil, and in some cases, criminal penalties for knowingly hiring, recruiting, referring for a fee or continuing to employ unauthorized aliens. Moreover, it is a violation for an employer to knowingly use a contractor to hire an unauthorized alien. That type of violation ordinarily carries a civil penalty consisting of fines. A fine of up to $10,000 can be imposed for each unauthorized alien on the third violation by the employer. However, if the employer engages in a "pattern or practice" of violating the law, criminal sanctions may be imposed. These include fines of up to $3,000 for each unauthorized alien, imprisonment for six months or both.[33]

3. Employment Verification

The law provides that employers must establish the identity and authorization to work of new employees. Concomitantly, new employees must provide the documents which verify their identity and employment authorization.[34] Some documents may be used to establish both identity and authorization to work. These include a U.S. passport, certificate of U.S. citizenship or naturalization, or an unexpired foreign passport with an endorsement which authorizes employment (work permit). A social security card or U.S. birth certification is sufficient to establish the work authorization and a drivers

496

license or state issued identification with a photograph is sufficient for identification only. The employee must attest that he or she is a citizen, a national of the United States, a lawfully admitted alien admitted for permanent residence, or a lawfully admitted alien authorized to work.[35] The employer must complete a form (Form I-9) at the time of hiring and formally attest that he or she has examined the documents to determine that the employee is eligible for employment.[36] The employer is required to retain the verification form and make it available for inspection by officers of the Immigration and Naturalization Service or the Department of Labor. The forms must be retained by the employer for three years from the date of hire or one year from date of termination, whichever is later.[37]

4. Accelerated Legalization

The Act included provisions for permitting aliens who entered the United States illegally before January 1, 1982 and who resided continuously in the country since that time to obtain legal temporary resident status.[38] Provisions were made for the adjustment of the temporary resident status to that of an alien admitted for permanent residence after 19 months from the date of the granting of legal temporary status. To be granted legal temporary resident status the application must have been filed within the twelve month period beginning May 5, 1987 and ending on May 4, 1988.

5. Special Agricultural Workers (SAWs)

One of the provisions of the new law directed the United States Attorney General to defer enforcement of IRCA provisions for an 18-month period commencing June 1, 1987 and ending November 30, 1988. The purpose of this is to allow seasonal agricultural workers the opportunity to receive lawful status.[39] This program was provided to workers who performed seasonal agricultural field work for at least 90 days during the period of May 1, 1985 to May 1, 1986. Proof of eligibility was to be supplied through employment records or other documentation.[40] The status of those individuals was adjusted to that of an alien lawfully admitted for temporary residence,[41] with the provision that it may subsequently be changed to permanent resident status. The change from lawful temporary resident status to permanent residence status is made on one of two possible dates. For some workers ("Group 1") the status may be changed one year after the alien was granted temporary residency status, or on November 1, 1989, whichever is earlier. Group 1 workers are those who performed seasonal agricultural services for at least 90 days during each of the 12 month period ending May 1, 1984, 1985 and 1986. Only 350,000 aliens may qualify under this section.[42]

Permanent resident status may be granted other aliens (those who do not meet Group 1 status or those who were not accepted within the 350,000 limit) two years after the alien was granted temporary residency or on November 1, 1990, whichever is later.[43] Group 2 aliens must have performed seasonal agricultural services for at least 90 days during the period of May 1, 1985 to May 1, 1986.

This special program is available only for workers who perform seasonal agricultural services. According to the Act, this means services which involve "the performance of field work related to planting, cultural practices, cultivating, growing and harvesting of fruits and vegetables of every kind and other perishable commodities as defined in regulations by the Secretary of Agriculture."[44]

6. Replenishment Agricultural Worker (RAWs) Admissions

If the Secretary of Labor and the Secretary of Agriculture determine that there is an inadequate supply of farm laborers in the United States, a new program - the Replenishment of Agricultural Workers Program - may be implemented commencing in fiscal year 1990 (October 1, 1989 to September 30, 1990). This program continues through fiscal year 1993.[45] A formula is designated for use in determining whether a shortage of workers exists. This formula takes into account both the anticipated need for and anticipated supply of SAW workers, and is based on the estimated number of "man days" worked by the average SAW worker in the previous year.[46]

498

$$\text{Shortage} = \frac{\text{Anticipated Need for SAW Workers} - \text{Anticipated Supply of SAW Workers}}{\text{"Man Day" Factor}}$$

The number of RAWs admitted each year is specifically limited by the number of SAWs admitted during the previous fiscal year.[47] However, an emergency procedure exists for increasing the shortage number upon the request of a group or association of employers (and potential employers) of individuals who perform seasonal agricultural services. If "extraordinary, unusual, and unforeseen circumstances have resulted in a significant increase in the shortage number" the Secretaries may increase the RAWs number for the fiscal year.[48]

Applicants under the RAWs admission program are subject to the same restrictions as are aliens who are seeking temporary resident status under the SAW program. Moreover, the same grounds for exclusion apply.[49] They may apply for permanent resident status after three years. However, in order to qualify they must perform 90 man-days of seasonal agricultural services each year during the time they are lawfully admitted for temporary residence.[50]

7. Non-Immigrant (H-2A) Temporary Guestworker Program

The new 1986 Act contains provisions which modify the former H-2 program to allow the admission of non-immigrant temporary agricultural workers into the United States. This program applies to non-immigrant foreign workers who may be admitted to perform temporary labor in the perishable commodities industry.[51] However, these workers are not limited to field work but can also be involved in other jobs which are associated with agriculture.

The crucial tests for determining whether those workers may be admitted into the United States are that:
  (A) there are not sufficient workers who are able, willing, and qualified, and who will be available at the time and place needed, to perform the labor or services involved in the petition; and
  (B) the employment of the alien in the relevant labor

or services will not adversely affect the wages and working conditions of workers in the United States who are similarly employed.[52]

The admission of H-2A workers is based on a determination that these tests have been met. The admission decision also requires a petition by an employer which attests that there is no strike or lockout, that the employer will provide the workers with worker's compensation insurance, that the employer has made "positive recruitment efforts within a multi-state region of traditional or expected labor supply" and that the employer has not violated the terms or conditions of a labor certification with respect to the employment of domestic or nonimmigrant workers within the past two years.[53] The application should be filed approximately 60 days before the first date on which the employer requires the services of an H-2A worker.[54] An association of agricultural producers which use agricultural services may file the application for the admission of H-2A workers.[55]

One new requirement for employers of H-2A workers is that housing must be furnished for the worker. Family housing must also be provided if the "prevailing practice" in the area or occupation is to provide family housing.[56]

8. Search Warrant Requirements

The law contains a new provision with regard to search warrants. Existing law requires either the consent of the proprietor or a properly executed warrant for an officer to obtain entry onto the premises of a farm or other outdoor agricultural operation for the purpose of interrogating a person who is believed to be an alien.[57] The Immigration and Naturalization Service retains the right to "enter private lands" which are located within 25 miles of the border for the purpose of patrolling to prevent illegal entry into the United States.

D. Occupational Safety and Health Act (OSHA)

Farming is considered one of the nation's most dangerous work activities. The Occupational Safety and Health Act (OSHA),[58] was enacted to promote safety in the workplace by requiring that employers eliminate recognized hazards that may adversely affect employees. The Act applies to an employer of one or more workers who is engaged in a business that affects interstate commerce. As a general rule, most agricultural enterprises are considered to affect interstate commerce and will therefore be potentially subject to the provisions of OSHA.

As a matter of administration, farming operations which employ fewer than ten employees during the relevant previous ten month period, are exempted from the Act unless they maintain a migrant labor camp. It should be noted that this exemption is not included in the terms of the Act but rather has been included in the annual funding authorization for OSHA.[59] Employers should check with their area OSHA office to determine whether the exemption is in force in a particular year.

Agricultural employers who are subject to OSHA must:

1. adequately inform employees of safety regulations and display OSHA-prescribed posters where employees will see them;
2. report accidents, within 48 hours, which result in the death of one or more employees or the hospitalization of five or more employees;
3. keep required records of occupational illness and injuries;
4. display in a prominent place the required Log and Summary of Occupational Injuries and Illness during February of each year;
5. comply with the "general duty" clause of OSHA which requires the workplace be free of recognized hazards. Specifically, this means that the employer may be required to perform the following:
   a. adequate supervision of the work site to insure proper or accepted practices in the field of work;
   b. proper supply and maintenance of necessary equipment;
   c. due care in the hiring of co-workers;
   d. use due care in informing himself or herself of hazards inherent in the work and in warning employees of the attendant risks; and
   e. maintain provisions for adequate sanitation, toilet facilities, clothing, or shelter where an

employee is unable to provide these amenities for himself, due to the work involved, and provide safe ingress and egress from the work area;[60]

6. comply with specific safety standards that apply to agriculture, including standards for:
   a. rollover protection structures (ROPS) and seat belts for certain tractors;
   b. guarding against hazards on farm machinery;
   c. preventing exposure to cotton dust in cotton gins;
   d. temporary labor camps;
   e. handling of anhydrous ammonia;
   f. pulpwood logging; and
   g. marking of slow moving vehicles.[61]

The employees themselves are also required to comply with a number of specific responsibilities. These include:

1. to read and understand the OSHA posters posted at their job sites;
2. to follow their employer's safety and health standards and rules;
3. to wear and use the protective equipment provided to them by their employers;
4. to report hazardous conditions to their employers or supervisors;
5. to report any job-related injuries or illnesses to their employers and seek prompt treatment when necessary; and,
6. to cooperate with the OSHA compliance officer when questioned about specific job conditions.[62]

The authority of OSHA to set safety standards has been restricted somewhat by the United States Supreme Court in Industrial Union v. American Petroleum.[63] In Industrial Union, the Supreme Court invalidated benzine regulations on the finding that OSHA did not demonstrate that the standard was reasonably necessary to provide for safety in the workplace. Noting that the intent of OSHA was not to regulate insignificant risks or to make the workplace risk-free, the Court held that there must be a finding by the Secretary that a significant risk of harm is present before safety standards can be promulgated. Therefore, as demonstrated by this opinion, not all health and safety issues in the workplace will be subject to OSHA. For example, OSHA originally had a policy of establishing standards to protect fieldworkers who re-enter the field after the application of pesticides. These standards were held invalid by the Fifth Circuit Court of Appeals in Florida Peach Growers Assoc. v. United States.[64] After this ruling, the Environmental Protection Agency promulgated fieldworker protection standards which were upheld and which are deemed to preempt OSHA from taking further action on this matter.[65]

The Supreme Court case of Whirlpool Corporation v. Marshall,[66] has potential implications for agricultural employees. In Whirlpool, the Court considered the ability of employees to refuse to undertake unsafe tasks. Specifically, two workers had been directed to remove objects from a suspended mesh guard screen. They refused, claiming the screen was unsafe. The foreman ordered them to leave the workplace without pay for the remaining six hours of the shift. A written reprimand was placed in their employment file as a result of the incident. The Secretary of Labor filed suit against the employer, alleging that the acts of the foreman constituted discrimination under provisions of OSHA which prohibit an employer from discharging or discriminating against an employee who exercises any right afforded by the Act. The Secretary had promulgated a regulation which protected the employee's right to refrain from performing his or her assigned task when there was a reasonable apprehension of death or serious injury and no reasonable and less drastic alternative for work performance was available. The Supreme Court reversed the District Court's opinion and held that the regulation was proper. Thus, it appears that an employee may justifiably refuse to perform certain dangerous tasks. The Whirlpool opinion suggests that if the following criteria are met, the refusal of an employee to work, based on safety reasons, is proper:

1. the danger must be ascertainable by objective tests;
2. the directive to perform the task must be urgent or require immediate action;
3. the decision by the employee to refuse work must be in good faith; and
4. the decision must be the decision a reasonable

person would make under the circumstances.

E. Social Security and Retirement

Several Federal laws affect the retirement plans of farmers. These include the Social Security Act of 1935,[67] the Self Employment Contributions Act,[68] and the Federal Insurance Contributions Act.[69]

As initially adopted, the Social Security Act and the Federal Insurance Contributions Act did not apply to agricultural labor. However, at present many farmers and farmworkers are within the coverage of those Acts. Regularly employed farm laborers were brought into the Social Security system in 1951 because they satisfied the statutory requirement of "regular employment". As the system is now structured, many farm employers must make Social Security deductions for employees.

1. Farm Employees

In 1955, the requirement of "regular employment" was dropped. Since then, as a general rule, the payment of wages from employment determines whether an employee is covered. "Wages" are defined as all remuneration for employment, including the cash value of all remuneration paid in a medium other than cash.[70] There are three exceptions, all of which apply to agricultural labor:

1. Remuneration paid in any medium other than cash for agricultural labor is not considered wages;
2. Amounts of cash or remuneration paid by an employer in any calendar year to an employee for agricultural labor which do not exceed $150 per year are also not considered wages; and
3. Remuneration in any amount paid for less than 20 days labor per year where remuneration is calculated on a time (hour, day, week, etc.) basis is not considered wages.[71]

The IRS has interpreted the meaning of the non-cash exception to include as wages those non-cash items that can be readily or immediately converted to cash. For example, if commodity storage receipts were given to employees in lieu of wages, they would be treated as cash. However, under this

504

analysis, items such as lodging, food, clothing, car tokens, transportation passes, farm products or other goods and commodities would not be included in the non-cash exception.[72]

The term "agricultural labor" has been defined in Internal Revenue Code regulations to generally include most work performed on a farm by anyone who is in the employ of any other person.[73] Work is deemed to be agricultural labor if it is performed in connection with the cultivation of soil or the raising or harvesting of any agricultural or horticultural commodity. The definition also includes work performed in connection with the operation, management, conservation, improvement or maintenance of a farm and its tools and equipment. However, this only applies if the work is done in the employ of the owner, tenant, or other operator of the farm and if the major part of the work is done on the farm.[74]

Members of the family are excluded as employees if:
1. the family member is a child under 21 in the employment of his father or mother;
2. the family member is in the employ of that person's spouse; or,
3. a parent is performing domestic service in the employ of a son or daughter in or about the private home of the son or daughter or does work not related to the son or daughter's trade or business.[75]

The family exclusion does not apply when the employer is a corporation or partnership, unless the family relationship exists between the employee and all the partners.[76]

The reporting and compliance requirements of the farmer-employer with respect to returns under FICA are set out in the Regulations.[77] As a general rule, these returns are required to be filed each calendar quarter. As an exception, the returns filed by agricultural employers must be filed on an annual basis.

2. Self-Employed Farmers

Self-employed farmers were included with the system as a result of the Self-Employment Contributions Act in 1954.[78] Persons who may be described as either an "owner-operator", a "tenant-operator", or a "share-farmer not a tenant" are deemed to receive "net earnings from self-employment". Rather than

505

paying FICA withholding, that farmer may be required to pay a self-employment tax.[79] By definition, the term "net earnings from self-employment" means the gross income which is derived by an individual from any trade or business carried on by that individual, less the allowable deductions attributable to that trade or business.[80] Similarly, if the individual is deemed to be an independent contractor, FICA has no application and self-employment rules govern.[81]

It may be difficult to determine whether someone has "net earnings from self employment." This is the case with many landlord-tenant relationships. The self-employment rules presume that all rental income, including income from crop or livestock share leases, is not self-employment income. This presumption may be rebutted as to income from crop or livestock share leases. Specifically, the rental income may be treated as self-employment income if there is "material participation" in the production of farm products or livestock. Where the status of the landowner is at issue, the material participation test may be satisfied in one of four alternative ways:

Test 1. The landowner may do any three of the following:

a. advance, pay or guarantee payment for half of the direct costs of producing the crop or livestock;

b. furnish half of the tools, equipment and livestock used in producing the crop or livestock;

c. advise and consult with the tenant periodically; and/or

d. inspect production activities periodically.

Test 2. The landlord may regularly and frequently make, or take an important part in making, management decisions which substantially contribute to the success of the enterprise;

Test 3. The landlord may work at least 100 hours or more over a period of five weeks or more in activities which are connected with producing the crop; and

Test 4. The landlord may do things which, in total

506

effect, show that the landlord is materially and significantly involved in the production of farm commodities.[82]

Case law suggests that local patterns of landlord interest and participation in crop production may be used to determine whether the landlord meets the material participation test.

It is sometimes difficult to determine whether an individual is a tenant or an employee for purposes of the self-employment tax. The criteria found in the Internal Revenue Code determine the individual to be a tenant if service is performed by an individual under an arrangement with the owner or tenant of land pursuant to which:

1. the individual undertakes to produce agricultural or horticultural commodities (including livestock, bees, poultry, and fur-bearing animals and wildlife) on the land;
2. the agricultural or horticultural commodities produced by the individual, or the proceeds therefrom, are to be divided between that individual and the owner or tenant; and
3. the amount of the individual's share depends on the amount of the agricultural or horticultural commodities produced.[83]

In the case of Sachs v. United States,[84] this ICC section was construed to allow some landlord participation in the farming operation as far as requirement one was concerned without destroying tenant status. In Sachs, the government argued that the individual who raised the crop had to perform or assume the entire responsibility for substantially all of the physical labor required. Therefore, since the farmworker did not actually plant the crop, it was argued that the agreement could not qualify as a share arrangement. The court rejected that position, largely because it found the facts to indicate that the return to the share farmer was directly related to the risk involved and the amount of crop or livestock produced. Therefore, the court held the workers to be share farmers or independent contractors rather than employees.

In the event that a self-employed farmer receives low income from his operations, the law provides that a cash or accrual basis farmer has an option to report as self-employment

507

income:

> (1) sixty-six and two-thirds percent (662/3%) of his or her gross income from farming, if the gross income from farming operations is not more than $2400; or
>
> (2) $1,600 if his or her gross income from farming operations is more than $2400, and his or her actual net earnings from those operations are less than $1600.[85]

This option is intended to benefit low income farmers by permitting them to report more than their actual net earnings from farming operations in order to receive a greater credit toward Social Security benefits. If the farmer qualifies under either of the previously-stated tests and wants to receive Social Security credit by reporting the optional amount, he or she can do so even though there may be an actual net operating loss from the farming operations.

The self-employed farmer receives special consideration by using the optional method of computing self-employment income. The non-farming business counterpart can only elect the optional method if his or her "regular" business activity has produced net earnings from self-employment of $400 or more in at least two of the three immediately preceding taxable years. There is no comparable "look-back" requirement applicable to farmers.[86] Furthermore, the non-farmer can only elect the optional method during any five taxable years during the individual's lifetime. In contrast, the farmer can elect the optional method an unlimited number of times during his or her lifetime.

3. Social Security Benefits

A farmer may become a recipient of benefits or payments under the Social Security system upon the occurrence of one of two events: disability or retirement. A disabled worker or a self-employed person under age 65 must be both fully insured and insured for disability benefits. At least six quarters of coverage are required to attain fully insured status. A worker of any age who has 40 quarters of coverage is fully insured for life. A "quarter of coverage" means a quarter in which an individual has been credited with self-employment income of a minimum amount. The minimum amount is increased each year and the amount of earnings credited for each quarter may be determined by contacting the local Social Security office.[87]

For disability benefits, the claimant:

1. must have been fully insured, using as a base the quarters of coverage necessary for a person age 62, filing a retirement benefit claim that month;
2. must have not less than 20 quarters of coverage during the 40-quarter period ending with the quarter in which the month occurred;
3. must show that he or she is, in fact, disabled. Disability is defined under the Act as an inability to engage in any substantial gainful activity by reason of any medically determinable physical or mental impairment that can be expected to result in death, or which has lasted or can be expected to last for a continuous period of not less than 12 months. If a worker meets the disability eligibility requirements, after a five month waiting period benefits can be paid to the insured and to his or her dependents. However, for a young disabled worker, there is a special maximum limit on the total family benefits.[88]

"Old age" or retirement benefits may begin at age 62 if the worker agrees to take a reduced benefit amount. There is no reduction in benefits if retirement is delayed until age 65. A farmer's spouse, of age 62 or over, and dependent children or grandchildren under age 18, are also entitled to receive retirement benefits through the farmer, provided he or she is a fully insured worker.[89]

To determine whether a farmer is retired, it is necessary to consider whether he or she still renders "substantial services" to the business. This requires that consideration be given to the following factors:

1. the amount of time the individual devotes to all trades and businesses;
2. the nature of the services rendered;
3. the extent and nature of the activity performed before the beneficiary allegedly retired, as compared

509

with that performed after retirement;
4. the presence or absence of an adequately paid manager, partner, or family member who presently manages the business;
5. the type of business establishment involved;
6. the amount of capital invested in the trade or business; and
7. the seasonal nature of the trade or business.[90]

It should be noted that the amount of earnings is not a controlling factor in determining whether a self-employed person performed substantial services in any given month. It is the person's work activity rather than his profit or loss that is critical in determining whether services are substantial. On the other hand, the fact that no work is done in connection with growing crops in certain months does not necessarily mean that the farmer is retired. The rate of incidence of all normal services must be examined. These include the repairing or constructing of fences, equipment, buildings, and machinery, fallow plowing, insecticide spraying, weed control, negotiation of the sale of crops, the buying of new farm equipment, etc.

If the farmer is a landlord, income which he or she receives in cash or crop share produced on their land by a tenant will generally be considered as rental income from real estate. This amount will be excluded from net self-employment earnings unless the farmer meets the "material participation" requirements.[91] If he or she does not meet these requirements, any services performed under the rental arrangement will be disregarded in determining whether substantial services were rendered. On the other hand, if he or she meets the material participation requirements, services rendered under the rental arrangement, including the time spent in managing, inspecting, advising, and consulting, and in performing physical farm work, will be considered time devoted to the business.[92]

IV. Miscellaneous Federal Acts Which Affect Farm Labor
    A. Civil Rights Act of 1964
The Civil Rights Act of 1964[93] prohibits discrimination on the basis of race, color, religion, sex and national origin. Under the provisions of Title II of the Act, employers may not discriminate on the basis of race or color under any

510

circumstances. They may discriminate on the basis of religion, sex or national origin only if it is a bona fide occupational qualification. The burden of proof is on the employer to show that the qualification is essential for the normal operation of the business. The Act applies if the employer hires 15 or more employees in at least 20 calendar weeks of the current or preceding year.

B. Age Discrimination in Employment Act of 1967
The Age Discrimination in Employment Act of 1967[94] prohibits discrimination against individuals aged 40 to 70 in hiring, discharge, wages and terms of employment, as well as employment privileges such as leaves, promotion, etc. This Act applies to employers of 20 or more employees during at least 20 calendar weeks in the current or preceding year.

C. Consumer Credit Protection Act
The Consumer Credit Protection Act,[95] sometimes called the Federal Wage Garnishment Law, limits the amount of an employee's disposable income which may be withheld in one week to satisfy creditors' claims. This limitation amount is the lesser of 25% of wages or the sum of thirty times the current minimum wages. The Act also provides that an employee may not be discharged because his or her earnings have been subject to garnishment.

D. Veterans Re-Employment Rights Act
The Veterans Re-Employment Rights Act[96] provides that any employee who enlists in or is inducted into the Armed Services, who for that reason leaves other than a temporary position, who receives a certificate of satisfactory service, and who applies for re-employment within 90 days of leaving the service, must be restored to the position he or she would otherwise have achieved but for the military service. This includes seniority status and pay if the individual is still qualified for the job. If the individual has become disabled during the military service, another appropriate position must be offered. This Act includes service in the National Guard and Reserves and applies to all employers in private industry.

V.   Major State Labor Statutes Affecting Farm Labor
      A. Unemployment Compensation
      Unemployment compensation is determined by both
Federal and state laws. At the federal level, the Federal
Unemployment Tax Act[97] (FUTA) applies to agricultural
workers if the employer meets a minimum payroll threshold in
any calendar quarter and employs a minimum number of
employees. At the state level, unemployment compensation
statutes implement the federal thresholds.
      For example, under the Kansas Act,[98] employers must:
      1. pay an unemployment compensation tax which
          includes the amount set by both Federal and state
          law. (For the Federal tax, if the rate is .7% on the
          first $7,000 of earnings, the state rate is calculated
          on the first $8,000 of earnings and varies with the
          experience the business has with claims. A new
          business is assigned a rate that is currently set at
          3.75%. An established business with a history of
          whether contributions exceed benefits paid may be
          assigned a rate which varies from .6% to 5.4%. A
          business with a negative account balance (that is,
          benefits exceed contributions) is assigned the 5.45%
          rate and is subject to an additional surcharge); and
      2. submit tax and wage reports.
      The eligibility of an employee depends on whether he or
she meets general eligibility requirements, is subject to specific
disqualifications and whether he or she has the necessary age
credits during the base period. Wage credits are based on the
average wages received during the base period. As a general
rule, to be eligible, the applicant must be unemployed and
available for work. A claimant may be disqualified if it is found
that the individual voluntarily quit his or her job without good
cause which could be attributed to the employer, was discharged
for misconduct connected with his or her work, or has failed to
apply for or accept suitable work.[99]

      B. Workers' Compensation
      Workers' compensation statutes have exempted
agricultural employees from coverage in most states since they
were initially enacted.[100] Over the years, however, the

rationale behind the exclusion has changed. Originally, public policy provided that workers' compensation should exist only to protect employees in inherently dangerous jobs. During that time period, agriculture was not considered to be hazardous, so agricultural workers were excluded.[101] Agriculture is still often excluded from coverage based on the apparent premise that the administrative burden that would be imposed on farm owners and operators would make agricultural worker coverage impossible to achieve.

Most statutes permit employees of excluded employers to opt into the system by purchasing workers' compensation insurance. Furthermore, since the state merely supervises the workers' compensation system to ensure that relevant laws are complied with, it would seem that the "administrative problems" arguments would be irrelevant in that situation when participation is voluntary. If an insurance carrier were willing to provide the coverage and to process agricultural employee claims, and an agricultural employer was willing to pay the requisite premium, there is no discernable rational basis for the state to seek to prevent that relationship from occurring.

The constitutionality of excluding farmers from workers' compensation laws has been litigated in various states, with inconsistent results. For example, the Michigan Supreme Court[102] held that the exclusion of agricultural workers violated the equal protection provisions of the Constitution. However, the New Mexico Supreme Court has reached the opposite conclusion.[103]

Where agriculture has been excluded from workers' compensation coverage, serious problems have arisen in regard to how agricultural employees can be identified and excluded. The typical workers' compensation act does not apply to "agricultural pursuits" or "employments incidental thereto".[104] However, whether an activity is an agricultural pursuit often has been difficult to determine. Although the term "agriculture" generally implies tillage or cultivation of the soil under traditional "family-farming" conditions, determinations may be difficult to make when the operation involves commercial production or processing activities related to agricultural commodities. A determination problem also arises where employees work partially in agricultural and partially in

513

non-agricultural pursuits. Furthermore, some of the agricultural activities at issue may be merely one stage in a commercial cannery or packinghouse operation. In most of these cases, the decisive question has been the nature of the employee's work activities rather than the nature of the employer's business. If the employee's work is agricultural in nature, then that person is considered to be an agricultural worker even though the employer is a factory or chemical company. At the same time, if the employer's business is agricultural in nature but the employee's work is non-agricultural, the agricultural exemption typically has been held not to apply. For example, Kansas courts have observed that where the employer was engaged in a trade or business subject to the Worker's Compensation Act, but also in an agricultural pursuit in which his workers sustained an injury, the injury was not compensable under the Act.[105] In other words, liability is to be determined on the basis of whether the injury results from work of an employee which is covered by the Act and not by whether the employer is engaged in a trade or business which is covered by the Act.

In many cases, if the character of the employee's work is ambiguous, there is a tendency to consider the nature of the employer's business, and to find that the labor is not agricultural unless the employer's business is agricultural as well. The decision is more difficult if the worker deals with an agricultural product which has already been harvested and could be considered "finished". For example, tomatoes being sorted at a packing house adjacent to the employer's farm where the tomatoes were grown could be considered a finished product. In a Florida decision the court held that an employee who was engaged in sorting agricultural commodities was entitled to workers compensation benefits since the actual work performed did not involve the agricultural production process.[106]

An employee who is generally engaged in ordinary farming activities does not leave the exempted class by engaging in activities such as fixing roofs on farm buildings, or repairing complicated farm machinery. This is justified by the common belief that these types of job departures are within the normal routine of running a farm. However, in reality, these departures may be radical enough to expose the employee to risks which are not normally associated with his or her usual employment.

514

Therefore, some courts have looked only at the nature of the work at the time of the injury.[107] Courts disagree as to how shifts in job duties should be handled. The Michigan Supreme Court in Guiterrez v. Glasser Crandell Co.,[108] found no basis for distinguishing the work of a laborer who drives a truck at a factory from a laborer who drives one on the farm. In general, the Court found no legal basis for any one of numerous other labor activities "on the farm" to be distinguished from the same activity which occurs in industry, wholesaling, retailing or building. More specifically, the Court found no basis for singling out for an exclusion piece work which was done "on the farm" but not elsewhere.

Similarly, there is no basis for a special definition of "weekly wage" for farm labor as distinguished from any other type of labor. This court used that argument to include all farm workers within the system. In contrast, the New Mexico Supreme Court in Cueto v. Stahman Farms,[109] determined a basis for excluding farm employees from workers' compensation. It found that if individual employees are continually changing their status under the Workers' Compensation Act the entire system would become unwieldy. As a result, employers might be discouraged from making effective use of their workers for fear of exposing themselves to uninsured claims. The Court held that the exempt status of the employee should be judged from the general character of his work rather than from his or her activity on any particular day. A recent Colorado case took a similar position and found that the delivery of a harvested crop by truck was part of the farming operation and therefore the agricultural exemption applied.[110]

The concept which is the basis of workers' compensation statutes is quite simple. This concept is that an employee is entitled to guaranteed compensation for work-related injuries without regard to fault. The amount of compensation is limited to a fixed schedule of recovery set by statute. In return for this guaranteed compensation, the employee forfeits the right to assert a common law claim against the employer. The cost of the system is born by the employer through insurance premiums.

In a significant sense, it probably makes more sense for the farm employer to opt for inclusion under the statute than to try to defend the exclusion. When the farmer is not covered <u>all</u> of his or her assets may be vulnerable to claims which result from death or injury to farm employees. In contrast, under the workers' compensation system, the remedy is exclusively provided by the statute. Thus, for the cost of the insurance premiums, the farmer may actually be protected from major liability awards.

C. Common Law Theories

When a farm employee is not covered by workers' compensation, a claim for damages which result from death or injury would be brought under common law theories. The Kansas Supreme Court, for example, has taken the position that it is the nondelegable duty of an employer to use ordinary care and prudence in providing his or her employees with a reasonably safe place in which to work, reasonably safe tools and appliances with which to work and reasonably safe and competent fellow employees with which to work. The failure of an employer to meet any of those duties will render the employer liable for damages which proximately result from such failure.[111] As a result, the farmer should inspect the working premises at reasonable intervals. The farmer-employer should pay particular attention to the tools used by workers. The employer will be generally responsible to see that the tools are in reasonable working condition. On the other hand, the farmer is not considered to be an insurer of the employee's safety, and therefore will not be responsible for design defects in the machines or tools themselves, or for latent defects which would not be known without specialized knowledge of the machine. A farm employee cannot recover damages from the farmer unless the farmer, as an employer, has been negligent. The employer must have breached a duty which he or she owed to the employee. The employer is not held liable for an injury to an employee simply because of danger which is inherent in the place of employment, since the employer is not an insurer against injuries which his or her employees may incur in the discharge of their duties.[112] To avoid being found liable for a breach of duty under negligence theory, the farmer should act in a reasonably prudent manner by inspecting all farm machines at regular intervals, and by replacing worn and defective parts when necessary.

When a farmer is sued as a result of work related injuries which are not covered by workers' compensation, the farmer may defend on the ground that no duty was breached through his or her lack of care. In addition, it may be possible to argue that the plaintiff's own negligence exceeded that of the farmer or that the plaintiff assumed the specific risk that caused the injury or harm. In the former situation, liability will be reduced to the extent the plaintiff is found to have been negligent. In the latter situation, the plaintiff may be precluded entirely from recovering for the injuries.

One Kansas court has described the doctrine of assumption of risk as resting upon:

> . . . the expressed or implied agreement of the employee that, knowing the danger to which he is exposed, he agrees to assume all responsibility for the resulting injury. To raise an implied agreement, the risk assumed must be known to the employee, or it must be of such nature as, by the exercise of reasonable observation and caution for his own safety, he should have known it. For it can never be said that one has agreed to assume responsibility for that of which he had no knowledge, or the existence of which he is not chargeable with notice.[113]

The word risk in this connection includes more than a knowledge of conditions. It also includes a knowledge, or an opportunity for knowledge, of the peril of the employee arising from the conditions.

Courts have consistently held that this knowledge may either be actual or implied. Implied knowledge may be found based on the training and farm experience of the employee. In Uhlrig v. Shortt,[114] an injured employee sued the farmer for a breach of his duty to provide a safe place in which to work. The farmer argued that the employee had assumed the risks involved. The plaintiff was working inside a silo keeping the ensilage level as it was blown in from the top. The distributor pipe feeding into the silo became obstructed and caused the ensilage to surround and impair the plaintiff's vision. As the plaintiff tried to reach the door to notify his co-workers of the emergency, he fell and lost an eye. The Uhlrig court cited Ivez

v. City of Ellsworth[115] as authority that there can be no
liability on the part of the employer where the employee's
knowledge of the danger was equal to or surpassed that of the
employer. Using this reasoning, the court in Uhlrig found an
assumption of risk.[116] Although the plaintiff in this case was
exposed to an unusual risk which the ordinarily prudent person
might not be able to comprehend and understand, he was considered to have assumed that risk and responsibility because his
knowledge of the danger was inferred from his years of experience with that type of work.

Other factors may be involved in determining the
farmer's liability and the extent to which the plaintiff has
assumed specific risks. One factor is the awareness of the
employee about adverse weather conditions which may result in
injury. In Conboy v. Crofoot,[117] the plaintiff was subjected
about severe cold which resulted in frostbite and amputation of
three toes. He claimed that his farmer-employer had a duty to
provide a safe work place. The court held that no duty existed.
Obviously, employees may be subjected to weather conditions.
However, when an employee is ordered to do a specified task,
but is free to adjust his or her efforts to the existing weather
and his or her own physical capacities, only the employee would
possibly know when his feet were cold and when the danger
existed. Until that danger becomes known to the employer, the
court held, there was neither a duty nor an opportunity for the
employer to protect the employee. Furthermore, "the laborer
must be presumed to have knowledge equal, if not superior, to
the employer's of the effect of cold upon his or her own body.
In other words, people are presumed to have ordinary common
sense, until the contrary is shown, and the law does not
speculate on degrees of knowledge about the weather."[118] In
this sense, the employee's own common sense is relevant and
the employer cannot be charged for the employee's lack of it.

D. Other State Legislation
State minimum wage, maximum hour and child labor
statutes may affect agricultural labor. However, these statutes,
like other labor legislation, often exclude agricultural workers
from coverage or apply only to certain types of employment.[119]
In addition, some states have laws which deal with collective

bargaining between employers and employees. In sum, it should be noted that agricultural employment disputes may be treated in special ways and that the general law of employment relations may not apply.[120]

FOOTNOTES

1. 29 U.S.C. §§ 151-169.

2. 29 U.S.C. § 203(f).

3. <u>See</u> Farmers Reservoir and Irrigation Co. v. McComb, 337 S. 755 (1949).

4. Guiterrez v. Glaser Crandall Co., 388 Mich. 654, 202 N.W.2d 786 (1972) at 791.

5. Cueto v. Stahman Farms, 608 P.2d 537 (N.M. 1980).

6. 29 U.S.C. § 201-219.

7. 29 U.S.C. § 202(a).

8. 29 U.S.C. § 206(a)(b).

9. 29 U.S.C. § 206(d).

10. 29 U.S.C. § 211(c).

11. 29 U.S.C. § 207(a).

12. 29 U.S.C. § 212.

13. 29 U.S.C. § 213(c).

14. 29 U.S.C. § 213(c).

15. 29 U.S.C. § 213(c).

16. 29 U.S.C. § 213(a)(6).

17. 29 U.S.C. § 213 (c)(1).

18. 29 U.S.C. § 213(c)(4).

19. Pub. L. 97-470, 96 Stat. 2583 (Jan. 14, 1983); 29 U.S.C. § 1801, et seq.

20. 29 U.S.C. § 1811.

21. 29 U.S.C. § 1803.

22. 29 U.S.C. § 1812.

23. 29 U.S.C. § 1813.

24. 29 U.S.C. § 1821(a).

25. 29 U.S.C. § 1821(d), (e).

26. 29 U.S.C. § 1855.

27. 29 U.S.C. § 1856.

28. 29 U.S.C. § 1841.

29. 29 U.S.C. § 1831, 1832.

30. 29 U.S.C. § 1851, 1853, 1854.

31. Donovan J. Gillmor, 535 F. Supp. 154 (N.D. Ohio 1982).

32. Pub. L. 99-603, 100 Stat. 3359 (Nov. 6, 1986).

33. IRCA § 101, 8 U.S.C. § 1324a.

34. IRCA § 101, 8 U.S.C. § 1324a(b).

35. IRCA § 101, 8 U.S.C. § 1324a(b)(1), (2).

36. IRCA § 101, 8 U.S.C. § 1324a(b)(1).

37. IRCA § 101, 8 U.S.C. § 1324a(b)(3).

38. IRCA § 201, 8 U.S.C. § 1255a(a).

39. IRCA § 302, 8 U.S.C. § 1160.

40. IRCA § 302, 8 U.S.C. § 1160(b)(3).

41. IRCA § 302, 8 U.S.C. § 1160(a)(1).

42. IRCA § 302, 8 U.S.C. § 1160(a)(2)(A).

43. IRCA § 302, 8 U.S.C. § 1160(a)(2)(B).

44. IRCA § 302, 8 U.S.C. § 1160(h).

45. IRCA § 303, 8 U.S.C. § 1161.

46. IRCA § 303, 8 U.S.C. § 1161(a)(4), (5) and (6).

47. IRCA § 303, 8 U.S.C. § 1161(b).

48. IRCA § 303, 8 U.S.C. § 1161(a)(7).

49. IRCA § 303, 8 U.S.C. § 1161(e).

50. IRCA § 303, 8 U.S.C. § 1161(d).

51. IRCA § 301, 8 U.S.C. § 1186(a).

52. IRCA § 301, 8 U.S.C. § 1186(a)(1).

53. IRCA § 301, 8 U.S.C. § 1186(b).

54. IRCA § 301, 8 U.S.C. § 1186(c).

55. IRCA § 301, 8 U.S.C. § 1186(d).

56. IRCA § 301, 8 U.S.C. § 1186(c)(4).

57. IRCA § 116, 8 U.S.C. § 1357(d).

58. 29 U.S.C. §§ 651 et seq.

59. Harl, 3 <u>Agricultural Law</u> Ch. 18, 18-6.

60. 29 U.S.C. § 654; 29 C.F.R. § 1904.

61. 29 C.F.R. § 1910 <u>et seq.</u> The specific safety standards that apply to agriculture are found at 29 C.F.R. §§ 1928.51-53 (rollover protection structures); § 1928.57 (hazard guards); §§ 1928.110 (field sanitation); § 1910.1043 (cotton dust exposure); § 1910.142 (temporary labor camps); § 1910.111 (anhydrous ammonia); 1910.26 (pulpwood logging); § 1910.145 (slow moving vehicles).

62. <u>See,</u> <u>A Safe and Healthful Workplace</u>, U.S. Dept. of Labor, Occupational Safety and Health Administration, OSHA 2263 (1976).

63. 448 U.S. 607 (1980).

64. 489 F.2d 120 (5th Cir. 1974).

65. Organized Migrants in Community Action, Inc. v. Brennan, 520 F.2d 1161 (D.C. Cir. 1975).

66. 445 U.S. 1 (1980).

67. 42 U.S.C. §§ 401 <u>et seq.</u>

68. 26 U.S.C. § 1401-1403.

69. 26 U.S.C. § 3101.

70. 26 U.S.C. § 3121(a)(8)(A).

71. 26 U.S.C. § 3121(a)(8)(B).

72. IRS Revenue Rul. 79-207, 1979-2 CB 351.

73. 26 U.S.C. § 3121(g).

74. Treas. Regs. § 31.3121(g)-1.

75. 26 U.S.C. § 3121(b).

76. See O'Byrne and Davenport, <u>Farm Income Tax Manual</u> § 1102 (1988) at 1007-1008.

77. Treas. Regs. § 31.6011.

78. 26 U.S.C. § 1403.

79. 26 U.S.C. § 1401-1403.

80. 26 U.S.C. § 1402; Treas. Regs. 1.1402(c)-1.

81. Rev. Proc. 85-18, 1985-1 CB 518.

82. IRS, <u>Farmers Tax Guide</u> (1988) at ___ ; Also see O'Byrne and Davenport, <u>Farm Income Tax Manual</u> § 1109 (1988).

83. 26 U.S.C. § 3102(b)(16).

84. 422 F. Supp. 1092 (N.D. Ohio 1976).

85. 26 U.S.C. § 1402(a).

86. 26 U.S.C. § 1402(a).

87. 42 U.S.C. § 402; O'Byrne and Davenport, <u>Farm Income Tax Manual</u> § 1119-20 (1988).

88. 42 U.S.C. § 402; O'Byrne and Davenport, § 1123.

89. 42 U.S.C. § 402; O'Byrne and Davenport § 1121.

90. 42 U.S.C. § 403; Treas. Regs. § 404.447(a); O'Byrne and Davenport § 1125.

91. See, 26 U.S.C. § 1402(a).

92. O'Byrne and Davenport § 1125.

93. 78 Stat 241, codified in scattered sections of U.S. Code.

94. 81 Stat 602, codified in scattered sections.

95. 11 U.S.C. § 523.

96. 38 U.S.C. § 2021.

97. 68 Stat. 454, codified in scattered sections.

98. K.S.A. § 44-701 et seq.

99. K.S.A. § 44-706.

100. See e.g., K.S.A. § 44-501 et seq.

101. See, e.g., Peters v. Cavanah, 132 Kan. 244, 295 P. 693 (1931).

102. Guiterrez v. Glaser Crandall Co., 202 N.W.2d 786 (Mich.1972).

103. Cueto v. Stahman Farms, Inc., 608 P.2d 535 (N. M. 1980).

104. See, e.g., K.S.A. § 44-505(a)(1).

105. See, Taylor v. Taylor, 156 Kan. 763, 137 P.2d 147 (1943); Campos v. Garden City Co., 166 Kan. 352, 201 P.2d 1017 (1949).

106. Dobbins v. S.A.F. Farms, Inc., 137 So. 2d 838 (Fla. 1962).

107. See, e.g., Campos v. Garden City Co., 166 Kan. 352, 201 P.2d 1017 (1949).

108. 202 N.W.2d 786 (Mich. 1972).

109. 608 P.2d 535 (N. Mex. 1980).

110. State Compensation Insurance Fund v. Indus. Commission, 713 P.2d 405 (Col. App. 1985).

111. <u>See</u>, <u>e.g.</u>, Ruggles v. Smith, 175 Kan. 76, 259 P.2d 199 (1953).

112. Uhlrig v. Shortt, 194 Kan. 71, 397 P.2d 321 (1964).

113. Blackmore v. Auer, 187 Kan. 434, 357 P.2d 765 (1960) at 773 quoting from Railway Co. v. Bancord, 66 Kan. 81, 71 P. 253 (1903) at 255.

114. 397 P.2d 321 (Kan. 1964).

115. 53 Kan. 751, 37 P 115 (1910).

116. 397 P.2d 321 (Kan. 1964).

117. 397 P.2d 326 (Kan. 1964).

118. 397 P.2d at 330, quoting Yazoo City Transp. Co. v. Smith, 78 Miss. 140, 28 So. 807 (1900) at 807.

119. <u>See</u>, <u>e.g.</u>, K.S.A. § 44-1201 <u>et seq</u>. (minimum wage and maximum hour) and K.S.A. § 38-601 (child labor).

120. <u>See</u>, <u>e.g.</u>, K.S.A. § 44-818.

CHAPTER 15
ORGANIZING THE FARM BUSINESS

I.   Introduction
The most common form of farm business organization is
the sole proprietorship. Approximately 80% of the farms in the
United States are organized as sole proprietorships.
Decisionmaking for the sole proprietorship is simple because
the proprietor makes all decisions and implements them.
Moreover, the proprietor is personally responsible for all
business debts and obligations of the business. Injury caused to
third parties by the proprietor or his or her employees while on
farm business are the owner's responsibility.
      Significant disadvantages are presented to an individual
who does business under this simple format. The major
disadvantages are:
      (1)   Unlimited personal liability;
      (2)   Lack of Continuity; and
      (3)   Difficulty of transfer.
For these reasons, farm owners often consider other forms of
organization, especially when one objective is to bring other
family members into the business.
      Organizing the farm business involves choosing the form
of business organization which meets the personal objectives of
the family and the business objectives of their farming
operation. Once a particular form of business is chosen it must
be structured in the manner which is most advantageous under
the circumstances. Both tax and non-tax factors are important
in choosing and structuring a farm business organization. These
include income tax planning, and more recently, structuring the
business to comply with federal farm program payment rules
under the various price and income support programs. Estate
planning has traditionally been a consideration in organizing the
farm business. Business continuity, as a goal, is often an
important consideration as a part of the estate plan as well.
These factors have led farmers to consider farm partnerships,
farm corporations and leasing arrangements as appropriate
business entities to achieve their objectives. Often, a

combination of these forms may be appropriate. In that case it becomes important to balance the various objectives with those structures which are most likely to achieve the goals of the family.

II.   Farm Partnerships
A partnership is defined in the Uniform Partnership Act (UPA) as "an association of two or more persons to carry on as co-owners a business for profit."[1]

There are two types of partnerships, (1) general partnerships and (2) limited partnerships. The main difference is that in a general partnership, all of the partners are personally liable for all of the debts and obligations of the partnership. In contrast, in a limited partnership only the general partner(s) has unlimited liability for the debts and obligations of the partnership. The limited partner(s) may incur liability only to the extent of their investment in the limited partnership.

A. Partnership Formation
The formation of a basic general partnership is relatively simple. No formal written agreement is required. In the absence of a partnership agreement, the Uniform Partnership Act sets forth the rules for organization and operation of the partnership. Partners may agree to arrangements which differ from those which are specified in the Uniform Partnership Act and such agreements are binding upon the partners. If no partnership agreement exists, the Uniform Partnership Act controls the terms of the partnership.[2]

Example:
Mabel and Ruby form a partnership to grow strawberries and sell them to the general public. Mabel simply wants to invest money in the operation, and not be involved in the daily activities of the partnership. On the other hand, Ruby is going to work full-time in the partnership business. Mabel is going to invest 10% of the money needed to start the business; Ruby will put up 90%. No partnership agreement exists other than to split the profits 10% to Mabel and 90% to Ruby. Under the

Uniform Partnership Act, since no partnership agreement exists to the contrary, both Mabel and Ruby will have equal right to determine the management decisions. Ruby cannot overrule Mabel on how many strawberries to plant or what to charge for them, even though Mabel is investing a much smaller amount of time and money than Ruby. If they had a written partnership agreement, they could give to Ruby the rights to make the management decisions for the partnership.

The definition of a partnership in the U.P.A. includes several elements. The first element is "association". This implies that two or more persons are acting voluntarily. it also implies that the intent of the parties may be the most important factor in determining whether a partnership exists. However, there will be situations in which the elements of a partnership are present even though the parties did not intend to form a partnership. If the elements are present, a court may construe the relationship to be a partnership, even though the parties call the relationship something else.[3]

The second element of the definition indicates that two or more persons are to be involved. "Persons" in this sense can include individuals, other partnerships, corporations, or other associations. However, minors, incompetents, and other specific classes of individuals may not legally qualify as capable parties to enter into a partnership arrangement.

The third element of the definition of a partnership is "business". Since the partnership is to carry on a business, it is necessary that the relationship be more than the mere co-ownership of property or joint undertakings for specific purposes. Co-ownership of the business is an essential element. In other words, the mere co-ownership of real estate or personal property does not create a partnership since those assets may be co-owned for purposes other than for conducting a business.

The carrying-on of a business implies the "profit" element of the definition. The sharing of profit (and losses) by two or more persons is prima facie evidence of the establishment of a partnership. This element, along with joint control, is a crucial aspect for establishing the partnership

529

relationship and gives some substance to the definition.[4]

The legal importance of determining whether a partnership exists usually arises when a third party alleges that individuals have been operating as partners. If the evidence clearly indicates a partnership, then all of the partners can be held personally responsible for debts and obligations of the partnership.

In addition to the elements considered in the definition of the partnership, a number of other items may be considered in determining whether or not a partnership exists. As indicated in Adams v. United States,[5] these include:

    (1) Mutual interest in profits;

    (2) Mutual liability, joint and several, for debts and loss of capital;

    (3) Mutual agency and responsibility in the conduct of the business;

    (4) Common contribution and ownership of partnership property; and

    (5) The rendition of service by all partners.

No single factor will conclusively establish the relationship between persons to constitute a legal partnership. In a particular case all of these elements may be considered in determining whether, in sum, the relationship is a partnership.

1. Partnership Distinguished From Other Business Forms

The joint venture is a business organization which is very similar to the partnership. The only real difference between a joint venture and a regular partnership is that the joint venture has a more limited scope and purpose. It is commonly used for a single undertaking, does not require the entire attention of the individuals involved, and is usually of fairly short duration. In most important legal aspects, it is treated as a partnership.[6]

It is often difficult to distinguish a partnership from a landlord-tenant relationship. This is particularly true if the business operation is a family enterprise. The strongest determining factors in distinguishing a landlord-tenant relationship from a partnership are the intent of the parties and the amount of control of the business which is exercised by the respective parties.[7] This is why clauses are normally included in a lease to exclude the possibility of a partnership being inferred from the relationship between the lessor and lessee. These clauses are not entirely effective, but they do serve as an expression of the intent of the parties. If the landlord retains joint possession of the real estate with a tenant, the possibility of joint control is more likely, and therefore, the existence of the partnership may be inferred. Another important aspect that is often used to distinguish the two relationships is that a partnership agreement normally includes an express agreement to share losses. This is not usually true in a landlord-tenant situation. The Uniform Partnership Act itself states that no inference of a partnership can be drawn in a situation where profits were received by a landlord as payment of rent.[8]

It is sometimes hard to distinguish between the partnership and the employer-employee relationship. Again, the Uniform Partnership Act indicates that no presumption of a partnership arises from profit-sharing which involves "wages of an employee."[9] Profit-sharing with employees is a fairly common practice. The distinguishing characteristic is the intent of the parties and the issue of control. If the employment contains the clear intent of the parties to establish an employer-employee relationship, it is difficult to prove the existence of a partnership. In addition, if the situation is one in which the alleged employer is clearly in control of the business operation, this is strong evidence that a partnership does not exist.

In common parlance, there is a tendancy to define a partnership by stating what it is not rather than by what it is. The Uniform Partnership Act attempts to correct this tendancy by providing some specific indications of what constitutes a partnership. However, the Act itself is subject to interpretation by courts. Therefore, it is necessary to analyze the facts of a particular case in determining whether or not sufficient evidence exists to infer a partnership relationship. Importantly, the burden of proving the partnership is on the person who asserts the existence of the partnership.

Example:

Opie graduates from State University and decides that he wants to return home to farm with his father,

Oscar. Opie and his father buy one tractor together and own it jointly; the rest of the farm machinery is owned by Oscar. Nothing is discussed or stated about whether the two are in partnership. Opie agrees to work full-time on Oscar's farm for what is termed "salary" equal to 20% of the net profits of the farming enterprise. Opie is not responsible for any losses of the farm business.

To determine whether Opie and Oscar are partners, several things must be considered. First of all, as a general rule, a person employed by another who receives a "wage" is not a partner. In other words, a person can hire employees and not create a partnership between the employer and employee. In this example, it must be determined whether Opie is truly a salaried employee receiving a wage. He and Oscar actually share the net profits of the farm 20%-80%. This gives rise to the presumption of a partnership. Furthermore, the two parties jointly own one piece of equipment. However, they do not share in the losses of the business, and the intent to create a partnership does not seem to be present. These two factors would suggest that there is not a partnership.

In conclusion, since Opie is receiving a share of the net profits rather than receiving a wage, there may be sufficient evidence to find that a partnership exists. This finding could be made despite the factors present that would indicate otherwise.

As stated at the outset, one of the fundamental features of a partnership is the unlimited personal liability of each partner. If partnership debt is incurred which cannot be paid with partnership assets, then each of the partners must provide personal assets to pay the debt. Even if a partnership is accidentally created, the "unintentional" partners are personally liable for all debts of the partnership.[10]

2. Partnership Property and Interests in the Partnership

In many partnership arrangements, the partners contribute the use of particular items of property to the partnership. This may be for a fixed rate of return, or it may be a contribution of the property with the expectation of sharing in a portion of the total returns of the partnership. In other cases, property will be transferred to the partnership as such. In most states, it is possible for a partnership to own both real and personal property.[11] In some states, this ownership is referred to as a "tenancy in partnership". In a fairly typical situation, property will be acquired during the operation of the partnership business by the expenditure of partnership funds. In such cases, this property is partnership property.

Sometimes there is a problem in distinguishing partnership property from property that is owned by the individual partners. This occurs most often at the time of the dissolution of the partnership or at a time when items of property are to be sold.

Any property owned by the partnership is required to be used for partnership purposes. Each partner has an equal right to possess and use the property for partnership purposes, but does not have a right to possess or use it for any other purpose without the consent of all partners.[12] In addition, no partner can assign or sell his or her right in specific partnership property.[13] To allow such an assignment or sale would, in effect, allow an assignee certain rights as a partner. This, of course, would be inconsistent with the characteristics of the partnership.

It is important to distinguish the interest of a particular partner in the partnership from his rights in specific partnership property. The interest in the partnership is, in and of itself, a property right of a partner, and is generally thought of as the partner's share of the profits and surplus.[14] Since this interest is personal property, it may be assigned. However, any such assignment entitles the assignee only to the profits to which the assigning partner would be entitled. The assignee does not become a partner.[15] A partner's interest in the partnership is similar in some ways to the ownership of shares of stock in a corporation. Creditors of a partner are entitled to attach or subject the partner's interest in the partnership to execution for any personal claims they have against the partner. However, the creditor does achieve an interest in the specific property owned by the partnership.[16] The economic value of the partner's interest is personal property, and can pass the same as any other personal property to those designated in the partner's will or to a person who is entitled to inherit when there is no will.[17]

The Uniform Partnership Act makes it clear that any one or more of the partners may be given the authority to transfer real property belonging to the partnership.[18] It is imperative that the partners agree on this matter in advance. If any special problems are anticipated, an effort should be made to inform innocent third parties as to the actual authority which is possessed by a partner who is dealing with those third parties. Another point that should be emphasized is that each partner may sell personal property in the regular course of the partnership business.[19] If the purpose of the partnership business does not include the selling of personal property, this rule would not apply to the transaction.

3. Powers of Partners

Since the partnership business is managed by the partners, they have the power to act for and by the partnership as long as they act within the scope of the business. For this reason, every partner is considered to be agent of the partnership for the purpose of the partnership business. The exception to this rule would be in a situation where the partner is not authorized to act and the person with whom he or she is dealing knows that the particular partner lacks authority to act on behalf of the partnership. In addition, if a partner's actions are not apparently for the carrying on of the business of the partnership in the usual way, then the other partners in the partnership are not bound by the partner's acts unless they have in fact authorized him or her to act.[20]

In all cases, the partnership agreement may include restrictions on the authority of partners to act and any act of the partner which is contrary to the restrictions will not bind the partnership if the person dealing with the partner has knowledge of the restrictions.

Just as certain limits and restrictions may be imposed on a partner's authority to act for the partnership, there are also situations in which the partnership is liable for acts of an individual partner. For example, if any partner acts in the ordinary course of business with the authority of the other partners and causes a loss or injury to another person, the partnership may be liable.[21] An important related rule is the provision that each partner is personally liable for all debts and obligations of the partnership.[22] The partnership agreement can determine the liability among the individual partners, but the partnership and the individual partners can not limit their liability in that manner as to third parties.

Important as a general rule of law notice to any partner, or knowledge by a partner of any matter relating to partnership business operates as notice or knowledge to the entire partnership.[23] (This would not apply in a case of fraud committed by or with consent of the partner who has notice or knowledge.) For example, suppose that the partnership acquired certain property under a financing arrangement in which payment was to be made when a statement or bill was sent to the partnership. However, instead of providing a statement to the partnership as such, the seller simply provided a statement to one of the partners. This would serve as sufficient notice of the debt to the partnership and the seller would be entitled to proceed accordingly against the partnership.

4. Rights and Duties of Partners

The partnership agreement is the basis for establishing the rights and duties of the partners. Unless the partnership agreement provides otherwise, the following rules prevail and determine the relationship of the partners to one another:

a. Each partner shares equally in the profits remaining after all liabilities for the partnership are satisfied. At the same time, each partner must contribute equally toward losses sustained by the partnership;[24]

b. Each partner is entitled to be repaid for any expenses incurred by him or her as personal liabilities arising from the ordinary and proper conduct of the partnership business;[25]

c. A partner is entitled to receive interest for any amounts contributed to the partnership over and above the amount originally agreed upon;[26]

d.   All partners have equal rights in the management and conduct of the partnership business;[27]

e.   No partner is entitled to any particular reimbursement for acting in the partnership business other than his or her share of the profits;[28]

f.   No person may become a member of the partnership without consent of all the partners. Thus, an assignment of a partnership interest to another person, such as from a father to a son, will not make the assignee a full-fledged partner unless the other partners in the association agree;[29]

g.   Differences that arise as to matters connected with the ordinary partnership business will be decided by a majority of the partners;[30]

h.   Partnership books must be kept at the principal place of business and all partners have access to and may inspect and copy any of the books at any time;[31]

i.   Partners must give true and full information of all things affecting the partnership to any other partner on demand;[32]

j.   Every partner must account to the partnership for any benefit or any profits derived by him for any transaction connected with the conduct of partnership business;[33] and

k.   Any partner has the right to a formal accounting as to the activities of a partner or a partnership.[34]

B.   Tax Treatment of the Partnership

Under Internal Revenue Code Section 701, a partnership is generally not a taxpaying entity and, normally is not required to pay income tax. The only requirement of a partnership is that it file an informational tax return.[35] The Internal Revenue Service (IRS) considers a partnership to be a conduit for a business to accumulate taxable income, deductions and credits and then pass these items along to the partners.

The individual partners are taxed according to their distributive share of the partnership's income, deductions and credits.[36] A partner's distributive share is the amount of

536

income, deductions or credits conveyed to him or her by the partnership. Normally, a partner's distributive share is established by the partnership agreement. The agreement sets forth what each partner is entitled to receive from the partnership. The partners, by and through the partnership agreement, can generally distribute the income, deductions and credits any way they want, as long as there is substantial economic effect in the way the tax attributes of the partnership are distributed.[37] "Substantial economic effect" means that one partner cannot contribute all the capital needed by the partnership and not receive any of the income from the partnership as a way to avoid income taxes. If the partnership distribution is merely for tax avoidance and not reflective of normal economic behavior, the arrangement can be set aside and the partners can be taxed according to the IRS determination of how the partnership would normally distribute income and losses without consideration for the tax consequences. To avoid problems in this area, the share of income received by each partner should be reasonably related to the contribution of capital or services to the partnership.

If there is no agreement concerning the distribution of partnership income, deductions or credits to the partners, then the IRS will consider these tax attributes apportioned according to the partner's capital interest.[38]

Example:

Pete, Pat and Peggy are in partnership. No agreement exists in regard to the distribution of partnership income, deductions and credits. The partners have contributed the following amount of capital to the partnership: Pete - $20,000; Pat - $30,000; and Peggy - $50,000. Since no agreement exists, the IRS will consider the income and deductions of the partnership distributed in the same proportion as the capital contribution of the partners. Thus, 20% of the income would be taxed to Pete, 30% to Pat, and 50% to Peggy. Furthermore, even if Pete, Pat and Peggy had a distribution agreement but it had no "substantial economic effect", the distributive share of each partner would be found by the IRS to be the same as the percentage of capital contributed.

C.   Termination of the Partnership

A partnership can be dissolved in a number of ways.
Typically, it is dissolved by agreement of the parties. Certain
partnerships exist for a fixed period of time with the partnership
automatically terminating at the end of that period. When no
partnership agreement exists concerning dissolution, any partner
may terminate the partnership at will.[39]

When dissolution occurs partnership debts frequently
remain to be paid. Partnership law provides for the payment of
those liabilities in the following order:

1st: Liabilities owed to creditors other than partners;

2nd: Liabilities to partners other than for capital and
profits;

3rd: Liabilities owed to partners in respect of capital;
and

4th: Liabilities to partners in respect of profits.[40]

Example:

The ABC partnership is ending with cash
and assets worth $130,000 and the following
debts:

$30,000   -   to Smith Elevator for fertilizer
<u>$10,000</u>   -   loan from Partner A to the Partnership
$40,000   -   Total Debt

The partners contributed capital to the
partnership in the following amounts:

$30,000   -   Partner A
$20,000   -   Partner B
<u>$10,000</u>   -   Partner C
$60,000   -   Total Capital Contribution

In distributing the assets of the partnership, the first item paid
is the debt to a creditor other than a partner, (Smith Elevator)
in the sum of $30,000. Next, loans made by partners to the
partnership are paid. Here it is the loan from partner A in the
amount of $10,000. The third item paid is the capital
contribution of the partners. Here, Partner A would receive
$30,000; Partner B, $20,000; and Partner C, $10,000. Absent
any agreement of the partners to the contrary, the $30,000

remaining would be divided equally between the partners as profits, with A, B, and C each receiving $10,000.

D. Advantages and Disadvantages of a Partnership
Partnerships are very flexible, easy to form and do not require the degree of record keeping and paperwork of a corporation. However, they do require more formality and paperwork than sole proprietorships. Partnerships can provide a business format for the easy transition of a farm enterprise from parent to child. Also, a partnership may be advantageous for a part-time farmer who needs to pool labor and resources with other farmers in order to accumulate necessary items for an economically feasible operation.

As to the disadvantages, the unlimited personal liability of each partner is a major problem. There is also a loss of management control and income by older family members when they transfer control of the partnership to younger members.

In a partnership, specific attention must be directed to the following questions before entering an agreement:

1) Will the partnership generate sufficient income to support the families of the partners?

2) What property will be transferred to the partnership? How much and by whom?

3) How will partnership income, debts, deductions and credits be divided?

4) Are there any present or future income tax problems involved in forming, continuing or dissolving the partnership?

5) Can the individuals involved work and operate a farm business together?

E. Elements of a Good Partnership Agreement
Below is a list of suggested areas to be addressed in a partnership agreement:[41]

* the name of the partnership or partnership business;
* the names and addresses of all partners;
* the address of principal place of business and any other business locations;
* the date of formation and, if applicable, the date of termination of the partnership;

539

* the capital contributions made and to be made by all partners listed by type and value;
* any salary to be paid to partners in addition to profit shares;
* special business work assignments of partners in addition to profit shares;
* how business decisions will be made;
* procedure and requirements for sale, exchange or liquidation of a partner's interest and for admission of new partners;
* each partner's share of partnership profits;
* each partner's share of partnership expenses and losses;
* any restrictions on any partner's authority to bind the partnership in business transactions;
* a list of all partnership-owned property and the source of the property;
* a list of property owned by partners separately and loaned to or used by the partnership;
* whether and how much interest may be paid for loans made by partners to the partnership;
* bookkeeping and accounting methods to be used by the partnership;
* all income tax elections to be made by the partnership;
* any special allocations of income tax deductions, depreciation, credits, gains or losses to be made to partners;
* dissolution notice requirements;
* whether a decedent partner's successor or estate may continue as a partner;
* any buy-sell agreements, including authorization for the purchase of insurance policies to fund the agreements and the method and conditions of use of insurance proceeds to purchase a deceased partner's interest;
* liquidation procedures for termination of one or more of all of the partner's interests and for termination of the partnership;
* how disputes between the partners will be solved (i.e.,

arbitration)
* the requirements and procedures for partners to continue the partnership business after dissolution; and
* the notarized signature of each partner.

III.   Limited Partnerships
   A. Definition
       A second type of partnership is the limited partnership.[42] A limited partnership is an association of two or more persons which has as members one or more general partners and one or more limited partners.[43] The general partner(s) in a limited partnership are in virtually the same position as partners in a regular partnership. However, the limited partner is only liable for the debts of the limited partnership to the extent of the investment in the limited partnership.[44] In this sense, a limited partner is more like a shareholder in a general corporation than a partner. Even though the limited partner has limited personal liability, the general partner does not enjoy such a protected status. The general partner in a limited partnership is personally liable for the debts and obligations of the partnership.

Example:
       Tom and Jerry form a limited partnership. Tom is the general partner and Jerry is the limited partner. Each puts up $10,000 in cash or assets. Due to crop failure, the limited partnership cannot survive and Tom and Jerry decide to dissolve the partnership. There remain outstanding debts to creditors in the sum of $50,000. Jerry, the limited partner, will be liable for those debts up to the amount he has invested in the limited partnership, that being $10,000 and thus will lose his $10,000 investment. On the other hand, Tom, as the general partner, is unlimitedly liable and will not only lose his $10,000 investment, but an additional $30,000 in order to meet the limited partnership's obligations to the creditors.

To obtain and retain limited liability, the limited partner

541

must not be involved in the management of the limited partnership's business.[45] The limited partner is, in essence, an investor, not a manager of the business. If the limited partner becomes involved in the daily management or control of the business then he or she will lose the limited liability status and will be personally liable for debts and obligations just like the general partner.

Example:
> Jed and Jethro form a farm limited partnership. Jed is the general partner and Jethro the limited partner. According to their partnership agreement, Jed and Jethro have equal authority in deciding what crops are to be planted. Each year they decide together what crops to grow.
>
> Will Jethro have limited liability for the debts of the business? The answer is no. He is involved in the management of the farming operation and thus loses his limited liability protection.

B. Use of Limited Partnerships

The features of control and management of the business by the general partner and limited liability for limited partners can be used very effectively in the proper farm business setting. For instance, a limited partnership can be used to bring in investor financing for a farm without risking all the resources of an investor, and retain farmer control of the farming operation. A limited partnership for a farming enterprise can be formed where an outside investor invests a certain amount of money to become a limited partner. In exchange, the investor receives a certain percentage of the net farm income plus a share of the farm's tax deductions. The farmer acts as the general partner and manager of the farm. The partnership of the farmer as general partner/manager and the investor as the funder and limited partner can be mutually advantageous. The farmer gains outside resources by changing from debt financing to equity financing. Typically, the investor would not receive interest on the investment and would be willing to accept a lower rate of return in the anticipation that the farm enterprise will appreciate over time. The farmer, as the general partner,

542

retains control of the operation, receives income from the partnership in the form of wages as manager and a share of the profits as a general partner.

Another situation in which a limited partnership can be effectively used is in estate planning. The parents or the parents and any on-farm children take the role of general partners and manage the business while the off-farm children are made limited partners. The parents and on-farm child remain owners of part or most of the business, and manage it. The off-farm heirs benefit as partial owners, are not involved in the management, and are not subject to unlimited liability. All children can receive equally from the assets of the parents while the parents and the child or children remaining on the farm operate the farming enterprise without interference from the off-farm heirs.

The following two examples show the usefulness of a limited partnership in different settings:

Example 1:

Stan has been in the cow-calf business for 10 years and still has to borrow substantially in order to finance his operation. The interest rates have negatively affected his farm. He decides to contact Laurel, a local businessman to see if he would like to become a limited partner in a cow-calf limited partnership. Stan and Laurel form a limited partnership. Laurel invests 75% of the capital and takes the role of a limited partner. Stan invests 25% of the capital and is the general partner and manager of the cow-calf herd. The receipts from the cow-calf operation are split 75% to Laurel and 25% to Stan. Stan receives a regular salary as manager of the herd. Also, he rents his pastureland and equipment to the limited partnership for a set rental fee. The income and deductions are split 75% to Laurel and 25% to Stan.

Example 2:

Betty and Barney have been farming for 30 years. They have three children, two have left the farm, the youngest son has stayed and intends to make farming his vocation.

543

Betty and Barney want to organize their estate in a way which enables their youngest son to retain control while all their children receive some value from the long-term growth of the business. They form a limited partnership with Betty and Barney and the son who has stayed on the farm as general partners and the other children as limited partners. This arrangement allows the family members on the farm to have control as general partners while all the children receive a share of the business.

C. Formation of the Limited Partnership

Limited partnerships are created by statute and can only be formed by following the guidelines set forth in the Uniform Limited Partnership Act and the Revised Uniform Limited Partnership Act, respectively. These Acts provide for the creation and operation of limited partnerships. A limited partnership is created by filing a Certificate of Limited Partnership or by filing the Limited Partnership Agreement, if it contains the necessary information, with the Secretary of State.[46] The Certificate or Agreement filed with the Secretary of State must contain the following information under the Revised Uniform Limited Partnership Act:

1) The name of the limited partnership;
2) The nature of the business to be conducted or promoted;
3) The address of the registered office and the name and address of the resident agent for the limited partnership;
4) The name and the business or residential address of each partner, specifying separately the general partners and the limited partners;
5) The amount of cash and a description and statement of the agreed value of the other property or services contributed, or agreed to be contributed in the future by each partner;
6) The times at which or events upon the happening of which any additional contributions agreed to be made by each partner are to be made;
7) The circumstances and conditions allowing a limited partner to assign his or her limited partnership

interest;

8) If agreed upon, the time at which or the events upon the happening of which a partner may withdraw from the limited partnership. Also the amount of, or the method of determining the distribution a partner would be entitled to and the terms and conditions of the withdrawal and distribution;

9) Any right of a partner to receive distributions of property from the limited partnership;

10) Any right of a partner to receive, or of a general partner to make, distributions to a partner which includes a return of all or any of the partner's contribution;

11) When, or what, would cause the dissolving of the limited partnership; and

12) Any right of the remaining general partners to continue the partnership upon the withdrawal of a general partner.[47]

The limited partnership becomes a separate legal entity once the Certificate or Agreement of Limited Partnership is filed with the Secretary of State. The limited partnership can be created on a date after the filing if this is stated in the certificate or filed agreement.

The name of the limited partnership must contain either the words "limited partnership" or the abbreviation "L.P." The name of the limited partnership generally cannot contain the name of any of the limited partners.[48]

D. Taxation of Limited Partnerships

A limited partnership is taxed like a regular partnership. The limited partnership files an informational tax return and is not ordinarily a taxpayer. Its taxable attributes of income and deductions are passed through to the partners. There are circumstances under which a limited partnership is treated like a corporation and thus must pay income taxes and retain its own deductions and credits.[49] In making a determination of whether to treat a limited partnership as a corporation for tax purposes, the Internal Revenue Service examines four key factors. If two of the four factors are present, then the limited partnership is taxed like a corporation. If none or only one of these characteristics are found, then the limited partnership is taxed like a regular partnership with all the income, deductions and credits passing through to the partners.

The four critical factors are:

1) centralized management;
2) continuity of life;
3) limited liability; and
4) free transferability of interest.[50]

Internal Revenue Code Section 465 limits loss deductions to the amount that a taxpayer-partner is "at risk" for the loss. A general or limited partner is considered "at risk" in the sum of:

1) the amount of money contributed to the limited partnership;
2) the adjusted basis of property contributed; and
3) any loans which the partner is personally liable for or for which he or she has pledged property.[51]

Furthermore, deductions from a limited partnership can only be taken by a passive investor to the extent of income the investor actually has from the activity.[52]

Example:

Buddy and Sally have a limited partnership with Buddy as the general partner and Sally the limited partner. Sally contributes $20,000 in cash plus machinery with an adjusted basis of $20,000. Buddy puts up $10,000 in cash. The limited partnership borrows $50,000 with Buddy being the only one liable for the promissory note. Sally is "at risk" in the amount of $40,000 and thus can take loss deductions of only $40,000.

E. Dissolution of Limited Partnerships

A limited partnership can be dissolved upon the happening of any one of the following events:

1) the arrival of the termination date set in the limited partnership certificate;
2) a written consent to dissolve signed by all the partners;
3) in certain situations, the withdrawal of the general

546

partner; or

4) the entry of a decree by a court dissolving the limited partnership.[53]

As with any business dissolution, tax implications are always present and must be considered.

F. Advantages and Disadvantages of Limited Partnerships

Some easily identifiable advantages of a limited partnership are:

1) Investor financing
   Farm financing is changed from debt to equity financing. With less borrowed money needed, interest expense is decreased. Profits and losses are spread over more individuals.

2) Use in estate planning

3) Full use of tax incentives
   In some situations the farm operator cannot take full advantage of tax deductions available. By bringing in an outside investor who can take full advantage of these deduction, the investor will receive a "return" that may be of little value to the farmer. This, perhaps, can be traded by the farmer for a greater share of the profits.

4) Limited liability for the limited partner

5) Stabilization of income
   Generally the farmer receives a salary for management of the business, thus insuring some income. The general partner can also rent facilities to the limited partnership.

Likewise, several disadvantage exist to doing business as a limited partnership. They are:

1) Complexity
   A limited partnership is a complex business form, more so than a regular partnership or a sole proprietorship. If outside investors are involved, they will want detailed records kept, quarterly reports filed, and explanations of actions and decisions by management. A limited partnership agreement and certificate of limited partnership are

necessary.
2) Cost of formation and reports
A filing fee and annual fees are required to form and maintain a limited partnership. Also, annual reports must be filed with the Secretary of State.
3) Loss of control
Even though a limited partner cannot become involved in the management of the business, the limited partner will request explanations for what is being done on the farm. The farm operator will lose some control of the business.
4) Unlimited liability for the general partner
The general partner remains personally liable for the debts and obligations of the business.

IV.   Corporations
    A. General
By definition, a corporation is an artificial person created under the authority of state law. As such, a corporation is considered to be a separate legal entity, a person, not a mere extension of its owners. The owners of the corporation must, in business transactions, treat the corporation as a separate person and not as merely an extension of themselves.

In most states, one person can own all the stock, be the president, sole employee and a member of the Board of Directors of a corporation. This may lead to charges that the corporation is merely an extension of its owner and cause the owner to lose some benefits of incorporating.

There are four types of stock generally recognized.
1) Common voting stock;
2) Common non-voting stock;
3) Preferred voting stock; or
4) Preferred non-voting stock.
Preferred stock is given priority in receiving dividends. If the corporation lacks sufficient income to pay dividends to all stockholders, the preferred stockholders are paid first. Furthermore, if the corporation is ever liquidated, the preferred stockholders are paid for their stock before the common stockholders receive payment. Often preferred stock is entitled to receive a set annual dividend while dividends paid to

common stockholders fluctuate depending on the profit of the corporation. Common stockholders assume a greater risk. The obvious difference between voting and non-voting stock is that voting stockholders are allowed to vote on the issues presented to the shareholders. A corporation can issue all four types of stock, or any combination.

Example:

> Herb and Zula, husband and wife, decide to incorporate their farming operation. They have three children, all under the age of 18. They decide to have two types of stock in their corporation; common voting and preferred non-voting stock. They decide to give their children part of the preferred non-voting stock with a set amount of dividends so that the children can have part ownership in the farm and receive dividends to use for college. Yet, Herb and Zula can retain control of the corporation by having all the voting stock.

B. Corporate Structure and Formation

State law generally provides that one or more persons may act as incorporators for the purpose of forming a corporation. In the case of farm corporations, the incorporators will usually be one or more family members involved in the business. These persons file articles of incorporation with the proper public agency or official. The articles of incorporation usually must detail: (1) The name of the corporation; (2) the purpose or purposes for which the corporation is organized; (3) the number of shares which the corporation will have authority to issue; (4) any special arrangements regarding the shares of stock, such as limitations on voting rights, preferences or classes; (5) an address of the initial registered office; (6) the name of the initial registered agent; (7) the number of directors constituting the initial Board of Directors, their names and addresses; (8) the period of duration of the corporation; and (9) any other provisions which incorporators choose to set forth regarding the internal affairs of the corporation.[54]

Once the above information has been submitted to the state, a determination is made as to whether or not the corporation is being organized for a legitimate business purpose.

Also, the state determines whether or not the name is the same or similar to that of an existing corporation. If no problems are evident, the state returns a certificate of incorporation to the registered agent signifying the creation of the corporation as a legal entity.

C. Restrictions on Farm Corporations

Nine states restrict entry into farming by corporations. The fear is that large corporations would enter farming and eventually displace "family farms".[55] For example, Kansas law prohibits a corporation from owning, acquiring, obtaining or leasing any agricultural land in the state unless the corporation qualifies as either a "Family Farm Corporation" or an "Authorized Farm Corporation."[56]

To qualify as a Family Farm Corporation the corporation must:

1) be founded for the purpose of farming and the ownership of agricultural land;
2) a majority of the voting stock must be held by, and a majority of the stockholders must be, persons related to each other; all of whom have a common ancestor within the third degree of relationship, or the spouses or the stepchildren of any such persons;
3) all stockholders must be natural persons or personal representatives of natural persons. This excludes corporations from being stockholders as a corporation is not a natural person; and
4) at least one of the stockholders must reside on the farm or be actively engaged in labor or management of the farming operation.[57]

To be an Authorized Farm Corporation the corporation must:

1) be a Kansas corporation;
2) all the incorporators must be Kansas residents;
3) the corporation must be founded for the purpose of farming and the ownership of agricultural land;
4) there can be no more than fifteen stockholders. Husband and wife are deemed to be one stockholder;
5) all the stockholders must be natural persons or

personal representatives of natural persons; and

6) at least 30% of the stockholders must be persons residing on the farm or actively engaged in the day-to-day labor or management of the farming operation.[58]

It is obvious from the restrictions that the intent is to have only certain types of corporations farm in Kansas. Similar legislation exists in the other states with various exemptions and exceptions.[59]

D. Corporate Taxation

Closely held family corporations have two options available under federal tax law. They may be taxed as regular corporations under the provisions of Subchapter C of the Internal Revenue Code, or they may elect to be taxed under the provisions of Subchapter S of the Code.

1. Subchapter S Corporations

Under Subchapter S, corporations may elect to be taxed in a manner similar to that of a partnership rather than as a regular corporation.[60] For some corporations this tax option will result in income tax advantages. Under this section, the business remains structured as a corporation for all purposes except taxation. For the purpose of taxation, each shareholder's portion of income, capital gains, operating losses, and undistributed taxable income is passed through in a manner similar to that of partners operating under a partnership agreement.[61] In this way the individual shareholders pay tax on any income generated by the corporation as part of their individual income.

In some cases, where there are shareholders involved in the corporation who render no services, there may be some income tax advantage to distributing income to all shareholders and allowing each to pay tax on a portion of the total income. This is because salaries could not be paid to those shareholders who do not render services to the corporation.

To qualify for Subchapter S treatment, a corporation must have 35 or fewer shareholders. For purposes of determining the number of shareholders, a husband and wife who own stock in the same corporation are treated as one shareholder. Generally, all shareholders must be individuals, estates of individuals, or lifetime trusts treated as owned by the grantor. A testamentary trust may be a shareholder for 60 days. Special rules apply to other types of trusts. No shareholders can be non-resident aliens, nor can there be more than one class of stock outstanding.[62]

Generally, all shareholders must consent to the election for Subchapter S treatment. However, the Subchapter S election will terminate if the owners of more than one-half of the voting stock revoke the election. If more than 25% of the corporation's receipts come from rent, royalties, dividends, interests, annuities, and sales or exchanges of stock or securities, for three consecutive years, the election terminates. Also, if the corporation has passive income in excess of 25% of gross receipts and has accumulated earnings and profits from pre-election years, a tax is imposed on the passive income. This provision of the law was designed to prohibit investment corporations from making the choice to be taxed under Subchapter S.[63]

If more than 35 people own stock in a corporation, it no longer qualifies for Subchapter S treatment. For those corporations that find Subchapter S advantageous as compared to Subchapter C or regular taxation, the dispersal of stock to a large number of shareholders could result in a loss of this tax option. This could happen after the property has passed from the older generation to the younger members. For example, in order to transfer as much of the estate as possible during life by use of lifetime gifts, many families transfer stock to the children, grandchildren, and other chosen family members. While this poses no immediate problems as long as the operating members remain in control, it may result in dispersal of shares to a large number of people. Not only may this result in management problems, but it can also affect the eligibility of the corporation to be taxed under the provisions of Subchapter S.

2. Subchapter C Corporations
Under the provisions regulating taxation of a regular corporation ("Subchapter C"), any income generated by the corporation in excess of all allowable business deductions is taxed to the corporation.[64] If distributions are made to the

shareholders in the form of dividends, these dividends are again subject to taxation as income to the individual shareholders.[65] This results in the so-called "double taxation" and in some cases may increase tax liability for the owners of the business.

Paying out most of the earnings as salaries may eliminate much or all of this disadvantage with the regular corporation form. All salaries, reasonable bonuses, interests, rent, and other business expenses are deductible at the corporate level. Therefore, a large portion of the total income of any farm corporation can be paid out in expenses. Obviously, if any of the owners are employees and receive salaries or bonuses from the corporation, these amounts will be taxed at the ordinary individual tax rate, even if no taxable income results at the corporate level.

Under the Tax Reform Act of 1986 the corporate tax rates were set at 15% for the first $50,000 of corporate taxable income, 25% on the next $25,000, 34% on the third $25,000, 39% on the income between $100,000 and $335,000 and 34% on all additional taxable income.[66] The effect of this rate structure is to phase out some of the benefits of the lower rates once the corporations income pushes into the fourth bracket ($100,000 - $335,000) and to make the tax on levels in the fifth bracket equivalent to a flat tax of 34% on taxable income. These provisions also allow some splitting of income between the individual and the corporation at certain levels of income. This is done by paying out part of the corporate income as salaries and retaining the balance in the corporation.

Other tax regulations provide that some accumulations of earnings and profits may be made without the imposition of tax. The Economic Recovery Tax Act of 1981 increased the limit on the amount of accumulated earnings and profits to $250,000 for tax years beginning after 1981. Beyond that level, the tax rate for accumulated earnings is 27 1/2% to 38 1/2%.[67] Naturally, accumulations can be made if it can be shown that they are justified by the reasonable needs of the business. Obviously, if money retained in the corporation for business purposes is later paid out to the shareholders, it will then be taxed to them as individuals either in the form of salary or as a taxable dividend.

3. Reducing Taxes When Forming The Corporation

At the time the corporation is organized, the shareholders may usually transfer assets to the corporation in exchange for stock without any federal income tax gain or loss to the shareholders or to the corporation. The corporation takes over the shareholder's depreciation schedule and income tax basis. No gain or loss is recognized on the exchange if the transfer is solely in exchange for stock in the corporation. A further requirement is that the shareholders who make the transfer of property to the corporation in exchange for stock must be in control of the corporation, as a group, immediately after the exchange.[68] This means that they must end up with at least 80% of the voting power and at least 80% of the total number of shares. If these requirements are not met, gain or loss may be computed and taxed to the individuals contributing property to the corporation.[69] With a family-owned corporation, this is usually no problem, because the people who transfer property to the corporation will be the same people who receive shares of stock and control of the corporation.

In general, those persons who form a corporation will not recognize gain or loss for income tax purposes on the transfer of property to the newly formed corporation if: 1) they only receive stock or securities of the corporation in exchange for the property transferred, and 2) they own at least 80% of each class of stock in the corporation.

Example:

Dick and Tracy want to form a small farm corporation. They convey to the corporation all of the farm equipment which they own and certain pieces of farmland. In exchange for this conveyance, they receive 100% of the stock in the corporation. The corporation does not pay them any money for the property, the only thing they receive is stock. Since Dick and Tracy own more than 80% of the voting and non-voting stock after the transaction, and they did not receive any extra money or "boot" for the equipment and land, they will not have to pay income tax on the transaction.

If the corporation assumes the debts of an individual at

the time of incorporation this may be considered a taxable gain for the individual.[70] If the corporation assumes liabilities in excess of the adjusted basis of all the assets transferred to the corporation, the excess will be treated as gain to the individual from the sale or exchange of the transferred assets. This problem frequently arises when a farmer conveys to the corporation zero or low basis assets such as growing crops, raised livestock, accounts receivable, or farmland purchased many years earlier at a low price. If these assets have a large debt against them which is assumed by the corporation the farmer may create an income tax problem by the transfer. Exceptions do apply, particularly if the debt being assumed gives rise to a deduction. Also, if a corporation transfers to a stockholder something other than stocks or securities, such as money ("boot") in exchange for the property conveyed to the corporation, the stockholder is required to show as gain the amount of the "boot" that is received for the transfer to the extent that it exceeds the basis of property transferred to the corporation.[71]

Example:

> Tyrus is changing his farm business organization from a sole proprietorship to a corporation. He transfers to the new corporation land worth $250,000 for which he paid $30,000. The land has against it an operating loan with an outstanding balance of $100,000. The loan is assumed by the corporation. For the land, Tyrus receives 100% of the stock in the corporation. Tyrus' basis in the land was $30,000. He transferred the land to the corporation for stock worth $250,000 and thus has a "gain" of $220,000, but must recognize and pay taxes on only $70,000. The reason is that the corporation assumed a debt of Tyrus' in the amount of $100,000. The assumption of debt over and above the basis in the property is considered by the IRS to be taxable income. If in addition to the stock, Tyrus had received $50,000 in cash for his land from the corporation, then this $50,000 would have been considered "boot" and he would be required to pay income tax on this gain to the extent that it exceeded his basis.

555

E. Dissolution of the Corporation

A corporation can be dissolved in one of two ways. It
may be dissolved either by the written consent of all the
stockholders entitled to vote or by the affirmative vote of the
majority of all the Board of Directors and who are stockholders
entitled to vote. Involuntary dissolution can result from the
failure to file state reports or to pay the required annual fees.

As with the formation of a corporation, when dissolution
occurs the potential for income taxes liability must be reviewed.
When a corporation dissolves it normally conveys its assets to
its stockholders. Generally, the cash and the value of property
received by a stockholder in excess of the basis he or she has in
the stock is taxable gain. In addition, the liquidating
corporation may accrue tax liability due to the recapture of
depreciation and investment tax credit. Under new distribution
rules the corporation will be treated as selling property to its
shareholders in either a liquidating or non-liquidating
distribution.[72] This means that the potential tax cost of getting
out of a corporation is a significant factor in whether to choose
the corporate form initially.

F. Advantages and Disadvantages of Corporations

As with other forms of doing business, the corporate
form has certain advantages and disadvantages.
Advantages:

1) Limited liability

Each stockholder's liability for corporate losses
is limited to the amount of his or her investment in
the corporation. In many situations this may be of
little benefit. For instance, most lenders will
require all stockholders to sign a personal
guarantee for the corporate debt. If this occurs, the
individual stockholders will be responsible for the
debts of the corporation to this particular lender,
thus eroding away some of the advantage of limited
liability. In addition, the value of the limited
liability feature is less when an individual is both an
employee and a stockholder of the corporation.
For example, if that person is in an accident which

556

causes personal injury to a third party, the corporation and the stockholder-employee will be required to pay for the injury because the stockholder-employee is responsible for his own actions. Furthermore, as an agent of the corporation, the corporation is also held responsible for the employees actions. Thus the stockholder-employee does not escape liability for the injury he caused by doing business as a corporation. Naturally, as to stockholders not involved in the accident, the corporation does give them some added protection.

Limited liability can also be lost by the stockholders if they abuse the corporate form by failing to have regular stockholder meetings or board meetings or by failing to make required filings with the state, and by otherwise not following the proper formality for doing business as a corporation. In this situation, the corporate veil can be "pierced" and the stockholder may be held responsible for corporate debts.

2) Continuity

Unlike a sole proprietorship which grows, flourishes, recedes and dies with its proprietor, a corporation has perpetual existence. This frequently aids the business in long-term growth and the ability to transfer the business from one generation to the next.

3) Estate planning and ease of transfer

A corporation offers many planning advantages for the farm estate. Heirs can be conveyed stock with less than 51% of the voting privileges so that the parents can remain in control of the corporation while still getting assets out of the estate. Also, on-farm heirs can be given voting stock and off-farm heirs non-voting stock. This allows control of the farm to reside with those who operate it, while all heirs share equally in the value and income from the corporation.

557

4) Tax deductible benefits

A corporation can deduct the expenses of providing certain benefits that individuals cannot. This area, however, was changed considerably with the passage of the 1986 Tax Reform Act.

Likewise, a corporation has several disadvantages which should be considered:

1) Formality and expense

Corporate record keeping normally requires greater detail than record keeping for most proprietorships and partnerships. Annual reports and fees are required by the Secretary of State. Annual shareholder and board of director meetings must be held. There are considerable costs in organizing and setting up the corporation.

2) Dissolution

Dissolution of the corporation can be difficult and sizable income taxes may be incurred.

3) Double taxation on dividends

V.   Farm Leases

Several types of leases have been developed to meet the divergent needs of various farming operations. For some a standard cash lease is sufficient. For others, a crop-share or crop-share-cash lease seems to work best. Special operations, such as a poultry or confined hog feeding operation, may involve the leasing of farm buildings. Those involved in livestock operations often operate on a pasture rental basis.

Leases can be simple, oral arrangements or complex, lengthy written instruments. Although the oral agreement may be legally enforceable, it is more desirable to place the details of an agreement in writing.

A.   The Landowner-Farm Operator Relationship

The relationship between a landowner and his or her farm operator may be classified as a landlord-tenant relationship, an employment contract, or a partnership. How the relationship is classified depends on the provisions of the agreement. The distinction is often crucial in resolving conflicts

558

that may arise out of the operating agreement.

1. Employee or Tenant

There are some definite distinctions between a tenant and an employee. An employee is paid a wage to produce a crop. The wages an employee receives may be a share of the crop or a share of the proceeds from the sale of the crop. The employee has no legal interest in the farm and usually no legal interest in the crops.

A tenant, on the other hand, is entitled to exclusive use and possession of the real estate. The tenant may sue other parties, including the landlord unless stated otherwise in the lease, for trespass on the premises. The crops, until divided, belong to the tenant exclusively. This is true even if the landlord is to receive a part of the crops as rent. As the operator of the real estate, the tenant is potentially liable in negligence cases for the injury of invitees or licensees, who come onto the rented property.

The distinction between an employee and tenant is less clear when a contract contains elements of both an employment contract and a lease. For example, a contract may use words such as "rentals" or "landlord-tenant." However, if the lease provides the owner with control of the operation, with the owner supplying the seed, fertilizer, and machinery, a court may determine that the relationship is one of employer-employee instead of landlord-tenant.[73]

2. Partnership or Landlord/Tenant Relationships

Legal problems may arise when the intent of the parties is not clearly expressed in their agreement. As a result, a court may interpret the relationship to be a partnership when the parties intended the relationship to be a landlord-tenant arrangement. The consequence of this distinction is that when a partnership exists, all partners are individually liable for all debts and obligations of the partnership. Generally, a landlord does not wish to assume the obligations of the tenant which arise from operation of the farming business. Therefore, it is important that the intent of the parties be expressed in the agreement.[74]

B. Types Of Leases

There are several types of leases which are commonly used in agriculture: (1) the crop share lease; (2) the cash lease; (3) the flexible cash lease; (4) the crop-share-cash lease; (5) farm building lease; and (6) the pasture lease.[75]

The type of lease selected depends on the type and condition of the farm, local custom, the preferences of the parties involved, and the business organization objectives. Also, the amount of time, interest and responsibility each party is willing to invest in the farming operation will influence the type of lease. For example, a landlord may not wish to be actively involved in the operation and may not want to share the risk of fluctuating income. If thess factors are present, the cash lease would likely be the most desirable lease for the farming operation. On the other hand, if the landlord wishes to be involved in the decision making process and is willing to bear some of the risk of fluctuating income, a crop-share lease may be the better alternative.

1. Crop Share Lease

The crop share lease is one of the most widely used types of farm rental arrangements. As its name implies, under the crop-share lease the landowner receives a share of the crops in return for contributing land to the farming operation. The actual share arrangement varies from area to area depending on the crops grown, soil quality and custom in the area.

The crop-share lease can be adapted to many different types of operations as long as the contributions of each party are appropriately evaluated. In the typical arrangement, the landowner furnishes land and buildings and shares the costs of certain inputs such as fertilizer, seed and pesticides. The tenant typically furnishes labor, machinery and equipment and fuel supplies. The tenant may also share costs for other inputs. The major problems facing the parties under this arrangement are to determine what share of the crops is a fair rent and what share of the costs will be paid by each party. In order for the agreement to be equitable, each party should contribute the same portion of annual investment as received in income.

The crop-share arrangement offers advantages and disadvantages to both the landlord and the tenant. For the landlord, the crop-share arrangement offers the opportunity to be relieved of labor and management responsibility, and at the same time to maintain an active interest in, and control over, the farming operation. At the same time, the landlord bears some of the costs associated with production and marketing but may also receive greater earnings potential than under a cash rental arrangement.

To the tenant the crop-share arrangement offers an opportunity to share some of the risks and some of the management responsibilities with the landlord and a chance to operate a farm with a lesser amount of capital and cash reserves than would otherwise be required. At the same time, the tenant may be subject to more control by the landlord and the arrangement may be less profitable to the tenant than under a cash lease, unless all contributions are fairly recognized and necessary adjustments are made on a regular basis.

2. Cash Lease

Cash lease arrangements are relatively simple. The tenant pays a set sum for the use of the farm. The tenants receives all of the income and often pays all of the expenses except for real property taxes, insurance and repairs directly associated with farm improvements and, of course, depreciation on the structures. The tenant has the major management responsibility. The landlord's involvement in management is limited to those areas stipulated in the agreement.

In the cash lease, the parties may agree, in advance, as to any restrictions on the use of the land and on the level of soil fertility that must be maintained by the tenant. Beyond this type of decision, the tenant usually has a free hand to plan and operate the business. The risks of the farming operation fall primarily upon the tenant. The landlord is assured of a steady income, is not concerned with variations in price or yield and does not have to be concerned with marketing choices. Obviously, the tenant stands to gain if a favorable market develops, and has the incentive to strive for high yields. The tenant may benefit from hir or her exercise of superior management ability, including decisions to adopt new technology.

One aspect of the cash lease which makes it attractive to

561

a retired landowner is that the cash lease reduces the likelihood of a reduction in social security benefits. Social security rules provide that a landlord who materially participates in a farming operation is considered to be self-employed and rentals are "earned income." For a landowner who is 62 to 70 years of age, earned income can result in a reduction in social security benefits if it exceeds the earnings limitation. This potential problem is avoided because the cash lease normally does not allow for material participation by the landlord.

The major difficulty in the cash lease arrangement is determining the amount of rent. Many rentals are based on the "going rate" in a particular community. However, this approach assumes that the current going rate is a fair reflection of the relative contributions of the parties. Two basic methods are used to determine an appropriate range for the rental amount. One is to estimate a maximum amount the tenant can afford to pay. This method estimates the tenant's return above all product costs, including a charge for labor and management. The difference between the tenant's estimated return and the production costs is an approximation of the maximum he or she could afford to pay to the landlord for use of the landlord's resources.

The second method approaches the problem from the landlord's side by determining the landlord's ownership costs as outlined earlier. The landlord's costs, including a fair return on his investment, give an indication of what the minimum rent might have to be in order to induce the landlord to enter the rental agreement. The costs include real estate taxes, insurance on buildings, repairs on productive improvements, depreciation on improvements and a return on the real estate investment.

Both of these approaches require information about costs, input values and expected yields and prices. Under either of these methods good farm records could provide useful information to determine an approximation of the rental rate. This approximation can serve as a basis for bargaining between the parties in order to determine a mutually satisfactory rental payment.

3. Flexible Cash Rent
Cash rent landlords do not share in the "windfall profits"

created by rapidly changing crop prices. At the same time, tenants' costs have risen rapidly and when crop prices drop or crop failure results, tenants find themselves in a position of possible net losses. Because of these fluctuations and uncertainties, the flexible cash rent arrangement has become more attractive to both landlords and tenants as a method of sharing price and production risks.

A flexible cash rental arrangement sets both a minimum and maximum rental for a given crop. A base rent is determined by procedures previously discussed. A base price and a base yield can be determined by historical records of "normal" years - perhaps on a five year average with adjustments for upward or downward trends. Adjustments can then be made for price variation or for price and yield variation by a simple calculation:

Adjustment for price variation:

$$\text{Current rent} = (\text{Base Rent}) \times \frac{\text{Current Price}}{\text{Base Price}}$$

Adjustment for price and yield variation:

$$\text{Current rent} = \text{Base Rent} \times \frac{\text{Current Yield}}{\text{Base Yield in Bushels}} \times \text{Current Price}$$

The "current price" to be used in such calculations must also be agreed upon by the parties in advance. This price may be the average cash grain price at the local elevator for a specific time period, a price in a particular month for a crop reporting district, a Board of Trade closing price for a particular date or any other method of estimating a fair current price agreeable to the parties.

4. Crop-Share-Cash Lease

A crop-share-cash lease is a variation of the crop-share lease in which the crop produced is shared according to the parties' agreement. In addition, a supplementary cash rental is paid to the landlord for land in hay or pasture and for use of farm buildings. Such an arrangement may be used when the parties wish to share in management decisions regarding the cropping program but where the tenant wishes to maintain sole management control of the livestock operation.

5. Farm Building Lease

Farm buildings may be rented specifically for the operation of an enterprise such as a poultry house for broiler production, a confinement swine feeding facility, or a dairy. Other farm buildings may be rented specifically for crop storage such as hay barns, grain bins, bulk airing barns, etc. And, when a crop-share cash lease is used the parties must arrive at a fair rental for farm buildings used by the tenant. In all these cases the building owner would like to be able to recover building ownership costs - interest, taxes, insurance, repairs and depreciation.

The tenant may not be willing to pay a rental amount for farm buildings which is sufficient to pay all of the ownership costs unless the building contributes directly to the farm operation. Even then, the tenant will be willing to pay no more than the value of the building in producing income. One approach to determine this is to calculate all other costs and subtract the total of all other costs from gross returns. The residual is the maximum the tenant could afford to pay and could be considered as the contribution of the buildings to the farming enterprise. Neither of these methods resolves the issue of how much rental is fair for the buildings but can serve as a basis for bargaining between the parties.

6. Pasture Leases

Rental rates for pasture are difficult to determine because the quality and quantity of production cannot be as easily measured as in the case of grain crops or even hay. In addition, stocking rates, fencing, water availability, grazing quality and fertility practices all have an impact on the value of the unit terms. These unit terms are (1) per head per month (2) per acre or (3) share of gain.

In arriving at a fair rental rate both the landowner's costs and the livestock owner's earnings from the pasture should

564

be considered. The landowner's costs include interest and taxes on the property plus repairs and depreciation on improvements such as fencing, buildings, handling facilities, etc. These ownership costs could serve as a basis for determining the amount of rent the landowner would desire.

The livestock owner's earnings can be the basis for determining the most the tenant can afford to pay. This is a residual calculation similar to that used for buildings. The tenants costs would include interest, taxes, insurance, death losses, purchasing, selling, hauling, labor, management and depreciation for cows or bulls. After returns are adjusted for all these items the residual can be attributed to gain due to the pasture.

Again, these calculations serve only as guidelines in arriving at a rate satisfactory to both parties.

C. Reasons For Having A Written Lease

Several of the advantages of having a written lease have already been stated. There are additional considerations as well. For example, a rental agreement that will not be performed within one year from the time of the making of the lease agreement must be in writing to be enforceable under the Statute of Frauds.[76] If a landowner and tenant orally agree to a two year lease of property, this agreement is unenforceable unless other legal arguments can be advanced which might require the parties to fulfill the two year agreement. Additionally, if a farm tenant decides to improve the leased land by erecting a building or sowing perennial crops, a written, long-term lease is necessary in order to protect the investment. Otherwise, the landowner may be able to terminate the agreement and benefit from the improvement.[77]

Any person in the possession of real property with the agreement of the owner is presumed to be a tenant at will. A tenant at will is one who has possession of the property by permission of the owner but without a fixed length of time under a lease term. When land is leased for one or more years and the tenant, with the consent of the landowner, continues to occupy the premises after the expiration of the agreed term, the tenant is deemed to be a tenant from year to year and holds the land for succeeding year-long lease periods until the landowner gives proper notice to terminate.[78]

Under all oral and written leases, except written leases which state a termination date, notice to terminate a farm tenancy must be given according to specific state law requirements. Any notice to terminate which does not comply with these requirements is inadequate to terminate the lease.[79] However, if the landowner and tenant, in a written lease signed by both, agree to a different notice of termination procedure and/or date, their agreement supercedes any state law regarding notice of termination.

A farm tenant who becomes a tenant from year to year by occupying the premises after the expiration of the term fixed in a written lease is not subject to notice of termination statutes. If a farm tenant becomes a tenant from year to year, the notice of termination of the tenancy must fix the termination to take place on the same day and month as was specified in the original lease under which the tenant first occupied the premises.[80]

In the event the landowner has given proper termination notice and the tenant, prior to receiving the notice, has tilled, applied or furnished fertilizers, herbicides, or pest control substances and has not planted the ground, in some states the landowner must pay the tenant for the fair and reasonable value of the services furnished. This value includes the cost of the fertilizers, herbicides, and/or pest control substances applied to the land.[81] In other states the tenant has no special rights in the absence of agreement or custom to the contrary.[82]

When the day of termination of the tenancy is stated in a written contract, a notice to vacate the premises is not necessary. The lease automatically terminates on the date stated in the lease. In some states both the landowner and tenant are required to deliver notice of termination when either is ending the lease. Other statutes may provide for notice to the tenant but not the landlord.[83]

The best way to serve notice of termination is normally by registered mail because the tenant must sign a receipt for the notice. If notice is given by mail, it must be done by registered or certified mail. Where service is by registered mail, it is important that the landowner keep the return receipt for proof of notice of termination.

566

D. Assignment of Farmland Leases

In most states a tenant may transfer or assign the lease to another person without the written consent of the landowner.[84] However, in some states assignment is permitted only if the lease is for more than two years.[85] When a tenant properly assigns his lease, the new tenant has the same legal rights as the prior tenant.

The tenant does not have to agree to become the tenant of a new landowner when the former landowner sells the property.[86] If the tenant has paid rent to the previous landowner before receiving notice of the sale, the tenant is not required to pay the new landowner for the same rent period. The tenant must pay rent to the landowner and not some other party unless the landowner has consented to the arrangement or a court has ordered payment to be made to another.[87]

If someone legally subleases property from a tenant, the person subleasing has the same rights and remedies against the landowner as they have against the original tenant.[88] Furthermore, a new landowner who purchases the property has the same rights against the tenant as the original landowner.[89] Also, a landowner, after selling leased property, may sue a tenant who abandoned the property before the sale for past due rent.[90]

E. Unpaid Rent and Ownership of Crops

If a tenant neglects or refuses to pay rent when due, the landowner may terminate the lease after giving written notice.[91] If a tenant is vacating or intending to vacate the premises, the landowner may get a court order and attach or seize the tenant's property for the rent, whether or not it is due.

In most states any rent due on farmland is an automatic lien or encumbrance on the crops growing or harvested off the leased premises.[92] This lien is superior to all other secured interests against the crops. It attaches to the entire crop and the landowner has a right to possession of the crop until the rent is paid.[93] The landowner should not enter the property and take the crop, but rather should seek a court order for possession. This encumbrance is enforceable against a purchaser of a crop who has actual or constructive notice of the lien.[94]

567

<u>Example:</u>
> Joe Tenant sells grain to the local elevator and then
> leaves for Las Vegas where he gambles his money away.
> When Joe returns, Bob Landowner asks for his rent
> money for the farmland. If the elevator that purchased
> the grain knew or should have known that the grain was
> from rented ground, Bob Landowner can force the
> elevator to pay him the rent that is due. Since the
> elevator knew that the grain was from rented ground,
> they bought the grain from Joe subject to any lien the
> landowner had on the grain for past due rent.

Thus, if a landowner suspects trouble in collecting rent
from the tenant it is wise to contact the area elevators by letter
and inform them of the lien and interest in grain from land
operated by a particular farmer. On the other hand, for the
grain buyer to be fully protected he should ask the landowner
to sign a written consent removing the landowner's lien and
allowing the tenant to sell the crop.

When rent is payable in a share of the crop, the
landowner is deemed to be the owner of that share of the crop.
If the tenant refuses to deliver the share owed to the
landowner, the landowner may enter upon the leased land and
take possession of his or her proportion of the crop.[95] The
landowner in a share crop arrangement has a distinct interest in
the crop from the time it is planted. However, absent an
agreement to the contrary, that interest does not become full
and complete until the crop matures.[96] This means that a
landowner cannot enter the premises and take his or her share
of a crop while it is still growing.

Rent is a lien only on the crop growing or harvested
from the rented ground. "Crop" has been defined as any
product of the soil that is grown and raised annually and that is
gathered during a single season.[97]

F. <u>Use of Leased Property</u>

Since a lease is a contract for the exclusive possession of
land for a definite period, the landowner cannot use the land
for his or her own purposes while it is leased. For example,
the landowner cannot hunt on the leased ground without the

permission of the tenant unless the landowner retained these rights in the written lease. A landowner may enter the premises to:

1) make reasonable inspections;
2) do repairs and/or installations;
3) show the premises to prospective buyers;
4) collect rent, and;
5) deliver a notice to terminate the tenancy.[98]

If mineral exploration or oil and gas drilling is to be pursued by the landowner, the written lease should contain a provision allowing the landowner or his agents and employees to enter and use the land for mineral exploration or drilling.

G.   Responsibility For Noxious Weed Control
State law often provides that certain weeds are noxious and that it is the duty of landowners and tenants to control the spread of, and eradicate, these weeds on lands they own or supervise. The noxious weeds typically are: 1) kudzu, 2) field bindweed, 3) Russian knapweed, 4) hoary cress, 5) Canada thistle, 6) quackgrass, 7) leafy spurge, 8) burragweed, 9) pignut, 10) musk (nodding) thistle, 11) Johnson grass, and 12) multiflora rose.[99]

It is often necessary to determine whether the landowner or the tenant, respectively, is responsible for noxious weed control? If there is no provision in the lease, those who own the land or supervise the use of the land have a duty to control noxious weeds. Thus, both the landowner and the tenant are responsible for noxious weed control. This is because, during the term of the lease, the tenant usually has exclusive supervision of the land. If noxious weeds are not properly controlled, the county has the authority to enter upon the infested land, perform the necessary treatment and charge the landowner for the services. The cost of the treatment is not charged against the tenant. If the county's cost for treatment is not paid it becomes a lien against the land. Therefore, both landowner and tenant are implicated in noxious weed control.

H.   Removal of Fixtures and Compensation for Improvements
Generally, a tenant who permanently improves the

leased property is not entitled to remove improvements when the lease terminates. Such improvements by the tenant would include constructing permanent buildings, installing terraces and improving existing structures. Furthermore, the tenant will not be entitled to reimbursement for expenditures on improvements unless this is specifically provided for in the lease agreement.[100]

I.   Death of Landowner or Tenant
If either the landowner or tenant dies while a farm lease is in effect, the decedent's executor or administrator is required to comply with the terms of the lease. For example, an administrator of the tenant's estate may be held responsible for the payment of rent under a long-term lease previously signed by the deceased tenant.[101]

If a landowner has a life estate interest in land, the holder of the life estate can only grant a lease for as long as he or she lives. Any lease of land held in a life estate terminates on the death of the life estate holder. However, a tenant can enter the land to cultivate and harvest crops planted before the owner's death.[102] In this situation, the estate of the life estate holder will receive the landowner's share of the crop.

Example:
> Bertha, an elderly woman with three children, has a life estate in a 160-acre farm. Her oldest son, Billy Bob has the remaining interest in the property. The land is leased to Clyde. Bertha dies after the crops are planted but before they are harvested. Her will states that all her property is to be divided equally between the three children. Immediately upon her death, the 160-acre farm belongs to Billy Bob, as the owner of the remainder interest. However, since the crops were planted before her death, the landowner's share will become part of her estate and be divided equally between the heirs. The crop does not follow the land.

J.   Elements of a Good Lease
A thorough farmland lease would cover the following topics:
1.   names of the parties involved;

2. the date the lease agreement is entered into;
3. accurate description of the property being rented, preferably a legal description;
4. beginning and ending dates of the lease;
5. how and when the "rent" is to be paid;
   a) Example: "Tenant will deliver Landowner's share of the crop to the Sunflower Elevator within five days after it is harvested;"
6. the amount of rent to be paid;
7. limitations on the use of the land;
   a) Example: "Tenant must employ contour farming practices and honor all soil conservation projects in use;"
8. the rights of the landowner to enter the leased premises;
9. who decides whether to participate in government farm programs;
10. who decides what is to be planted;
11. what each party is to furnish;
    a) Examples: "Landowner will allow tenant unlimited use of irrigation wells on the premises." "Landowner will pay for one-third (1/3) of the chemical cost, tenant will pay two-thirds (2/3);"
12. who is responsible for accidents;
13. who has hunting rights;
14. who gets to use the buildings;
15. who insures the buildings;
16. what happens in case of the sale of the premises;
17. if tenant makes permanent improvements, how is he or she to be compensated;
18. what improvements made by the tenant will be removable;
19. who is responsible for noxious weed control;
20. tenant must farm in a workmanlike manner;
21. if a dispute arises about the terms of the lease, how is the conflict settled;
22. maximum number of livestock which can be placed in a particular pasture;
23. renewal of the lease;
24. how amendments or alternations to the lease are

made;
25. the lease does not create a partnership between landowner and tenant;
26. allowing or prohibiting subleasing;
27. who pays for damages to the land or improvements;
28. who pays for fencing materials and labor if needed;
29. who pays for liming if needed;
30. who decides if capital improvements are necessary and who pays for them;
31. what happens if either party does not perform under the contract;
   a) Example: "If either landowner or tenant fails to perform their duties under this contract for a period of 30 days, then the injured party, at their option, may terminate the lease;"
32. whether Federal Crop Insurance to be used;
33. what happens in case of financial failure and/or bankruptcy to either party; and
34. notarized signature of the parties and their spouses.

K. Taxation and Leasing Arrangements

Generally, most farmers report net farm profit as "self-employment income" for tax purposes. Self-employment income normally would not include rental income from farm real estate or personal property which is leased along with the farm real estate.[103] Under some circumstances, the landlord participates in the operation. In that case, the landowner may be subject to tax as a self-employed individual. The key in these cases is the "material participation" test applied to the landowner. Material participation may come about in a variety of ways. An agreement which specifies participation by the landlord will serve as evidence that the income is self-employment income. In cases where there is no agreement for the landlord to participate, but the landlord does, in fact, materially participate in the production of agricultural products, the income received may be considered self-employment income. This actual participation may be in the form of physical labor or by a management contribution. The factors that are involved in determining whether or not a landlord materially participates in the operation include the actual amount of work done, the participation in management decisions, the tools, equipment, and livestock furnished, and production expenses advanced, among others.[104]

In those situations where self-employment income is involved, it is subject to tax, and also generates social security benefits. Therefore, there may be circumstances under which an owner will wish to show material participation in order to qualify for social security benefits at a later date.

In the converse situation, an individual may wish to avoid material participation in order not to reduce current social security benefits. Often a direct lease agreement will provide that the decision making in the operation is left to the tenant. However, if the landowner continues to be involved and renders substantial services to the farming operation, his or her income may be considered as self-employment income and serve to reduce current social security benefits. Up to age 70, any farmer who draws above a statutory maximum of earned income will incur the possibility of reduced social security benefits. The test in this case is "substantial services rendered in self-employment."[105] This test is slightly different than the "material participation" test used to determine whether or not the income is subject to self-employment tax. Substantial services arise only from the actual participation by the landlord and cannot occur through the acts of an agent. Basically, the Social Security Administration will look at the nature of the services rendered and the amount of time devoted to the entire operation. They will also compare the amount of work the individual landowner is contributing compared to the amount contributed prior to retirement in order to determine whether or not there has been a substantial change. These problems emphasize the benefit of having a carefully drawn and effective agreement which limits the activities of the landowner. In cases where it is effectively done, the landowner may be able to avoid taxation under self-employment and at the same time receive full social security benefits.

The tax treatment of leasing arrangements is significantly affected by "passive loss" rules of the 1986 Tax Reform Act. Under these rules deductions from passive trade or business activities are limited to the income attributable to those activities and may not be deducted against other income.

Credits are limited to the taxes attributable to passive activities. Rental activity is considered a "passive activity," but under the Act up to $25,000 of passive activity losses from rental activity (exceeding rental income) may be deducted against other income.[106]

An "active management" test is applied to determine if the limits of the act are applicable to a particular rental situation. This "active management" test is roughly the equivalent of "material participation" and there are indications that the Internal Revenue Service will look for similar activity to determine if the test has been met. If an activity involves active management (material participation) then the passive loss rules would not be applicable. However, the individuals would be subject to the self employment tax and a possible reduction in social security benefits. A purely cash lease, on the other hand, would not involve material participation by the landlord. In such cases the $25,000 limit on passive losses (above rental income) would be applicable.[107]

VI.   Tax Planning and Form of Business Organization
Changes in tax rates made in the Tax Reform Act of 1986 make the rates for a regular corporation ("Subchapter C") potentially higher than for individuals or for operations taxed under Subchapter S or for partnerships. In the past regular corporate tax rates have often been lower. The risk of "double taxation" of dividends could be reduced by delaying payments as dividends and allowing some planning by payment of salaries or rental payments to individuals involved in the business. However, since the new corporate tax rates are potentially higher than the individual rates (15%, 28%, 33%, and 28% brackets) the splitting of income must be planned more carefully if the taxable income is to be taxed at the lowest possible rates. The use of multiple corporations to gain the advantage of lower rates is also limited by rules which may result in their treatment as a single entity for tax purposes.[108]

Another change in the tax law makes the farm corporation less attractive as a vehicle for business operation as well. This change concerns the taxation of distributions of appreciated property by a corporation to its shareholders. These rules generally treat such distributions as a sale of the property to the shareholders for fair market value. Therefore, the distribution may result in taxable gain to the corporation to the extent the fair market value of the property exceeds the corporation's tax basis in the property. In addition, the same distribution may be taxed to the shareholder either as a dividend or as gain if the fair market value of the property exceeds the shareholder's basis in stock. This increases the potential tax consequences of transferring property out of a corporation, even at the time of liquidation.[109]

Another problem area involves getting property into the corporation at formation. It is generally easier to get property into a partnership without tax consequences than into either a C or S corporation. Special problems arise if property is transferred in exchange for services or if property is transferred subject to indebtedness. While the problems are similar if a partnership is being formed, the rules are considerably more complicated if the corporate form is used. The "control" requirement (80% of the combined voting power of all classes of stock and 80% of the total of all shares must be in the hands of the same shareholders who contributed the property) for corporations is somewhat restrictive but does not exist for partnerships.[110]

Because of these problems, special effort may be necessary to plan a structure which allows for the leasing of property to a corporation for the purpose of avoiding the potentially adverse tax consequences of getting property into and out of the corporation. Rental payments (bona fide) would be deductible to the corporation and, of course, taxable to the lessor. Leasing arrangements may also be used in combination with partnerships to achieve other objectives since the tax consequences are not of particular concern.

VII. Organizing The Farm Business to Comply With Farm
      Program Payment Limitations
The general requirements for entitlement to separate program payments under the payment limitation provisions are that the individual or entity qualify as a separate "person" and that "person" be "actively engaged in farming" with respect to the particular farming operation.[111] To be "actively engaged in farming" generally requires a significant contribution of capital,

equipment, land, or a combination thereof, <u>and</u> a significant contribution of active personal labor or active personal manage or a combination of both.[112] However, special rules, may make it easier for a lessor and lessee to separately qualify.

It is likely that special consideration will be given to leasing arrangements in order to qualify both the lessor and lessee as separately entitled to program payments. It may also be possible to structure lease arrangements so as to be consistent with some of the likely tax goals, such as leasing to a corporation rather than transferring ownership to the corporation.

Separate requirements are imposed on a lessor and lessee in order to qualify for program payments. If both lessor and lessee meet the requirements, they should separately qualify for such payments.

The special landowner rule[113] would seem to make it relatively easy to insure that a landowner-lessor "person" is "actively engaged in farming" so as to qualify for program payments. As long as a landowner-lessor "person" receives rentals based on production or the operation's operating results, and satisfies the commensurate profits/losses and at risk tests, the landowner-lessor should be considered as "actively engaged in farming" so as to qualify for program payments. On the other hand, if the landlord receives a cash rent or a crop share guaranteed as to amount, the landlord would not be considered as actively engaged in farming under the special landowner rule.[114] Even if the landowner-lessor qualifies for program payments, the lessee must meet separate requirements if the lessee is to qualify for program payments separately from the landowner-lessor.

As to the landowner-lessor, the special landowner rule (where rents are based on production) means that a landowner should not have to provide significant active personal management and/or labor in order to qualify for program payments. A production lease could therefore be structured so as to avoid "material participation" on the part of the landowner-lessor. This could render the rentals payment as self-employment income for self-employment tax purposes.[115]

This special landowner rule could apply to a sole owner as well as multiple owners who have undivided interests in the land.[116] Thus, for example, if land owned by two (or more) tenants in common were leased on a crop-share basis, each tenant in common could be considered as actively engaged in farming and (assuming each qualified as a separate "person") separately qualify for program payments.

If the land is owned by a general partnership-lessor, with rent based on production, the partnership would not separately qualify for program payments since it is not a separate "person". However, individual partners qualifying as "persons" could be separately considered as actively engaged in farming under the landowner rule if the partnership agreement provides that the partners will receive an interest in the land on dissolution of the partnership.[117]

If the landowner-lessor is a limited partnership, corporation (whether Subchapter "C" or "S"), irrevocable trust, or estate, the entity itself could qualify as the "person" entitled to program payments under the special landowner rule. This at least leaves open the possibility that the individual partners, shareholders, or beneficiaries might separately qualify for program payments with respect to other farming operations.

The program payment restrictions make the corporate form less attractive since an individual is restricted to an interest in no more than three such entities (the individual plus two entities or three separate entities). The difficulty of getting land into and out of the corporation without adverse tax consequences coupled with the potentially higher tax rates generally make the Subchapter C corporation an unattractive vehicle, from a tax standpoint, to act as a landowner-lessor. Other significant tax concerns would include the possibility of a personal holding company tax or an accumulated earnings tax at the corporate level in addition to the regular income tax.

As a business operating entity the Subchapter S corporation may have some appeal but only as an operator - not as landowner. If it is used it may lease land from the individual landowners, all of which may be considered to be actively engaged in farming if the lease agreement is on a crop share lease basis (not cash or guaranteed share as to amount of the crop.) Partnerships offer the same appeal and they are separately provided for in the payment limitation regulations. Properly designed, the Subchapter S corporation itself could

577

achieve separate person status unlike a partnership. But, because of the tax implications the Subchapter S corporation will, no doubt, be used most often for operating purposes - not landholding.

If used for operating reasons the Subchapter S corporation will likely lease land from the individuals who hold the ownership interest in the land. From a review of both the new tax provisions and the farm program payment rules, it can be concluded that crop share leasing arrangements will likely become more popular in structuring entities to comply with both tax rules and farm program payment limitations.

FOOTNOTES

1. Uniform Partnership Act 6(1) (hereinafter "UPA").

2. UPA §§ 9(3), 18, 19, 22(2), 25(2), 37, 40, 42.

3. See, e.g., Lee v. Slovak, 81 App. Div. 2d 98, 440 N.Y.S.2d 358 (1981); Rizzo v. Rizzo, 3 Ill. App. 291, 120 N.E.2d 546 (1954).

4. See, e.g., Tex-Co Grain Co. v. Happy Wheat Growers, Inc. 542 S.W.2d 934 (Tex. Civ. App. 1976).

5. Adams v. United States, 328 F. Supp. 228 (D. Neb. 1971).

6. See, Falker v. Falker, 24 Mich. App. 633, 180 N.W.2d 491 (1970).

7. Roach v. Rector, 93 Ark. 521, 123 S.W.2d 399 (1909).

8. UPA § 7(2),(3),(4)(b).

9. UPA § 7(4)(b).

10. UPA § 15.

11. UPA § 8.

12. UPA § 25(2)(a).

13. UPA § 29(2)(b).

14. UPA § 26.

15. UPA § 27.

16. UPA § 28.

17. UPA § 25(d).

18. UPA § 10.

19. UPA § 9.

20. UPA § 9(1).

21. UPA § 13, 14.

22. UPA § 15.

23. UPA § 12.

24. UPA § 18(a).

25. UPA § 18 (b).

26. UPA § 18(c).

27. UPA § 18(e).

28. UPA § 18(f).

29. UPA § 18(g).

30. UPA § 18(h).

31. UPA § 19.

32. UPA § 20.

33. UPA § 21.

34. UPA § 22.

35. Form 1065, Treas. Reg. 1, 761-2(b)(2).

36. IRC § 702.

37. Treas. Reg. § 1.704-1(b)(2).

38. David A. Foxman, 41 T.C. 535 (1964) aff'd 352 F.2d 466 (3rd Cir. 1965).

39. UPA § 31.

40. UPA § 40(b).

41. See Bock, "Formalizing the Farm Partnership, 34 Neb. L. Rev. 558 (1975).

42. Most states have enacted the Uniform Limited Partnership Act (hereinafter ULPA) on the Revised Uniform Limited Partnership Act (RULPA).

43. ULPA § 1; RULPA § 101.

44. ULPA § 17(1)(a); RULPA § 502(a).

45. ULPA § 7; RULPA § 303.

46. ULPA § 2; RULPA § 201. The ULPA also permits local filing.

47. RULPA § 201. A similar certificate is required under the Uniform Limited Partnership Act. See ULPA § 2.

48. ULPA § 2; RULPA § 102, 103.

49. Treas. Reg. § 301.7701-3(b).

50. Larson v. Comms., 66 T.C. 159 (1976); Treas. Reg. § 301.7701-2.

51. IRC § 465.

52. IRC § 469.

53. ULPA § 20; RULPA § 801.

54. See, e.g., K.S.A. § 17-6002.

55. These nine are Iowa, Kansas, Minnesota, Missouri, Nebraska, North Dakota, Oklahoma, South Dakota and Wisconsin. See Morrison, "State Corporate Farm Legislation" 7 Toledo L.Rev. 961 (1976).

56. K.S.A. § 17-5904.

57. K.S.A. § 17-5903(i).

58. K.S.A. § 17-5903(j).

59. See Smart and Hoberg, Corporate Farming in the Anti-Corporate Farming States, National Center for Agricultural Law Research and Information (1989).

60. I.R.C. § 1361-1379.

61. I.R.C. § 1373, 1374, 1375.

62. I.R.C. § 1361.

63. I.R.C. § 1362.

64. I.R.C. § 11.

65. I.R.C. § 316.

66. I.R.C. § 11.

67. I.R.C. § 531-537.

68. I.R.C. § 351.

69. I.R.C. § 368.

70. I.R.C. § 357(c).

71. I.R.C. § 357.

72. I.R.C. § 311(b), 336(a).

73. See Johnson v. Mantooth, 108 Ark. 36, 1567 S.W. 448 (1913); Campbell v. Anderson, 189 Ark. 671, 74 S.W.2d 782 (1934).

74. Roach v. Rector, 93 Ark. 521, 123 S.W. 399 (1909).

75. These are described in more detail in Looney, "Legal and Economic Considerations in Drafting Arkansas Farm Leases" 39 Ark. L.Rev. 395 (1981).

76. See, e.g., Ark. Code Ann. § 4-59-102.

77. National Housewares Corp. v. Trakin, 247 Ark. 1, 444 S.W.2d 68 (1969); Gocio v. Day, 51 Ark. 46, 9 S.W. 433 (1888).

78. See, Looney, 35 Ark. L.Rev. 395 (1981) at 422-431 and cases cited therein.

79. See, e.g., Ark. Code Ann. § 18-16-105.

80. Felder v. Hall Bros. Co., 151 Ark. 182, 235 S.W. 789 (1921); K.S.A. § 58-2506.

81. See, K.S.A. § 58-2506A.

82. See, Huckaby v. Walker, 141 Ark. 477, 217 S.W. 481 (1920).

83. Smith v. Pritchett, 168 Md. 347, 178 A.113 (1935).

84. Keith v. McGregor, 163 Ark. 203, 259 S.W. 725 (1924).

85. K.S.A. § 58-2511.

86. K.S.A. § 58-2513.

87. K.S.A. § 58-2514.

88. K.S.A. § 58-2515.

89. K.S.A. § 58-2516.

90. Erickson v. O'Leary, 127 Kan. 12 (1929).

91. K.S.A. § 58-2507.

92. See, e.g., K.S.A. § 58-2524.

93. Dale Wessley and Co. v. Taylor, 63 Kan. 674 (1901).

94. Mailzer v. Swan, 75 Kan. 496 (1907).

95. Finley v. McClure, 222 Kan. 637 (1977).

96. Wyandt v. Merrill, 107 Kan. 661 (1920).

97. Kennedy v. Spalding, 143 Kan. 67 (1935).

98. See, e.g., Sprout v. Gilbert, 226 Or. 392, 359 P.2d 543 (1961); Flanders v. New Hampshire Savings Bank, 90 N.H. 285, 7 A.2d 223 (1939).

99. See, e.g., K.S.A. § 2-1301-1332.

100. Choate v. Kimbell, 56 Ark. 52, 19 S.W. 108 (1892).

101. In re Speare's Estate, 349 Pa. 76, 36 A.2d 489 (1944); Jewell v. MacFarland, 41 Kan. 40 (1935).

102. Spreck v. Beach, 188 Kan. 296 (1961); Finley v. McClure, 222 Kan. 637 (1977).

103. 42 U.S.C. § 411(a).

104. O'Byrne and Davenport, Farm Income Tax Manual (1988) § 1109.

105. Treas. Reg. § 404.447(a).

106. I.R.C. § 469(i).

107. I.R.C. § 469(i).

108. See I.R.C. § 1561.

109. I.R.C. § 311(b), 336(a).

110. I.R.C. § 351(a), 368(c).

111. Pub. L. No. 100-203, § 1302, 101 Stat. 1330 (1987) 7 U.S.C. § 1308.

112. 7 C.F.R. § 1497.7.

113. 7 C.F.R. § 1497.13.

114. 7 U.S.C. § 1308-1(b)(4)(A).

115. I.R.C. § 1402(a)(1).

116. 7 C.F.R. § 1497.13.

117. 7 C.F.R. § 1497.13.

CHAPTER 16
LIABILITY WITH RESPECT TO LAND USE

I. Introduction

Farmers are faced with a variety of potential liability claims which arise out of the use of their farmland. This includes use by the farmer and use by others. These claims may involve damage to the property of others arising from activities conducted on the farmer's land, such as the misapplication of chemical herbicides or pesticides. Other common forms of liability involve claims of nuisance or claims of personal injuries to trespassers, licensees or invitees who are present on the farmland. Claims may also involve the action of a landowner with regard to trespassing animals or involve damage caused by trespassing animals which escape from a farmer's property. While these claims will ordinarily be resolved by using traditional principles of common law, special statutory provisions may also affect the degree of liability that may be imposed, or may restrict liability claims in other significant ways.

II. Nuisance

The legal principle which underlies the doctrine of nuisance is that one must use property in a manner which does not injure the property of another, or impair its use. Certain types of farming operations such as feed lots generate offensive odors. Other farming operations may be dusty or noisy, or may involve the use of machinery or structures that are unattractive to neighbors. Agriculturally-related industries also contribute to the problem. For example, rendering plants emit odors, feed mills are noisy and dusty, and other establishments pose specific traffic hazards.

Land development that is incompatible with farming is often permitted, and even encouraged, in agricultural areas. Ironically, when the more established farming operations are found to be incompatible with the new non-farming neighbors, the farming operation may be alleged to be a nuisance.

A precise definition of nuisance is difficult to formulate. For example, the Kansas Supreme Court in the case of <u>Wilburn</u>

<u>v. Boeing Airplane Co.,</u>[1] observed that:

> Briefly stated, the word "nuisance", while perhaps incapable of precise definition, generally is held to be something which interferes with the rights of citizens, whether in person, property, or enjoyment of property or comfort, and also has been held to mean an annoyance, and that which annoys or causes trouble or vexation, that which is offensive or noxious, or anything that works hurt, inconvenience or damage.[2]

As the concept of nuisance is applied, it operates as a restriction on the right of an owner to make use of his or her own property in any way they please. The objective of nuisance law is to prevent the injury that results to another person's enjoyment of their own land from an unreasonable, unwarranted or unlawful use by a person of his or her own property. In other words, a nuisance is created when a person's use of their land interferes with another person's use of their own land. The law will assess damages for material annoyance, inconvenience, discomfort or hurt that is caused by these activities. Because of the potential for farming operations to be considered nuisances by persons who are engaged in non-farm activities in farm areas, many states have adopted so-called "right to farm" statutes. These statutes limit the circumstances under which a farm operation may be considered a nuisance. The statutes tend to be of four basic types:

1. Those which establish a specific time after which an agricultural operation may be declared a nuisance because of changed conditions within the locality;
2. Those which create a presumption that the operation is not a nuisance;
3. Those which exclude specific, but not all, agricultural operations from nuisance suits; and
4. Those which provide protection against only certain types of nuisance claims.[3]

The most widely-used statute appears to be the first type. According to this approach, courts cannot hold that a farming operation is a nuisance if it finds that (a) the operation was not a nuisance when it began; (b) the only basis for the nuisance claim is the changed conditions within the locality surrounding the farm; (c) the farming operation was in existence for at least a year before the lawsuit was filed; (d) the alleged nuisance did not result from negligent or improper activities on the farm; and (e) the alleged nuisance does not involve water pollution or flooding.

Statutes of the second type appear to be the next most popular. According to this approach, there is a presumption that no nuisance exists if the farming operation is conducted according to generally-accepted agricultural practices, and was established prior to the existence of the surrounding non-farming activities. These statutes do not protect the farm operator from claims that relate to aspects of the farming operation that are adverse to public health and safety.

The significant difference between these first two approaches is that the second type merely creates a rebuttable presumption of the reasonableness of the operation, whereas the first type actually bars the nuisance litigation on a statute of limitations basis. It may be argued that the second type does not give farming operations much more protection than they would receive under the common law. However, these statutes articulate a number of specific factors, not addressed in the common law, that are relevant to the question of whether the farming operation is actually a nuisance. These statutes also suggest that only public health and safety interests can negate the presumption that the farm activity is reasonable and therefore not a nuisance. Further, the statutes indicate a strong public policy interest in protecting the existence of agricultural operations. In a close case, this interest may promote a liberal application of the statute.

It should be noted that not all farms qualify for this statutory protection. In other words, a "farming operation" must meet a specific statutory definition. The statutes typically define agricultural activity as the "growing or raising of horticultural and agricultural crops, hay, poultry and livestock, and livestock, poultry and dairy products for commercial purposes".[4] Similarly, farmland is normally defined as land devoted primarily to an agricultural activity.[5]

It should also be noted that even though right-to-farm statutes may limit a farmer's civil liability, they do not eliminate criminal liability. For example, it is a criminal offense to maintain a public nuisance. According to case law, certain agricultural activities may constitute a public nuisance.[6]

Most farm nuisance litigation has involved confined animal feeding operations, commonly known as "feedlots". However, there are relatively few cases in which feedlot operations have been held to be nuisances. In part, this is probably an indication that the majority of feedlots are deliberately located in isolated areas so that their adverse affects are minimized. Furthermore, there seems to be a prevalent court attitude that persons who locate in an agricultural area must accept the disadvantages associated with living in that particular setting. According to this view, the farming activity must have impacts beyond those reasonably expected in rural areas. Finally, there is specific statutory nuisance protection for feedlots in some states. This is separate and distinct from the "right to farm" statutes.

For example, the Kansas legislature has created a presumption that feedlots will not be considered a nuisance if certain basic requirements are met by feedlot operators. These requirements are that the feedlot:

1) have reasonable methods for the disposal of animal excrements;
2) have chemical and scientific control procedures for the prevention and eradication of pests;
3) have adequate drainage to control pollution of streams and lakes;
4) have adequate veterinarian services to detect, control and eliminate livestock diseases;
5) have available for use at all times the mechanical means for scraping, cleaning and grading the feedlot premises;
6) provide weather-resistant aprons adjacent to feed bunks, water tanks and feeding devices; and
7) conduct the operation in conformity with established practices in the industry, with regulations promulgated by the state livestock sanitary commissioner, and with statutory guidelines.[7]

The Kansas statute specifically provides that when a feedlot is operated in compliance with these standards there is prima facie evidence that a nuisance does not exist.

III.   Misapplication of Agricultural Chemicals
Agricultural chemicals are widely-used for the control of weeds, insects, rodents and other pests that damage farm crops. Arguably, the bounty of United States' agricultural production would not be possible without the use of these potent chemicals. However, pesticides (including herbicides) may cause harm if their effects reach land areas other than their targeted destinations. For instance, if a pesticide which is designed for application to pastures for weed control "drifts" to a neighbor's cotton field, the cotton may be destroyed.

A.   Rights and Responsibilities of the Farmer Applicator
The farmer must exercise "reasonable precautions" in the application of farm chemicals or else be liable for damages. While a farmer has a right to use dusts or sprays upon his or her land for the control of pests, weeds, insects, etc., liability may result to adjoining owners, and also to more distant owners, for injuries which they suffer as the result of negligent chemical application(s).[8] A number of factors must be considered in determining whether a farmer has used due care in his or her chemical application. Several of these factors are: "1) weather conditions present; 2) the degree and direction of the wind at and after the time the chemicals are applied; 3) whether the chemical spreader was shut off at the end of the field; 4) the concentration of the chemical applied; and 5) how close to adjacent land is the chemical applied".[9]

A few states have imposed strict liability (liability without fault) on farmer-applicators whose chemicals have caused damage to others.[10] A more typical approach is that exemplified by the Kansas Supreme Court in Binder v. Perkins.[11] In Binder, the court required applicators to exercise "a high degree of care, not liability without fault," in preventing chemical pesticides from causing damage to others. Terms such as "high degree of care" and "reasonable precautions" are not easily defined. As a result, courts have wide latitude in determining whether a farmer-applicator should be held liable for damages. One legal scholar found that, except under unusual circumstances, the injured plaintiff will almost always win if the following two factors can be established:

1) the drifted or misapplied chemical caused injury, and
2) the plaintiff was damaged.[12]

For instance, in states where the plaintiff must prove some degree of negligence before they can recover, defendants have been held liable for dusting in adverse weather described as a light wind, light breeze, and breeze.[13] Other factors which have also been identified as constituting negligence include the improper selection, mixing or application of a pesticide, the use of defective or improperly adjusted sprayer heads, the failure to notify adjoining landowners in advance of the spraying and the dropping of pesticide on adjacent property.[14]

B.   Liability for the Actions of an Individual Hired to Apply Pesticides

When a third party is hired by a farmer to apply a pesticide and it causes damage to a neighbor, courts are split on the issue of which party may be held liable. Under those circumstances consideration will be given to whether the person applying the pesticide is an independent contractor or an employee of the farmer. If the applicator is an employee of the farmer, the farmer-employer is generally liable for the actions of the employee. If the applicator is an independent contractor, the farmer is normally not held liable for damages caused by the negligent action(s) of the independent contractor. However, a major exception to this rule exists. If the activity is inherently or abnormally dangerous, the farmer-employer may be held liable for damages caused by the independent contractor. For example, the majority of courts which have considered this issue have ruled that aerial chemical crop dusting is abnormally dangerous. Thus, the farmer may be held responsible for damages caused by the negligence of an independent aerial chemical applicator.[15]

However, even in those jurisdictions which take the minority view that the application of chemical pesticides is not inherently or abnormally dangerous, a situation could arise where a particularly potent chemical is applied and therefore the activity is deemed to be abnormally dangerous. This would result in the applicator and the farmer being held jointly liable for the resulting damages. Simply put, a farmer may not delegate the work of spraying a crop with poisonous insecticides to an independent contractor and automatically avoid liability for those actions.[16]

Commercial pesticide applicators in some states are required to obtain and maintain either a surety bond or liability insurance to cover damages they might cause.[17] As a practical matter, a landowner whose property is damaged will probably seek to collect under the bond or insurance policy before seeking compensation from the employer-farmer.

IV. Responsibilities to Farm Visitors

The extent of the farm landowner's duty to protect persons who enter the land from injury is an important concern. This is true whether those persons are trespassers, business visitors, social guests or sportsmen. In most states, the standard for determining legal liability to the injured party depends on whether the visitor is a trespasser, licensee (examples - social guest or hunter with permission) or invitee (example - farm employee), and whether the farmer has undertaken sufficient measures to protect the visitor from injury. The legal status of a particular visitor determines the standard of care that the farmer must use to protect the visitor and the standard of liability which will be imposed upon the failure to use the proper care.

An invitee is a person who is present on another's property through the invitation of the owner for some kind of business purpose.[18] A licensee is a person who is privileged to enter or remain on another's land by virtue of the express or implied consent of the owner.[19] In contrast to invitees and licensees, trespassers are persons who enter or remain upon the land or premises in the possession of another without the possessor's consent.[20] Different degrees of care and responsibility are owed to visitors based on whether they are an invitee, a licensee, or a trespasser, respectively.

A. Duty to Invitees

The standard of care owed to a visitor is directly related to the economic benefit that a farmer receives by the visitor's presence. The greater the benefits, the more the farmer must do to protect the visitor from harm. Thus, the highest degree of care is owed to an invitee. This is because an invitee is a person who is permitted or invited to enter or remain on the farmer's land for a business purpose which benefits the farmer. Some examples of an invitee are: 1) a person who comes to the farm to purchase milk or eggs; 2) a cattle buyer coming to the farm to buy cattle; and 3) an employee. More specific examples of situations in which persons have been held to be invitees include: 1) a visitor who was requested to help a farmer catch a bull; 2) a person in the hay business who fell through a hole in a hayloft; 3) a deliveryman gored by a farmer's bull, and 4) a man who fell from a ladder at a berry farm open to the public.[21]

A farmer owes an invitee the duty to use ordinary care to keep those portions of the premises used by business visitors in a reasonably safe condition. This includes the duty to warn an invitee against any dangerous condition that exists on the premises of which the owner knows or should know. In certain situations this duty will require the owner to inspect the premises periodically to discover defects. The reason for the landowner's liability is his or her superior knowledge of any dangerous condition and his failure to warn of the risk.[22]

Despite this high standard, the law does not expect the farmer to insure the invitee's safety. In other words, an express invitation is not a guarantee that the premises are absolutely safe. The invitee must still exercise due care while on the land. However, the farmer has the duty to warn an invitee of a concealed danger which the farmer knows, or should know, exists.[23] Thus, the farmer is best advised to periodically inspect heavily traveled areas of the farm for concealed dangers. If the farmer fails to warn an invitee of a dangerous condition or otherwise fails to exercise ordinary care in keeping the premises safe, he or she may be liable for any injury the invitee suffers as a result of the dangerous condition.

A good example of the care owed to an invitee is illustrated by Guenther v. Hawthorn Mellody Inc.,[24] an Illinois case in which a man in the hay selling business was injured while delivering hay to a farmer. The hay seller fell through a hole in the farmer's hayloft when boards covering the hole broke. The court barred the hay seller from recovering from the farmer for his injuries because the court determined that the farmer had exercised reasonable care for the plaintiff's safety

594

by putting boards over the hole. Furthermore, it was not proven that the defendant farmer knew about or should have discovered the defect in the boards by the exercise of reasonable care.

B. Duty to Licensees

A lesser degree of care is owed to a licensee, which is an individual who is privileged to enter or remain upon land or premises by the owner's consent. This consent may be obtained by invitation, permission or by operation of law.[25] A licensee, in contrast to an invitee, enters the premises for his or her own personal gain, benefit, convenience or pleasure and not to benefit the owner. In other words, a person who enters land by invitation does not enjoy the status of an invitee unless the entry is made in connection with the business or purpose of the landowner.[26] To convert a licensee to an invitee, ordinarily a business or commercial benefit must accrue to the landowner from the entry.[27] Examples of licensees include social guests-- even though expressly invited, unsolicited salespersons, and hunters with permission.

The standard of care which is owed to licensees is to refrain from committing willful, reckless, or malicious actions which cause injury to another.[28] A farmer will be held liable for injuries to a licensee which are caused by the farmer's willful or wanton conduct. Willful conduct is an intentional act performed with a purpose or intent to do wrong or to cause injury to another.[29] Wanton conduct is an act performed with a realization of imminent danger and with a reckless disregard or complete indifference to the probable consequences of the act.[30] Under these standards the farmer must refrain from intentionally exposing a licensee to danger or willfully "setting a trap" that will cause injury to the licensee.[31] The failure of the landowner to warn the licensee of a concealed danger which is known to the owner may also be grounds to impose liability for damages.[32] In addition, active negligence by the landowner may result in liability for injuries caused to a licensee. For example, in Montague v. Burgerhoff,[33] the owner of a building knocked a man down in a such manner as to injure a third party who was entering the building on a lawful errand. The court found the owner liable for the injuries to the third party.

595

C. Duty to Trespassers

The final category of visitors is trespassers. A trespasser is a person who enters or remains upon land in possession of another without the possessor's consent.[34] The standard of care owed by a farmer to a trespasser is to refrain from committing willful, malicious, or reckless injury. There is no general duty to put the land in a condition which is safe for trespassers.[35]

However, if a trespasser is injured by a trap, the farmer is subject to liability for the injury. A trap is a hazard that is known to the owner but concealed from others. A farmer cannot set traps for trespassers. The following have been held to be unlawful traps for which the owner was held responsible: 1) setting a spring gun; 2) creating obstacles on a public roadway; and 3) installing a cable gate across a private road known to be used by the public.[36]

A leading case in the area of setting traps is the Iowa case of Kato v. Briney.[37] In Kato, the plaintiff was a trespasser who had broken into a vacant house on the defendant's property in order to steal antique bottles. The defendant's property had been broken into numerous times in the past. The defendant placed a spring gun on the bedroom door of the house. It was designed so that the gun would fire when the door was opened. When the plaintiff-trespasser entered the bedroom, the gun discharged and caused the plaintiff severe injury. Even though the trespasser was violating the law by breaking and entering, the farmer was held liable for the injury because it was willful and malicious on his part to set the spring gun.

D. Liability To Recreational Entrants

In recent years, there has been a dramatic increase in public interest in outdoor leisure and recreation. In many states (especially in the midwest and east) there is relatively little publicly owned land. Therefore, public recreation often occurs on private agricultural or rural land, usually with the express permission of the landowner. The standard of care which is owed to recreational land users is analyzed under the general liability principles outlined above. Therefore, the duties owed by an owner or occupier of land to a person who is

596

accidentally injured while on the premises depends on the nature of the relationship between the parties at the time of the accident. Although there have been modifications to this rule in several jurisdictions[38] the standard of care required is that the landowner exercise reasonable care toward the entrant, depending on whether the person on the premises is an invitee, a licensee or a trespasser. In most instances, the status of the visitor is determined by the purpose of the entry and whether the entrant is present with the permission or consent of the landowner or occupier. Hunters, fisherman, and other recreational entrants will often be found to have the implied consent of the landowner and will therefore be considered either invitees or licensees.[39]

The standard of care owed by the landowner to invitees and licensees is generally greater than that owed to trespassers. This standard may require that the landowner keep the premises free of hazards and warn the entrant of dangers. Because of the liability risks, landowners are often reluctant to give permission. For many landowners, the alternative is to "post" public notice the land should not be entered. This is commonly known as posting a "No trespassing" sign. In this way landowners expect not to owe any person a higher duty of care than that which is owed to trespassers.

To encourage landowners to allow their lands to be used for recreation, some states have adopted legislation which limits the liability of the landowner. These statutes apply to private land which is opened to the public, without charge, for purposes such as nature study, water skiing, winter sports, and viewing or enjoying historical, archeological, scenic, or scientific sites. They provide that the standard of care owed to the public is that the landowner must refrain from intentionally, or through gross neglect, creating a condition which causes injury.[40]

E. Who is Liable: Landowner or Tenant?

If a trespasser, licensee or invitee is injured while on leased property, the question arises as to which party is liable--the landowner or the tenant. Traditionally, the tenant has the responsibility of maintaining the premises in a reasonably safe condition to protect persons who come upon the land. This is because the tenant is the person in possession of the land. When land is leased to a tenant, the lease is regarded as equivalent to a sale of the premises for the term of the lease. The tenant acquires an estate in the land and all of the responsibilities of a person in possession. Therefore, as a general rule, the landowner is not liable to the tenant or to others who are injured while the land is leased to the tenant.[41]

This general rule of the non-liability of the landowner has several specific exceptions. These exceptions provide that the landowner is liable when there is: 1) an undisclosed danger known to the landowner and unknown to the tenant (for example, a hidden well); 2) a condition which is dangerous to a person not on the premises (for example, a low hanging tree branch across a public road which causes injury); 3) land retained in the landowner's control which the tenant is entitled to use (for example, outer hallways in an apartment complex); 4) premises leased for the admission of the public (for example, an area leased for a rummage sale); and 5) an agreement by the landowner to repair a condition on the premises and a negligent repair is performed by the landowner. Unless the liability of the landowner arises from a defective condition under one of these exceptions, the landowner will generally not incur liability when an injury occurs on the property.[42]

F. Liability to Children

A farmer may be liable for injuries to young children who are attracted to or lured onto the property by some hazardous condition, place or thing created by the farmer. This rule is commonly known as the "attractive nuisance doctrine". The farmer's liability is based on his or her negligence in failing to protect the children.[43]

A possessor of land is subject to liability for bodily harm to trespassing children when the injury is caused by some object or condition that the landowner maintains on the premises if:

(a) the possessor knows or should know, that young children are likely to trespass upon the premises;

(b) the owner knows, or should know, that an object or condition exists on the premises that involves an unreasonable risk of bodily harm to young children;

(c) the children, because of their youth, either do not discover or understand the danger which the object,

598

condition or area presents; and

(d) a person who used ordinary care would not have
maintained the object or dangerous condition after he or
she considered:

(1) the usefulness of the object or condition, and

(2) the expense or inconvenience involved in remedying
the situation in comparison to the risk of harm it
posed to children.[44]

As is evident, the attractive nuisance doctrine has a
number of conditions which must be met in order to cause
liability to be incurred by the landowner. In other words, the
owner of an object which is determined to be an attractive
nuisance is not always liable to a child who is injured by that
object. The owner's liability depends on what the attraction is,
the comparative ease or difficulty of preventing the danger
without destroying the object's usefulness, and the reasonableness of the owner's conduct under the specific circumstance.[45]

A good illustration of how courts consider all these
factors is provided by the Kansas case of McGaughey v.
Haines.[46] In McGaughey, a four-year-old boy was seriously
injured by a disk which was attached to a tractor on which the
boy had been playing. The tractor and disk had been left
overnight by the defendant's farm employee in a field adjacent
to the boy's residence. The key was left in the tractor's
ignition. The injured boy and his stepbrother were playing on
the tractor. The stepbrother started the tractor and moved it.
This caused the four-year-old to fall off the tractor and into the
path of the disk, which severely injured him. The trial court
returned a verdict in favor of the injured boy. The appellate
court reversed, holding that the tractor and disk were not an
attractive nuisance.

In McGaughey, the issue before the appellate court was
whether the tractor and disk left in an area near where children
live is an attractive nuisance. The appellate court's holding
seems to be based on farm necessity since the court noted that
the "agricultural pursuits of the farmers of the state of Kansas
should not be handicapped by their being required, at the end
of each day's work, to remove their farm machinery, over busy
highways, from the fields in which they have been working to

some sheltered place away from the eyes of farm children".[47]

The attractive nuisance doctrine also generally does not apply to private ponds or other similar bodies of water.[48] An exception to this general rule exists when an inherently dangerous condition is present in or around the body of water or where the landowner knows or had reason to know that children habitually play around the body of water.[49]

It is important to note that the attractive nuisance doctrine applies only to dangers which are not understood by the injured child. It does not apply to obvious dangers that a child should recognize.[50] As a practical observation, the younger the child, the less likely he or she is to understand and appreciate a danger. Therefore, a farmer will be held to a higher standard of care when anticipating the protection of young children from danger.

In summary, under the attractive nuisance doctrine the circumstances often determine whether the farmer will be held liable. Liability depends on what the farmer knows about the activities of children around his or her property and whether the farmer is aware that there is something on the property that may attract them. Finally, liability may be determined by what the farmer has done or could have done to remove or lessen the nuisance in comparison to the apparent danger involved.

V.   Trespassing Animals

Many farmers have had animals trespass on their land and cause damage to their property. Many agricultural states have specific statutes which determine when and under what conditions it is legal to kill or injure a trespassing animal. These statutes also prescribe the remedies which the farmer has against the owner of the animal. Typically, under statutes which pertain to cruelty to animals, it is illegal to intentionally kill, maim, torture, or mutilate any animal.[51] These laws would make it illegal for a farmer to shoot a trespassing animal merely because it is trespassing.

A typical exception to these animal protection statutes exists when a domestic animal is discovered causing or attempting to cause damage or injury to a person or their property. Many state statutes permit an animal, such as a dog, to be killed if it is found outside the property of its owner and

600

it is injuring or threatening to injure a person, farm animals, or property.[52]

Similarly, state statutes often permit a person to kill a dog which is injuring or attempting to injure cattle, hogs, or sheep.[53] This action can be taken at the time the dog is discovered causing or attempting to cause the damage. In addition a farmer may, for a reasonable time after the damage was done, pursue the dog and shoot it. However, the farmer cannot trespass on another's land without permission in order to kill a dog. In other words, the statute which grants a person the authority to shoot a dog would not make the trespass legal.[54]

Whether the killing of a domestic animal is justified depends on the circumstances of each case. Relevant factors include the animal's past history of violent acts and whether the animal was injuring or threatening a person or property. Further consideration must be given to local county or city ordinances which relate to trespassing dogs.

In regard to trespassing cattle, it is usually lawful for a landowner to retain the trespassing animals until the owner pays for the damage they have caused, including feeding expenses.[55] A typical statute addresses liability in these situations as follows:

> If any of the animals mentioned in this act (domesticated livestock primarily) break free of their lawful enclosure, and trespass on land owned by another person, the owner or occupant of the land may take into possession such animal trespassing, and keep the same until damages, with reasonable charges for feeding and keeping, and all cost of suit, be paid, to be recovered in any court of competent jurisdiction.[56]

This type of statute, in essence, gives the victim a possessory lien against the trespassing livestock. The assertion of this lien can be used in some situations to quickly and effectively resolve minor disputes regarding property damage which was caused by the trespass.

In some states there are other statutes which provide a procedure for removing stray animals from a person's property.[57] A typical provision allows the county sheriff to confiscate livestock which are found running at large and hold them in custody. After securing the animal, the sheriff must notify the owner that the animals have been confiscated. The owner of the animals may claim the livestock by paying the costs which were incurred in gathering, keeping, and feeding the livestock. If the owner of the animals fails to claim them, the sheriff may take the animals to a public livestock market and sell them.[58]

In many states, another procedure provides for the gathering and sale of stray animals.[59] A "stray" is typically defined as "any domestic animal which is found running at large, contrary to law, or which may be found in an enclosure other than that of its ownership, and whose owner is not known in the community or whose owner cannot be found."[60]

VI.   Fence Laws

The common law rule in regard to fences is that owners and keepers of livestock are under the duty to restrain their animals from trespassing on real property. Persons are held strictly liable for the acts of their trespassing livestock.[61] Under the common law, if livestock escape their confines and damage another person's property, the owner is liable for the resulting damage regardless of attempts by the owner to restrain the livestock or to properly maintain the condition of the fences. Liability is imposed on the owner of the livestock regardless of whether negligence has occurred.[62]

Many states have enacted so-called "fencing out" statutes. These statutes require a landowner to construct a lawful fence around property before being able to collect damages from the owner of straying livestock. Thus, the landowner is required to "fence-out" livestock which belong to others. If the landowner did not have a legal fence around his or her land, they could not recover for damages caused by another's straying livestock.[63]

Under these fencing-out statutes, which are still in effect in some states, if livestock trespass within a lawful enclosure, then the livestock owner is strictly liable for the damages caused by his or her livestock. No proof of negligence is needed. The simple fact that the livestock trespass within a lawful enclosure is enough to find the stock owner liable.[64]

Other statutes provide that farm animals cannot run at large and that they have to be enclosed by a lawful fence.

602

However, these statutes make it clear that the livestock owner has to be negligent in some way before he or she can be held responsible for the damages caused by their trespassing animals. These statutes do not eliminate but merely limit strict liability. Strict liability still exists where land is surrounded by a legal fence and animals trespass into the enclosure.[65]

As a general rule, livestock owners must avoid negligent acts through the exercise of "reasonable care" and "reasonable precautions" in confining livestock. The courts examine a number of factors to determine whether an individual has been negligent. Some key factors in determining liability are:

1. The quality of the owner's fence;
2. Whether his or her animals are habitual roamers;
3. Whether the owner caused the animals to escape (i.e., by running the animals or shooting around them);
4. Whether the owner adequately feeds the animals; and
5. Whether the owner makes immediate attempts to recapture the animals.[66]

FOOTNOTES

1. 188 Kan. 722, 366 P.2d 246 (1961).

2. 366 P.2d at 254.

3. See generally, Hand, "Right to Farm Laws: Breaking New Ground in the Preservation of Farmland" 45 U. Pitt. L. Rev. 289 (1984).

4. See, e.g., K.S.A. § 2-3203(a).

5. See, e.g., K.S.A. § 2-3203(b).

6. For further discussion, see Note, "Agricultural Law: Suburban Sprawl and the Right to Farm," 22 Washburn L. J. 448 (1983).

7. K.S.A. § 47-1505.

8. See, "Agriculture", 3 AmJur 2d, § 47.

9. 3 AmJur 2d, § 47 at 814.

10. See, e.g., Gotreaux v. Garg, 232 La. 373, 94 So. 2d 293 (1957); Young v. Darter, 363 P.2d 829 (Okla. 1961); Cross v. Harris, 230 Ore. 398, 370 P.2d 703 (1962); Langans v. Valicopters, Inc. 88 Wash. 2d 855, 567 P.2d 278 (1977).

11. 213 Kan. 365 (1973).

12. Jensen, "Crop Dusting: Two Theories of Liability?", 19 Hastings L. J. 476 (1968).

13. 19 Hastings L. J. at 482.

14. Harl, 1 Agricultural Law, Ch. 2, at 2-35 (1984), note 13.

15. Harl, 1 Agricultural Law, Ch. 2, at 2-28 (1984).

16. 19 <u>Hastings L. J.</u> at 482.

17. <u>See</u>, <u>e.g.</u>, K.S.A. 2-2448. Commercial applicators must have either a surety bond for no less than $6,000.00 per year <u>or</u> liability insurance of not less than $25,000.00 for bodily injury and not less than $5,000.00 for property damages. The amount of the surety bond or insurance may be adjusted upward as deemed necessary by the Kansas Secretary of Agriculture.

18. <u>Pattern Instructions for Kansas</u> 2d § 12.01; <u>also see</u> <u>Restatement, Second, Torts</u> § 332.

19. <u>Restatement, Second, Torts</u> § 330.

20. <u>Restatement, Second, Torts</u> § 329.

21. Harl, 1 <u>Agricultural Law</u>, Ch. 4, at 4-29.

22. Little v. Butner, 186 Kan. 75 (1960).

23. Graham v. Loper Electric Co., 192 Kan. 558, cited in Smith v. Board of Education, 204 Kan. 580, 586 (1970).

24. Guenther v. Hawthorn Mellody, Inc., 27 Ill. App. 3d 214 (1975).

25. Gerchberg v. Loney, 233 Kan. 446 (1978); cited in Britt v. Allen Co. Community Jr. College, 230 Kan. 502, 638 P.2d 914 (1982).

26. Britt v. Allen Co. Community Jr. College, 230 Kan. at 508.

27. Zuther v. Schild, 224 Kan. 528, 529 (1978).

28. <u>Pattern Instructions for Kansas</u> 2d § 12.11.

29. <u>Pattern Instructions for Kansas</u> 2d § 3.03.

30. <u>Pattern Instructions for Kansas</u> 2d § 3.02.

31. Harl, 1 <u>Agricultural Law</u>, Ch. 4, 4-38.

32. Harl, 1 <u>Agricultural Law</u>, Ch. 4, 4-37.

33. 150 Kan. 217 (1939).

34. <u>Pattern Instructions for Kansas</u> 2d § 12.20; <u>Restatement Second, Torts</u> § 329.

35. <u>Restatement, Second, Torts</u> § 333.

36. Harl, 1 <u>Agricultural Law</u>, Ch. 4, 4-48, 4-49.

37. 183 N.W.2d 657 (1971).

38. <u>See</u>, <u>e.g.</u>, Rowland v. Christian, 69 Cal.2d 108, 70 Cal. Rptr. 97, 443 P.2d 561 (1968).

39. <u>See</u> <u>Restatement, Second, Torts</u> § 330, Comment C; § 332, Comment b.

40. <u>See</u>, <u>e.g.</u>, Ark. Code. Ann. § 18-11-302 to 307.

41. Harl, 2 <u>Agricultural Law</u>, Ch. 8, 8-4 to 8-7.

42. <u>See</u> <u>generally</u>, Harl, 2 <u>Agricultural Law</u>, Ch. 8, 8-11 to 8-33.

43. <u>Albanese v. Edwardsville Mobile Home Village, Inc.</u>, 214 Kan. 826, (1974).

44. <u>Pattern instructions for Kansas</u> 2d § 12.40; <u>Gerchberg v. Loney</u>, 223 Kan. 446 (1978).

45. <u>Brittain v. Cubbon</u>, 190 Kan. 641 (1963).

46. 189 Kan. 453, 370 P.2d 120 (1962).

47. 370 P.2d at 124.

48. See, e.g., Jones v. Comer, 237 Ark. 500, 374 S.W.2d 465 (1964).

49. See note, "Liability Resulting from Artificial Books of Water" 48 Iowa L. Rev. 939 (1963).

50. Bartlett v. Marinas Heersche, et al, 204 Kan. 392 (1969).

51. See, e.g., K.S.A. § 21-4310.

52. See, e.g., K.S.A. § 21-4310 (2) (g).

53. See, e.g., K.S.A. § 47-646.

54. See, McDonald v. Bauman, 199 Kan. 628 (1967).

55. See, e.g., K.S.A. § 29-408.

56. K.S.A. § 47-123.

57. See, e.g., K.S.A. § 47-122a.

58. See, e.g., K.S.A. § 47-122a (b).

59. See, e.g., K.S.A. § 47-229 to 47-239.

60. Chasteen v. Childers, 218 Kan. 519 (1976) and K.S.A. § 47-229 (b).

61. Harl, 1 Agricultural Law, Ch. 3, 3-2, 3-3.

62. Lindsey v. Cobb, 6 Kan. App. 2d 171 (1981).

63. Harl, 1 Agricultural Law Ch. 3, 3-10 (1984) note 4, see, e.g., N.M. Stat. Ann. § 47-17-1.

64. See, e.g., Bates v. Allison, 186 Kan. 548, 352 P.2d 16 (1960).

65. See, e.g., Tenn. Code Ann. § 44-1401, Overbey v. Poteat, 206 Tenn. 146, 332 S.W.2d 197 (1960).

66. See Harl, Agricultural Law, Ch. 3, particularly the state by state analysis commencing at 3-14.

Acceleration clause, in
    security agreement, 75
Acreage Conservation
    Reserve, 204-5
Acreage reductions, 201-2
"Active management" test,
    and farm leasing, 574
Adams v. United States,
    530
Administrative Procedure
    Act, 21
  adjudicatory procedures
    under, 23-27
  judicial review under,
    27-29, 135-37
  notice and comment
    procedures of, 23
  notice provisions of, 22
  and oral presentations,
    23
  rulemaking provisions
    in, 22
Administrative remedies,
    exhaustion of, 28
A Gay Jenson Farms Co. v.
    Cargill, Inc., 58
Age Discrimination in
    Employment Act (1967),
    511
Agricultural Act (1949),
    11, 194
Agricultural Act (1956),
    240
Agricultural Adjustment
    Act, 476
Agricultural Adjustment
    Act (1933), 11
Agricultural Adjustment
    Act (1938), 10-11,
    193-94
Agricultural agencies,
    handling of information
    requests by, 30-31

judicial review of,
    27-29
response of, to
    information requests,
    31-33
Agricultural chemicals,
    liability in,
    misapplication of,
    591-93
Agricultural Conservation
    Program, 223
Agricultural cooperatives,
    4
Agricultural Credit Act
    (1987), 60, 103, 115,
    117-18, 131
  administration of loans
    under, 157
  borrower's rights
    under, 155-56
  regulations under,
    120-22
  right of first refusal
    under, 157-58
  and use of loan
    servicing in cases of
    financial distress,
    152-53
Agricultural Fair
    Practices Act, 13
Agricultural law, 1-3
  application of general
    law in, 2, 3-4
  specialized, as
    exception to general
    law, 2, 4-8
  specialized regulating
    agriculture, 2, 8-16
  under federal agencies,
    17
Agricultural Marketing
    Agreement Act (1937),
    11, 13, 38, 341-42,

and consumer credit
  protection, 511
definition of, 487-89
and the Fair Labor
  Standards Act, 489-91
and immigration law,
  495-500
and migrant and seasonal
  worker protection,
  491-95
and Occupational Safety
  and Health Act, 500-4
and social security and
  retirement, 504-10
and state labor
  statutes, 512-19
and unemployment
  compensation, 512
and veterans
  reemployment rights,
  511
and workers'
  compensation, 512-16
Agriculture and Consumer
  Protection Act (1973),
  194-95
Agriculture and Food Act
  (1981), 201
Allison v. Block, 117, 137
Allotment Programs for
  Cotton, 223
Allotment Programs for
  Peanuts, 223
Allotment Programs for
  Rice, 223
Allotment Programs for
  Wheat, 223
American Fruit Purveyors,
  Inc. v. United States,
  343
Anderson v. Blackfoot
  Livestock Commission
  Co., 315

Anderson v. Farmer's
  Hybrid Companies,
  Inc., 316-17
Animal and Plant Health
  Inspection Service
  administration of
  inspection and control
  programs by, 396-402
  rules for information
  requests, 31
Animal Disease Control
  Statutes, 311-13
Animal Quarantine Act, 38
Animal Welfare Act, 38
Anticipatory repudiation,
  303-4
Antitrust exemptions, for
  farm cooperatives,
  475-81
Appeals, under Farmers
  Home Administration,
  131-35
Appraisals, for farm
  loans, 110-11
Arbitration, in commodity
  litigation, 443-44
Archaeological Resources
  Protection Act, 38
Arkansas Valley Industries
  v. Freeman, 393-94
Armstrong v. Corn Belt
  Bank, 169
Army Corps of Engineers,
  17
Assembly of God v.
  Sangster, 80
Associated person, 434
Attractive nuisance
  doctrine, 598-600
Authorized farm
  corporation, 550-51

Bache Halsey Stuart, Inc.

income support
programs, 198-99
Taxation
of farm corporations,
551-55
and farm leasing, 572-74
of general partnership,
536-38
of limited partnerships,
545-46
Tax planning, and form of
business organization,
574-75
Tax Reform Act (1986),
240, 553
passive loss rules of,
573-74
Tenant
death of, and farm
leases, 570
distinction between
employee and, 559
Tendency determination,
333
Tennessee Protection
Agency, 17
Terminal markets, 363
Tigner v. Texas, 478
In re Tim Wargo & Sons,
Inc., 170
Tort theories, and sales
of diseased or
defective livestock,
314-17
Treasure Valley Potato
Bargaining Association
v. Ore-Ida Foods,
Inc., 480-81
Treasury, U.S. Department
of, 17
Trespassers, duty of farm
landowner to, 596
Trespassing animals, 600-2

Tuepker v. Farmers Home
Administration, 136
"Two funds" rule, 91
Two Rivers v. Curtiss
Breeding Service, 316,
317

Uhlrig v. Shortt, 517-18
Unemployment compensation,
for agricultural
workers, 512
Unequal relationship
theory, 57
Uniform Commercial Code
and sales of farm
products, 3, 4,
297-305
and protection for
buyers of livestock,
402-3
Uniform Partnership Act,
528-29, 531
United Corp. v. Federal
Trade Commission, 368
U.S. Cotton Standards Act,
39
U.S. Grain Standards Act,
24, 39
U.S. Grain Warehouse Act,
11
U.S. Warehouse Act, 24, 39
U.S. v. Batson, 29
U.S. v. Borden Company,
478
U.S. v. Butler, 194
U.S. v. Carroll, 28
U.S. v. Frame, 410
U.S. v. Garth, 116
U.S. v. Kimball Foods,
Inc., 13-14
U.S. v. Maryland
Cooperative Milk
Producers, Inc.,